I0213105

STUDIES IN JEWISH BIBLIOGRAPHY AND MEDIEVAL HEBREW POETRY

Menahem H. Schmelzer

STUDIES IN JEWISH BIBLIOGRAPHY AND MEDIEVAL HEBREW POETRY

Collected Essays

The Jewish Theological Seminary of America
New York and Jerusalem 2006 - 5766

ISBN 965-456-043-7

Photo Typesetting: Shulamit Yerushalmi, Jerusalem
Plates and Offset Printing: Shlomo Natan Ltd, Jerusalem

CONTENTS

FORWORD

This handsome volume of Professor Menahem Schmelzer's widely scattered published essays carries with it a profound expression of gratitude for his unstinting services to the Seminary and to Jewish scholarship. According to the Hasidic master, Reb Levi Yitzhak of Berditchev, piety comes in two forms. The first is personified by those pious individuals who spend their lives devoutly worshiping God. They divert no energy to bringing those estranged from God and besotted with sin closer to their Maker. The second is personified by those individuals who seek to share their love of God with others. If Noah exemplifies the first type, Abraham does the second, of whom it can be said, in the words of the Talmud that he was of benefit to humanity as well as to heaven.

Great scholars, like true pietists, are life-long practitioners of self-deprivation. But few among them, in their devotion to advancing the frontiers of their field, find the time to facilitate the work of others. About Professor Schmelzer, though, it can be said that he has truly been of inestimable benefit to his field precisely because he has given so much of himself to aiding the work of his colleagues. His generosity of spirit consistently matches his erudition. As Seminary librarian from 1964 to 1987 and as the editor of Aron Freimann's *Union Catalogue of Hebrew Manuscripts and Their Location* and of Alexander Marx's *Bibliographical Studies and Notes on Rare Books and Manuscripts in the Library of the Jewish Theological Seminary of America*, he set aside his own research to bring to fruition the labor of scholars both living and deceased.

His superb editing of Shalom Spiegel's *Avot ha-Piyyut* recalls the role that Leopold Zunz once played in bringing Nachman Krochmal's literary torso, *Moreh Nevukhei ha-Zeman*, to print in 1851. Both were feats of vast learning and stark self-effacement to salvage from oblivion the unfinished work of a lifetime. Indeed, I suspect that the disordered and unhewn state of Spiegel's papers required of Professor Schmelzer a degree of imagination, ingenuity and sheer hard work that exceeded what Krochmal's more complete and cohesive manuscript demanded of Zunz. And there can be no doubt as to the superiority of the final product in terms of physical beauty and the absence of errors. Its pervasive high quality and good taste are an enduring monument to the greatness of its author and the humanity of its editor.

One year after the 150th anniversary of the founding of the Breslau Seminary in 1854, Professor Schmelzer represents a living link to that seminal font of *Jüdische Wissenschaft*. Born in Hungary, he still had the chance before his departure in 1956 to study at its institutional offspring, the Jewish Theological Seminary of Budapest among whose founders in 1877 were several graduates of Breslau. The most formative influence on his young life came from the last laudable embodiment of that spirit in Hungary, Professor Alexander Scheiber, who single-handedly sustained a greatly diminished seminary through the nightmare of the Holocaust and its oppressive Communist aftermath. In that lonely and lugubrious setting, Professor Schmelzer learned to value the building blocks of *Wissenschaft des Judentums* – a thorough command of Bible and Talmud, knowledge of foreign languages, mastery of philology and paleography, recourse to the archives in search of unknown legacies and the application of a historical perspective. Above all, he relished the thrill of discovery that marked the pioneers of *Wissenschaft* who first glimpsed the vast landscape of a Jewish past still largely unimagined.

Like the scholarship of those same pioneers, Professor Schmelzer's own research ranges over the enormous expanse of literary Jewish creativity from rabbinics to the history of Hebrew publishing in the eighteenth century, often through the lens of piyyut. To collect this rich harvest in a single silo is an act of recompense that will perpetuate in our midst a source of unending nourishment and comfort.

Ismar Schorsch
New York 2005 - 5765
The Jewish Theological Seminary of America

PREFACE

The articles published in the present volume are the fruit of some four decades of my interest in two areas of learning: medieval Hebrew poetry and Jewish bibliography and booklore. They appear here, with the exception of minor editorial changes and of a few essential bibliographical additions, in their original version.

As a graduate student in the early 1960's, I wrote a dissertation on the poetic work of the great Spanish rabbi, Isaac ibn Giat, who lived in Lucena, Spain in the eleventh century. His liturgical poetry exercised a great influence on future generations of Spanish Hebrew poets, chief among them Moses ibn Ezra. My original plan was to prepare a critical edition of all of his poems, but unfortunately, for various reasons, I was unable to realize my plan. Still, I published a few articles about ibn Giat, which also included some unpublished poems by him.

From the mid-1960's until the mid-1980's, my main energies were directed to my position as librarian of the Seminary. During those years I was also active in the professional organization of Judaica librarians in the United States: I delivered some lectures and wrote some articles relating to the history of the Seminary Library and on various themes in Jewish bibliography. A few studies on specific Hebrew manuscripts and rare books were also the result of my good fortune of having had access to the treasures of the Seminary Library, and, of course, also to the holdings of other institutions.

Later, beginning with the 1990's, my interest turned to medieval Hebrew poetry in Ashkenaz. I was fascinated to realize that medieval Ashkenazi rabbis were also prolific in composing occasional poems, many of them on weddings. This somehow stood in contrast with the stereotypical impression of them being the authors of exclusively lachrymose poems on tragic events. A few of my later articles deal with Ashkenazi Piyyutim.

Finally, I published a few biographical appreciations. These are devoted to the much admired great scholars and leaders at the Seminary, Alexander Marx and Louis Finkelstein, and to my teacher Alexander Scheiber of Budapest, who inspired me to embark on a career in Jewish Studies.

The articles gathered in this volume reflect on these interests and topics.

Preface

It is my pleasant duty to express my thanks to those who made my work possible over the years and to those who were instrumental in the publication of this volume.

I thank Professor Shmuel Glick and Mr. Israel Hazani of the Schocken Institute in Jerusalem for their highly skilled professional efforts and expertise in the preparation of the articles for a uniform and pleasing collective re-issue. Without their work, this book could not have been published; Many thanks also for Mr. David Kerschen for preparing the indeces, Hebrew and English. Professor Jack Wertheimer, Provost of the Jewish Theological Seminary and Professor Alan Cooper, chair of its Publication Committee, supported this project from its inception until its completion.

For 45 years the Jewish Theological Seminary of America and its Library have been my professional and academic home. I had the privilege of serving under three chancellors, Professor Louis Finkelstein and Professor Gerson D. Cohen, of blessed memory, and *yibbadel lehayyim*, Professor Ismar Schorsch. I am most grateful to them for the trust they placed in me, for their support and for the many kindnesses they have shown me.

But, of course, my most profound thanks are due to my family. To my wife, Ruth, for her patience, understanding and love. To our children, Naomi and Ely Stillman, Shai Schmelzer and Lisa Rotmil and Becky and Mark Benisz who made us proud with their achievements, and to our grandchildren, Avinoam, Lydia and Alexander who are a source of joy for us. I pray for their well-being and happiness.

Menahem H. Schmelzer
New York 2006 - 5766

Personal Recollections

It was Sunday, March 19, 1944, when German soldiers entered Hungary—the last country to be invaded by the Nazis. Until this date, Hungarian Jews were quite optimistic. The Nazis were losing the war. At Stalingrad, the Germans had lost 330,000 troops by February 1943, when the few remaining German soldiers surrendered. In North Africa, it became clear that by May 1943 Germany's drive had failed. And in July of that year, the Allies invaded Sicily; Mussolini was overthrown. Even Hungary, one of Nazi Germany's most faithful allies, was flirting with the idea of extricating itself from the war in March of 1944. No one, of course, knew yet of D-Day—to happen two and a half months later on June 6—but everyone was hoping for an imminent landing of the Allies in Western Europe.

While most Jews in German-occupied lands already had been massacred, Hungarian Jewry, in the midst of this terrible annihilation, was still relatively intact during the early months of 1944. Families were living in their homes, Jewish institutions and organizations were functioning, and Jewish schools were operating normally.

Yet business and professional activities were severely curtailed and restricted by the Hungarian government's anti-Jewish legislation that began in 1938. Soon after the promulgation of these anti-Jewish laws, tens of thousands of Jewish men were drafted into forced labor companies attached to the Hungarian Army, which, after June of 1941, were fighting on the Russian front alongside the Germans. The Jews in these forced labor formations were assigned to the most dangerous and menial tasks. They were forced to wear yellow armbands (Jews converted to Christianity wore white ones). They served as a kind of buffer between the Russians and the Hungarians. Their tasks included clearing minefields. Jews were also required to dig ditches to prevent the Russian advance. Many were killed or maimed during these operations.

Yet the biggest danger came not from the fighting but from the officers and soldiers of the regular Hungarian army. Their cruelty and sadism raised the eyebrows of even the German Nazis. Poorly clad, exposed to the elements, many Jews froze to death, including those whom Hungarian soldiers doused with water until they turned to ice sculptures. Jews were ordered to climb trees, sit on the branches, and shout "I am a dirty Jew," as Hungarians shot at them. On April 30, 1943, the last day of Passover, Hungarian soldiers herded eight hundred Jews into a shed, ignited the structure, and shot anyone who tried to flee the flames. The suffering and fate of these Jewish victims served as entertainment and amusement for a number of the Hungarians. Out of some fifty thousand Jews in the forced labor companies, only between six and seven thousand returned. Most of the deaths occurred on the Russian front, but many other Jews in these units met their deaths elsewhere. In late 1944 and early 1945, just weeks before the end of the war in Hungary, Jewish men were forced to dig antitank ditches on the western border of Hungary, not far from Vienna, in a totally senseless effort to prevent the Red Army's rapid advance. Jews died there of beatings, shootings, typhoid fever, and exhaustion, but principally of starvation. My father was there, but miraculously survived. One of his brothers was not so fortunate.

Miklos Radnoti, a great Hungarian poet of Jewish origin, though completely assimilated, was among the victims of the forced labor. Poems that he had composed during these brutal days were found on his body. In a fragment written on May 19, 1944, he said:

I lived on this earth in an age
when man became so debased
that he killed on his own, with lust,
not just on orders.

I lived on this earth in an age
when in informing lay merit, and murderers,
backstabbers, and muggers were your heroes.

I lived on this earth in an age
when a mother was a curse to her child
and the woman was happy to miscarry,
the living envied the worm-eaten dead their prison.

I lived on this earth in an age
when the poet too just kept his silence
and waited, maybe to find his voice again,
for surely, no one else could utter a worthy curse
but Isaiah, learned master of terrible words.

[Miklo's Radnóti, *The Complete Poetry*; ed. and tr. by Emery George. Ann Arbor, Ardis, 1980, p. 267]

Still, with all these sufferings, there was hope in the air during the spring of 1944. Hungarian Jews believed that as they had survived until then amidst all the destruction, it was unlikely that anything would happen to them now, so late in the war. The Nazis would not want to expend energy to liquidate hundreds of thousands of Hungarian Jews at a time when the Germans were so busy fighting for their own survival. The Jews of Hungary lulled themselves into a false sense of security. This is not an accusation; it merely describes their mood—a mood that was not completely irrational.

Two examples demonstrate this point, one trivial, the other more significant. In a newspaper that appeared around the date of the Nazi invasion of Hungary, March 19, 1944, an uncle of mine placed an advertisement, looking for a nanny for his daughter. The same issue carried advertisements for Passover products. Clearly, this was an expression of a certain measure of normalcy. A more significant example of the atmosphere prevailing in the preinvasion days in Budapest, and in Hungary in general, can be found in the reaction to a speech delivered on January 16, 1944, by the brother of the famous Hasidic Rebbe, the Belzer. The Belzer Rebbe and his brother were passing through Hungary on their way to Palestine. Their followers were able to arrange for the Rebbe's escape from a Polish ghetto, as well as for their own safe passage. In the presence of thousands of Orthodox Jews in Budapest, the Rebbe was quoted as saying that only goodness and mercy would pursue and reach the Jews of Hungary. The address was published in February of 1944 in a special brochure; it was republished a few weeks later, practically days before the invasion. Clearly, the Rebbe most likely meant a blessing, a wish, and not a prophecy or assurance. However, it is clear from the number and fast distribution of the published brochures that Orthodox Jews in Hungary considered the Rebbe's words, in terms of their relevance for the future of Hungarian Jewry, as encouraging and reassuring. This interpretation was supported by a previous announcement by an earlier Belzer Rebbe. He was quoted as saying that when the Messiah arrived, he would choose members of the Sanhedrin [rabbinical parliament] mainly from among Hungarian Jews. This was a great compliment to Hungarian Orthodox and Hasidic Jewish leaders. With Jewries to the north, south, east and west of Hungary virtually destroyed by early 1944, the two statements were taken to mean that Hungarian Jewry would not only avoid the horrors that had befallen their brethren, but that it would also become a remnant—and a source of renewal—for Jewry in general.

This fatal self-delusion was shattered on March 19, 1944. By April 5, all Jews were required to wear yellow stars. I remember how my mother had sewn the stars on my jacket and coat and how scared I was to go into the street for the first time branded with the yellow badge. I remember the hushed whispering of adults—I was then ten years old—as they prepared to bury our silver candlesticks in the courtyard of our house. I remember the day in May when Hungarian gendarmes, in their distinct feathered caps, rounded us up, put us and our meager belongings on horse-drawn wagons, and drove us to a ghetto in the neighboring town of Bacsalmas. In this ghetto, 2,793 Jews from the towns, villages, and hamlets of the countryside (specifically the Szeged District) were concentrated—to await deportation. From the ghetto days, I remember vividly the cries of people who were beaten by the gendarmes, and the screams and bizarre behavior of Jewish former inmates of a mental asylum who were ghettoized together with us.

On June 25, 1944, we were taken to the railroad station and placed into cattle cars, which began their journey to the north—destination Auschwitz. At a certain station in northern Hungary a few cars were directed to the west, to a concentration camp called Strasshof, near Vienna. My mother, my brother, and other members of my family happened to be in those cars, and we survived the next ten months, until the end of the war in Austria. All my classmates were in the section of the train that continued to Auschwitz—none returned.

Long after the Holocaust I found out the reason for our survival. About twenty thousand Hungarian Jews, out of the more than four hundred thousand deported, were "put on ice," to await the outcome of the famous bargaining between Adolf Eichmann and various Jewish leaders and organizations on trading "trucks for blood"—a proposal to let Jews go in exchange for a supply of trucks and other goods badly needed by the Germans. As a goodwill gesture, the Nazis stopped the deportation of twenty thousand Jews headed to Auschwitz, who were to be kept alive in concentration camp conditions until the completion of the negotiations.

The selection of the twenty thousand was arbitrary. In this connection falls my painful and traumatic postwar experience. One of my uncles and his family lived in the western Hungarian city of Gyor. His wife and two children were murdered in Auschwitz. After the war, we, the surviving Schmelzer children, tried to avoid the uncle because we sensed that whenever he saw us he was reminded of his own children. He told us that when he returned to Gyor after the war he could not pull himself together to go to the main street because all along the street he could see photos of his daughter, taken before the Holocaust, used as an advertisement for a photography store. Many years after the war, I read in Randolph Braham's book, *The Politics of Genocide: The Holocaust in Hungary*, that it was the deportation train from Gyor that was supposed to be taken to nearby Austria. As a result of a switching error, the train was directed to Auschwitz. To substitute for the missing Jews, our train was stopped on its way to Auschwitz, with the appropriate number of cattle cars detached and routed to Austria—and it was we who survived and not our cousins from Gyor.

By the end of June 1944, three months after the invasion, the Germans, with the help of Hungarian gendarmes, deported hundreds of thousands of Jews to Auschwitz from every locality in Greater Hungary, with the exception of Budapest. The Hungarian countryside became *judenrein*.

There used to be a kind of morbid competition between Hungarian and Polish Jews—the latter's fate more protracted, more brutal, more tragic. Polish Jews had suffered for years before 1944, while their Hungarian brothers and sisters were still enjoying relative tranquility. When, in May and June of 1944, the large transports of Hungarian Jews were arriving in Auschwitz, well-dressed and well-fed, with neat bundles and suitcases, the Polish Jews were totally emaciated. Resentment was harbored toward Hungarian Jews, who seemed to have fared much better than other Jewries under German occupation. The Hungarian Jews, on the other hand, were crushed by the suddenness, swiftness, and completeness of their liquidation. The collapse of their world in such a short time, in less than three months, was so cruel that Hungarian Jews felt that no other Jewry could match the enormity of their tragedy. One is reminded of the elegy, recited on the eve of the Ninth of Av, in which Ohola and Oholiva, symbolic representatives of the ancient kingdoms of Israel and of Judea, debate whose suffering was greater.

If one wants to understand the state of mind of Hungarian Jewry on the eve of its destruction, one should take a brief glance at its history. When compared to other Jewries, Hungarian Jewry is young, at least in regard to the beginnings of its creativity and assumption of distinct characteristics. German Jewry was at a creative peak in the eleventh and twelfth centuries; Polish Jewry in the sixteenth century; but Hungarian Jewry only in the nineteenth and twentieth centuries.

The expanding importance of Hungarian Jewry coincided with Hungary's first steps toward extricating itself from Austria and feudalism. Jews became leaders in the Hungarian modernization and capitalization process. They were the middle class—in the middle between the decadent Hungarian nobility and the downtrodden serfdom. An unprecedented dynamic burst of economic, social, political, cultural, and religious activity made this period the Golden Age of Hungarian Jewry—lasting until 1944.

Jewish participation was immense in commerce, industry, agriculture, music, arts, literature, and the sciences. In the 1920s Hungarian Jews constituted 5 percent of the total population, but 50 percent of all lawyers, 46 percent of physicians, 41 percent of veterinarians, 39 percent of engineers and chemists, 34 percent of journalists and editors, and 40 percent of all industrial-firm owners were Jews, and, most surprising: almost 20 percent of all large-landed estates were in Jewish hands, while 26 percent of those who either owned or rented small estates were Jews.

It is quite well known that in the late 1930s and early 1940s a group of Hungarian Jewish scientists, including Edward Teller, Leo Szilard, and Janos von Neumann, played a pioneering role in the development of the American nuclear bomb. All of them were refugee Jews from Budapest who studied at the same high school, attended mainly by extraordinarily talented Jewish students. Probably much less well known is the fact that seventy-six Jews won Olympic medals for Hungary before 1968, compared to the forty-seven who did the same for the United States. Large numbers of Hungarian Jews were ennobled and carried the title "baron." One can say that there was no Jewry, including German Jewry, that was more a product of, or a contributor to, its environment than was Hungarian Jewry. A great non-Jewish Hungarian writer once said: "No nationality was more loyal to us than the Jews." Another writer observed: "No one could out-duel, out-ride, out-drink, or out-serenade an assimilated Hungarian Jew!" Indeed, Hungarian Jews were great patriots. Rabbi Simon Hevesi, the rabbi of the famous Dohany Temple in Budapest, the grandfather of New York City Comptroller Alan Hevesi, would say in a prayer in the early 1940s: "I believe that Thou hast worked wonders with Hungary, our beloved nation, and shalt work wonders with her forever." Immanuel Loew, the learned rabbi of Szeged, looked upon Hungary as the land of Canaan. Abraham von Freudiger, head of the national Orthodox organization of Hungarian Jews, was photographed in Hungarian folk costume with the family coat of arms, received when his family was ennobled in Hungary. The coat of arms is engraved on the tombstones of family members in a Jerusalem cemetery.

I have referred previously to the city of Szeged. Many people confuse it with Sighet. There can be no greater difference than that between these two cities. Szeged is in southern Hungary, on the Hungarian Great Plain. In and around it lived Jews who became very successful and wealthy by introducing modern methods into agriculture and the marketing of agricultural products. Indeed, the rich soil of the "Land of Canaan" provided its inhabitants, including the Jews, with milk and honey. In behavior, manners, and language, the Jews of Szeged were greatly assimilated. In religion they followed the liberal Neolog branch of Hungarian Judaism. Immanuel Loew, Szeged's great rabbi, led his congregation in designing and building a synagogue, dedicated in 1903, that in his day was perhaps the most beautiful synagogue in the world. It is like a cathedral and it is the sight that perhaps most characterizes the city of Szeged. The community and Loew intended it to be a monument to the prosperity and permanence of Szeged Jewry. What a sense of security and self-confidence those people must have possessed to build such an edifice!

In contrast to the rich, assimilated, magyarized Jews of Szeged, the Jews of Sighet, in northeastern Hungary, had many poor among them. Their language was mainly Yiddish; they were Orthodox, with a large Hasidic element. The life of the Jews of Sighet was not much different from their brethren in Galician shtetls: full of *cheders* (religious schools), *talmidei chakhomim* (learned teachers and students), rebbes and rabbis, among them members of the Teitelbaum rabbinical dynasty, from whom the Rebbe of Satmar descends.

In the Golden Age of Hungarian Jewry there were many shades of communities and individuals, representing all colors of the rainbow between these two extremes—Szeged and Sighet. Jews in Budapest and Jews in the smallest of rural settlements, German-speaking Jews in the west, Yiddish-speaking in the east, with the great majority in the middle speaking Hungarian and looking down upon and loathing those whose language was Yiddish; rigidly Orthodox and liberally Neolog, totally assimilated and Zionistic—following the movement founded by the Budapest Jew Theodor Herzl—all were part of a multicolored tapestry.

The Hungarians and the Germans did not differentiate between them. Immanuel Loew at the age of ninety was placed in a cattle car to be deported. Through highest-level intervention he was removed from the train to be taken to a hospital in Budapest where he mercifully died shortly thereafter. The 1932 Olympic gold medal winner in fencing, Attila Petschauer (notice the *very Hungarian* first name!) was beaten to death by Hungarian murderers. And our neighbors from across the street, a veterinarian who converted to Christianity and his family, died in Auschwitz.

Out of 825,000 Hungarian Jews of all persuasions, 565,000 were murdered. The rich tapestry of what was once a great community was completely destroyed.

How should we remember the Jews of Hungary and what happened to them? Mourning, crying out, reminding, warning, or perhaps most eloquently, silence, are all ways of remembering. But so is searching and studying their brilliant lives and dark deaths. Not to forget means we must first know. We must know about their lives *before* the Holocaust as we must know about the Holocaust itself—so that we should be able to incorporate into our own lives the rich traditions of those who were martyred. We shall never be able to make sense of what happened. But perhaps we can make the lessons of their lives part of ours, and of our children's and of our children's children's, so that their tragically extinguished lives will be bound up with the life of the people of Israel for all generations to come.

The Hebrew Manuscript as Source for the Study of History and Literature

The mention of a Hebrew manuscript often conjures up the image of an object relevant only to select *cognoscenti* or highly trained specialists. In reality, most Hebrew manuscripts, books written by hand (*libri manuscripti*) in Hebrew characters, are ready and eager to yield the manifold information contained among their leaves. After all, Hebrew manuscripts were read and studied by ordinary people, not only by scholars, during the time before printed books (*libri impressi*) were made and sometimes even after the invention of printing.

Hebrew manuscripts can teach us a great deal about the reading and study habits of each generation in the various Jewish communities and about the authority and popularity of certain works. Of course, they are equally important because they often preserve significant unpublished religious, literary, historical, philosophical, and scientific texts. Furthermore, manuscripts may serve as objects of study in themselves, as artifacts and physical remnants of the culture in which they were created. As such, manuscripts teach us about Hebrew scribal traditions, book manufacturing, and aesthetic tastes, as well as offering genealogical and biographical facts concerning the scribes and owners by whom and for whom they were written.

Our principal and primary access to the study of Hebrew manuscripts is provided by the numerous catalogs of public and private collections of Hebrew manuscripts to be found in Europe, Israel, and America. Rather complete lists of these catalogs may be found in Shlomo Shunami's *Bibliography of Jewish Bibliographies* (1965 and supplement in 1975) and in Aron Freimann's *Union Catalog of Hebrew Manuscripts and Their Location* (volume I, 1973). [See now: B. Richler, *Guide to Hebrew Manuscript Collections*, 1994.] Needless to say, the quality of the various catalogs is uneven; some are extremely careful, detailed, and scholarly, while others display opposite characteristics.

The pioneering project of the Institute of Microfilmed Hebrew Manuscripts at the Jewish National and University Library in Jerusalem was initiated in 1950 by David Ben-Gurion and has as its goal "to systematically collect microfilms of Hebrew manuscripts scattered in libraries and collections throughout the world, catalogue the manuscripts and make them available to readers who come to the Institute." This goal has been substantially achieved and, at present, records relating to well over forty thousand Hebrew manuscripts and countless fragments are at the service of Jewish scholarship.

Despite this progress, there is still no textbook that provides solid, comprehensive, up-to-date information on Hebrew manuscripts and the various aspects of their study. The last guide to the subject is Moritz Steinschneider's *Vorlesungen über die Kunde hebräischer Handschriften* (1897; with supplementary notes by A.M. Habermann and in a Hebrew translation, 1965). [See now: B. Richler, *Hebrew Manuscripts A Treasured Legacy*, 1990.]

For one, albeit extremely significant area of Hebrew manuscript study, we have now at our disposal the fundamental work by Malachi Beit-Arie, *Hebrew Codicology* (1976). Thanks to Beit-Arie's book, we are able to supply some statistical information on the early centuries of medieval Hebrew manuscripts. The oldest known dated Hebrew manuscript was written in Tiberias, in 895 C.E., and it contains a portion of the Bible. Although there are undated fragments that may be older, their existence does not alter the basic situation, which is that there is a huge gap of centuries separating the Dead Sea Scrolls from the appearance of the earliest medieval Hebrew manuscripts. The rabbinic inclination against writing down rabbinic and liturgical texts may partially explain this phenomenon, but it does not explain the lack of surviving copies of the Bible from that period. Even after the ninth century, Hebrew manuscripts remain very scarce. In Beit-Arie's words: "Of some 2,700 extant dated Hebrew manuscripts until 1540, 6 dated codices from the tenth century, 8 from the eleventh century and 22 from the twelfth century are known to us" (*Hebrew Codicology*, p. II). These figures are in sharp contrast with the large number of Latin and Greek manuscripts that are extant from the fifth century onward.

* These manuscripts, with palaeographical and codicological descriptions and representative reproductions, are now in the process of being published by the Comité de Paléographie Hébraïque, a joint Israeli-French project. Several volumes have already appeared.

Some change in this respect may be expected once the approximately two hundred thousand fragments of the Cairo *Genizah* are thoroughly researched. The Cairo *Genizah*, a treasure trove of manuscript leaves written in Hebrew characters, was discovered in an old synagogue in Fostat, near Cairo, toward the end of the nineteenth century. The *Genizah* owes its existence to the traditionally respectful attitude of Jews toward the written Hebrew word, even after the book or document that carries the Hebrew script has become worn out or otherwise outlived its usefulness. The contents of the *Genizah* represent the literary as well as economic and social creativity and activity of the Jewish community in the Mediterranean era, covering a period of many centuries. The *Genizah* fragments are now scattered in the libraries of the world, the largest collection of them being held by the Cambridge University Library in England. Despite the great advances in *Genizah* research, there is still hope that further systematic study will shed light on Hebrew manuscript scholarship, especially in the earlier medieval period.

If we now turn our attention to the broad subject areas within collections of Hebrew manuscripts, we arrive at widely varying situations.

First, let us look at manuscripts of the Hebrew Bible. There are extant hundreds, if not thousands, of medieval and later Hebrew Bible manuscripts. Given the care taken with the transmission of a sacred text, one expects and finds few significant textual variants among them. On the other hand, these manuscripts have great scholarly importance for the study of Hebrew orthography, pronunciation, systems of vocalization of Hebrew, cantillation, and the entire range of the so-called masoretic literature that deals with scribal instructions and the rules for the transmission of the text. Some Bible codices, especially the older ones, were considered, in their times, as models by scribes who used them for copying other Bibles with as much care and exactitude as possible. That some of the manuscripts are richly illuminated adds to their significance. The recent reproduction in facsimile editions of some of the finest codices, for example, the *Aleppo*, *Damascus*, and *Kennicott Bibles*, allows even the non-specialist to enjoy the beauty and antiquity of these monuments of the Jewish heritage.

Arabic and Aramaic as well as other versions of the Hebrew Bible are found in large numbers among Hebrew manuscripts. These reflect local traditions and serve as research materials for linguists and historians of Bible exegesis.

Works of Bible commentators of all ages are richly represented in this group. They may be divided into two categories: copies of classic commentaries that are also found in many printed editions, such as the works of Rashi, Abraham ibn Ezra, and Naḥmanides, and texts that are preserved only in manuscripts. In both categories one may discover important elements for the critical understanding of the long history of Jewish Bible interpretation.

Let us look at two works as examples: the Pentateuch commentary of Rashi and that of his grandson, Samuel ben Meir (the *Rashbam*). Rashi's commentary has been the staple of elementary education for Jewish children throughout the centuries and it has also been an extremely popular text for lay adults. As a result, throughout the Jewish Diaspora, in the east and in the west, in Spain and in Germany, in Yemen and in Italy, numerous manuscripts of this beloved work were written, containing local variants. Although attempts have been made to collate large numbers of manuscripts and printed editions in order to present the scholar with the various traditions of the Rashi text, the classification of all available manuscripts according to families of tradition is still a *desideratum*. Accordingly, here it is not so much individual manuscripts, but rather the totality of all the sources, that are valuable for their contribution to an understanding of the history of the transmission of this standard text. On the other hand, if someone were to discover in our day a hitherto unknown manuscript of the Pentateuch commentary by Samuel ben Meir, high expectations would arise, for the commentary by Rashi's grandson is available in only a very few manuscripts, some poorly preserved. Thus, any new material would be eagerly explored for a better understanding of and insights into the mind of the commentator who, in contrast to most medieval Jewish Bible exegetes, radically adhered to the so-called simple meaning of the Bible. It is interesting to note that the first edition of this work was not published until 1705, when the greatest Jewish bibliophile of all time, Rabbi David Oppenheim, printed it on the basis of a defective manuscript that he had discovered in the *genizah* of the synagogue of Worms. The fates of these two works could serve as models for the evaluation of the intellectual and, perhaps even, religious preferences and tastes of generations of Jewish students and readers.

When we turn to manuscripts of the Talmud, we find that they are of utmost scarcity. The medieval Church regarded the Talmud as the source and symbol of what it considered to be the perfidy of the Jews. As a result, the Talmud became a constant target and victim of persecution, defamation, censorship, confiscation, and book burning. The relationship between the number of surviving copies of the Talmud and that of the Bible can best be illustrated by pointing out that in the catalog of the outstanding collection of Hebrew manuscripts at the British library are listed 161 manuscripts of the Bible and its translations, while the collection includes only five fragmentary Talmud manuscripts. At the Bibliothèque Nationale in Paris the ratio is 132:0.

The situation is not as bleak in the field of commentaries to the Talmud, Midrashim, halakhic codes, and responsa. These works, although related to and dependent on the Talmud, survived in large numbers of manuscripts, and their study yields valuable insights in many areas of Jewish studies. Some highly important texts have been discovered and published only relatively recently, for example, the now popular commentary to the Talmud by Menahem Meiri (Provence, thirteenth century) which was edited for the first time on the basis of manuscripts at the Palatine Library in Parma. The large number of extant manuscripts of the halakhic codes *Sefer Mitsvot Gadol* (*SeMaG*) by Moses of Coucy (France, thirteenth century) and of the *Sefer Mitsvot Katan* (*SeMaK*) by Isaac of Corbeil (late thirteenth century) indicate that these works were much more popular in the Middle Ages than in later times, when the *Shulḥan 'Arukh*, the authoritative code by Joseph Caro (sixteenth century), began to be published in an almost unending stream of printed editions. Because the first edition of the *Shulḥan 'Arukh* was printed in 1564-65, in the lifetime of its author, any eventual manuscript of the work, except for a most unlikely autograph, would be almost redundant and of little significance. Responsa manuscripts are frequently of great usefulness for not only the halakhic but also the historical materials they contain.

The intensive institutional and individual efforts that are being diligently devoted to the publication of rabbinic texts from manuscripts contribute significantly to our understanding of personalities and trends in the history of rabbinic literature.

Liturgical manuscripts are perhaps the most colorful representatives of Hebrew manuscripts. In the words of Shalom Spiegel, "the standard prayers, the oldest nucleus of the liturgy, always and everywhere became the center of Jewish worship, a bond of union despite geographic dispersal...

[while] new compositions, called *piyyut*, or poetry, constitute... an ever changing and restless element in the Jewish liturgy" (*The Jews, Their History, Culture, and Religion*, ed. L. Finkelstein, 3rd ed., 1960, p. 866). The extant manuscripts faithfully reflect this description. From all the countries of the Jewish Diaspora and from all ages, manuscript prayerbooks for local usage provide us with a wealth of information about the history of the standard prayers but even more about the immense literature of religious poetry. Among the multitudes of *piyyutim* one finds many by the great Hebrew poets of the Middle Ages such as Judah ha-Levi, but also large numbers of liturgical compositions by local talent. Although the literary quality of the poems in the latter category may not be exquisite, they still are important for the study of local tastes and traditions.

Liturgical instructions, frequently in the vernacular—Judeo-French, Judeo-Greek, Judeo-Persian, and, of course, Judeo-Arabic, Yiddish, and Ladino—offer rich research opportunities for linguists and for historians of liturgy. In this group we are also blessed with many beautifully illuminated and decorated codices, as lavish Haggadah and prayerbook manuscripts demonstrate. Prayerbooks of smaller communities often remained in manuscript and, accordingly, are our only source for their particular liturgy. This was the case with the rite of the small communities of Asti, Fossano, and Moncalvo of Northern Italy (usually referred to by the acronym APAM), of which there are many fine manuscripts but no printed editions.

While liturgical manuscripts display great variety, mainly dictated by the geographical dispersal of the Jews, manuscripts in Jewish thought, philosophy, ethics, mysticism, and homiletics reflect the vast differences of interest conditioned by the changing intellectual preoccupation among the Jews during their long history. In the Middle Ages, up to approximately the fifteenth century, the works of Aristotle, accompanied by the commentaries of Averroës, in Hebrew translation, dominated the field. Large collections of these works are preserved on the shelves of the great libraries of the world, and they are studied for what they contribute to the general, not only Jewish, history of medieval philosophy. The classic works of Jewish philosophers and ethicists, Bahya, Maimonides, Albo, and others, are available in many manuscripts. Interestingly, some codices containing Maimonides' *Guide to the Perplexed* are richly illuminated, for example, the *Copenhagen Codex*.

Toward the fourteenth century, manuscripts containing mystical works began to appear. The sixteenth and seventeenth centuries produced more and more manuscripts in this field. The majority of these texts of the Kabbalah remained in manuscript form until recent centuries. There was reluctance among the leaders of the Jewish community to allow wide circulation for esoteric, mystical writings and, accordingly, many kabbalistic works were copied only privately. The popular *Ets Hayyim* by the famous sixteenth century kabbalist Hayyim Vital was not printed until the end of the eighteenth century, when many handwritten copies of it were produced in Europe and in North Africa.

It should be pointed out that there were other reasons as well for the continued use of handwritten books at a time when printing was widespread. In distant places, for example, Yemen, the art of printing was never practiced and the rich and ancient literature of Yemenite Jews was transmitted in manuscript form from generation to generation. This explains why, among Yemenite manuscripts, there are many of late vintage, some even from the twentieth century. When such manuscripts contain standard texts, their significance for scholarship or even as collectors' items is minimal. On the other hand, they often preserve older traditions. Only individual examination will determine a given manuscript's importance, if any.

Alongside well-known works of Jewish philosophy and ethics, one finds many manuscript collections of homiletical materials. These must be judged individually and considered frequently as no more than private notebooks. Works on medicine and the sciences, especially astronomy, a subject which was important beyond its intrinsic merit for calendar calculation, are common among the older libraries of Hebrew manuscripts. These include the works of Greek, Latin, and Arabic physicians, mathematicians, and scientists in Hebrew translation. As in philosophy, Jews played a prominent role in the Middle Ages as translators of the classical and Arabic scientific heritage; thanks to their activity, works by Galen, Hippocrates, Euclid, Ptolemy, Avicenna, and others are preserved in Hebrew versions. Toward the beginning of modern times, these works became all but obsolete and were rarely copied or reprinted; historians of the sciences must therefore rely mainly on medieval manuscripts.

Manuscripts also contain diverse materials of a belletristic nature. Poems, both secular and religious, stories, folktales, dramatic works, parodies, etc., in Hebrew, or in the vernacular but in Hebrew characters, constitute a large segment of Hebrew manuscript collections, especially those assembled more recently. Many of these works were intended for private or local use, and the works of even famous poets were rarely collected in complete manuscripts and survive in fragmentary sources, often only among the leaves of the Cairo *Genizah*.

There are, of course, other groups of manuscripts of great importance. Karaite manuscripts, some older ones in a mixture of Hebrew and Arabic characters, Hebrew dictionaries and grammars, polemical works that were composed for the frequent disputations between Jews and Christians or Muslims, all provide material for the interested scholar. Manuscripts of the record books of the various Jewish communities and societies, containing minutes, by-laws, and personal and financial records, were by nature intended for local use and were preserved in community, society, or family archives. With the destruction of old Jewish communities, the surviving, scattered examples of this type of document assumed a highly important place in libraries of Hebrew manuscripts. These handwritten records became the primary source for the study of the political, economic, and social history of the Jews throughout the ages. Furthermore, they serve as a mine of genealogical and biographical information. Since some of these sources require expertise in many disciplines as well as familiarity with languages and many types of script, relatively few have been published in full scholarly editions. Thus, a great deal of painstaking, systematic work still awaits the attention of the competent historian.

Since the Holocaust, the appreciation of Hebrew manuscripts as testimony to the spiritual and historical greatness of destroyed Jewish life has assumed new dimensions. The overwhelming loss of Jewish treasures during the Third Reich has made the survivor generation much more conscious of the need for the preservation and exploration of what remains. The dramatic upsurge in Jewish studies, in Israel and in the United States, has led many scholars to the study and publication of Hebrew manuscripts. Through the ready availability of modern technology, microfilming, computerization, and the growth of the reprint industry, scholars have built upon the advances that had already been achieved. Progress will undoubtedly continue, and still-hidden treasures preserved among the leaves of Hebrew manuscripts will come to light: to enrich, to instruct, and to add to our understanding of the Jewish heritage.

Hebrew Manuscripts and Printed Books Among the Sephardim Before and After the Expulsion

The production of Hebrew manuscripts[1] and printed books[2] flourished in the second half of the fifteenth century in Spain and Portugal. Indeed, several features of Hebrew bookmaking were unique to Sephardic Jewry at the time and not found in other Jewish centers. These features made the decades prior to the expulsion extraordinary in the history of the Hebrew book.[3]

1 There are no monographs, to the best of my knowledge, that deal with Hebrew manuscript making in Sepharad in the second half of the fifteenth century. There are, however, a number of relatively recent publications that offer valuable information on Hebrew paleography and codicology in general, including many aspects of the subject under discussion here. See Malachi Beit-Arié, *Hebrew Codicology*, 2nd ed. (Paris, 1981); and *idem*, *The Makings of the Medieval Hebrew Book* (Jerusalem, 1993); Binyamin Richler, *Hebrew Manuscripts: A Treasured Legacy* (Cleveland, 1990); Colette Sirat, *Min ha-Ketav 'el ha-Sefer* (Jerusalem, 1992) [See now: Colette Sirat, *Hebrew Manuscripts of the Middle Ages* (Cambridge, 2002); and Michael Riegler, "Colophons of Medieval Hebrew Manuscripts as Historical Sources" (in Hebrew), Ph.D. diss., Hebrew University, Jerusalem, 1995. Of course, the most important source for the study of medieval Hebrew manuscripts is the multivolume, still unfinished work by Colette Sirat and Malachi Beit-Arié, eds., *Manuscrits médiévaux en caractères hébraïques* (Jerusalem-Paris, 1972). For illuminated manuscripts, see Bezalel Narkiss, *Hebrew Illuminated Manuscripts in the British Isles*, vol. I: *The Spanish and Portuguese Manuscripts*, 2 parts (Jerusalem and London, 1982).

2 On Hebrew printing in Spain and Portugal in general, see the old survey by Joshua Bloch, "Early Hebrew Printing in Spain and Portugal," in Charles Berlin, ed., *Hebrew Printing and Bibliography* (1938; repr. New York, 1976), pp. 7-56. On Hebrew printing in Portugal, see Arthur Anselmo, *Les origines de l'imprimerie au Portugal* (Paris, 1983). For thorough and detailed treatments of some aspects of Hebrew printing on the Iberian Peninsula, see H.Z. Dimitrovsky, *S'ridei Bavli: Fragments from Spanish and Portuguese Incunabula and Bibliographical Century Printing of the Babylonian Talmud and Alfasi: An Historical and Bibliographical Introduction* (in Hebrew) (New York, 1979); Eleazer Hurvitz, *Mishneh Torah of Maimonides* (in Hebrew) (New York, 1985), introduction, esp. pp. 39-44; and Peretz Tishby, "Hebrew Incunabula: Spain and Portugal (Guadalajara)" (in Hebrew), *Kiryat Sefer* 61 (1986-87), pp. 521-46.

3 Eleazar Gutwirth's forthcoming article, "Jewish Readers and Their Libraries in Late-Medieval Spain" is expected to shed light on the subject [I was unable to determine whether this article was published or wasn't]. See Eleazar Gutwirth and Miguel Ángel Motis Dolader, "Twenty-Six Jewish Libraries from Fifteenth-Century Spain," *Library* 18 (1996), pp. 27-53, esp. note 4.

One of these features was the assumed existence of a workshop for creating Hebrew manuscripts in Lisbon. Unlike Christian manuscripts, the production of which took place mostly in scriptoria, Hebrew manuscripts in the Middle Ages were written by individual scribes and not in workshops.[4] A possible exception is a Lisbon workshop that flourished between the 1460s and the 1490s. This atelier produced attractive illuminated Hebrew manuscripts, mainly Bibles and prayer-books, but also a *Mishneh Torah* of Maimonides and calligraphically beautiful, although nonilluminated, manuscripts of Kimḥi's grammar, Naḥmanides' commentary on the Pentateuch, and Joseph ibn Shem Tob's commentary on Aristotle's *Ethics*.[5] Unfortunately, there are no external sources about the history of this atelier, its inner workings, and its personnel. The evidence is in the manuscripts themselves, in their style and in the occasional laconic statements in the colophons relating to the place and date of their writing and to the identity of the copyists. It is noteworthy that it was on the Iberian Peninsula that the appreciation for aesthetically pleasing, fine manuscripts led to what was apparently the only institutionalized undertaking among medieval Jews for the production of Hebrew codices. Manuscript making in Lisbon also influenced the newly introduced art of printing by movable type, which began there in the 1480s. The Hebrew manuscripts of the Lisbon school and the printed books of the Lisbon Hebrew press bear some similarity in the character of letters and in the layout and decoration of the pages.[6]

Another phenomenon found among Sephardic Jewry was perhaps similar to the organized effort for the writing of Hebrew manuscripts in

4 Beit-Arié, *The Makings of the Medieval Hebrew Book*, p. 78.

5 See Gabrielle Sed-Rajna, *Manuscrits hébreux de Lisbonne: Un atalier de copistes et d'enlumineurs au XVe siècle* (Paris, 1970); and Thérèse Metzger, *Les Manuscrits hébreux copiés e décorés à Lisbonne dans les dernières décennies du Xve siècle* (Paris, 1977). The fact that some famous scribes worked with apprentices (Richler, *Hebrew Manuscripts*, p. 41) and that many manuscripts were written by more than one scribe in stereotype scripts (Beit-Arié, *The Making of the Medieval Hebrew Book*, pp. 78-79), does not necessarily mean that these were institutional efforts. As Beit-Arié points out: "Hebrew manuscripts in the Lisbon workshop and in the various Rabbinic academies (see below), may have been the exception and may have been initiated by the workshop or the academy." See also Riegler, "Colophons." p. 107.

6 See Sed-Rajna, *Manuscrits hébreux*, pp. 51, 107; but see Metzger, *Les manuscrits hébreux*, pp. 14-17, according to whom the influence was not as pronounced as it was proposed by Sed-Rajna. On the affinity between Hebrew manuscripts and the first products of the Hebrew press in general, see Beit-Arié, *The Making of the Medieval Hebrew Book*, pp. 251-77.

the Lisbon workshop. There are some references in colophons to manuscripts copied in the rabbinic academies of Spain.[7] In Seville, the scribe Jacob ben Joshua Frontino copied manuscripts in 1471 and 1474 in the synagogue called Ibn Yaish. One manuscript contained a halakhic work, *Ḥazeh ha-tenufah*, and the other the Book of Proverbs, with commentaries by Ibn Ezra, Kimḥi, and Gersonides. Joseph ben Joshua Frontino, most likely a brother of Jacob, was active as a scribe of Hebrew manuscripts in the Jewish quarter of Fez, probably after the expulsion.[8] Fez, as we shall soon see, was the site of organized scribal and printing activity in the second decade of the sixteenth century. The involvement of the Frontino brothers in scribal work in the Ibn Yaish synagogue in Seville and later in the *mellah* of Fez, seems to indicate not only the continuation of a family tradition but also that of an established and perhaps institutionalized endeavor of Hebrew book production. In Saragossa, in 1471, Moses Narboni's commentary on al-Ghazzali's *The Intentions of Philosophers* was copied in the academy of Rabbi Abraham Bibago.[9] A manuscript of Judah Halevi's *Kuzari* was written in 1490 by a Spanish scribe in the academy of Rabbi Moses ibn Habib of Lisbon, in the Southern Italian city of Bitonto.[10] The Responsa of Asher ben Jehiel were copied in the academy of Rabbi Isaac Aboab in Guadalajara in 1491.[11] Guadalajara was the site of a Hebrew press, too.[12] This tradition was apparently transported by the exiles from the Iberian Peninsula to their new home in Fez. Members of a society of scholars (*ḥavurah*) that was established in Fez by a Castilian exile, Rabbi Judah Uzziel, were engaged as scribes of Hebrew manuscripts.[13] Other Iberian traditions of book-making were carried out in this city. It is well known that Abudraham's commentary on the prayerbook, originally printed in Lisbon in 1489, was reprinted in Fez in 1516 and followed the layout and typographical arrangement of that of the Lisbon edition to the letter.[14] Similarly,

7 On manuscripts copied in study houses and yeshivot, see Riegler, "Colophons," pp. 162-72.

8 Sirat and Beit-Arié, *Manuscrits médiévaux*, 3:3 and nn. 2,4.

9 *Ibid.*, 3:5.

10 British Library, Harley 5779 (Catalogue Margoliouth, no. 901).

11 Manuscript R 1351 in the Library of the Jewish Theological Seminary.

12 See Tishby, "Hebrew Incunabula"; A.K. Offenberg, *Hebrew Incunabula in Public Collections* (Nieuwkoop, 1990), p. 187.

13 Sirat and Beit-Arié, *Manuscrits médiévaux*, 3:62 and n. 1; Riegler, "Colophons," p. 169.

14 Dimitrovsky, *S'ridei Bavli*, pp. 61-70.

fragments of editions of the Talmud published in Fez closely resembled their earlier Iberian counterparts.[15]

In one of the few elegies on the expulsion that has come down to us, the author, Abraham ibn Bukrat, mourns the destruction of book-filled academies. He referred probably to the existence of extensive libraries in the yeshivot of Sepharad. Still, he may have wanted to imply that the yeshiva had also served as a place for the organized production of Hebrew books.[16]

There seem to have been two kinds of scriptoria in Sepharad, the Lisbon type, on the one hand, and various academic types, on the other hand. Further, the Lisbon atelier served the needs of well-to-do laypeople, producing mainly lavish illuminated Bibles and prayerbooks, while the academies provided manuscripts for scholars in the areas of halakhah, philosophy, and other disciplines.

The introduction of one of mankind's greatest inventions, printing by movable type, occurred in Spain and Portugal in the waning years of Jewish life there. As a result of the abrupt end of the Jewish community on the Iberian Peninsula, Hebrew printed books from there are far less known and far more scarce than Hebrew books printed in the same period in Italy. Generally, Italy is regarded as the cradle of the Hebrew printed book and the name of the Soncinos, the pre-eminent Hebrew printers, is familiar even to the lay public. Hebrew incunabula from Italy have been thoroughly researched for a long period of time, whereas the history of Iberian Hebrew incunabula is much more obscure. If not for the expulsion, Hebrew printing in Sepharad would have become as significant as that of Italy. The first Hebrew book in Spain was probably printed in 1476, just one year after the printing of the first dated Hebrew book in Italy.[17] In the following years, Hebrew presses were established in Zamora, Hijar, Leiria, Faro, and Lisbon, and perhaps also in Montalbán and Toledo.[18] The products of these presses yield considerable knowledge on various aspects of Jewish life and learning. In addition

15 *Ibid.*, p. 25 ff., p. 58 ff.

16 Published by Hayyim Hillel Ben-Sasson, in *Tarbiẓ* 31 (1961), p. 68 (line 53).

17 Both books contain Rashi's commentary to the Pentateuch, testimony to the popularity of this work among Jews. The Italian edition was printed in Reggio di Calabria (Offenberg, *Hebrew Incunabula*, no. 112), the Spanish one in Guadalajara (Offenberg, *Hebrew Incunabula*, no. 113).

18 See the literature listed in note 2.

to the names of the printers, frequently members of well-known families, and the dates and places of printing,[19] the colophons also reveal attitudes toward the new art. The Iberian printers, like their Italian colleagues, expressed their amazement about the seemingly miraculous quality of the new art to which they refer as a divine gift, heavenly work, and deriving from God.[20]

Allusions to historical events are also found in the colophons. In a Leiria incunabulum, the 1494 Bible, there is explicit mention of the expulsion and its effects on Hebrew printing. The printer speaks about the great anguish that befell the Jewish community as a result of the decree of expulsion. Among its devastating results he counts the decline of Hebrew printing: this glorious, heavenly work suffered its downfall when the Jews were compelled to leave Spain.[21]

Because of this dislocation, alongside easily identifiable incunabula from Spain and Portugal, there exists a puzzling load of unidentified printed fragments of Sephardic origin. Among these are leaves from tractates of the Babylonian Talmud, of Isaac Alfasi's *Halakhot*, and of Maimonides' *Mishneh Torah*. The first discovery of these Sephardic fragments was made at the end of the nineteenth century, and since then they have continued to pose a scholarly quandary. Because of the fragmentary nature of these remnants and because of the similarity between paper and type used on the Iberian Peninsula and that used by exiles in Fez, Constantinople, and Salonika, scholars could not determine which of the fragments were pre-expulsion and which were post-expulsion. Recently, however, as a result of painstaking research, new

19 A list of places, dates, and printers is found in Offenberg's *Hebrew Incunabula*, pp. 186-94.

20 Jacob ben Asher, *Tur Yoreh De'ah* (Hijar, 1486-1487), colophon: *le-nes hi' be-khol peh* (see A. Freimann, *Thesaurus typographie hebraicae saeculi XV* [Berlin, 1924-31; repr. Jerusalem, c. 1967], B. 9,2; Offenberg, *Hebrew Incunabula*, no. 72); Pentateuch (Hijar, 1490), colophon: *re'u sefer ve-'ein kofer le-mofetav, mattan 'elokim* (Freimann, B 11,4; Offenberg, *Hebrew Incunabula*, no. 16); Rashi on Pentateuch (Zamora, 1492 [?]), colophon: *'ale deyo neyyar she-lo ke-derekh* (Freimann, B 13,3; Offenberg, *Hebrew Incunabula*, no. 114 bis); Former Prophets (Leiria, 1494), colophon: *mel'ekhet shamayim* (Freimann, B 27,5; Offenberg, *Hebrew Incunabula*, no. 28); Pentateuch, colophon, from the Genizah, quoted by Hurvitz, *Mishneh Torah of Maimonides*, 30, end of n. 101: *me-'et h[a-shem] hayeta zot.*

21 In the colophon of Former Prophets (Leiria, 1494) (Freimann, *Thesaurus*, B 27,5; Offenberg, *Hebrew Incunabula*, no. 28). The relevant passages from the colophon are quoted and discussed by Isaiah Tishby, *Messianism in the Time of the Expulsion from Spain and Portugal* (in Hebrew) (Jerusalem, 1985), p. 25, n. 41.

criteria were established for classifying the material with greater accuracy. This made it possible to know what tractates of the pre-expulsion Sephardic editions of the Babylonian Talmud are extant and to identify printed editions of various other works, among them printed fragments of pre-exilic editions of the *Mishneh Torah*.[22] The latter were printed in square letters resembling the monumental square Hebrew script so familiar from medieval Spanish synagogue inscriptions and from formal biblical codices. The anonymity of these leaves, the lack of any identifying features such as place, date, and name of printer, led to the suggestion that the books represented by these fragments were produced clandestinely by Marranos. In archival sources mention is made of a Marrano, Juan de Lucena, and his daughters who, according to the accusations of the Inquisition, were producing Hebrew books set in Hebrew type. Although no actual book from this alleged press can be identified with certainty, the assumption that the anonymous *Mishneh Torah* fragments were the work of Juan de Lucena is quite alluring.[23]

Other fragments, most significant among them leaves of the first illustrated printed Haggadah, may have been produced in Spain before the expulsion and not, as was previously assumed, in Constantinople in the second decade of the sixteenth century.[24]

Despite some of the uncertainty regarding the attributions of these unidentified fragments as the products of the Hebrew printing presses of Spain and Portugal, there is no doubt that right up to the expulsion there existed on the Iberian Peninsula a rich and varied printing activity, alongside the continued making of Hebrew manuscripts. Indeed, as Joseph Hacker has amply documented,[25] the exiles mention an abundance of Hebrew books possessed by Jews of Spain and Portugal, but they also refer to the fact that they were able to take their books with them on their

22 Dimitrovsky, *S'ridei Bavli*; Hurvitz, *Mishneh Torah of Maimonides*.

23 Bloch, "Early Hebrew Printing," pp. 9-16; Hurvitz, *Mishneh Torah of Maimonides*, pp. 39-44.

24 Yosef Hayim Yerushalmi, *Leaves from the Oldest Illustrated Printed Haggadah* (Philadelphia, 1974), pp. 7-18, supplement to Yosef Hayim Yerushalmi, *Haggadah and History* (Philadelphia, 1974).

25 Joseph Hacker, "Patterns of Intellectual Activity of Ottoman Jewry in the Sixteenth and Seventeenth Centuries" (in Hebrew), *Tarbiẓ* 53 (1984), pp. 569-606, esp. 579 and n. 25.

wanderings. Abraham ibn Yaish[26] and Abraham Saba[27] both speak about innumerable books that were lost during the flight from the Iberian Peninsula. David ibn Yahya, another exile, relates that he had lost three-quarters of his collection of four hundred books.[28] Isaac Abravanel tells us that he had sent "whatever the hail has left" (Exodus 10:12) from his books to Salonika.[29]

The combined number of Hebrew manuscripts from the Iberian Peninsula and of Hebrew codices written in Sephardic script by scribes from Spain and Portugal in Italy and in Byzantium is, surprisingly, greater than the number of Hebrew books copied by native scribes in Italy, long considered to be the "homeland" of Hebrew manuscripts.[30] The popularity of Spanish Hebrew manuscripts in Italy can be seen from the humorous description by Immanuel of Rome of the Italian adventures of a bookseller from Toledo in the fourteenth century.[31] The basic point of the story, that Hebrew manuscripts from Spain were highly desirable in Italy and that Italian Jews were ready even to commit mischief in order to obtain them, is probably valid for the fifteenth century as well.

The expulsion put an end to a rich and productive tradition in the area of scribal and printing activity. Hebrew books became the target of banning, burning, and confiscation or were victims of loss and abandonment.[32] Despite these adversities, as mentioned above,[33] many exiles managed to take their books with them.

26 In the colophon to the 1505-1506 Constantinople edition of the Bible, see Abraham Yaari, *Hebrew Printing at Constantinople* (in Hebrew) (Jerusalem 1967), p. 60. He says that the books were lost on "dryland and on the sea." Similarly, in a report by Joseph ibn Shraga, it is mentioned that books were lost at sea. Hacker, "Patterns of Intellectual Activity," p. 579.

27 Dan Manor, "Abraham Sabba: His Life and Work" (in Hebrew), *Jerusalem Studies in Jewish Thought* 2 (1982-83), p. 227. He refers to his books as his writing instruments.

28 Hacker, "Patterns of Intellectual Activity," p. 579.

29 Isaac Abravanel, *She'elot le-Rabbi Sha'ul ha-Kohen* (Venice, 1574), p. 18a.

30 See the interesting statistics in Beit-Arié, *The Makings of the Medieval Hebrew Book*, p. 49. About Italy as the "homeland" of Hebrew manuscripts, see Abraham Berliner, *Ketavim Nivḥarim* 2 (Jerusalem, 1949), p. 83.

31 *The Cantos of Immanuel of Rome*, ed. Dov Jarden (Jerusalem, 1957), 1:161-66.

32 On King Manuel's decree to seize Hebrew books, see report of Abraham Saba, William Popper, *The Censorship of Hebrew Books*, introduction by Moshe Carmilly-Weinberger (New York, 1969), p. 20; Manor, "Abraham Sabba," pp. 212-13; Meir Benayahu, "A New Source Concerning the Spanish Refugees in Portugal and Their Move to Salonika" (in Hebrew), *Sefunot* 11 (1971-77), pp. 244-45.

33 See note 23.

There are two manuscripts in the library of the Jewish Theological Seminary that include on their pages the account of having been taken from Spain and from Portugal at the time of the expulsion. A manuscript Bible records the following colophon:

> This volume, which contains the twenty-four sacred books, was written by the learned Rabbi Abraham Calif in the City of Toledo, in Spain. It was finished in the month of Nissan 5252 [1492]. And on the seventh day of the month of Av in the selfsame year, the exiles of Jerusalem who were in Spain, went forth dismayed and banished by the royal edict. And I, Ḥayyim ibn Ḥayyim, have copied therein part of the Masorah and the variants in the year 5257 [1497] in the city of Constantinople.[34]

Hence, it is clear from this colophon that the unfinished manuscript was taken from Spain in 1492 and was completed five years later in Constantinople. The other manuscript is Shem Tob ben Shem Tob's *Sefer ha-'Emunot*, an anti-Maimonidean polemic against philosophy. Because of its controversial nature, this work had been copied only rarely. In 1497 the Portuguese ruler, King Manuel, issued a decree forbidding Jews to possess Hebrew books. He ordered that they be surrendered and deposited in synagogues. The JTS manuscript of *Sefer ha-'Emunot* was among books that ended up in a synagogue in Lisbon, where it was locked up and made inaccessible to its former Jewish owners. Somehow, exiles managed to remove the manuscript and take it with them on the journey to Constantinople or Salonika. Thus was the manuscript of *Sefer ha-'Emunot* saved. The story of its vicissitudes is told on the margin of the manuscript, concluding with the words: "It was brought here to the Ottoman Empire by the exiles from Spain and Portugal."[35]

The exiles not only tried to save their books and bring them to their new homes, but also, very soon after their arrival — indeed, even at a time when they had not yet had a permanent home — they resumed their activities as scribes and printers, as preservers and transmitters of knowledge.

34 JTS Manuscript, Bible collection, L 6. See *Illuminated Hebrew Manuscripts from the Library of the Jewish Theological Seminary* (New York, 1965), no. 6.

35 JTS Manuscript no. 1969. See Benayahu, "A New Source," p. 236 ff., esp. 262, where the marginal inscription is quoted. On King Manuel's decree, see note 30 above.

The manuscript of Joseph ibn Shoshan's commentary on the *Sayings of the Fathers* was written in Tunis, in 1496. The scribe, an exile from Spain, states in the colophon: "I, the unfortunate, a man of suffering, copied these commentaries, while on the shores of Tunis, in the house of eminent and righteous people in a room in the attic that they put at my disposal. And as we were expelled from our homeland..."[36] There are other testimonies in which scribes mention the fact that they were exiles from Spain and Portugal, and in a few instances they indicate the year the manuscript was copied by counting from the expulsion, for example, "year two of the Spanish exile."[37]

Hebrew manuscripts continued to be written in the new communities, but the introduction of printing by Iberian exiles in Constantinople, Salonika, and Fez made the printing press the dominant instrument of publishing, with far-reaching effects on Jewish religious and cultural life. Perhaps the most telling example of the introduction of printing in the newly established communities is the story of the printing, by Spanish exiles, of Jacob ben Asher's *'Arba'ah Turim* in Constantinople. Despite the fact that there is an explicit date, 1493, in the colophon, scholars have long debated when this edition was actually published. Alexander Marx and his brother, Moses Marx, took the date at face value and emphasized its meaning for demonstrating how speedily the Spanish exiles began the reconstruction of their cultural and religious life. After all, to print a bulky volume such as the *'Arba'ah Turim* just one year after the expulsion, in a faraway location, is a sign of great vitality and a proof of strong determination to start the rebuilding of the community. Others, however — De Rossi, Steinschneider, Goldschmidt, and Yaari — doubted that it was possible to print such a major work just one year after the expulsion. They argued that the printers needed time to arrive in the Balkans from the Iberian Peninsula, and considerable time was also required for setting up an operation capable of carrying out a project of such magnitude. Accordingly, these scholars maintained that the explicit date was a typographical error, and they suggested a later date: 1503. A.K. Offenberg, on the basis of the evidence of the paper and its watermarks and the typographical material, proved that

36 Sirat and Beit-Arié, *Manuscrits médiévaux*, 3:51.

37 *Ibid.*, 3:49, also 55. Cf. Joseph Hacker, "New Chronicle on the Expulsion of the Jews from Spain: Its Causes and Results," *Zion* 44 (1979), p. 202, n. 6.

the book was indeed printed in 1493, and this is the year when Hebrew printing in Constantinople started.[38]

After the printing of the *'Arba'ah Turim*, the nascent Hebrew press of Constantinople issued a series of major works: the Bible with commentaries by Rashi, David Kimḥi, and Abraham ibn Ezra, in 1505-1506,[39] the *Halakhot* by Isaac Alfasi in 1509,[40] and the *Mishneh Torah* by Maimonides in the same year.[41] These were monumental undertakings, large, multivolume, copious folio productions, efforts that required a great deal of technical skill, scholarship, and financial investment. The printers and the people associated with them were fully aware of the importance of their historical mission: transplanting Jewish learning from the Iberian Peninsula to the new Jewish centers established by the exiles. This sense of mission is clearly expressed in the lengthy colophon of the 1505-1506 Bible. The colophon was written by Abraham ben Joseph ibn Yaish, the editor and corrector of the work, an exile from Spain and a well-known rabbi:

> From the day that God had confounded the speech of the whole earth through the bitter and impetuous exile, the exile from Sepharad, all good things have abandoned us... The few survivors were compelled to wander from country to country... In the wake of the terror of the persecutions the books, too, were gone... People neglect to teach their children because of the vicissitudes of the times and the unavailability of books... When one finds a copy of the Torah, the Targum will be lacking, and if there is available a copy of the Targum, the Commentary [that is, Rashi's] will be missing... Suddenly, God provided a remedy. A few survivors, coming from many directions... found their way to Constantinople, among them two brothers, David and Samuel Nechamias, who were blessed by

38 On the influence of Hebrew printing in the Ottoman Empire and the literature about it, see Hacker, "Patterns of Intellectual Activity," pp. 576-77, and n. 13. On the Constantinople *'Arba'ah Turim*, see A.K. Offenberg, "The First Printed Book Produced at Constantinople," *Studia Rosenthaliana* 3 (1969), pp. 96-112, where the literature on the subject is reviewed. [See now: A.K. Offenberg, *A Choice of Corals* (Nieuwkoop, 1992), pp. 102-132.]

39 Yaari, *Hebrew Printing*, no. 2; Nigel Allan, "A Typographical Odyssey: The 1505 Constantinople Pentateuch," *Journal of the Royal Asiatic Society*, ser. 3, I,3 (1991), pp. 343-51.

40 Yaari, *Hebrew Printing*, no. 5.

41 *Ibid.*, no. 6.

> God to be great experts in the art of printing... They decided to spread the knowledge of Torah among Israel, to make up, even though only to a small extent, for the innumerable books that were destroyed on land and on sea.[42]

In the 1509 edition of Maimonides' *Mishneh Torah*, the printers bemoan the destruction of the Jewish communities of Sepharad, the forced exile imposed upon them, and the consequences of these dislocations, including the loss of books and the diminution of learning and scholarship. In view of these vicissitudes, they regard their own activities in spreading knowledge through printing as the "restoration of the fallen tabernacle of the Torah."[43]

In the subsequent decades, the printing presses of the cities of the Ottoman Empire, operated mainly by Iberian exiles, were churning out Hebrew books in large number and in many subject areas. Again, a comparison with Italy may be helpful. It is noteworthy that it was in Constantinople and Salonika that the first editions of midrashim and midrashic anthologies appeared in print.[44] The *Midrash Rabbah*, the halakhic midrashim, the *Tanḥuma*', the Midrash on Psalms and Proverbs, *Pirke de-Rabbi 'Eliezer*, the '*Ein Ya'akov*, the *Haggadot ha-Talmud*, and so on, all were printed for the first time by Spanish exiles in Constantinople and Salonika, followed only decades later by Italian editions. The reason for including these titles among the early editions produced by Sephardic printers may have been related to the importance of sermons in the newly established exile communities. Sermons provided solace and guidance following the recent traumas. Indeed, a large number of collections of sermons, some printed but many more in manuscripts, have come down to us from this period.[45] Since the sermons were, of course, based on midrashic sources, it is plausible to assume that the practical needs of the rabbis for appropriate source material for their homiletic activity was what prompted the printing of midrashim and midrashic anthologies in the first two decades of the establishment of Hebrew presses in the Ottoman Empire.

42 *Ibid.*, no. 2, p. 60; Allan, "A Typographical Odyssey," p. 350.

43 Yaari, *Hebrew Printing*, no. 6, p. 63.

44 Hacker, "Patterns of Intellectual Activity," p. 585, n. 39.

45 *Ibid.*, pp. 583-93.

Alongside the traditional literature — Bible and commentaries, rabbinic classics and their commentaries, codes, philosophy and ethics — other subject matter, such as belles lettres, responsa, poetry, grammar, medicine, mathematics, history, and travel, were also represented among the books published. The wide-ranging intellectual interest of the exile communities is attested to also by the report that many copies of al-Ghazzali's writings were circulating in Salonika in the sixteenth century.[46] Al-Ghazzali's works on logic may have been much in demand because of the dominance of the philosophical-logical method of Talmud study that was practiced by many talmudists in the period.[47] This prolific printing activity was aided and stimulated by the existence of great private collections of Hebrew manuscripts and printed books. Jacob ibn Habib, in the introduction to his *'Ein Ya'akov*, writes that although he had planned to publish this collection of talmudic *aggadot* for a long time, he had to delay his work on it because he lacked the books needed for it. But in Salonika, with the help of the extensive libraries owned by members of the Benveniste family, he could finally carry his project to completion.[48] Samuel di Modena and Joseph ben Leb also mention books that they had found in the private libraries of the same family.[49] An elegy included in the Ninth of Av liturgy of an Ashkenazic *maḥzor* printed in Salonika mourns the losses from a great fire that devastated Salonika in 1545. Among these, the destruction of Samuel Benveniste's collection of books occupies a prominent place. We learn from this elegy that Don Samuel used to hire scribes to copy for him "innumerable" copies of the books of the Talmud, codes, and commentaries. The author, Benjamin ben Meir ha-Levi Ashkenazi, refers to "ḥibburim... penimiyyim ve-ḥiẓoniyyim," perhaps meaning writings not only by Jewish but also by non-Jewish authors, such as al-Ghazzali, just mentioned. He also speaks about the physical beauty of the books, some of which were copied on fine parchment.[50] Indeed, it is noteworthy that among the earliest books printed in Constantinople and Salonika, a disproportio-

46 *Ibid.*, p. 578, n. 20.

47 On this method, see Daniel Boyarin, *Ha-'Iyyun ha-Sefaradi: Le-Farshanut ba-Talmud Shel Megorashe Sefarad* (Jerusalem, 1989).

48 Hacker, "Patterns of Intellectual Activity," pp. 577-79.

49 *Ibid.*

50 *Maḥzor*, Ashkenazi rite. Salonika c. 1555-1556 (no pagination), in the *kinah*, "Le-Mi 'Oy le-Mi Hoy" (Israel Davidson, *Thesaurus of Medieval Hebrew Poetry* [New York, 1970], *lamed*, 1085).

nately large number were produced on parchment, a clear sign of interest in bibliophilic, aesthetically pleasing editions.[51] In this connection, mention should also be made of Rabbi David ibn Zimra, the Radbaz, who possessed a large library in Cairo and who encouraged scholars to copy works that he owned.[52]

This survey has attempted to demonstrate the centrality and diversity of the Hebrew book in the life of Sephardic Jews in a time of great historical upheaval. The Hebrew book, in its physical form and as an idea, became, as at so many other times in Jewish history, a symbol of memory, survival, continuity, and vitality.

51 See A. Freimann, "Die hebräischen Pergamentdrucke," *Zeitschrift für hebräische Bibliographie* 15 (1911), pp. 46-57, nos. 31, 32, 34, 35, 37, 40, 41, 42, 45, etc.

52 Hacker, "Patterns of Intellectual Activity," p. 578, n. 20; Yaari, *Hebrew Printing*, pp. 122-23.

Hebrew Incunabula: An Agenda for Research

The first questions in Hebrew incunabula research are most basic: how many incunabula are there, what are they, and where are they? The answers to these simple questions are by no means easy. Since incunabula were printed without title pages, and some without colophons, and since there are many early Hebrew printed books that survive only in a most fragmentary state, the identification of certain early Hebrew books as incunabula is doubtful and, at times, hotly debated.

There was a colorful and rather cantankerous scholar in the last generation by the name of Lazarus Goldschmidt who is perhaps best known as the translator of the Babylonian Talmud into German and who, incidentally, admitted in his old age that in his youth he had fabricated a work in the style of an ancient Aramaic Midrash in order to perpetrate a prank on his scholarly colleagues.[1] Goldschmidt was the author of a small book on Hebrew incunabula[2] in which he poked fun at collectors and dealers who purposely inflate the number of Hebrew incunabula to make their wares more attractive. He maintained that there are no more than 100 Hebrew books which can beyond doubt be claimed as dating back to the 15th century. This figure is the most conservative estimate; the most generous one is made by Herrmann Meyer in the *Encyclopaedia Judaica*, listing 175 books.[3] Current scholarship by Perez Tishby puts their number at 140.[4] Be that as it may, the total number of Hebrew incunabula known to us today does not amount to even one-half percent of the approximately 40,000 non-Hebrew incunabula. Even in the 16th century, their number was very low. The extensive booklists prepared in Italy for the use of Church censors of Hebrew books demonstrate that, e.g., in

1 See *Areshet* (added t.p.: *Aresheth*), vol. 1, 1958, pp. 484-485.

2 Lazarus Goldschmidt, *Hebrew Incunables; a bibliographical essay* (Oxford, 1948).

3 *Encyclopaedia Judaica*, vol. 8, 1971, col. 1335-1344.

4 In the first part of his definitive study on Hebrew incunabula, see *Kiryat Sefer*, vol. 58, 1983, p. 808.

1595, among 20,000 Hebrew printed books, there were only about 100 copies of various incunabula.[5] There is no easy explanation for this. Perhaps one reason for the scarcity of 15th century Hebrew printed books is that they were produced in small editions, normally not exceeding 300 to 400 copies. Also, since many Hebrew incunabula contained basic and much studied texts, they were worn out quickly and, when new editions became available, the older, worn copies were put away as "shemot" [lit. *names* — referring to names of God in Hebrew sacred texts. Worn copies of such texts may not be discarded, and must be buried. — *Eds.*]

No wonder, therefore, that the number of Hebrew incunabula preserved today, even in the most prestigious institutions, is relatively small. The Vatican Library contains 42, the Rosenthaliana in Amsterdam 27, and the Bibliotheque Nationale in Paris 39.[6] Accordingly, the 29 titles represented in a total of 40 copies at Yeshiva University's library place it among the ranking institutions holding 15th century Hebrew printed books, and the publication of Gershon Cohen's catalog[7] of this collection calls the attention of the scholarly world to it for the first time. This publication thus corrects the anomaly found in Goff's census of incunabula in American libraries,[8] in which the Hebrew incunabula of Yeshiva University were completely ignored. Cohen's catalog does more than just put this library on the map of incunabula research; it also proposes to enlarge the number of known Hebrew incunabula. He describes a certain Italian *Mahzor* as having been printed shortly after 1486 and not in 1504 as previously assumed — thus making it an incunabulum.[9]

The first task of the study of Hebrew incunabula remains the establishment of a solid, reliable corpus of the books that belong to this category. This can be achieved by careful and thorough scrutiny of all physical aspects of each book, such as paper, parchment, watermarks, type size, type shape, decorative graphic materials, text arrangement, and

5 See Sh. Simonsohn in *Kiryat Sefer* (added t.p.: *Kirjath Sepher*), vol. 37, 1961, pp. 106-107.

6 On the Vatican, see Tishby's article quoted in note 4, pp. 853-857; on the Rosenthaliana, see A.K. Offenberg in *Studia Rosenthaliana*, vol. 5, 1971, p. 125; and on the Bibliothèque Nationale, see Israel Adler, *Les incunables hébraïques de la Bibliothèque Nationale* (Paris, 1962).

7 Gershon Cohen, *Hebrew Incunabula; Mendel Gottesman Library of Hebraica-Judaica, Yeshiva University* (New York, 1984).

8 F.R. Goff, *Incunabula in American libraries; a third census* (New York, 1964), pp. 316-325.

9 Cohen, *op. cit.*, pp. 39-43.

composition of sheets. Equally important is the study of all statements found in the book itself regarding its printing. The language of these statements, located mostly in the colophons, is often obscure or ambiguous and must be closely analyzed. Let me cite one example. In what is, perhaps, the most beautiful incunabulum that Yeshiva University possesses, the Mantua 1476 *Orah Hayyim*, the printer, Abraham Conat, states:

> And mastered this craft so as to print properly, juxtaposing one forme to another, one thousand columns each day [printing each sheet by processing it twice with] devotion and commitment; [printing] in one process four columns which are on one side of the large folio sheet...

Michael Pollak interprets the colophon as meaning that Conat printed 2,000 columns on 250 sheets each day. Abraham Rosenthal, in a rejoinder, reduces this to mean 1,000 columns, namely, 125 sheets daily, while Gershon Cohen agrees with Rosenthal as to the number of sheets printed each day, but disagrees with him concerning other details of the interpretation.[10]

Information about Hebrew incunabula may also be found in later sources. Again, just one example: an Italian rabbi in a responsum dated 1566, quotes a passage from the Responsa of Rabbi Solomon ibn Adret that he identifies as having been printed in Rome. The discovery of this quotation, and the identification of the book to which it refers, was the first step that led to the conclusion that 9 books — otherwise lacking any indication of place and date — were the products of the very first Hebrew presses in the world that were active in Rome, presumably between the years 1469-1475.[11]

The correct and painstaking description of incunabula in catalogs of public or private collections provides the foundation for a further stage of incunabula research which deals with the cultural, historical, literary, and religious significance of early Hebrew printing.

10 *ibid.*, p. 11; see Michael Pollak, "The daily performance of a printing press in 1476, evidence from a Hebrew incunable," in: *Gutenberg Jahrbuch*, 1974, pp. 66-76 and Avraham Rosenthal's remarks in *Gutenberg Jahrbuch*, 1979, pp. 39-50 (the translation of the colophon is on p. 42).

11 Moses Marx in *The Alexander Marx Jubilee Volume*, English section (New York, 1950), pp. 481-501 and see now Tishby's article quoted in note 4.

The questions that exercise the curiosity of scholars in these areas are the following: who were the first printers of Hebrew books; from whom did they learn their trade; on what basis did they select the books to be printed; what manuscripts did they use; what method did they employ for establishing the text; what was the religious status of books produced by the new craft; and — perhaps the most interesting one — in what ways did the introduction of printing change and affect Jewish life?

It is now generally accepted that the very first Hebrew books produced by movable type were printed in Rome between 1469-1475. These books resemble in all physical aspects the non-Hebrew incunabula produced in Rome at the same time by the Christian printers Sweynheym, Pannartz, and Han.[12] As their names betray, these early typographers were of German origin, as were many later printers of Hebrew books in Italy — the most prominent among them being members of the Soncino family. One may assume, therefore, that the printers of the Hebrew Roman incunabula were also Ashkenazi Jews and that their Christian counterparts may have originally belonged to a circle of apprentices and assistants who had worked with Gutenberg, and parted with him in order to become independent. But there is another line of speculation, not necessarily contradicting or excluding the one mentioned just now. Isaiah Sonne was the first to suggest that with the return of the Pope to Rome from his exile in Avignon, a number of wealthy and learned Jews from Provence also settled in the Papal State.[13] As pointed out by David B. Ruderman, there was a large number of Italians in the Provencal city of Avignon and some Jews, influenced by personal contact with them, may have chosen to try their luck in Italy.[14] There is an isolated piece of information about the Jew, Davino de Caderousse, who, in 1444, in the city of Avignon, was involved in some kind of activity that may have been a precursor of printing.[15] Incidentally, Davino was also an expert in dyeing, an occupation that he shared with one of the first printers of Hebrew books, Abraham ben Hayyim the Dyer of Ferrara, who printed the *Yoreh Deah* in that city in 1477. The craft of dyeing was apparently related to printing.

12 See Tishby, *op. cit.*, p. 815.

13 See *Studies in Bibliography and Booklore*, vol. 2, 1955, p. 12 and esp. p. 19, note 22.

14 David B. Ruderman, *The world of a Renaissance Jew: the life and thought of Abraham ben Mordecai Farissol* (Cincinnati, 1981), pp. 10-11.

15 See Sonne in his article quoted in note 13, p. 19, note 23.

Another datum may be added: a Renaissance Jew by the name of Abraham Farissol worked as a scribe of Hebrew manuscripts, among his many activities and talents. From a highly plausible reconstruction by Ruderman, we know that Farissol left Avignon for Italy in the year 1468 or 1469.[16] As noted above, 1469 was the year in which, in all probability, the first printed Hebrew book appeared in Rome. Farissol lived for a while in Ferrara, where Abraham ben Hayyim the Dyer was engaged in operating a printing press using the type of Abraham Conat from Mantua. Furthermore, Farissol's handwriting — which we know from numerous examples — was similar to the printed type employed in 1476-1477 by the Mantua and Ferrara printers. Ruderman therefore suggests that Farissol may have been one of the scribes whose manuscripts served as a model for the Conat type.[17] On the basis of Ruderman's study, one may further consider Farissol's career as having a bearing on the history of the infancy of Hebrew printing.

It is common knowledge that the early printers encountered opposition by practitioners of the ancient art of the scribes. The scribes had a vested interest in protecting their craft from the new invention that many considered to be the devil's work. We do not have any explicit sources in Jewish literature, as far as I know, about such tension between new printers and old scribes. Farissol's case may, however, suggest the existence of such tensions. At first, as just mentioned, Farissol may have been involved in the pioneering stage of printing by Conat. Conat still refers to the new art of typography as *ketivah*, writing. Also, he considers it *avodat kodesh*, holy work, probably indicating that printed works in Hebrew deserve the same amount of respect and possess the same sanctity as their manuscript counterparts. Interestingly, the question of the sanctity of printed books was the subject of numerous responsa.[18] Conat also states that what he does as a printer is like "writing with many pens," but "*be-lo ma'aseh nisim*" (not through miracles).[19] In these words, one hears an echo of the rejection of the notion that printing is the devil's work. We may thus speculate that Farissol at first saw printing as just another form of writing, and thought that his skills and talents as a scribe

16 See Ruderman, *op. cit.*, *ibid.*

17 *ibid.*, p. 22.

18 See Isaac Zeev Kahana, *Ha-defus be-halakhah*, in: *Sinai*, vol. 16, 1944-45, pp. 49-61.

19 Quoted by Cohen, *op. cit.*, p. 11.

would continue to be in demand. But as typography developed and spread rapidly as an independent instrument of producing books, Farissol realized that the new technique would inevitably render his craft obsolete. His reaction was to disassociate himself from printing, and his name never occurs in any early printed book. Farissol continued to write beautiful manuscripts by hand well into the 16th century. His scribal activity, at a time when printing was already highly developed, may have been an act of protest, as if to demonstrate the excellence and superiority of the scribe's art above the mechanical skills of the printer.

The happy convergence of Provencal, as well as German scholars and artisans to prosperous Italy — in Rome, Mantua and Ferrara — in the third quarter of the 15th century, gave the impetus to the quick emergence and rapid growth of Hebrew printing.

When we turn our attention to questions concerning the kinds of books that were selected to be printed by the first printers and the manuscripts that were used for establishing the texts, we are dealing with a topic that has a bearing on the general cultural, intellectual, and religious profile of the period. The scope of this type of inquiry must encompass not only Italy, but also Spain and Portugal, where Hebrew printing was practiced during a shorter period, beginning a little later than in Italy, and coming to an end with the expulsion of the Jews from Spain in 1492 and from Portugal in 1497. In a recent publication, Robert Bonfil deals with the nature and contents of the libraries of Renaissance Jews.[20] Bonfil emphasizes the importance of comparing the degree of popularity of certain works with others, in order to determine the cultural interests of the community. A work that was rarely copied or printed, even if very learned and important in itself, could not have left its imprint on society. Bonfil, as did other scholars before him, examined some extant library inventories from that period and found that there were very few books on philosophy and Kabbalah in Jewish libraries in the second part of the 15th century. Indeed, among the incunabula, the most commonly found categories are: Bible; Bible commentaries by Rashi, Nahmanides, Kimchi, Gersonides and ibn Ezra; codes by Maimonides, Jacob ben Asher and Moses of Coucy; several tractates of the Babylonian Talmud; liturgical works; certain popular ethical works; and works on grammar (e.g.,

20 R. Bonfil, *The Rabbinate in Renaissance Italy* (Jerusalem, 1979), pp. 174-179.

Kimchi's *Sefer ha-shorashim* that saw 3 editions in fewer than 20 years). On the other hand, we have only two books on philosophy — the *Guide to the Perplexed* by Maimonides and the *Ikarim* by Albo — and none on Kabbalah.[21]

In this connection, one must also raise the problem of book distribution and book trade. Strangely, many of the rarest Hebrew incunabula, especially the Iberian ones, survived in remote places such as Persia and Yemen, and among the fragments of the Cairo *Genizah*. We know very little about how they got there.

Let us now turn to what is, in my view, the most fascinating area of research in connection with early Hebrew printing. What was the impact of Hebrew printed books on Jewish life in the generation in which it was introduced and in the period following it? The only comprehensive article on the subject was published by Abraham Berliner about a century ago.[22] There are, however, in the works of Isaiah Sonne,[23] and, in our generation, those of Sh.Z. Havlin,[24] H.Z. Dimitrovsky,[25] and others, discussions that offer many valuable insights about the decisive influences of printing on the mind of the Jews.

A number of practices were significantly changed as a result of Hebrew printing. In manuscripts, the order of Biblical books was not uniform. In most manuscripts, the Prophets were copied according to the order mentioned in the Talmud: Jeremiah, Ezekiel, Isaiah. The sequence in early printed Bibles is Isaiah, Jeremiah, Ezekiel. In manuscripts, the book of Ruth usually precedes Psalms; in early printed books, it is Psalms that stand at the head of Hagiographa. In both cases, all subsequent editions followed the arrangements found in early printed Bibles.

Perhaps the greatest influence of printing is on the standardization of liturgical texts. Many of the minor local variations disappeared once a

21 See A. Marx, "The Choice of books by the printers of incunabula," in: *To Dr. R.* [A.S.W. Rosenbach] (Philadelphia, 1946), pp. 154-173.

22 Abraham Berliner, *Ueber den Einfluss des ersten hebraeischen Buchdrucks auf den Cultus and die Cultur der Juden*, published originally in 1893-1894 and translated and published in his *Ketavim nivharim*, vol. 2 (Jerusalem, 1949), pp. 113-143.

23 See his "*Tiyulim be-historiyah u-ve-bibliyografiyah,*" in: *The Alexander Marx Jubilee Volume*, Hebrew Section (New York, 1950), pp. 209-235.

24 See introduction to *Responsa of R. Solomon ben Abraham Adret; first edition, Rome ca. 1470* (Jerusalem, 1976).

25 See his *S'ridei Bavli; an historical and bibliographical introduction* (New York, 1979).

small local community acquired a printed *Mahzor* or *Siddur*. The more generalized customs were adopted, and the local usage went out of practice. In addition, the role of the *hazan* as the person who had the authority of excluding or including certain non-obligatory *piyyutim* or private prayers was assumed by the printer, and once his prayerbooks were distributed, they became accepted as standard by worshippers.

The form and direction of Talmud studies, ever since the end of the 15th century, were shaped in a most decisive way by the first printed editions of the Talmud. H.Z. Dimitrovsky gathered and studied all the surviving fragments of the Spanish and Portuguese Talmud incunabula. He then pointed out the substantial variants that exist between the Iberian and Italian traditions.[26] The Iberian tractates preserve the textual traditions of the Spanish academies, whereas the Italian Soncino tractates reflect those of Ashkenaz. Since the Soncino volumes became the foundation of all later editions, and since the Iberian prints disappeared or were destroyed as a result of the expulsion, it was the Ashkenazi tradition of transmitting the text of the Talmud that became the dominant one for all Jewry. Similarly, the decision of the Soncino printers to print Rashi on one side of the Talmud text and certain kinds of *Tosafot* on the other side changed the learning habits of all students of Talmud for all times.[27]

The publication by Yeshiva University of Gershon Cohen's fine and beautiful catalog is surely an event worth celebrating. It carries incunabula research substantially forward, and we hope that it will help to provide inspiration and serve as the stimulus for further study of this multifaceted topic.[28]

The people who made this great achievement possible deserve the gratitude of all lovers of the Hebrew book.

26 *ibid.*

27 See E.E. Urbach, *The Tosaphists*. 4th edition. vol. 1 (Jerusalem, 1980), pp. 29-31.

28 [There is a rich literature on Hebrew incunabula that appeared after the publication of this article. I would like to single out here A.K. Offenberg's *Hebrew incunabula in Public Collections* (Nieuwkoop, 1990), with its rich bibliography as well as the various publications of S.M. Iakerson. See e.g. his "Hebrew incunabula in the Asiatic Museum of St. Petersburg", in: *Judaic in the Slavic Realm*, ed. by Z.M. Baker (Binghamton, N.Y., 2003), pp. 37-37, and his *Catalogue of Hebrew Inconabula from the Collection of the Library of the Jewish Theological Seminary of America*, New York and Jerusalem, 1-2, 2004-2005.]

Hebrew Printing and Publishing in Germany, 1650-1750. On Jewish Book Culture and the Emergence of Modern Jewry

There was a century in early modern Jewish cultural and religious history in Europe that perhaps could best be characterized as an orphan. The approximately one hundred years that fall between the Chmielnicki massacres and the events surrounding the appearance of the pseudo-messiah Sabbatai Zvi at one end, and the emergence of *Hasidism* and Enlightenment at the other end, i.e. the second half of the seventeenth and the first half of the eighteenth century, are usually accorded scant treatment and are denied the kind of scholarly attention given to other, more spectacular periods in European Jewish cultural and religious history.[1] In contrast to the times that begin with Mendelssohn, the century preceding him is relegated into a kind of twilight zone that is regarded as the end of the vanishing Jewish Middle Ages. On the other hand, the years between 1650 and 1713 were recently characterized as a time when Jews, in the realm of economic and political activity, exerted "the most profound and pervasive impact on the West which they were ever to exert, whilst still retaining a large measure of social and cultural cohesion."[2] Culturally and religiously,

1 This paper is based on lectures delivered in 1986 at the Leo Baeck Institute, New York and at Yeshiva University, in conjunction with the latter's exhibition, *Ashkenaz: The German Jewish Heritage*. I wish to express my deep gratitude to Mr. and Mrs. Ludwig Jesselson for encouraging me to explore this subject during a sabbatical year that I spent at Yeshiva University in 1985-1986. I would also like to thank Yehudah Mirsky for his helpful comments on a draft of this paper.

2 Jonathan I. Israel, *European Jewry in the Age of Mercantilism, 1550-1750* (Oxford, 1985), p. [1]. Israel explicitly states that he has "not attempted to say anything new, or import any substantially new emphases, on the religious history of the period." Surprisingly, Israel does not even mention in his bibliography any of Jacob Katz's books that are relevant to the period. Attention should be called here to Azriel Shohet's *Im hillufei tekufoth (Beginnings of the Haskalah among German Jewry)* (Jerusalem, 1960) (in Hebrew) that deals with the first half of

however, the period still remains to be looked upon as inward-directed, self-contained, stagnating and rigid. It seems that a systematic and extensive study of the intellectual life of the German-Jewish community in the century preceding the entry of Jews into modern society could lead to substantive change in this perception. By choosing to explore, albeit tentatively, some aspects of Hebrew printing and publishing in Germany during this period, we hope to gain new insight into the cultural, intellectual and religious conditions of the Jews. This activity, although it may look peripheral now, occupied central stage then, and therefore may serve as a good instrument to be used for drawing a cultural profile of pre-emancipation German Jewry. After the Thirty Years' War, in the middle of the seventeenth century, the rulers of the numerous small sovereignties on German territory were eager to reconstruct the land and to develop strong, independent principalities. Large numbers of Jews from Polish and Russian localities devastated by Chmielnicki, others who were expelled from Vienna in 1670, as well as co-religionists who fled the turmoil in Buda that resulted from recapture of the city from the Turks in 1686, gravitated towards the German lands, where prosperity and relative protection awaited them. In the wake of this movement Hebrew printing in Germany rapidly expanded and, by the end of the seventeenth century, a steady and ever increasing flow of Hebrew and Yiddish books left the recently established printing presses.[3] In order to demonstrate the multifaceted nature of this activity, a few personalities and trends have been selected for describing the phenomenal expansion of Hebrew printing in a relatively short period of time. Through these selections we hope to illustrate the interplay of many factors which were responsible for this development.

the eighteenth century, mainly from the point of view of the social background. See Jacob Katz's discussion of Shohet's book in *Out of the Ghetto* (Cambridge, Mass., 1973), pp. 34ff.

3 See Moritz Steinschneider and David Cassel, *Jüdische Typographie und Jüdischer Buchhandel*, originally published in Ersch und Gruber, *Encyclopädie der Wissenschaften und Künste*, Teil 28 (Leipzig, 1851, reprinted in Jerusalem 1938), pp. 57-70. This is still the most comprehensive survey on the subject. See also *Encyclopaedia Judaica* (German), vol. 6, cols. 66-70: *Druckwesen* and *The Hebrew Book; An Historical Survey*, ed. by Raphael Posner and Israel Ta-Shema (Jerusalem, 1975), pp. 106-111. [See now: The brief chapter on Hebrew printing in Germany by Mordechai Breuer, in *German-Jewish History in Modern Times*, Ed. by Michael A. Meyer, Vol. I (New York, 1996), pp. 222-226; For comprehensive lists of Hebrew books printed in varivos German localities see now: Y. Vinograd, *Thesaurus of the Hebrew Book*. Part II, *Places of Print*, Jerusalem, 1993.]

Our first example is Shabbetai Bass,[4] printer, bibliographer and rabbinic scholar. Bass was a native of Kalisz, Poland, where his parents were killed in a pogrom in 1655. He and his brother survived and fled to Prague. There he became an assistant to the cantor of the *Altneuschul.* After a while, he moved to Amsterdam. The Amsterdam Sefardi community made a tremendous impression on Bass to which he gave expression in the introduction to his book, *Siftei Yeshenim.*[5] In a glowing portrayal of the advanced, progressive ways of the Sefardim, Bass described the organized, graduated, communally financed educational system of the Sefardi Jews of Amsterdam and contrasted them with what he considered to be the backwardness of the Eastern European Jews. *Siftei Yeshenim* is the first Hebrew bibliography compiled by a Jewish author and in it Bass provided not only lists and classifications of books, but also a programme for the establishment of a Jewish educational system which could properly serve the cultural and religious needs of all elements of Jewish society: the learned, the simple, the child, those who were familiar with Hebrew as well as those who only knew Yiddish. In this book, Bass demonstrated openness towards secular subjects, such as mathematics and medicine, and he even included a list of rabbinic works which were available in Latin translations.

The various interests of Bass and his concern for the raising of the educational level of the Jews, prompted him to acquire the technical knowledge required for the establishment of a Hebrew printing press. In 1689, Bass took up residence in a small Silesian town, Dyhernfurth. The town was founded just shortly before this time and the authorities, in order to promote the development of the new locality, granted Bass and a number of Jewish assistants the right to settle in the town and to start operating a Hebrew printing house.[6]

He and his assistants, mainly Jewish craftsmen from Prague and Cracow, constituted the foundation of the Jewish community in the new town. In the foreword to the first book that Bass published in

4 On the life and personality of Bass see the bibliography in Herbert C. Zafren, "Dyhernfurth and Shabtai Bass: a Typographic Profile", in *Studies in Jewish Bibliography, History and Literature in Honour of I. Edward Kiev* (New York, 1971), pp. 546-547.

5 Amsterdam, 1680, f. 8a-b.

6 See Markus Brann, "Geschichte und Annalen der Dyhernfurther Druckerei," in *Montasschrift für Geschichte und Wissenschaft des Judentums (MGWJ)*, vol. 40 (1896), pp. 474-477.

Dyhernfurth, he thanked God for making the heart of the local prince favourably inclined towards him by granting him the privilege to settle there and to establish a Hebrew printing press.[7] Bass eagerly availed himself of the new opportunity. His first publication, *Beith Shemuel*, a commentary on *Even Haezer*, a section of Joseph Caro's *Shulhan Arukh*, composed by Samuel ben Uri Shraga, was ready even before the agreed deadline.[8] Samuel himself was of Polish origin, he studied in Cracow and served as rabbi in Szydlowiecz. He came to Dyhernfurth in 1689 in order to supervise the printing of his book. Soon afterwards, he was invited to become rabbi and head of the famous *yeshiva* in one of the most important Jewish communities in Germany, in Fürth. It was there that Samuel published a second edition of his work,[9] incorporating into it comments and suggestions that emerged as a result of his learning together with his pupils in the Fürth *yeshiva*. Subsequently, Samuel returned to Poland permanently.[10] These brief sketches of the lives of Bass and Samuel may serve as typical illustrations of the steady flow of two-way traffic between East and West[11] and of the mutual enrichment derived from this mobility. The basic commodity of the Jews was easy to transport: it consisted of knowledge, or as Bass formulated it: "wherever Samuel went, his house [the House of Torah] went with him."[12] Bass' first effort was followed by many more and during the existence of the press, operated by him and by his descendants until 1762, hundreds of Hebrew and Yiddish books were published. The output included Bibles, Talmuds, codes, responsa, prayerbooks, sermons, ethical and kabbalistic works, but also books of popular entertainment in Yiddish, and even a book on arithmetic.[13]

Let us now turn to another Hebrew publishing and printing venture. In Anhalt-Dessau, we find the Court Jew, Moses Benjamin Wulff,[14] in the

7 *Beith Shemuel* (Dyhernfurth, 1689), afterword by Bass, f. 106b.

8 *Ibid.*

9 Fürth 1694.

10 See *Encyclopaedia Judaica*, vol. 14, cols. 814-815.

11 See Moses A. Shulvass, *From East to West, The Westward Migration of Jews from Eastern Europe during the Seventeenth and Eighteenth Centuries* (Detroit, 1971).

12 See note 6.

13 See the list in Moses Marx's "A Bibliography of Hebrew Printing in Dyhernfurth, 1689-1718," in *Studies in Jewish Bibliography*, etc. (cited above in note 4), pp. 221-234, esp. numbers 45, 82, 94 and 108.

14 See Max Freudenthal, *Aus der Heimat Mendelssohns* (Berlin, 1900). A large part of

service of King Leopold I. The King was one of the pioneers of modernisation and Wulff was perhaps the most capable, dynamic, influential and wealthy Jew of his time. Wulff was deeply interested in Jewish matters. He established a *Klaus*, but also a Hebrew printing press in Dessau, in 1694. The privilege granted to him by the Duchess Henrietta Katherina included most liberal conditions: the new firm was to enjoy complete tax and duty freedom and these freedoms were to be extended to the staff, too.[15] More than 30 books were published between 1696 and 1704.[16] Wulff himself, because of his entanglements in stormy financial and legal affairs, relinquished his role as the principal of the firm and transferred his press, equipment and stock to one of his relatives.[17] The press continued to operate in the neighbouring cities of Halle, Jessnitz and Köthen.[18] The highlight of this press was its Jessnitz period. Not only standard biblical, rabbinic and liturgical works were published in large numbers, but also important books in other areas of learning. Mention should be made of a few: a new, etymological dictionary of the Hebrew language by an Ashkenazi author, Yehudah Aryeh Loeb, who settled in Provence, included an introduction that dealt with the history of languages in general and in which the author had also announced his plan to compose a book on French glosses found in Rashi's commentary on the Pentateuch.[19] Another interesting book printed in Jessnitz was the second edition of the medical and scientific encyclopaedia, *Maaseh Tuviah*, by Tobias Cohen. The work of this famous physician contained the latest information on medicine and the natural sciences.[20] *The Guide for the Perplexed* by Maimonides was published in Jessnitz in 1742, for the first time after two hundred years, the previous editions having been published in the middle of the sixteenth century in Italy.[21] The

Freudenthal's book deals with Wulff and his family. See also Selma Stern, *The Court Jew. A Contribution to the History of Absolutism in Central Europe* (Philadelphia, 1950), index; and Alexander Altmann, *Moses Mendelssohn, A Biographical Study* (Philadelphia, 1973), pp. 5-8.

15 Freudenthal, *op. cit.*, pp. 157-160.

16 *Ibid.*, pp. 163-173 and pp. 235-246.

17 *Ibid.*, p. 174 and p. 181.

18 For a list of books printed in Halle, see Freudenthal *op. cit.*, pp. 246-249, for Jessnitz, *ibid.*, pp. 251-270 and for Köthen, *ibid.*, pp. 249-251.

19 *Oholei Yehudah* (Jessnitz, 1719), f. [4b].

20 Printed in 1721.

21 Freudenthal, *op. cit.*, pp. 219-221 and p. 259, No. 82. See also Altmann, *op. cit.*, pp. 10-11.

astronomical work, *Nehmad ve-naim*, by David Gans, remained in manuscript for one hundred and thirty years until the Jessnitz printers issued it for the first time in 1743.[22] In the field of rabbinical studies, an outstanding achievement was the Maimonidean code, *Mishneh Torah*, which included the text of previously unpublished commentaries as well as geometrical figures specially etched for the new edition, all arranged in a pleasing typographical harmony.[23]

Back in Dessau, the son of Moses Wulff, Elijah, re-opened the printing house for a short time in 1742.[24] Among the most important publications leaving the renewed Dessau press was a commentary on the Talmud of Jerusalem by David Fränkel,[25] the teacher of Moses Mendelssohn. The interest in the Jerusalem Talmud, usually neglected by traditional students of rabbinics, is another indication of the widening horizons characterising the period. The importance of the intellectual atmosphere that prevailed in Dessau for the shaping of Mendelssohn's personality and the role of Hebrew printing in that city and vicinity in creating that atmosphere were fully recognized by Max Freudenthal who devoted more than half of his book, *Aus der Heimat Mendelssohns*, to the printing history of the Dessau, Halle, Jessnitz and Köthen presses.[26]

Hebrew printing presses in many other places were opened up one after the other. Some were established because of scholarly interests, others owed their existence to commercial ambitions. In Sulzbach, Northern Bavaria, Prince Christian August allowed the printer Moses Bloch to settle there and to open a Hebrew printing press.[27] The prince was strongly drawn to mysticism and deeply interested in *Kabbalah*. He invited the Christian theologian and poet, Baron Knorr von Rosenroth, to join his court and encouraged him to publish his *Kabbala Denudata*, a study of the

22 Freudenthal, *op. cit.*, pp. 222-223 and p. 264, No. 87. See also André Néher, *Jewish Thought and the Scientific Revolution of the Sixteenth Century. David Gans (1541-1613) and his Times* (Oxford, 1986), pp. 67-71.

23 Freudenthal, *op. cit.*, pp. 214-219 and pp. 261-263, No. 85.

24 *Ibid.*, p. 219.

25 Printed in 1743, see Freudenthal, *op. cit.*, pp. 229-230 and pp. 240-241, No. 19; see also Altmann, *op. cit.*, pp. 13-14.

26 Freudenthal, *op. cit.*, pp. 155-276 and 291-304.

27 See Magnus Weinberg, "Die hebräischen Druckereien in Sulzbach," in *Jahrbuch der jüdisch-literarischen Gesellschaft*, vol. I (1903), pp. 19-202, vol. 15 (1923), pp. 125-155 and vol. 21 (1930), pp. 319-370.

theosophical teachings of the Jews which contained many passages from the *Zohar* in Latin translation. The publication of *Kabbala Denudata* was completed in 1684 and in the same year Moses Bloch printed a magnificent, folio edition of the *Zohar* in the original, accompanied by a Latin dedication to Christian August composed by Baron Knorr von Rosenroth. There can be no doubt that Christian August's motives in granting Bloch the privilege to print Hebrew books were intellectual: namely, his desire to become familiar with Jewish mystical teachings.[28] Bloch took advantage of the grant and launched Sulzbach as one of the most prolific of Hebrew presses in Europe. From 1684 until 1851, Bloch, his successors, as well as other printers produced well over seven hundred Hebrew and Yiddish titles bearing the imprint Sulzbach, thereby making the name of this small Bavarian city well known in every Jewish community.[29]

In contrast to Sulzbach, the Wilhermsdorf Hebrew press was founded as a result of economic interests. Wolfgang Julius, Count of Hohenlohe, granted the privilege to establish a Hebrew press to Isaac Cohen, for the purpose of supporting the production of the local paper mills. The first Hebrew book left the Wilhermsdorf press in 1670 and in subsequent years many important, elegant and large format books were produced by the Hebrew printers of the city.[30] The convergence of various factors, chief among them the involvement of wealthy Court Jews who were ready to supply the initial financing, and the interest of local rulers in the large and active Jewish book market, encouraged the flourishing of more than twenty independent Hebrew presses in Germany in the period under consideration. The consumers were members of the German-Jewish communities and, to a smaller extent, German Christian Hebraists, but to a large measure it was the Eastern European community that had the capacity of absorbing a considerable portion of the production. Russia and Poland had no printing presses in the second half of the seventeenth

28 On *Kabbala Denudata* and its influence see *Mishnath ha-Zohar*, by I. Tishby, vol. 1 (Jerusalem, 1971), p. 48 and pp. 113-114.

29 See Weinberg, *loc. cit.*, vol. 1 (1903), pp. 19-202, vol. 15 (1923), pp. 125-155 and vol. 21 (1930), pp. 319-370.

30 See Aron Freimann, "Annalen der hebräischen Druckerei in Wilhermsdorf," in *Festschrift zum siebzigsten Geburtstage A. Berliner's* (Frankfurt a. Main, 1903), pp. 100-115. [See now: Moshe Nathan Rosenfeld, *Jewish Printing in Wilhermsdorf*, London, 1995.]

century, with the exception of the fledgling Zolkiew press that was established in 1692.[31] Accordingly, the needs of Russian and Polish Jews had to be supplied from abroad and the German Hebrew presses were eager to do so.

As an excellent illustration of this state of affairs, mention should be made of the 1697-1699 Frankfurt an der Oder edition of the Babylonian Talmud.[32] This major publication effort was the result of a combination of forces that joined together to produce the first complete Talmud in Germany. Behrend Lehmann,[33] the famous and influential Court Jew, who was Polish Resident to the Court of Brandenburg, underwrote the expenses of this major undertaking. According to some sources, Lehmann spent 50,000 talers to produce the work. He was also instrumental, through his excellent connections, in obtaining the required permission for the Talmud. Indeed, such permissions were granted by Frederick III of Brandenburg and by King Leopold I. The application for the privilege was drafted by a Christian scholar, perhaps Johann Christoph Beckmann, professor at the University of Frankfurt an der Oder and business associate of the Gentile bookdealer, Michael Gottschalck. The latter operated a Hebrew printing press and had sufficient technical means and adequate staff to carry out such a major undertaking as the printing of the Talmud. Gottschalck also used the services of M. Berninger, a Christian engraver, who was the artist in charge of the figures that were incorporated into the edition. The background of this venture was described by Rabbi David Oppenheim in his approbation.[34] Oppenheim referred to the burnings of the Talmud

31 See Hayyim Dov (Bernhard) Friedberg, *History of Hebrew Typography in Poland* (Tel-Aviv, 1950) (in Hebrew), p. 41 and esp. note 2 there; pp. 59-60, 62-63 and esp. note 4 on p. 63. See also I. Heilprin, "The Council of Four Lands and the Hebrew Book," in *Kiryat Sefer*, vol. 9 (1932-1933), pp. 373-374 (in Hebrew).

32 See Max Freudenthal, "Zum Jubiläum des ersten Talmuddrucks in Deutschland," in *MGWJ*, vol. 42 (1898), pp. 80-89, 134-143, 180-185, 229-236 and 278-285 and Raphael Nathan Rabinowitz, *Maamar al hadpasath ha-Talmud*, ed. by Abraham Meir Habermann (Jerusalem, 1952), pp. 96-100. See also Manfred R. Lehmann, "A Jewish Financier's Lasting Investment," in *Tradition*, vol. 19 (1981), pp. 340-347; Stern, *op. cit.*, p. 225 and see also Hans Joachim Schoeps, *Philosemitismus in Barock*, (Tübingen, 1952), pp. 188-189 with quotations from an eyewitness report describing the scene in the printing house during the printing of the Talmud.

33 See Stern, *op. cit.*, pp. 73-85 and *passim*.

34 His approbation on the verso of the title-page of Tractate *Berakhoth*.

and other Hebrew books in the wake of the Chmielnicki massacres, to the frequent fires that destroyed Jewish books and the resulting dire need for Talmud volumes so that the study of Talmud in the *yeshivoth* could be continued. According to Oppenheim, the entire Jewish educational system was endangered because of the lack of sufficient copies of the Talmud. Needless to say, Oppenheim heaped praise on Lehmann for his generosity and mentioned that Lehmann distributed half of the edition to needy scholars, free of charge. As a result of the involvement of Christian scholars and businessmen in this venture, the text of the Talmud itself was cleansed from some of the corruptions that had previously disfigured it as an outcome of the intervention of Church censorship. Although the title-pages of this edition bear a statement that the volumes were printed in accordance with the regulations of the Council of Trent and that they followed the censored Basel Talmud (1578-1581), in actual fact, many passages and the entire Tractate *Avodah Zarah* (on idolatry), which had been omitted in Basel, were restored in Frankfurt.[35] The publication of the Frankfurt Talmud was rightly considered an event of major importance for the Jewish community and, apparently, the edition was rather rapidly sold out. Soon, other complete editions of the Talmud were printed, in Frankfurt a. Main, in Berlin and Sulzbach, and the resulting fierce competition and occasional infringements of prior privileges and copyrights kept many secular and rabbinic courts busy.[36] In any case, the first complete edition of the Talmud ever printed in Germany demonstrates the cooperation of Jew and Gentile, scholarly and financial, as well as Eastern and Western European Jewish forces.

More limited in nature, serving narrower interests and smaller geographic areas, were the printing presses established by a Christian and a rabbinic scholar, respectively. Heinrich Jacob Bashuysen, a Calvinist theologian and accomplished Hebraist, in addition to his translations of rabbinic works into Latin, had also operated a Hebrew

35 See Rabinowitz, *op. cit.*, p. 100.

36 On the various editions of the Talmud printed in German cities see Rabinowitz, *op. cit.*, p. 101, pp. 108-112, 115-117, 120-124, on legal controversies see *ibid.*, pp. 106-107, 111, 121 and 123-124; see also Nahum Rakover, *Ha-haskamoth li-sefarim ki-yesod li-zekhuth ha-yotzrim* (Jerusalem, 1970), pp. 25-39. [See now also: Marvin J. Heller, *Printing the Talmud; A History of the individual Treatises Printed from 1700 to 1750*, Leiden, 1999.]

printing press in his native Hanau, beginning in 1708.[37] It is worthwhile to call attention to the fact that Bashuysen printed not only such standard commentaries to the Bible as that of Don Isaac Abarbanel, but also difficult and very technical books on Talmud. In 1712, Bashuysen published the pilpulistic novellae on various tractates of the Talmud written by Rabbi Yona Teomim (*Kikayon de-Yona*) and in 1714 issued a book called *Sugyoth ha-Talmud* by Moses of Rohatyn, in the original Hebrew, with a Latin translation, under the title *Clavis Talmudica*. This work was an important methodological introduction to the pilpulistic way of Talmud study as it was practiced in many Polish and German *yeshivoth*.[38] Apparently, Bashuysen believed that without an understanding of the rules governing the specific method of *pilpul*, one could not understand the mentality of the contemporary rabbis. Such deep familiarity with rabbinic writings must have developed through personal contacts, and the interaction between scholars of different faiths and scholarly backgrounds must have exerted an influence on both sides. The large number of Latin dissertations produced in German universities on Jewish topics by non-Jews shows one side of the coin.[39] It is less obvious to observe the other side, namely the influence of Christian scholars on the rabbis. One may speculate that the exposure of rabbinic scholars to Christian orientalists may have led some of the former to become more inclined toward a historical, methodological and more critical approach to their own heritage. A thorough re-examination of rabbinic literature produced during this period may detect such influences even in the traditional fields of learning and may point to the existence of a subtle, perhaps hardly discernible phenomenon which could be

37 Ernst J. Zimmermann's "Die Hanauer hebräischen Drucke (1610-1744)" in *Hanauisches Magazin* (Supplement to *Han. Anzeiger*), Jg. 3, Nr. 7 (1. Juni 1924) lists 52 entries according to Shlomo Shunami's bibliography (cited in note 43), number 2880. Unfortunately, Zimmermann's work was not available to me. On an earlier period in Hebrew printing in Hanau see Herbert C. Zafren, "A Probe into Hebrew Printing in Hanau in the 17th Century or How Quantifiable is Hebrew Typography," in *Studies in Judaica, Karaitica and Islamica presented to Leon Nemoy* (Ramat Gan, 1982), pp. 273-285.

38 On the nature of *pilpul* in Germany around this time see Hayyim Zalman Dimitrovsky, "Al derekh ha-pilpul," in *Salo W. Baron Jubilee Volume*, Hebrew section (Jerusalem, 1974), pp. 128-130; see also his "Leket Yosef and Sugyot ha-Talmud," in *Alei Sefer*, vol. 4 (1977), pp. 90-98.

39 See the extensive literature and list in Raphael Loewe's article in *Encyclopaedia Judaica*, vol. 8, cols. 9-71 ("Hebraists, Christian").

regarded as some kind of precursor of nineteenth-century *Jüdische Wissenschaft*.[40]

Let us now turn to another scholarly press, the one which was established by the famous Rabbi Jakob Emden in Altona.[41] In 1743, Emden received a royal privilege from Christian VII of Denmark that allowed him to print Hebrew books. The privilege contained two restrictive conditions: Emden must refrain from printing books in German and in Latin and he must submit all books printed by him for approval to the local rabbinic and lay authorities. The first condition, apparently imposed on Emden at the insistence of a Christian publisher who feared that the new press would compete with his, was fulfilled. We have no knowledge of any non-Hebrew book ever printed by Emden. On the other hand, the second condition was flouted by the controversial rabbi. Emden published a stream of polemical pamphlets against his great foe, Rabbi Jonathan Eibeschütz, without proper approbation. Emden realized the power of the press as a political tool and used it with great enthusiasm. Many of his tracts were published without a prepared manuscript, improvising while setting the type and camouflaging the fact that they were produced in Altona.[42] The fact that a scholar of Emden's stature invested his time and effort in learning the printing craft himself and the trouble he took to acquire the equipment and the type, as well as his skillful use of the press in his polemics against his adversary, indicate that Emden had recognised the potential of the printing press as an effective and quick instrument in furthering his cause. In this respect, Emden may be compared to other eighteenth-century public figures in Europe and in the American colonies who made similar use of the press. In addition to the Hebrew printing presses mentioned above there existed many others, some major and some minor. The very prolific Fürth press should be singled out, but others, in Berlin, Hamburg, Leipzig, Wandsbek, Homburg vor der Höhe, Karlsruhe,[42a] Neuwied, Offenbach, Rödelheim

40 Compare Altmann's remarks on David Fränkel's commentary on the Palestinian Talmud in his work cited above (note 14), top of p. 14.

41 On Emden's activities as printer of Hebrew books see Bernhard Brilling, "Die Privilegien der hebräischen Buchdruckerien in Altona (1726-1836)," in *Studies in Bibliography and Booklore*, vol. 9 (1969-1971), pp. 155-156 and vol. 11 (1976), pp. 41-56.

42 *Ibid.*, vol. 9, p. 156 and p. 165, note 16.

42a [See now: Moshe Nathan Rosenfeld, *Jewish Printing in Karlsruhe* (London, 1997).]

and elsewhere deserve to be remembered, too.[43] Despite some recent, important scholarship on the subject,[44] much more remains to be done and it is to be hoped that the history of Hebrew printing in Germany in the period will soon attract the kind of scholarly attention that it deserves.

Beyond the study of the history of the various printing presses, there are other areas that could offer insights into the life of the Jewish community, especially in the cultural and religious realm. In the following, we shall briefly refer to some such aspects. The existence of well-run printing establishments served as a stimulus to many authors to publish their works and to migrate to places where such presses operated. On the title-page of a book on talmudic *aggadoth, Zinzeneth Menahem*, by Menahem Mendel ben Zevi Hirsch, we find the text of a letter issued by the Council of the Four Lands in Yaroslav in 1691. The signatories recommend the publication of the book and urge that the printer who will undertake the printing of the book, should proceed efficiently and quickly, in order to enable the author to return to his home without delay, otherwise the students in his *yeshiva* would be forced to be idle in their Talmud study. For some reason, the admonition of the Council was not heeded and the book remained unpublished until 1719 when printers in Berlin completed its 100 folios in four months. Rabbi Menahem Mendel enjoyed the

43 See the literature cited above in note 3. See also Aron Freimann, *A Gazetteer of Hebrew Printing* (New York, 1946) reprinted in *Hebrew Printing and Bibliography*, ed. by Charles Berlin (New York, 1976), pp. 255-340; see also Sh. Shunami, *Bibliography of Jewish Bibliographies*, 2nd ed. (Jerusalem, 1965), pp. 510-514; and also H.B. Friedberg, *History of Hebrew Typography of the Following Cities in Central Europe: Altona, etc.* (Antwerp, 1935) (in Hebrew).

44 See especially Bernhard Brilling's articles in *Studies in Bibliography and Booklore*, Kirjath Sepher, and elsewhere. Mosche N. Rosenfeld of London has published a large number of articles on Hebrew printing in Fürth in the bulletin of the *Israelitische Kultusgemeinde Fürth*. I understand that he is also planning to publish a comprehensive work on the history of Hebrew printing in Fürth. His paper on centres of Hebrew printing in the seventeenth and eighteenth centuries is scheduled to appear in a book to be published by the New York Public Library in 1988 [=Moshe N. Rosenfeld, "The Development of Hebrew Printing in the Sixteenth and Seventeenth Centuries", in: *A Sign and a Witness: 2000 Years of Hebrew Books and Illuminated Manuscripts* (New York, 1988), pp. 92-100.] On Yiddish books printed in the period, much important material is found in the works of Chone Shmeruk and his school at the Hebrew University in Jerusalem. See his *Yiddish Literature. Aspects of its History* (Tel-Aviv, 1978); and his *The Illustrations in Yiddish Books of the Sixteenth and Seventeenth Centuries* (Jerusalem, 1986); and Sarah Zfatman, *Yiddish Narrative Prose* (Jerusalem, 1985); as well as Chava Turniansky, "The 'Bentsherel' and the Sabbath-Hymns," in *Alei Sefer*, vol. 10 (1982), pp. 51-92 (all in Hebrew).

hospitality of the son-in-law and daughter of the influential Court Jew, Joseph van Geldern, during the time that he was engaged in the supervision of the printing in Berlin.[45]

Rabbi Yair Haim Bacharach also dealt with the significance of the availability of efficient printing facilities for Hebrew works. He described the devastation of his city, Worms, in 1689, and his decision to settle in Frankfurt a. Main, among whose attractions he singled out the existence of a good, well-organized printing press. Once in Frankfurt, Bacharach began the publication of his book which was due to the favourable circumstances in the new domicile.[46] In a similar vein, Rabbi Ezekiel Katzenellenbogen, of Altona, Hamburg and Wandsbek, in the introduction to his collection of responsa, counted among his blessings the establishment of a printing press for Hebrew books in Altona which provided him with the opportunity to publish his work.[47]

An important aspect of the history of Hebrew publishing was the issue of freedom of the press, or rather the lack of it, namely censorship.[48] Control over publishing rested not only with the civil authorities but also with the rabbinate and internal Jewish communal leadership. These authorities had the right to regulate the flow and contents of Hebrew and Yiddish books. The privileges extended to Jewish printers included, as a matter of course, the requirement that expressions that might be construed as offensive to Christianity be excluded from the text of the works to be produced. The enforcement of this provision, however, was not as strict as it had been when it was in the hands of centralised Church censorship which originated in sixteenth-century Italy. As an example of less stringent attitudes, reference should again be made to the Frankfurt 1697-1699 Talmud edition as well as to subsequent editions of the Talmud produced in various German cities.[49] Despite the more liberal times, accusations against Hebrew books continued to be levelled and confiscation of

45 Verso of title page of *Zinzeneth Menahem* (Berlin, 1719).

46 *Havvoth Yair* (Frankfurt a. Main, 1699), f. [2a].

47 *Keneseth Yehezkeel* (Altona, 1732), f. [2a].

48 On censorship of Hebrew books in general see William Popper, *The Censorship of Hebrew Books* (New York, 1899), reprinted, with an introduction by Moshe Carmilly-Weinberger (New York, 1969). Also Carmilly-Weinberger, *Censorship and Freedom of Expression in Jewish History* (New York, 1977).

49 See above note 36.

Hebrew books took place in Fürth in 1702,[50] and Shabbetai Bass was forced to face trials in Dyhernfurth in 1694 and again in 1712, having been accused by Jesuits for not excising from the Hebrew books published by him passages that allegedly contained anti-Christian statements.[51] Internal Jewish control was exercised through the instrument of rabbinic approbations, the *haskamoth*.[52] These served multiple purposes: they provided copyright protection, contained praise and recommendation for the author and attested to the reliability of the work from the point of view of religious beliefs and laws. The granting of *haskamoth* was one of the functions of the local rabbinate, but was also entrusted to the Council of Four Lands.[53] Accordingly, in many Hebrew works printed in Germany, the *haskamoth* were divided into two groups, one by German rabbis and the other by their Polish and Russian colleagues. *Haskamoth* occasionally were issued with reservations. Rabbi Ezekiel Katzenellenbogen of Altona granted an approbation to Rabbi Efraim Heckscher's *halakhic* work, but took exception to one of his particular rulings, depriving it of its validity.[54] There are Hebrew and Yiddish books that lack *haskamoth* completely. Usually, their absence is a clear indication of either a copyright violation or questionable contents.[55] The latter applies especially to the area of popular literature, mainly works of belletristics that were issued in Hebrew characters, many originally composed in High German.[56] Despite the fact that in such works, containing popular German novels, the explicitly

50 See Leopold Löwenstein, "Zur Geschichte der Juden in Fürth," in *Jahrbuch der jüdische-literarischen Gesellschaft*, vol. 10 (1912), p. 51.

51 See Brann's article cited above in note 6, pp. 560-562, 572-573.

52 See Rakover's book cited above in note 36 and, on an earlier period in Italy but containing much important general material as well, M. Benayahu's *Copyright, Authorization and Imprimatour for Hebrew Books Printed in Venice* (Jerusalem, 1971) (in Hebrew).

53 See Yisrael Heilprin, "The Council of Four Lands and the Hebrew Book," in *Kiryat Sefer*, vol. 9 (1932-1933), pp. 367-378; and his "Approbations of the Council of Four Lands in Poland," *ibid.*, vol. 11 (1934-1935), pp. 105-110, 252-264; and also ibid., vol. 12 (1935-1936), pp. 250-253. It would be useful to investigate the differences between the Polish and German *haskamoth*, although it seems that they were basically similar and concerned with more or less the same issues.

54 *Adnei Paz* (Altona, 1743), verso of title-page.

55 See s.v. "Approbation," *Jewish Encyclopedia*, vol. 2, esp. p. 28.

56 See Arnold Paucker, "Yiddish Versions of Early German Prose Novels," in *The Journal of Jewish Studies*, vol. 10 (1959), pp. 151-167, and his "The Yiddish Versions of the Schildbürgerbuch," in *Yivo Belter*, vol. 44 (1973), pp. 59-77; and his other articles cited there in notes 18-19. See also Zfatman's book cited above in note 44.

Christian expressions were neutralised (instead of cathedrals, fortresses, instead of Christian pilgrims, merchants were substituted, etc.), the lack of rabbinic approbations betray the displeasure of the rabbis with the dissemination of secular literature.[57]

The proliferation of Hebrew and Yiddish books provides an opportunity for research in various related areas, such as the reading and study habits of the Jewish population, the practices of the booktrade, the status of books in Jewish society, the book as a commodity, the book as an artifact, etc. Since, to the best of this writer's knowledge, no systematic study has ever been conducted concerning these and related subjects,[58] the observations that follow must remain, at this time, of very tentative nature. First of all, on the basis of available lists of Hebrew printed books produced in various localities, one may venture to suggest that during the approximately one hundred years under discussion, at least 2,500 separate editions of Hebrew and Yiddish books appeared,[59] and if we assume that the average size of each edition was 1,000, we arrive at a total of two and a half million copies of books printed in Hebrew characters. Moritz Steinschneider and David Cassel estimated that about one third of all Hebrew books printed up to the beginning of modern times came from German-Jewish presses.[60] The average size of each edition, of course, is only an estimate, although we do have information on the size of some specific editions, e.g. Behrend Lehmann's 1697-1699 Talmud was published in 5,000 sets,[61] the Yiddish *Maasse-bukh* was issued in 3,500 copies in 1708-1709, while, at the same time, the bulky *Yalkut Shimoni* was

57 Approbations are lacking in most of the books containing narratives that are listed in Zfatman's work.

58 See, however, Zafren's various articles on the typographical aspects of Hebrew printing and esp. his statement in his paper cited above in note 4, pp. 543-544. [See now also: Zeev Gries, *The Book as an Agent of Culture: 1700-1900* (Tel Aviv, 2002, in Hebrew).]

59 We arrived at this figure by using the number of books listed in some of the bibliographies, e.g. Sulzbach (*Jahrbuch der Jüdische-literarischen Gesellschaft*, vol. 21 [1930], p. 348) has 701 items, Fürth (*ibid.*, vol. 10 [1912], p. 167) lists 533 entries, for Dyhernfurth (see Marx as cited in note 13, p. 234) we have 132 books, for Wilhermsdorf (Freimann, *op. cit.*, see above note 30, p. 113) 150, for Dessau, Jessnitz, etc. (Freudenthal, *op. cit.*, above note 14, p. 270) 104 books are listed. Using these figures and extrapolating the rest, it seems that 2,500 for more than twenty presses is a rather conservative estimate. [See now: Vinograd's *Thesaurus*, above note 3.]

60 *Op. cit.*, (above note 3), p. 57.

61 Rabinowitz, *op. cit.* (above note 32), p. 98, end of note 1; but see Freudenthal, *MGWJ*, vol. 42 (1898), p. 84, note 3.

printed, by the same publisher who issued the popular *Maasse-bukh*, in 1,600 copies.[62]

As to the subjects on which Hebrew and Yiddish books were published, one immediately observes that the largest proportion of them were of a liturgical nature. Prayerbooks of all kinds, *siddurim*, *mahzorim, Haggadoth, selihoth, tehinnoth*, etc., amount to at least half of all books published.[63] The standard editions of the Pentateuch, with Rashi's commentary, Targum Onkelos, *Haftaroth* and the Five Scrolls were also issued frequently and often they included the Sabbath prayers as well. Very popular were books on *mussar*, such classics of ethics as *Hovoth ha-levavoth, Menorath ha-maor*, and later works such as *Simhath ha-nefesh, Kav ha-yashar* and *Lev tov* saw dozens of editions.[64] Rabbinic works, besides the Talmud itself, i.e. codes, responsa, novellae, etc. occupy a significant portion of this production. Popular entertainment, in the form of stories as well as transcriptions of German novels into Yiddish, also appeared in large numbers.[65] Philosophy, mysticism, medicine and astronomy were also represented, but in smaller numbers than the above mentioned categories. It would be rewarding to examine this area carefully and, at the same time, to pay attention to the relation between the number of original works by contemporary authors and that of the re-issues of older works. One can judge the taste of the public also by the frequency of the editions of particular works. Books that had a practical bearing on *halakhic* matters, especially commentaries on those parts of the *Shulhan Arukh* that deal with the dietary laws, were re-published over and over again. Still, works on *Midrash* and *aggadah* were also in demand as may be seen from the fact that the *Midrash rabba* and the aggadic *Yalkut Shimoni* and *Ein Yaakov* appeared frequently.[66] *Aggadic* works were considered potentially more profitable because of the wider readership and authors

62 See Bernhard Brilling, "Letters of a Jewish Publisher in Frankfurt on the Oder, 1708-1709," in *Studies in Jewish Bibliography and Booklore*, vol. 8 (1966-1968), p. 25.

63 See e.g. the index (compiled by Joseph Prys) of books printed in Sulzbach, in *Jahrbuch der Jüdische-literarischen Gesellschaft*, vol. 21 (1930), pp. 368-370 and see also, *ibid.*, pp. 366-367.

64 On *Hovoth ha-levavoth* see the bibliography by A. M. Habermann in *Sinai*, vol. 28 (1950-1951), pp. 320-329; the editions of *Menorath ha-maor* are listed in Naftali Ben-Menahem's introduction to the Jerusalem 1952 edition of the work and Jacob Shatzky listed the editions of *Simhath ha-nefesh* in his New York 1926 facsimile reprint of the work, pp. 23-29.

65 See the literature cited in note 56.

66 See their respective entries in H. D. Friedberg's *Bet Eked Sepharim* (Tel-Aviv, 1951-1956).

preferred to publish their *aggadic* books first in order to obtain the funds needed for subsequent publication of more technical *halakhic* or rabbinic works. As one rabbi puts it succinctly: *aggadah* is more appealing and therefore more people buy it![67]

It is generally assumed that a certain type of book, especially the very popular *Zena Ur'ena*, was directed towards the female reading public. Women were avid readers and also patronesses of publishing ventures, workers in the printing trade and accomplished scholars. Behrend Lehmann's wife, Haenele, urged her husband to lend hundreds of talers to the Jessnitz printers in 1721 to cover the cost of the printing of Rabbi Moses Alsheik's commentary on various biblical books.[68] Alsheik's works were very rare in central Europe because they had not been published for over a hundred years, since their first edition in Venice at the beginning of the seventeenth century. Among women who were accomplished scholars mention should be made of the grandmother of Yair Haim Bacharach,[69] and the wife of Joseph Steinhardt (who was Isaiah Pick Berlin's sister).[70] Women printers are mentioned from time to time, among them a nine-year-old girl who worked as a typesetter in Dessau at the end of the seventeenth century.[71]

Another aspect of the role that books played in this era is the question of book prices. It would be interesting to compare the prices of books to that of other commodities. In the meantime, it suffices to record some prices that are known: e.g. the scholarly *Beith Shemuel*, consisting of 160 folios, was sold for 1 taler and 10 groschen, while four copies of the liturgical book, *Shaarei Zion*, which contained 48 quarto leaves, were priced at ten groschen.[72] The main channels of book distribution were the fairs. Jewish merchants from East and West used to meet at the fairs of Königsberg, Leipzig, Breslau and Frankfurt an der Oder, and large

67 In Zevi Hirsch Bialeh's (*Hirsch Harif's*) approbation to Jehiel Michael Glogau's *Nezer ha-kodesh* (Jessnitz, 1719), f. 2a.

68 See *Rommemuth el* (Jessnitz, 1721), verso of title-page.

69 See the introduction to his *Havvoth Yair* (Frankfurt a. Main, 1699), f. [3a-b].

70 See *Zikhron Yoseph* (Fürth, 1773), f. [3a].

71 See Abraham Yaari, *Studies in Hebrew Booklore* (Jerusalem, 1955), pp. 256-302 (in Hebrew). On the nine-year-old girl see *ibid.*, p. 262 and also Freudenthal, *op. cit.* (above note 14), p. 271 and Alexander Marx, *Bibliographical Studies and Notes on Rare Books and Manuscripts in the Library of the Jewish Theological Seminary of America* (New York, 1977), p. 326.

72 See M. Marx, *loc. cit.*, (cited above in note 13), p. 221, Nos. 1 and 5.

quantities of books exchanged hands there.[73] Of course, there were also local booksellers and various other methods of promotion and sale.

The rabbinate in Poznań, in 1733, imposed upon the Jews of the district the compulsory acquisition of copies of *Even ha-shoham*, by the local rabbi, Eliakum Goetz ben Meir.[74] In a different vein, the Gentile printer, Johann Koelner of Frankfurt a. Main, planned to finance his edition of Alfasi's *Halakhoth* by selling lottery tickets that entitled the purchaser to a set as well as to a prize.[75] For some unknown reason, Koelner's edition of this work never appeared. It is to be assumed, on the basis of general impressions and especially because of the large quantities of Hebrew books available, that the Hebrew book occupied a central place in the average Jewish household. Again, the data are very scarce and not collected, but some limited observations may be appropriate. It was pointed out in a recent study that, in the estate of normal, seventeenth-century Gentile German citizens, book collections did not constitute, either relatively or absolutely, a quantifiable portion; books are rarely mentioned in estate inventories and if they are included, their value is usually less than 1% of the total estate.[76] This state of affairs could be compared to what is known to us about the estates of Viennese Jews in the seventeenth and eighteenth centuries, where books are regularly included.[77]

Although the following is a far from typical example, it is significant to single out the estate of Samson Wertheimer in whose household articles were valued at 6,000 florins at the same time that the value of his book collections, kept in his houses of study in Nikolsburg and Frankfurt, was estimated at 13,000 florins.[78]

73 See esp. in Brilling's article, *loc. cit.*, note 61, p. 25 and see *Encyclopaedia Judaica*, s. v. "Market Days and Fairs," vol. 11, cols. 1000-1005.

74 See Heilprin, *loc. cit.*, *Kiryat Sefer*, vol. 9, p. 377.

75 See Steinschneider and Cassel, *op. cit.*, cited above p. 59, note 3.

76 See *Stadt im Wandel. Kunst und Kultur des Bürgtums in Norddeutschland, 1150-1650*, hrsg. von Cord Meckseper. Ausstellungskatalog, Band 3 (Stuttgart-Bad Cannstatt, 1985), pp. 653-659, esp. p. 655: "...die privaten Büchersammlungen weder absolut noch relativ einen besonderen Anteil an den bürgerlichen Vermögen des 17. Jahrhunderts hatten."

77 Israel Taglicht, *Nachlässe der Wiener Juden im 17. und 18. Jahrhundert* (Wien-Leipzig, 1917), p. 44.

78 *Ibid.*, p. 45, end of note 1.

The proliferation of Hebrew and Yiddish books carried with it negative phenomena as well. Criticism was levelled against some rabbis who published their work, of limited scholarly or educational value, mainly for reasons of self-aggrandisement and financial benefit. Rabbi Joseph Samuel of Cracow, who was active in Frankfurt a. Main, advocated the prevention of the publication of books of homilies and novellae on codes, at least for a period of ten years, because the quality of the books in those areas had declined and their authors were only interested in promoting themselves. Rabbi Joseph Samuel was quite blunt: "there are sufficient books in existence and we do not need any more."[79] Rabbi Hirsch Charif of Halberstadt was perhaps even more outspoken about the work of some of his contemporaries: "the publication of books of inferior quality is actually harmful, they cause students to neglect the study of Talmud and their publication should be prevented."[80]

It was not only the contents of the books that was found wanting, but also their external appearance. The Council of Four Lands thundered against those printers who produced shabbily printed, inaccurately proof-read books, on cheap paper. The poor readability and the corrupt text were considered to be detrimental, especially in teaching children proper reading and understanding of the basic Jewish texts.[81]

Perhaps as a reaction to the deterioration of mass-printed books, especially in the area of liturgical books, some of the affluent Court Jews began to commission beautifully written and decorated calligraphic manuscripts and expensively printed books produced on vellum or on blue paper.[82]

79 In his approbation to Hayyim Krochmal's *Mekor hayyim* (Fürth, 1697), f. [3a].

80 In his approbation to *Nezer ha-kodesh* (see above note 67) and elsewhere. See Benjamin Hirsch Auerbach, *Geschichte der israelitischen Gemeinde in Halberstadt* (Halberstadt, 1866), p. 66. In general, see also Heilprin, *loc. cit.*, *Kirjath Sepher*, vol. 11 (1934-1935), pp. 105-110 and Rakover (note 35), index, s. v. *nimmukim neged mattan haskamah.*

81 See Heilprin, *loc. cit.*, *Kirjath Sepher*, vol. 9, p. 373.

82 On eighteenth-century manuscript illumination, a very popular topic lately, still the best survey is Ernest Naményi, "La miniature juive au XVIIe et au XVIIe siècle," in *Revue des études juives*, vol. 116 (1957), pp. 27-71 and its English version in *Jewish Art*, ed. by Cecil Roth, rev. edn. (Jerusalem, 1971), pp. 149-162. See also Chaya Benjamin, Introduction to the facsimile edition of the *Copenhagen Haggadah*, 1986, and my list, "Decorated Hebrew Manuscripts of the 18th Century in the Library of the Jewish Theological Seminary of America," in *The Alexander Scheiber Memorial Volume* [in the present volume, pp. 58*-82*]. On books printed on vellum and on coloured paper in this period, esp. those commissioned by David Oppenheim, see Alexander Marx, *Studies in Jewish History and Booklore* (New York, 1944) (reprint: 1969), pp. 217-218.

One more aspect of the period's great interest in publishing was the discovery and utilisation of Hebrew manuscripts for the editing of texts which had been unpublished previously. The most significant personality in this respect was David Oppenheim. His great collection of manuscripts served not only antiquarian interests, but also furthered the publication, for the first time, of important works. It was Oppenheim who published the first edition of Samuel ben Meir's commentary on the Pentateuch, and we have evidence that he made available his manuscript collection to contemporary scholars.[83] Many manuscripts were utilised for the various Talmud editions and, in general, old Hebrew manuscripts were used for critical text studies and for the establishment of an apparatus of variant readings.[84] This trend culminated in the activities of Rabbi Isaiah Pick Berlin in the second half of the eighteenth century.[85]

The interaction of many social, economic and political forces, the prominence of Court Jews in the community and outside of it, the contacts between Jews and Gentiles in the commercial as well as in the scholarly realm, the mobility of Jewish scholars and the migration from East to West and back, the growth of *yeshivoth* and the establishment of the *Klaus* in many communities where rabbis had the opportunity of undisturbed study, made the period outstandingly productive in many areas of Jewish learning. The phenomenal development of Hebrew printing in a relatively short period of time in so many German cities is a testimony to this vitality. Accordingly, the second part of the seventeenth and the first part of the eighteenth century were not only crucial, economically and socially, but also culturally and religiously. Further competent and detailed research in the diverse aspects of the history of the Jewish book in Germany in the period before the emancipation may reward us with many new insights and with a reappraised image of the intellectual profile of pre-modern German Jewry.

83 See Yitzchok Dov Feld in his introduction to Oppenheim's *Nishal David*, vol. 2 (Jerusalem, 5736 [1976]), pp. 36-39.

84 See Rabinowitz, *op. cit.*, pp. 103-105, note 1, quoting at length from the Introduction to the Frankfurt a. Main 1720-1722 edition of the Talmud.

85 See Abraham Berliner, *Rabbi Jesaja Berlin; eine biographische Skizze* (Berlin, 1879).

Decorated Hebrew Manuscripts of the Eighteenth Century in the Library of the Jewish Theological Seminary of America

An important segment of Alexander Scheiber's multifaceted and prodigious scholarly activity has been his contribution to the study of eighteenth century[1] Hebrew manuscript art. In scores of articles,[2] he focused on the systematic description of the *oeuvre* of Jewish scribe-artists of Central European origin who, in the eighteenth and early nineteenth century, created an amazing and imposing corpus of calligraphic and decorated Hebrew manuscripts. Building on the foundations laid by his Hungarian Jewish scholarly predecessors, David Kaufmann[3] and Ernest Naményi,[4] Scheiber expanded the field and stimulated a growing scholarly and bibliophilic interest in this manifestation of Jewish artistic creativity.[5]

The following list, containing a brief description of 47 Hebrew manuscripts in this area of study, is offered in deep gratitude by one of Scheiber's students as a modest tribute to the Master.

* The author wishes to express his thanks to Evelyn N. Cohen, Curator of Graphic Materials at the Library of the Jewish Theological Seminary, for her assistance during the writing of the present article and for her many valuable suggestions and corrections.

1 An exception is his work on Marcus Donath who was active in the nineteenth century. Accordingly, the present article also includes a work by Donath, see number 11.

2 See the bibliography compiled by Robert Dàn (in Scheiber's *Folklór és Tàrgytörténet*, vol. 2, 2nd ed. (Budapest, 1977), pp. 507-573), numbers 530, 601, 619, 633, 649, 741, 794, 808, 827, 830, 835, 842, 856, 875, 888, 894, 930, 954, 956, 963, 976, 1000, 1001, 1018, 1036, 1044, 1065, 1142.

3 "Zur Geschichte der juedischen Handschriftenillustration," in *Die Haggadah von Sarajevo*, ed. Dav. Heinr. Mueller and Julius v. Schlosser (Wien, 1898), pp. 253-311.

4 "La miniature juive au XVIIe et au XVIIIe siècle," *REJ*, v. 116 (1957), pp. 27-71.

5 See the most recent survey of this activity in the introduction by Iris Fishof to *Grace after meals and other benedictions: facsimile of Cod. Hebr. XXXII in the Royal Library, Copenhagen* (Copenhagen, 1983). [See now: Iris Fishof, *Jüdische Buchmalerai in Hamburg und Altona* (Hamburg, 1999). A comprehensive inventory and study of 18th century Hebrew manuscript illumination will be found in the forthcoming book of Emile G.L. Schrijver on this Subject.]

Books of Blessings

(1) *Seder birkath ha-mazon u-birkoth ha-nehenin we-tikkun keriath shema al ha-mitta.*
Vienna 1724.
Scribe: Aaron of Gewitsch (f. la: *wa-yaas ken Aharon me-k[ehillath] Gewitsch*).
For Hanna, daughter of Isaac Oppenheim, *Rosh Hodesh Nissan* 1725, Frankfurt.
Vellum. 17 f. 8.5 x 6.5 cm. Original leather binding.
Decoration: Colored miniatures. Frontispiece: Moses and Aaron; 3a: lighting of *Hannukah menorah*; 3b: hanging of Haman and his sons; 8a: meal; 9b: blessing on king; blessing on seeing strange creatures; 10a: prayer on visiting the sick; 10b: prayer before retiring; 14a: Isaac's sacrifice; 18b: Solomon's couch encircled by warriors (Song of Songs 3:7); 16a: David.
JTS 8232. Acc. Number: 0588. Benguiat collection.

(2) *Seder birkath ha-mazon we-tikkun keriath shema u-birkoth ha-nehenin.*
Mannheim 1735.
For Fradche (?), wife of Jacob Kalman.
Vellum. 76 f. 8.5 x 6 cm. Original velvet binding. The original part of this manuscript consists of ff. 1-31. Folios 32-76 containing prayers for women in Judeo-German were added. The first part is written in square characters, the second part in "weiber Deutsch."
Decoration: colored miniatures. Frontispiece: Moses and Aaron; 1b: meal; 2b: *Hannukah menorah* and hanging of Haman; 4b: Jerusalem; 11a: the guardian angel (Genesis 48:16).
JTS 4432a. Acc. number: 01051. Gift of Harry G. Friedman.

(3) *Seder birkath ha-mazon... im tikkunei keriath shema.*
Mannheim 1736.
For Bella from Frankfurt.
Vellum. 23 f. 10 x 7.5 cm. Original leather binding.
Decoration: colored miniatures. Frontispiece: Moses and Aaron; David and Solomon; 3a: meal; 4a: *Hanukkah menorah* and hanging of Haman; 6b: Jerusalem; 10b: prayer before retiring; 14a: the

guardian angel (Genesis 48:16); 16a: David; 20a: the blessing of the moon.

JTS 8230. Acc. number 01160. Gift of Harry G. Friedman.

(4) *Seder birkath ha-mazon... im birkoth ha-nehenin we-tikkun keriath shema al ha-mittah im s[efirath] ha[-omer] u-perek shirah.*
Vienna 1736.
Given by the bridegroom Asher Anshel to... Inscriptions on frontispiece as well as the colophon erased.
Vellum. 46 f. 8 x 5.5 cm. Original tortoise-shell binding.
Decoration: Colored miniatures. Frontispiece: Moses and Aaron; 3a: Judith and Holofernes; 4b: Purim scene; 11a: blessing on vegetables (basket of vegetables); 12a: blessing on fruit of trees; on sweet scented wood; 12b: on fragrant plants; on spices and herbs (man in pharmacy); 13a: on seeing strange creatures; on beholding the sea (sea and boat); 13b: prayer for the sick (patient and doctor); prayer on recovery of sick; 14a: blessing on seeing lightning; on hearing thunder; 14b: on seeing rainbow; blessing on king; 15a: the taking of *Hallah*; 16a: *mikveh*; 16b: lighting of Sabbath candles; 29a: prayer before retiring; 33b: Solomon's couch encircled by warriors (Song of Songs 3:7); 35b: the starry sky; 39a: forest; 41a: fowl; 44a: animals.
JTS 4789. From the library of Dr. H. Adler.

(5) *Seder birkath ha-mazon ...u-birkoth ha-nehenin u-keriath shema u-birkath ha-levanah we-seder hadlakah niddah hallah u-sefirath* [ha-omer].
Fuerth 1793.
For Braindel, wife of Seckel Z' B' (=Sulzbach?).
Vellum. 65f. (the last three folios on paper). 8.5x6.5cm. Original velvet binding.
Decoration: Colored miniatures. 7a: *Hanukkah menorah* and hanging of Haman; 32b: the guardian angel (Genesis 48:16); 43b: the blessing of the moon.
JTS 8252, Acc. number: 01286.
Gift of Harry G. Friedman.

(6) [*Seder birkath ha-mazon*].
Inscriptions and some miniatures on frontispiece erased.
Vellum. 20f. 6 x 4.5 cm.
Decoration: Frontispiece: Moses and Aaron; 3a: meal; 4b: *Hanukkah menorah*; 5a: hanging of Haman and his sons; 7a: Jerusalem; 10a: blessing on grape (vineyard); 11a: blessing on fruit of trees; on vegetables; 11b: blessing on drinking water; on seeing strange creatures; 12a: on hearing good news; 12a: on hearing thunder; 12b: on seeing lightning; on seeing rainbow; 13b: prayer before retiring; 16b: the guardian angel (Genesis 48:16); 19b: David.
JTS 4432h. Acc. number: 01963.

Circumcision Books

(7) *Sefer sod ha-shem we-sharvit ha-zahav... we-seder birkath ha-mazon... we-seder pideyon ha-ben.*
Hamburg 1728.
Scribe: Jacob Sofer ben Judah Loeb Shammash from Berlin, presently in Hamburg, 1728 (colophon on f. 17b).
Vellum. 18 f. (f. 18 blank). 14 x 9 cm.
Decoration: Ink drawing of portal with columns on frontispiece; gilded initial words; 6b: blank space, probably intended for circumcision scene.
JTS 4428. Acc. number 2863.

(8) *Dinim u-tefilloth we-seder birkath ha-mazon la-berith milah*. 1758.
3 f. (on paper); 10 f. (on vellum); 9 f. (on paper). 14 x 9.5 cm. Original leather binding.
Decoration: Colored miniatures. Frontispiece: Moses and Aaron; 4a: circumcision.
Contains 273 circumcision entries, 1781-1809.
JTS 4433e. Acc. number: 01497. Gift of Harry G. Friedman.

(9) *Sefer sod ha-shem we-sharvit ha-zahav.*
Hamburg 1763.
Scribe: Nethanel ben Aaron ha-Levi Segal (see colophon, f. 20b).

For Itzig ben Solomon ben Azriel in Hamburg (see flyleaf). 22 f. (on vellum); 8 f. (on paper). 13.5 x 9.5 cm. Original leather binding.
Decoration: Colored miniatures. Frontispiece: Moses and Aaron; 9a: circumcision.
Contains 78 circumcision entries, 1763-1782.
JTS 3697. Acc. number: none. Benguiat collection.

(10) *Dinim u-tefilloth we-seder ha-berakhoth... la-berith milah*. 1770.
Scribe: Zevi Hirsch Segal Sofer.
Owner: Judah Loeb ben Azriel Joseph Segal of Pappenheim. 12 f. (vellum); 4 f. (paper, last three blank). 12 x 9 cm.
Original leather binding.
Decoration: Colored miniatures. Frontispiece: Moses and Aaron. Birds, lions and putti.
JTS 4432d. Acc. number: 01592. Gift of Harry G. Friedman.

(11) *Sefer sod ha-shem we-hu oth berith kodesh*.
1817(?).
Scribe: Mordecai ben Josel Sofer of Nyitra.
For Lipman ben Saul [Ehrenfeld] משאפעדני (=of Sopron?). 18 f. (on vellum); 9 f. (on paper). 16.5 x 10.5 cm. Original leather binding, stamped in Hebrew: Lipman ben Saul.
Decoration: Ink drawings and micrography, some colored. 3a: David; 3b: calligraphic inscription written in five different types of script, signed: Mordecai ben Josel Sofer of Nyitra; 4a: Solomon, micrography of Song of Songs, signed: Mordecai ben Josel Sofer of Nyitra; 5a: Isaac and Jacob and geometrical figures in micrography of the text of the evening prayers, signed: Mordecai ben Josel Sofer; 5b: Abraham and the three angels; 6b: Moses, micrography of the text of the Blessing of Moses (Deuteronomy 33); 12a: circumcision; 14b: meal.
Circumcision entries, 1814-1841.
Folio 19a:... I acquired this book from my brother-in-law, Lipman Ehrenfeld...
Ownership entry on flyleaf: Hayyim Gruenfeld.
JTS 8273. Acc. number: 01494. Gift of Harry G. Friedman.

(12) [*Milah book*].
No place, no date.
Vellum. 25 f. 10.5 x 7 cm. Original leather binding.
Decoration: colored miniatures: 1a: Outline of portal, no text; 3a: *mohel*, with box containing tools for circumcision; 6a: circumcision; 10a: meal; 22b: blessing of the moon.
JTS 8740. Acc. number: 0823. Gift of Harry G. Friedman.

Haggadahs

(13) *Seder haggadah shel pessah*. With Judeo-German translation. 1729.
Vellum. 26 f. 33 x 19.5 cm. Original parchment binding.
Decoration: Colored miniatures. Most of the miniatures are very crude and poorly preserved. Scenes of preparations for Pessah, scenes depicting the conducting of the seder; Biblical scenes from the lives of the Patriarchs and of the Exodus; scenes relating to text of Haggadah.
On frontispiece: *hamtzaah hadashah arukha be-kol ammud we-ammud u-le-kol ha-nimtza bi-ketav naasu tzuroth*... (a novelty—with pictures on each page illustrating what is written there).
JTS 4478. Acc. number 40663.

(14) *Seder haggadah shel pessah*.
1732.
Scribe: Joseph ben David Aaron [*mi-Leipnik*] *bi-medinath Maehren* (of Leipnik in Moravia).
Written in the house of Moses Freudenburg.
On frontispiece: *be-otiyyoth Amsterdam*.
Vellum. 19 f. 20 x 14 cm. Original leather binding, stamped: 492 (=1732).
Decoration: Colored miniatures. Frontispiece: Moses and Aaron; David. Scenes relating to the text of the Haggadah; Biblical scenes from the lives of the Patriarchs and of the Exodus; the Temple of Jerusalem; miniatures for each verse of *Ehad mi yodea* and *Had gadya*.
JTS 4446. Acc. number 0286. Gift of Harry G. Friedman.

(15) *Seder haggadah shel pessah.*
Darmstadt 1733.
Scribe: Joseph Leipnik.
Vellum. 23 f. 18 x 13.5 cm. Original leather binding, stamped on front and on back: 1733.
Decoration: Colored miniatures. Frontispiece: Moses and Aaron; David; Sacrifice of Isaac. Scenes relating to the text of the Haggadah; Biblical scenes from the lives of the Patriarchs and of the Exodus; the Temple of Jerusalem; miniatures for each verse of *Ehad mi yodea* and *Had gadya.*
On flyleaf: Formerly property of Scholem Asch.
JTS 4452a (8253). Acc. number: 0527. Gift of Felix M. Warburg.

(16) *Seder haggadah shel pessah.*
1739.
Scribe: Issachar Baer ben Jacob Hayyim of אליק.
Vellum. 46 f. 10.5 x 8.5 cm. Original leather binding.
Decoration: Colored miniatures. Frontispiece: Moses and Aaron; 2a: searching for *hametz*; 2b: *eruv*; 6a: meal; 7b: meal; 8b: invitation to needy; 10b: a wise man; 11a: the four sons and a wise old man; 13b: building Pithom and Ramses; 15b: the defeat of Sennacherib (with explanation on f. 15a); 19b-20b: *pessah, matzah* and *maror*; 21b: David; 26b: Messiah; 37b: the Temple of Jerusalem; 38a-42b: miniatures for each verse of *Ehad mi yodea*; 43a-45b: miniatures for each verse of *Had gadya.*
1b: Ownership entry: Belongs to Moses ben Abraham Bukim Katz in Duesseldorf. He presented it to his wife, Elle on the 13th of Nissan 509 (=1809).
JTS 8896. Acc. number: 0621. In memory of Rebecca Elsberg.

(17) *Seder haggadah shel pessah.*
Vienna 1751.
Scribe: Aaron Schreiber Herlingen.
Vellum. 13 f. 23 x 15 cm. Original leather binding.
Decoration: Ink drawings. Gilded initial words. Frontispiece: Moses and Aaron. Scenes relating to the text of the Haggadah; Biblical scenes from the lives of the Patriarchs and of the Exodus; the Temple

of Jerusalem; miniatures for each verse of *Ehad mi yodea* and *Had gadya*.
Inscribed in medallion on top of frontispiece: Koppel Segal of Reschin.
JTS 4477. Acc. number: 01171. Gift of Harry G. Friedman.

(18) *Seder haggadah shel pessah.*
Vienna 1751.
Scribe: Aaron Schreiber Herlingen.
Vellum. 14 f. 24 x 15 cm. Original gilded leather binding.
Decoration: Ink drawings. Gilded initial words. Frontispiece: Moses and Aaron. Scenes relating to the text of the Haggadah; Biblical scenes from the lives of the Patriarchs and of the Exodus; the Temple of Jerusalem; miniatures for each verse of *Ehad mi yodea* and *Had gadya*.
Ownership entries: belonged to S. Prag in Duesseldorf (great-grandfather of Alexander Marx); Alexander Marx; Jacob Benjamin Marx (son of Alexander Marx).
JTS 8963. Acc. number: 04086.

(19) *Seder haggadah shel pessah im perush Abrabanel.*
Altona 1766.
Scribe: Elkanah P' H' ben Meir ben Elkanah, *Shammash* and *Sofer* in Altona.
On frontispiece: *be-otiyyoth Amsterdam.*
Vellum. 24 f. 28 x 16 cm. Original leather binding, stamped on front: *Haggadah shel pessah.*
Decoration: Colored miniatures, many of them very crude. Frontispiece: Moses and Aaron; Passover lamb. Scenes of preparations for Pessah, scenes depicting the conducting of the *seder*; Biblical scenes from the lives of the Patriarchs and from the Exodus; scenes relating to the text of the Haggadah.
Ownership entries: Ber Urschel (?); Itzig ben Nathan London.
JTS 8183. Acc. number: 01327. Gift of Harry G. Friedman.

(20) *Seder haggadah shel pessah.*
Kittsee 1772.
Scribe: Hayyim ben Asher Anshel of Kittsee.
Vellum. 21 f. 29 x 20 cm. Original gilded leather binding.
Decoration: Colored floral panels surrounding initial words. Frontispiece: Moses and Aaron.
Ownership entries: Elijah (?) ben Loeb... (frontispiece); Samuel Singer (flyleaf); Selig Singer of Bonyhád; Betty Singer (flyleaf and 3b).
JTS 4453. Acc. number: 01543. Gift of Harry G. Friedman.

(21) *Haggadah shel pessah.*
Pressburg 1788.
Scribe: Phinehas ben Pessah Hazzan(?) of Trebitsch, *Sofer* in Pressburg.
Paper. 20 f. 28 x 20.5 cm. Original leather binding.
Decoration: Ink drawings. Calligraphic letters. On frontispiece: David; the Rabbis of Bne Brak; Moses and Aaron.
Ownership entry: Solomon ben Hirsch Sacherles of Pressburg.
JTS 4467. Acc. number: 130857. Gift of Harry G. Friedman.

(22) *Seder haggadah shel pessah.*
1797.
Scribe: Raphael Neckarsulm.
Paper. 31 f. 20.5 x 15 cm. Original leather binding.
Decoration: Ink drawings (pasted on). 6a: the four sons; 10b: *pessah* meal with Passover lamb; 12b: meal; 18a: woman opening door, woman's dress made of cloth pasted on paper; 23a: David.
Ownership entries: Itzig ben Ber(?) of Ergersheim(?); Baruch ben Itzig of Ergersheim(?); Baruch ben Itzig of Kobersdorf(?).
JTS 8338. Acc. number: 01253. Gift of Harry G. Friedman.

Perek Shirah

(23) *Seder perek shirah.*
1719.
On frontispiece: *be-otiyyoth Amsterdam.*
Vellum. 16 f. 13 x 7.5 cm. Original leather binding.

Decoration: Ink drawings. Frontispiece: Moses and Aaron; 2a: heaven; 5b: vegetation; 6a: trees; 7a: reptiles; 9a: birds; 13a: animals.
Ownership entry: Baruch Moses Gomperz.
JTS 4376. Acc. number: 62225.

(24) *Seder perek shirah.*
1719.
For Herz (Hirz) ben Loeb Darmstadt of Frankfurt.
On frontispiece: *be-otiyyoth Amsterdam.*
Vellum. 23 f. 9.5 x 7 cm. Original leather binding.
Decoration: Ink drawings. Frontispiece: portal with columns; 6a: vegetation; 7a: trees; 8a: reptiles; 9a: birds; 15a: domestic animals; 17a: wild animals.
Folios 21-23 contain the *kiddush* for holidays.
Ownership entry: Perez Deutsch.
Ivan F. Boesky and Seema Boesky Manuscript Collection.

Sabbath Prayers

(25) *Seder tikkunei shabbath... me—...Yitzhak Luria...*
[Vienna] 1719.
Scribe: Meshullam Zimmel of Polin [=Polna].
For Joseph Nathan, the son-in-law of Isaac Oppenheim.
Vellum. 53 f. 11 x 7.5 cm. Original leather binding.
Decoration: Ink drawings. Frontispiece: Scenes from the story of Joseph (alluding to the name Joseph Nathan for whom the manuscript was written); top: Joseph's dreams; right: Joseph and his brethren; left: Jacob is shown Joseph's coat; bottom: Joseph's goblet found in Benjamin's bag; 13a: Solomon on his throne; 23a: Sabbath meal; 33a: Sabbath meal; 40b: Sabbath meal; 47a: Jacob and the angels (Genesis 32:4); 49b: *havdalah*; 52b: blessing of the moon.
Ownership entry: Marcus Nathan Adler. With list of *pideyon ha-ben* ceremonies performed by Adler.
JTS 4259. E.N. Adler Collection.

(26) *Seder tikkunei shabbath... me—...Yizhak Luria... im zemiroth we-gam kiddush levanah.*
Vienna 1724.
On frontispiece: *be-otiyyoth Amsterdam.*
Vellum. 61 f. 9.5 x 6.5 cm. Original leather binding.
Decoration: Ink drawings. Frontispiece: Moses and Aaron; 10b: lighting of Sabbath candles; 11b: Solomon; 20b: *kiddush*; 21a: Sabbath meal; 35a: Sabbath meal; 48a: the blessing of the moon; 54a: *havdalah.*
JTS 8269. Acc. number: 01326. Gift of Harry G. Friedman.

(27) *Seder tikkunei shabbath... me—...Yizhak Luria... im zemiroth... hanhagoth.*
Vienna 1725.
On frontispiece: *be-otiyyoth Amsterdam.*
Vellum. 43 f. 11.5 x 8.5 cm. Original leather binding.
Decoration: Ink drawings. Frontispiece: Moses and Aaron; 8b: lighting of Sabbath candles; 9a: Solomon; 14b: *kiddush*; 15b: Sabbath meal; 25b: Sabbath meal; 36 b: *havdalah.*
Folios 42-43: ceremony for the blessing of the moon.
JTS 8093. Acc. number: 01375.

(28) *Seder olath shabbath: tefilloth u-zemiroth le-arvith we-shaharith shel shabbath we-yom tov we-rosh hodesh we-tikkunei shabbath im perush... al mishnayoth massekheth shabbath we-seder hanhagoth... u-pirkei avoth im perush...*
Berlin 1742.
Scribe: Wolff Hirschel von Tikotschin in Pohl[en] (in Roman characters). On frontispiece, within the contours of letters forming the words: *seder olath shabbath*: Benjamin Zeev ben Zevi Hirsch of Sanok.
Vellum. 125 f. 10 x 6.5 cm. Original leather binding.
Decoration: Ink drawings. Frontispiece: Moses and Aaron. Initial words surrounded by panels consisting of human, zoomorphic and floral figures and designs. 96a: micrography forming portal and lion from letters of I Kings 17 ff (the story of Elijah); 101b: David; 108b: zoomorphic figures within the contours of letters.
100b: mention of Rabbi Bunem ha-Levi, rabbi of Rymanow.

Ownership entry: Bd (Bernard) Beer Eskeles, who inherited manuscript from his father, Hirschel Beer Kann (hence the initials H B on the spine of the binding). Hirschel Beer Kann died on *Rosh Hodesh Nissan* 1819.
JTS 8264. Acc. number: 01052. Gift of Harry G. Friedman.

(29) *Seder tikkunei shabbath... seder hanhagoth shabbath... me-Yizhak Luria... [im] zemiroth le-shabbath we-esrim we-arbaah perakim mi-massekheth shabbath...*
Pressburg 1744.
Vellum. 29 f. 10.5 x 6 cm. Original leather binding, stamped: I.H.
Decoration: Ink drawings and gilded initial words. Frontispiece: Moses and Aaron.
Ownership entries: Eliezer Mermelstein; Zvi Ackerman; Samuel Silberman.
JTS 9498. Acc. number: 04359. Gift of Jennie C. and Martin P. Kasofsky.

(30) [*Seder ha-tefillah shel shabbath*].
The Hague 1744.
For Menahem Mendel.
Vellum. 107 f. 17 x 11 cm. Original leather binding.
Decoration: Ink drawings. 5b, 9b, 11b, 14a, 26b, 28b, 31b: zodiac signs (on all these pages total erasures next to the zodiac signs of texts that must have been dedications); 20a: lighting of Sabbath candles; 86a: grape; 104b: *shiviti*, with *menorah* and lions. Additional frontispieces: 32a: *seder ha-tefillah shel shabbath shaharith mussaf u-minhah u-motzaei shabbath.* Portal, with books and figure of David. 59a: *Seder tehillim u-maamadoth we-shir ha-yihhud shel shabbath... be-otiyyoth defus Amsterdam* 504 (=1744). Moses and Aaron.
Ownership entries: 70b: belongs to Zalman ben Elhanan Elkan from Frankfurt am Main, 1839; 106b: Solomon Zalman ben Elhanan Elkan from Frankfurt am Main presented this prayerbook to the synagogue, 1840. This dedication written by Lipman ben Aaron, *sofer* of Amsterdam; 107a: this prayerbook belongs to Zalman Elkan from Frankfurt am Main, in Paris, 1836. On flyleaf: Presented by A. Kosmann to the master E. Adler on the day of his confirmation.
JTS 4558. E.N. Adler 429.

(31) *Seder tikkunei shabbath... me... Yizhak Luria...*
Place and date erased.
On frontispiece: *we-nikhtav ki-defus Amsterdam.*
Vellum. 59 f. 9.5 x 7 cm.
Decoration: Colored miniatures. Frontispiece: David and Solomon; 38b: Sabbath meal; 56a: *havdalah.*
JTS 4433g. Acc. number: 01287. Gift of Harry G. Friedman.

Siddurim

(32) *Tefillah mi-kol ha-shanah.*
Vienna 1712-1714.
Scribe: Aryeh Judah Loeb ben Elhanan Katz of Trebitsch.
For Simon Wolf ben Daniel Moses Oppenheim from Worms and his wife Vogel bath Moses Zunz of Frankfurt.
On first frontispiece: *be-otiyyoth Amsterdam.*
Vellum. 3 + 2 + 155 + 57 f. 33.5 x 23 cm. Original leather binding.
Decoration: Colored miniatures, ink drawings and gilded letters. 1b: Wolf and scorpio, alluding to name of Simon Wolf Oppenheim; bird and libra, alluding to his wife's name: Vogel; hands in posture of priestly blessing, alluding to scribe's name: Katz; 3b: *shiviti*, with geometric design of ten *sefiroth*; frontispiece: Moses and Aaron; hand of scribe, writing in a book; 2a: *shiviti*, with *menorah*; f. 79a: second frontispiece: angels and crown; 127b: wolf and bird; 128a: third frontispiece: angels with crown; after f. 155: fourth frontispiece: Judgement of Solomon and other Biblical scenes relating to David and Solomon.
Dedications by the scribe are found on f. 1b and 2a: scribe states that his father, Elhanan, passed away in Jerusalem on Iyyar 28, 1708; a long acrostic poem giving the names of the Oppenheims, mentioning the great fire in the Frankfurt ghetto on Teveth 24, 1711. Date of dedication: Vienna 1713. On f. 127b: in small letters, within the contours of the letters forming the words: *selik* and *b'y'l'a'* (*barukh ha-shem le-olam amen*): this prayerbook belongs to Simon Wolf ben Daniel Moses Oppenheim and his wife, Vogel bath Moses Zunz of Frankfurt; signed: Aryeh Judah Loeb ben Elhanan Katz of Trebitsch, Kislev 14, 473 (= December 13, 1712).
There are four frontispieces in this manuscript: 1: see title above; 2:

Yotzeroth mi-kol ha-shanah. Vienna 1714 (f. 79a); 3: *Selihoth*. 1712 (f. 128a); 4: *Seder tehillim*. 1712 (after f. 155). At end of volume: Wolf Oppenheim of Vienna.
JTS 9340. Acc. number: 01929. Gift of Miriam Schlessinger.

(33) *Tefillah mi-reshith ha-shanah ad aharith ha-shanah*.
Forchheim 1717-1720.
Scribe: David ben Elijah Segal of Forchheim.
Vellum. 198 f. 10 x 6 cm. Original leather binding.
Decoration: Colored miniatures. First frontispiece: Moses and Aaron, David, Jacob tending his sheep; second frontispiece (f. 128a): 7 Biblical scenes and miniature depicting *seder* table; numerous miniatures throughout the volume depicting various synagogue practices; ff. 35b-40a: *Perek shirah*, with many miniatures of animals, birds, trees, etc.; ff. 128a-151b: Haggadah, with many miniatures relating to the Haggadah and to the lives of the Patriarchs and to the Exodus.
Date on first frontispiece: faded; on second frontispiece: 1717; date of colophon (f. 195b): 1720.
Ownership entry: Lipman Janowitz, who acquired it from Herschel Neu...
JTS 9507. Acc. number: 03487. Gift of Harry K. Cohen.

(34) *Tefillah shel kol yemoth ha-shanah*.
1729.
Scribe: Perez ben Naftali Moses Abraham, *sofer* of Bingen.
For Uri Feivish ben Joseph Moses ha-Cohen and his wife, who presented it to the Synagogue of Abraham G'B' (?).
Vellum. 178 f. 33 x 26.5 cm.
Decoration: Some initial words in elaborate decorated panels, calligraphic letters.
F. 179b: Acrostic poem with name of Uri Feivish ben Joseph Moses ha-Cohen. Also: colophon: completed before *Pessah*, 1729, Perez ben Naftali Moses Abraham, *sofer* of Bingen.
JTS 9346. No acc. number. Gift of Rabbi T.E. Sandrow and Louis M. Rabinowitz.

(35) *Tefillah mi-kol ha-shanah*.
Metz 1660 (f. 224a); restored: 1797 (frontispiece).

Scribe: Abraham ben Mordecai Israel מְוְיא (on the original text, see colophon); Gerson ben Zanwel Katz, *sofer* of Metz (frontispiece).
For the Society for the Study of Mishnayoth through the generosity of Isaiah ben Herz Segal.
On f. 224b: list of 8 members of the Society for the Study of Mishnayoth who donated volume to the synagogue.
Vellum. 224 f. 32 x 26 cm.
Decoration: Frontispiece: columns and lions; some initial words in elaborate decorated panels; calligraphic letters.
JTS 9345. Acc. number: 01720. Gift of Rabbi T.E. Sandrow and Louis M. Rabinowitz.

Tikkun Erev Rosh Hodesh (Yom Kippur Katan)

(36) *Tikkun erev rosh hodesh.*
1723.
Scribe: Nathan Sofer of Mezeritsh.
On frontispiece: *be-otiyyoth Amsterdam.*
Vellum. 21 f. 12.5 x 7.5 cm. Original leather binding.
Decoration: Ink drawings. Frontispiece: two allegorical figures; at bottom: personification of Time, with book and sandglass (allusion to passing of time marked by the renewal of the new moon); 17a: two miniatures depicting men in posture of confession.
JTS 4432c. Acc. number: 76639. Gift of Louis Bamberger.

(37) *Erev rosh hodesh.*
No place, no date (ca. 1728).
Scribe: Judah Loeb ben Samson Segal.
Vellum. 16 f. 17 x 11 cm. Original leather binding.
Decoration: Colored miniatures. Frontispiece: Moses and Aaron. On top: well with pail and two pitchers; 13b: man in posture of confession.
Ownership entry: Jacob ben Moses Neuwit (born on first night of *Pessah*, 1728) and his brother Nahum (born 1733).
JTS 4411. Acc. number: 01055. Gift of Harry G. Friedman.

(38) *Tikkun erev rosh hodesh.*
1728.

Scribe: Nathan ben Samson of Mezeritsh in Moravia.
For Kossman ben Judah Jeremiah Segal of Leinz.
On frontispiece: *be-otiyyoth Amsterdam.*
Vellum. 16 f. 16 x 10 cm. Original leather binding. Ink drawings.
Decoration: Frontispiece: David and Solomon; decorated calligraphic letters.
Ownership entry: Gift of Benjamin Zeev ben Jacob Coopman to Judah Loeb ben Moses Dr. Landsberg, Maastricht 1870.
JTS 4433f. Acc. number: 01585. Gift of Harry G. Friedman.

Varia

(39) *Seder yotzeroth... gam... massekheth avoth.*
1717.
Scribe: Moses Loeb of Trebitsch.
On frontispiece: *be-otiyyoth Amsterdam.*
Vellum. 38 f. 15.5 x 9.5 cm. Original leather binding.
Decoration: Ink drawings. Frontispiece: portal with columns. Initial words in decorated panels, calligraphic letters.
JTS 4866. Acc. number: 01294. Gift of Mr. and Mrs. Bernard Katz.

(40) *Seder ha-selihoth shel kol yemoth ha-shanah.*
Metz 1725.
Scribe: David ben Josiah Isaac Moses ha-Levi (colophon, f. 111a).
Corrector: Solomon *Hazzan* Lipschuetz, *Hazzan* of Metz (f. 111b).
Vellum. 111 f. 36 x 28 cm. Original leather binding.
Decoration: Colored miniatures and ink drawings. Frontispiece: David; elaborate decorated panels surrounding initial words; calligraphic letters; 8b: hand holding cup; 9b: building surrounding word: *meshiah*; 10a: hand holding pen (above word: *sofer*); 26b: *shofar*; 36b: sacrifice of Isaac; 75a: hands holding candles; 80b: hand holding crown; 82a: hands in posture of priestly blessing; hand pouring water on hands of priest; hand holding incense; 97b: preparation for circumcision; 106a: outstretched hand with rod (Ahasuerus' hand?); bust and hand with hammer (meaning uncertain); 11a: breaking of two tablets of Law; Temple of Jerusalem.
Dedications on front flyleaf: Acrostic poem with name of Feiverl ben Simon Boaz Treni from Metz who donated manuscript; donor's

name is also indicated on frontispiece; f. 111b: Manuscript is donated to synagogue by Joshua Feiverl ben Simon Boaz Treni and his wife, Vogel.
JTS 9343. Acc. number: 01720. Gift of Rabbi T.E. Sandrow and Louis Rabinowitz.

(41) *Tikkun lel shavuoth ha-seder she-sidder ha-SheLaH... hoshana rabba... we-tikkun lel shevii shel pessah.*
Mannheim 1740.
On frontispiece: *be-otiyyoth Amsterdam.*
For Gabriel May Segal.
Vellum. 84 f. 19.5 x 14 cm. Original leather binding.
Decoration: Ink drawings. Frontispiece: Moses and Aaron (faces erased), angels and lions.
JTS 4385. Acc. number: 01512. Gift of M. Zagayski.

(42) *Seder birkath ha-kohanim.*
Berlin 1741.
Scribe: Nathan ben Joseph of זלאטדרי, in Berlin (f. 10b). 24 f. (1-10: vellum; 11-24: paper).
Vellum and paper. 11 x 7.5 cm. Original leather binding.
Decoration: Ink drawings, gilded letters. Frontispiece: hands in posture of priestly blessing, lions and crowns.
Includes other prayers, too.
Ownership entries: Frontispiece: Abraham ben Aaron Katz; Front flyleaf: Judah Rosenthal of Cologne presented it to his father, Aaron Rosenthal of Wuerzburg, in 1905.
JTS 4334. Acc. number: 01789. Gift of Harry G. Friedman.

(43) *Seder me-arvith... be-lel simhath torah.*
Kittsee 1747.
Scribe: [Hayyim ben Asher Anshel of Kittsee].
Paper. 25 f. 15 x 9.5 cm.
Decoration: Ink drawings. Frontispiece: Moses and Aaron; 8a: man handing *Sefer Torah* to other man.
Ownership entry: Samuel ben David Hils (?) of...
JTS 8337. Acc. number: 03470.

(44) *Tikkun keriath shema al ha-mittah we-seder ha-mizmorim mi-kol yemoth ha-shavua we-gam tefillath ha-derekh.*
1760.
Scribe: Levi Offenbach.
Vellum. 27 f. 10 x 7.5 cm. Original leather binding, stamped: Belongs to Mendele
Decoration: Ink drawings, calligraphic letters. Frontispiece: portal with columns; initial words in elaborately decorated panels; 16a: in panels of initial letters: David; synagogue building.
Ownership entries: Klerche Schweich (on frontispiece); Loeb ben Kalman Schweich bought it from the estate of his mother, Esther bath Nathan Berkessel, 1846 (on flyleaf); received from Meshullam Katzenbogen, Marseille 1937.
JTS 4432g. Acc. number: 01054. Gift of Harry G. Friedman.

(44a) *Seder keriath shema al ha-mittah... u-mizmorim...*
זנקיווערט 1775.
Scribe: Baruch Bendet ben Samuel Segal of Werlau (?) (ווערלה), being with Lezer N'S' (Neustadt?) of זנקיווערט (colophon).
For the bride Gittele bath Zelig Wilneritz.
Vellum. 20 f. 9.5 x 5 cm. Embroidered silk binding.
Decoration: Colored miniatures and ink drawings. Frontispiece: Moses and Aaron; 1b: drawing: portrait of a lady with violin (portrait of the bride, Gittele?); 11a: the guardian angel (Genesis 48:16).
JTS 4426. Acc number: 01962. Gift of Harry G. Friedman.

(45) *Sefirath ha-omer im tefillath minhah u-maariv u-mizmorim we-keriath shema al ha-mittah u-birkath ha-levanah.*
1771.
On frontispiece: *be-otiyyoth Amsterdam.*
Vellum: 33 f. 9 x 6 cm. Original leather binding.
Decoration: Colored miniatures. Frontispiece: Moses and Aaron. Days for counting of *omer* in colored roundels; 19a: *menorah*, formed from words of Psalm 67; 19b: *menorah*, formed from words of prayer: *ana be-koah*.

Ownership entries: On frontispiece: Brentelche, wife of Samuel in Mainz (?)... Karlsruhe...; Taube, wife of Joseph Gunzenhausen of Bonn (?).
JTS 4430. Acc. number: 01948.

(46) *Four scrolls (Song of Songs, Ruth, Lamentations, Ecclesiastes*).
No place, no date.
Vellum. 22f. 17 x 9.5 cm. Original leather binding.
Decoration: Colored miniatures. 1b: Judgement of Solomon; 5b: Ruth gleaning in the field; 9b: Temple of Jerusalem in flames; 14a: Satan in chains in front of Solomon.
Ownership entries: Herz of Medelsheim (=Herz Cerfberr); Mordecai ben Moses Engelmann.
JTS 8222. Acc. number: 01165. Gift of Florence Sutro Anspacher.

Indices

Places

Dates

Scribes

6 [For literature on the scribes see the forthcoming book by Schrijver, above note 5.] See A. Naményi, "La miniature juive au XVIIe et au XVIIIe siècle, *REJ*, vol. 116 (1957), pp. 61-63 and the English version of the above, in: Cecil Roth, *Jewish Art; An Illustrated History*, rev. ed. B. Narkiss (New York, 1971), pp. 158-159; A.N.Z. Roth, *Yeda Am*, v. 5 (1958), pp. 73-79; *Illustrated haggadot of the eighteenth century* (Jerusalem, 1983), pp. 30-31 and passim; see Scheiber's bibliography, compiled by Róbert Dán (in Scheiber, *Folklór és tárgytärténet*, 2nd ed, v. 2 (Budapest, 1977), pp. 507-573, numbers 875, 894, 930.

7 See Naményi, *op. cit.*, pp. 60-61; English version, *ibid.*, p. 158; *The book and its cover: an exhibit guide*, New York, The Jewish Museum, [1981], numbers 23-24.

8 See Scheiber's bibliography, *op. cit.*, numbers 436, 741, 1001, 1018, 1036 and his article in *Journal of Jewish Art*, v. 7 (1980), pp. 44-49; *Illustrated haggadot*, p. 31 and passim. For a facsimile reproduction of one of Hayyim's works see *The Kittsee Haggadah*, The Orphan Hospital Ward of Israel (New York, 1975), with an introduction by Tovia Preschel.

9 See Naményi, *op. cit.*, pp. 66-67; *Illustrated haggadot*, p. 31 and passim. For facsimiles of two of Jacob's works see *First printed edition of Haggadh etc.*, The Orphan Hospital Ward of Israel (New York, 1961) with an introduction by Moses Lutzki and *The Hamburg-Amsterdam Haggadah of 1728*, The Diskin Orphan Home of Israel (New York, 1980), with an introduction by Tovia Preschel.

10 See Naményi, *op. cit.*, pp. 64-65; English, *ibid.*, pp. 159-160; *Illustrated haggadot*, p. 31 and passim. For a facsimile of one of Leipnik's works see: *The Leipnik-Rosenthaliana Haggadah*, The Orphan Hospital Ward of Israel (New York, 1977) with an introduction by Tovia Preschel.

11 See Naményi, *op. cit.*, p. 63; English version, *ibid.*, p. 159; *Illustrated haggadot*, p. 31 and passim; Scheiber's bibliography, numbers 530, 956.

Iconography

12 See Scheiber's bibliography, numbers 842, 856, 1044, 1065, 1142.

13 See Naményi, *op. cit.*, pp. 59-60; English version, *ibid.*, p. 158.

14 See Naményi, *op. cit.*, p. 64; English version, *ibid.*, p. 159; *Illustrated haggadot*, p. 32 and passim.

15 For facsimiles of two of his works see *The Tel Aviv Haggadah* (1971) and *The Moshe Bamberger Haggadah* (1972), both published by The Orphan Hospital Ward of Israel, with introductions by Tovia Preschel.

16 See Y. Shahar, Askolath Moravia, in: *Third World Congress of Jewish Studies* (Jerusalem, 1965), p. 359.

Owners, patrons and donors

Manuscript numbers

The following are numbers of manuscripts in the Library of the Jewish Theological Seminary of America

A Fifteenth Century Hebrew Book List

Among the many achievements of Professor Herbert Zafren is his editorship, over the many years since its inception, of *Studies in Bibliography and Booklore*. In the first volume of the journal, the late Isaiah Sonne published and analyzed some Hebrew book lists.[1] It seems appropriate to contribute an article on the same subject to the volume of *Studies* that is dedicated to honor Herbert Zafren. Sonne was not the first to publish such book lists.[2] It was he, however, who emphasized the significance of the inventories of Hebrew books from the Middle Ages and the Renaissance as not merely sources for bibliographical knowledge, but also as documents that shed light on "general cultural patterns and trends."[3] Other scholars also worked on book lists, particularly the late Nehemia Allony who systematically collected relevant material on the subject and planned the publication of an entire *corpus* of Hebrew book lists. Unfortunately, the *corpus* has not yet been published and its present status is unknown.[4]

More recently, Robert Bonfil had been examining Hebrew book lists from Italy for knowledge that they can provide on the "cultural ambience" of Italian Jewry.[5] Another scholar, Shifra Baruchson, had

1 Isaiah Sonne, "Book Lists through Three Centuries," *Studies in Bibliography and Booklore* 1 (1953), 55-76; 2 (1955), 3-19. According to Sonne's original plan, six such lists should have been published.

2 For a list of such publications, including book lists from the Cairo Genizah, see Robert Bonfil, רשימת ספרים עברים מאימולה, *Scritti in Memoria di Umberto Nahon* (Jerusalem, 1978), pp. 48-49, notes 1-3.

3 *Studies* 1 (1953), 55.

4 See Robert Bonfil, *Rabbis and Jewish Communities in Renaissance Italy* (Oxford, New York, 1990), p. 275, note 18. Three of Allony's articles in which he published book lists are included in his *Studies in Medieval Philology and Literature*, vol. 5; *Bibliography and Book Art* (Jerusalem, 1979), pp. 185-227.

5 Bonfil, *Rabbis* pp. 272-280, for quotation see p. 272. In the original Hebrew of Bonfil's work, הרבנות באיטליה בתקופת הריניסאנס (Jerusalem, 1979), pp. 295-298, there is an appendix containing a list of 41 published and unpublished book lists from Italy, until 1540.

chosen this area as the focus of her scholarly interest. Her book on the significance of the inventories of Hebrew books confiscated in Mantua in 1595 for the understanding of the reading habits of Mantuan Jews is very important.[6] Still, Bonfil's assertion that "this entire area may still be considered as virgin territory"[7] is basically true even today and a comprehensive search for Hebrew book lists, their study and interpretation is still a *desideratum*. Accordingly, every new find of a medieval Hebrew book list is welcome, particularly if it originated from a Jewish community about whose cultural life very little is otherwise known. The list published here, as will be shown soon, represents a collection of Hebrew manuscripts that were assembled in southern Italy, a geographical area that was excluded from Bonfil's study "due to the almost complete lack of internal Jewish documents pertaining to the Rabbinate in Sicily and the Kingdom of Naples."[8] Our document, therefore, lifts the veil of darkness a little from an obscure corner of Jewish cultural history.

The list, published here for the first time, is found on f. 89b of Manuscript 2601 (E.N. Adler 1743) at the Library of the Jewish Theological Seminary [JTS]. The volume lacks beginning and end, as well as any explicit information about where, when, and by whom it was written. It contains translations into Hebrew of a number of Arabic and Latin astrological and astronomical treatises,[9] copied in various

6 Shifra Baruchson, *Books and Readers; The Reading Interests of Italian Jews at the Close of the Renaissance* (Ramat-Gan, 1993) (in Hebrew).

7 Bonfil, *Rabbis*, p. 275.

8 See esp. Bonfil, *Rabbis*, p. 275 and note 18.

9 The late Alexander Marx, in a handwritten note on the flyleaf of the manuscript identified the contents as follows:

1-72: Abu Ma'shar, מבוא הגדול לחכמת התכונה, II-VIII. *H.Ueb*. 570.

73-80: List of Constellations.

81-82: Arnald de Villa Nova, *De judiciis astronomiae*, abridged by the translator, Jacob ben Judah Cabret. *H.Ueb* 783. End missing.

83-85: Pseudo-Hippocrates, *De esse aegrotorum secundum lunam*. Leon Joseph's translation, without introduction? *H.Ueb*. 666.

86-88: *Sefer ha-Tekufah* = Neub. 2028,3. Notes.

89b: List of MSS.

90-147a: Levi Abraham, ספר הכולל, chs. 36-40.

147-151: Arnald de Villa Nova, *De judiciis astronomiae*, פנים במשפט, trans. by Sol Abigdor. *H.Ueb*. 782/783.

152: Immanuel, Notes on Ibn Ezra's astrol. writings.

153-155: Ptolemy, *Centiloquium*, ס הפרי, trans. by Jacob ben Elijah. *H.Ueb*. 530.

fifteenth century Provencal and Italian cursive and semi-cursive scripts.

In the booklist itself there appear three entries that are identified as orders of prayer according to the rite of ליצי (Nos. 12-13, 15). I consulted Dr. Seth Jerichower of JTS, who kindly and immediately identified the word as standing for the southern Italian city of Lecce. In searching for information about the Jews of Lecce in the fifteenth century, I learned that it was the birthplace of the well-known grammarian and physician, Abraham de Balmes, author of the grammatical work מקנה אברם. In Hebrew and Italian sources, the names of members of the Balmes family are also given. Three sons of an Abraham de Balmes in Lecce in the fifteenth century are recorded in Italian documents as Mayr, Moyses, and Struch. In the Seminary manuscript, on the page preceeding the book list, there is a register of births of children. The entries are in the first person singular, written by the father, without identifying his name, and are in the same hand as the book list. This register records the births of three sons: Moses, in 1440, Meir, in 1442, and Astruc, in 1444. There can be no doubt that these three sons are the same as the sons whose names were recorded in contemporary Italian documents.[10]

The Abraham de Balmes who authored מקנה אברם died in 1523. Accordingly, it is impossible that the father of the three sons whose births are registered in the 1440s should still be alive in 1523. It is clear, therefore, that there were two persons by this name, probably grandfather and grandson, and that the writer who registered the births of three sons in our manuscript was Abraham de Balmes, the elder.[11] As

10 On Abraham de Balmes and family see Nicola Ferorelli, "Abramo de Balmes di Lecce," *Archivio Storico per le Province Napoletane* 31 (1906), 632-654; on the sons, see esp. 637; Giovanni Guerrieri, "Gli Ebrei a Brindisi e a Lecce," *Studi Senesi nel Circolo Giuridico della R. Universita* 17 (1900), pp. 225-252; H. Vogelstein and P. Rieger, *Geschichte der Juden in Rom* (Berlin, 1895-1896), vol. 2, pp. 20, 22-23. In the beginning of the introduction to his grammatical work, מקנה אברם, Abraham de Balmes gives his genealogy as follows:
נאום... אברהם... בן קדוש... מאיר דבלמש בן... אברהם בן... משה בן... מאיר בכר חזקיה מציף דבלמש.
See also A.M. Habermann, *The Printer Daniel Bomberg and the List of Books Published by His Press* (Safed, 1978) (in Hebrew), p. 23, note 30. For a recent bibliography on him, see Daniel Carpi, *Between Renaissance and Ghetto* (Tel Aviv, 1989), p. 106, note 26 (in Hebrew).

11 Joseph Perles, *Beitraege zur Geschichte der hebraeischen und aramaeischen Studien* (Munich, 1884), p. 194 assumes that there was only one Abraham de Balmes who reached a very old age. The entry: "Balmes de, Abraham ben Meir," in the German *Encyclopaedia Judaica* (vol. 3, Berlin, 1929, 1008-1009) also speaks about only one scholar by that name and gives his dates as ca. 1440-1523. We know that the younger Abraham de Balmes died in 1523 from the Venice 1523 edition of his book, מקנה אברם, f. l. IIIb. [Profesor Daniel Carpi called by attention to a

mentioned above, the book list and the birth register are written in the same script. Therefore, we may identify the person who made these notes, the owner of the books and the father of Moses, Meir, and Astruc, as one and the same; namely, Abraham de Balmes, the elder, of Lecce. The fact that the script of these notes is a Provencal cursive should not be surprising; we know that Abraham de Balmes came to southern Italy from Provence.[12]

There is additional support for placing our entire manuscript, and not only the book list and book register, in Lecce. The watermark in the paper, a pair of scissors, is documented from southern Italy (Palermo) and Provence from the years 1446 and 1448.[13] But even more interesting is the fact that some of the treatises copied in the manuscript are connected elsewhere with Lecce. According to Moritz Steinschneider, Abu Ma'shar's מבוא הגדול, that appears as the first treatise in the JTS manuscript, had been known previously in only one manuscript, written in 1439 in Lecce, of all places.[14] Alexander Marx, in a handwritten comment on Steinschneider's statement, notes the existence of two additional manuscripts: the one discussed here and one in Vienna.[15] The connection of the JTS manuscript with Lecce was established above. The Vienna manuscript also leads to the same city: there is a reference in it to a natural phenomenon that took place in Lecce in 1473.[16] The JTS manuscript (f. 165b) contains a similar entry concerning the observation of some strange natural apparition in Lecce in the same year. And if the above is not sufficient, it should be pointed out that the astrological work *Centiloquium*, the last treatise in our manuscript in the translation of Jacob ben Elijah, is included in the same Vienna manuscript to which we just referred.[17] On the basis of all this, one can state with a great degree of certainty that the JTS manuscript was written in Lecce in the middle of the

document published by him in his *Between Renaissance and Ghetto* (Tel Aviv, 1989), p. 105 (in Hebrew). According to that document Abraham de Balmes, the Younger, died before 1520.]

12 Perles, *Beitraege*, p. 194.

13 C.M. Briquet, *Les Filigranes*, v. 3 (Amsterdam, 1968, Facsimile of the 1907 ed.), nos. 3665-3666.

14 Moritz Steinschneider, *Die hebraeischen Uebersetzungen des Mittelalters* (Berlin, 1893), p. 570.

15 The note is found in the copy of Steinschneider's work mentioned in the previous footnote (Z 7070 S83 v.2. c.2). About the Vienna manuscript, see Arthur Zacharias Schwartz, *Die hebraeischen Handschriften der Nationalbibliothek Wien* (Leipzig, 1925), pp. 227-231 (no. 196).

16 Schwartz, *Hebr. Handschriften*, p. 231.

17 Steinschneider, *Hebr. Uebersetzungen*, p. 530 and Schwartz, *Hebr. Handschriften*, p. 227.

fifteenth century and that the book list published here represents the books owned by Abraham de Balmes, the elder, of the same city. That Balmes was interested in Hebrew manuscripts can also be attested to by the fact that in 1452 he commissioned the copying of a compendium of Galen's medical works in Hebrew translation.[18] These facts seem to indicate that Lecce in the mid-fifteenth century had a Jewish community whose members were actively engaged in commissioning, owning, and studying manuscripts of scientific and philosophic works.

Let us now turn to the book list itself. It is divided into subject categories: [Bible], [Prayer-books], Bible commentaries, Talmud and Codes, Philosophy, and Mathematics.[19] "Classified" book lists are rather uncommon otherwise. The list identifies the material on which the manuscripts were written as parchment, paper, or a combination of the two.[20] The condition of the manuscripts is stated occasionally (nos. 6 and 10), as well as the fact that a certain manuscript was incomplete (no. 56). In this particular case, the owner added that he himself completed the book. The compiler remarks about two items (nos. 44 and 45) that they were with a certain R. David. It is not clear whether this R. David was a dealer in books, a scribe, or someone with whom these manuscripts were deposited for safekeeping as a pledge.

The size of the manuscripts is usually given as folio or half-folio. Some of the manuscripts did not contain complete texts, as noted in connection with entries no. 66 and no. 75. Number 11 was a "multi-layered" manuscript, containing a prayerbook in the middle surrounded by various Biblical texts.[21] The first item in the various subject categories is designated as ראשונה (nos. 1, 16, 42, 64). Similar designations for the first book appearing

18 Aaron Freimann, "Jewish Scribes in Medieval Italy," *Alexander Marx Jubilee Volume*, English section (New York, 1950), p. 284 (no. 246a). About other Hebrew manuscripts written in Lecce, see nos. 100 ab.; 111 ab.; 164a; 295a; 477a. [See now: the Parma Catalogue, below note 29, numbers 1472, 1507.] The manuscripts listed under no. 100 are repeated under no. 111 as a result of a variance in the name of the scribe. Jacob ben Elijah, the translator mentioned above, may have had some connection with Lecce, too. See also note 29.

19 The numbers were added by me. Part of the page is water-damaged and some spots are illegible. Still, I was able to decipher some lines, especially 1-5, 35-41, with the aid of an ultra-violet lamp.

20 On the latter, see Malachi Beit-Arié, *Hebrew Codicology* (Paris, 1976), pp. 37-39.

21 On this kind of Manuscript, see Malachi Beit-Arié, *Hebrew Manuscripts of East and West; Towards a Comparative Codicology* (London, 1992), (The Panizzi Lectures, 1992) pp. 86-88. A very beautiful fifteenth century manuscript in two volumes, at JTS (Ms. 4501-4502), contains the *Mahzor* according to the Roman rite, surrounded by the text of the Pentateuch, the Haftaroth, Psalms, Proverbs, Job, the Five Scrolls, Ezra, Daniel, and Chronicles.

on a list are found elsewhere as well.[22] The phrase בקובץ אחד [in one volume] occurs in nos. 7, 44-45, 47-48, 50, 52-53, indicating that several works were included in one volume.

The first item on the list, a Bible, is called מקדשיה,[23] and it, as well as no. 9, are characterized as belonging to the Toledan type of Hebrew Bible manuscripts. Toledo was the home of the famous so-called Hilleli model codex of the Bible.[24] Other manuscripts are identified as having been written in square script (nos. 19 and 43) or in the script called *Mashq* or *Mashait*, a semi-cursive Rabbinic script (no. 8).[25]

In the second division, six prayerbooks are listed. The rite of two of them is unidentified, although it may be assumed that they were of the usual Italian rite. Number 11 also contained Biblical texts on the margin.[26] Number 14 is a *Mahzor* following the usage of Provence.[27] Most interesting is the mention of three prayerbooks according to the order of Lecce. Very little information has come down to us about the prayerbooks of Sicilian and southern Italian Jewish communities[28] and there is no reference, to the best of my knowledge, to any prayerbook as following the order of the Jews of Lecce.[29] On the basis of this brief mention, it is impossible to determine whether the Lecce rite was indeed

22 E.g., קודם in the lists published by Sonne (see above, note 1), p. 11 and by Allony (see above, note 4), 198, p. 201.

23 On this term, see Allony, *op. cit.*, pp. 298-310 (originally published in *Studies in Bibliography and Booklore*, 14), esp. p. 299, note 11 where Allony refers to Naftali Wieder's article, "Sanctuary as a Metaphor for Scripture," *Journal of Jewish Studies* 8 (1957), 165-175.

24 On the Toledan Hilleli codex, see Nahum M. Sarna's introduction to the facsimile edition of *The Pentateuch; Early Spanish Manuscript (Codex Hillely)* (Jerusalem, 1974). About Hebrew Bibles written in Toledo, see also Bezalel Narkiss, *Hebrew Illuminated Manuscripts in the British Isles* 1 (Jerusalem and London, 1982), p. 20.

25 Beit-Arié (see above note 21), p. 116, note 40. The term occurs in other book lists too. See e.g. in the lists published by E.E. Urbach, קרית ספר, 15 (1938-1939), 238-239 and by S. Assaf, קרית ספר, 24 (1947-1948), 248.

26 See above note 21. The repetition of וסביב הס' is simply due to dittography.

27 Stefan Reif, *Judaism and Hebrew Prayer* (Cambridge, 1993), pp. 167-168.

28 J. Sermoneta, "נוסח התפילה של יהודי סיציליה", *Jews in Italy; Studies Dedicated to the Memory of U. Cassuto* (Jerusalem, 1988), Hebrew Section, pp. 131-217, esp. 131 and 157, note 53.

29 But see manuscript Parma 89 (Freimann, "Jewish Scribes," p. 321, no. 477). In De Rossi's catalog, this manuscript is identified as *Seder, seu Ordo precum totius anni.* Freimann identifies it as a manuscript of Pentateuch and Psalms. The manuscript was written in Lecce in 1485. [See now in *The Biblioteca Palatina in Parma*, Ed. by B. Richler (Jerusalem, 2001), number 1089, where the rite is identified as "Romanian (south Italian) rite".]

different from other rites, to what degree, and in what way. However, the mere fact that the existence of Lecce prayerbooks is recorded is an interesting addition to what we know about the prayer rites of medieval Jewish communities.

The next division includes Rabbi Jonah ibn Janah's Hebrew dictionary (no. 23),[30] his grammar, ספר הרקמה (no. 36),[31] and the grammatical work פתח דברי (no. 36).[32] A glossary on Psalms and the latter Prophets is listed under no. 24.[33] The standard Bible commentators are represented by Rashi (nos. 16, 17, 18), Abraham ibn Ezra (no. 19), Levi ben Gershon (Gersonides) (nos. 21 and 22), David Kimhi (no. 25), and super-commentaries on Rashi (no. 39). It is interesting to note that this division, Bible commentaries, includes, besides Bible commentaries proper, also grammatical and philosophical works. The compiler of the list considered works of Jewish philosophy and ethics, and grammatical works, as being, ultimately, instruments of Bible exegesis. On the other hand, Aristotelian and similar works are classified by him as philosophy, as distinct and separate from Jewish philosophical books. Maimonides' *Guide to the Perplexed* occurs three times in this section. Besides a parchment manuscript without commentary (no. 27), there are two other copies of the *Guide* on the list; one with the commentary of Maestre Vidal (no. 31), who is better known as Moses Narboni,[34] and another one by Zerahiah (no. 32), who is identical with Zerahiah ben Isaac ben Shealtiel Gracian (Hen).[35] The commentary of Narboni is accompanied by some Kabbalistic matters (דברים אחדים מקבלה). It is well known that Narboni had an inclination toward mysticism. Therefore, it makes sense that a manuscript containing his works on the *Guide* should also contain additional Kabbalistic matters, although it is impossible to determine whether these were by Narboni himself or were drawn from some other source.

30 See Michael Wilensky's edition (Jerusalem, 1964) (2nd edition).

31 *ibid.*

32 See *Enc. Jud.* (Jerusalem, 1972), 16, 1389. no. 81A.

33 It mentions four (!) latter Prophets. Probably, under the fourth the Minor Prophets were meant as one unit.

34 Maestre Vidal is Moses Narboni, see *Enc. Jud.*, 12, 422.

35 See *Enc. Jud.*, 7, 842-843.

36 See Levi ben Gershon (Gersonides), *The Wars of the Lord*. Translated with an introduction and notes by Seymour Feldman (Philadelphia, 1984-1987).

In this section one also find Gersonides' מלחמות השם (no. 28),[36] Albo's עקרים (no. 29),[37] Bahya's חובות הלבבות (no. 30),[38] Judah Halevi's כוזרי (no. 33),[39] as well as Samuel ibn Tibbon's מאמר יקוו המים (no. 34),[40] and an unidentified philosophical work (no. 26). The work זכרון טוב (no. 20) is probably Nathan ben Samuel Tibbon's mystical commentary on the Pentateuch.[41] Finally, it is most likely that the entry סוד ה' (no. 41) refers to Ezra Gatigno's book by the same title.[42] Now, it is interesting to note that the last two works are known to have been copied by a scribe who was active in Lecce. This scribe, Elijah ben David, copied a manuscript of זכרון טוב in 1381 (the place of copying is not mentioned) and Gatigno's סוד ה' in Lecce in 1414 and 1423.[43] These two works appearing on our list actually may have been the ones that were written by this Lecce scribe but, of course, this is just speculation. In any case, a link exists among the titles entered on our list and the products of known scribal activities in Lecce.

The next group contains Talmudic and Rabbinic works: a full set of the Mishnah (no. 42), various Talmudic tractates (nos. 43, 44, 46), unidentified commentaries on various Talmud tractates (nos. 45 and 49), Rashi's commentary on some Talmudic tractates (nos. 51 and 54), Isaac Alfasi's הלכות on some Talmud tractates (nos. 47 and 48), parts of Maimonides' משנה תורה (nos. 50, 52, 53), the first two parts of Jacob ben Asher's ארבעה טורים (nos. 55 and 56), and two books on the Commandments, probably both by Isaac of Corbeil (nos. 57 and 58).[44]

37 In many manuscripts and printed editions.

38 In many manuscripts and printed editions.

39 In many manuscripts and printed editions.

40 Published in Pressburg, 1837, the book is a philosophical treatise dealing with the first chapter of Genesis, esp. the creation of waters.

41 See on this work, Abraham Berliner, "Aus Handschriften," *Festschrift zum siebzigsten Geburtstage David Hoffman's* (Berlin, 1913), p. 290.

42 The full title of this work is סוד ה' ליראיו, but occasionally it was quoted as סוד ה'. See M. Steinschneider, *Gesammelte Schriften* (Berlin, 1925), p. 5, note 13.

43 Berliner (see note 41) describes the Parma manuscript of זכרון טוב as having been written by Elijah ben David in 1381. [See now Parma Catalogue, above note 29, number 632.] On the two manuscripts of סוד ה' written in Lecce, see Freimann (above note 18), p. 256, no. 100. Freimann has separate entries for the scribe of the זכרון טוב, no. 99, and the scribe of סוד ה', no. 100. There is no doubt that they are one and the same person.

44 All these works are known in many manuscripts and printed editions. עמודי גולה (no. 59) is the title of Isaac of Corbeil's ספר מצוות קטן, the סמ"ק.

The last five entries in this category (nos. 59-63) refer to works on Talmudic orders or tractates by authors who are designated as "רב הגדול" or "[רב] השני", respectively. There is no doubt that by these references the compiler meant Rabbi Isaiah di Trani, the Elder, and his grandson, Rabbi Isaiah di Trani, the Younger. This is the way these authors had been referred to in many medieval sources.[45] The relatively prominent place these works occupy on our list is an indication of their popularity in Lecce; after all, Trani and Lecce are two communities not too far from each other on the Adriatic Coast in southern Italy.

The next division contains general philosophical works, mainly parts of Aristotle's philosophical *oeuvre*, with the commentaries of Averroes. Mentioned here are: Aristotle's *Physica*, with Averroes' middle commentary (no. 64), *De Caelo*, with the short commentary (Epitome) (no. 65), *De Generatione et Corruptione, Meterologica*, and parts of *De Anima* (no. 66), *Metaphysica*, with short commentary (Epitome) (no. 73); *Metaphysica*, with middle commentary (no. 74), and parts of *Metaphysica*, with long commentary (no. 75).[46] Also mentioned are two copies of the commentary on *Physica* by Levi ben Gershon (Gersonides) (nos. 67 and 71).[47] Other philosophical works listed here are the following: Al-Ghazali's *Intentions of the Philosophers*, in Isaac Albalag's translation (no. 68)[48] and, finally, Ibn Tufayl's חי בן יקטן and Averroes' *Epistle on the Possibility of Conjunction* (no. 76), perhaps both with Moshe Narboni's commentary.[49] Albalag's translation was "read with interest in the Jewish intellectual

45 See Zedekiah ben Abraham min ha-anavim, שבלי הלקט, ed. S. K. Mirsky (New York, 1966), p. 29, esp. notes 1-2. These works are now in the process of being published under the title פסקי הרי"ד and פסקי הריא"ז, Makhon ha-Talmud ha-Yisra'eli ha-shalem (Jerusalem, 1964) ff.

46 For a listing of these (and other) commentaries by Averroes on Aristotle, see H.A. Wolfson, "Plan for a Corpus Commentariorum Averrois in Aristotelem," *Speculum* 6 (1931), 415-416.

47 See Levi ben Gershon (Gersonides), *The Wars of the Lord*; translated with an introduction by Seymour Feldman (Philadelphia, 1984), vol. 1, 25.

48 See G. Vajda's article about Albalag in *Enc. Jud.*, vol 2, pp. 520-521. See also Vajda's introduction to his edition of Albalag's ספר תיקון הדעות (Jerusalem, 1973), pp. 9-13 (and the literature listed there).

49 See *The Epistle on the Possibility of Conjunction with the Active Intellect by Ibn Rushd with the Commentary of Moses Narboni*; a critical edition and annotated translation by Kalman P. Bland (New York, 1982). For Narboni's commentary on חי בן יקטן, see pp. 1 and 14, note 12.

circles" of southern Italy; it is known that the work had been copied in southern Italy several times.[50]

In the last category, mathematics,[51] Abraham ibn Ezra's ספר המספר[52] appears in two copies. The list closes with a manuscript by Al-Farghani, probably one of his astronomical works.[53]

To summarize: this book list, containing manuscripts probably owned by Abraham de Balmes, the elder, in Lecce, southern Italy, from the middle of the fifteenth century, bears testimony to the wide intellectual interests of the owner. The fact that the number of books of general philosophy more or less equals that of Talmud and Codes is an indication of an intriguing balance of cultural and religious interests. The inclusion of Jewish works of philosophy in the division of Bible commentaries not only shows the owner's interest in the subject, but also the high value he placed on these works, putting them on the same level as the most popular and respected Bible commentaries. Finally, the book list and, for that matter, the entire JTS manuscript 2061, reflects local, southern Italian cultural tastes and interests, particularly those of the city of Lecce.[54]

...אשר לי בשנת אלף...

[מקרא]

1. ראשונה מקדשיה אחת... מכתיבה (!) טולידאנו עם מסורה גדולה וקטנה
2. חומש אחר קטן עם הפטרות וה' מגילות
3. חומש אחר עם הפטרות וחמש מגילות
4. חומש עם חמש מגילות
5. חומש עם חמש מגילות
6. כתובים שלימים מטושטשים
7. איוב ומשלי בקובץ אחד
8. נביאים ראשונים מנייר וקלף מכתיבת משקה
9. נביאים אחרונים מקלף מכתיבה (!) טולידנו עם מסורה גדו' וקטנ'

50 See above, note 47.

51 Mathematics is called החכמה הלימודית in medieval sources, see Jacob Klatzkin, אוצר המונחים הפילוסופיים, v. 2 (Berlin, 1928), p. 121.

52 See Israel Levin, *Abraham ibn Ezra Reader* (New York-Tel Aviv, 1985), pp. 23, 397 (in Hebrew).

53 See Moritz Steinschneider, *Hebr. Uebersetzungen* (Berlin, 1893), pp. 554-557.

54 Upon completion of my article I came across: Gerard E. Weil, *La Bibliotheque de Gersonides: d'apres son catalogue autographe* (Louvain-Paris: E. Peeters, 1991). It was too late to refer in detail to the points of mutual interest that exist between the book list of *Gersonides* and the one published here, but I want to call the attention of the reader to this important publication.

[תפילות]

10. תפילות שלימות עם עניינים אחרים מטושטשות
11. תפילות אחרות שלימות עם משלי ואיוב ואיכה ורות ושיר השירים וסביב הספר וסביב הספ׳ תלים ורות
12. עוד תפילות אחרות כפי סדר ליצי
13. עוד תפילות אחרות כפי סדר ליצי
14. מחזור מסודר כפי סדר פרובינצא מקלף
15. עוד מחזור מסודר כפי סדר ליצי מקלף

מביאורי התורה

16. ראשונה פי׳ רבינו שלמה בקלף
17. [בצד]: עו׳ רב׳ שלמה מבראשית שמות (?) ויקרא
18. [בצד]: עוד אחד מקלף ונייר וה׳ מגילות
19. ר׳ אברהם ן׳ עזרא בקלף בכתיבה מרובעת
20. זכרון טוב מחצי פול׳
21. מר׳ לוי גרשום ביאור על דניאל ואיוב מקלף ונייר מחצי פול׳
22. פי׳ שיר השירים ומשלי מר׳ לוי בן גרשום מחצי פול׳
23 שרשים מר׳ יונה מפולייאה שלימה
24. מלות מתילים וד׳ נביאים אחרונים
25. פי׳ משמואל ומלכים מקמחי מקלף ונייר מחצי פול׳
26. ספרים תורניים מעורבים עם עיון פילוסופי
27. מורה הנבוכים מקלף מפול׳
28. מלחמות השם מנייר מפול׳
29. ר׳ יוסף אלבו מקלף ונייר מחצי פול׳
30. חובת הלבבות מחצי פול׳
31. פי׳ מאי׳ וידאל על מורה הנבוכים מנייר וקלף עם דברים אחרים מקבלה
32. קצת מביאור ר׳ זרחיה על מורה הנבוכים מחצי פול׳ מק׳ ונייר
33. ספר כוזר מקלף
34. מאמר יקוו מנייר וקלף
35. ...
36. ... הרקמה פתח דברי מחצי פול׳
37. מבראשית עד קדושים תהיו פול׳
38. ... מחצי פול׳
39. פירושים על רבנו שלמה מקלף ונייר חצי פול׳
40. ביאורים אחרים (?) מקלף ונייר
41. ... סוד ה׳ ועניינים אחרים

מספרי התלמוד ופסק

42. ראשונה משניות כל התלמוד
43. מסכת עירובין ויומא מקלף מרובעת ופולייה גדולה
44. מסכת בכורות וערכין בקובץ אחד מקלף והוא ביד ר׳ דוד
45. פי׳ מבכורות וערכין בקובץ אח׳ מקלף והוא ביד ר׳ דוד
46. ברכות ותעניות מקלף
47. מסכת יבמות וגיטין וכתובות וקידושין מקלף בקובץ אחד מר׳ יצחק אלפסי
48. תלתא בבות וסנהדרין ושבועות וע״ז בקובץ אחד מקלף מהאלפס
49. מסכת כתובות ויום טוב מנייר מפול׳ הפי׳ מפול׳ ג״כ
50. מדע אהבה זמנים מקלף בקובץ אחד
51. פי׳ מרש״י בערובין פסחים מקלף מפולייה קטנה
52. ספר זרעים עבודה וקרבנות בקובץ א׳ מקלף
53. ספר משפטים ושופטים מנייר וקלף בקובץ אחד
54. פי׳ מרש״י מיבמות מפול׳ קלף ונייר
55. אורח חיים מנייר מפול׳
56. יורה דעה מנייר ואינו שלם השלמתיו
57. קיצור א׳ ממצוות מקלף
58. עמודי גולה מקלף
59. סדר מועד מרב הגדול מקלף ונייר מפול׳
60. סדר נשים מרב הגדול מקלף ונייר מפול׳
61. מסכת שבת וערובין מרב הגדול מקל׳ מנייר מפול׳
62. פסחים סוכה מגילה תעניות מרב הגדול מפול׳ מנייר
63. סדר נשים מרב השני מקלף... סדר נזיקין מקלף

מפילוסופים

64. ראשונה שמע טבעי האמצעי מקלף ונייר מחצי פול׳ בקובץ אחד
65. שמים והעולם הקצר
66. הויה והפסד אותות עליונות ספ׳ הנפש ממאמר י״ג מס׳ כ״א עד סוף הס׳ מקלף ונייר בקובץ אחד
67. פי׳ משמע מר׳ לוי בן גרשום מקלף ונייר מחצי פול׳
68. כונות מאבוחמד מהעתקת אלבלג
69. [בצד]:... מפול׳...
70. [בצד]: ...מחצי פול׳ מהעתקת...
71. פי׳ משמע מר׳ לוי בן גרשום מקלף ונייר מפול׳
72. העיוניות (?)
73. הקיצורים ממה שאחר מחצי פול׳
74. האמצעים ממה שאחר מחצי פול׳

75. המאמר הז׳ והח׳ והט׳ והי׳ ממה שאחר הארוך מחצי פול׳
76. חי בן יקטן ואגרת אפשרות הדבקות

מלמודיות

77. מספר מן עזרה אחד מקלף ואחד מנייר וקלף מחצי פול׳
78. אלפרגני מפול׳ מנייר

Rashi's *Commentary on the Pentateuch and on the Five Scrolls*, Venice, Bomberg, 1538

The Hebrew Union College Library in Cincinnati owns a very rare printed edition of Rashi's *Commentary on the Pentateuch and on the Five Scrolls.*[1] There are only three other copies known of this book: one in the British Museum,[2] another in the Schocken Institute in Jerusalem, and a third in a private collection in the same city.[3]

The late Isaiah Sonne, in an article on the text-criticism of Rashi's *Commentary on the Pentateuch*, has called attention to this rare, 1538 edition and to its many interesting features.[4] An examination of the volume, indeed, reveals some new information and, at the same time, raises some questions relating to the activity of Daniel Bomberg's famous Venetian printing house.

On the title page we read:

פירוש רש״י על התורה ועל
חמש מגילות נדפס שנית עם רב העיון ע״י
השר דניאל בומבירג מאנוירש״ה
בשנת רצ״ח לפ״ק
פה ויניציאה

The book, in small quarto, contains 197 leaves. At the end there is the following colophon, in rhymed prose:[4a]

1 I wish to express my thanks to Prof. H. Zafren for providing me with a microfilm copy of the book.

2 Cf. M. Steinschneider, Supplement to *CB*, p. 506; Van Straalen, p. 225.

3 I am grateful to Mr. A. Rosenthal of the Schocken Institute in Jerusalem for calling these copies to my attention.

4 י. זנה, לביקורת הטכסט של פירוש רש״י על התורה, *HUCA*, v. 15, p. 40 (Hebrew section).

4a The rhymes are indicated by a slash.

בהיות כי כל השכנים/ אשר סביבותי ישנים/ ושבחי לא יגידו/ ועל טובי לא יעידו/ לשבח את עצמי אתעורר/ אף שאמר המשורר/ יהללך זר ולא פיך/ אקרא מלת ולא במשיכה/ ועם פיך אותו לא אחבר/[5] והישר אדבר/ ואגיד מישרים/ ודברי אמת נכרים/ הנה כאשר זממתי/ ובלבי הסכמתי/ להדפיס הספר הזה שהוא באור תורתנו הקדושה מהנשר הגדול הרב המובהק רבינו שלמה יצחקי ז"ל כי באמת על כל דברי התורה הזאת/ פירוש זולת פירושו לא יאות/ וכל המפרשי' שפירשום ודרשום/ נחשבים כנגדו כקליפת השום/ כי כל התלמוד הארוך/ היה לפניו כשלחן ערוך/[6] לכן פירוש המצוות ודקדוקם/ לא יצאו מתחת ידו רקם/ ועליו אמרו המושלים/ בדרך מליצה אלו המלים/ כל פרש"תא תרמוס לאשפתא/ חוץ מן פרש"נדתא ופר"תא/[7] והנה אף כי נדפס הספר הזה כמה פעמים בכל המקומות אשר נמצא שם בית דפיסה/[7א] אכן לרוב טובו ותועלתו/ ושאין מי יעמוד בלתו ספו תמו מן הארץ וכל מבקשיו לא ימצאונהו ואני בראותי כי כן/ ולעמוד בלתו לא יתכן/ שנסתי את מתני לרגל המלאכה אשר לפני ואמרתי עת לעשו' לה'/ והסכמתי להדפיסו/ אף הפעם והשתדלתי בהגהתו/[7ב] בעיון רב וקבצתי העתקו' היותר מוגהות וטובות/ מן המחוקקות ומן הנכתבו'/ אך מצאתי בהם שנוי והפרדה/ שניין דא מן דא/ יש שבא בארוכה/ ויש שבא בקצרה/ וזה לסיבת מיעוט ידיעת המגיהים ושלא הבינו עצתו ומה טובו/ שמו בו דברים אשר לא צוה ולא עלו על לבו/ וכן קם אחד מבני שונצי"ן/ חשב עצמו ראש וקצין/ והתפאר לאמר כי הוא ידפיס פירוש רבינו שלמה/ שבכל העולם לא יהיה דומו/ וכל שלפניו נחקקו ונכתבו/ מאפס ותהו לו נחשבו/ והנה ראיתי את אשר כבר עשהו/ והב"ל הביא גם הוא/ ובמקומות אין חקר/ העיד עדות שקר/ ובמקצת מקומות

5 On this well-known, humorous interpretation of Proverbs 27,2, cf. Eshtori Farhi, כפתור ופרח, ch. 44, ed. J. Blumenfeld, v. 2, p. 833; Ratner, אהבת ציון וירושלים, v. 12, p. 231; cf. also Zohar, v. 3, f. 193b and N. S. Libowitz, פניני הזהר, pp. 23-4.

6 Cf. Moses ibn Danon, כללים, MS. JTS, Rab. 959, f. 101a-b and MS. JTS, Rab. 955, f. 68a: כת' גברא רבא על ר"ת וז"ל שאני ר"ת דרב גובריה והיה כרש"י ור"ח ובה"ג והיה כאחד מהם ואולי יותר מהם בחריפות ובקיאות לפי מה שנראה ממה שחידש בתלמוד וכל חכמי ישראל הנמצאים היום כלם כקליפת השום וכגרגיר שומשין נגד אחד מתלמידיו הקטנים וכו';
cf. also Responsa of R. Isaac bar Sheshet, no. 394:
המאור הגדול רבינו שלמה זכר צדיק לברכה גלה עמוקות התלמוד מני חשך לא עממוהו כל סתום ובזולת פירושו היה כדברי הספר החתום והמאור השני רבינו יעקב איש תם אשר כמוהו בפלפול לא נהיה מאחר שהתלמוד נחתם תלמוד ערוך בפיו וכו'.

The first statement is quoted, the second is mentioned by Azulay in his שם הגדולים s.v. R. Jacob ben Meir, י' no. 241.

7 This saying is found in a slightly different version in Moses ibn Danon's כללים, MS. Oxford, no. 850, f. 14b (this section is missing in the two JTS MSS. mentioned in the preceding note). Azulay, op. cit., s.v. Rashi, ש' no. 35 quotes it from Ibn Danon's work. Cf. Aptowitzer, *Bitzaron*, v. 2, p. 324 note 1; Wellesz, *Rasi* (Budapest, 1906), p. 111, 187 (in Hungarian); A. Geiger, פרשנדתא p. 5.

7a Apparently the writer, who was from Germany, rhymes "tav" with "samekh" according to the Ashkenazi pronunciation.

7b See n. 7a.

חשב לתקן המעוות והוא עות את המתוקן ויצא משפטו מעוקל/ והוא לא פנים קלקל/ ובדרך הזה הלכו שאר המגיהים/ ואני לא עשיתי כן מפני יראת האלהים/ ועוד יתרון לפירושי זה על פירוש השונצי״ן כי הוא לא הדפיס רק פירוש חמשה חומשי תורה לבד ואנכי הוספתי עליו פירוש של חמש מגלות ואת כלם הגהתי ושפטתי משפט צדק/ עד שלא נמצא שם בדק/ ובמקומות שהיתה ידיעתי קצרה/ מלהבין ראייה או סברא/ על בינתי לא נשענתי/ ושאלתי מה שלא הבנתי/ ועל הרוב על דברי רבי אליהו המדקדק נסמכתי/ ובו יתדותי תמכתי/ כי במקרא ובפירושי׳ יש לו יד ושם/ והוא ידע ולא אשם/ ובכן אודה לאל אשר עד הנה הגיעני והחייני וקיימני להשלים הספר הזה עד תומו/ ולהעביר חסרונו ומומו/ כן יהיה עוד בעזרי להגיה בתלמוד כאשר החלותי ועד הנה נדפסו מסכתות ששה/ היינו בבא קמא בבא בתרא שבועות חגיגה תענית מגילה ואגיע בע״ה להגיה עד תשעה/ ויהיו נקיות מכל טעות ורשעה/ כאשר עיינתי בהעתקות מוגהות וצודקות/ אשר למדו בהם ראשי ישיבות/ בעיון רב ובחשיבות/ והנה היתה השלמת הספר הזה בחדש תשרי שנת רצ״ט לפר״ק פה ווינציייה בבית השר דניאל בומבירגי יר״ה אנכי המגיה הצעיר מבית אבי יהודה המכונה ליביא ב״ר יצחק הלוי המכונה אייזק קולפא מורנקבורט.[8]

After this lengthy and interesting colophon, we find a poem by Elijah Levita:

ויהי כאשר ראה רבי אליהו הלוי האשכנזי את המלאכה והנה היא עשויה כהלכה מערכה לקראת מערכה לא נעשה כן בכל ממלכה ולא נשאר בה טעות או מבוכה וישם על המגיה ברכה ויפתח את פיו בשירה ערוכה וישא משלו ויאמר ככה

את ליב״א קולפ״ה יודה כל פה   כי טוב עושה הוא תוך עמו
לבו תואב אל ספרי בין   אל כל אחד קורא בשמו
יתן למבקש למודו   וספרים אתו אינימו
הוא המשביר אל כל העם   יפתח אוצרו ואסמו
ובתוכו כל ספרי משנה   גם המקרא עם תרגומו
לו פירושים גם מדרשים   מה טוב לאכול את פרימו
ובסדורים ובמחזורים   ימציא כל עם מנהגימו
יש נחקקים יש נכתבים   יש נקשרים בעבותימו
המה לרוב אך מקרוב   נעדר פירוש של שלמה
היצחקי הרב בקי   על כל אדם תטוף נואמו
כל הגולה שותה מימיו   כל ישראל לוחם לחמו
ופעמים רבים נדפסו   אכן תמו אזלו למו
לכן בחר ליב״א הנזכר   גם הפעם בדפוס שמו

8 Part of this colophon is quoted by Sonne, ibid. See also: M. Marx, in *HUCA*, v. 11, p. 481.

הוא הגיהו והכינהו שלם מראשו עד תומו
כי בספרים הראשונים הסופרים שנו את טעמו
יש הוסיף בו יש גרע בו יש בשגגה יש באשמו
אך זה נמצא בלתי שמצה מעולם לא נעשה דומו
רובו הגיע הוא עצמו גם לפעמים ידי עמו
אותו הכשיר בעל השיר ובראשי בתיו חותמו
ובשם האל צור ישראל היום היה יום תשלומו
ששת תשרי בשנת פטר״י ליצירת אל את עולמו
ווינציייה בית דניאל ולאנווירשה שב למקומו[9]

Jehudah ben Isaac ha-Levy of Frankfort, called Loeb Kulpa, the corrector of this Rashi edition, was active in the Hebrew printing of Italy. His name appears in a number of books printed in Venice and Mantua between the years 1538 and 1561.[10] M. Horovitz mentions him briefly among sixteenth-century Frankfort scholars.[11]

From a study of the colophons signed by Kulpa, we can gain some knowledge, although fragmentary, of his life and work. He originates from a well-known family in Frankfort. The Kulpas (Kulps), a branch of the Gehlhaeuser family, are traced back by Alexander Dietz to the sixteenth century. Members of this family were affluent and some were known as learned and active men in the community. The first bearer of the Kulp name appears in 1592 with a certain Loeb (Jehudah) Kulp, the son of Samuel Gehlhaeuser.[12] The corrector of the 1538 Rashi edition bears the

9 On Elijah Levita in general and on his role in Bomberg's publishing house see: G. Weil, *Elie Levita* (Leiden, 1963) (where this poem is not mentioned). A few lines of the poem are quoted by Steinschneider, *ibid.* Reference to the last line is made by A. Freiman, in *ZfhB*, vol. 10, p. 34; D.W. Amram, *The Makers of Hebrew Books in Italy*, p. 193; J. Bloch, *Venetian Printers of Hebrew Books*, p. 14; Ch. B. Friedberg, תולדות הדפוס העברי באיטליה, p. 66 note 16; I. Mehlman, in ארשת, v. 3, p. 98. [See now: A.M. Haberman, *Ha-madpiss Daniel Bomberg u-reshimath sifre beth defusso. The Printer Daniel Bomberg and the first of Books Published by his Press*. Zefat, Museum of Printing Art [1978], p. 20 and p. 71, number 154 (in Hebrew).]

10 Cf. Steinschneider, CB, col. 2937; Nepi-Ghirondi, תולדות גדולי ישראל, p. 182; Mortara, מזכרת חכמי איטליא, p. 33 (Levi Jehuda ben Isaac); Rabinowitz, מאמר על הדפסת התלמוד (ed. A.M. Haberman), p. 53, note: Friedberg, op. cit., pp. 67-68; Amram, op. cit., pp. 201, 253; Bloch, op. cit., p. 17; A. Yaari, *Kirjath Sepher*, v. 15, pp. 377-380; I. Sonne, *ibid.*, v. 16, pp. 134-7; the rejoinder by Yaari, *ibid.*, pp. 137-9 and the latter's דגלי המדפיסים, pp. 129-131.

11 In his *Frankfurter Rabbinen*, v. 1, p. 23.

12 Alexander Dietz, *Stammbuch der Frankfurter Juden*, pp. 102-3, 174-4. Dietz's assumption that the Kulps were not Levites (*ibid.*, p. 103) is contradicted by the fact that our Jehudah Kulpa always signs his name as Ha-Levy.

same name—apparently it was common in that family—and now the beginnings of the Kulp family can be dated at least some fifty years earlier than the date offered by Dietz. Kulpa was involved in many branches of the book business. Elijah Levita seems to refer to his activities as a book dealer who had in his stock a wide assortment of manuscripts and printed books.[13] Whether the printed books were all products of Bomberg's press or also included other books cannot be determined.[14]

As a corrector, Kulpa started his work prior to the printing of Rashi. In his colophon to this book, he mentions six tractates of the Talmud which he had already corrected and printed. Elijah Levita also seems to refer to his previous work as a printer.[15]

The richest information about Kulpa is to be found in a number of books printed by him and his associate, Jehiel ben Jekuthiel ha-Cohen Rapa,[16] between the years 1544 and 1548. In 1544 they worked for the Christian printers, the Brothers dei Farri and, from 1545, for Marc Antonio Giustinian. The books printed by them are listed by M. Steinschneider,[17] R.N. Rabinowitz[18] and D.W. Amram.[19] Kulpa, the initiator of the enterprise, and his partner Rapa, announce their plans in the following words:

בהיות כי ראה ראינו כי הזמן הולך וסוער עלינו ולומדי התורה הולכים ומתמעטים... לכן אנחנו השותפים אשר בשמינו רשומים... קנא קנאנו לה׳ צבאות... והקרה ה׳ לפנינו איש גדול ורם מבחר הנוצרים והדרם... ובלשונינו הקדוש ידו גברה... הוא השר והאדון נקרא בשם מארקו אנטוניאו יושטיניאן ובראותו כי כמה שנים אנחנו עמלים בתקונים לעשות אותיות וכלים ובעזר האלהי מעולם לא מצאנו בעל מלאכה שנצחנו עם כי לטורח גדול ורב ההוצאה לא השגחנו והשכיל והבין ענינינו כי יש לנו שכם אחד על אחינו המדפיסים אשר

13 See above in his poem, 11, 4-8.

14 A book-list of Daniel Bomberg's firm, compiled after 1541, contains books from Bomberg's press as well as books printed in Constantinople and Bologna, cf. *ZfhB*, v. 10, pp. 38-42.

15 In his poem, 1, 13.

16 On Rapa, cf., Steinschneider, *CB*, col. 2933 and the works by Rabinowitz, Friedberg, Amram, Yaari, Sonne and Bloch quoted in note 10. Cf. also Friedberg, *op. cit.*, p. 23, note 7; Y.T. Eisenstadt, דעת קדושים (St. Petersburg, 1897-98), p. 136. On the role of the Rapa and Kusi families in introducing Hebrew printing to Italy, cf. A. Friemann in *Journal of Jewish Bibliography*, v. 1, pp. 9-11.

17 See above, note 10.

18 See above, note 10.

19 *Op. cit.*, p. 201 (above note 9).

היו לפנינו... ולכן את בן משק ביתו צוה להדפיס כל הספרים אשר עד הנה היו נסתרים... ואף כי זה הספר נעשה במלאכה חדשה וכל התחלה קשה...[20]

The administrator of Giustinian's firm (בן משק ביתו), probably Cornelio Adelkind, also speaks about the partners:

בהתעדן מאד מאד גבירי הנעלה בלשון הקדש לדבקה בו... פקד עלי... לחבר לולאות הזריזות בקרסי המפעלות להשתדל לתת התחלות להדפיס כל מיני הספרי' רבי התועלות והיו למאורות ברקועים פחי הדפוסיות באותיות חרותות בעט ברזל ועופרת חקוקות בכתיבות היותר מאושרות ויפות ונוירות ישרות ביותר מעולות וטובות אשר מעולם לא היו בפעל נדפסות... ויד הנכבדים באמצע כהן ולוי הנלוים להצדיק את הרבים... רבי יהודה הלוי ורבי יחיאל הכהן השותפים... מי בכם אוהבי התורה ולומדיה... והכינו עצמכם להשיג ממנו בקוצר זמן כל חפצכם עם התלמוד ערוך כלו והעשרי' וארבע קטן כגדול עם כל המתיחס לו ורב אלפס עם חדר שכלו יחפש וכל חפץ מחופש משאר החבורים חדשים גם ישנים בשכבר נדפסו או לא נדפסו...[21]

From the above it is evident that the partners were engaged for many years in improving printing machinery and types and had introduced a new method in typography.

In addition to his technical and business skills, Kulpa had scholarly interests, too. Already in the 1538 edition of Rashi, he describes his method of establishing the text by using many manuscripts and printed editions. In the colophon to the same book, he also mentions his efforts in the printing of Talmud tractates. For the publication of these texts he claims to have used "correct and true copies such as those being studied by the heads of Yeshiboth" (ההעתקות מוגהות וצודקות אשר למדו בהם ראשי ישיבות). Kulpa's introduction to the 1548 Venice edition of *Halakhoth Gedoloth* was recorded as a proof of his scholarship by R.N. Rabinowitz and M. Horovitz.[22] In this introduction, Kulpa tackles the problematic authorship of the book, reviewing the conflicting opinions of early Rabbinic authors.

In 1547 he published a commentary to the Pentateuch, culled from the Pentateuch commentaries of Rashi, Nahmanides, Abraham ibn Ezra, and

20 In the colophon to ביאור על התורה להרמב"ן (Giustinian, Venice, 1545). It also appears in other books printed by them, cf. Rabinowitz, *op. cit.*, p. 52, note 11, where excerpts from this colophon are quoted; on the phrase: מעולם לא מצאנו וכו' see Responsa of R. Simeon Duran, I, 72.

21 *Ibid.* On the identity of בן משק ביתו, see the works by Yaari and Sonne cited in note 10.

22 See above, note 10 and 11.

David Kimhi. In addition to this interesting and useful anthology of selected comments, Kulpa included in his book notes to the Masorah and the order of the 613 precepts. He also planned to append at the end an index of all the Biblical passages mentioned in the Talmud.[23]

It is to be assumed that Kulpa, during his association with the Bomberg, dei Farri, and Giustinian printing houses, helped in the publication of numerous other books, though his name is not explicitly mentioned in them.

Some of the information contained in the colophon of the 1538 Rashi edition adds to the complexity of problems relating to the activities of the Bomberg press. Though the history of Bomberg's press was dealt with frequently,[24] we are still in the dark in regard to the chronology of events and to many aspects of the work done under Bomberg's auspices.[25] From 1516 to 1533, there is a continuity in Bomberg's work. This period can be divided into two: the "golden age" of his activities, between 1516 and 1525, when the most important editions, e.g., that of the *Biblia Rabbinica*, of the Babylonian and Jerusalem Talmud, and of important Rabbinic texts were printed, and the second period, from 1525 to 1533, when mainly second editions, frequently unchanged, were produced.

Bomberg resumed his activities in 1537 and issued a few minor books again until 1539. In the latter year, the only anti-Jewish book ever to be printed by Bomberg was published.[26] According to Elijah Levita's poem in the 1538 Rashi, dated Tishre 6, 5239 (1538), Bomberg returned to his native city of Antwerp.[27] Two years later, Levita again refers to Bomberg

23 ארבעה ועשרים עם באור כל מלה קשה... נעתק אות באות מלשון גדולי המפרשים... והם רש״י והרמב״ן וראב״ע ורד״ק ז״ל... ובחתימת כל הכ״ד ספרים יהיה מורה מקום מכל הפסוקים הנדרשי׳ והמבוארי׳ בתלמוד...
Cf. Steinschneider, CB, col. 23, no. 123; Zedner, p. 17; Van Straalen, p. 26; Roest, בית הספר, p. 175, no. 2425. According to all these bibliographies, the title page reads: ארבעה ועשרים. The same title appears in the copy seen by Sonne. See the latter's comments on this book in the *Alexander Marx Jubilee Volume*, Hebrew part, pp. 218-219. However, in the copy at the Library of the Jewish Theological Seminary, the title page is different; it reads: חמשה חומשי תורה וחמש מגילות והפטדך(!)ות עם באור כל מלה קשה וכו׳ ובחתימת החומש וחמש מגילות יהיה מורה מקום וכו׳. Apparently, the printers, after realizing that they will not be able to complete the entire Bible, changed the title page of some copies.

24 See the bibliography in *Encyclopaedia Judaica*, vol. 4, col. 930.

25 Mehlman, ארשת, v. 3, pp. 93-98, establishes the date of the first book printed by Bomberg as 1511 instead of the generally accepted date of 1516.

26 *Ibid.*

27 l. 22.

as having stopped his work, "and he will not work again."[28] However, there are quite a large number of books printed between the years 1543 and 1548 bearing Bomberg's imprint.[29]

A special problem is presented by the different editions of the Talmud on which Bomberg's name appears. R.N. Rabinowitz was at a loss to explain the confusion of dates, sequence, number, and designation of editions of the Babylonian Talmud after the first one.[30] He also refers to the contradiction relating to the printing of the Jerusalem Talmud.[31] According to Rabinowitz's suggestions, it seems likely that tractates of the Talmud with the imprint 1538-9 were actually printed between 1526 and 1531 and that in 1538-9 Bomberg removed the old title pages and printed new ones with the current date. Rabinowitz admits that he cannot find a reason for this fact and for the lack of Bomberg's activity between 1533 and 1538.[32] About a hundred years have passed since Rabinowitz expressed his aforementioned views and we are still in no better position to solve these problems. In fact, the 1538 Rashi colophon only adds to the confusion. Kulpa mentions there that he had finished the careful correction of six tractates of the Talmud: *Baba Kama, Baba Bathra, Shebuoth, Hagiga, Taanith* and *Megilla*, and that he plans to print an additional three (unnamed) tractates. Indeed, we know of the tractates *Baba Kama, Hagiga, Taanith, Megilla, Makkoth, Moed Katan* and *Aboth*, bearing the imprint date 1538-9. Rabinowitz lists also an undated second (or third?) edition of *Baba Bathra* and *Shebuoth*.[33] This brings the total of tractates from 1538-9 to nine (including the two undated ones), thus equalling the nine tractates mentioned by Kulpa (six finished in 5238 = 1537/8 and three more in preparation at the beginning of 5239 = 1538). This, and the fact that four of the tractates bearing the

28 Cf. Elijah Levita in his introduction to his תשבי, Isny: 1541.

29 Cf. *ZfhB*, v. 10, pp. 86-88. Incidentally, an interesting testimony to the rather chaotic conditions of Hebrew printing in Venice in the 1540s is the edition of *Midrash Rabba* (Venice, 1545). There are copies of this book with Bomberg's title page and others with that of Giustinian. Cf. *Bereshit Rabba*, ed. Theodor-Albeck, introduction, p. 129; *ZfhB*, vol. 9, pp. 61-62, 159; *Kirjath Sepher*, vol. 4, p. 227.

30 *Op. cit.*, pp. 43-45 (above note 10); cf. also Rivkind, *Alexander Marx Jubilee Volume*, Hebrew section, pp. 410-414. [See now: Marvin J. Heller, *Printing the Talmud; A History of the Earliest Printed Editions of the Talmud* (Brooklyn, 1992) and see now also the detailed study of Bomberg's Talmud editions by Milton McC. Gatch and Bruce E. Nielsen, "The Wittenberg Copy of the Bomberg Talmud", in: *Gutenberg-Jahrbuch* 78 (2003), pp. 296-326.]

31 *Op. cit.*, p. 44.

32 *Ibid.*

33 *Ibid.*

imprint 1538 and the other two undated ones are all mentioned by Kulpa, tend to invalidate Rabinowitz's view that no real printing of these tractates took place in 1538-9. On the other hand, a cursory examination of three editions of tractates *Aboth* (1521, 1526, 1539), *Moed Katan* (1521, 1526, 1538/9) and *Makkoth* (1520, 1529/30, 1538/9) shows that there is no significant textual difference between the second and third(?) editions.[34]

Similar problems arise in connection with the 1538 edition of the Rashi text. Kulpa boasts in his colophon about the superiority of his text in relation to all previous editions. He also mentions Elijah Levita's assistance in the establishment of the text. He especially singles out the 1525 Soncino Rashi as being full of mistakes.[35] Now, on the title page, we read that this is the second Bomberg edition of Rashi. The first one was printed in 1522, i.e., three years before Soncino's. A comparison between the three editions shows that the first and second Bomberg editions are almost identical, and that of Soncino is different from the two. Is there any merit, then, in Kulpa's claim of presenting a new text? Similarly, why does he claim that his edition is far better than Soncino's because it also contains Rashi on the Five Scrolls, when the commentary on the Five Scrolls is already printed in the first, 1522, Bomberg edition? Furthermore, the two texts are again identical.[36] Is it possible that Kulpa, counting on the naiveté of his contemporaries, was only praising his

34 The third edition of *Aboth* contains a number of misprints in passages where the first and second editions are correct; e.g. f. 2a: אז תבין ירתא (!) ה׳; 2b: הצריך מן העינים (!) (read: העניים); 5c: כעבדים שאינם מקוים להטהבה (read: להטבה); 9c: שלא תעשה התובה (!) (read: התורה).

35 See above, note 8.

36 A few examples will show the almost complete identity of the two Bomberg texts versus the Soncino text (the passages are taken from Genesis, 25. 19ff.), the text being used by Sonne, *HUCA*, v. 15, pp. 49-56 (Hebrew part), for his model of a new edition of Rashi on Pentateuch:

Soncino 1525	*Bomberg 1522*	*Bomberg 1538*	
ומשנולד יצחק עד שמתה שרה שלשים ושבע היו ובת צ׳ היתה כשנולד ובת קכ״ז כשמתה שנאמ׳ ויהיו חיי שרה וגומר הרי ליצחק ל״ז שני׳ ובו בפ׳ נולדה רבקה המתין לה עד שתהא ראוי׳ לביאה שלש שנים ונשאה	ומשנולד יצחק עד שמתה שרה ל״ז היו ובת צ׳ היתה כשנולד ובת קכ״ז כשמתה שנאמר ויהיו חיי שרה וגומר הרי ליצחק ל״ז שנים ובפ׳ (!) נולדה רבקה המתין לה עד שתהא ראוי׳ לביאה שלש שני׳ ונשאה	ומשנולד יצחק עד שמת׳ שרה ל״ז שנה היו בת צ׳ היתה כשנולד ובת קכ״ז כשמתה שנ׳ ויהיו חיי שרה וגו׳ הרי ליצחק ל״ז ובו בפרק נולדה רבקה המתין לה שתהא ראויה לביאה שלש שנים ונשאה	20.

ware without actually doing any work in presenting a new text?

In view of our limited knowledge of the events in Venetian Hebrew publishing in the fifteen-twenties and fifteen-thirties, no definitive answer can be given to the many questions relating to apparent contradictions, conflicting designations, and sequence of editions of the period.

Only a thorough new investigation, and the possibility of discovering hitherto unknown documents, perhaps in the archives of Venice, can throw much needed new light on this very important period of early Hebrew publishing history.[37]

21.	ויעתר לו, ולא לה	ויעתר לו, לו ולא לה	ויעתר לו, לו ולא לה
22.	לדרש את ה׳, להגיד מה תהא בסופה	לדרוש את ה׳, להגיד לה מה תהא בסופה	לדרוש את ה׳, להגיד לה מה תהא בסופה
30.	ואין זו שיבה טובה שהב־טיחו הקב״ה לפיכך קצר ה׳ שנים משנותיו של יצחק חי ק״פ וזה קע״ה	ואין זו שיבה טובה שהבטיחו הקב״ה לפיכך קצר הקב״ה ה׳ שנים משנותיו שיצחק חי קפ׳ שנה וזה קע״ה	ואין זו שיבה טובה שהבטיחו הקב״ה לפיכך קצר הקב״ה ה׳ שני׳ משנותיו שיצחק חי קפ׳ שנה וזה קע״ה
32.	הנה אנכי הולך למות, אמר מה שכר של עבודה זו	הנה אנכי הולך למות, אמר עשו מה טיבה של עבודה זו	הנה אנכי הולך למות, אמר עשו מה טיבה של עבוד׳ זו

37 It was only after this article was set in type that Meir Benayahu's important book, *Copyright, authorization and imprimatur for Hebrew books printed in Venice* (Jerusalem, 1971, in Hebrew), appeared. Therefore, it was not possible for me to make use of his materials and conclusions. However, it should be pointed out that Benayahu's suggestion that Judah Kulpa converted to Christianity. [Actually, Benayahu only suggests that Kulpa may have been demanded that be converts.] around the year 1545 (p. 23, note 2), is not convincing. Cf. the colophon to ס׳ יחוס הצדיקים, Mantua 1561:

והוגה בעיון רב ע״י כמ״ר יהודה הלוי יצ״ו בכמ״ר יצחק הלוי זצ״ל מברנקבורט המכונה ליבא קולפה אשכנזי

It is obvious that an apostate could never have been referred to in this manner.

Guides to the Perplexed in the Wilderness of Hebraica: From Historical to Contemporary Bibliographies and Catalogs of Hebraica

In it you shall find the names of the books of Scripture and of all the commentators, designated by their names, and the titles of all books, arranged in the order of the alphabet, their authors and the subjects upon which they deliberated. I listed them in two main divisions and prepared twenty indexes, each in brevity. The books of the Mishnah, commentators, novellae—old and new—responsa, Talmud, Tosafot and codes, astronomy, philosophy and grammar, ethics, kabbalah, stories, reference works and prayerbooks, all are there. Anyone who wishes to study, do research or find something, should turn to them and shall find everything, the root and the branch. O dear reader, read my introduction carefully and you will realize that my aim is to serve you with all my soul and all my might.

At the outset I would like to dispel any possible misunderstanding: the above quotation is not a description of the *Catalog of the Hebrew Collection of the Harvard College Library*! Rather, it is a translation, almost verbatim, of the rhymed foreword of the first Hebrew bibliography, *Siftei Yeshenim* by Shabbethai Bass, published in Amsterdam in 1680.[1] More than three hundred years later, the substantial message of these words could equally apply to the catalog whose publication we celebrate.[1a] Both were created to provide easy access, to offer guidance, service, and help, and to present a bewildering

1 For a bibliography on Bass, see Herbert Zafren in *Studies in Jewish Bibliography, History and Literature in Honor of I. Edward Kiev* (New York: Ktav, 1971), pp. 546-47.

1a The Catalog of the Hebrew Collection of the Harvard College Library (Munich, 1995), 11 volumes.

array of data in well-arranged order. These works and many others of a similar nature have an identical aim. Their technique, scope, dimension, and mode of presentation, however, are as different as a horse drawn wagon is from a spaceship. Furthermore, the motivation for creating these instruments of information reflects the spirit and culture of their times and the corresponding ideologies of their authors.

In general I shall refrain from rattling off either titles, authors, places, and dates or lots of statistics, though I cannot resist mentioning that in the 1680 bibliography 1,900 Hebrew titles were listed, while in the new Harvard Catalog there are entries for more than a hundred thousand Hebrew monographs, plus thousands of sound recordings, videotapes and scores. Size alone would make it a monumental work, and here, in honor of the new Harvard Catalog, I shall call attention to the other monumental landmarks in the field, locate them on the map of Jewish intellectual and scholarly history, and characterize their specific features briefly.

All general bibliographies and catalogs of Hebraica, old and new, face a series of common problems and challenges. One of the major problems results from the dispersion of the Jewish people. Hebrew book production through the ages took place in many localities over the globe. Under pre-modern communication and transportation conditions it took a long time for a book printed in one part of the world to reach another part, and it might never do so. Even as late as the nineteenth century, Rabbi Bezalel Ranschburg, in his commentary to the Talmudic tractate *Horayoth*, reports that he had heard rumors of the existence of a similar commentary by Rabbi Hayyim Yosef David Azulai, printed some thirty years earlier in Italy, but that he could not obtain a copy.[2] The maps of Europe, North Africa, and the Middle East, as well as those of India and America, are dotted with places, large and small, where Hebrew books were printed. Collecting information on books from all these places, even identifying the names of strange, exotic localities, occasionally distorted in Hebrew characters, was and remains a formidable task. Another difficulty relates to a characteristic feature of much of traditional Hebrew literature: a book's title often conveys no meaning whatsoever about its subject matter or content. Thus, the title of the first Hebrew bibliography, *Siftei Yeshenim*, is a quote from the Song of Songs (7:10), which reads in

2 *Sefer Horah Gever* (Prague, 1802), introduction, paragraph beginning "u-va-sheviith."

translation, "the lips of those who slumber." Hebrew books with such titles as *Penei Yehoshua* (The Face of Joshua), *Mahatzit ha-Shekel* (Half a Shekel), *Hafetz Hayyim* (One who Desires Life), *Hazon Ish* (The Vision of Man), and thousands similar, are still common today. Who were their authors? What were their names? Furthermore, to distinguish among authors bearing common Jewish names is not so simple. How many Isaacs and Cohens, and how many Isaac Cohens do we have? In how many countries and in how many different periods did they live? And how can we distinguish between the Shapiras and the Rabinowitzes whose names appear in so many variant forms, depending on the country in which they lived? Indeed, the author of the first Hebrew bibliography found it necessary to establish rules for the entry of authors with Sefardi and Ashkenazi names. Ashkenazim with double names, such as Abraham Aron, are entered under the second name, while Sefardim, for example, Moses Rafael, are entered under the first, according to their respective customs in referring to a person.

Subject classification and added entries posed other problems. A single edition of a Hebrew Bible or of a Haggadah for Passover could have multiple commentaries, some seeking to explain the so-called simple meaning, others the philosophical, homiletical, or mystical; some contain illustrations, and some music. Translations may call for dozens of author, title, and subject entries. A particularly complex example is the standard Vilna edition of the Babylonian Talmud, in which there are 243 various commentaries.[3] Add to these complexities the fact that Hebrew characters have been used for Yiddish, Ladino, Judeo-Arabic, and other languages, and the number of bibliographical challenges multiply exponentially. In 1680, as well as in 1995, creators of Hebrew bibliographical records have had to strive to bring order to this huge array of deceptively similar data, albeit never in a totally and absolutely satisfying way.

Let us now, turning to the widely differing attempts to create general bibliographies and catalogs of Hebraica, examine the motivation that led their authors in their labors.[4] In the case of the first Hebrew bibliography, already referred to, it is quite easy to know the aims of its author,

3 Y.S. Weinfeld, *Mavo le-shas Vilna* (Jerusalem, 1994), p. 403.

4 Among the secondary literature on Hebrew bibliographies and their authors, first and foremost is Simeon Brisman's relatively recent and most excellent and reliable *A History and Guide to Judaic Bibliography* (Cincinnati and New York: Hebrew Union College Press and Ktav, 1977).

Shabbethai Bass Meshorer, in compiling his book, the *Siftei Yeshenim*. I followed the author's admonition, emphatically stated on the title page, and read his lengthy introduction carefully. There, Bass enumerated the "benefits," ten in number, that one may derive from his book, and he explained what it contained and how it is arranged.

The practical benefits of the *Siftei Yeshenim* are obvious. It provides help to authors, scholars, publishers, printers, and booksellers in identifying various editions of Hebrew titles and informing them about what exists in the field. Because Bass himself was an author, printer, and bookseller, he must have known from his own experience how useful such a bibliography could be, especially one in Hebrew, as opposed to the earlier bibliographies in Latin.[5]

Every scholar who writes about Bass and his *Siftei Yeshenim* observes that the so-called first benefit is based on a pious, mystical, almost magical concept, quoted from one of the most influential Jewish books of the last three centuries, the bulky *Shnei Luhoth ha-Berith* (The Two Tablets of the Covenant), by Isaiah Horowitz (1555-1630).[6] (Incidentally, the public, with its healthy sense of proportion and propriety, refused to refer to this book by its full title, feeling that The Two Tablets of the Covenant by Rabbi Horowitz was presumptuous, using instead the acronym, *Shelah*.) The concept borrowed from the *Shelah* is that the recitation and remembrance of titles of sacred books and their saintly authors by lay people, especially the ignorant, may be regarded by the Almighty as worthy of reward. Those who are not capable of learning themselves, should at least pronounce the names of the holy books, as a kind of substitute for learning, and God will grant them merit for their sincere effort despite their deficiency. Bass adds that these acts are recommended to the pious as instruments of intercession with the deceased, and he offers the prayer: "and may the recitation of your names and the names of your books that you composed be considered as if I had studied and understood them and may my prayer be counted as more than even a visit to your graves."[7] In the scholarly literature this benefit is discounted as self-serving. It is claimed that Bass advanced it to prove his own piety as a

5 Brisman, *History and Guide*, pp. 3-8.

6 First edition: Amsterdam, 1649. On Horowitz see the forthcoming book by Miles Krassen, *Isaiah Horowitz: The Generations of Adam* [Published by the Paulist Press (New York 1996)].

7 *Siftei Yeshenim* (see above note 1), f. 9a.

means of helping to convince the reader that bibliography, though a new genre of Hebrew literature, ought not to be rejected as a non-religious innovation: it does fulfill a religious purpose and therefore can be recommended even to a deeply traditional and conventional audience.[8]

In my view, the matter is much more complicated. A comparison of the subject divisions in *Siftei Yeshenim* with the structure of the *Shelah* yields some surprising similarities. Bass divides all Hebrew books into two categories: Written Law and Oral Law. Within each category there are ten sub-divisions, alluding to the Ten Commandments. The *Shelah* is similarly structured, having two main divisions called Oral Law and Written Law, hence the allusion in the title to the Two Tablets of the Covenant. Within the two main divisions are various sub-sections, some further divided into chapters of ten, others arranged alphabetically. Rabbi Isaiah Horowitz's highly influential book is an encyclopedic work, containing an enormous amount of mystical, homiletical, liturgical, and halakhic materials, and likewise the bibliography of Bass is encyclopedic in scope, with references to all sorts of books on a variety of subjects. Although Bass mentions the works by their titles alone, do we not know by now, from the *Shelah*, that the mere mention of a title or an author serves as a substitute for the understanding and study of the books themselves? I hope to develop fully this argument elsewhere; here it suffices, to suggest further that Bass, who came from Prague, tried to imitate Horowitz, the famous Rabbi of Prague. One additional point: Bass frequently refers to his brother, a kabbalist who settled in the Land of Israel, as did the kabbalist Horowitz. According to my line of reasoning, the first Hebrew bibliography was a product of the religious-mystical atmosphere of its times under the impact of the *Shelah*, and it was produced with the goal of being an instrument of religious efficacy and teaching.[9]

Exactly two hundred years later, in 1880, the second major general Hebraica bibliography appeared.[10] During these two centuries, the center of Jewish publishing activity shifted from the West to the East, from

8 See M.M. Slatkine, Reshith bikkurei ha-bibliografiyah be-sifruth ha-ivrith (Tel Aviv, 1958), pp. 65-68; A.M. Habermann, *Anshei sefer ve-anshei maaseh* (Jerusalem: R. Mass, 1974), pp. 6-7.

9 For the classification according to Written and Oral Law and for fitting the books into the scheme of the Ten Commandments, see *Siftei Yeshenim*, ff. 6b-7a; for the brother of Shabbathai Bass, see Slatkine, *Reshith bikkurei*, p. 12.

10 *Otzar ha-sefarim*, by Isaac Benjacob (Vilna, 1880).

Amsterdam to Vilna. The new bibliography bore the imprint of Vilna in more than one sense. Its author, Isaac Benjacob, was born in 1801 in a small town near Vilna, was educated in that city, and spent much of his life there. When he died in 1863, his only son, Jacob, who was also living in Vilna, completed the Hebrew bibliography that his father had started. When Jacob Benjacob submitted his father's work for publication, he obtained the approbations of members of the rabbinical court of his city. In them the *dayyanim* of Vilna heap praise on the author for his scholarship, diligence, and piety, calling his book *melekheth shamayim*, "heavenly work." These rather lengthy statements contain arguments that the bibliography is important because of its benefits to serious scholars of Talmud. Rabbi Shelomo ben Yisrael Moshe ha-Cohen, the author of one of the approbations, lists ten instances in various rabbinic works where the standard editions contain errors that may be corrected upon consultation with other, rare editions of the same works. For example, he points out that twelve lines are omitted from the common editions of Josef Karo's commentary of Jacob ben Asher's code, which can be restored by using the early Venice edition of the same work.[11] Since such reconstructions can be achieved only with the aid of a good Hebrew bibliography, the rabbis are placing Benjacob's bibliography in a religious framework: a help in arriving at correct interpretations of passages in Rabbinic literature.

Originally Benjacob planned to revise and supplement the *Siftei Yeshenim* of Bass. The son's German preface states this explicitly: "The author, of blessed memory, had originally intended to publish as complete a revision as possible of the only Hebrew bibliography, the *Siftei Yeshenim*."[12] In preparing for his work, Benjacob also issued a rearranged edition of the bio-bibliographic *Shem ha-Gedolim* by Rabbi Hayyim Yosef David Azulai.[13] In his conception, he was only extending the work of Rabbis who preceded him; rather than offering something radically new, his work was just another link in the chain of Rabbinic literature. But in truth, Benjacob's work differs significantly from the *Siftei Yeshenim*. The title pages alone are testimony to the great differences that divide this work from its predecessor. Gone is the flowery, Biblical title of Bass's work. Benjacob's title is simple and describes the contents accurately: *Otzar ha-Sefarim*, a

11 *Ibid.*, xi.

12 *Ibid.*, "Vorbemerkung" (immediately following the title pages).

13 Vilna, 1852.

thesaurus of books. Moreover, besides the Hebrew title page are three others: in Latin, in German and in Russian. The Latin title is *Thesaurus librorum hebraicorum*, and the German and Russian ones read (in translation): A Bibliography of the Entire Hebrew Literature. But even more significant is a letter printed in German on the verso of the German title page: signed in Berlin in 1880 by Leopold Zunz, the founder of modern Jewish scholarship, it states that Jacob Benjacob's father deserves for his *Otzar* the highest possible praise and that the work will become indispensable to every scholar who occupies himself with Jewish literature.

Indeed, although *Otzar* formally follows earlier models, it incorporates in its entries the accomplishments of decades of modern Jewish scholarship. The father of modern Jewish bibliography, Moritz Steinschneider, a friend of Zunz, and together with him a founder of "jüdische Wissenschaft," shared with Benjacob the results of his own research. Information forwarded by Steinschneider, and signed Ramshash, i.e., the initials of Rabbi Moshe Steinschneider, is on practically every page of the *Otzar*. Thus, Benjacob's work integrates modern Jewish scholarly information with traditional learning. Benjacob himself, deeply steeped in Talmud studies as a youngster, pursued the study of Hebrew language and poetry and became an advocate of Enlightenment (*Haskalah*). Accordingly, *Haskalah*, modern Jewish scholarship, and traditional Rabbinic learning shaped Benjacob and led him to the labor of many decades that resulted in his "indispensable" bibliography of the entirety of Hebrew literature.

It is instructive to spend a moment comparing the so-called benefits that are enumerated in Benjacob with those found in Bass. Bass lists ten, Benjacob six, but the most striking difference is that the *Siftei Yeshenim* emphasizes the religious-mystical value of recording the works of saintly authors, whereas in Jacob Benjacob's first benefit, history replaces religion: "It is well known that every person should know the history of his country and land. A nation without history cannot be counted among the nations. This is even more so in regard to the nation of Israel. The only remnant of its glorious history is its literature; it is its land, its government, it is its only monument of the past. From it one can learn the sacred and secular history of the Jewish people."[14] The "turn to history," in the

14 *Otzar ha-sefarim*, xviii (the translation is a slightly abbreviated version of the original).

phrase of Ismar Schorsch, is one of the most important developments in the nineteenth-century movement of the Jews toward emancipation and modernization.[15] Jacob Benjacob sees bibliography as a discipline that provides the foundation for study, understanding, and appreciation of Jewish history. It is, to him, an essential element in the move toward emancipation of the Jews, because it will foster Jewish historical consciousness. Some of the subsequent points of Benjacob must be understood against the background of the times as well. Becoming acquainted with the entire range of Hebrew literature, that is, with the sciences, philosophy, and literature, and not only Rabbinic works, will fill the Jews with pride; no more will they stand embarrassed before other nations, and the common human heritage of the Jewish people with other peoples will lead to an era when *kineath amim ve-shinnuye ha-datot taavir [taavor] min ha-aretz*, "jealousy among nations and differences among religions will be removed from the earth."[16] What a difference in ideology between the professed motivation of this general Hebrew bibliography and that of its older model and predecessor!

Ideology is, of course, not the only difference between the two works. The *Otzar* is immeasurably richer and better than the *Siftei Yeshenim*. Books were more carefully examined and more precisely described, and the resources at Benjacob's disposal were much greater than those of Bass. The most significant of these were the catalogs of two major collections of Hebraica, those at the Bodleian in Oxford and the British Museum (now British Library) in London. The Judaica sections of both of those libraries grew throughout the seventeenth, eighteenth, and, especially, the nineteenth centuries into the most comprehensive and richest collections of Hebraica heretofore assembled. Great care was also extended to the proper cataloging of these collections. The Bodleian invited Steinschneider himself to catalog its Hebraica; in the British Museum, the scholarly and precise Joseph Zedner prepared the catalog of Hebrew books.[17] Steinschneider's catalog, in Latin, is regarded, in Solomon Schechter's words, as "the *Urim*

15 See Ismar Schorsch, *From Text to Context; The Turn to History in Modern Judaism* (Hanover, N. H.: Brandeis University Press, 1994). See also Y. H. Yerushalmi, *Zakhor; Jewish History and Jewish Memory* (Seattle and London: University of Washington Press, 1982).

16 *Otzar ha-sefarim*, xviii

17 *Catalogus librorum hebraeorum in Bibliotheca Bodleiana* (Berlin, 1852-1860); *Catalogue of the Hebrew Books in the Library of the British Museum* (London: British Museum, 1867).

ve-Tumim (oracle) of every Jewish student."[18] It was considered to be "the reference tool on all questions of Jewish literature."[19] It was this work, along with others, that was utilized by Benjacob. No wonder then that the *Otzar* has remained up to our own days an important and reliable tool of research. Still, despite its great value, the *Otzar* is an imperfect instrument. It is arranged alphabetically by title, and it did not originally have indexes by author, subject, or place of publication. One of these deficiencies was corrected as recently as 1965 by Menahem Mendel Slatkine's author index.[20] Jacob Benjacob, the son, who died in 1926, spent many years on the preparation of a new edition, but his vast manuscript fell victim to the Holocaust.[21]

The third general Hebrew bibliography is Bernhard Friedberg's *Bet Eked Sefarim*, which has gone through two editions, the first published from 1928 to 1931, the second in 1956. Friedberg was a dealer in books and later in diamonds. Recording Hebrew books was for him more a hobby and a means of livelihood than a scholarly pursuit, so his bibliography, though quantitatively much larger than that of Benjacob, is less accurate. Friedberg was not an ideologue, he was simply interested in the book trade and in printing history. Still, despite its limitations, until recently the *Beth Eked* has served as the most frequently consulted general Hebrew bibliography.[22]

After the Holocaust, and particularly after the establishment of the State of Israel, new justifications were advanced for the creation of an inclusive, general Hebrew bibliography. In 1954, Israeli governmental and educational institutions joined in a partnership to plan and produce a bibliography of all printed Hebrew-language books before 1960. Gershom Scholem formulated the goals of the project and the reasons for carrying it out. He wrote: "The catastrophe which overtook European Jewry during the Second World War and the mass exodus of the Jews living in the Moslem countries have created an entirely new situation. Great treasuries

18 Solomon Schechter, *Seminary Addresses* (New York: Burning Bush, 1959), p. 122 (quoted by Brisman, *History and Guide*, p. 277, note 33).

19 Alexander Marx, *Essays in Jewish Biography* (Philadelphia: Jewish Publication Society, 1947), 150 (quoted by Brisman, *History and Guide*, p. 42).

20 *Otzar ha-sefarim, helek sheni* (Jerusalem, 1965).

21 Brisman, *History and Guide*, pp. 22-23.

22 Brisman, *History and Guide*, pp. 24-26.

of books have been destroyed while centres in which important discoveries might have been expected have been liquidated... Under these circumstances the renaissance of the Jewish people in its own country made it mandatory for it to undertake a task which, by its very nature, could not be performed by individuals. Thus took shape the idea of compiling a comprehensive National Bibliography."[23] Of course, we do not claim that Scholem did not realize that the primary function of a comprehensive bibliography is to be a research instrument. Much of his early work was bibliographical in nature, and he knew full well that without systematic, solid bibliographies, research only limps along. Still, it is quite interesting to note Scholem's articulation of the aims of the comprehensive Hebrew bibliography project. First, it should serve as a memorial to the destroyed and dispersed Jewish books in the wake of the Holocaust and the exodus of Jews from Islamic countries. At the same time, it should become a symbol of the revival of the Jewish people in its national home. A national home demands a national bibliography.

Three centuries, three centers, three bibliographies, three motivations. Amsterdam, Vilna, Jerusalem, each with its own goals and aspirations. The compilation of Hebrew bibliographies sprang from emotions of piety in the seventeenth century, was promoted by historical consciousness and a striving for emancipation in the nineteenth, and in the twentieth century was inspired by the need of erecting a memorial and by a national renaissance.

The technological revolution of our own days has brought immense changes to the field of Hebrew bibliography and cataloging. It has reached an entirely new stage of development with the publication in 1995 of the *Catalog of the Hebrew Collection of the Harvard College Library*.

Other prestigious libraries have over the years published very fine catalogs of their Hebraica holdings. Steinschneider's catalog of the Hebrew books in the Bodleian Library in Oxford has already been mentioned. This highly detailed and scholarly work adds to the description of each entry a full bibliography relating to the work, its author, place of publication, and other relevant matters. It is not just a catalog, but a bio-bibliographical encyclopedia. The catalogs of the Hebrew collections of the British Museum in London, of the Rosenthaliana in Amsterdam, of the Academy

23 Institute for Hebrew Bibliography, *Specimen Brochure* (Jerusalem, 1964), p. 47.

of Sciences in St. Petersburg, of the Jewish Community in Vienna,[24] have all been modeled, to a greater or lesser degree, on Steinschneider. Their Hebrew collections consisted of traditional, older, and rarer literature assembled before the publishing explosion of the twentieth century. The number of books in them was relatively small, and they were treated with great scholarly precision. Similarly, a few private collections established in the second part of the twentieth century, such as Yisrael Mehlman's, now at the Jewish National and University Library in Jerusalem, or Manfred Lehmann's private collection in New York, were cataloged with all scholarly detail.[25] The authors of these catalogs were motivated by academic aspirations: to contribute by full bibliographical documentation to scholarly research in the field of the history of Hebrew printing and booklore.

This orientation changed in the 1960s in the United States. The availability of new technology made it possible to reproduce entire card catalogs in book form. The New York Public Library, Hebrew Union College, the Harvard College Library, and YIVO all made available to the public a reproduction of their cards in multi-volume sets.[26] In these cases the purpose was not to create original scholarly works, but, instead, to provide help to a wide audience. The card catalogs of these collections represented much larger quantities of books than those mentioned before, and they also offered more access points, both of which aspects well compensated for what they lacked in scholarly apparatus.

The next stage in the progress of recording, processing, and making accessible large collections was reached by the introduction of computer technology. How this has changed the creating of bibliographies and catalogs may perhaps be best illustrated by the fate of the National Hebrew Bibliography Project to which I have referred previously.

24 For the British Museum see above, note 16; for the Rosenthaliana, see M. Roest, *Catalog der Hebraica and Judaica aus der L. Rosenthalscher Bibliothek* (Amsterdam, 1875); for the Academy of Sciences in St. Petersburg, S. Wiener, *Kehilloth Moshe*, (St. Petersburg, 1893-1936).

25 *The Israel Mehlman Collection in the Jewish National and University Library; An Annotated Catalogue*, by Isaac Yudlov (Jerusalem: The National and University Library, 1984) and *Ohel Hayim: A Catalogue of Hebrew Manuscripts of the Manfred and Anne Lehmann Family: vol. 3: Printed Books, Incunabula and Sixteenth Century Books*. Prepared by Shimon M. Iakerson (New York: Manfred and Anne Lehmann Foundation, 1996).

26 The New York Public Library in 1960; Hebrew Union College in 1964; Harvard University Library in 1968; and YIVO in 1990.

In the early 1950s, a team of scholarly catalogers started to describe the books in the Jewish National and University Library. The work was done by hand, each volume was painstakingly examined, every detail was recorded, and the secondary literature was searched for references to each item. Lengthy notes dealt with disputes concerning attributions and datings. The staff knew that their labors would take a long time, but they were quite optimistic that sooner or later the printing of the multi-volume bibliography would begin and that the project would be finished. A very nicely typeset sample brochure was issued, containing a few well-chosen entries.[27] The promise of the beautiful brochure was, however, never fulfilled. More than thirty years after the start of the project, the people and institutions involved were in despair over ever being able to bring it to publication in the form originally planned.

Fortunately, the thirty years passed at a time when it became feasible to transfer the information from the cards onto CD-ROM. A project that began in the traditional, conventional mode and that was supposed to produce an elegantly printed, multivolume national bibliography, turned into an electronic publishing venture. For book lovers some of the original appeal was lost, but for the average librarian, user, and reader much has been gained. The bibliography, which currently contains Hebrew books printed before 1960, became an open-ended project, one that can be instantly updated. Moreover, the retrieval of information became immeasurably more flexible and rapid than it would have been in the traditional book format. Thus, the National Hebrew Bibliography has turned into a practical instrument that serves a large constituency of scholars, students, and librarians.[28]

Computerization is a tremendous lure to the initiation of ambitious undertakings. The Institute for Computerized Bibliography in Jerusalem, a private enterprise under the directorship of Yeshayahu Vinograd, launched a project called *Otzar ha-sefer ha-ivri* (Thesaurus for the Hebrew Book). The result of the enterprise is a book that is presented as a continuation and modernization of Benjacob's *Otzar ha-sefarim*. It contains Hebrew books printed until 1863, the cut-off date of Benjacob's *Otzar*. The entries are accompanied by short bibliographical references,

27 See above, note 22.

28 *The Bibliography of the Hebrew Book: 1473-1960*. From the Institute for Hebrew Bibliography, User manual, Temporary Edition (Jerusalem: C. D. I. Systems, 1994).

and the volumes are attractively produced.[29] The most innovative feature of this publication is that it contains a listing arranged by places of printing, in addition to the title listing. Thus, almost simultaneously, we have two computer-produced bibliographies, besides the one whose appearance we celebrate, the *Catalog of the Hebrew Collection of the Harvard College Library*.

This latter is unique and extraordinary. The Harvard Catalog is the culmination of two major processes. I have in mind the process of Harvard's collection development, on the one hand, and its pioneering use of technology, on the other hand. Building on a solid historical foundation, the Harvard College Library, over the last three decades and more, under the leadership of Dr. Charles Berlin, has systematically and wisely strengthened its holdings of older material, but it has at the same time endeavored—successfully—to collect Israeli publications as extensively as possible. As a result, Harvard has become the most comprehensive depository of all kinds of Israeli publications, not only those relating to literary, religious, and cultural matters, and not only ones in the field of Jewish studies, but also publications relating to the scientific, political, economic and other aspects of Israeli life. These newer areas of interest, beyond Jewish and Rabbinic studies in the more traditional sense, have also been covered by collecting related materials from outside of Israel, from the Jewish diaspora in general. A cursory perusal of randomly selected pages of the new catalog easily demonstrates the variety and wealth of the collection. The subject section provides access to topics ranging from *afforestation* to *rock music* and from *aeronautics* to *kitchen utensils*. At the same time, it takes more than eighty columns to list the works in Jewish ethical literature, for there are at least 1,500 of them.

A very useful and highly significant index of the printing places occupies a large part of the catalog. If, for example, one looks up Fano, one finds that Harvard has six books printed in that small Italian city; produced in the first decade of the sixteenth century, they represent some of the rarest of Hebrew books. Does one want to know whether Hebrew books were ever published in Oran, Algeria? The answer is five books, all from the

29 Yeshayahu Vinograd, *Thesaurus of the Hebrew Book; Listing of Books Printed in Hebrew Letters Since the Beginning of Hebrew Printing circa 1469 through 1863*, 2v. (Jerusalem: The Institute for Computerized Bibliography, 1993-1995).

nineteenth century. What was the book production in Tel Aviv in 1956? Look it up in the catalog, under the appropriate heading in the place index, and you will find an amazing quantity of publications. The panorama of Jewish and Israel publications is as fascinatingly diverse as life itself. What distinguishes this catalog from other similar works is that it exhibits strengths in so many areas, from the rare to the standard, from the ephemeral to the central, from the old to the new, from seminal to the trivial. This was achieved by good and careful planning, not chance. As stated in the brochure describing the catalog, this is the "first Hebraica catalog of its type and magnitude to be produced from machine readable cataloging data." An extraordinary rich collection was made accessible by the most advanced current technology.

The catalog has other features that make it valuable in ways that other bibliographical works lack. The Harvard Catalog covers materials published up to the 1990s, while Vinograd's bibliography extends until 1863 and the Jerusalem project until 1960. Neither of the latter has a subject index. The subject index points up the most important and unique aspect of the Harvard Catalog: its all-encompassing nature. It cannot be emphasized too strongly that the Harvard collection goes well beyond traditional Hebrew literature to cover material that does not even touch directly upon Jewish studies, as long as it is in Hebrew. The Hebraica collections of other major universities limit themselves to materials relating mainly to traditional, Rabbinic works. Harvard, by including secular works, becomes the first university that truly integrates its Hebraica collection into the university's general program. Jewish studies are no longer segregated, and Hebrew language publications have become an integral part of the general collecting profile of a great university library.

In conclusion, the Harvard Catalog is a complete, faithful record of the holdings of a great collection. Its aim is to serve and to stimulate scholarship. By grouping together by author, place, subject large segments of related materials, the scholar is invited to partake of the delicacies of a *Shulhan Arukh*, that is, a set table. Using another metaphor, the catalog provides the building blocks; the researcher can use them as he or she wishes to create new knowledge, new learning, and new scholarship. And as to the rest: go and study!

On Judaica Research Services

In the last twenty-five years, Jewish studies in this country, in Israel, and elsewhere have experienced tremendous growth, and Judaica librarianship, in its own manner, has tried to keep up with the giant strides of the discipline it serves.

Obviously, it is impossible to enumerate all the achievements of the last quarter of a century here; therefore, my mention of a few outstanding accomplishments in this field should be regarded as a highly selective sampling. The multivolume dictionary catalogs of the Jewish Division of the New York Public Library (1960), of the Klau Library of Hebrew Union College (1964), and the *Catalogue of Hebrew Books of Harvard University Library* (1968) have put at the disposal of scholars and librarians the records of hundreds of thousands of Hebraica and Judaica publications. *The Index of Articles of Jewish Studies* (1969 ff.) has become an indispensable reference tool. Shlomo Shunami's standard *Bibliography of Jewish Bibliographies* (2nd edition enlarged, 1965) was enhanced in 1975 by a *Supplement* that includes over 2,000 entries (the 1965 volume has 4,751 entries). In other words, the *Supplement* that represents basically the bibliographical output of only ten years contains almost half of the total number of bibliographies published over a period of some 300 years, since the first Jewish bibliographies started to appear in the seventeenth century! The Hebrew Paleography Project (established in 1965) has published a number of volumes of pioneering importance for the study of medieval Hebrew manuscripts. The two volumes of Shimeon Brisman's *Jewish Research Literature* (1977, 1987) [there is now a third volume (Volume Three, Part One), 2000] place in the hand of the interested and serious reader the best, most reliable and concise guide to the subject.

Not only the published bibliographies and reference works bear testimony to progress in Judaica librarianship. Sophisticated new technologies such as automation and microfilming, on site in Judaica libraries, the wide availability of library materials through these measures as well as through facsimiles and reprints, and the proliferation of special collections of Judaica throughout the world are all to be credited for making the present period the best of times for researchers in Jewish studies. If one considers Manhattan alone, from 4th Street to 185th Street one finds an unprecedented accumulation of Judaica books in such fine libraries as that of Hebrew Union College, New York Public Library, Yivo, Leo Baeck Institute, Jewish Theological Seminary, and Yeshiva University.

Therefore, the celebration of the twenty-fifth anniversary of the establishment of the Judaica Department of the Harvard College Library, an exemplary model for innovations and substantial contributions, provides us with an opportunity to rejoice in the remarkable development of the field. More significantly, it allows the practitioners of Judaica librarianship to look forward and assess the *desiderata* for the future.

The difficulties a Judaica bibliographer faces in his or her tasks are succinctly formulated by Robert Singerman in the introduction to his *Jewish Serials of the World* (1986):

> At first glance, it is somewhat surprising to note that there does not yet exist an authoritative, book-length study of the three-hundred-year-old history of Jewish serials and press since the founding of the *Gazeta de Amsterdam* in 1675. This lacuna, while regrettable, is certainly understandable when the linguistic diversity of the thousands of Jewish serials is recalled. Undoubtedly, a command of at least eight languages (Hebrew, Yiddish, Judezmo, German, French, English, Russian and Polish) would be required of the ideal historian of Jewish journalism. The expert would also need to be fully knowledgeable in Jewish culture and intellectual history with additional training in modern Jewish history, content analysis, and the historical development of journalism. Another major handicap, while not insurmountable, is the lack of a comprehensive, global checklist of all known Jewish serials with their publishing and editorial genealogies fully described and with the titles located in holding repositories.

Similar demands could be placed on bibliographers in Jewish studies in many other areas and the status of available resources is not always different from the situation that Singerman describes.

A quotation from another recently published book demonstrates the tentativeness in many other aspects of Jewish bibliography and booklore. Malachi Beit-Arie, in the foreword to his *Specimens of Medieval Hebrew Scripts* (1987), states, "We have not yet forged a clear methodology, morphological or quantitative, for differentiation between models of the same type [of Hebrew script], and even our classification into types is tentative." In short, two challenges confront the Jewish bibliographer and scholar of Jewish booklore: the complexity of the field of Jewish studies, in general, and the frequent lack of authoritative reference books and handbooks that are commonly available in other disciplines. Accordingly, despite the significant achievements, many ambitious and innovative new projects in research services still await the attention and dedication of competent Judaica librarians.

In a broader sense, Judaica librarianship research services may be divided into two major categories: direct services, such as bibliographies, indexes, catalogs, guides and reference works; and indirect services, of a more abstract scholarly nature, that encompass works dealing with the history of the Hebrew manuscript and printed book, the history of publishing, Jewish book collections, etc. Obviously, in some ways the two areas overlap.

The following are examples of a few projects that seem worthy of being continued and completed or planned and carried out.

The National Hebrew Bibliography Project began in 1964 at the Jewish National and University Library in Jerusalem. This most ambitious, first national Hebrew bibliography is now nearing completion of its editorial stage. The international Jewish library community is eagerly awaiting the publication, in one form or another, of this monumental work and should be ready to offer any help needed to promote its speedy completion and distribution.

A systematic and sustained effort should be applied to the consistent, periodic updating of standard Jewish bibliographies and reference works. Some important examples are: Shunami's *Bibliography of Jewish Bibliographies*, the last edition of which is from 1975; M.M. Kasher and J.B. Mandelbaum's *Sarei ha-elef* (a millennium of Hebrew authors [500-1500 C.E.]; a complete bibliographical compendium of Hebraica... new edition, 1978); Abraham Yaari, *Bibliography of the Passover Haggadah*, 1960, for which a number of supplements have been compiled by various bibliographers, but which has not been issued in a new, cumulative, revised edition [See now: Isaac Yudlov, *The Haggadah Thesaurus: Bibliography of Passover Haggadoth from the Beginning of Hebrew*

Printing until 1960 (Jerusalem, 1997)] and Nahum Rakover's *Otsar ha-mishpat* (a bibliography on Jewish law), published in 1975.

There are also *desiderata* in the field of periodical indexing. All users appreciate the comprehensiveness and the detailed and easy classification of the *Index of Articles on Jewish Studies*, but the fact that there are now twenty-seven volumes of this important work makes cumulative indexes, arranged by author and subject and published at regular intervals, desirable. [There are now 50 volumes and a cumulative index is available on-line.] Passage indexes to classical Jewish literature in periodicals, going back to the emergence of modern Jewish scholarship, are also important. The Saul Lieberman Talmudic Research Institute of the Jewish Theological Seminary in Jerusalem is in the process of preparing such a passage index to Talmudic literature, and it is to be hoped both that the work will be completed soon and that other similar projects will be planned and carried out.

Annotated critical bibliographies on well-defined subjects or influential authors would also fill gaps. Louis Feldman's masterly bibliography on Josephus (1986) could serve as a model, and one hopes that Jacob Dienstag's labors in the field of Maimonides bibliography will ultimately be published in a suitable form.

The field of Jewish studies needs an up-to-date, accurate, comprehensive biographical encyclopedia. The most comprehensive one available is in German, is not always accurate, and is hopelessly outdated (S. Wininger's *Grosse juedische National-biographie, 1925-1936*). As Shimeon Brisman writes:

> The number of Jewish biographical encyclopedias and lexicons, arranged in alphabetical order, is substantial. Unfortunately, some are incomplete, defective, or unreliable. This situation prompted some scholars, beginning in the early 19th century, to propose the production of a national Jewish biography. Several attempts to produce such a work were made, none too successful. A national Jewish biography is still a dream of the future. (*Jewish Research Literature*, vol. 2, pp. 253-254)

Obviously, such a project could be carried out only as a cooperative venture and over a long period of time.

A large number of publications in the post-Holocaust period have dealt with the history of Jewish communities in various geographical locations. Though good bibliographies are available on the history of the Jews in many countries, there are still some areas where reliable, accurate, comprehensive works would be helpful. Just as one example, the history of the Jews in Hungary is not bibliographically well documented, and a "Hungaria Judaica," modeled after the excellent *Germania Judaica* (1917-1968), would be an important contribution. The same applies to individual, important Jewish communities of the past and the present.

The standard and still extremely useful encyclopedia of beginning lines of Medieval Hebrew poetry (*Otzar ha-shira ve-ha-piyyut*), the work of Israel Davidson (published in 1924-1938), has never been updated. [For a partial update see: *J. Schirmann's Bibliography of Studies in Hebrew Medieval Poetry 1948-1978*, Compiled and edited by E. Adler, G. Davidson, A. Kehath and P. Ziv (Beer-Sheva, 1989).]

Accordingly, in all areas of bibliographies and reference works in Jewish studies, one could suggest projects to complement the many fine tools already at our disposal or to bring such tools to fields that lack them.

Bibliographical work and thoughtful indexing could also facilitate the work of students through study guides and bibliographies to such monumental achievements of scholars of the previous generation as Saul Lieberman's *Tosefta ki-feshuta* or M.M. Kasher's *Torah shelema*. These works embody an immense number of references to Rabbinic and other literature, and their use is quite complicated for those who are not well versed in this type of literature.

Similarly, there are great gaps in the field of cataloging important collections of Hebrew manuscripts and rare books. The collections of Hebrew manuscripts in the library of the Jewish Theological Seminary, Hebrew Union College, and the Jewish National and University Library are not described in printed catalogs, while great and famous collections of Hebrew manuscripts in the old European libraries are frequently known only through nineteenth- and eighteenth-century catalogs (e.g., Florence, Parma [see now: *Hebrew Manuscripts in the Biblioteca Palatine in Parma*, Edited by Benjamin Richler, Palaeographical and codicological descriptions by Malachi Beit-Arié (Jerusalem, 2001)] and such German libraries as Hamburg and Munich, which had their collections of Hebrew manuscripts cataloged by the great Moritz Steinschneider). Hebrew manuscripts could be cataloged not only according to the depository where they are kept but also by country of origin. In this manner, manuscript collections stemming from a particular culture and tradition can be brought together. Examples of this kind of catalog are Amnon Netzer's *Manuscripts of the Jews of Persia in the Ben Zvi Institute* (1985) and Norman Golb's *Spertus College of Judaica Yemenite Manuscripts* (1972). The foundation for the preparation of catalogs of Hebrew manuscripts is already in place through the efforts of The Institute of Microfilmed Hebrew Manuscripts of the Jewish National and University Library, the Hebrew Paleography Project, and the Index of Jewish Art: Iconographical Index of Hebrew Illuminated Manuscripts, the latter two joint Israeli-French projects. These projects, when completed, will undoubtedly make the task of anyone setting out to catalog individual, public, or private collections of Hebrew manuscripts much easier.

It would also be desirable to publish catalogs of the rare printed Hebraica holdings of major Judaica libraries (similar to the fine catalog of the Mehlman Collection [*Ginzei Yisrael*], in the Jewish National and University Library in Jerusalem, prepared by Isaac Yudlov, 1984). Furthermore, good, reliable guides to individual collections should be made available so that a researcher can know what kind of materials to expect in each library.

On a more general level, Hebrew manuscripts and printed books deserve scholarly exploration in their own right. Studies in paleography, in scribal traditions and practices, in the selection of works to be copied, the dissemination of manuscripts, the textual traditions they reflect, the esthetic aspect of the handwritten book and its survival—or unfortunately, frequently, its destruction—are all challenging fields for investigation. The first and last general introduction to all aspects of the lore of Hebrew manuscripts is still Moritz Steinschneider's *Vorlesungen ueber die Kunde hebraeischer Handschriften* (1897, Hebrew translation with additions by A.M. Haberman in 1965) [see now: B. Richler, *Hebrew Manuscripts: A Treasures legacy*, Cleveland, 1990 and of B. Richler, *Guide to Hebrew Manuscript Collections*, Jerusalem, 1994]. Undoubtedly, in view of the great advances and changes in the field, a new handbook providing information on Hebrew manuscripts is needed.

The history of the Hebrew printed book also offers many research opportunities. Histories and records of local printing presses, publishing, booktrade, illustration, censorship, technical and esthetic aspects of typography, copyright and Rabbinic approbation, Christian-Jewish relationships in the scholarly and commercial aspects of Hebrew publishing and printing, and the impact of the introduction of printing of Hebrew books on the various Jewish communities and on the Jewish mind are subjects that should invite the curiosity of the researcher.

In our times, when interest in the Jewish book is so keen, careful thought should be given to planning, coordinating, and executing worthy projects in the field of Judaica bibliography and booklore. In addition to supporting the few single-minded, highly dedicated individuals who devote themselves to research in this area, we must make provisions for directing promising young scholars toward Judaica bibliography and booklore as worthy, stimulating, and challenging scholarly endeavors. In the words of Shimeon Brisman:

> During his years as a Jewish Studies librarian and lecturer in Hebrew bibliography, the author has noticed with disappointment that the average Jewish scholar, student, or even librarian is totally unaware of the existence of such [reference] tools; but he has been pleasantly surprised as a lecturer to notice students' fascination with Jewish bibliography, a subject usually considered "dry." It seems that Jewish bibliography when presented in the realm of Jewish cultural and literary history, can become an exciting topic for scholars and students. (*Jewish Research Literature*, vol. 1, p. IX)

The time may have come for considering the establishment of an Institute for Judaica Bibliography and Booklore that would serve as an international clearinghouse for the field and eventually grow into a center for the training of scholars and for the realization of some of the projects that would benefit Jewish studies the world over. The great progress achieved in the last quarter of a century, so dramatically symbolized in this country by the magnificent contributions of the Judaica Department of the Harvard College Library to the field of Judaica librarianship, should serve as an inspiration to the entire profession when it looks to the future.

One Hundred Years of Genizah Discovery and Research in the United States

Not long ago, Frank Rich wrote an interesting column in *The New York Times*. It was called "Reverse Exodus" and was subtitled "American Jews go back downtown."[1] The main thrust of the article was that American Jews should not have to seek their roots or identity in the "old country" or Israel or the Holocaust, because there is pride to be derived from their rich American Jewish heritage. He pointed out that the past of American Judaism could well serve as a source of inspiration for younger generations of Jews. The story told here of a little known chapter of American Jewish scholarship, is for sure glorious, rich of great achievement, and part of the proud American Jewish past.

Nineteen ninety-seven marked the centennial of the removal of hundreds of thousands of old and worn Hebrew manuscript fragments from a chamber—the *Genizah*—of the ancient Ben Ezra synagogue in Old Cairo.[2] This feat is forever tied to Solomon Schechter,[3] whose name has indeed become a household word, mainly because of the success of the network of Schechter schools named after him. However, Solomon Schechter's name is memorable for the reasons of his own watershed achievements. Schechter, a hundred years ago, was a teacher of Rabbinics at Cambridge University in England, enjoying fame as a scholar, whose pioneering publications made a great impression on Jews and non-Jews

* [See now: Jacob Lassner, "Geniza Studies in the United States", in: *A Gateway to Medieval Mediterranean Life: Cairo's Ben Ezra Synagogue* (Chicago, Spertus Institute, 2001.]

1 *New York Times*, May 15, 1997 (Op Ed Page).

2 On the Ben Ezra Synagogue see Phyllis Lambert (ed.), *Fortifications and the Synagogue: The Fortress of Babylon and the Ben Ezra Synagogue, Cairo* (London: Weidenfeld and Nicolson, 1994).

3 For a biography of Schechter, see Norman Bentwich, *Solomon Schechter: A Biography* (Philadelphia: The Jewish Publication Society, 1938). [See now also: Ismar Schorsch, "Schechter's Seminary: Polarities in Balance", in: *Conservative Judaism* 55 (2003), pp. 3-23.]

alike. It is well known how two Scottish tourist ladies, returning from a trip to Egypt, showed Schechter some old Hebrew manuscript fragments that they had acquired there, and how Schechter, in great excitement, identified these fragments as part of the long-lost original of the ancient Hebrew work, the Book of Ben Sira. Schechter, with the full support of the authorities of Cambridge University, journeyed to Cairo and removed the contents of that old chamber, called the *Genizah*,[4] and transferred it to Cambridge.[5] With this event, a century of exciting discoveries began.

Solomon Schechter was the most influential figure in *Genizah* discoveries, but he was not the only one.

Cyrus Adler, an American scholar and public leader, played an important role as well in this endeavor. Grace Cohen Grossman recently painted an intricate portrait of Cyrus Adler, who, among his many public Jewish and non-Jewish roles, was instrumental in acquiring Judaica items for the Smithsonian Institution, where he served as secretary. In 1890, Adler became involved in the preparation of a large scale exposition to take place in Chicago to celebrate the four hundredth anniversary of the discovery of America. He was asked to travel to the Orient to secure objects for the exposition.[6] On his way to the Middle East, he stopped for a few days in England where he met, for the first time, two men who later became important in *Genizah* history, Solomon Schechter and Elkan Nathan Adler. Cyrus Adler, no relation to Elkan, proceeded on his trip and spent the spring of 1891 in Cairo. In his memoirs, he recorded his acquisition of *Genizah* fragments:

> I was always looking out for Museum specimens that could be bought within reason, and I wandered about the shops very often. I happened one day to find several trays full of parchment leaves written in Hebrew, which the merchant had labeled *anticas*. I saw at a glance that these were very old. As I wore a pith helmet and khaki suit, like every other tourist, he thought I wanted one as a souvenir.

4 The *Genizah* was the repository for Jewish religious texts — Torah scrolls, prayer books, Bibles, rabbinic literature, and other religious and ritual Judaica — which under religious law must not be destroyed.

5 *Ibid.*, pp. 140-144.

6 Grace Cohen Grossman with Richard Eighme Ahlborn, *Judaica at the Smithsonian: Cultural Politics as Cultural Model* (Washington, D. C.: Smithsonian Institution Press, 1997), esp. pp. 28-31, 42-61.

> But indicating an interest in the whole lot I purchased them, big and little, some of the pieces only one sheet, some of them forty or fifty pages, at the enormous price of one shilling per unit and thus brought back to Europe what was probably the second largest collection from the *Genizah*, certainly the first to America, out of which has come at least one book and several important articles. These are now in the Dropsie College... I showed these documents to Dr. Schechter of Cambridge in 1892. He promptly borrowed a few, and I have always flattered myself that this accidental purchase of mine was at least one of the leads that enabled Dr. Schechter to make his discovery of the Cairo *Genizah*.[7]

That Adler did a good job of arousing Schechter's interest in the *Genizah* is obvious. When Adler returned to Cairo in 1929 and wanted to see the *Genizah*, the *shammash* told him: "Schechter carried it away."[8] But what did Adler carry away? Fortunately, we do have a catalogue of the Dropsie College *Genizah* fragments, now at the University of Pennsylvania. This relatively small collection is a kind of microcosm of the *Genizah* as a whole. By the way, in the Dropsie collection, in addition to the Cyrus Adler acquisition, there were also manuscripts that several other American collectors, Mayer Sulzberger, Herbert Friedenwald, David Werner Amram, and Camden M. Cobern obtained in Cairo. In the Dropsie collection there are fragments of Bible and Talmud, liturgy and poetry, documents and letters, amulets and philosophical texts.[9] The oldest known text of the Passover Haggadah is the proud possession of the collection, as is a 4,000 word letter from Sicily, from the year 1064, in which various business matters and a civil war in Tunisia where the writer faced death, are described. The Dropsie Haggadah is not only old, but also very different from the text that we are using today.[10] The

7 Cyrus Adler, *I Have Considered the Days* (Philadelphia: The Jewish Publication Society, 1941), pp. 116-117.

8 *Ibid.*, p. 364.

9 See B. Halpern, *Descriptive Catalogue of the Genizah Fragments in Philadelphia* (Philadelphia: Dropsie College, 1924).

10 On the Haggadah see *The Passover Haggadah: Its Sources and History*, ed. by E.D. Goldschmidt (Jerusalem: Bialik Institute, 1960), pp. 73-84 (in Hebrew); on the letter see S.D. Goitein, *A Mediterranean Society*, Volume 1 (Berkeley and Los Angeles: University of California Press, 1967), plate 1 (after p. 20).

availability of this collection in the United States spurred great activity among scholars in this country, who devoted themselves to studying the treasures hidden in these fragments.

Solomon Schechter's arrival in New York as president of the Jewish Theological Seminary in 1902 made New York into a capital of *Genizah* research. Schechter himself continued to publish his discoveries, and others joined him. Many of these discoveries were first published in the scholarly journal, *The Jewish Quarterly Review*, which was issued since 1910 under the auspices of Dropsie College in Philadelphia, and was edited by Adler and Schechter. The transfer of the prestigious journal from England, where it had been published from its inception in 1889 until 1910, to the United States, was another important step in the development of Jewish studies in this country.[11] Schechter also brought with himself several important fragments that were owned by him personally. One of them was a famous letter signed by Maimonides' own hand. In the letter, Maimonides pleads for funds for the redemption of Jewish prisoners who were captured in a caravan in *Erez Yisrael* and were held for ransom by the Crusader King of Jerusalem. Maimonides describes how he and the *dayyanim* (the judges of Rabbinical courts), the elders and learned people (*talmidei hakhamim*), worked day and night, in the synagogues, in the market places, and in private homes, to gather together the sums needed to ransom the captives.[12] At Schechter's death, his own *Genizah* fragments became part of the library of the Jewish Theological Seminary.

There is an interesting episode that is connected with Schechter's coming to America and the *Genizah*. The manuscripts that Schechter removed from Cairo in 1897 had become part of the library of Cambridge University in England. When Schechter prepared his move to New York, he borrowed from the library more than a hundred documents on which he intended to work; the manuscripts were given call numbers as Cambridge Loan Fragments. Some of them were indeed published. In the 1920s and 1930s, the Cambridge authorities turned to the Seminary Library in New York and asked for the return of the original of these "Loan" manuscripts. Despite diligent searches by the then Librarian, Alexander Marx, the originals could

11 See *The Seventy Fifth Anniversary of the Jewish Quarterly Review*, ed. by Abraham A. Neuman and Solomon Zeitlin (Philadelphia: *Jewish Quarterly Review*, 1967), pp. 62-64.

12 See S. D. Goitein, *Palestine Jewry in Early Islamic and Crusader Times in the Light of the Genizah Documents* (Jerusalem: Yad Ben Zvi, 1980), pp. 312-314.

not be located. They were rediscovered in the Seminary Library in the late 1960s among huge, long sheets of paper on which Schechter himself transcribed the original texts. The late Professor Louis Finkelstein asked me to return them, in person, to Cambridge, which I did; and obviously, I received a royal treatment at the Cambridge University Library as the bearer of such treasures.

In the first two decades of our century, Detroit joined Philadelphia and New York as a depository of *Genizah* fragments. Charles Freer, the famous collector of oriental art objects, purchased *Genizah* documents in Egypt from a dealer. In all likelihood, the dealer had acquired them earlier from the *Genizah* synagogue. An alternative source could have been an ancient cemetery where they had been originally buried. Be that as it may, the documents are now in the Freer Gallery of the Smithsonian in Washington, D.C. A detailed and elegant catalogue of the fragments was published, describing some fascinating aspects of Jewish life in the Middle Ages, relating to trade, travel and marriage. The Freer catalogue is, in itself, a model work, as it includes photographs, transcriptions, and full translations of the texts.[13]

The major boost to the *Genizah* collection in America came in 1922 through the purchase by the Seminary Library of the library of Elkan Nathan Adler, the famous British traveler, collector and scholar, who was mentioned above. Elkan Adler traveled to Cairo in 1888 and again in 1895-1896, still before Schechter's 1897 trip. On Adler's second journey, "The Cairo synagogue authorities accompanied me to the *Genizah* and permitted me to take away the first sackful of fragments from that famous hoard. Neubauer[14] rated me soundly for not carrying the whole lot away, Schechter admired my continence but was not foolish enough to follow my example."[15] Elsewhere, Elkan Adler wrote the following on his visit to the Cairo *Genizah* synagogue: "I... was conducted... to the extreme end of the ladies' gallery, permitted to climb to the topmost rung of a ladder, to enter the secret chamber of the *Genizah* through a hole in the wall, and to

13 See Richard Gottheil and William H. Wottel, *Fragments from the Cairo Genizah in the Freer Collection* (New York: Macmillan, 1927), esp. p. XIV.

14 Adolf Neubauer (1831-1907), a well-known Jewish scholar, librarian at the Bodleian Library in Oxford, England.

15 *Catalogue of Hebrew Manuscripts in the Collection of Elkan Nathan Adler* (Cambridge University Press, 1921), p. V.

take away with me a sackful of paper and parchment writings—as much in fact as I could gather up in the three or four hours I was permitted to linger there."[16]

What was in the sack that Adler called a very Benjamin's sack?[17] The best description of the original state and contents of the *Genizah* is still one that comes from the pen of Schechter:

> One can hardly realize the confusion in a genuine, old *Genizah* until one has seen it. It is a battlefield of books, and the literary productions of many centuries had their share in the battle, and their *disjecta membra* are now strewn over its area. Some of the belligerents have perished outright, and are literally ground to dust in the terrible struggle for space, whilst others, as if overtaken by a general crush, are squeezed into big, unshapely lumps, which even with the aid of chemical appliances can no longer be separated without serious damage to their constituents. In their present condition these lumps sometimes afford curiously suggestive combinations; as, for instance, when you find a piece of some rational work, in which the very existence of either angels or devils is denied, clinging for its very life to an amulet in which these same beings (mostly the latter) are bound over to be on their good behavior and not interfere with Miss Jair's love for somebody. The development of the romance is obscured by the fact that the last lines of the amulet are mounted on some I.O.U., or lease, and this in turn is squeezed between the sheets of an old moralist, who treats all attention to money affairs with scorn and indignation. Again, all these contradictory matters cleave tightly to some sheets from a very old Bible. This, indeed, ought to be the last umpire between them, but it is hardly legible without peeling off from its surface the fragments of some printed work, which clings to old nobility with all the obstinacy and obstructiveness of the *Parvenu*.[18]

Another interesting collection of *Genizah* fragments in the United States

16 *Jewish Quarterly Review*, old series, IX (1897), pp. 672-673.

17 *Ibid.*, p. 673.

18 Solomon Schechter, *Studies in Judaism*, Second Series (Philadelphia: The Jewish Publication Society, 1908), pp. 6-7.

was once owned by Johann Krengel, who served as rabbi in several Central European communities.[19] Krengel received these fragments in the early years of the century and wrote an article on some of them.[20] They disappeared during World War II and were found in the Seminary Library in the 1970s in an old, worn, leather briefcase, mixed up with Krengel's typewritten sermons in German. The collection is now called the Krengel *Genizah*.

The easy availability of these collections in American libraries, combined with the great impact of the magnetic personality of Solomon Schechter and the lure and challenge of the opportunity for a veritable treasure hunt among the dispersed leaves, inspired many leading Jewish scholars in the United States to devote their lives to the exploration of this immense accumulation of old Hebrew, Aramaic, and Judeo-Arabic fragments.

I would like to single out four great scholars who were closely associated with American institutions of learning most of their lives and whose work had an immense impact on *Genizah* scholarship. There were others, whose names I can only mention: Henry Malter, S.L. Skoss, Benzion Halper, Richard Gottheil, Moshe Zucker, Shalom Spiegel, all deceased; and Norman Golb, Marc Cohen, Norman Stillman, the Friedman brothers, Shamma and Mordecai (now in Israel), Elazar Hurvitz, and Neil Danzig, who fortunately are still with us and continue to be active in *Genizah* research.

Let us start with Louis Ginzberg, best known in the general community for his monumental *Legends of the Jews*. A native of Lithuania, a descendant of the Gaon of Vilna, a student of Lithuanian *yeshivoth* and German universities, he came to this country in 1899. For the next half a century, he taught at the Jewish Theological Seminary in New York and was regarded as the foremost scholar of his generation.[21] In 1909, Ginzberg published a two volume work, *Geonica*. In the first volume he provided a synthesis of the Geonic era, an approximately 500 year period in Jewish history, mainly in Babylonia. This span of time, between the end of the Talmudic period and the beginning of the emergence of the great

19 See the brief entry about him in *Encyclopaedia Judaica*, (German), vol. 10, col. 405-406.

20 See *Festschrift zu Israel Lewy's Siebzigsten Geburstag* (Breslau: Marcus, 1911), pp. 36-46.

21 On his life see the personal memoir by his son, Eli Ginzberg, *Keeper of the Law: Louis Ginzberg* (Philadelphia: Jewish Publication Society, 1966) [with a new afterword, 1996].

European Jewish centers in Spain, Italy, France and Germany, contained the seeds of many later developments in Jewish life, culture and religion. The knowledge on this period was meager, scattered and fragmentary. Ginzberg, in the second volume of *Geonica*, entitled *Genizah Studies*, published and analyzed for the first time many manuscripts relating to this subject. In Ginzberg's words: "There is no exaggeration in maintaining that the discovery of the *Genizah* by Prof. Solomon Schechter was in no other department of Jewish learning so epoch making as in the history of the Geonim."[22] Ginzberg continued to enrich this field and, in 1929, published a further volume of *Genizah* studies on Geonic Halakhah. In the introduction to this volume, Ginzberg maintained that the results of his 1909 publications were still valid and listed some of the major scholarly challenges posed by the Geonic period: "the evolution of the Talmud from a literary compilation to the molder of Jewish thought and feeling, the hegemony of Babylonian Jewry over all Israel, the rise of sects, the growth of mysticism, and the attempts at an interpretation of Talmudic Judaism by the light of Graeco-Arabic philosophy."[23]

The *Genizah* documents, as deciphered and analyzed by Ginzberg, and others, played a major role in contributing to the solution of these scholarly challenges. Ginzberg also published a major work containing *Genizah* manuscripts that elucidate many obscure passages of the Talmud of Jerusalem.[24] Ginzberg consciously chose to write his Geonic history in English: "having cast in my lot with American Jewry, I felt myself bound to write in the language of the land of my adoption, and trust I shall not suffer in regarding myself as an American Jew."[25] This remark must be understood against the background of his times: most modern Jewish scholarship in the first decades of our century was written in German, often referred to as the second-most-used Jewish language. The important discoveries of Ginzberg, achieved in America and published in English, placed American Jewish scholarship into the mainstream of the academic

22 Louis Ginzberg, *Geonica*. Volume 1 (New York: The Jewish Theological Seminary, 1909), pp. VIII-IX.

23 *Genizah Studies in Memory of Doctor Solomon Schechter*. Volume 11: *Geonic and Early Karaitic Halakha* by Louis Ginzberg (New York: The Jewish Theological Seminary, 1929).

24 *Yerushalmi Fragments from the Genizah*. Edited by Louis Ginzberg (New York: The Jewish Theological Seminary, 1909).

25 Eli Ginzberg, *Keeper of the Law* (see above note 21), p. 94.

study of Judaism and contributed toward the gradual transfer of Jewish learning from Europe to America, already in the pre-Holocaust period. In subsequent *Genizah* research of Rabbinics, particularly Geonic literature, Ginzberg remained the pioneering authority, whose work still constitutes the starting point in every serious study of the topic. Historical, Halakhic and sociological research of the Geonate builds on the foundations Ginzberg had laid.

Another major American figure in a different discipline of *Genizah* research was Israel Davidson.[26] He was also a native of Lithuania, who arrived in America in 1888. Among various occupations of his early career, being a chaplain in the Sing Sing prison deserves mention. A product of City College and Columbia University, Davidson became a professor at the Jewish Theological Seminary of America and specialized in medieval Hebrew literature. His best known work is the four volume *Thesaurus of Medieval Hebrew Poetry* in which he listed more than 35,000 poems.[27] In terms of originality, however, his discovery of Yannai was most decisive. Yannai's name as a composer of liturgical poems had been known for a long time. His poetry, however, was unknown and no facts were available about his life or times until Davidson published his findings in 1919.[28] About twenty years before Davidson's book appeared, one of the first and more sensational *Genizah* finds was made by the English scholars, F. Crawford Burkitt and Charles Taylor. In one of the fragments at Cambridge University, the two scholars identified, underneath some Hebrew script, remnants of a lost Greek translation of the Bible. They edited the Greek, without paying attention to the Hebrew written over it. Davidson, observing the facsimiles of these manuscripts, became attracted to the Hebrew text and found, to his great amazement, that it contained poems that were connected to the weekly Bible sections, divided according to the ancient triennial cycle of public Torah reading. He recognized in the texts the signature of Yannai and was able to reconstruct the structure of these poetic compositions. The language was innovative, fresh and supple;

26 On his life see his wife's memoirs: C. Davidson, *Out of Endless Yearnings: A Memoir of Israel Davidson* (New York: Bloch, 1946).

27 The work was published in New York by the Jewish Theological Seminary, between the years 1924-1933.

28 Israel Davidson, *Mahzor Yannai: A Liturgical Work of the VIIth Century* (New York: The Jewish Theological Seminary, 1919).

the content mirrored the conditions of *Eretz Yisrael* toward the end of the Byzantine period; and the function revealed a synagogue practice of including creative new poetry into the weekly Shabbat service. Davidson's discovery opened up a new area of study of ancient Hebrew poetry. Scholars expressed their admiration for Davidson's work and stood in awe of the rich and beautiful poetry discovered by him; one scholar remarked that Yannai's work belongs alongside the folio volumes of the classics of Talmud and Midrash.[29] In the last seventy years and more, the field of Hebrew poetry in *Eretz Yisrael* has indeed exploded with many important new discoveries, which were ultimately started by Davidson's initial identification and publication of Yannai. Davidson received the recognition of his colleagues in Europe and *Eretz Yisrael*, was honored by the Bialik Prize,[30] and a street was named after him in Jerusalem.[31] The immigrant boy, the City College graduate, the American scholar became a central figure in the still unfolding scholarship of *Genizah* poetry.

The third scholar I want to mention is Jacob Mann. For a change, Mann was not from Lithuania, but from Galicia. He came to England in 1908 and then to the United States in 1920. First Mann taught at the Baltimore Hebrew College and later, until the end of his life, at the Hebrew Union College in Cincinnati.[32] Examining the holdings of *Genizah* in the various libraries, he became, in the words of Gerson D. Cohen, "an insatiable investigator of manuscripts" and "a hunter who was determined to confine his quest to new game,"[33] the new game being the *Genizah*. While Ginzberg and Davidson were mainly interested in literary and halakhic texts, Mann wanted to find and utilize documentary evidence: letters, contracts, court records. These shed light on the communal life of the Jews in Babylonia, Palestine and Egypt in the classic *Genizah* centuries, namely, from ca. 900 until ca. 1200. The non-literary fragments of the Cairo *Genizah* moved into the forefront through the work of Jacob Mann. He organized the huge quantities of data in

29 Saul Lieberman, *Studies in Palestinian Talmudic Literature* (Jerusalem: Magnes, 1991) (in Hebrew), p. 152.

30 C. Davidson (see above note 26), pp. 174-177.

31 In the *Nayot* section.

32 On Mann see Victor E. Reichert in volume 2 of Mann's *The Bible as Read and Preached in the Old Synagogue* (Cincinnati: Hebrew Union College, 1966), pp. XI-XVII.

33 Gerson D. Cohen, *Reconstruction of Gaonic History*, Introduction to Jacob Mann, *Texts and Studies in Jewish History and Literature*. Two volumes (New York: Ktav, 1972), p. XLVII.

chronological sequence in three monumental works, each of two volumes: *The Jews in Egypt and Palestine,*[34] *Texts and Studies in Jewish History and Literature,*[35] and *The Bible as Read and Preached in the Old Synagogue.*[36] Mann reconstructed events, restored forgotten names, and described the communal, political and organizational aspects of the life of the Jews, both Rabbinites and Karaites. Mann provided the raw materials for the continuing exploration of the history of the Jews in those areas. From Cincinnati, Jacob Mann dominated the field and provided the solid bricks needed for future work. As he himself put it: "The more the material stored up in manuscripts is made accessible in a scientific manner, the better will the history of the Jewish life and activities in the course of the past ages be reconstructed anew."[37]

With his familiarity with all aspects of the *Genizah*, literary, Halakhic, and documentary, Jacob Mann avoided the pitfalls of narrow specialization and provided the outlines of a synthesis of the life of the Jewish communities in the Near and Middle East that would later serve as the foundation of the scholarly achievements of the fourth scholar, S.D. Goitein.[38] Goitein, where the G could stand for *Genizah*, has spent his life, more or less equally divided, between Germany, Israel and the United States. A native of Germany, the son of a rabbi, he was trained in traditional Jewish sources, and also acquired highly advanced knowledge in Semitic and classical philology. In Palestine, in the 1920s and later, Goitein immersed himself in Arabic studies, especially Islamic law, as well as in research on the Yemenite communities. Around 1950, his single-minded devotion to *Genizah* studies had begun, a preoccupation that lasted until his death in 1985. In the United States he was associated with the University of Pennsylvania and, later, with the Institute of Advanced Studies at Princeton University. He was also the recipient of a MacArthur Fellowship. Before turning to the majestic

34 Jacob Mann, *The Jews in Egypt and in Palestine under the Fatimid Caliphs*. Two volumes (Oxford University Press, 1920-1922). New edition with Preface and Reader's Guide by S. D. Goitein (New York: Ktav, 1970).

35 See above note 33. Original edition: Cincinnati, Hebrew Union College, 1931-1933.

36 Jacob Mann, *The Bible as Read and Preached in the Old Synagogue*. Volume 1 (Cincinnati: Union of American Hebrew Congregations, 1940). Volume 2: with Isaiah Sonne (Cincinnati: Hebrew Union College, 1966).

37 *Texts and Studies* (see above note 33 and 35), vol. 1, p. VIII.

38 On his life and work see *Shelomo Dov Goitein 1900-1985* (Princeton: The Institute for Advanced Study, 1985).

volumes containing Goitein's brilliant *Genizah* research, a word is in place on Goitein's role in cataloging, classifying and organizing *Genizah* fragments and the data derived from them. Goitein himself regarded this aspect of his activity "not less vital than [his] published work."[39] He acquired an almost complete collection of photostats of the fragments and arranged them in order of the manuscript collections, creating a subject catalog, arranged around groups such as letters on trade between the Mediterranean and India, accounts, and marriage contracts. The following indexes were devised: persons, families, honorific titles, Arabic words and phrases, dated manuscripts in chronological order, and occupations.[40] This catalogue is now at Princeton University, where *Genizah* research is being continued by Goitein's student, Professor Marc Cohen.

The undisputed crowning achievement of 100 years' non-literary *Genizah* research is Goitein's five volume *A Mediterranean Society: The Jewish Communities of the Arab World as Portrayed in the Documents of the Cairo Genizah.*[41] These large volumes provide a panoramic sweep, based on the most minute attention to detail, of the life of the Jewish communities and their coexistence with the Arab world. Goitein created a new term to describe his scholarly specialization: he called himself a sociographer.[42] The main feature that grabs the reader is the liveliness of the society described through his discussions. In the masterly portrayals, his subjects, their lives, and their mentalities become vivid and palpably concrete. Goitein presents a picture of the totality of an active, dynamic, living community, or rather communities: the Jewish, the Arab and the Christian. As Amitav Ghosh, the author of a semi-fictional, semi-anthropological book, inspired by the *Genizah*, writes: "a trapdoor into a vast network of foxholes where real life continues uninterrupted" was opened by Goitein and his colleagues.[43]

Just a brief glance at the table of contents of the five volumes gives an idea of the richness of this work. Here are some chapter headings: "The working

39 See *Religion in a Religious Age*, edited by S. D. Goitein (Cambridge, Mass: Association for Jewish Studies, 1974), p. 143.

40 *Ibid.*, pp. 141-146.

41 Published by the University of California Press, 1967-1988 [Volume 6, the index volume was published in 1993].

42 See *Shelomo Dov Goitein* (above note 38), p. 9.

43 Amitov Ghosh, *In an Antique Land* (New York: Knopf, 1993), pp. 15-16.

people: craftsmen, wage earners, agriculture and fishery; professions of women;" "The world of commerce and finance: producers, dealers, brokers, auctioneers, travel and sea faring, types of vessels;" "Communal organization and institutions, medieval democracy, social services, education, interfaith relations;" "The family: marriage, the nuclear family, the extended family, the world of women;" "Daily life: the city, domestic architecture, clothing and jewelry, food and drink;" "The individual: gatherings, poverty, illness, death, awareness of personality, the ideal person, rank and renown, sex, the true believer, the prestige of scholarship." At the end of the fifth volume, Goitein paints the portrait of seven prominent personalities, among them that of Abraham, the son of Maimonides.

Besides the brilliance and hard work, what made this monumental achievement possible? Goitein himself was not reticent in speaking and writing about the forces that shaped him. Among other things, he wrote:

> Last, and strangest of all, I believe I would have missed many aspects of the *Genizah* documents had I not been granted the opportunity of observing the American scene for many years. Authoritarian Germany, where I spent my childhood and youth and the Jewish society in Palestine and later Israel with its socialist, welfare and protectionist tendencies which saw most of my working life, were utterly different from the *Genizah* society, which was loosely organized and competitive in every aspect. This vigorous free-enterprise society of the United States, which is not without petty jealousies and often cheap public honors, its endless fund-raising campaigns and all that goes with them, its general involvement in public affairs and deep concerns (or lip service, as the case may be) for the under dog all proved to be extremely instructive. We do not wear turbans here; but while reading many a *Genizah* document one feels quite at home.[44]

American institution-building, collecting zeal, scholarly ambition, concern for the preservation of our heritage—all contributed to *Genizah* research world-wide and made American Jewish scholarship a proud partner in the ongoing effort of unraveling the multitude of documents preserved among the treasures of the *Genizah*.

44 *A Mediterranean Society* (see above note 41), vol. 2, p. IX.

Building a Great Judaica Library—at What Price?

Among scholars and laypeople alike, the Seminary library has, for a long time, enjoyed a reputation as one of the most important collections of Hebraica and Judaica not only in the United States, but also in the world. In the highly complimentary, albeit well-justified characterizations of the library, it has been customary to describe the thousands of outstanding rare and valuable manuscripts, books, and graphic materials—in other words, the great treasures of the collection.[1] With the exception of some random remarks, however, very little has been said about the conception that lay behind the ambitious endeavor of creating a major research library and book museum at the Seminary. The library, almost from the onset, was envisioned as an institution that transcended the needs of the

1 Among the descriptions of the library and its history, the following should be mentioned: Alexander Marx, in *The Jewish Theological Seminary of America; Semi-Centennial Volume*, ed. Cyrus Adler (New York: Jewish Theological Seminary, 1939), pp. 87-120 (henceforth cited as *Semi-Centennial Volume*); Marx's library reports and some of his other writings on the library were collected and published as Alexander Marx, *Bibliographical Studies and Notes on Rare Books, and Manuscripts in the Library of the Jewish Theological Seminary of America*, ed. Menahem H. Schmelzer, foreword by Gerson D. Cohen (New York: Jewish Theological Seminary and Ktav Publishing, 1977) (cited hereafter as *Bibliographical Studies*). Not included in that volume are A. Marx, "What Our Library Offers to Our Students," in *Students Annual of the Jewish Theological Seminary of America* I (1914), pp. 218-26. For other smaller publications by Marx relating to the library, see the bibliography of his writings in *Alexander Marx Jubilee Volume*, English section (New York: Jewish Theological Seminary, 1950), pp. 35-59, nos. 106, 114, 173, 174, 203, 209, 219, 233. Of course, Marx's volume, *Studies in Jewish History and Booklore* (New York: Jewish Theological Seminary, 1944) also contains many references to the library's holdings. See also Boaz Cohen in *Jewish Forum* 17 (1934), pp. 20-22, 26, 58-61. On later developments, see Nahum M. Sarna, in *Jewish Book Annual* 21 (1963-64), pp. 53-59; and Menahem Schmelzer, in *Jewish Book Annual* 42 (1984-85), pp. 183-88 [pp. 182*-187* in the present volume]. For an overview of the library's history, see Herman Dicker, *Of Learning and Libraries: The Seminary Library at One Hundred* (New York: Jewish Theological Seminary, 1988). The recent library exhibition catalogue, *Great Books from Great Collectors* (New York: The Library of the Jewish Theological Seminary, 1996), provides information on the private collectors whose books became part of the Seminary library. Various other catalogs of sections of the library's collections will be cited below.

Seminary's instructional program. Rather, its avowed purpose was to collect manuscripts, printed books, and other materials to serve the emerging research projects of Jewish scholarship in the United States and to provide materials on all aspects of the Jewish experience. Unabashedly, the Seminary's lay and professional leaders proclaimed their goal of creating in the Seminary's library the foremost, first-ranked, strongest possible collection of Hebraica and Judaica ever assembled by a Jewish institution. We shall examine the forces that motivated this plan and try to determine to what degree the library succeeded (or failed) to achieve the ideal.

Despite the fact that the public statements about the library always emphasized its greatness as the premier collection for original research, internal reports and correspondence between the various officers of the Seminary reveal a tension concerning the library's central mission. Some argued that the library must be more responsive to the day-to-day demands of students and less concentrated on the abstract idea of creating an all-inclusive collection of books and manuscripts. Still, the conception of the Seminary library as a research center prevailed, although occasional doubts continued to be voiced about the wisdom of investing in yet more expensive acquisitions.

This essay will demonstrate how the one-sided, sometimes obsessive orientation toward expansion and acquisition diverted attention, energy, and resources from other aspects of library service—chief among them preservation, cataloging, classification, and the publication of library catalogs. Over the decades an imbalance developed: the library became an immensely rich depository of the rarest and most valuable materials and a deplorably poor place for a properly classified and cataloged, accessible collection of Hebraica and Judaica. This imbalance lasted until the 1950s, when the reorganization of the library was begun.[2]

Prior to that reorganization, the library provided few tools for scholars to find their way around the collection. One frustrated researcher quipped

2 The reorganization of the library that began in 1959, the 1966 fire, the opening of the new library building in 1983, and the entry into the era of computerization of library services, which reached advanced stages in the 1990s, form an entirely new period in the history of the library. This period deserves to be studied, but the present writer, who served in the library from 1961 to 1987, feels that the task of writing the history of the second half century of the library, is better left to others.

in the 1960s that the Seminary library in New York served as a *genizah* (a storage place for books that have become unusable) for the Cairo *Genizah* fragments it housed. The library's inadequacies in the areas of library technology and organization, coupled with its surprising riches, rendered it a hunting ground where the curious and adventurous scholar was rewarded by many new finds—but at the cost of much frustration. Despite this situation, it was providential that the Seminary library had the wisdom to acquire its vast treasures prior to World War II, at a time when this was still possible. Gaining bibliographical control, however essential, could be achieved later, as indeed it was in the postwar years.

What Is a Great Judaica Library?

The best-known formulation of the ambitious plans set for the library was publicly expressed in an address by Judge Mayer Sulzberger, delivered at the dedication of the Seminary's new building in 1903:

> The Bodleian Library at Oxford and the British Museum at London are, and perhaps will always remain, the most magnificent and complete Hebrew book museums in the world. But it is our business on this side of the Atlantic to hope and to work, undaunted by the magnitude of others' achievements; we should hold in view the purpose to make our collection as nearly complete as the resources of the world may render possible, and in so doing, we should spare neither thought nor labor nor money.[3]

Two things stand out in this statement: the naming of the most accomplished, most famous, and richest collections of Hebraica as models for the fledgling Seminary library and the declared goal of creating a "Hebrew book museum." Although the Bodleian Library is situated at Oxford and serves Oxford University, it is not conceived of as a university library, and the British Museum, now the British Library, is not a university library either, but rather a *universal* library. These two major libraries do not serve the instructional needs of any single institution but stand as depositories of the written record of the past in all

3 *Semi-Centennial Volume*, p. 91.

its possible fullness. The Seminary library, according to the vision of Judge Sulzberger, should aspire to the same breadth in the area of Jewish culture. It should become a Hebrew book museum, containing everything available and accessible in the field.

It is noteworthy that Sulzberger's examples were not taken from collections under Jewish auspices. Although at the time of Sulzberger's address, European Jewish life, learning, and scholarship were at a peak and full of great achievements and plans, no European Jewish library existed that met this stated ideal. There were Jewish communal libraries and collections at seminaries in Vienna, Berlin, Budapest, Paris, Cracow, Vilna, Warsaw, and elsewhere, and the library of the Breslau seminary was quite well known for its good collection of Hebrew manuscripts and printed books, containing, in 1904, eighteen thousand printed books and four hundred manuscripts.[4] Still, neither of these libraries matched the major Hebraica collections nor could have aspired to rival those of the Bodleian or the British Museum. Libraries of Jewish organizations and institutions could not and did not reach the level of Hebraica collections in royal, ecclesiastical, state, or university libraries in Europe. Historically, no public Jewish libraries existed before the 18th century; Hebrew books were owned by individuals, and frequently, significant private collections of Jewish owners were acquired by non-Jewish libraries. Thus, two of the finest private Jewish collections, David Oppenheimer's and Heimann Michael's, were purchased in the 19th century by the Bodleian and by the British Museum; the important private collection of Abraham Merzbacher was acquired by the City Library of Frankfurt and that of David Kaufmann by the Hungarian Academy of Sciences—both at the beginning of the 20th century.[5] Jewish scholars and institutions simply lacked the desire to establish "complete" collections of Hebraica and Judaica in Jewish hands: they were surrounded in Europe by numerous large general libraries with rich Jewish holdings.

4 Dov Schidorsky, *Libraries and Books in Late Ottoman Palestine* (Jerusalem: The Magnes Press, 1990), p. 191 (in Hebrew); on Breslau, see M. Brann, *Geschichte des jüdisch-theologisches Seminars (Fraenckel'sche Stiftung) in Breslau* (Breslau: Jüdische-Theologisches Seminar, [1905]), p. 79.

5 Marx, *Studies*, pp. 238-55 (on the Oppenheimer Library), pp. 221-24 (on Michael's collection). On Merzbacher and Kaufmann, see *Encyclopaedia Judaica*, vol. 11, col. 1395 and vol. 10, cols. 842-43.

Accordingly, while in the 19th and early 20th centuries Jewish scholars were engaged in a great many original scholarly endeavors to gather and interpret information on practically all aspects of the Jewish experience, there was no attempt to assemble under one roof the sources of this information, namely, the books and the manuscripts themselves. The recovery, collection, organization, and preservation of knowledge were primary goals of the pioneers of modern Jewish scholarship, but the establishment of "complete" collections of the written and printed word was not among those ambitions. The leading scholars of *jüdische Wissenschaft* focused their attention on the utilization of the Jewish resources in general libraries. Moritz Steinschneider devoted much of his scholarly life to the cataloging of the collections of the Bodleian, the Royal Library in Berlin, the City and University Library of Hamburg, the State Library of Munich, etc.[6] Abraham Berliner studied the Hebrew manuscript collections of the Vatican and the Biblioteca Palatina in Parma.[7] Jewish copyists were hired by scholars to copy Hebrew manuscripts in the Bibliothèque Nationale in Paris and elsewhere. Baer Goldberg and others earned their living by providing scholars of the period with transcripts of Hebrew manuscripts found in various European collections.[8] Leopold Zunz, in the introduction to his *Literaturgeschichte der synagogalen Poesie*, refers to twenty libraries in Europe where he had worked during the preparation of the volume and to an additional thirteen places from which he obtained manuscripts or copies.[9] The labors of Zunz, Steinschneider, and others resulted in many basic and monumental works: comprehensive surveys of various aspects of Jewish literature and history were produced, with extensive, almost full utilization of manuscript and printed sources; bibliographies were compiled and journals launched; organizations for the collection and publication of archival

6 *Catalogus librorum hebraeorum in Bibliotheca Bodleiana*, 1852-60; *Verzeichnis der hebraeischen Handschriften der Königlichen Bibliothek zu Berlin*, 1878-97; *Catalog der hebraeischen Handschriften in der Stadtbibliothek zu Hamburg*, 1878; *Die hebraeischen Handschriften der K. Hof-und Staatsbibliothek in München*, 1875.

7 Abraham Berliner, "Siyyur be-sifriyot Italia," in his *Selected Writings* (Jerusalem: Mosad Harav Kook, 1969), vol. 2, pp. 83-105 (in Hebrew).

8 On Baer Goldberg and his copying activity in Oxford and Paris, see *Encyclopaedia Judaica*, vol. 7, col. 700.

9 L. Zunz, *Literaturgeschichte der synagogalen Poesie* (Berlin: L. Gerschel, 1865), pp. VI-VII.

materials, folklore, and ethnography were established.[10] This accumulation of knowledge was pursued almost exclusively on the basis of Jewish resources preserved in European institutions under non-Jewish auspices.

In the United States, where original research in the field of Jewish studies just started at the end of the 19th and the beginning of the 20th centuries, the situation was entirely different. There were simply no libraries of Judaica and Hebraica comparable to the European collections. No wonder then that plans for the emancipation of American Jewish scholarship from Europe also encompassed the establishment of comprehensive Jewish libraries.[11] Such libraries would make it possible for American Jewish scholars to work independently, without having to rely upon the major collections of Hebraica and Judaica in Europe. This was a concern of the Seminary leaders, already prior to Sulzberger's address in 1903. When, in 1893, the old Seminary marked the seventieth birthday of Sabato Morais, arrangements were made for establishing a library carrying his name. This library incorporated Morais' own valuable books, and it was concieved of as a "centre of Hebrew learning and research."[12] Other donations of collections and of individual items came to the library, including three thousand volumes of the German Jewish scholar David Cassel; the goal was to make it "the most perfect collection of Hebraica and Judaica in this country."[13] This policy served as the basis on which Sulzberger and Alexander Marx, who arrived at the Seminary in

10 On Jewish historical societies, see A. Marx, "Societies for the Promotion of the Study of Jewish History," in *Publications of the American Jewish Historical Society* 20 (1911), pp. 1-9. On the efforts to collect and preserve Jewish historical documents in Eastern Europe, see David E. Fishman, *Embers Plucked from the Fire* (New York: Jewish Theological Seminary, 1996), pp. 1-3.

11 On the beginnings of Jewish studies in America, see Jonathan D. Sarna, *JPS: The Americanization of Jewish Culture, 1888-1988* (Philadelphia: Jewish Publication Society, 1989); Shuly R. Schwartz, *The Emergence of Jewish Scholarship in America: The Publication of the Jewish Encyclopedia* (Cincinnati: Hebrew Union College, 1991), and Paul Ritterband and Harold S. Wechsler, *Jewish Learning in American Universities: The First Century* (Bloomington: Indiana University Press, 1994). Very little, if any, attention was paid by these authors to the emergence of Jewish libraries in America. Schwartz (p. 14) quotes Cyrus Adler: "At the present we have no libraries, no publications and no independent scholars."

12 Letter of trustees to Morais, 17 April 1893. *Proceedings of the Fourth Biennial Convention of The Jewish Theological Seminary Association 1894*, p. 14 (excerpted in librarian's reports to Board of Directors, 1904-14, summary of pre-1904 reports), JTS library.

13 On Cassel, see *Encyclopaedia Judaica*, vol. 5, col. 229. On his library, see *Semi-Centennial Volume*, p. 89. For the quote, see the source cited in the previous note, p. 15.

November 1903, developed their blueprint for the future of the Seminary library. Sulzberger's donation of his library of eight thousand volumes and seven hundred fifty manuscripts in 1904 made the library the "largest... in the Western Hemisphere and one of the largest and most valuable in the world." With this gift, "the Seminary library" came to be regarded as "one of the notable Hebrew libraries of the world."[14] Sulzberger himself expressed his hope for the library in a letter formally presenting the collection to the Seminary: "My hope is that the Seminary may become the centre for original work in the science of Judaism, to which end the acquisition of a great library is indispensable."[15] This hope was quickly fulfilled. In 1907, Marx wrote that the library was "the greatest Jewish library in the world in Jewish hands" and "the most important on the American continent."[16] In the words of Schechter: "It [the Seminary] is in the possession of a library, collected and donated by Judge Sulzberger, a book collector with the best of judgement and with the greatest of sacrifices, such *as no other seminary in the world* can show [emphasis added]."[17]

Besides laboring to make the library the "centre for original work in the science of Judaism,"[18] there was another motivation that drove the Seminary's leadership in the direction of building a comprehensive library. With the awakening of nationalism among the Jews of Europe, the idea of creating a national library in Jerusalem came into being. By the turn of the century, activities on behalf of such a library intensified. Solomon Schechter served on an international committee on behalf of a Jewish national library in Jerusalem.[19] The need for libraries under Jewish auspices gained in importance for an additional reason: the dissolution of many small communities in Eastern and Central Europe and the assimilation of many Jewish families released large numbers of Hebrew

14 Librarian's report, 14 March 1904; *Semi-Centennial Volume*, pp. 89-90; Board of Directors' reports, 1903, p. 9. For a partial catalog of the Sulzberger collection, see E. Deinard, *Or Meir* (New York: n.p., 1897) (in Hebrew); see also *Biblical Manuscripts and Books in the Library of Jewish Theological Seminary* (New York: Jewish Theological Seminary, 1913 and 1914).

15 *Semi-Centennial Volume*, p. 90.

16 Librarian's report, 24 May 1907, p. 4.

17 See the essay on the Schechter era by Mel Scult in *Tradition Renewed*, ed, by Jack Wertheimer, vol. I (New York: Jewish Theological Seminary, 1997), pp. 43-102. The quote is on p. 75.

18 *Semi-Centennial Volume*, p. 90.

19 Schidorsky, *Libraries and Books*, pp. 236, 288.

books from private possession into the public realm. Also, manuscripts and books from the Mediterranean and the Middle East started to reach Europe and America in large numbers. Libraries were created in order to assure that these books, some of them precious, would be preserved in Jewish hands.

The emergence of a large population center of Jews in the United States and the growth of Jewish settlements in Palestine made it desirable to create Jewish cultural centers, including a "public library on Jewish topics" at the Seminary "to be free for the use and for the benefit of all interested" persons.[20] Such a library would serve the wider community as well as scholars and would be a place where materials becoming abundantly available would be preserved. In Palestine and in the United States, the idea of a national Jewish library was vigorously promoted. The Seminary library was never officially called a national library, but its aims, as carried out by Marx and others, were so comprehensive in the area of collecting Jewish manuscripts, books, and related materials that little doubt remained about its ambitions to serve not only one institution but also the Jewish people at large. Marx came closest to formulating this purpose when he wrote: [The Library] "performs today a distinct national function in American Jewish life."[21]

How the Library Grew

The growth of the library came at a propitious time. Andrew Carnegie was spending many millions of dollars for the building of public libraries across the nation. A Jewish public library, providing free access to books for all, corresponded to the general mood of the period. The availability of materials, thanks to Jewish bookdealers who roamed the Jewish communities of Europe, North Africa, and the Middle East acquiring many Hebrew books, and the desire to build libraries for the masses as well as for scholars, came together in this period. The results were the laying of plans for a library which, if not in name but in function, was to assume the role of a

20 *Proceedings of the Fourth Biennial Convention of the Jewish Theological Seminary Association, 1892*, pp. 32-33 (excerpted in librarian's reports to Board of Directors, 1904-14, summary of pre-1904 reports).

21 *Semi-Centennial Volume*, p. 120.

"national" library, serving "all" people and preserving and making available "all" books. The collection development policies of the library betray these purposes and ambitions. From its beginning the library attempted to cover areas of contemporary Jewish concern as well. It received books issued by the Jewish Publication Society, and a reference collection, for which funds were donated by the Ottinger brothers, prominent New York lawyers and politicians, was created.[22] In a report to the Board of Directors, Solomon Schechter wrote in 1903:

> There is still, and will for a long time remain, the need of securing the recent modern literature which is constantly growing... and I recommend the appropriation of $1,000 for the coming year, this of course, to include payment for current periodicals.[23]

In an estimated budget submitted by Marx in 1910, he requested $1,280 for current purchases (new works, periodicals, reference books) and $1,010 for special collections.[24]

When Marx argued the need for new quarters for the library in 1916, the library's holdings had already surpassed fifty thousand books. He referred to the library as one "which is destined to supply the wants of this ever-increasing center of Judaism." In the same report, he mentioned that Eliezer Ben-Yehudah had used the library regularly, "collecting material for his great Hebrew dictionary."[25] In 1917, Marx reported the receipt of "an important collection of Russian newspapers dealing with the Jewish question during the time of the war until the outbreak of the revolution, including sets of the important anti-semitic Russian dailies."[26] In 1920, the library received $50 from the class of 1919 to purchase books dealing with sociology.[27] In the same year, large numbers of anti-Semitic and pro-Semitic publications, many of them of an ephemeral nature, were

22 *Proceedings of the Fourth Biennial Convention of the Jewish Theological Seminary Association, 1894*, pp. 15, 21-22 (excerpted in librarian's reports to Board of Directors, 1904-14, summary of pre-1904 reports); *Semi-Centennial Volume*, p. 95. On the Ottinger brothers' relation to the new Seminary, see Mel Scult, above note 17, pp. 54-55.

23 Board of Directors' reports, 1903, p. 9.

24 Librarian's report, 16 February 1910, pp. 3, 5.

25 Board of Directors' reports, 15 November 1916, p. 6.

26 Librarian's report, 20 April 1917, p. 2.

27 Librarian's report, 10 May 1920, p. 5.

incorporated into the collection at the advice of the board. Marx explained that these books and pamphlets were important for "the defence [*sic*] of Judaism against the recent anti-semitic attacks" and that, unfortunately, the subject, the Jewish question, had become timely again. The same report mentioned the acquisition of Hebrew periodicals published in Palestine under English rule.[28] In this post-World War I period, the library also endeavored to acquire publications dealing with the participation of Jewish soldiers of the various armies in the Great War.[29] In 1925, a substantial collection on Palestine and Zionism was received.[30] The class of 1922 donated money for the purchase of books in modern Hebrew, and, in 1937, the Morris Levine Memorial Collection, consisting of modern Hebrew literature, was created.[31]

These acquisitions suggest that, despite reports that the library was interested only in rare and esoteric books and manuscripts, current issues affecting the state of the Jewish people were not overlooked. The numerical growth of the holdings of the library reflected the systematic addition of materials on modern and contemporary Jewish affairs. Thus, over the years, the library came to serve multiple purposes: it was the library of the school, of the students and faculty, as well as a center of scholarly research in *jüdische Wissenschaft* and a depository of materials on current Jewish affairs for the public at large. Those who guided the Seminary library wanted to catch up and even supersede the European libraries as repositories of Hebrew manuscripts and rare books, but they also sought to create an information center on current Jewish affairs, providing reference services to all. A statement in the librarian's report in 1920 spoke clearly about these all-encompassing goals:

> The growth of the library has involved the creation of new lacunae which ought to be filled. By the nature of things these lacunae are greater in a collection as important and many-sided as ours has become in its field, than they are in a lesser library since people expect to find in our library all the important Jewish publications they may

28 Librarian's report, 26 October 1920, p. 2.

29 Librarian's report, 10 May 1920, p. 2.

30 Librarian's report, 19 October 1925, p. 5 (also in *Bibliographical Studies*, p. 70).

31 Librarian's report, 19 October 1925, p. 5 (also in *Bibliographical Studies*, p. 72) and librarian's report, 1 April 1937, p. 4 (also in *Bibliographical Studies*, p. 270).

> be looking for. Negative answer to an inquiry whether we possess a certain book of Jewish interest in many instances means that the scholar desiring to consult it will not be able to obtain it anywhere in this country. We therefore ought to continue in our efforts to make our library as rich and therewith as useful as possible.[32]

The shift of the population center of the Jews to America, the awakening of Jewish nationalism, the crises that befell European Jewry, first in Russia and Poland and later in Germany and in the rest of Central Europe, the growing interest in the exploration of the Jewish past in all its aspects, the increasing awareness of Jewish scholarship of the great cultural wealth and diversity of North African and Middle Eastern Jewish communities, all combined, were driving the expansion of the Seminary library in many directions.

The realization of this vision required a great deal of thought, labor, and, particularly, money. Fortunately, the American scene at the turn of the century was conducive to the achievement of these goals. America at that time had many "obsessed" collectors who used their new wealth to buy up great European libraries and bring them to the United States. Philanthropic book collectors cooperated with scholars and established vast libraries containing bibliophilic treasures and immense research collections. Private libraries were acquired en bloc; bookdealer emissaries were authorized to trace and purchase rare treasures. Henry E. Huntington, Henry C. Folger, Walter L. Newberry, and J. Pierpont Morgan assembled at the end of the 19th and the beginning of the 20th centuries the most valuable, expensive, and extensive libraries of rarities, treasures, and special collections. These collections later were opened to the public as book museums and research libraries.[33] Thanks to these activities by American magnates, public and university libraries experienced immensely rapid expansion in this period. Academic libraries in America doubled in size every sixteen years. Columbia University, for example, owned 750,000 books in 1898 and three million in 1934.[34]

32 Librarian's report, 10 May 1920, p. 10.

33 See the recent popular book by Nicholas A. Basbanes, *A Gentle Madness: Bibliophiles, Bibliomanes and the Eternal Passion for Books* (New York: Holt, 1995), index and chaps. 4 and 5.

34 Elmer D. Johnson and Michael H. Harris, *History of Libraries in the Western World*, 3rd ed. (Metuchen, N.J.: Scarecrow Press, 1976), p. 275.

The New York Public Library was founded in 1895, and it grew by leaps and bounds in the first decades of the 20th century, due to the support and influence of philanthropists, among them Jacob Schiff.[35] Schiff was, of course, also one of the main supporters of the Seminary and its library. Schiff's interest in the acquisition of major collections of Hebraica and Judaica preceded his commitments to the Seminary library. In 1898, Schiff acquired the library of Dr. Moritz Steinschneider of Berlin for ten thousand marks with the understanding that the books would remain with Steinschneider during his lifetime. Schiff did not decide until 1899 which American institution would receive the Steinschneider collection. Sulzberger, in 1899, responding to an inquiry from Schiff, presented him with a number of options as to the appropriate library in the United States that could serve as the right place for Steinschneider's books. These included the New York Public Library, the Cincinnati [Hebrew Union] College, the not yet established but planned Dropsie College in Philadelphia, and the Jewish Theological Seminary. Sulzberger anticipated the possibility of a union between the last two. He advised Schiff to defer the ultimate disposition of the Steinschneider library until a center for Jewish scholarship in America, and in New York in particular, became a reality:

> New York, too, is, and I think is destined to remain, the centre of Jewish population in this country. Whatever may be its shortcomings at present I have a firm faith that it will in time be a great rallying-place for Jewish learning and thought. There it is wise to build up a treasure-house of Jewish lore ready for the generation that will rise to use it.

Across the first page of Sulzberger's letter, Schiff wrote diagonally over Sulzberger's script: "My intention is to give the Steinschneider collection to the N. York Public Library, unless the Seminary herein referred has become established prior to either Professor Steinschneider's or my own death, and is approved by myself or my inheritors."[36] Ultimately, Schiff decided to

35 See *Biblion: The Bulletin of the New York Public Library* 3, no. 2 (Spring 1995), 100th Anniversary Commemorative Issue.

36 Correspondence concerning the Steinschneider collection, JTS archival Group 62, box 6; see also Dicker, *The Seminary Library*, p. 23. There reference is made to Schiff's plans of giving the Steinschneider library to the New York Public Library, Columbia University, or Harvard University. See also Rebekah Kohut in her appreciation of Marx, mentioned in note 42, pp. xiv-xv.

present the Steinschneider collection to the Seminary library, and it was incorporated into its holdings in 1907.[37] In addition to this gift, Schiff provided funds for other acquisitions as well. In 1911, the collection of the German Christian Bible scholar, Emil F. Kautzsch, was offered for sale and was purchased with funds provided by Schiff.[38] In 1914, he pledged the bulk of the sum needed for the purchase of the Hebrew manuscript collection of Baron David Gunzburg, a transaction that was not consummated due to the outbreak of World War I.[39] Jacob Schiff and Mayer Sulzberger, examples of philanthropists and bibliophilic collectors, played the most pivotal role in the shaping of the Seminary library. Although Sulzberger expressed his reservation about unlimited purchases, "until some Carnegie or Rockefeller turns up,"[40] he, Schiff, and others were generous in expanding funds for the acquisition of individual items and of collections. Again, in the words of Marx:

> I am deeply grateful for the generosity with which the library has been treated, both by the Board as a whole and by its individual members, especially Judge Sulzberger and Mr. Schiff, whom I have so frequently had occasion to mention in previous reports... Hitherto, we have been dependent, in large measure, for the magnificent growth of our collection, on the generosity of private benefactors, like Judge Sulzberger and Mr. Schiff.[41]

The examples of Sulzberger and Schiff inspired others as well. Felix Warburg, Louis Marshall, and somewhat later, Mortimer Schiff were generous supporters of the library. Besides their numerous gifts, they jointly contributed $70,000 of the total $100,000 in 1922 for the purchase of the Elkan Nathan Adler library, and Mortimer Schiff gave $4,000 annually for special acquisitions in the 1920s.[42]

37 *Semi-Centennial Volume*, pp. 92-93.

38 *Ibid.*, p. 95.

39 Michael Stanislawski, "An Unperformed Contract: The Sale of Baron Gunzburg's Library to the Jewish Theological Seminary of America," in Herman Dicker, *The Seminary Library*, pp. 89-106.

40 *The Mayer Sulzberger — Alexander Marx Correspondence, 1904-1923*, edited and annotated by Herman Dicker (New York: Sepher-Hermon, 1990), p. 46.

41 Librarian's report, 16 February 1910, pp. 2 and 4.

42 Board of Directors' reports, 1923, p. 4. See also note 113. On Mortimer Schiff's annual allocation to the library, see library committee minutes, 13 February 1947.

These people held the view that part of the endeavor of making the Seminary an institution of great influence in American Jewry was the developing of its library to dimensions that surpassed the ordinary function of an institutional library. Inspired greatly by the fervor of Alexander Marx for such an expanded, broad vision, the lay leaders of the Seminary were willing to lend support to Marx's activities as he proceeded to augment the holdings of the library energetically and rapidly.

The Role of Alexander Marx

Although historical circumstances were right for the development of the library, a personal factor played a role as well. Alexander Marx, through his personality, his scholarly orientation, his relationship with practitioners of Jewish studies in Europe—especially with his teacher, Moritz Steinschneider—was singularly equipped and inclined to be the driving force behind the growth of the library.

Without Marx's conception of what *jüdische Wissenschaft* entailed and what a library that was supposed to serve it should contain, the Seminary library would not have become what it did. Marx was a product of German Jewish scholarship. He was well connected through family ties and friendship to many prominent European Jewish scholars. He was greatly devoted to Steinschneider. His father-in-law was David Zvi Hoffman, the head of the Orthodox rabbinical seminary in Berlin. S.Y. Agnon was his brother-in-law. Marx was deeply rooted in traditional Jewish life, in the *Wissenschaft des Judentums*, and in the methodology of German philological and text-critical scholarship. His attachment to Steinschneider and the similarity of their scholarly goals prompted the quip: "Europe had its Steinschneider and America now has its Marx."[43]

For Marx, the study of Judaism encompassed, besides rabbinical sources, the history of sciences, philosophy, medicine, and mathematics as pursued and practiced by Jews, mainly in the Middle Ages. These were subjects of Steinschneider's many studies, and Marx was deeply influenced

43 On Marx's life, see Rebekah Kohut's and Solomon Goldman's appreciation in *Alexander Marx Jubilee Volume*, English section (New York: Jewish Theological Seminary, 1950), pp. xi-xxiii and pp. 1-34. For the quip, see A.S.W. Rosenbach's foreword to Marx's *Studies*, p. ix. See also A.S. Halkin in *American Jewish Year Book 56* (1955), pp. 580-88.

by them. Cultural and intellectual contacts between Jews, Christians, and Muslims were at the center of Steinschneider's interest. The study of mutual influences, of translations from one culture into another, became significant aspects of the *Wissenschaft des Judentums*.

These new preoccupations among Jewish scholars in the 19th century in Europe denoted a cardinal shift from previous, inward directed scholarly pursuits, and it broadened the parameters of Jewish studies immensely. It was not only "indigenous" Jewish works that fell under the category of Jewish literature but also translations into Hebrew, mainly from the Arabic and to a lesser extent from Latin. These works, frequently going back to Greek originals, were widely studied by learned Jews in the Middle Ages, and it was Steinschneider who mapped the vast literature of this extensive philosophical, scientific, medical, and mathematical activity. Marx regarded these works as highly important and, as librarian, he tried to acquire medieval manuscripts and books relating to these areas. The library became a rich depository of such materials. It was with great pride that Marx pointed out from time to time that the American scholars working on the history of the sciences and medicine made use of the Seminary library. It brought him a great deal of satisfaction when George Sarton, the prominent historian of medieval science, acknowledged the library's importance in the field. In a report in *Isis*, the journal of the History of Science Society, Sarton wrote that the Seminary library "will soon be one of the greatest centers of information on Judaica and Hebraica."[44] When, in 1913, manuscripts of Maimonides' medical works from the Seminary library were requested on loan by a German scholar, Sulzberger remarked: "Not only is it to the credit of our institution that its treasures should be used in the interest of science, but it contributes to the cultural reputation of our country that scholars living in Europe should come to America as a source of instruction."[45]

Similarly, the work of early Christian Hebraists and, later, non-Jewish scholars on the Bible, Hebrew grammar, and any other Jewish subject in all languages became targets of the collection development policy of the library. As a result of this policy, the library's collection of Hebrew grammars and dictionaries, particularly of the 16th century, is extra-

44 *Isis* 11 (1928), p. 513.

45 *Sulzberger-Marx Correspondence*, pp. 85-86.

ordinarily full and strong. The interest in the use of Hebrew by Christians went so far as to cover the occasional use of Hebrew type in general works. In one of Marx's reports we read:

> Dr. A.S.W. Rosenbach presented a fine, beautifully bound copy of *Hypnerotomachia Poliphili*, printed by Aldus in Venice, 1499. This is perhaps the most famous book ever issued from the Venice presses and attracts our special attention by over 150 remarkable illustrations. In one of these *a few words of Hebrew* [emphasis added] were found together with Arabic, Greek, and Latin and in two places Aldus, perhaps for the first time, uses Hebrew characters. It is for this reason that the volume is of special significance for our library.[46]

A good illustration of this broad conception is evident in the decision to purchase the Kautzsch library. Already in the early years of the library, the books of Christian scholars of Bible and Semitic philology, such as the libraries of Bernhard Stade and of Theodore Noeldeke, were mentioned as possible acquisitions, but ultimately, it was Emil Kautzsch's that was purchased.[47]

In 1911, a bookdealer in Leipzig, Gustav Fock, offered Kautzsch's library for sale. Marx brought the matter to the attention of the Seminary's Board of Directors immediately. He described the Kautzsch library as "probably the finest private collection of modern works and pamphlets on Biblical literature and Hebrew philology." The collection consisted of twenty-five hundred books and twenty-seven hundred pamphlets. Fock offered the collection for $2,400; Marx estimated that it could be obtained for $1,800. In support of his recommendation Marx added:

> Now, it has been the avowed policy of President Schechter to look out for such a collection in order to obtain a proper apparatus of modern works on Bible and Hebrew... The Kautzsch Collection would at once place the Biblical section of our Library on the same high level as our post-biblical departments... I trust, therefore, that

46 *Bibliographical Studies*, p. 70.

47 On Stade's library, see *Sulzberger-Marx Correspondence*, p. 23 (26 January 1907); on Noeldeke's, *Cyrus Adler — Marx Correspondence*, 30 November 1909 and 7 December 1909.

> the Directors will see their way to seize this valuable opportunity, and place the Biblical section of our library, which is, naturally, of utmost importance to a theological institution, in the position it ought to hold.

Marx's appeal to the board was persuasive and, as already mentioned, Jacob Schiff provided the funds for the purchase. By September 1911, the boxes containing the Kautzsch books were delivered to the Seminary.[48]

The Kautzsch collection, indeed, was especially strong in its holdings of works by German Protestant Bible scholars in the fields of biblical criticism, biblical archaeology, the geography of Palestine, and biblical Hebrew linguistics. Interestingly, no one expressed reservations about this acquisition, and the proximity of Union Theological Seminary and Columbia University did not play any role in the decision that led to the purchase of the collection. Parenthetically, the library endeavored to add to its shelves translations of the Bible in as many languages and dialects as possible. These translations were close to the heart of Judge Sulzberger, and he purchased such from time to time for the Seminary library.[49]

Another aspect of Jewish-Gentile relations always served as a focus of collecting for the library. This was, to some extent, the mirror image of the positive cultural and intellectual cross-fertilization that existed between Jews and non-Jews. Polemics, apologetics, anti-Semitism, and the defense of Judaism were phenomena that manifested themselves throughout the Middle Ages as well as in modern times. Source materials dealing with these issues, from everywhere and in any language, constituted a large section of the library, and no effort was spared when appropriate opportunities for acquisitions arose. Again, the library's holdings of manuscripts, books, pamphlets, documents, broadsides, and graphic materials—especially older ones—on this painful subject became extraordinarily rich.[50]

48 Librarian's report, 12 February 1911, pp. 2-4 and supplements; 16 April 1911, p. 2, and 20 October 1911 (supplement).

49 For a partial list, see *Bibliographical Studies*, index, pp. 554-56; *Sulzberger-Marx Correspondence*, pp. 11, 40, 97, 121, etc.

50 On anti-Semitic caricatures in the JTS library, see the exhibition catalogue, *The Jew as Other: A Century of English Caricature, 1730-1830* (New York: Library of the Jewish Theological Seminary, 1995); on inquisition materials, see *Bibliographical Studies*, pp. 62, 226-31, and index. As an example of the wealth of the library's collection in this area, I mention the extensive and

Marx, the historian, of course, had an abiding interest in collecting in the area of Jewish history. We have an explicit and detailed programmatic statement from him about what he thought to be the aims and tasks of Jewish historiography, especially as it pertains to political, economic, and social history.[51] Against the background of 19th and early 20th-century developments, Marx outlined an ambitious research agenda for Jewish historical scholarship. Historical consciousness and the awakening of interest in preserving historical documents became prevalent in Europe in the 19th century. Societies were established and archives founded for the gathering of documents such as communal record books, decrees, laws, letters, *memorbooks*, records of commercial transactions, etc.[52] These types of source materials were not usually among the items that were well represented in the great Jewish departments of general libraries. Many of these documents were still in situ: in synagogues, community archives, and family collections and not in public depositories. They were still fulfilling a living function, as record books of active Jewish communities. With assimilation and emancipation and the transfer of many registerial and record-keeping functions from religious to secular bodies, these documents became more the subject of historical and antiquarian interest than active, practical records. The diminution of various communal functions and the focus on the synagogue and the temple as loci for religious worship services, but not as autonomous bodies of self-government, made some of these documents superfluous in their original setting. The Seminary library, along with collecting printed books, medieval manuscript codices, and other materials, also started to concentrate on the acquisition of communal and individual records. *Pinkasim* (record books), *memorbooks*, broadsides, letters, laws, etc. were acquired whenever possible. Marx valued these sources greatly: "The basis of all historical investigation is free access to all sources. To attain this end large collections of historical records for all the countries of the world are necessary."[53]

rare holdings of the library on the case of Jud Süss. See the recent *From Court Jews to the Rothschilds: Art, Patronage, and Power, 1600-1800*, ed. Vivian B. Mann and Richard I. Cohen (Munich and New York: Prestel, 1996), catalog numbers 206, 210-212, 216, 217a, 218, 220, 222.

51 A. Marx, "Aims and Tasks of Jewish Historiography," *Publications of the American Jewish Historical Society* 26 (1918), pp. 11-32.

52 Marx, *ibid.*; Fishman, *Embers Plucked from the Fire.*

53 Marx, *ibid.*, p. 18.

By this, Marx did not mean the actual physical collecting of these records, but rather their publication. In the framework of the library, however, he worked on the acquisition of the records themselves. Many of these materials were archival in nature, and, indeed, after many decades, it became necessary to separate them from the rest of the collection, and a special archival division was created within the library. The historian's ken came to the fore also in Marx's reports on these sources, which were often miniature gems of original scholarship.[54]

The energetic and successful drive by Marx to develop the library's collections in areas of the history of science, mathematics, and medicine, the works of Christian Hebraists, polemics and apologetics and historical sources in general, was his way of translating Steinschneider's pioneering ingathering of knowledge into the ingathering of the physical evidence itself. The sources that Steinschneider analyzed, recorded and described in his publications were the kinds of manuscripts and books that Marx wanted to have in the library. *Hebraische Übersetzungen*[55] (Hebrew Translations in the Middle Ages), *Bibliographisches Handbuch*[56] (Bibliography of the Works of Christian Hebraists), *Polemische und apologetische Literatur*[57] (Polemical and Apologetical Literature), and *Geschichtsliteratur der Juden*[58] (Historical Literature of the Jews) became blueprints for the holdings of the Seminary library.

If Steinschneider's works may be seen as guiding Marx in acquiring materials in the areas mentioned above, Zunz's studies on *Midrash* and Jewish liturgy served the same purpose in the departments of Rabbinics and liturgy. The reports of the library are full of recording the acquisition of liturgical books, not only from the more general, well-known rites, such as Ashkenaz, Sefarad, Italy, and Yemen, but also from local and lesser-known ones, such as Aleppo, Algiers, Sicily, Tripoli, and many others. These liturgies covered the standard services as well as services for special events. They also contained thousands of *piyyutim* (liturgical poems),

54 For example, in *Bibliographical Studies*, pp. 54-55, 102-03, 152-53.

55 Published in Berlin, 1893.

56 Leipzig, 1859.

57 Leipzig, 1877. Marx published a catalog of the Seminary's polemical manuscripts; see *Bibliographical Studies*, pp. 444-75. While Steinschneider's work is on polemics with Islam, Marx's catalog lists polemics with Christianity.

58 Frankfurt am Main, 1905.

added to or inserted within the standard prayers.[59] Zunz cataloged them comprehensively in his *Literaturgeschichte der synagogalen Poesie* on the basis of manuscript and printed sources. Marx wanted to make as many of them accessible to American Jewish scholarship as possible. The liturgy department of the library grew so rapidly that when, in the 1910s, Israel Davidson set out to work on his monumental four-volume *Thesaurus of Medieval Hebrew Poetry*, the library's resources made it possible for him to bring it to completion as one of the greatest achievements of Jewish scholarship in the United States.[60] In 1910, Marx enumerated eight areas which "are, so far as I am aware, the largest of their kind in the world."[61] Of course, liturgy was one of them. Passover *Haggadahs* constituted the strongest component of the liturgy section. In 1908, it was reported that the Seminary's *Haggadah* collection was "almost equal in numbers to the St. Petersburg collection," a collection which at that time was considered to be the richest in the world, including 116 items "of which no other copy is known."[62]

In the same statement, the sections on responsa, codes and hasidic literature were identified as being "the largest of their kind in the world," while Jewish history, Talmud commentaries, and Talmud editions were not singled out as such. Still, there are many references in the reports and elsewhere to the acquisition of classical rabbinic texts, in various editions and versions, to facilitate another important item on the agenda of *jüdische Wissenschaft*. Since the 19th century, Jewish scholars in Europe had become heavily engaged in the publication of the texts of rabbinic

59 For a small sampling of the variety of liturgical books in the library, see *Bibliographical Studies*, index, under *Mahzor, Selihot, Siddur*.

60 The four volumes of the *Thesaurus* were published between 1924 and 1933. Most of the liturgical books listed as sources for the *Thesaurus*, in vol. 1, pp. liii-[xcvi], and in vol. 4, pp. 1-23, were owned by the Seminary library. See Davidson's remarks in vol. 2, p. xvii: "My indebtedness to the library of the Jewish Theological Seminary of America is, of course, self-evident, since the greater part of this work is based on the literary treasures gathered by my friend and colleague, Professor Alexander Marx."

61 Librarian's report, 16 February 1910, p. 5.

62 Librarian's reports, 15 January 1908, p. 1, and 1 June 1908, pp. 1-2; *Semi-Centennial Volume*, p. 94. Testimony to the excellence of the library's *Haggadah* collection is Yosef Hayim Yerushalmi's *Haggadah and History: A Panorama in Facsimile of Five Centuries of the Printed Haggadah from the Collections of Harvard University and the Jewish Theological Seminary of America* (Philadelphia: Jewish Publication Society, 1975). In this book most of the oldest and rarest pre-19th-century *Haggadot* are from the Seminary library.

literature, both published and unpublished, in critical editions, based on all available manuscript and printed materials. The editions, at least in principle, followed the models established by German classical philological scholarship. Solomon Schechter's edition of *Aboth de Rabbi Nathan* was a pioneering work in this field. Schechter determined that this early Rabbinic work was transmitted in two distinct versions and, in his introduction, dealt with the history of this transmission. Alexander Marx, while still a student, became personally acquainted with Schechter as a result of his interest in preparing critical editions of two fundamentally important Hebrew works: the *Seder Olam Rabba* and the *Seder Rav Amram Gaon*. Schechter's reputation as the editor of *Aboth de Rabbi Nathan* and his proximity to the treasures of the great libraries of England, attracted Marx to Schechter. Ultimately, Marx followed Schechter to America.[63] In the sources about the development of the Seminary library's collections, the need for assembling books that would serve as the basis for text editions is repeatedly stressed. Sulzberger encouraged Marx to "keep on buying" rare Talmud editions so that, in time, the library would have complete sets of them all.[64] He urged Marx that copies of tractates of the rare Pesaro (early 16th century) and Constantinople (late 16th century) Talmud editions, "ought to be got."[65] In the exchange between Marx and Sulzberger, the Bible Commentary of Immanuel of Rome, covering Genesis and Exodus, was raised. This manuscript was offered to the library, and Marx, unable to agree with the bookseller on the price, was reluctantly ready to return it. Schechter strongly opposed allowing "such a valuable manuscript to leave our library," and Marx asked Sulzberger's advice on how to proceed. Sulzberger replied: "If Dr. Schechter thinks it wise, buy the Immanuel manuscript for £40 and charge it to me."[66] Schechter himself, in emphasizing the library's prominence, pointed out that there were in the library five different commentaries to the Tannaitic Midrash *Sifre*, when "ordinarily" he would have been able to find only one.[67]

63 See Goldman's article on Marx mentioned in note 43. See also Marx, *Studies*, pp. 380-81 and pp. 393-94.

64 *Sulzberger-Marx Correspondence*, p. 20.

65 *Ibid.*, p. 47.

66 *Ibid.*, p. 67.

67 See Mel Scult, *Tradition Renewed* (above note 17, p. 75.

Wearing a different hat, not as librarian but as a member of the board of the Jewish Publication Society, Marx discussed with Sulzberger, Henry Malter's critical edition of the Talmudic Tractate *Taanith*. Marx described the nature of Malter's work as the "first serious effort to produce a critical text of a part of the Talmud according to modern scientific principles" and urged the publication of the work: "It will be no mean matter for our community if the first serious work along this line will be undertaken by American scholars."[68] It was the view of Marx that work that is held to be so important must be supported by making primary sources available to the largest possible extent. In 1919, Marx wrote to Cyrus Adler: "The possession of different manuscripts of important works enables us to prepare critical editions without having in every instance recourse to the great European libraries."[69] After the acquisition of the Adler collection in 1923, Marx clearly formulated the utility of various manuscripts and printed books for producing critical editions:

> I have mentioned above [in his description of books and manuscripts in the Adler collection] quite a number of books which are often printed but it is a fact that our editions, even of the most important works, are so full of mistakes and misprints that it is of the greatest importance that their text should be carefully revised and corrected on the basis of old manuscripts. The classics should be as carefully and correctly edited as is being done since a century and longer with the Greek and Roman classics.[70]

It was in this spirit that the library attempted to collect extensively *all* editions of *all* Jewish texts, resulting in many manuscripts and multiple printed editions of one and the same biblical, rabbinical, philosophical, ethical, and other works.

In addition to the concentration on relatively well-defined subject areas, the library's development policies were also driven by other considerations. According to Marx and Sulzberger, the library needed a strong

68 *Sulzberger-Marx Correspondence*, pp. 143-44.

69 *Adler-Marx Correspondence*, 24 February 1919.

70 Copy of letter to Mr. Dolidowsky (dated 10 August 1923), apparently a correspondent of the Yiddish newspaper, *Tageblatt*, bound with a copy of *Catalog of Hebrew Manuscripts in the Collection of Elkan Nathan Adler* (Cambridge: Cambridge University Press, 1921) JTS library SRR Z 6605 H4A19 c.8.

Judeo-Spanish section,[71] or as the latter put it, the library should buy "Judeo-*anything*" [emphasis added].[72] The geographic dispersion of the Jewish Diaspora and its linguistic diversity invited the ingathering of documents originating in distant Jewish communities. Interest in far-flung Jewish groups grew in the 19th century as Western European Jewish travelers reached exotic places where they discovered Jews living in communities with their own language, culture, and religious customs. One of these travelers was Elkan Nathan Adler, who diligently and skillfully tracked down the books and manuscripts of the places that he had visited. Many treasures in his collection were acquired during his trips to North African and Asian Jewish communities.[73] Judah Magnes was also among those Jewish scholars who acquired literary remnants of Jews living in faraway places.[74] Encouraged by the interest of scholars and collectors, such learned booksellers as Ephraim Deinard, the Toledano Brothers, Lippa Schwager, David Fraenkel, and Jacob Halperin (who traveled for eight months in search of books and manuscripts) went on long trips to obtain objects, manuscripts, and other materials of remote and exotic Jewish communities.[75] As a result of these efforts, the knowledge about the Jews of Yemen, Persia, Bukhara, Morocco, Algiers, Tunis, Kurdistan, and China had greatly increased. The Seminary library availed itself of the services of these itinerant booksellers and tried in many ways to enrich its collections with materials pertaining to and originating in non-European Jewish communities. Thus, books were bought from Tiberias and Aleppo and from the Orient, notably Damascus and Southern Arabia, including "a large number of hitherto unknown books."[76] Marx reported about his negotiations with a bookdealer in Aleppo "for several very important books and mss, the expenses of which Mr. Louis Marshall kindly

71 See above, note 60, and *Semi-Centennial Volume*, p. 94.

72 *Sulzberger-Marx Correspondence*, p. 47.

73 See preface to *Adler Manuscript Catalog* (above, note 70), p. v.

74 *Bibliographical Studies*, p. 44.

75 See *Adler Manuscript Catalog*, p. v; *Bibliographical Studies*, pp. 411-412, *Semi-Centennial Volume*, p. 102. The Marx papers contain extensive files of correspondence, invoices, and lists relating to these booksellers. They provide important source materials about the provenance of some of the library's holdings, their prices, rarity, etc., and they deserve to be studied for their value for bibliographical information. JTS library archives.

76 Librarian's reports, 1 June 1908, p. 4, and 30 October 1910, pp. 1-2.

promised to defray."[77] Wilhelm Bacher in Budapest utilized, in his pioneering studies of Yemenite Jewish literature, manuscripts lent to him by the Seminary.[78] In 1915, the library received an illuminated Judeo-Persian manuscript, its first manuscript of this kind, and, when the Adler collection arrived, it became one of the largest, if not the largest, depository of Hebrew and Judeo-Persian manuscripts from Persia and Bukhara.[79] Materials relating to the Jews of China, including a Sefer Torah used in Kaifeng, were also added to the collection and were proudly mentioned and displayed.[80]

The largest and most diverse collection of this kind of manuscript was added to the library in 1932. Eleven hundred Hebrew and Judeo-Arabic manuscripts, assembled by the Viennese bookseller Jacob Halpern, were bought for the library by Linda Miller in honor of Hyman G. Enelow, rabbi of Temple Emanu-El in New York. Mrs. Miller desired to remain anonymous at the time of the purchase and only later did her identity as the donor become public. The collection was gathered together in Yemen, Persia, Asia Minor, and North Africa. The manuscripts were purchased in, among other places, Fez, Mequinez, Agadir, Oran, Algiers, Jerba, Tripoli, and Gardaia (in the Sahara), Tokat (Anatolia), Aleppo, and Damascus. The Yemenite manuscripts largely stemmed from Sanaa.[81] As a result of this purchase, the global coverage of cultural treasures of the far-flung Jewish communities was enlarged and brought closer to being as extensive as possible. The Enelow collection, added to the library's already existing holdings, especially the Adler collection that was bought exactly a decade earlier, expanded the chronological span of the materials considerably. While the Adler library, particularly the part that contained the famous collection of Cairo *Genizah* fragments, provided sources for

77 Librarian's report, 20 May 1910, p. 2.

78 Librarian's report, 4 February 1912, p. 3.

79 Board of Directors' report, 21 November 1915, p. 3, and W. Bacher, "Zur jüdisch-persischen Litteratur," in E.N. Adler, *About Hebrew Manuscripts* (London, 1905; reprint New York: Hermon Press, 1970), pp. 136-68.

80 On the Kaifeng Torah Scroll, see Michael Pollak, *The Torah Scrolls of the Chinese Jews* (Dallas: Bridwell Library, Southern Methodist University, 1975), esp. pp. 49-53. On other Kaifeng materials, see *Bibliographical Studies*, p. 2.

81 *Bibliographical Studies*, pp. 411-43. See also Jacob Halpern's file in the Marx papers. Librarian's reports, 1 December 1932, pp. 10-11, 18-25; 23 May 1934, pp. 1-2; minutes of the library corporation, 23 May 1934, p. 3, and 21 April 1936, pp. 1-2.

the history of Jewish culture and life around the Mediterranean and in the Middle East in medieval times, the Enelow manuscripts covered modern times, ranging from the 16th to the 19th centuries. Through these efforts, the Seminary library became one of the most important places for the study of Yemenite, Judeo-Persian, and Moroccan manuscripts. It was fortunate that the biblical commentaries and *Midrash* manuscripts of the Yemenite holdings found utilization very soon in the work of Rabbi M.M. Kasher, who incorporated in his *Torah Shelemah*, an encyclopedic commentary to the Pentateuch, the new discoveries from the Seminary's Yemenite materials.[82]

The library, from its inception, tried to assemble as full a collection as possible of printed Hebrew books. Hebrew books printed in the 15th century, the first products of Hebrew presses, the incunabula, were especially sought out. Marx included in his reports statistics on Hebrew incunabula. He counted them, compared their numbers with the holdings of other libraries until, finally, he was able to declare that the Seminary's collection of Hebrew incunabula surpassed that of every other library.[83]

A further bibliographical consideration in assembling books for the library was the desire to own books from each and every place where Hebrew books were ever printed. "I do like to have gradually represented as many different presses as I can in our collection if they produced books in our line."[84] Marx made this statement in connection with Latin incunabula, but it applied even to a greater degree to Hebrew presses. Next to the products of major centers of Hebrew printing, such as Constantinople, Venice, Amsterdam and many others, particular attention was paid to books printed in tiny towns and villages, especially in Russia where, at the end of the 18th and the beginning of the 19th centuries, Hebrew books were printed in very small editions in order to elude Czarist censorship. Books produced through these short-lived

82 First volume published in 1949.

83 *Semi-Centennial Volume*, p. 98. See also F. Goff, *Incunabula in American Libraries*, 3rd census (New York: The Bibliographical Society of America, 1964), pp. 316-25. Of the 127 items listed there, only one was not represented in the Seminary library. A detailed catalog of the library's collection of Hebrew incunabula, prepared by Shimon Iakerson of the Institute of Oriental Studies, Russian Academy of Sciences, St. Petersburg, will be published in the near future. [Sh. Iakerson. *Catalogue of Hebrew Inconabula from the Collection of the Library of the Jewish Theological Seminary of America*, New York and Jerusalem, 1-2, 2004-2005.]

84 *Sulzberger-Marx Correspondence*, p. 191.

efforts are extremely rare and Sulzberger encouraged Marx to acquire them for the library: "The Russian prints are desirable too" and "missing Russian prints... I am also willing to buy, provided you think the prices right." As a result, Marx could write: "Our Russian division is growing very satisfactorily and in a few years we may excel all in this line."[85]

Another dimension of collection building at the Seminary library was dictated by the bibliophilic passion for collecting of Sulzberger, E.N. Adler, Mortimer Schiff, H.G. Enelow, later Harry G. Friedman, and, of course, Marx himself. Not only "ordinary" books but also special editions were sought out. Deluxe editions of books printed on parchment or on colored paper (mainly on blue—an expensive paper considered to be particularly attractive), large paper copies, artistic bindings (including silver ones), and association copies (signed or owned by distinguished people) were constantly added to the library. It was with great enthusiasm that Marx included acquisitions of this type in his reports. Characteristic is a short note by Marx in 1911 about the library's holdings of Hebrew books printed on parchment and his mention of "a unique copy of the third edition of Maimonides' Code, Constantinople 1509, printed on vellum, which was found in the interior of Yemen."[86] Similarly, in his reports on the library there are special sections on "Luxus Editions:" "To our collections of Editions deluxe one on vellum, seven on blue paper and ten large paper copies were added by Mr. [Mortimer] Schiff," "the collection of deluxe editions of Hebrew books was enriched this year by eight volumes printed on blue paper, one on yellow and eight large paper copies."[87]

References to decorative bindings, including silver ones that were usually given as presents by bridegrooms to brides, are also quite frequent in the reports, as are descriptions of association copies. One of the features of the Steinschneider collection, repeatedly emphasized by Marx, was that it contained "numerous dedication copies showing Steinschneider's relationship with Jewish and non-Jewish scholars." The following is a characteristic example of both dedication and annotation: To D. Cassel's dedication of his *Kore ha-Dorot*, 1846: "Meinem lieben Freunde M. Steinschneider—der Herausgeber" [To my dear friend M. Steinschnei-

85 *Ibid.*, pp. 26, 47, 73.

86 *Bibliographical Studies*, pp. 409, 413.

87 *Ibid.*, pp. 194-95, 244-46.

der—the Editor], Steinschneider added "(nur bis 1865!)" above the word "Freunde." Underneath there is another note by Steinschneider stating that this was a special copy printed for him on large paper.[88]

Finally, the library under Marx also diligently collected broadsides, etchings, woodcuts, photographs, and postcards. In 1921, with the Israel Solomons collection, eleven hundred prints were acquired. The Solomons collection, a gift of Mortimer Schiff, was particularly famous for its pamphlets relating to the history of the Jews in England. Among these pamphlets were many of great rarity, some not found even in the British Library, and equally rare prints: portraits of Jewish personalities, depictions of Jewish scenes and sites, and anti-Semitic caricatures.[89] The library at once turned into a central place of research for such graphic materials. In the division of broadsides, the large collection of wedding and other poems and riddles from Italy, collected by the Italian scholar, Moise Soave, should be singled out.[90] The Jewish marriage contracts, many of them profusely decorated, constitute one of the finest such collections in the world.[91] In the first decades of the library, all of these categories, as well as ceremonial objects, were handled by the administration of the library as a unit. The aim of the library's leadership was to collect and preserve under one roof all printed, handwritten, graphic, and artistic manifestations of the Jewish past. It was only in 1943 that the museum part of the library was physically removed from the Seminary to the Jewish Museum on Fifth Avenue. A distinct graphic collection was, at least administratively, separated from the rest of the library first in the 1970s.

In conclusion, the library's policy of acquisition resulted in the accumulation of materials in practically all forms of the written or graphic media of the Jewish past.

88 *Semi-Centennial Volume*, pp. 93, 114.

89 *Ibid.*, pp. 96-97. See also *The Jew as Other* (cited above, note 50), introduction.

90 *Ibid.*, pp. 94-95. Many of these broadsides were analyzed by Dan Pagis, *A Secret Sealed: Hebrew Baroque Emblem-Riddles from Italy and Holland* (Jerusalem: The Magnes Press, 1986) (in Hebrew).

91 A detailed catalog of the Seminary library's marriage contract collection is presently being prepared by Dr. Shalom Sabar, Hebrew University, Jerusalem.

The Library's Mission

This broad understanding of the mission of the library was never challenged nor formally and publicly debated, and it was generally accepted by subsequent Seminary administrations, at least tacitly. There was no written acquisition policy in existence: "There never has been any official book-buying policy adopted by the library" wrote Gerson D. Cohen.[92] Neither was there any open opposition to the comprehensive conception of the library's mission, except at the very beginning of its history:

> Originally some of the Trustees were of the opinion that the library should be limited to the immediate needs of the Seminary and should be kept within the bounds of an ordinary college library. We are grateful to Judge Sulzberger that such a policy was not accepted.[93]

Echoes of a more limited conception of the library's mission may also be detected in what Marx wrote to Sulzberger in 1918:

> When American Jewish scholarship in time will take the rank it ought to in proportion to the number of American Jews, your name will always be connected with its advance as the one who furnished the tools *at a time when no one else foresaw that they might ever be needed"* [emphasis added].[94]

Or in the words of Boaz Cohen:

> The library was originally founded for the purpose of serving the Seminary faculty and students, but it soon outgrew its original design and began to minister to the wider circle of scholars who are engaged in scientific research. In addition, the library was to be a storehouse where everything printed in Hebrew or Hebrew characters, as well as anything published in any tongue pertaining to the Jews and Judaism, was to be preserved forever against the ravages of time.[95]

92 Maurice F. Tauber, *A Report on the Library of the Jewish Theological Seminary* (New York: mimeographed, 1959) p. 79. Quoted as *Tauber Report*.

93 *Semi-Centennial Volume*, p. 92.

94 *Sulzberger-Marx Correspondence*, p. 148.

95 *Jewish Forum* 17 (1934), p. 20.

Indeed, the first decades of the library's existence were marked by the dominance of Judge Mayer Sulzberger's vision of building a great bibliographic center at the Seminary and by the massive acquisitions efforts of the library. Sulzberger's determination and Marx's scholarship and contacts won the blessing of Jacob Schiff, Felix Warburg, and Louis Marshall. The scholarly interests of Schechter, Ginzberg, Friedlander, Davidson, and Marx himself helped shape the perception of the library as an indispensable agency for advancing the Seminary's standing as the leading Jewish academic institution in the United States.

By the 1920s and early 1930s, the library's reputation was already firmly established. This was the time when attempts were made to lend an independent identity to this great collection. Mortimer Schiff, especially, wanted the library to become an institution that, although connected to the Seminary, stood on its own organizationally, financially, and even architecturally. In 1924, the library was incorporated as a separate organization.[96] In 1932-34, major bequests from members of the Schiff family were made for the library: $25,000 from the estate of Mortimer Schiff and a fund of approximately $227,000, to be turned over to the library for its general purposes, by Felix Warburg and John Schiff, Mortimer's son.[97]

By this time the new building of the library was already erected, and it was an architectural symbol of the library's relationship to the Seminary. The tall library tower, flanked by two lower buildings of Seminary classrooms, offices, and a dormitory, signaled the dual status of the library: a part of the larger Seminary, but also distinct from it. Cyrus Adler articulated this ambiguity in 1923:

> With regard to the library building, I have had a further interview with Mr. [Mortimer] Schiff... Mr. Schiff agrees with you and me that [Arnold W.] Brunner's plan is inadequate and something more comprehensive ought to be created. There is no thought of

96 *Semi-Centennial Volume*, pp. 105-8.

97 Minutes of the library corporation, 12 December 1932, pp. 2-5; 23 May 1934, pp. 1-2. See also minutes of the Board of Directors, 9 June 1933. In the latter, mention is made of $150,000 left for the general purpose of the library by Therese Schiff, Jacob's widow. It is not clear whether or not this sum is included in the $227,000 turned over to the library by Warburg and John Schiff. See also Cyrus Adler, *Selected Letters*, ed. Ira Robinson (Philadelphia: Jewish Publication Society, 1985), vol. 2, p. 147.

> separating the library from the Seminary by any physical distance, but I feel that in view of the fact that this is not merely an ordinary working library, but a great collection of books and manuscripts, it should be used in such a way that students and scholars who desire to use it for research purposes should be able to do so without encountering the almost necessary distraction that occurs in a building which is used by students, who may sometimes even have the right to shout and sing.[98]

Decline and Reorganization

The library's dynamic expansion during these years, and the plans for a semi-independent or perhaps totally autonomous library, came to a halt in the 1930s. The Great Depression, the rise of Nazism in Germany, as well as personal circumstances — such as Marx's growing anguish over the fate of his family and friends in Germany and his only daughter's illness, and also the death of Mortimer Schiff in 1931 — dissipated the tremendous energy that was invested in the great vision for the library.

The phenomenal growth of the library also caused severe problems. As new collections and individual items continued to pour in, the library gradually became unmanageable. Ever since the early years of his association with the Seminary, Marx had continually complained about the fact that the catalog of the library was not complete and the staff not adequate. As time passed, and especially after the receipt of the Adler collection in 1923 and the Enelow collection in 1932, the situation assumed crisis proportions. Not only the cataloging, but also binding, shelving, reader services, and ordinary acquisitions suffered.

The library could not keep pace with the demands imposed upon it by its unprecedented, spectacular growth. In 1911, we find the first serious admission about the staff's inability to cope:

> Owing to the constant increase of our library, the rapidity with which accessions are being made and the much greater use by the students and other scholars and institutions, the library staff is only

98 *Ibid.*, vol. 2, p. 75.

> able by the greatest exertions to cope with the regular work... As a consequence, the cataloging, for the first time, is getting behind.[99]

In 1913 Marx pointed out that the library lacked a subject catalog: "At present there are no subject catalogs of Hebraica and Judaica, and the man interested in research work must inevitably lose a great deal of time before he is able to gather together his material."[100]

Subsequently, we read about the "considerable" number of uncataloged Judaica and the "even larger" number of such Hebraica.[101] A few years later there is a report about finishing "the cataloguing of the accumulation of the past years" and beginning "the difficult work of cataloguing the rare broad sheets and occasional publications." But, in the same year, the complaint about the large number of uncataloged books recurs: "Owing to the constant influx of new books," the cataloging lags behind.[102] At one point, Cyrus Adler requested funds from the board to hire an assistant and a secretary to help out Marx, because:

> Professor Marx is so entirely engrossed with the detail of the library that his bibliographical and scientific work in general perforce suffers... it seems almost a waste of energy for a man of his excellent capacities to give so much of his time to ordinary routine.[103]

Marx, after the receipt of the Adler collection in 1923, described the difficulties in unpacking and checking the books and the time-consuming comparison of Adler's copies with copies of the same editions already in the library, and he concluded: "It is a duty of honour after we have received this wonderful gift to attend to it properly and promptly."[104] Unfortunately, the backlog remained with the library for a very long time. The reasons for this situation were manifold: the small and non-professional staff, a fact to which Marx called attention constantly, could not handle the numerous library tasks adequately. Marx's obsession with bibliographic detail was also a contributing factor. When the Adler

99 Librarian's report, 20 October 1911, pp. 3-4.

100 Librarian's report, 16 November 1913, p. 10.

101 Librarian's report, 25 November 1914, p. 5.

102 Librarian's report, 15 May 1918, p. 6; and librarian's report, 7 November 1918, p. 5.

103 Board of Directors' report, 19 May 1918, p. 15.

104 Librarian's report, 10 May 1923, p. 6.

books arrived, he appointed Isaac Rivkind,[105] a scholarly member of the staff, to examine the Adler copies of rare Hebrew books and compare them with the older copies of the very same books already in the library. Rivkind discovered a number of important typographical differences in these copies of rare Hebraica, in the title pages and elsewhere, and Marx observed, "Mr. Rivkind has become a real expert in these matters... Owing to the large number of rare Hebraica and the necessity of carefully comparing the copies *page by page* [emphasis added] this work is naturally proceeding very slowly."[106] True, Rivkind's discoveries created a new area of bibliographical inquiry, because until that time few, if any, bibliographers had at their disposal two or more copies of extremely rare Hebrew books from the same edition for comparison. Still, the preoccupation with such tedious scholarly detail slowed considerably the integration of the Adler collection into the library and contributed greatly to the increase in the backlog. With the receipt of the Enelow collection, the situation further deteriorated. In 1934, Marx anticipated that "it will take years" before the Enelow collection could be made accessible to readers.[107]

Other aspects of the library's management also suffered. Significantly, the catalog of manuscripts to which Marx himself devoted many years of labor was never completed.[108] As early as 1916, the librarian reported that

105 On Rivkind (1895-1968), see *Minha L'yitshaq: A Bibliography of the Writings of Isaac Rivkind*, compiled by Mordechai Kosover and Abraham G. Ducker (New York: Jewish Librarians Association, 1949), English section v-xv, Hebrew section 7-26.

106 Librarian's report, 15 May 1924, p. [7]; on Rivkind's publications based on these comparisons, see his article "*Dikdukei Sefarim*" in *Alexander Marx Jubilee Volume*, Hebrew section, pp. 401-32.

107 Librarian's report, 23 May 1934, p. 2.

108 Librarian's report, 10 November 1913, p. 9, and repeatedly in subsequent years. Interesting is a statement in the librarian's report, 1 December 1932: "A catalogue of the manuscripts possessed by the library ten years ago... was also copied... The... Adler manuscripts are roughly listed in the printed catalogue of the former owner. The most important manuscripts received in recent years have been recorded annually in the Registers... A copy of the bookseller's catalog of the recent donation [Enelow collection]... has also been deposited." Marx's difficulties in describing the manuscripts are frequently mentioned in his letters to Aron Freimann, see e.g., Freimann file, Marx papers, 13 January 1921, 27 March 1923, 27 April 1923. The first full, albeit very tentative and brief, list of the Seminary library's Hebrew manuscript collection was first published in 1991: *A Guide to the Hebrew Manuscript Collection of the Library of the Jewish Theological Seminary of America*, 5 vols. (New York: Library of the Jewish Theological

the Bible and liturgy sections had to be revised because they "had become considerably disarranged owing to the constant additions and the great lack of space."[109] And again, in 1924:

> Leaving aside the question of a proper building which, I understand will be taken up as soon as feasible, there is a most urgent necessity for an increase in the staff of the library. Many important branches of the library are being neglected at the present time on account of the inadequacy of our staff. Thus we are not able to go over our shelves in order to ascertain whether the books are all in their proper places and how many have been lost in the course of years.[110]

When the new building was erected in 1932, the space situation improved immeasurably, but some of the problems plaguing the library's management remained unsolved. Freshly settled in the new quarters, Marx submitted the following report to the board:

> After having worked under the most unfavorable conditions in the congested quarters of the old building, it is a great relief to have the spacious stacks where all the books can be placed to the best advantage. A considerable rearrangement was necessary after the books had been transferred in order to place them properly.
>
> Because of lack of space in the old building it was necessary to separate many divisions, limiting them to books most frequently in demand and placing others on less accessible shelves. Now all the books have been put together in their proper places. While the division between Hebrew and non-Hebrew books has been maintained, care has been taken to keep on one floor all the books of the same subject in all languages. Only the Hebrew liturgical collection which offers a particularly difficult problem is still in the process of being arranged, but this task will be finished very soon.

Seminary, 1991). See Jay Rovner's introduction, vol. 1, pp. v-x. This list does not include the manuscript fragments of the *Genizah* collection. For these, one still must use the *Adler Manuscript Catalog*. A catalog of halakhic and midrashic *Genizah* fragments, prepared by Neil Danzig, is, however, forthcoming. [See now: Neil Danzig, *A Catalogue of Fragments of Halakhah and Midrash from the Cario Genizah in the Elkan Nathan Adler Collection of the Library of the Jewish Theological Seminary of America*, New York-Jerusalem, JTSA, 1997.]

109 Librarian's report, 15 November 1916, p. 5.

110 Librarian's report, 15 May 1924, p. [9].

> The other divisions are all in order, although it is necessary to go over the books from time to time. Since the books are placed according to authors, *but are not numbered* [emphasis added], such revision at regular intervals is indispensable...
>
> A great many pamphlets, fragments, incomplete volumes of periodicals and duplicates have gradually accumulated. All these which had been scattered in various places in the old building have now been brought together on the 8th and 9th floors of the stacks. Doctor [Boaz] Cohen uses his spare time in going over this accumulation, sifting and arranging them...
>
> We are handicapped by the lack of funds for binding which prevents us from placing these volumes in their proper places. The longer these papers are left unbound, the more they deteriorate.
>
> The cataloging has also greatly progressed. In the Judaica department there are very few books left uncatalogued, and many of the smaller pamphlets have already been attended to... In the Hebraica division the number of uncataloged books is larger.[111]

This state of affairs was characteristic of the Seminary library for the next two decades.

Early in the Seminary's history, some voices called for a different approach to the library and for a change in its priorities. In 1905, Schechter wrote to Cyrus Adler: "I intend altogether to interest myself a little more with library matters. As it seems to me a little more discipline and a little more exactness might be productive of good results."[112] It is not clear to what situation Schechter was actually referring, but one could surmise that he was unhappy with the lack of direction in the collection policy of the library as well as with the inadequate service provided to students and other users. In 1908, Marx was mildly apologetic and defensive when he tried to explain "the large number of purchases" and the fact that he "was obliged somewhat to anticipate the appropriation of the coming year."[113]

It was not only the question of internal library priorities that from time to time occupied the minds of the people who were entrusted to lead it.

111 Librarian's report, 1 December 1932, pp. 4-6.

112 Schechter to Adler, 15 September 1905.

113 Librarian's report, 1 June 1908, p. 4.

Another issue that surfaced had to do in general with the appropriateness of spending huge amounts of monies for the purchase of large collections of manuscripts and rare books. This must have been a point of discussion at the time of the deliberations about the purchase of Baron Gunzburg's library (1914) and again when the acquisition of the Adler collection was considered in 1919. Here is how Marx presented Jacob Schiff's (and quite clearly, his own) point of view:

> When Mr. Schiff had decided to purchase the Gunzburg Library he told me at the next graduation, shortly afterwards, that just then a request for $100,000 for Jewish primary education had been made, but that he had decided rather to buy the library which no one else would do, while for education funds would be made available through others. While one cannot know how Mr. Schiff feels now towards this question, I think his interest in the growth of our library is quite strong and that he looked at the Gunzburg collection from a broader point of view than Mr. Warburg seems to assume.[114]

As the years went by, Cyrus Adler gave vent to his opposition, although somewhat mutedly, to Marx's policies: "The Library is not simply intended as an aid to research. It is of course, also for the use of students."[115] This statement must be understood against the background of Marx's practice of including in his reports, at least since 1924, extensive sections entitled "The Library as an Aid to Research,"[116] which listed publications based on the library's manuscripts and other rare materials. The number of such publications over a period of twenty years, ending in 1947, reached seven hundred.[117] Adler apparently felt that too much emphasis was placed on the research aspect of the library and that insufficient attention was paid to general library service.

In 1931, we have the following two statements from Adler:

> I am sure you know that I want and always have wanted the library to grow as fast as possible, but I somehow have the feeling at the

114 Marx to Adler, 7 Sept. [1919]. See also Cyrus Adler, *Selected Letters*, vol. 1, pp. 390-91; vol. 2, pp. 55-58.

115 Adler to Marx, 3 May 1926.

116 *Bibliographical Studies*, pp. 476-548.

117 Librarian's report, 6 May 1947, p. 3.

> moment that the best thing we can do now is to concentrate on getting it in good running order in our new building and make it as accessible as possible.[118]
>
> I do not feel that we have a moral right to have assembled the greatest collection in the world and then deal with it as though it were only available to a privileged class... In the old building, our principal effort was at collection and conservation. In the new building, our principal effort must be in the direction of use.[119]

Although Felix Warburg had supported the library generously, he also expressed reservations about the race to become the largest collection: "The argument that we would, at least in numbers, be far ahead of other collections of Hebrew manuscripts, does not appeal to me."[120] Marx, of course, did not give in, and he replied to Warburg, "I am of the opinion that since here is the largest Jewish community that ever existed in one place, it is our duty to establish a spiritual center and that we ought to have a library as complete as we can make it of all the treasures of our past."[121]

Warburg continued to support the library and participated in the drive for the purchase of the Adler collection in 1922.[122] Still, he remained concerned with the one-sidedness of the library's policy: "I feel that until our library has caught up in every respect in regard to cataloging, binding, etc., we had better leave new things alone."[123] Warburg's advice was not followed and, actually, could not have been followed. "New things" always surfaced and the acquisitions could not be stopped, although they continued to contribute to the ever growing backlog of uncataloged and unbound books.

In the 1930s, the rescue of European Jewish treasures also moved onto the agenda. The transfer of the ritual objects and *Sifrei Torah* of the Danzig Jewish community to the Seminary in 1939 is well known.[124] In the

118 Adler to Marx, 18 May 1931.

119 Adler to Marx, 25 September 1931.

120 Felix Warburg to Marx, 19 February 1919, Cyrus Adler Papers, JTS library archives.

121 Marx to Warburg, 20 May 1919, Cyrus Adler Papers, JTS library archives.

122 Warburg's role in the acquisition of the Adler collection is documented in note 42.

123 Warburg to Marx, 29 January 1935.

124 See *Danzig 1939: Treasures of a Destroyed Community*, catalog for the Jewish Museum exhibit by Vivian B. Mann and Joseph Guttman (New York: The Jewish Museum, 1980).

same year, other collections that could possibly be saved were mentioned:

> I take this opportunity of bringing to your attention a proposal of Leo Winz, former editor of *Ost und West* in Berlin, and now a resident of Tel-Aviv, Palestine. Mr. Winz, in a letter recently received, states that the Jewish library in Vienna was burned by the Nazis, and that other great Jewish libraries and cultural collections in the Reich stood in similar danger.
> Mr. Winz suggests that such valuable collections as those in the Rabbinical Seminary at Breslau, the *Hochschule für die Wissenschaft des Judentums* and the Hildesheimer Seminary in Berlin, as well as the library of the *Jüdische Gemeinde* in Berlin could be ransomed for a moderate sum and brought to this country or to Palestine. He cites the German need for foreign exchange as a probable inducement for the Nazis parting with these collections at a reasonable figure, and thinks a committee should be formed in this country to collect the monies. I do not know whether you have already been approached on this matter or you thought it practicable.[125]

These salvage efforts never succeeded and it is not known what steps, if any, were taken by the Seminary or other organizations in this direction.[126]

Other collections also became available in this period. Thirteen thousand books from the personal libraries of Louis Ginzberg and Alexander Marx were added in 1953 and, prior to that, many collections reached the library as gifts.[127] In the post-World War II years, thousands

125 Extract from letter of Dr. Israel Schapiro of the Library of Congress to Marx, 15 February 1939.

126 On 16 May 1938, Adler wrote to Marx about the fate of the collection of the Berlin Jewish Community. Adler did not see a possibility to intervene with the American ambassador in Berlin. In the minutes of the Board of Directors, 31 May 1939, it is related how Louis Finkelstein met with a Mr. Teterka who stated that he could bring the library of the Breslau Seminary to the United States for 75,000 marks. The following remark is added to this report: "It would be understood that the Breslau community would not ask any compensation for the transaction." On 21 February 1939, Marx wrote to Adler: "I heard the other day that the Museum of the Berlin Jewish Community could be ransomed for $25,000." Stating that he realized it "was absolutely against our policy to send American money to Germany." Marx suggested that perhaps steps could be taken to salvage the "irreplaceable treasures" by individuals.

127 Some of these collections, since they were not cataloged, were stored on the upper floors of the library tower, and the bulk of them were destroyed or damaged in the 1966 fire. A partial list of

of books were given to the Seminary library by the Jewish Cultural Reconstruction Organization. This organization, headed by Salo W. Baron and administered by Hannah Arendt, was responsible for the distribution of tens of thousands of Judaica and Hebraica works looted by the Nazis and recovered after the war by the allied forces in a warehouse in Offenbach.[128]

In 1955, the librarian, Gerson D. Cohen, reported that twenty-eight thousand volumes arrived in the library in one year.[129] No wonder then that in 1958, the new librarian, Nahum Sarna, referred to fifty thousand uncataloged books and an equal number of books in need of binding.[130]

Efforts toward Reorganization

The challenge of the library's reorganization, the adjustment of its direction to changed circumstances in the postwar period, became the task of a new, young leadership. Under the direction of Gerson D. Cohen and, later, Nahum Sarna, the late 1940s and especially the 1950s[131] were years of renewed and bustling energy, growth, and, most significantly, careful, well-thought-out, long-range planning for the library. The long-standing problems of the library were confronted and tackled even as the collections were considerably enhanced.

After the end of World War II, major departments in the library were expanded through important acquisitions. A large collection of French documents relating to the history of the Jewish communities in France in the 18th and 19th centuries was purchased. Some of the documents were of great rarity, but particularly important was the fact that they represented primary source materials for the understanding of the history of the Jews of France and Europe particularly during the period of emancipation and enlightment. Indeed, in subsequent years much original research was

the collections is found in my article in *Jewish Book Annual* 42 (1984-85), pp. 183-84 [see in the present volume, pp. 000-000.]

128 Dicker, *The Seminary Library*, pp. 54-58; 107-12.

129 Library committee minutes, 6 October 1955, p. 1.

130 Library committee minutes, 26 March 1958.

131 Gerson D. Cohen served as librarian from 1950 to 1957. In the years between 1950 and 1953, Marx's title was Director of Libraries. Nahum Sarna was appointed librarian in 1957 and he served until 1963. On the Cohen and Sarna years, see Dicker, *The Seminary Library*, pp. 64-69.

generated on the basis of the Seminary library's highly significant collection of Franco-Jewish historical documents.[132] Another major purchase was that of the collection of old Yiddish books from Judah A. Joffe, a scholar of Yiddish language and literature. He had assembled over the years an outstanding collection of rare printed books and some manuscripts in Yiddish, mainly from the 16th to the 18th centuries. Early Yiddish books are of the utmost rarity. They were printed for the use of the community at large and not only for the community of scholars. They covered popular fields, translations from Hebrew, ethical works, and literature for entertainment and reading pleasure. Since they were intended for popular use, they quickly became worn out and, often, no great care was taken to preserve them. Through the Joffe collection, the library became one of the foremost centers of scholarship in the field of Yiddish.[133]

In 1947 a library committee was formed. Representatives of the Seminary administration and the library, as well as lay leaders, participated in the regular meetings of the committee. Its members—Julius Silver, H.G. Friedman, Harry K. Cohen, Arthur Rosenbloom, Louis Silver—and others provided the funds for the purchase of the French and Yiddish collections as well as important and expensive individual rare books and manuscripts. But more important, the minutes of the meetings of the library committee reveal that its members realized, fundamental changes would have to be introduced in the library in order to cure the many ills that had affected it over the years. It is most illuminating to read the minutes of a committee meeting from 1947. Alexander Marx and members of the library staff who had been associated with the library for many years called attention to the situation in the library. Marx pointed out that, during the depression, the library's budget for buying current books dropped from $4,000 to $250(!) annually, and even in 1947, the allocation was only $2,000. Boaz Cohen, who at the time had been with the library for twenty three years, and Isaac Rivkind, after twenty four years of service, complained that throughout all their years,

132 See Roger S. Kohn, *An Inventory to the French Jewish Communities Record Group 1648-1946* (New York: Library of the Jewish Theological Seminary, 1991). Rabbi Arthur Herzberg was instrumental in raising the funds for the acquisition of this collection.

133 On the negotiations leading to the purchase of the Joffe collection, see librarian's report, 1 March 1959 — 12 May 1959, pp. 4-5.

the staff remained the same, except for one additional *page*, while the collection more than doubled in size. The library had to compete with the Seminary's many other expanding activities. Moshe Davis and Simon Greenberg, representing the library administration on the library committee, expressed opposing views as to the policy to be followed. Davis advocated a "complete overhauling," while Greenberg recommended that the changes be carried out gradually.[134] It appears that Louis Finkelstein supported Greenberg's position because, until 1953, the year of Marx's death, drastic steps to reorganize the library never were taken. Despite much deliberation over the problems facing the library, it was only in 1958 that Nahum Sarna, then the librarian, persuaded the Seminary administration to invite Maurice F. Tauber, a professor of library service at Columbia University, to undertake a thorough survey of the library and to submit his evaluation and recommendations. His 153-page report and its recommendations marked a distinct turning point in the library's history.[135]

Tauber worked carefully for about a year on his report. He conducted extensive interviews with the library staff, Seminary administrators, faculty, students, members of the library committee, and general users of the library. Questionnaires were distributed to students and faculty. The preambles of these questionnaires are revealing of a new orientation: in the questionnaire intended for the faculty, the claim was made that the purpose of the survey was "to assist [the library's] staff in developing services to meet more fully the needs of the faculty, students, and the various academic departments in carrying out their instructional and research programs."[136] The student questionnaire began with these words: "It is the purpose of the Jewish Theological Seminary to make the best possible library available for its students. Consequently, as part of the

134 Library committee minutes, 16 February 1947.

135 On the situation in the library prior to the commissioning of the Tauber Report and on Sarna's efforts to invite Tauber, see excerpts from a letter by Sarna in Dicker, *The Seminary Library*, pp. 67-68. Simon Greenberg, representing the Seminary administration on the library committee, continued to express his cautious policy. When Tauber presented his report to the library committee on 22 October 1959, Greenberg made the following statement, according to the minutes of the meeting: "We must view the needs of the library against the background of the total needs of the Seminary as a whole. Priorities must be established, and it is possible that the sums required for a new library building may not be forthcoming immediately."

136 Tauber Report, p. 133.

continuing *study* of the Seminary to *study* its educational program, the Chancellor has approved a *study* of the functions, services, facilities and operation of the library."[137]

The purpose, as formulated here, is distinctly service-oriented. Indeed, Tauber devoted most attention to this aspect. Although he did describe the resources of the library, his main concern was to determine how the library could be reorganized to become an effective instrument in fulfilling the Seminary's objectives. The report's summary of recommendations,[138] in itself quite extensive, included many salient points. The library, despite its collections and great strengths, "has definite weaknesses in its current acquisition policy."[139] Deficiencies were noted in "such areas as modern Hebrew literature, current Jewish life, educational practices and problems, and music."[140] The report observed that there were many other institutions in Manhattan with large holdings in various areas of Jewish studies and it suggested that the Seminary library formalize its relations to the other institutions "so that reciprocal use may be developed to the utmost."[141] Most important were the report's recommendations for new library quarters, a modern system of circulation and acquisition, a total reclassification and recataloging of the collection according to the rules of the American Library Association and the Library of Congress, a huge preservation and binding operation, and the appointment of professional librarians to the staff. Tauber also wrote extensively about the relations between the library and the Seminary administration and about the involvement of the faculty, especially in the development of an acquisition policy for the library.

The tone and thrust of the Tauber Report were a far cry from the optimistic pronouncements early in the library's history, when the great treasures of the collections and its global importance were highlighted. So many things had changed since then. Other Jewish libraries had developed and grown; in Manhattan alone there existed a number of collections that, if combined, probably would constitute the largest conglomeration of Jewish books in the world. From downtown Manhattan to uptown, the

137 *Ibid.*, p. 138.

138 *Ibid.*, pp. 3-14.

139 *Ibid.*, p. 6.

140 *Ibid.*

141 *Ibid.*, p. 7.

libraries of Hebrew Union College, Yeshiva University, New York Public Library, Columbia University, YIVO (the Yiddish Scientific Institute), and the Leo Baeck Institute provide materials that render the Seminary library less central and less responsible for the acquisition of a "complete" collection of Judaica and Hebraica. The establishment of the State of Israel and the explosion of publishing activities in Hebrew in the new country made it impractical to try to collect "all" books printed in Hebrew. So, it was not only necessary in the 1950s to turn attention to the reorganization of the library's services, but also prudent.

The new realities forced a reassessment of the mission of the Seminary library. With full recognition of the importance of the collections, the library began its move toward the modernization of its functions and the cataloging of its resources. With this, the first half century of the library's history came to a close—a glorious history of great dreams, daring visions, and tremendous achievements, but also one that left as a bequest to the next half century very taxing tasks.

The New Jewish Theological Seminary Library

Twenty years ago, the *Jewish Book Annual* (vol. 21, 1963-1964, pp. 53-59) published an article on the Library of the Jewish Theological Seminary of America by the then librarian, Professor Nahum Sarna. In it, Sarna described the main features of the Seminary Library and its significance. In the twenty years that have elapsed since then, the Seminary Library's history has been marked by tragedy and renewal. In 1966 a fire occurred in the Library stacks. Ten stories of book stacks were located in the Library tower and the fire struck the three upper floors destroying approximately 70,000 books. Particularly tragic was the loss of the following collections:

Cyrus Adler Papers, representing a great portion of his papers and correspondence during his presidency of the Seminary (1915-1940).

Benaim Collection. This collection was acquired in 1965 and it contained books and manuscripts from North Africa. The majority of the 2,000 printed books was completely destroyed. About 105 manuscripts were partially damaged but can still be used for scholarly purposes. Of the remaining 45, only fragments have survived.

Danzig Collection of Torah Scrolls. Some forty scrolls, formerly the property of the Jewish Community of Danzig, deposited with the Seminary in 1939.

Israel Davidson Collection (on permanent loan from the College of the City of New York). The great scholar's complete collection of 8,000 volumes, which was especially rich in rare liturgical and poetical material.

Louis Ginzberg and Alexander Marx Collection of Books. Many of the books had the learned owners' marginal notes. Their papers, and those books which were in the Ginzberg-Marx Faculty Library and the Manuscript Room, remained intact.

Graduate School for Jewish Social Work. The collection of 5,000 books and pamphlets in the fields of social science, education, and psychology and much rare typewritten material, as well as about 145 bound, typewritten theses and the school's student records and correspondence files, were completely destroyed. This collection had been transferred to the Seminary Library in 1940 and became the Seminary's property in 1950.

Jewish Cultural Reconstruction Collection. After the Second World War, the Seminary received about 5,000 books from European collections whose owners could not be located. Many of these had been incorporated into the regular collections and suffered water damage, but the remaining volumes, mostly duplicates, were destroyed.

Moritz Steinschneider Collection. With the exception of his correspondence, his own works with handwritten notes, and his manuscript collection, the irreplaceable library of some 5,000 volumes of the great scholar was completely burned.

Tausner Collection. Several thousand Hebrew, Yiddish, and Russian books and pamphlets, published mainly in Russia and Poland.

Zemachson Collection. Manuscripts of music and scores of liturgical compositions.

Zilberts Collection. Manuscripts and liturgical manuscripts.

The rest of the collection suffered considerable water-damage and the entire stacks, containing approximately 150,000 volumes, had to be evacuated. The books were dispersed into various locations. After the evacuation, the arduous task of drying out the books began. Although some of the water-damaged books were beyond repair, the great majority of them could be restored, rebound, and returned to use.

As a result of the fire, it was decided to recatalog the entire collection according to the Library of Congress system and to abandon the old classification scheme based on the system devised by A.S. Freidus.

Special Treasures

Fortunately, the rare book and manuscript collection of the Library, which was housed in a different part of the building, remained intact. Immediately after the fire, arrangements were made with University Microfilms for the microfilming of the collection of manuscripts containing some 10,000 items, including 40,000 *Genizah* fragments. Certain sections of the rare book collection, especially the Hebrew incunabula, were also included in this project. University Microfilms has issued printed reel guides, arranged by subjects, to most of the collection, and these now provide, for the first time, lists to most of the Seminary's rich holdings of Hebrew and related manuscripts. The overwhelming majority of the Seminary's manuscripts have been made commercially available on microfilm to interested libraries and scholars. A complete set is on deposit at the Jewish National and University Library in Jerusalem, and microfilms of the *Genizah* collection, in its entirety, were acquired by Cambridge University Library. Through this measure, the manuscript collection of the Seminary Library is now widely available to the scholarly world in Europe, Israel, and throughout the United States.

As an additional guide to the rare books and manuscripts, a reprint of the late Alexander Marx's annual reports on unusual acquisitions was published (A. Marx, *Bibliographical Studies and Notes on Rare Books and Manuscripts in the Library of the Jewish Theological Seminary of America*, N.Y. 1977).

New Acquisitions

Although preoccupied with the task of reconstructing its damaged holdings, the physical restoration of the volumes, and the modernization of library practices, the Library continued to acquire important collections of books, and individual rare and unusual volumes. Among these collections thus acquired, mention should be made of those assembled by Rabbi Solomon Goldman, Rabbi Felix Levy, both of Chicago, and the Yiddish writers, Yehoash and N.M. Minkoff. Recently, the library received, as a gift, the collection of books that had belonged to Rabbi Hayyim Wasserzug (Filipower), a Lithuanian rabbi of the 19th century, whose library had been moved to this country a long time ago. This may be among the very few private libraries that remained together as a unit over such a long period of time, thus preserving a scholarly Eastern European rabbinic library relatively intact. Important Hebrew manuscripts, as well as rare printed books, were consistently acquired on a selective basis. Special mention should be made of such major manuscript acquisitions as the gift to the Library of the *Rothschild Manuscript*, a beautifully illuminated Hebrew codex written in Florence,

Italy in 1492; a Spanish *Haggadah*, written and illuminated around the year 1300; and a richly illuminated prayerbook, written in Pforchheim, Germany in 1720. Selected pages of the magnificent *Rothschild Manuscript* were reproduced and published in 1983, with an introduction and essays in honor of the dedication of the new Library building.

During its attempts to modernize its collections and bring the richness of its holding under bibliographical control, the Library initiated a number of projects. It received funding for two such projects from the National Endowment for the Humanities: *Recording and Microfilming of Newspaper and Periodical Collections* and *Support for the Archival Activities at the Library of the Jewish Theological Seminary of America*. As a result of these projects, the Seminary's archival holdings and periodicals collection became more easily accessible to the scholarly public. The latter grant also provided funds for the preservation on microfilm of some runs of rare titles. A recent grant from the Perlow Foundation will make it possible for the library to catalog and preserve its old Yiddish and hasidic books from Eastern Europe. The publication of a catalog is planned upon the successful completion of the project.

For a period of seventeen years, most of these activities took place in a temporary prefabricated structure that was erected in the courtyard of the Seminary for the reconstruction effort. The erection of this structure became imperative as a result of the total internal damage that the Library tower suffered at the time of the fire. Soon after 1966, planning began for a new Library building. In fact, plans for such a building were made even before the fire and Nahum Sarna's above-mentioned article concludes with the following words: "It is hoped that the greatest Jewish Library of all time, and one of the great cultural assets of the United States, will, in the not too distant future, be housed in a building worthy of its importance and fully equipped to fulfill its role as the mecca of Jewish scholars." Still, it was not until the year 1980 that ground was broken for the erection of a new Library structure. In 1983 the building was completed and the Library's holdings were moved into the new quarters. At the dedication, the Library was named the Ivan F. & Seema Boesky Family Library. [Subsequently, its original name: The Library of the Jewish Theological Seminary, was restored.]

Modern Facility

The new Library, which adjoins the Seminary's old buildings, occupies 55,000 square feet, has a book capacity of close to 400,000 books, and a seating capacity of 300. The first floor is used by the Library staff for acquisition, cataloguing and technical activities. It also provides space for a large room for sorting and storing duplicates. Next to this room is a bookstore for the sale of surplus duplicates to students and faculty. The staff offices also include facilities for computer terminals. The next two floors house the Library's regular collection which is available to the public on open shelves. This part of the collection contains some 100,000 books. Large desks for reference and circulation services dominate the center of the second floor. Around them are to be found the reference, bibliography, and periodical collections. On the same floor are shelved books in the fields of language and literature. The third floor houses the circulating, open-shelf collection of the Library, mainly in the areas of Philosophy, Religion, Bible, Rabbinics, Liturgy, and History. On both floors, a variety of types of seating is available for the readers. In two corners of each floor there are semi-enclosed reading rooms. Along the perimeters of the two floors, rows of carrels for individual study are located. In addition, lounge tables and chairs are available on both floors, with many in the area of the periodical display cases and newspaper racks. The second floor also includes office space for the public services staff as well as two large rooms for microfilm and music centers. On the third floor, in an enclosed area, space-saving, high density shelving is installed for the storage of lesser used materials.

The top floor is reserved for the special collections. These include: manuscripts, *Genizah* fragments, incunabula, rare printed books, archives, and graphic materials (prints, photographs, *Ketubbot*, etc.). Readers may use these materials in a reading room adjacent to the special collections stacks. The stacks are equipped with the most up-to-date safety devices and are temperature and humidity controlled. The shelving provides space for a variety of forms and sizes; there are map cases, scroll cabinets, and shelves of a diversity of width and height for folio, regular size, and miniature books. On this floor there are also library offices, individual private studies that will be made available, upon application, to visiting scholars, a small auditorium for lectures, which is equipped with projection facilities, and rooms for binding and photography.

On all the floors there are provisions for display areas of different kinds, enabling the Library to exhibit its holdings in a variety of settings.

With the completion of the new building, it became necessary to strengthen the Library staff. Therefore, the positions of assistant librarian, administrative librarian for public services, administrative librarian for technical services, and curator of graphic materials were established.

Looking to the future, we hope that the excellent collection of materials relating to all aspects of Jewish studies, now housed in an attractive, comfortable, and modern building, will enable the Seminary Library to develop and adopt systems of information retrieval and bibliographical control through automation. This would make available to scholars, as well as the general public, all the accumulated knowledge stored among the pages of the treasures of the Library. This endeavor, as well as the equally important efforts of preserving and restoring the precious originals, will be planned and carried out, whenever possible, in friendly cooperation with other major Jewish libraries in this country. Thus, it is to be hoped that the vast resource of materials relating to the Jewish past, accumulated in American institutions, will become a major source of knowledge and renewal in the life of generations to come.

The Contribution of the Genizah to the Study of Liturgy and Poetry

One hundred years ago, David Kaufmann, a giant of a scholar, whose genius and manifold scholarly contributions place him among the most outstanding representatives of modern Jewish scholarship in the nineteenth century,[1] foretold the immense research potential of the then freshly discovered treasures of the Cairo Genizah. In a Hebrew article, prompted by Solomon Schechter's removal of the Genizah from Cairo to Cambridge, and by Kaufmann's own acquisition of a significant collection of Genizah fragments, Kaufmann wrote:

> At the time when the publication of these treasures will begin, my words will be proven to be true and it will become evident that I did not err and my hope will not remain vain. There will come to light matters about which we did not even dare to dream in our wildest dreams. After long periods of time, when all the treasures of the Genizah will become revealed, it will become possible to match the discoveries against my expectations, and then it will be seen what has become of my dreams.[2]

After a century of Genizah research, Kaufmann's expectations of undreamt of discoveries have become a reality. If some *jinn* would remove all knowledge derived from the Genizah from the works on Jewish

1 On Kaufmann's life and work see Samuel Krauss, in David Kaufmann, *Meḥkarim be-sifruth ha-ivrith shel yeme ha-beinayim* (Jerusalem: Mosad Harav Kook, 1962), pp. 7-35. Dov Schwartz, "On the Contribution of David Kaufmann to the Study of Medieval Jewish Philosophy," in *Jewish Studies*, vol. 36 (1996), pp. 163-173; H.I. Schmelzer, "David Kaufmann (1852-1899): Denker, Gelehrter, Visionar," in: *Judaica*, vol. 55 (1999), pp. 212-219.

2 *Ginzei Kaufmann*, vol. 1, ed. by D.S. Loewinger and A. Scheiber. Budapest, (n.p., 1949), Hebrew dedication page, quoting from Kaufmann's article, "Or ha-ganuz," *Hashiloaḥ*, vol. 2, 1897, pp. 385-393, 481-490. The quotation is on p. 489.

studies, we would not be able to recognize our field. Many fundamental conceptions in the various disciplines of Judaic studies would have to be altered and immense black holes would gape at us in history, literature, Rabbinics, linguistics, and other areas of learning.

In no field would the gap be larger than in the study of liturgy and poetry, for since the earliest days of Genizah publications, these fields have been continuously enriched by discoveries that revolutionized them.

The contributions of the Genizah to various branches of Jewish studies have been examined previously. Fifty years ago, the American Academy for Jewish Research held a series of lectures on the subject. Louis Ginzberg presented a paper on the importance of the Genizah for Talmud and Rabbinics, Shalom Spiegel on its value for religious and secular poetry and Alexander Marx on its significance for Jewish history. Unfortunately, only Marx's paper was published.[3] In 1976, a conference was held at Tel Aviv University devoted to Cairo Genizah research and the papers delivered at the conference were published in book form.[4] In 1996, Tel Aviv University and the Hebrew University arranged jointly to commemorate the centennial of Genizah discoveries with a three-day conference. Finally, in the summer of 1997, the World Congress of Jewish Studies, during its sessions in Jerusalem, celebrated the centennial by a number of lectures and keynote addresses.[5] Inevitably, any attempt to survey Genizah contributions to any field of Jewish studies will have to rely heavily on similar surveys and summaries presented previously. This, of course, applies with equal force to a review of the milestones of Genizah research over the last one hundred years in liturgy and poetry.[6]

3 See *Proceedings of the American Academy for Jewish Research*, vol. 16, 1946-1947, VII-VIII, pp. 183-204.

4 *Te'uda; I. Cairo Geniza Studies*. Ed. by Mordechai A. Friedman (Tel Aviv: Tel Aviv University, 1980). The volume contains the following relevant articles: Ezra Fleischer, "The Contribution of the Geniza to the Study of Medieval Hebrew Religious Poetry" (pp. 83-87); Menahem Schmelzer, "The Piyyutim of Isaac ibn Giat" (See in the Hebrew Séction, pp. 93-98); J. Schirmann, "Secular Hebrew Poetry in the Geniza Manuscripts" (pp. 97-123). All articles are in Hebrew, with English summaries.

5 See the articles listed in the *Program* of the *Twelfth World Congress of Jewish Studies*. Jerusalem, 1997, p. 232.

6 On the *Genizah* and its significance for the history of Hebrew poetry, see the various articles by Menahem Zulay, now collected in his: *Eretz Israel and its Poetry: Studies in Piyyutim from the Cairo Geniza*, ed. by Ephraim Hazan (Jerusalem: Magnes, 1995), pp. 3-124 (in Hebrew). See also: Hayyim Schirmann, *New Hebrew Poems from the Genizah* (Jerusalem: The Israel Academy of Sciences and Humanities, 1965) (in Hebrew). For Fleischer's lecture on the subject see note 19.

Among the first sensational publications from the Genizah was Solomon Schechter's modestly titled "Genizah Specimens."[7] In a short sentence, Schechter introduced the publication of the fragments by claiming that the "fragments represent as it seems portions of the liturgy *in their oldest form*"[8] (emphasis mine). Thus, Schechter immediately catapulted the newly discovered fragments into a position of central importance for the early history of Jewish liturgy. The new texts included, among others, versions of the *Amidah* for weekdays, which in their brevity and economic, concise style clearly ring with the tone of antiquity. Schechter identified the fragments as reflecting the rite of Eretz Yisrael and with this he launched the long efforts of the reconstruction of its standard liturgy. In subsequent years and decades, leading scholars such as Israel Levi, Ismar Elbogen, Jacob Mann, Simha Assaf, Alexander Scheiber and Naftali Wieder[9] discovered and published many new texts that changed the scholarly perception of the development of Jewish liturgy. Elbogen, in his history of Jewish liturgy, first published in 1913,[10] offers a synthesis of its development, utilizing the newly discovered materials for the first time. The emergence of the contours of the Palestinian rite was greeted with great curiosity and enthusiasm, since this rite, in juxtaposition to the Babylonian one, had become almost totally forgotten during the Middle Ages. The new Genizah texts did not only reveal unknown prayer texts, but also showed how Palestinian prayers offered a much livelier variety of parallel liturgical formulations than anything that was known previously. This variety was taken as an indication of an ongoing, somewhat unchecked, creativity and flexibility and it was looked upon as a welcome change from the more frozen and canonized manifestations of liturgical practice.[11]

7 *The Jewish Quarterly Review*, vol. 10, 1898, pp. 654-659. Reprinted in: *Contributions to the Scientific Study of Jewish Liturgy*, ed. by Jakob J. Petuchowski (New York: Ktav, 1970), pp. 373-378. This was Schechter's second publication in this series, the first being his publication of the famous Ben Sira fragments, *ibid.*, pp. 197-206.

8 *Ibid.*, p. 654 (= *Contributions*, 373).

9 See Ezra Fleischer, *Eretz-Israel Prayer and Prayer Rituals as Portrayed in the Geniza Documents* (Jerusalem: Magnes, 1988), pp. 9-11.

10 Ismar Elbogen, *Der juedische Gottesdienst in seiner geschichtlichen Entwicklung* (Leipzig: Fock, 1913). A Hebrew translation, with additional notes, was published in 1972. The book appeared in Raymond Scheindlin's English translation as *Jewish Liturgy: A Comprehensive History* (Philadelphia-New York: JPS-JTS, 1993).

11 See Fleischer, *Eretz-Israel* (above note 9), p. 14, and his criticism of this view.

Alongside the discoveries and studies of the liturgy of the Jews in Eretz Yisrael, fragments relating to other rites and other aspects of liturgical history came to light from the Genizah. Our knowledge and understanding of the liturgy of the Jews of Babylonia, and other later rites, were deepened by Genizah discoveries, made mainly by Wieder.[12] Besides texts relating to individual prayers or liturgical practices, the Genizah enabled scholars to reconstruct entire prayerbooks. Most important of such reconstructions was that of the prayerbook of Saadiah Gaon in the original Judeo-Arabic, although based on a conventional manuscript, but complemented and completed by an extensive array of Genizah fragments.[13] Another discovery of great importance was that of a polemical work by a scholar named Pirkoi ben Baboi, a staunch defender of Babylonian customs, many of them in the area of liturgy, who harshly criticized the customs of the Palestinians. Pirkoi ben Baboi's treatise is a very important source, shedding light on various liturgical practices.[14] A later, but equally fascinating document from the Genizah, deals with a covenant signed by members of a Fostat synagogue who pledge in the year 1211 that they will continue to adhere to their particular Palestinian customs.[15] In the various works emanating from the Geonic period, many of them first published or reconstructed on the basis of Genizah fragments, there are many passages that deal with liturgical matters and ultimately contribute to our knowledge of liturgical phenomena.[16] Needless to say, the rich literature of *piyyut* from the

12 "*Leḥeker minhag Bavel ha-kadmon,*" in: *Tarbiz*, vol. 37 (1968), pp. 135-157, 240-264; his *The Formation of Jewish Liturgy in the East and the West* (Jerusalem: Ben-Zvi Institute, 1998) vol. 1, pp. 13-64 (in Hebrew).

13 *Siddur R. Saadia Gaon*, ed. I. Davidson, S. Assaf, B.I. Joel (Jerusalem: Mekize Nirdamim, 1941). Naftali Wieder published additional fragments of the Siddur, see his "Fourteen New Genizah Fragments of Saadya's Siddur." In: *Saadya Studies*, ed. by E.I.J. Rosenthal (Manchester: Manchester University Press, 1943). See also his *Formation* etc. (above note 12), vol. 2, pp. 648-658.

14 On Pirkoi see now: Robert Brody, *The Geonim of Babylonia and the Shaping of Medieval Jewish Culture* (New Haven: Yale, 1998), pp. 113-117, and the literature mentioned there, p. 113, note 45.

15 Fleischer, *Eretz-Israel*, (above note 9), pp. 218ff.

16 See, e.g., Neil Danzig, *Introduction to Halakhot Pesuqot with a Supplement to Halakhot Pesuqot* (New York: The Jewish Theological Seminary, 1993) (in Hebrew), index, s.v. "*tefillot u-verakhot u-keriath ha-tora,*" pp. 654-655. See now also Neil Danzig, *A Catalogue of Fragments of Halakhah and Midrash from the Cairo Genizah in the Elkan Nathan Adler Collection of the Library of the Jewish Theological Seminary of America* (New York: JTS, 1997), p. 72 (introduction), pp. 328-329 (index). Compare, however, Fleischer, *Eretz-Israel*, (above note 9),

Genizah, about which more later, touches upon many aspects of the standard liturgy, directly or indirectly.

It is legitimate to ask at this point: Where do we stand today in the full utilization of Genizah fragments, particularly in the study of the liturgical practices of Eretz Yisrael? Ezra Fleischer, in his major study of this topic, evaluates and surveys the research and takes account of the major advances and great strides taken since the initial publications of Schechter. Still, Fleischer is blunt in pointing out the limits of what had been achieved and presents the *desiderata* for a future agenda of research that still requires attention. Fleischer explicitly states about his own book — a book containing the richest collection of relevant Genizah materials, much of it discovered by Fleischer himself — that it does not offer a synthesis on the subject. He writes that "a legitimate summary of the subject is still very far away."[17] The reason for this, after 100 years of scholarly research, is that there are still large quantities of unpublished materials in the Genizah, and even the published ones are often so enigmatic that they defy proper interpretation.[18] This situation, of course, is characteristic of other fields of Genizah research as well. The enormous amount of material, its fragmentary and scattered nature, the lack of comprehensive catalogues,[19] make it impossible, even after a century of diligent labor, to gain and to give a full picture of the significance of the Genizah for liturgical (and other) study. Perhaps this explains why there were no papers devoted to a survey of this branch of learning at the Genizah conferences mentioned above and why even Fleischer omitted a discussion of this issue in his address delivered before the plenary session of the Twelfth World Congress of Jewish Studies.[20]

pp. 15-16, who urges caution in using Geonic halakhic materials for the understanding of the actual practice and text of liturgy.

17 Fleischer, *ibid.*, p.11.

18 *Ibid.*, Recently, under the direction of Dr. Uri Ehrlich at Ben Gurion University in Beer Sheva, a project was launched for the purpose of collecting and identifying the information on liturgical fragments from the Cairo Genizah.

19 See now Danzig, *Catalogue* (above note 16), pp. 3-31, for an extensive discussion of the various Genizah collections and the literature about them. Also, recently, the Friedberg Genizah project at New York University was established for the study and cataloging of all Genizah collections.

20 Published in *Haaretz*, October 22, 1997 (*Tarbut ve-sifrut* section, 3). See now: *Jewish Studies*, vol. 38 (1998), pp. 253-265 (Hebrew section).

On the other hand, there exist a number of important papers evaluating the significance of the Genizah for the study of medieval Hebrew poetry, and *piyyut*, liturgical poetry, in particular.[21] The sheer quantity of poetic texts in the Genizah made scholars focus on them from the very beginning of Genizah research. The internal catalogue of the Institute for Medieval Hebrew Poetry at the Hebrew University, under the directorship of Ezra Fleischer, contains references to 56,000 items.[22] And this number does not yet include all the poetic Genizah texts! There is no doubt that the Genizah had added tens of thousands of poems to the corpus of Hebrew poetry. Such a huge mass of new texts commanded the attention of scholars and a constant flow of publications has kept appearing from the very beginning of Genizah scholarship. The vast quantity of poetic pieces in the Genizah is a testimony to the central importance of poetry in the society that is mirrored by it.

Arguably, the most revolutionary discovery in this respect was Israel Davidson's reconstruction of the liturgical poetry of the ancient Palestinian poet, Yannai.[23] The publication of *Mahzor Yannai* by Davidson in 1919 startled the scholarly community. One of the chief features of the surprising character of Yannai's poetry was the fact that it included lengthy, elaborate and intricate poetic compositions for each and every Shabbath of the year. Before Yannai's weekly *piyyut* compositions were published, only poetic embellishments for the holiday services were known. The regular recitation of extensive religious poetry on a weekly basis was taken as an indication of a true appreciation of, and taste for, poetic creativity in Hebrew language and literature. That such creativity existed in Yannai's time, sometime toward the end of Byzantine rule in Palestine, speaks volumes on the cultural conditions of the community. Other Genizah discoveries produced additional rich materials that bear testimony to the popularity of the *genre* in the various Jewish communities. These texts were used as frequent, sometimes daily, insertions (or perhaps in earlier times substitutions) in the standard liturgy.[24] The seemingly insatiable desire for new *piyyutim* is documented

21 See above notes 4-6.

22 Fleischer (above note 9), p. 253.

23 Israel Davidson, *Mahzor Yannai: A Liturgical Work of the VIIth Century* (New York: Jewish Theological Seminary, 1919).

24 See Zulay, *Eretz Israel*, (above note 6), pp. 65-118.

not only by their quantity, but also by a curious document found in the Genizah. True, this document is from a much later time than the period of early *piyyut*, still it shows the demands a community placed on a cantor to produce new compositions in order to please his audience. The document, a letter from 1214, probably written in Alexandria, tells about the efforts of obtaining new poems, even surreptitiously, from as far as Marseilles.[25] This letter, but, of course, much more the evidence of tens of thousands of poems, written by hundreds of poets, most of them totally unknown before the discovery of the Genizah, clearly prove the popularity and centrality of poetic creativity in medieval Jewry.

With the publication of *Mahzor Yannai* in 1919, the interest in the subject increased. The 1920s, but especially the 1930s, may be considered as a most influential period in Genizah research in medieval Hebrew poetry, both religious and secular. A pivotal figure in sponsoring and promoting scholarship in this area was Salman Schocken, a visionary patron of art and culture.[26] First in Germany, and later in Palestine, Schocken enabled young scholars to devote their time and talent to the study of medieval Hebrew poetry. A precondition of such study was the exploration of the thousands of Genizah fragments scattered in the various libraries. In 1930, Schocken established the Institute for the Study of Medieval Hebrew Poetry in Berlin and engaged the services of Hayyim Brody, Hayyim Schirmann, Menahem Zulay and A.M. Habermann to assemble the manuscript materials, mainly in photographs, to carry out research and to publish the poetic texts. The productivity of the Institute was amazing. In a relatively short period of time, many volumes and studies of ancient *piyyut*, of medieval Hebrew poetry in Spain, Germany and Italy appeared.[27] Mention should also be made of another factor that promoted interest in the field. In the post-World War I years, Paul Kahle, a German gentile scholar, attracted some Jewish students to his seminar at the University of Bonn. Kahle was mainly interested in Masoretic studies,

25 See S.D. Goitein, *Jewish Education in Muslim Countries Based on Records from the Cairo Geniza* (Jerusalem: The Ben-Zvi Institute, 1962), pp. 97-103 (in Hebrew).

26 On Schocken see Volker Dahm, *Das juedische Buch im Dritten Reich*, 2nd ed. (Munchen: Beck, 1993), pp. 220-501 and *Der Schocken Verlag/Berlin. Juedische Selbstbehauptung in Deutschland. 1931-1938*. Hrsg. von Saskia Schreuder und Claude Weber (Berlin: Akademie Verlag, 1994).

27 See Zulay, *Eretz Israel*, (above note 6), pp. 41 and 78, note 4 and Peter S. Lehnardt, "Das Forschungsinstitut fuer hebraeische Dichtung und sein Beitrag zur Kenntnis der hebraeischen Dichtung des Mittelalters," in: *Der Schocken Verlag* (above note 26), pp. 299-320.

to a large extent based on Genizah manuscripts. While studying Genizah fragments in search of materials relevant to Masoretic studies, Kahle and his assistants encountered many poetic texts, some of them employing the system of Palestinian vocalization, a subject of great interest to them. Zulay started out working with Kahle and probably it was in Kahle's seminar that his involvement in the research of ancient Palestinian *piyyut* began.[28] As a consequence of the work in Kahle's seminar, a number of doctoral dissertations in early *piyyut* were published in the 1930s.[29]

The crowning achievement of this scholarly activity was the publication, by Schocken, of Zulay's edition of Yannai's poems, in Berlin, in 1938, one of the last Hebrew books to appear in Nazi Germany.[30] While Davidson's edition in 1919 contained the text of ten compositions, Zulay's included 138, albeit most of them fragmentary. The major feat of Zulay's work was the reconstruction of the text, as far as it was possible, out of hundreds of Genizah fragments, many of them tiny scraps. Building on Davidson's pioneering work, Zulay provided the corpus of Yannai's poems, but he did not write a commentary to the poems. Soon after Zulay's edition appeared, Saul Lieberman published a major study on it, in which he discussed the affinity between Yannai's poetry and Talmudic and Midrashic literatures. Lieberman regarded these newly discovered texts as primary sources for new insights into Rabbinic literature and he expressed the hope that the day will come when Yannai's poetry will occupy its rightful place among the folio volumes of Talmud and Midrash, because, as he put it, that is where it belongs![31] Some forty years after Zulay's edition, Zvi Meir Rabinovitz had at least partially fulfilled the hope expressed by Lieberman. He prepared an edition of Yannai's poems, including some unpublished texts, and accompanied it by a detailed commentary and introductions.[32] Through these long decades of scholar-

28 Zulay, *op. cit.* (note 27), p. 40.

29 E.g. Zulay's dissertation, *Zur Liturgie der babylonischen Juden* (Stuttgart: Kohlhammer, 1933) and R. Edelmann, *Zur Fruehgeschichte des Mahzor* (Stuttgart: Kohlhammer, 1934).

30 *Piyyute Yannai. Liturgical Poems of Yannai.* Collected from Geniza Manuscripts and other sources and published by Menahem Zulay (Berlin: Schocken/Jewish Publishing Company, 1938).

31 *Hazzanut Yannai*, now included in Saul Lieberman, *Studies in Palestinian Talmudic Literature* (Jerusalem: Magnes, 1991), pp. 123-152, (in Hebrew). The quote is on p. 152.

32 *The Liturgical Poems of Rabbi Yannai according to the Triennial Cycle of the Pentateuch and the Holidays.* Critical edition with introductions and commentary by Zvi Meir Rabinovitz, 2 volumes (Jerusalem: Bialik Institute, 1985-1987).

ship, Yannai emerged as a central figure in ancient Jewish literature. A great innovator, the one who introduced rhyme into Hebrew poetry in a systematic and consistent fashion, Yannai, through his language, poetry, use of Rabbinic material, presentation of religious belief and practice, polemics with Byzantine Christianity, and references to the realia of his times, offers a fresh, new picture of the life of the Jewish community in Eretz Yisrael, some time around the fifth-sixth century. Shalom Spiegel, in his inimitable Hebrew, characterized Yannai as follows:

> זה כחו של ינאי, ששרשיו משולחים אל מעמקי הדורות ויונקותיו יוצאות על עיינות בראשית. מקורות המורשה הקדמונית טרם דללו בימיו... עוד יש בהם כדי לרוות נפש הדור ולכלכל צרכי תקופה. כמעט כל הניצוצות, שנתחלקו מתורותם של ראשונים, מבריקים בזיום ומבהיקים בעיזוזם עוד גם מתחת פטישו של ינאי, יורש הגדת חז״ל, ויוצר בצלמה ובצביונה... תום של כיבוש ראשון לו... זה חינו של ינאי, שהוא כלו ישן ואינו אלא חדש, וצמודים ילכו בו אחרון וגם ראשון. קשי זריעה ורינת קציר נפגשו, בשורת מחרשה וברכת חרמש נשקו.[33]

Yannai had some predecessors and, of course, many successors. It was again the Genizah that yielded the works of many poets and that enabled scholarship to establish criteria for classifying their poetry as pre-classical, classical, and late. The activity spans half a millennium, from ca. 500 to ca. 1000, in Eretz Yisrael, Babylonia and other Mediterranean centers. The names and works of poets during this long period of time were totally unknown before the Genizah discoveries revealed them. Today, we have scholarly editions of the works of such poets as the Anonymus,[34] Simeon berabbi Megas,[35] Yehudah,[36] Eleazar berabbi Kilar,[37] and others, as well as editions of related materials.[38] The work continues and the liturgical

33 Shalom Spiegel, *The Fathers of Piyyut: Texts and Studies Toward a History of the Piyyut in Eretz Yisrael.* Selected from his literary estate and edited by Menahem H. Schmelzer (New York: Jewish Theological Seminary, 1996), pp. 385-386 (in Hebrew).

34 *The Pizmonim of the Anonymus.* Critical edition with introduction and commentary by Ezra Fleischer (Jerusalem: The Israel Academy of Sciences and Humanities, 1974).

35 *Liturgical Poems of Sim'on bar Megas.* Critical edition with commentary and introduction by Joseph Yahalom (Jerusalem: The Israel Academy of Sciences and Humanities, 1984).

36 *Wouter Jacques Van Bekkum, Hebrew Poetry from Late Antiquity; Liturgical Poems of Yehudah.* Critical edition with introduction and commentary (Leiden: Brill, 1998).

37 Shulamit Alizur (sic!) [= Elizur], *The Piyyutim of Rabbi El'azar birabbi Qillar* (Jerusalem: Magnes, 1988).

38 Joseph Yahalom published, among others: *Mahzor Eretz Israel: A Geniza Codex* (Jerusalem:

poetry of various poets is in the process of being assembled and prepared for edition, among them the poems of Pinehas ha-Kohen of Tiberias and of the Babylonian poet, Joseph Al-Baradani.[39]

Along with the discovery of brand new texts by hitherto unknown authors, Genizah scholars have also unearthed unknown works by well-known writers. The work of the enigmatic poet, Eleazar Kalir (or Kilir), to be distinguished from that of a poet with a deceptively similar name, Eleazar berabbi Kilar, mentioned above, has been part of the synagogue liturgy throughout the Middle Ages and into modern times. Numerous poems of his were recited on holidays and fastdays in Italy, France, Germany, and, later, in Eastern Europe. The Genizah, however, contains many unknown compositions by him, and although some have been published, many of them still await editing, and a critical edition of all his poems, from conventional as well as Genizah sources, is still a great *desideratum* and is a long time away.[40] The poetic work of Saadiah Gaon and Hai (Hayya) Gaon became known to a great extent as a result of Genizah discoveries; and the role played, especially by Saadia, in the emergence and development of a new style of Hebrew poetry in tenth and eleventh century Spain, forced scholars to re-evaluate previous conceptions concerning the birth of Golden Age Hebrew Poetry.[41] Before Saadia's poetry was published, mainly from Genizah fragments, Dunash

Magnes, 1987) and *Palestinian Vocalised Piyyut Manuscripts in the Cambridge Genizah Collections* (Cambridge: University Press, 1997). Among Shulamit Elizur's publications are: *Rabbi Jehuda Berabbi Binjaminis Carmina Cuncta* (Jerusalem: Mekize Nirdamim, 1988); *Shiv'atot for the Weekly Tora Readings* (Jerusalem: World Union of Jewish Studies, 1993); *Poet at a Turning Point: Rabbi Yehoshua bar Khalfa and his Poetry* (Jerusalem: Ben Zvi, 1994); *She'erit Yosef: The Piyyutim of Rabbi Yosef Ha'levi he-haver* (Jerusalem: Magnes, 1994).

39 "Pinehas" by Shulamit Elizur, see *Tarbiz*, vol. 66 (1997), p. 586, note 11 and Al-Baradani by Tovah Beeri, see Fleischer (above note 9), 260. [See now: Tova Beeri, *The "Great Cantor" of Baghdad; Ther Liturgical Poems of Joseph ben Hayyim al-Baradani* (Jerusalem, Ben-Zvi Institute, 2002), The edition of Pinehas' *Piyyutim* by Elizur, is scheduled to be published in 2004.]

40 See the various publications of Shulamit Elizur, among them: *Kedushah ve-Shir: Kedushatoth le-Shabbatoth ha-Nehamah le-Rabbi Eleazar berabbi Kilir* (Jerusalem: n.p., 1988) and *Be-Todah ve-Shir: Shivatoth le-Arba ha-Parashiyoth le-Rabbi Eleazar berabbi Kalir* (Jerusalem: R. Mass, 1991). See also Ezra Fleischer, *The Yozer: Its Emergence and Development* (Jerusalem: Magnes, 1984), pp. 29-30 (in Hebrew).

41 On Saadia's poetry see Menahem Zulay, *Ha-Askolah ha-Paytanit shel Rav Saadya Gaon* (Jerusalem: The Schocken Institute, 1964) and the various works published by Joseph Tobi, listed by Ezra Fleischer in his "Mekomo shel Rav Saadya Gaon be-Toledoth ha-Shirah ha-ivrith," in: *Pe'amim*, 54 (1993), 4, note 2. On the poetry of Hai Gaon see Ezra Fleischer, "Studies in the

ibn Labrat and other Spanish Hebrew poets were regarded as the founders of a new school of poetry, shaped and influenced by Arabic poetical form and contents. Now, Saadia's poetic work is considered to have been path-breaking in introducing new forms and subjects and is judged to have been the foundation on which his followers in the Spanish school developed their work. Saadia is thus credited with having exerted lasting influence on poetry as he did in Jewish philosophy, exegesis and law.[42]

The Genizah has also been the source of new texts and new understandings in the field of Hebrew poetry, liturgical as well as secular, during the Golden Age in Spain. Poems by famous as well as obscure poets came to light and documentary evidence on some of the major figures of the period have surfaced from the Genizah. The best known of such discoveries in this respect is the material identified by S.D. Goitein on the life of Judah Halevi and on his pilgrimage from Spain via Alexandria on the way to the Holy Land. Besides Goitein, who discovered and published autograph letters by Judah Halevy, Shraga Abramson and Hayyim Schirmann contributed greatly to the reconstruction of minute details of the great poet's life.[43] The poetic oeuvres of the classic poets, Samuel ha-nagid, Solomon ibn Gabirol, Moses ibn Ezra and Abraham ibn Ezra were enlarged and transformed quantitatively and qualitatively.[44] The work of less famous poets, such as Joseph ibn Abitur and Isaac ibn Ghiyat and many others, especially those who were active in the generation of Moses ibn Ezra and Judah Halevi, has also become much better known and understood as a result of the large number of poems added to their oeuvres

Poetry of R. Hai Gaon," in: *Papers on Medieval Hebrew Literature Presented to A.M. Habermann* ed. by Zvi Malachi (Jerusalem: R. Mass, 1977), pp. 239-274 (in Hebrew).

42 Fleischer, *ibid.*, 4-17.

43 See S.D. Goitein, *A Mediterranean Society.* Volume V: *The Individual* (Berkeley: University of California Press, 1988), pp. 448-468. These materials are collected and analyzed in a forthcoming book by Moshe Gil and Ezra Fleischer. [See now: Moshe Gil and Ezra Fleischer *Yehuda ha-Levi and his Circle: 55 Geniza Documents* (Jerusalem, World Union of Jewish Studies, 2001; in Hebrew.]

44 *Divan Shmuel Hanagid*, ed. by Dov Jarden (Jerusalem: Hebrew Union College Press, 1966), List of Genizah Manuscripts: pp. 345-346; *Solomon Ibn Gabirol: Secular Poems*, ed. by H. Brody and J. Schirmann (Jerusalem: The Schocken Institute, 1974), List of Manuscripts: pp. 315-318; *The Liturgical Poetry of Rabbi Solomon ibn Gabirol*, ed. by Dov Jarden (Jerusalem: n.p., 1972), List of Manuscripts: pp. 665-686; *Moses ibn Ezra, Shirei ha-Hol*, ed. by H. Brody (Jerusalem: Schocken, 1942), vol. 2, List of Manuscripts: pp. 17-24; *The Religious Poems of Abraham ibn Ezra*, ed. by Israel Levin (Jerusalem: The Israel Academy of Sciences and Humanities, 1975), vol. 1, List of Genizah Manuscripts: pp. 17-18.

through a steady stream of Genizah discoveries.[45] It is also significant to note that even in the case of poems that had been known previously from conventional sources, the Genizah has often yielded manuscripts, written in the lifetime of the authors, that changed readings and supplied information on the circumstances in which they were composed, the latter mostly through the Arabic superscriptions appearing at the head of the poems.[46]

There is one particular *genre* of Hebrew poetry for which the Genizah is the main source. Hebrew *muwashshahs*, metrical strophic poems (also called girdle poems), many with a final strophe in Arabic or in a mixture of Arabic and Romance vernacular, are richly represented among the Genizah fragments. An extensive literature deals with the artistic, linguistic and cultural import of this popular form. This typical Andalusian poetic composition, first used for secular poetry only, later became part and parcel of religious and liturgical poetry as well, albeit without the vernacular endings, and it spread from Spain to other centers of Jewish creativity.[47]

The steady flow of new information, the constant enrichment of the field with new discoveries, some revolutionary and some more routine, enabled scholars to produce large and significant syntheses.

Ezra Fleischer's history of liturgical Hebrew poetry in the Middle Ages, and the history of Hebrew poetry in Spain, by Hayyim Schirmann, complemented by Ezra Fleischer's up-to-date notes, would not be the books that they are, if not for the drastic transformation of the discipline of both secular and religious Hebrew poetry, caused by the century-long intensive Genizah scholarship.[48]

45 See J. Schirmann, "Poets Contemporary with Mose ibn Ezra and Jehuda Hallevi," in: *Studies of the Research Institute for Hebrew Poetry = Yediot ha-Makhon le-Heker ha-Shira ha-Ivrit*, vol. 2 (1936), pp. 117-212. On Ibn Abitur see Ezra Fleischer, "Beḥinoth be-shirato shel Rabbi Yosef ibn Abitur," in: *Asufoth*, 4 (1990), pp. 127-188. On Ibn Ghiyat's work see Menahem H. Schmelzer, *The Poetic Work of Isaac ibn Giyat*. Doctoral dissertation (New York: Jewish Theological Seminary, 1965) (unpublished) and his article, above note 4.

46 See Schirmann in his article mentioned above in note 4, pp. 101-102.

47 *Ibid.*, pp. 102-105.

48 Ezra Fleischer, *Hebrew Liturgical Poetry in the Middle Ages* (Jerusalem: Keter, 1975) (in Hebrew); Jefim Schirmann, *The History of Hebrew Poetry in Muslim Spain*. Ed., supplemented and annotated by Ezra Fleischer (Jerusalem: Magnes, 1995) (in Hebrew).

Where do we go from here? Is there still room for further Genizah studies? As in the area of standard liturgy, so in the field of *piyyut*-literature, in Eretz Yisrael and in the Orient, there are still untold unedited fragments of the work of known as well as unknown poets. Zulay once wrote about his dream of 30 volumes of poetry that could be published on the basis of the Genizah.[49] Much of it still awaits identification, analysis and publication. As mentioned above, a critical edition of the *piyyutim* of Eleazar Kalir is still to be accomplished. New editions of Golden Age Hebrew poetry in Spain should also be undertaken. Judah Halevy's religious and secular poetry and Moses ibn Ezra's religious poems are chief candidates for such new editions. The accessibility of Genizah collections from the former Soviet Union, particularly that of the Firkovich collection in St. Petersburg,[50] pose new opportunities in Genizah research as do the advanced technologies of photography and computer science.[51]

The dreams of David Kaufmann and Menahem Zulay are still far from being completely fulfilled. If we could come back for a celebration of the bi-centennial of the Genizah, we would still possibly be told that the long journey of research in the inexhaustible treasure trove of the Genizah is not yet quite over.

49 Zulay, *Eretz Israel* (above note 6), p. 34.

50 Joseph Yahalom, "Ginzei Leningrad ve-ḥeker shirath ḥayyav shel Rabbi Yehudah ha-Levi," in: *Pe'amim* 46-47 (1991), pp. 55-73. Ezra Fleischer, "Shirim ve-shivrei shirim hadashim le-Rabbi Yehudah ha-Levi," in: *Meḥkerei Yerushalayim be-sifruth ivrith* 13 (1992), pp. 65-94.

51 The Friedberg Genizah Project (see above note 19) will utilize these new technologies.

Some Examples of Poetic Reformulations of Biblical and Midrashic Passages in Liturgy and Piyyut

It is a commonplace that newer layers of Hebrew literature are stylistically dependent on quotations from Bible and Rabbinic literature. Sometimes the later work quotes the Biblical verse or the Rabbinic passage word for word, sometimes it reworks it. When the text is reworked, it is interesting to examine what the principles are, if any, which guide the authors when they substitute new words for the ones that appear in the original.

Several scholars gave examples of this practice in the literature of *piyyut*[1] A few more examples, from standard liturgy as well as from early *piyyut* are provided in the following, with the hope that perhaps in the future a more comprehensive treatment of the subject could be offered.

I

In the blessing over the new moon, we read אשר במאמרו/ ברא שחקים/ וברוח פיו/ כל צבאם/ חוק וזמן/ נתן בהם/ שלא ישנו/ את תפקידם.[2] These lines are composed in one of the favorite meters of ancient Hebrew poetry, namely

1 On the uses of the Biblical idiom in the works of early *payyetanim* in general, see: Ezra Fleischer, *Shirath ha-Kodesh ha-Ivrith Bimei ha-Benayyim* (Jerusalem, 1977), p. 98-104; esp. pp. 103-104; *Piyyutei Yosse ben Yosse*, ed. by Aharon Mirsky (Jerusalem, 1977), p. 42ff, where he formulates four basic rules which characterize Yosse ben Yosse's employment of Biblical language. On the language of *piyyut* in general, see: Yosef Yahalom, *Sefat ha-Shir Shel ha-Piyyut ha-Eretz Yisraeli ha-Kadum* (Jerusalem, 1985). The particular phenomenon which is the subject of this paper is discussed in connection with Yannai's poems by Z.M. Rabinovitz in the introduction to his edition of *Mahzor Piyyutei Rabbi Yannai* (Jerusalem, 1985), vol. 1, pp. 30-33. See also: A. Mirsky, "Mahazavtan Shel Zuroth ha-Piyyut," in *Yedioth ha-Makhon le-Heker ha-Shira ha-Ivrith*, vol. 7, 1958, p. 29 and Yahalom, *op. cit.* p. 145.

2 This is an early text which is already found in the Babylonian Talmud, Sanhedrin 42a.

two words in each verse of a poetic line which divides into four parts.[3] The lines are based on the following biblical verses.

1. Psalms 33:6: בדבר ה׳ שמים נעשו/ וברוח פיו כל צבאם
2. Psalms 148:3-6: הללוהו שמש וירח/ הללוהו כל כוכבי אור/ הללוהו שמי השמים...כי הוא צוה ונבראו/ ויעמידם לעד לעולם/ חק נתן ולא יעבר

They contain two word-for-word quotations, וברוח פיו כל צבאם and חק נתן. The rest is paraphrase.

Now let us analyze the text: the usual liturgical blessing formula requires that it begins with אשר. One would expect this word to continue with a slightly adjusted first part of Psalms 33:6, such as e.g.: אשר בדברו שמים נעשו, however, this is not the case. Instead of בדבר ה׳ we have במאמרו; the common שמים is replaced by the loftier שחקים, while ברא becomes a substitute for נעשו. The choice of ברא is predicated on the frequent use of this verb in liturgical blessings, on its occurrence in the just quoted Psalms 148:5, and perhaps on such Rabbinic models as e.g.: בעשרה מאמרות נברא העולם[4] which parallels the phrase במאמרו ברא of the blessing. The second part of Psalms 33:6 fortuitously contains exactly four words: וברוח פיו כל צבאם and accordingly it fits into the poetic scheme perfectly. The next line חק וזמן נתן בהם/ שלא ישנו את תפקידם paraphrases Psalms 148:6: ויעמידם לעד לעולם חק נתן ולא יעבר, wherein the phrase שלא ישנו is in the liturgical style of the Rabbis.[5] Otherwise the line retains two key words from the Biblical verse: חק נתן.

We may formulate the principles emerging from the above reworking:

1. The use of the common two word/four part poetic line and the clever embedding of a verbatim quote from the Biblical verse into it.
2. The use of "loftier" words instead of "common" ones.
3. The mixing of Biblical, Rabbinic and liturgical vocabulary.

3 See: Mirsky, *Piyyutei Yosse ben Yosse*, p. 47ff; Benjamin Hrushovski "Note on the Systems of Hebrew Versification," *The Penguin Book of Hebrew Verse*, edited and translated by T. Carmi (New York, 1981), pp. 60-61.

4 Pirkei Avoth 5:1.

5 Cf. Mirsky's analysis of the style of the Alainu prayer in his: *Piyyut: Hitpathuto be-Eretz Yisrael* (Jerusalem, 1990), pp. 72-73 (originally published in the periodical *Jerusalem*, Vol. 2, 1967, pp. 161-179). He calls attention to שלא וכו׳ constructions in liturgical passages.

II

In the *Amidah* for *mussaf* for the New Moon we read זכרון לכולם יהיו/ ותשועת נפשם מיד שונא. This is based on Numbers 10:9: ונזכרתם לפני ה׳ אלקיכם ונושעתם מאויביכם. The author of the prayer subtly reworks the verse. He changes the text from the second person plural to third person plural, the verbal forms ונזכרתם and ונושעתם to the nominal forms: זכרון and ותשועת נפשם, he adds the word נפש and substitutes מיד שונא for מאויביכם. In Numbers it is God who is speaking to Israel and the context, although it mentions the New Moon, is God's delivery of Israel from its enemies. In the liturgical passage a statement is made in the third person plural about Israel and New Moon is associated with atonement. Atonement for sins, and not delivery in battle, is the subject of the prayer. This is then the reason for the introduction of נפש, which appears in: ותשועת נפשם. Perhaps the substitution of שונא for אויב takes place so as to create phonetic assonance with תשועת נפשם. This example shows us how a liturgical-Rabbinic reformulation shifts the emphasis of the Biblical verse and gives it a new, midrashic, meaning.

III

We read in one of the *Avodah* poems of Yose ben Yose: קדושים יבדילו איש מנוהו.[6] This line is, of course, a paraphrase of Mishna Yoma 1:1: מפרישין כהן גדול מביתו. For the Rabbinic מפרישין the poet gives us the Biblical יבדילו and the grammatical form is changed from the participle, which is common in Rabbinic style, to the Biblically favored imperfect.[7] The word איש designates the High Priest, according to Mishna Yoma 1:3: ואומרים לו אישי כהן גדול. Finally, the prosaic מביתו becomes the poetic מנוהו.[8] Thus, the simple statement in the Mishna is transformed into a quasi-Biblical and allusive poetic line.

6 *Piyyutei Yosse ben Yosse*, ed. Mirsky, p. 183.

7 See Rabinovitz, *Mahzor Piyyutei Rabbi Yannai*, Vol. 1 pp. 30-31 and note 21.

8 In Isaac ibn Ghiyyat *Seder Avodah*, we read: לשבעה לקחתיך להטהר וכו׳ מן הנוה אני לקחתיך. *Shirei Rabbi Yizhak ibn Ghiyyat*: tentative edition by Yonah David (Jerusalem, 1987), p. 144. This, of course, is based on 2 Samuel 7:8, but it seems that ibn Ghiyyat also had Yosse ben Yosse's passage in mind.

IV

Eleazar birabbi Qilir, commonly known as Kalir, in one of his compositions which deals with matters concerning the red heifer and which is recited on *shabbath parah*, says:

רָעַד כְּהִסְכִּית טַעַם תְּחִלַּת מִשְׁנָתָה,/ פָּרָה בַּת שְׁתַּיִם עֶגְלָה בַּת שְׁנָתָהּ
בְּצֵר צִיר תַּחַן כְּקָשַׁב שְׁמוּעָתָהּ/ נָא מֶנִּי יִפְרֶה מוֹרֶה הֲלָכָה לְשַׁעְתָּהּ
...
רֶמֶז בְּוְיִקְחוּ אֵלֶיךָ הֱיוֹת פָּרָתוֹ מִתְמֶדֶת/ שֶׁכָּל־הַפָּרוֹת כָּלוֹת וְשֶׁלְּךָ לָעַד עוֹמֶדֶת.[9]

Compare this to the following passage in *Pesikta Derav Kahana*:

ויקחו אליך פרה... א״ר יוסי בר׳ חנינה רמזו שכל הפרות בטילות ושלך קיימות. ר׳ אחא בשם ר׳ יוסי בר׳ חנינה בשעה שעלה לשמי מרום שמע קולו של הקב״ה יושב ועוסק בפרשת פרה ואומ׳ הלכה משם אומרה, ״ר׳ אליעזר או׳ עגלה בת שנתה ופרה בת שתים״, אמ׳ משה לפני הקב״ה, רבון העולמים, העליונים והתחתונים ברשותך ואת יושב ואו׳ הלכה משמו של בשר ודם? אמ׳ לו הקב״ה, משה, צדיק אחד עתיד לעמוד בעולמי ועתיד לפתוח בפרשת פרה תחילה, ״ר׳ אליעזר אומ׳ עגלה בת שנתה ופרה בת שתים״. אמר לפניו, רבון העולמים, יהי רצון שיהי׳ מחלציי וכו׳[10]

There is no doubt that Kalir used Rabbi Yosef berabbi Hanina's statement and adopted it poetically. He composed it in rhyme and employed acrostics. He further enhanced the poetic character of the piece by exchanging Rabbinic expressions for Biblical ones and by using rare, lofty words instead of common ones. בטילות in the phrase שכל הפרות בטילות[11] thus became the Biblical כלות and קיימת turned into לעד עומדת alluding to such Biblical verses as Psalms 19:10: עומדת לעד and Ecclesiastes 1:4: לעולם עומדת. The reworking of the rest of the passage is even more interesting. Here Kalir does not refer to Moses by name, but calls him by the emblematic expression ציר. Instead of the simple שמע we have קשב, a poetic synonym of the former. The word order of the statement of R. Eliezer is reversed for the sake of the rhyme: in place of עגלה בת שנתה ופרה

9 *Atzurah u-Mufrashah*, Davidson, *Thesaurus*, alef 7260 [*Seder Avodath Yisrael*, ed. S. Baer, Berlin 1937, pp. 692-693].

10 Ed. Mandelbaum, pp. 72-73.

11 Leopold Zunz, *Literaturgeschichte der synagogalen Poesie* (Berlin, 1865), p. 19 mentions the passage שכל הפרות וכו׳ as one in which Kalir reworks a certain *pesikta* almost word for word.

בת שתים Kalir has פרה בת שתים עגלה בת שנתה. Finally, יהי רצון שיהי׳ מחלציי is expressed as נא מני יפרה. For the Rabbinic יהי רצון we have the Biblical נא and for שיהי׳ מחלציי we find the Biblical מני יפרה. יפרה occurs in this particular grammatical form only once, in Isaiah 11:1. We can detect here a subtle allusion to the contents of the Isaiah verse and the one following it, ונצר משרשיו יפרה ונחה עליו רוח ה׳ וגו׳, and we can relate it to the message of the midrashic passage in which Moses prays for and is promised an offspring upon whom the spirit of wisdom shall rest. Despite this conspicuous use of the Biblical idiom within the confines of the *piyyutic* genre, the overall midrashic mood and contents of the passage are retained, as are some phrases from the Midrash (שמועה, מורה הלכה).

Kalir presented us here with a *piyyutic* fusion of Biblical and Rabbinic allusions and vocabularies.

V

In another *piyyut* by Kalir dealing with the red heifer we read:

אֲצִילֵי עַם עוֹלֵי גוֹלָה
כְּחָשׁ בּוֹא קֵץ גְאוּלָּה
עָלוּ בְנוֹת בַּיִת בְּגִילָּה
...
זָמְמוּ בְנוֹת בָּתֵּי חֲצֵרִים
עַל צְחִיחַ סֶלַע מְבֻוצָּרִים
...
בְּתוֹכָם נוֹלָדִים וְשָׁם בָּרִים
עַד יֻוגְדְּלוּ בְּכֹחַ כְּגִיבּוֹרִים
בְּעֵת יִפְרְחוּ כְּבַעֲלֵי דְבָרִים
יַגִּישׁוּ לָמוֹ אֵיתָנֵי שְׁוָרִים
...
יָבִיאוּ אַיִל מוּקְרָן כְּמַטָּרָה[12]

This poem is based on Mishna and Tosefta Parah, chapter 3. It is instructive to examine how Kalir transforms these legal texts into a *piyyutic* one. There is a brief statement of Rabbi Yehuda in the Tosefta: מעשים אלו עשו כשעלו מן הגולה, which refers to the ingenious methods

12 Ed. by Shulamit Elizur in *Kobez al Yad*, vol. 10 (20), 1982, pp. 36-38.

invented by the rabbis at the time of the return of the exiles from Babylonia. These methods were used by them when they were confronted with the problem of preparing the first red heifer, an act which requires ritual purity, at a time when the exiles were in a state of ritual defilement. The anonymous authorities alluded to by Rabbi Yehuda become אצילי עם in the *piyyut*. Their behavior is described as joyous when they learn about the impending redemption. Nothing of this is found in Rabbi Yehuda's statement. Again we find the substitution of simple phrases by more unusual ones, the phrase על גבי סלע of the Mishna and Tosefta source appears in the poem as על צחיח סלע quoting Ezekiel 24:7. In the Tosefta we read about שוורים שכריסם רחבה, a rather crass expression. Kalir turns this into a much more elegant איתני שוורים, hinting at the Biblical quote איתן מושבך in Numbers 24:21. Similarly, for the Mishna's זכר של רחלים Kalir prefers איל מקורן (cf. Psalms 69:32 מקרין).

The passage בעת יפרחו כבעלי דברים is not only stylistically new, but is also useful for the proper understanding of the sources on which it is based.

According to Tosefta Parah 3:2 children were reared in isolation until they reached the age of 18 so that they should not be ritually defiled and should be mature enough to perform the tasks required of them. The late Professor Saul Lieberman, on the basis of the text as quoted by some *Rishonim*, emended the passage to read 7 or 8 years old instead of 18 years old. He explained that the error crept into the text as a result of misreading the original ז' ח' for י"ח.[13] Why was the age 7 or 8 established for these children for this particular ritual action? Elsewhere in the Mishna (Gittin 5:7) we read: הפעוטות מקחן מקח וממכרן ממכר במטלטלין. Lieberman explained the meaning of the word פעוטות deriving from the Greek and meaning seven-year-old children.[14] At that age minors were deemed capable of transacting certain kinds of business with some degree of competence. The same age was chosen for the children who were involved in the preparations for the red heifer. Kalir knew an uncorrupted version of the Tosefta passage according to which the required age of the children was to be 7 or 8. Being aware of the Mishna passage in Gittin and of the fact that in Talmudic literature parties to a business transaction are

13 *Tosefeth Rishonim*, vol. 3 (Jerusalem, 1939), pp. 215-216.

14 *Siphre Zutta* (New York, 1968), pp. 137-139 and *Tosefta ki-Fshutah, Nashim* (New York, 1973), pp. 847-848.

frequently referred to as בעלי דברים, Kalir rephrased ומגדלות שם בניהן עד שיהו בני שבע או שמונה as בעת יפרחו כבעלי דברים. Thus Kalir's *piyyut* provides further testimony to the correctness of the Tosefta emendation.

In this example, in addition to the features which were already mentioned, we find an attempt by the *payyetan* to provide some kind of setting for an event which the sources mention in the most rudimentary fashion only and we see him trying to replace some crass phrases by more elegant ones. Finally, his rephrasing helps us to understand the original passage properly.

VI

A section of Kalir's composition for Passover[15] is clearly based on an old Midrash. In the Mechilta[16] (and parallel sources) we read: וכן אתה מוצא בכל מקום שגלו ישראל כביכול גלתה שכינה עמהם, גלו למצרים... גלו לבבל... גלו לעילם... גלו לאדום. For גלו, repeated four times, we find in Kalir's composition: הובאו, נדו, נעו and only once: ובגלותם. Through this simple change, Kalir avoided monotonous uniformity.

VII

The *silluk* to Kalir's *kerova* for Sukkoth[17] is based on a midrash in *Pesikta Derav Kahana*[18] and parallels. Both sources contain a series of analogies concerning the four species.

Let us examine a few of these. In the Midrash we read: פרי עץ הדר, זה הקב"ה דכתיב ביה הוד והדר לבשת (תהלים ק"ד א'). Kalir, on the other hand, has: פרי עץ הדר/ לְבַקֹּדֶשׁ נאדר. It is possible that Kalir here had a different version of the statement. Instead of the prooftext just quoted, he may have had a version with a prooftext: מי כמכה נאדר בקדש (Exodus 15:11). Accordingly, Kalir's formulation may be an indication of a variant text of the Midrash. Kalir continues: ענפי הדסים/ לצג בין ההדסים. The midrashic source has: וענף עץ עבות, זה הק' והוא עומד בין ההדסים (זכרי' א' ח'). Despite the fact that the word עומד

15 *Be-Eser Makoth Patrusim Hifrakhta*, *Mahzor Pessah*, ed. Y. Fraenkel (Jerusalem 1993), p. 123.

16 Ed. Horovitz-Rabin, pp. 51-52.

17 *Ekekha ba-Rishon*, *Mahzor Sukkoth*, ed. D. Goldschmidt and Y. Fraenkel (Jerusalem, 1981), pp. 106-107.

18 Ed. Mandelbaum, pp. 414-415.

is part of the Biblical prooftext, the *payyetan* changes it. Since עומד is too pedestrian, the *payyetan* prefers to avoid it. He chooses instead a word for which *payyetanim* have a special fondness: the verb נצג and uses it in its shortened forms, hence צג for עמד.[19] When Kalir uses his own *payyetanic voice*, even a Biblical quotation is subject to his stylistic transformation.

Further in the same *piyyut* we read: בהדר לחשוב בְּלוּיַת עֶדְנָה. The corresponding passage in the Midrash has: פרי עץ הדר, זו אמנו שרה שהידרה הקב"ה בשיבה טובה דכתיב ואברהם ושרה זקנים (בראשית י"ח י"א). The Midrash makes good sense in playing on הדר which is used in connection with old age (cf. Leviticus 19:32) (and therefore applies to matriarch Sarah) and which is also a keyword in the passage dealing with the four species (Leviticus 23:40).

On the other hand, Kalir's בְּלוּיַת עֶדְנָה not only lacks the element of analogy, but also creates a contrast (דבר והיפוכו)[20] with הדר of the four species. It seems that Kalir here chose to use an emblematic expression, בְּלוּיַת עֶדְנָה, instead of following the analogy of the Midrash, because his esthetic sense demanded an adherence to deep-rooted *payyetanic* practice. This practice preferred an emblematic expression, often riddle-like and surprising, even though it was not connected to the midrashic analogy directly. Exactly the same applies to another line in the *piyyut*: בערבה להזכיר וערבי נחל, זה יוסף. מה ערבה זו כמושה אח לעבד הוקנה which replaces the midrashic: יבישה בפני שלשה המינים, כך מת יוסף לפני אחיו.

It is to be hoped that a systematic, comprehensive study of liturgical and *payyetanic* texts for search of patterns of stylistic reworkings of Biblical and Rabbinic sources will yield results for further understanding of the esthetic standards which guided their authors.

19 On the frequent use of this verb by the *payyetanim*, see: Yahalom, *op. cit.*, pp. 87-88, where he also quotes our passage.

20 On the use of the hermeneutical rule דבר והיפוכו in *piyyut* see: Mirsky, "Mahazavtan" etc., (see above, note 1), pp. 68-80.

How Was the High Priest Kept Awake on the Night of Yom Ha-Kippurim?

The late Professor Saul Lieberman, of blessed memory, in his commentary on Tosefta Kippurim utilized the texts of the *sidrei avodah* (liturgical poems describing the Temple Service on the Day of Atonement) whenever these shed light on a relevant Tosefta passage. His comments gave new meaning to many lines of *avodah* poems and scholars in their respective works routinely quote Professor Lieberman's observations when trying to elucidate the often obscure sense of these liturgical/literary texts.[1]

The Rabbinic sources, Mishnah, Tosefta, the Jerusalem and the Babylonian Talmud report briefly on how the High Priest was kept awake on the night preceding the Day of Atonement, so as to avoid accidental ritual defilement. In the Mishnah we read:

יומא פ"א מ"ו-ז:
אם היה חכם דורש ואם לאו תלמידי חכמים דורשין לפניו
ואם רגיל לקרות קורא ואם לאו קורין לפניו.
ובמה קוראין לפניו?
באיוב ובעזרא ובדברי הימים.
זכריה בן קבוטל אומר:
פעמים הרבה קראתי לפניו בדניאל.
בקש להתנמנם, פרחי כהונה מכין לפניו באצבע צרדה,
ואומרים לו:
אישי כהן גדול, עמוד והפג אחת על הרצפה!
ומעסיקין אותו עד שיגיע זמן השחיטה.

1 E.g. Ezra Fleischer in his commentary to Shelomo ha-Bavli's *seder avodah*, in his: *The Poems of Shelomo ha-Bavli* (Jerusalem: The Israel Academy of Sciences and Humanities, 1973), pp. 153-189 (in Hebrew); Aharon Mirsky in his edition of Yosse ben Yosse's poems, 2nd ed. (Jerusalem: Bialik Institute, 1991), p. 127ff.; Joseph Yahalom in his: *Priestly Palestinian Poetry: A Narrative Liturgy for the Day of Atonement* (Jerusalem: Magnes Press, 1996) (in Hebrew).

The Tosefta cites the following on this subject:

כפורים פ״א ה״ט, מהד׳ הגר״ש ליברמן, עמ׳ 223-224:
אי זהו אצבע הצרדה?
זו אצבע גדולה של ימין.
בפה, לא בנבל ולא בכנור.
מה היו אומ׳:
שיר המעלות לשלמה אם ה׳ לא יבנה בית וגו׳.
לא היו ישנין כל הלילה אלא שוקדין כנגד כהן גדול
כדי לעסקו בהבראה.
כך היו נוהגין בגבולין אחר חורבן הבית, זכר למקדש,
אבל חוטאין היו.

The Jerusalem Talmud's discussion is as follows:

ירושלמי, פ״א ה״ו-ה״ז, ל״ט ע״ב:
תני: במשלי ובתילים
מפני שטעמן מפיג את השינה.
...
רב הונא אמר:
באצבע צרדה — בפה
ור׳ יוחנן אמר: באצבע צרדה — ביד.
מתניתא פליגא על ר׳ יוחנן:
בפה, לא בנבל ולא בכנור!!
פתר לה:
נעימה הנאמרת באצבע צרדה
אומרה בפה, לא בנבל ולא בכנור.

Finally, in the Babylonian Talmud the relevant discussion includes:

בבלי יומא י״ט ע״ב:
תנא:
לא היו מעסיקין אותו לא בנבל ולא בכנור אלא בפה.
ומה היו אומרין:
אם ה׳ לא יבנה בית שוא עמלו בוניו בו.
מיקירי ירושלים לא היו ישנין כל הלילה
כדי שישמע כהן גדול קול הברה
ולא תהא שינה חוטפתו.

תניא:
אבא שאול אומר:
אף בגבולין היו עושין כן, זכר למקדש,
אלא שהיו חוטאין.

In *Tosefta ki-fshuta*, Professor Lieberman deals with the Tosefta passage in all its aspects.[2]

In this note, I shall first focus on a section of this Mishnah that has no parallel in the Tosefta but to which there are many allusions in the *sidrei avodah*. The earliest known *seder avodah* is called *shivath yamim*.[3] Unlike the later *Avodah* texts, this one is not yet in poetic form and in language and content it quite closely adheres to Mishnah Yoma. In *shivath yamim* we read:

אם היה חכם דורש ואם לאו תלמידי חכמים דורשין לפניו
אם רגיל לקרות קורא ואם לאו קוראים לפניו. ובמה קוראים לפניו?
באיוב ובעזרא ובדברי הימים
ואם עם הארץ הוא מסיחין לפניו סיחת מל׳ סיחת חסידים הראשונים וכו׳.

The last line is not found in the Mishnah nor in other rabbinic sources. The question whether the author of *shivath yamim* had before him a different version of the Mishnah or rather added this line on the basis of other traditions, cannot be answered. As noted by Joseph Yahalom, this line introduces an additional degree of ignorance to what is listed in the Mishnah.[4] If the High Priest is not even capable of understanding Scripture as read before him, let his entourage tell him stories about the royal and pious heroes of the distant past. The expression *siah melakhim*[5] appears repeatedly in subsequent *avodah* poems. In the early Palestinian *seder avodah, az be-ein kol*, we read[6]

וּבְאַרְבַּעַת סְפָרִים   חוֹקְרִים לִימּ[וּ]דוֹ
אִם לֹא יֶחְכַּם   בְּסִיחַ מְלָכִים יְשַׁעַשְׁעֻהוּ.

2 *Tosefta ki-fshuta*, vol. 4, pp. 731-733.

3 Ismar Elbogen, *Studien zur Geschichte des juedischen Gottesdienstes* (Berlin: Mayer & Mueller, 1907), p. 104. See Yahalom (above note 1), pp. 16-17 and p. 142 comments to line 721.

4 *Ibid.*

5 The phrase סיחת חסידים הראשונים that appears in *shivath yamim* is not found, as far as I can determine, in later *sidrei avodah*. Compare, however, Nehemiah ben Shlomo Ha-Nassi's *seder avodah* (below note 10) where נביאים, קצינים, כהנים are mentioned in this context.

6 Yahalom, *op. cit.*, p. 142. See also Spiegel (below note 10), p. 35 note 24.

Yahalom, in his notes to this text, calls attention to the fact that it represents an extension of the original (Mishnah) tradition and he refers to *shivath yamim*, as well as to a *seder avodah* by Yosse ben Yosse, *azkir gevuroth*, where the same extension occurs.

Azkir gevuroth[7] recounts the "entertainment" of the High Priest as follows:

נְעִימוֹת מִדְרָשׁ וּמִקְרָא יְשׂוֹחֲחוּ אוֹ בִּכְתָבֵי קֹדֶשׁ הֵם יַעֲסִיקוּהוּ
נַפְשׁוֹ יְשׁוֹבְבוּ בְּשִׂיחַ מַלְכֵי קֶדֶם אִם בַּעַר הוּא וְלֹא לָמַד לֶקַח

Aharon Mirsky notes the discrepancy between these lines and the tradition in the Mishnah and suggests that the poet's version may indicate that not only the four books enumerated in the Mishnah, but also other Biblical books as well, used to be recited for the High Priest. Secondly, he comments that the phrase *siah malkei kedem* may be a poetic designation for the Book of Daniel, the book that Zekhariah ben Kabutal used to read before the High Priest on the eve of the Day of Atonement. Mirsky does not explain why he equates *siah malkei kedem* with the Book of Daniel. Of course, one can justify this identification, because of the role that King Nebuchadnezzar plays in Daniel. Accordingly, it would be fitting to call the book *siah melakhim,* perhaps best translated as *royal chronicle.*[8]

Still, other Biblical books could also qualify for this designation, particularly the books of Ezra and Chronicles which are mentioned in our Mishnah, too.[9] So, the exact meaning of this phrase is not clear.

That the High Priest was kept awake by the telling of *siah melakhim* is mentioned in a number of other *sidrei avodah* as well:[10]

7 Mirsky (as above note 1), p. 151.

8 In an incomplete, anonymous *avodah* we read: דברי חכמים. נחת דברי חכמים/ בין דברי הימים... refers to דורשין of the Mishnah while דברי הימים seems to stand for all the Biblical books mentioned there, and not only for the Book of Chronicles. For the quote see Z. Malachi (note 10), p. 168.

9 In a poem doubtfully attributed to Shimon bar Megas we find the following lines: נער אם יהי או בער במורשה/ לפניו יסוחחו ספרים שלושה. It seems that this poet understood *siah [melakhim]* to mean the three Biblical books mentioned in the Mishnah. For the quote see Joseph Yahalom, *Liturgical Poems of Sim'on bar Megas* (Jerusalem: The Israel Academy of Sciences and Humanities, 1984), p. 281 (in Hebrew).

10 The first two citations are from Yosse ben Yosse's *sidrei avodah,* see Mirsky, *op. cit.,* pp. 189, 233. Most of the other texts are found in Zvi Malachi's unpublished doctoral dissertation, *The*

1 שַׁעֲשׁוּעַ מִדְרָשׁ   וְהֶגֶא כִּתְבֵי קֹדֶשׁ   אִם יֶחְכַּם   לְפָנָיו יְשׂוֹחֲהוּ
שִׁנּוּן שִׂחוֹת   מְלָכִים קַדְמוֹנִים   אִם יִהְיֶה בַעַר   בָּם יַעֲסִיקוּהוּ

2 גָּשׁ לִדְרוֹשׁ שֵׂכֶל   כְּחָכָם וְנָבוֹן   [וְלִפְנֵי] גְדוֹלִים   אַל יַגְבִּיהַּ לֵב
בִּהְיוֹת לִבּוֹ   צָפוּן מִשֵּׂ[כֶל]   בְּהֶגֶיה כִּתְבֵי קֹדֶשׁ   בְּפֶה יַעֲסִיקוּהוּ
בַּעַר אִם יִהְיֶה   וְלֹא לָמַד לֶקַח   בְּשִׂיחַ מַלְכֵי קֶדֶם   לִבּוֹ יָפִיגוּ

3 ...עוֹד הֵם פָּרְשׁוּ וְנָהוּ וּבְשִׂיחַ מְלָכִים עוֹרְרוּהוּ

4 עָנוּ וּבַשֵּׁם הִשְׁבִּיעוּהוּ   וּבְשִׂיחַ מְלָכִים עוֹרְרוּהוּ

5 פִּיתּוּהוּ בְּסִיחַ טוּב זִקְנֵי שִׁבְטוֹ   וְעִינְּגוּהוּ בְּשִׂיחָה...

6 ...נִיגַּשׁ לְהִשְׁתַּעְשֵׁעַ בַּחֲוּקִים וְלֹא כְבַעַר
סִיחוֹת יְפִיגוּהוּ...

7 נְכוֹחִים פִּילֵשׁ הַדְּרוּשִׁים לְכָל חֵפֶץ   נמוגותם בְּטַעַם אֲמָרָיו יִפֶּץ
נִמְצָא שִׁיכֵחַ אוֹ לֹא בֶן שְׁמוּעַ   נִיב פֶּה הִמְתִּיקוּ בִּכְתָב קוֹדֶשׁ לְהִשְׁתַּעְשֵׁעַ
נְבוֹנֵי סוֹד שִׂיחַ מְלָכִים יַרְגִּילוּ   נֶגְדּוֹ בְּכָבוֹד וְנַפְשׁוֹ הִיגִילוּ

8 נפש וּבִיאֵר שִׁינּוּן מִדְרָשׁ   נוֹאֵם... קוֹדֶשׁ עַל פֶּה פֵּרַשׁ
נַחַת תּוּשִׁיָּה אִם [לֹא הִי]תְבוֹנָן   נֶגְדּוֹ מִפְעַל מַלְכֵי קֶדֶם יְשׁוֹנָן

9 נָאֳמוֹ יַנְעִימוּ תַחְכְּמוֹנִים   בְּשִׁינּוּן מְלָכִים קַדְמוֹנִים
נִיצּוּחַ אַרְבָּעָה כתב...אֱמוּנִים   קוֹרְאִים לְפָנָיו נֶאֱמָנִים

Avodah for Yom Kippur (Jerusalem: The Hebrew University, 1973), vol. 2. #3 is on p. 108 (from *ekra be-garon* by Pinchas ha-Kohen, see Yahalom (above note 1), p. 57, note 79); #4 is from a fragmentary *avodah* by the poet Joshua, see in the unpublished file in the archives of Shalom Spiegel, folder 183. #5 is in Malachi, p. 157 (from the anonymous tenfold *avodah*); #6 see *ibid.*, pp 173-174 (from an incomplete, anonymous *avodah*, cf. Elbogen, above note 3, pp. 96, 163); #7 see *ibid.*, p. 179 (from an incomplete, anonymous *avodah*, cf. Elbogen, *op. cit.*, pp. 97-98, 175); #8, *ibid.*, p. 184 (from another anonymous, incomplete *avodah*); #9, *ibid.*, p. 193 (from the second *avodah* of Shlomo Suleiman al-Sangari, cf. Jefim (Hayyim) Schirmann, *New Hebrew Poems from the Genizah* (Jerusalem: Israel Academy of Sciences and Humanities, 1965), pp. 46-47, in Hebrew); #10 see Nehemiah ben Shlomo Ha-Nassi's *seder avodah*, see M. Zulay's edition in *Studies of the Research Institute for Hebrew Poetry in Jerusalem* (= *Yedioth ha-makhon leheker ha-shira ha-ivrith bi-yerushalayim*), 4, 1938, p. 230; #11 see Meshullam ben Kalonymus in *Mahzor* for Yom Kippur, ed. D. Goldschmidt (Jerusalem: Koren, 1970), p. 439; #12 see Solomon ibn Gabirol, *Liturgical Poetry*, ed. Dov Jarden (Jerusalem, 1971), p. 267. See also Shalom Spiegel, *The Fathers of Piyyut*, ed. M. Schmelzer (New York-Jerusalem: Jewish Theological Seminary, 1996), p. 35, note 24 (in Hebrew), where Spiegel first calls attention to the phrase *siah melakhim* and lists its repeated appearance in *sidrei avodah*.

10 מֻורְגָּל הָיָה בְּמִקְרָא/ קוֹרֵא בְּדָת מִקְרָא
וְאִם נִמְנַע מִסִּיבְרָה/ קוֹרְאִים לְפָנָיו לְיַקְּרָה
נוֹאֲמִים לְפָנָיו קַדְמוֹנִים/ חִידוֹת נְבִיאִים וּקְצִינִים
מִפְּעַל יוֹשֶׁר כֹּהֲנִים/ הָיוּ לְפָנָיו מְשַׁנְּנִים

11 שִׂיחַ מִדְרָשׁ בְּפֶה וּבִכְתָב הִגָּיוֹן   סְבִיבָיו יְשַׁנְּנוּ לְעוֹרְרוֹ עַד חֲצוֹת

12 מְכֻבָּד נְכוֹחִים יֶהְגּוּ לְפָנָיו   בְּסִפְרֵי קֹדֶשׁ אוֹ בְשִׂיחִים

The repetition of *siah (sihat) melakhim* in so many works, either exactly in these words or in a close paraphrase, indicates that the original source used by the *payyetanim* did indeed contain this phrase. It is not likely that the *seder avodah shivath yamim* was the original source from where *siah melakhim* was derived; it is much more plausible to assume, as Shalom Spiegel suggests, that it may have been part of a rabbinic text which is not extant anymore.[11]

Another phrase, *kitvei kodesh*, Scripture, in general, or Hagiographa, in particular—instead of the enumeration of the three (or four) Biblical books that are explicitly named in the Mishnah—occurs in several of the texts quoted above. Interestingly enough, Maimonides, in this context, also speaks about *kitve kodesh* and not about the books mentioned in the Mishnah by name.[12] Whether this choice of language reflects some old, alternative Rabbinic variant relating to the Mishnah or, rather, it is an interpretation offered by the *payyetanim* and by Maimonides, albeit independently from each other,[13] remains unclear.[14]

11 *Op. cit., ibid.*: דומה, ניתותר בפי פייטנים שריד ממקור חז״ל... שלא הגיע אלינו?

12 *Mishne Torah, Hilkhot avodath yom ha-kippurim*, chapter 1, *halakhah* 8.

13 It is well-known that Maimonides was not favorably inclined toward poetry, see Jefim Schirmann, *The History of Hebrew Poetry in Christian Spain and Southern France*, edited, supplemented and annotated by Ezra Fleischer (Jerusalem: Magnes, 1997), pp. 281-283 (in Hebrew). Accordingly, it is not to be assumed that Maimonides borrowed this phrase from a liturgical poem. See, however, the recent article by Joseph Yahalom, הרמב״ם והמליצה העברית, *Pe'amim* 81, 1999/2000, pp. 4-18, where Yahalom presents a more complex picture about Maimonides' attitude to poetry, in general. Still, this does not change the basic truth about Maimonides' aversion to *piyyut*.

14 Some commentators also find the use of *kitve kodesh* difficult. They point out that it would have been expected that Maimonides names the books, Job, Ezra and Chronicles (and Daniel) as it is done in the Mishnah. The question, apparently, is first asked in the *Lehem Mishneh* by Rabbi Abraham di Boton (16th century) and various attempts at resolving the difficulty are being offered by later commentators. See *Sefer ha-mafteah* at the end of the Shabse Fraenkel edition of the *Mishneh Torah*, vol. 7, *Avodah*, p. 885.

If the use of *kitve kodesh* is interpretive in nature, which is quite likely, we may resort to an explanation of the phrase offered by a relatively late Rabbinical commentator, Isaac Nunez-Vaez (Leghorn, 18th century). In connection with the Maimonides passage, Nunez-Vaez suggests[15] that Maimonides, in using *kitve kodesh*, wanted to combine two traditions: that of the Mishnah and that of the Jerusalem Talmud. As we recall, the Mishnah names Job, Ezra and Chronicles as the books read before the High Priest, while the Jerusalem Talmud quotes a *baraita* according to which Psalms and Proverbs were the books read to keep the High Priest awake. The existence of these two traditions may have been the impetus for the *payyetanim*, too, for their employment of the phrase *kitve kodesh*, rather than just mentioning the books by name as in the Mishnah.

Now, if we examine the two Tannaitic traditions, we may first ask whether they are independent from each other, contradicting each other, or rather they complement each other. In the Mishnah's statement it is strange that the historical books of Ezra and Chronicles (and Daniel, according to Zekhariah ben Kabutal) were joined by Job as the reading materials for the occasion. The historical books have much in common, not only in their very nature of being chronicles of events, but also in their concentration on the Second Temple period and on the service of the priests and Levites in the Second Temple.[16]

The book of Job is different altogether. It would be more fitting to group it with the other two books, Psalms and Proverbs. Much is in common among these three: they are poetic, ethical and fully or partially belong to Wisdom literature. Therefore, perhaps, one may suggest that originally Psalms and Proverbs (the books mentioned in the Jerusalem Talmud) were listed together with Job (the book mentioned in the Mishnah) and these three served as one type of book read before the High Priest. At some point, however, Job was detached from the original group of three and was added to the group of historical books about which the Mishnah reports.

The three books, Job, Proverbs and Psalms, are also regarded as a unit

15 In his *Siah Yitzhak* (Leghorn, 1766; reprinted in Tel Aviv 1969, as part of the collection: *Asefat Zekenim* on Yoma), f. 23a.

16 The practices relating to the High Priest, reported in Rabbinic literature, reflect the situation at the end of the Second Temple period. See Shmuel Safrai, *In Times of Temple and Mishnah: Studies in Jewish History*, vol. 1 (Jerusalem: Magnes, 1994), p. 36 (in Hebrew). Books dealing with this period may then have served eminently as amusing to the High Priest.

in Masoretic literature, as seen from the expression ספרי אמ"ת, where אמ"ת stands for איוב משלי תהלים. These three have a common cantillation system, different from that of other Biblical books. When one reads in the statement in the Jerusalem Talmud that Psalms and Proverbs were chosen to be read מפני שטעמן מפיג את השינה, because their טעם dispels sleep, the suggestion comes to mind that טעם here may mean the tune of recitation of these books, as in טעמי המקרא. Now, this suggestion may sound anachronistic, but we should bear in mind that the term טעמים, in connection with the mode the Bible was recited, does occur both in the Jerusalem as well as the Babylonian Talmud.[17] What the exact meaning of the term in the Talmud is and what its connection to its later Masoretic sense is, remain, however, unclear.[18]

The proposal that in our passage טעם may refer to some kind of musical rendering may be strengthened by other statements in the sources that bear testimony about the role music and noisemaking had played in the attempts at keeping the High Priest awake on the night of the Day of Atonement.

As seen above, some kind of noise was produced with a finger (אצבע הצרדה)[19] or vocally, imitating the snapping of a finger, by young priests (or Levites)[20] to keep the High Priest awake. The Rabbinic sources emphasize that this was vocal and not instrumental music (בפה, לא בנבל ולא בכנור). It was necessary to point this out because, apparently, there was a tradition according to which the noise making was "by hand" (Rabbi Yohanan's view in the Jerusalem Talmud). So, as a conclusion, the latter source establishes that the נעימה (tune, song, melody) produced through the finger was not accompanied by harp and lyre.[21]

17 On the earliest mentions of טעמים in this sense in Talmudic literature see *Encyclopaedia Mikraith*, vol. 3, col. 395-396 (in Hebrew). On the טעמים for Job, Proverbs and Psalms see *ibid.*, col. 400-401. See also Israel Yeivin, *Introduction to the Tiberian Masorah* (Scholars Press, 1980), pp. 157-158, 163-164.

18 *Ibid.*

19 See about the various definitions of אצבע הצרדה in Lieberman's *Tosefta ki-fshutah*, vol. 4, pp. 731-732.

20 In the standard Mishnah editions we read: פרחי כהונה, but in manuscripts and in some *sidrei avodah* the reading is: פרחי לויה. See Yahalom (above note 1, p. 142, comments to line 722). This is also the reading of the Mishnah with the commentary of Maimonides, see Yosef Kafih's edition, *Moed* (Jerusalem: Mossad Ha-Rav Kook, 1964), p. 240.

21 See the commentary of Professor Lieberman on these passages in his *Tosefta ki-fshutah*, vol. 4, pp. 731-732. Zvi Malachi, in his dissertation (see above note 10), vol. 1, chapter 6 [pp. 351ff] collected and discussed the passages in *piyyutim* where the matter of אצבע הצרדה is included.

The passage in the Jerusalem Talmud, נעימה הנאמרת באצבע צרדה, influenced the authors of *sidrei avodah* to write that whatever was done through אצבע הצרדה was tied to singing:[22]

1 נָטָה לָנוּם שְׁנָתוֹ יַפְרִידוּ בְּנוֹעַם שִׁיר צְרָדָה בְּפֶה וְלֹא בְכִנּוֹר

2 שִׁיר יְשׁוֹרְרוּ לוֹ פִּרְחֵי כְהֻונָּה בְּפֶה וּבְחֵיךְ עָרֵב וּבִנְעִימַת צְרָדָה

3 מַכִּים בְּאֶצְבַּע מְשׁוֹרְרִים לְעוֹרְרוֹ עַד נֶחֱלַק לַיְלָה וְאֻוסְּפוּ בְרוּרִים

4 אִם תִּגְבַּר עָלָיו שֵׁנָה וּבִקֵּשׁ לְהִתְנַמְנֵם בְּחֵיךְ נוֹעַם צְרָדָה מְשׁוֹרְרִים יְעוֹרְרוּהוּ

5 נוֹעַם צְרָ[דָה] בְּפֶה מְשׁוֹרְרִים יַמְתִּיקוּ

6 נוֹגְנִים צְרָדָה בְּאֶצְבַּע הִיכּוּ

7 לְנוֹעַם צְרָדָה וְקוֹל זֶמֶר רוֹגְנִים יִלְמְדוּ לֶקַח

8 נוֹגְנֵי דוּכָן גַּם הֵם יַשְׁמִיעוּ
נְעִימַת צְרָדָה בְּפֶה וְלֹא בְּכִינּוֹר

9 נִצָּנֵי לְוִיָּה, מְנַצְּחֵי עַל שׁוֹשַׁנִּים
נִמְנוּמוֹ לְהַעֲבִיר, קוֹל צְרֵדָתָם יַשְׁפִּירוּ
...
נֵבֶל וְכִנּוֹר לְהַעֲסִיקוֹ לֹא יְנַעְנְעוּ,
נוֹצֵר וּבַנַּאי אָדוֹן שִׁיר יְנַגְּנוּ

10 נְעִימוֹת צְרָדָה יְסוֹבְבוּהוּ...
נֶצַח נוֹעַם מַנְעִימִים לְפָנָיו...

11 וִיעוֹרְרוּהוּ מְשׁוֹרְרִים מַכֵּי בִּצְרָדָה...

12 מִזֶּה מְכֻבָּד בְּקוֹל תְּשׁוּאָה וְנֹעַם צְרָדָה בַּפֶּה בִלְבַד

13 ...וּבִצְרָדָה מַכִּים לְפָנָיו פִּרְחֵי נוֹגְנִים

22 For #1-4 see Yosse ben Yosse (note 1), pp. 152, 190, 207, 233; #5-6 are from the poems quoted above (see note 10, #6-7); #7 is from Saadia Gaon, see *Siddur Rav Saadia Gaon*, ed. I. Davidson, S. Assaf, B.I. Joel (Jerusalem: Mekize Nirdamim, 1941), p. 284; for #8 see Nachum Weissenstern, *The Piyyutim of Johanan ha-Kohen Birabbi Jehoshua* (Jerusalem: Hebrew University Dissertation, 1983), p. 138; for #9 see Shlomo ha-Bavli (note 1), p. 174; #10 is by Joseph ibn Abitur, see *Kovetz maasei yedei geonim kadmonim*, ed. by Y. Rosenberg (Berlin: 1856), part 2, pp. 22-23; #11 is by Meshullam ben Kalonymus, see *Mahzor* for Yom Kippur, ed. Goldschmidt (note 10), p. 453; #12 is by Ibn Gabirol, see ed. Jarden (note 10), p. 266; and #13 is by Isaac ibn Giat, see his *seder avodah* in Yonah David, *The Poems of Rabbi Isaac ibn Ghiyyat: A Tentative Edition* (Jerusalem: Ah'shav, 1987), p. 146.

According to the Tosefta and the Babylonian Talmud, it was Psalm 127 that was said (sung?) to the accompaniment of the sound produced by אצבע הצרדה. It is, of course, just speculation, but perhaps there existed some connection between the reading of the Biblical books, including the book of Psalms, perhaps to some special tune, and the melodic recitation of Psalm 127.

There is an additional "musical" event associated with keeping the High Priest awake. The Tosefta and the Babylonian Talmud report that some of the nobility of Jerusalem (מיקירי ירושלים) did not sleep the entire night and produced some kind of noise (קול הברה).[23] The section containing this statement is found in some versions as part of the Mishnah itself.[24]

The nature of this noise is not described explicitly in the sources. Still, we can learn something about it from the statement reported in the name of Abba Shaul. Abba Shaul relates that the practice of staying up all night and creating קול הברה was continued even after the destruction of the Temple, to keep the Temple's memory alive. According to Abba Shaul's statement, this observance led to sinful behavior and we may presume that it was stopped not too long after the destruction of the Temple. Rashi, to the passage in the Babylonian Talmud Yoma 19b, comments that the sinful behavior consisted of משחקין אנשים ונשים יחד ובאין לעבירה, men and women were participating together in amusement which led to sinful behavior.[25] One may assume on the basis of this meager information that toward the end of the Second Temple period some merriment took place on the night of Yom ha-Kippurim in Jerusalem. When this practice continued afterwards, it led to lewdness. One may surmise that human behavior during such merriment may not have been much different at the time when the Temple still stood.

Interestingly, there was another Day of Atonement observance of merriment about which the Mishnah reports. The Mishna in Taanith 4:8 tells us that on the Day of Atonement the maidens of Jerusalem used to go out to the vineyards to dance in order to induce eligible young men to marry them. We have no source to indicate that this observance had anything to do with the noise created at night in Jerusalem to keep the High Priest awake, but, one may surmise, that during the end of the

23 See on this phrase Lieberman, *op. cit.*, pp. 732-733.

24 *Ibid.*, and Y.N. Epstein, *Mavo le-nussah ha-Mishnah*, p. 967.

25 See Lieberman, *ibid.*, p. 733 who explains the Tosefta passage according to this interpretation of Rashi.

Second Temple period the celebration of the Day of Atonement included a merriment at night (that at a later period may have turned improper) and another one during daytime that was considered to be praiseworthy. These two events may have lent to the Day of Atonement a character totally different from what we normally associate with that day.

The creating of קול הברה in Jerusalem was understood by the *payyetanim* to mean an uproar generated on the streets of a tumultuous city (cf. Isaiah 22,2) and some *payyetanim* hint at joyous singing as part of the practice:[26]

נוֹתְנִים שָׁאוֹן עִיר הוֹמִיָּה לְהַשְׁבִּיעוֹ נְדוּדִים עֲדֵי נָשֶׁף

שָׁאוֹן יַגְבִּירוּ הֲמוֹן רַבָּתִי עַם כִּי מִקּוֹלָם שְׁנָתוֹ תְּפוֹרָר

אֵת קוֹל שָׁאוֹן מֵעִיר יִשְׁמַע וְתִפָּרֵד שְׁנָתוֹ עַד יֶחֱצֶה לַיְלָה

צְעִירֵי שָׁלוֹם הֲבָרָה יַשְׁמִיעוּ   בִּרְחוֹבוֹת עִיר עֶרֶב יוֹם כִּפּוּר

צְעִידוֹת יָרֹבּוּ בְּכָל פִּנּוֹתֶיהָ לְהַשְׁמִיעַ לַכֹּהֵן לְבַל יִתְנַמְנֵם

נִיצוּחֵי הֵיכָל שָׂשׂוּ לְשׁוֹרֵר   נְדוּדִים בְּשָׂבְעוֹ וּמִשְּׁאוֹנָם יִתְעוֹרֵר

נוֹתֵן בְּרַבָּתִי קוֹל הנחת גַּהַץ   נָדְדָה שְׁנָתוֹ [עַד?] לַיְלָה יֶחֱץ

נִיהֲלוּהוּ רוֹבֵי קְהִילָּה   בַּהֲבָרָה כָּל הַלַּיְלָה

מַשְׁמִיעִים שִׁיר וּתְהִילָּה   לָאֵל נוֹרָא עֲלִילָה

וְהָעִיר תֵּהוֹם שְׁנָתוֹ לְנַדְּדָה

In a concise manner, Meshullam ben Kalonymus combines the various attempts at keeping the High Priest awake at the night of the Day of Atonement in one brief stanza:[27]

וִיעוֹרְרוּהוּ מְשׁוֹרְרִים מַכֵּי בִּצְרָדָה/ וְיוּפַג בַּמִּדְרָשׁ וּכְתָבֵי תְעוּדָה
וְעַל הָרִצְפָּה יְהַפֵּךְ לְקוֹדָה   / וְהָעִיר תֵּהוֹם שְׁנָתוֹ לְנַדְּדָה

The question of the nature of the correspondence of the *avodah* poems to the Rabbinic sources, especially in the realm of the halakhic passages, the problem of deviations between the poems and the Talmud (mainly the

26 For the first three quotes see Yosse ben Yosse (note 1), pp. 152, 190, 233. The next three are found in Malachi's dissertation (note 10), pp. 157, 179, 184. The last two are by Nechemiah (note 10, p. 230) and Meshullam ben Kalonymus (note 10, p. 453), respectively. For the word גהץ = joy, light, in the quote from Malachi, p. 184, see Menahem Zulay, *Eretz Israel and Its Poetry* (Jerusalem: Magnes, 1995), pp. 465-466, 518, in Hebrew.

27 *Ibid.*

Babylonian), was the subject of frequent inquiry among the commentators.[28] In the present note, the examination of one aspect of the Day of Atonement service by the High Priest demonstrates the complexity of the poetic traditions as they reflect the rabbinic texts. On the one hand, there is a great deal of uniformity and faithfulness in following the sources, but, on the other hand, we see how the poems contain elements lacking in our sources and also, how the poets adapt, interpret and change them.

28 See Weissenstern (note 22), p. 64ff.

Penitence, Prayer and (Charity?)

The triad, תשובה, תפילה, צדקה is familiar to the Jewish worshipper from the liturgy of the Days of Awe. It is found in the liturgical poem, ונתנה תוקף, which is recited according to the present Ashkenazi rite on both days of Rosh ha-shanah as well as on Yom Kippur.[1] The full sentence, in which these three nouns are found, reads:

ותשובה ותפילה וצדקה מעבירין את רוע הגזרה

and repentance, and prayer and charity remove the evil decree.

This statement reaches back (over the rather long section beginning with the words בראש השנה) to the closing words of the first paragraph of the poem:

ותכתוב את גזר דינם

and you will inscribe their decree

All commentators point to a passage in *Bereshith Rabba* as the source of the statement. We read there:[2]

ר׳ יודן בשם ר׳ לעזר: שלשה דברים מבטלין את הגזירה ואילו הן: תפילה וצדקה ותשובה ושלשתן בפסוק אחד: ויכנעו עמי אשר נקרא שמי עליו ויתפללו (דה״ב ז יד), הרי תפילה, ויבקשו פני (שם שם), הרי צדקה היך דאת אמר אני בצדק אחזה פניך (תהלים יז טו), וישובו מדרכם הרעה (דה״ב שם), הרי תשובה וכו׳.

R. Yudan in the name of R. Eleazar: Three things annul the decree: Prayer, *sedaqah* and repentance. We learn this from one and the

1 The poem was originally for Rosh ha-shanah only. It is not found for Yom Kippur in the old French and German rites. See *Mahzor le-yamim noraim. I. Rosh ha-shanah*, ed. D. Goldschmidt (Jerusalem, 1970), pp. 169-71, esp. the variant reading to line 1. See also *op. cit.*, II. Introduction, pp. 41-43.

2 *Bereshith Rabba* 44.12 (ed. Theodor Albeck), p. 434 and parallels.

> same verse: "When My people, who bear My name, humble themselves, pray" (II Chronicles 7.14): this means prayer, "and seek My face" (*ibid.*) this is *sedaqah*, as it is written "Then I, *be-sedeq*, will behold Your face" (Psalms 17.15) "and turn from their evil ways" (*ibid.*): this is repentance, etc.

This saying of R. Eleazar is quoted in various contexts in rabbinic literature. Its original setting seems to be in connection with astrology or dreams; *gezerah* means one's fate as determined by stars or foretold by dreams. In *Bereshith Rabba* R. Eleazar's words are recorded immediately following the assertion that Abraham, the patriarch, was a prophet and not an astrologer, and that the stars had no power over him. In *Koheleth Rabba* (and in its parallels), R. Yudan's statement is quoted in connection with the verse:

> There is much dreaming and futilities and superfluous talk, but you should fear God (Eccl. 5.6): Rabbi says: If you dreamt difficult dreams and had difficult and contradictory visions and (or) you are scared because of them, hasten to do three things and you will be saved, as stated by R. Yudan in the name of R. Eleazar, three things annul bad decrees, etc.[3]

In both sources, then, the *gezerah* is not the result of actions by man, but rather of superhuman or unconscious forces. To counteract these forces, the Rabbis urge the individual to resort to three things, which, for sure, will act as an antidote to ill fate destined by astrology or predicted by dreams.

There is, however, a third midrashic context, in which R. Eleazar's saying appears. In the *Tanhuma* the triad is recommended as an antidote to the evil inclination, the *yeṣer ha-ra*.[4] Thus, in the *Tanhuma*, the belief in the effectiveness of the triad shows affinity for the liturgical theme, as it appears in the hymn ונתנה תוקף. The statement becomes appropriate for the Days of Awe: sin (caused by the evil inclination) results in an unfavorable, severe divine decree. This decree may be annulled and atonement may be attained by employing the three things recommended by R. Eleazar. Here it is the evil inclination, and not the stars or dreams, that determines man's fate.

3 *Midrash Koheleth Rabba* on Eccl. 5.6.

4 *Tanhuma, Noah*, paragraph 8.

In the Babylonian Talmud, R. Yitzhak suggests four remedies for averting the severe decree:

צדקה, צעקה, שינוי השם, שינוי מעשה

sedaqah, crying out (prayer), change of name, change of deed.[5]

The original context of R. Yitzhak's statement is not indicated, but it is likely that he said it in connection with averting destiny declared upon an individual by the stars, and not brought upon himself by his evil deeds. Otherwise, it would be difficult to explain why שינוי השם would be considered useful to change the divine judgment.

Three of R. Yitzhak's four things match the triad of R. Eleazar. צעקה (crying out) obviously corresponds to תפלה, as does שינוי מעשה (changing of deed) to penitence (תשובה). צדקה. is the same in both sources. Still, there is an important difference: in R. Yitzhak's statement the prooftext for צדקה is וצדקה תציל ממות (Prov. 11.4, But *sedaqah* saves from death), while, as we recall, R. Eleazar's prooftext is Ps. 17.15, "Then I, *be-sedeq* will behold Your face." We shall return to this discrepancy below. It is obvious that various strains are discernible in these traditions about *gezerah* or *gezar din*. They include destiny determined by stars, foretold by dreams, caused by the evil inclination or declared in God's annual judgment of human beings according to their deeds. The recommended acts to avert fate resulting from any of the above, however, always include prayer, penitence and *sedaqah*. That these matters are commingled in the various sources indicates, the complexity of the concept of destiny on the New Year in Ancient Israel and in rabbinic Judaism. It is obvious that the change of year brings with it a change of fate. At first, this fate was probably conceived as determined by astrology, and only later by the individual's good (or evil) ways.[6] It would be interesting to attempt to trace the evolution of this concept in the literature, but let us instead turn our attention to some other matters relating to the occurrence of the triad in the liturgy of the Days of Awe.

5 *B. Roš. Haš.* 16b.

6 See N.H. Snaith, *The Jewish New Year Festival: Its Origins and its Development* (London, 1947), esp. pp. 73ff; 165ff; 217f. The various meanings of *gezerah* are also discussed in traditional Jewish sources, see, e.g. Samuel Ashkenazi, *Yefeh Toar*, a commentary on *Bereshith Rabba* (Fuerth, 1692, reprint Jerusalem, 1989), f. 262b. In his comments on our passage, he differentiates between גזר דין דראש השנה and גזירות המערכה, the latter meaning destiny determined by the constellations.

In R. Eleazar's homily, based on 2 Chron. 7.14, the sequence of the triad is: first תפלה, followed by צדקה, and concluded by תשובה. Whether by design or by chance, the sequence of the words in the *Tanhuma* is different. Here we find תשובה, תפלה, צדקה. It is the order of the *Tanhuma* which has found its way into the liturgical hymn, ונתנה תקף. We recall that it is also the *Tanhuma* that connects the three to the evil inclination. Since ונתנה תקף follows the order of the *Tanhuma*, and not that of the other sources, and, furthermore, since in the liturgical setting of Rosh ha-shanah judgment of sins (caused by evil inclination) plays such a central role, it is plausible to suggest that the anonymous author of ונתנה תקף used the *Tanhuma* (or a source similar to it) as his inspiration.

The deviation from the sequence of the three things as enumerated in the original midrashic exegesis did not escape the attention of medieval liturgists. On the other hand, in modern times the issue has been forgotten completely. No trace of it is left in present liturgical practice and for that matter, it is hardly even mentioned in scholarly literature.[7] A cursory examination of just a few medieval and early modern manuscripts as well as printed *mahzorim* yields some interesting information relating to a debate among Rabbis concerning the proper sequence of the triad. In some *mahzorim* we find small letters above the three words, indicating a different order.[8] The text in these sources looks like this:

ג	א	ב
ותשובה	ותפלה	וצדקה

There is no doubt that the superimposed letters try to restore the order of the original homily, as derived by R. Eleazar from the Biblical verse. Still, in no *mahzor* was the conventional sequence changed in the body of the text itself. It was only some commentator, owner or scribe who indicated the "correct" sequence by superimposing letters, thereby disapproving of the order as normally found in ונתנה תקף. The sources also give explicit explanation for the graphic signs. It is reported in the name of Rabbi Abraham Klausner (Austria, 14-15th century):

7 W. Bacher, *Die Agadah der palaestinischen Amoraer*, II (Strassburg, 1896), p. 13 n. 3 refers to the different sequence in the *u-netanneh tokef*. Bacher's observation is quoted by Theodor in his *Minhath Yehuda* to *Bereshith Rabba*, top of p. 435.

8 Ms. Oxford, Opp. 166, Neubauer, Catalogue, 1160, f. 49a; JTS, Ms. 4843, f. 85b; *Mahzor* (Prague, 1522-25) (printed), I, for *mussaf* for first day of Rosh ha-shanah.

וכת׳ הרא״ק שיש לומר ותפלה וצדקה ותשובה כסדר הפסוק ואין לשנות כלל.[9]

On the other hand, Rabbi Jacob Moellin (the Maharil; Germany, 14-15th century) advocates the conventional order. Since he is aware of the weighty argument against the common reading, which is based on the original sequence of the Midrash, he has to defend the prevalent practice and find justification for it. Accordingly, he advances the following explanation:

ותשובה ותפלה וצדקה ודלא כסדר הקראי ואמר ותשובה ותפלה ר״ל ע״י התשובה הקדומה לתפלה ולצדקה על דרך נירו לכם ניר (ירמ׳ ד ג).[10]

תשובה, placed before the two others, alludes, according to Maharil, to the need of "preparing the ground" for the effectiveness of תפלה וצדקה. As if תשובה would be needed to break the untilled ground (Jer. 3.4) so that sowing (and not amidst thorns) may follow.

The controversy about the proper order of the words cannot be documented before the 14-15th centuries. Therefore, it should be assumed that the appearance of superimposed letters in older *mahzor* manuscripts indicates later additions.[11]

The origin of another tradition in connection with this triad may be explained as a result of the controversy concerning its proper sequence. Worshippers are familiar with the way תשובה ותפלה וצדקה appear in the printed editions of most *mahzorim*. Above each of the words, in smaller type, a kind of identification appears. It looks like this:

ממון	קול	צום
צדקה	**תפלה**	**תשובה**

9 Handwritten marginal note in the printed *Mahzor* (Prague, 1522-1525), see previous note. This remark is not found in *Minhagim* of Rabbi Abraham Klausner (ed. Y.Y. Dissen; Jerusalem, 1978).

10 See *Sefer Maharil: Minhagim shel R. Yaakov Moellin*, ed. Sh. Y. Spitzer (Jerusalem, 1989), pp. 294-95.

11 That the suggestions for changing the order are late may also be seen from the comments of R. Moses Mat (Poland, 16th cent.). In his *Matteh Mosheh* (Cracow, 1591), 144a, paragraph 819 (in later editions: 818) he writes:
ואומר ונתנה תקף ואח״כ ותשובה ותפלה וצדקה, כך נמצא בכל המחזורים, חדשים גם ישנים. רק חדשים מקרוב באו אומרים ותפלה וצדקה ותשובה על פי המדרש, אמר ר׳ יודן וכו ונראה דאין לשנות כלל כמו שכתב בדרשות מהרי״ל וזה לשון מהרי״ל שגגה היא ביד המגיהים את הספרים של הצבור וכו׳... ומי יודע מה היא כוונת המסדר ואפשר שהיה כוונתו על דרך הנעלם סוד... לכן אין לשנות, וכן ראיתי כל רבותיי נוהגים... וכל המשנה ידו על התחתונה.

This phenomenon is, of course, quite odd. There is no other passage in the prayerbook with a similar attempt of definition. Why the superimposition of these "explanations"? It is suggested here that the placing of the three words on top of the original triad is connected with the issue of its sequence, namely, that the three superimposed letter-numerals that originally indicated the "proper" sequence ultimately evolved into the three superimposed words. In at least two printed commentaries to ונתנה תקף, we read:

ומהר״י היה אומ׳ ותשובה ותפלה וצדקה ודלא כסדר הפסוקים ושקולים זה כזה
דכל א׳[חד] בגי׳[מטריא] קל״ו: צו״ם קו״ל ממו״ן.[12]

Mahari, probably identical with Maharil, justified the deviation of the liturgical text from that of the midrashic one in the following ingenious way: since the numerical value of three words, which are "synonymous" with the original three words of the triad, comes to the same amount, it does not actually matter in what order one recites them; ignore the superimposed *letter-numerals*, which try to tell you that the sequence is wrong. Pay attention, instead, to the superimposed *words* and their numerical value. Since it is the same for all three, 136 for צום and קול as well as for ממון there is no need to worry about the sequence of תשובה ותפלה וצדקה. Apparently, the previous explanation, about "preparing the ground" was found wanting, and, therefore, a supplemental reason, based on *gematria*, was advanced.

The identification of צדקה as ממון (money) seems natural. After all, the word means giving charity in rabbinic and post-rabbinic parlance. This is how the word, as it appears in the midrashic passage and in ונתנה תקף, is universally understood. There is only one possible exception: a passage in Solomon ibn Gabirol's *Kether Malkhuth*. This religious poem was intended as a private devotion for Yom Kippur. In it we read:

קטנתי מכל החסדים ומכל האמת אשר עשית את עבדך... כי נתת בי נפש קדושה...
וביצרי הרע חללתיה... יצרי האכזר נצב על ימיני לשטני... וכמה פעמים יצאתי
להלחם עמו וערכתי מחנה עבודתי ותשובתי ושמתי מחנה רחמיך לעמתי לעזרתי:

12 *Mahzor* (Cracow, 1585) f. 21a and *Mahzor* (Venice, 1600), with commentary *Hadrath Kodesh*, f. 72b. The same comment is found in a marginal manuscript note in the copy of a *Mahzor Ashkenaz* (Salonika, 1555-1556), the verso of quire 8.1, in the Library of JTS, 1758.2. In this *Mahzor* one also finds the superimposed letters over the three words.

כי אמרתי: אם יבוא יצרי אל המחנה האחת והכהו — והיה המחנה הנשאר לפליטה, וכאשר חשבתי, כן היה: והנה גבר עלי, והפיץ חילי, ולא נשאר אלי, כי אם מחנה רחמיך.[13]

> I am unworthy of all the mercies and of all the truth that Thou hast dispensed to Thy servant... for Thou hast put a holy soul in me... and with my evil imagining I profaned it... my cruel temper stands firm by my right hand... how many times did I go forth to fight against him and order the company of my worship and my penitence, putting the company of Thy mercies before me to help me. For I said: if my temper "comes to the one company and smites it, then the other company which is left shall escape." And as I thought, so it was. For he prevailed over me, and scattered my warriors, and nothing remained to me but the company of Thy mercies. [14]

It seems that this passage alludes to R. Eleazar's statement. The three "companies" are worship, penitence and God's mercy. They are the ones that are mobilized against the evil inclination (evil imagining or temper, in the above translation). In the *Tanhuma*,[15] too, the triad serves as an antidote against the evil inclination. It seems plausible to suggest that ibn Gabirol's source is the *Tanhuma*. Ibn Gabirol, however, understood צדקה in R. Eleazar's statement as God's mercy and not as the giving of charity. This can easily be done if one understands the word according to one of its many biblical nuances. While in rabbinic literature צדקה denotes charity, in the Bible it may mean many things, including God's love, compassion, mercy, etc.[16]

However, a question remains: is it appropriate to interpret צדקה, occurring in a midrash, in its biblical sense? Let us now take a look at the midrash again. Two of the phrases in 2 Chron. 7.14 easily support their

13 Paragraph 36 (Jerusalem: Y. A. Seidmann, 1950), pp. 76-78.

14 Solomon ibn Gabirol, *The Kingly Crown*, trans. B. Lewis (London, 1961), p. 58. See also R. Loewe, *Ibn Gabirol* (New York, 1990), pp. 150-51.

15 See above, p. 292 n. 2.

16 See the various biblical dictionaries. See also A. Hurvitz, "The Biblical Roots of a Talmudic Term: The Early History of the Concept צדקה (=charity, alms)," in *Mekharim be-lashon* (Jerusalem, 1987), pp. 155-60. I am grateful to David Marcus for calling this paper to my attention.

rabbinic exegesis: ויתפללו: הרי תפלה and וישובו מדרכם הרעה: הרי תשובה. These are very simple, straightforward "midrashim". This is not so, however, in the case of the third phrase: ויבקשו פני: הרי צדקה. Indeed, for this exegesis the midrash needs a prooftext: היאך דאת אמר אני בצדק אחזה פניך (תה' יז טו). לבקש פני ה' means to seek the face of God, that is, to gain God's attention and favor;[17] in other words, to seek God's mercy. Therefore, צדקה, as the rabbinic exegesis of ויבקשו פני, may be interpreted by Ibn Gabirol as mercy in the abstract sense, and as God's mercy.[18] That צדקה and רחמים are equated is known from the Babylonian Talmud: חסד זו גמילת חסדים רחמים זו צדקה, but there צדקה clearly means the giving of charity.[19] In the statement by R. Eleazar, as interpreted by Ibn Gabirol, it refers to God's mercy. Possibly, this could have been the original intent of the midrashic passage as well.

Now the prooftext makes sense, too. Ps. 17.15 (אני בצדק אחזה פניך) was chosen to "prove" that ויבקשו פני means צדקה in the sense of God's mercy. If one would want to bring a prooftext to indicate that צדקה means charity, Prov. 10.2 (וצדקה תציל ממות) would be more to the point. This is, indeed, the prooftext in R. Yitzhak's statement, quoted above,[20] and it serves to demonstrate the merit of charity in rabbinic literature.[21]

Through this interpretation, Ibn Gabirol lends a new dimension to the midrashic statement and to its liturgical derivation. Man can do two things to combat the *gezerah* (in Ibn Gabirol's understanding, the machinations of the evil inclination): engage in worship (תפלה-עבודה) and repent. If these two fail, one can only rely on God's mercy. Although the giving of charity is a great and meritorious deed, it is not in the same category as prayer and penitence. One could argue that some other deed could easily be substituted for charity, but not for prayer and penitence. Instead of singling out just one good deed, we would rather expect a more general category, such as for example the frequently used מעשים טובים, as in the expression תשובה ומעשים טובים.[22] In light

17 See C.L. Mayers and E.M. Mayers, *Haggai, Zechariah 1-8* AB, 25B (New York, 1987), p. 438.

18 It may be just a coincidence, but it is interesting to note that in a poem by Yannai for Rosh hashanah (*The Liturgical Poems of Rabbi Yannai* [ed. Z.M. Rabinovitz; Jerusalem, 1987], p. 199, line 13) we read ותרועה מפרשת צדקה מבקשת. The sense of the line is that Israel seeks צדקה (from God). Does the midrashic passage, ויבקשו פני: הרי צדקה, reverberate here? Does Yannai understand the passage in the Midrash the same way as Ibn Gabirol?

19 *B.B. Bat.* 10a.

20 See above, n. 5.

21 E.g. in *b. Sab* 156b.

22 E.g. in *m. Ab.* 4.11; 4.17; *b. Ber.* 17a; *b. Sab.* 32a, etc.

of the above, Ibn Gabirol's treatment of the passage provides a better understanding of the original intent of R. Eleazar.

Ibn Gabirol's surprising interpretation should not be attributed to poetic license alone; he may have possessed a tradition according to which the word צדקה in the passage in *Bereshit Rabba* (and parallels) referred to God's mercy and not to the giving of charity. Ibn Gabirol's *Kether Malkhuth* is the only surviving testimony of this interpretation.

Sefer Or Zarua and the Legend of Rabbi Amnon

A highly important Hebrew manuscript at the Bibliotheca Rosenthaliana is a late thirteenth-century copy of the famous halakhic work *Sefer Or Zarua* by Rabbi Isaac ben Moses of Vienna (c. 1180-c. 1250). It was from this manuscript, one of only two surviving medieval copies, that the first edition of the work was published in Zhytomir in 1862. The *Or Zarua* preserves one of the earliest, if not the very earliest version of the story of Rabbi Amnon. At the end of the laws concerning Rosh Ha-Shana, Rabbi Isaac of Vienna recorded in the name of Rabbi Ephraim of Bonn (1133-after 1197) that a great and pious scholar in Mainz, Rabbi Amnon, had been the target of a conversion attempt by the local ruler. Under the continued enticement of the ruler, Rabbi Amnon once faltered in his steadfastness. He deeply regretted this momentary hesitation and henceforth refused to appear before the ruler, whereupon the latter ordered his mutilation. With his last ounce of strength, Rabbi Amnon asked to be carried to the synagogue on Rosh Ha-Shana. When the cantor reached the Kedushah prayer, Rabbi Amnon interrupted him and recited the hymn *u-netanneh tokef*. He passed away immediately afterwards. Three days later he appeared in a dream to Rabbi Kalonymos ben Rabbi Meshullam and taught him the hymn that has since become a regular component of the Rosh Ha-Shana liturgy for Ashkenazi and Italian Jewry.

Much has been written about this story, about whether or not Rabbi Amnon was a historical figure; about the liturgical-literary problem concerning the hymn, the text of which antedates the time in which Rabbi Amnon was supposed to have lived; and about the historical setting that gave birth to the story, all of which have been subject to scholarly inquiry.

The attribution of the story to Rabbi Ephraim of Bonn is of special relevance. Rabbi Ephraim was the author of a chronicle, *Sefer Zekhirah*, on the Crusades and other anti-Jewish persecutions; of liturgical poems, some of which commemorate the martyrdom of Jewish victims; and of a commentary on liturgical hymns. In a recent article, Ivan Marcus has argued convincingly that the Amnon story reflects the social and cultural reality of Ashkenazi Jewry in the late twelfth century, the time of Rabbi Ephraim.[1] The connection between the contents of *u-netanneh tokef* and martyrology, however, is unclear. In *u-netanneh tokef* there are no references to events or circumstances in the story itself, and it is devoid of any allusions to martyrology. Also deserving scrutiny is the problem of tracing the route or transmission of the Rabbi Amnon story through the ages.

On the basis of a very limited and preliminary search, it seems that unlike the standard printed machzorim, medieval manuscripts did not routinely place the Rabbi Amnon story alongside *u-netanneh tokef*. A.N.Z. Roth in his study mentions only one manuscript, a machzor (Jewish National and University Library, 8⁰ 3037, beginning of the fourteenth century) in which the commentary to *u-netanneh tokef* includes the story, although in a version different from the one in the *Or Zarua*.[2] Roth refers to a Hamburg manuscript, dated 1317, where *u-netanneh tokef* is identified as the *silluk* (a type of *piyyut*) of Rabbi Amnon, but without the story itself. In printed editions the story first appears in the Bologna 1540 Roman Machzor and in the Venice 1600 Ashkenazi Machzor.

The occurrence in an edition of *selichot* published in Prague in 1587 of a somewhat different version of the Rabbi Amnon story from the one commonly circulating presents a surprising twist. In this source, the story appears before the selichah *ta shema*, written by the previously mentioned Ephraim of Bonn. We are told that before he died as a result of the mutilation he had suffered, Rabbi Amnon composed two poems, *ta shema* and *u-netanneh tokef*. The chronicles *Shalshelet Ha-Kabbalah* by Gedaliah ibn Yahya (1515-1578) and *Tzemach David* by the Prague rabbi and scholar David Ganz (1541-1613) also mention *ta shema* along with *u-netanneh tokef* as having been authored by Rabbi Amnon. In fact, on the basis of the content of *ta shema*, it may make more sense to attach the Rabbi Amnon story to it than to connect it to *u-netanneh tokef*.[3]

1 I.G. Marcus, "Kiddush ha-shem be-ashkenaz we-sippur Rabbi Amnon mi-Magenza," in: I.M. Gafni *et al.*, eds., *Sanctity of Life and Martyrdom: Studies in Memory of Amir Yekutiel* (Jerusalem, 1992), pp. 131-147 (in Hebrew).

2 A.N.Z. Roth, "U-netanneh tokef ve-ha-ir Magenza," *Hadoar* 44.36 (1964) pp. 650-651.

3 Menahem H. Schmelzer, "Maaseh Rabbi Amnon ve-ha-selicha ta shema", *Hadoar* 44.38 (1964) p. 734 [see Hebrew section, pp. 188-189].

Whether we find the story connected with *ta shema* or *u-netanneh tokef* or both, many literary and liturgical questions and problems remain. A search for versions of the Rabbi Amnon story in other manuscripts of the *Or Zarua*, in collections of stories, in liturgical commentaries, and in machzor manuscripts as well as printed editions, may one day yield some solutions to the puzzles posed by this widely known martyrological story. For now, the Amsterdam manuscript of *Sefer Or Zarua* continues to serve as the starting point of all inquiry into the history of the story of Rabbi Amnon of Mainz.

READING

E.G.L. Schrijver, "Some Light on the Amsterdam and London Manuscripts of Isaak ben Moses of Vienna's 'Or Zarua'," *Bulletin of the John Rylands University Library Manchester 73.3* (1993).

E.E. Urbach, [Introduction to] *Sefer Arugat Ha-Bosem* 4 (Jerusalem, 1963), p. 40, n. 92.

Two Philosophical Passages in the Liturgical Poetry of Rabbi Isaac Ibn Giat

Abraham ibn Daud, in his *The Exalted Faith*,[1] regularly quotes Scripture to bear testimony to the various philosophical opinions expounded by him. It is quite amazing that Abraham ibn Daud's prooftexts rarely, if ever, contain references to post-biblical sources, but, on the other hand, include two passages as prooftexts from Isaac ibn Giat's poetry. This clearly indicates that, in the view of Abraham ibn Daud, Ibn Giat's poetry offers valid and authoritative statements relating to metaphysical themes.

In the nineteenth century, the father of modern research in the history of medieval Hebrew poetry, Leopold Zunz, pointed out that Isaac ibn Giat's religious poetry contains interesting information on Jewish philosophy, as well as on the history of sciences among the Jews.[2] Other nineteenth century scholars, Leopold Dukes,[3] Michael Sachs[4] and David Kaufmann,[5] also used Ibn Giat's poetry as a source of philosophical and scientific knowledge.

In 1962, Ibn Giat's Arabic commentary on Ecclesiastes was published for the first time, although the existence of the work had been known previously. With the publication of this work, new insights were gained into

1 Abraham ibn Daud, *The Exalted Faith*; translated with commentary by Norbert M. Samuelson. Translation edited by Gershon Weiss (London and Toronto: Associated University Presses, 1986).

2 Leopold Zunz, *Literaturgeschichte der synagogalen Poesie* (Berlin, 1865), p. 195.

3 Leopold Dukes, "Die naturhistorischen Hymnen des Isak ibn Gioth," in: *Monatsschrift für die Geschichte und Wissenschaft des Judentums*, vol. 8 (1859), pp. 118-121.

4 Michael Sachs, *Die religiöse Poesie der Juden in Spanien*. 2nd ed. (Berlin, 1901), pp. 262-263.

5 David Kaufmann, *Die Sinne* (Budapest, 1884), pp. 30, 40, 44, 51, 84, 93, 124, 139. Also in his *Gesammelte Schriften* (Frankfurt, 1908-1915), vol. 1, p. 246 and in his *Studien über Salomon ibn Gabirol* (Budapest, 1899), p. 102 and in his notes to S.J. Halberstamm's edition of Judah bar Barzillai al-Bargeloni's commentary to *Sefer Yezira* (Berlin, 1885), p. 345.

the philosophy of Ibn Giat, and the commentary could now also be utilized for the understanding of some difficult poetic passages in his work.[6]

Ibn Giat's religious poetry received very scant attention in recent times and very little, if anything, is published about him in English.[7] This, of course, is to be regretted, since Ibn Giat was a central figure in eleventh century Spanish Jewry and was highly regarded as a halakhist and as a poet.[8]

In the present paper, the two passages quoted by Abraham ibn Daud will be examined.

Abraham ibn Daud's first quotation is from Ibn Giat's monumental composition for the morning service of the Day of Atonement. It reads:

אמרו קצת חשובי אומתנו וחכמיה ומשורריה׳ גִזְרֵי חָכְמוֹת גָבְהוּ/ גָזַר וּמְקוֹרֵיהֶם
גָבְרוּ וְלֹא לָהוּ/ גַל עֵינוֹת שֵׂכֶל יָצָא מֶנְהוּ/ וְהוּא/ רֵאשִׁית דַרְכֵי אֵל.[9]

In order to understand this passage, we must look for aid in other places in Ibn Giat's compositions, which will, perhaps, shed light on this rather difficult sentence. Elsewhere in the Day of Atonement liturgy, Ibn Giat writes:

מַעֲשֶׂיךָ זָהֳרֵי חָכְמָה רֵאשִׁית יְצִירוֹת נָצְרוּ/ חֻקֵּי תָכְנִיתָם מֵהַשִּׂיג גָבְרוּ/ טוֹעֲמֶיהָ טָעֲמוּ
וְרָאוּ וְאָמְרוּ/ לֵאלֹהִים מַה נּוֹרָא מַעֲשֶׂיךָ.

מַעֲשֶׂיךָ יְסוֹד שֵׂכֶל מֵאוֹר חָכְמָה נִמְצָא/ כְּנֹגַהּ אֵשׁ וּמִן הָאֵשׁ בָּרָק יָצָא/ מַעֲשֶׂיךָ מִנֹּגַהּ
הַשֵּׂכֶל נְבוּנֹתִי/ נִמְצְאוּ נְשָׁמוֹת עַד לֹא נִמְצֵאתִי.[10]

6 In *Hamesh Megillot 'im Perushim 'Atikim*, edited by Joseph Kafih (Jerusalem, 1962), pp. 161-296. See S. Pines in *Tarbiz*, vol. 33 (1964), pp. 212-213; G. Vajda in *Historia Judaica*, vol. 2 (1963), p. 450; S. Abramson, *Rav Nissim Gaon* (Jerusalem, 1965), p. 305, note 1.

7 See the brief selections from his poetry in *The Penguin Book of Hebrew Verse*, edited and translated by T. Carmi (Middlesex, England and New York: Penguin Books, 1981), pp. 103-104; 317-320.

8 See Abraham Ibn Daud, *The Book of Tradition (Sefer ha-Qabbalah)*, Critical edition and notes by Gerson D. Cohen (Philadelphia: Jewish Publication Society, 1967), Hebrew Section, pp. 60-61; English section, pp. 81-82 and Moshe ibn Ezra, *Kitab al-Muhadara wal-Mudhakara*, edited by A.S. Halkin (Jerusalem: Mekize Nirdamim, 1975), pp. 72-73.

9 *The Exalted Faith* (see above, note 1), Hebrew section, p. 324 (160b, 11.7-9); English section, p. 179. The composition begins: "וארץ אכף", see: Israel Davidson, *Thesaurus of Mediaeval Hebrew Poetry*, 4 volumes (New York: Jewish Theological Seminary, 1924-1933) (reprint: New York: Ktav Publishing, 1970), letter vav, number 66. The quotation is from the first section; see also: Yonah David, *The Poems of Rabbi Isaac ibn Ghiyyat*; a tentative edition (Jerusalem: Akhshav, 1987), p. 7.

10 Davidson, *op. cit.*, letter mem, number 2056; David, *op. cit.*, p. 41.

The latter passage can best be understood by comparing it to the following statement that occurs in Isaac Israeli's *Chapter on the Elements*:

> Aristotle the philosopher and master of the wisdom of the Greeks said: The beginning of all roots is two simple substances: one of them is first matter, which receives form and is known to the philosophers as the root of roots. It is the first substance which subsists in itself and is the substratum of diversity. The other is substantial form, which is ready to impregnate matter. It is perfect wisdom, pure radiance, and clear splendour, by the conjunction of which with first matter the nature and form of intellect came into being, because it [intellect] is composed of them [matter and form]. After the nature, form, and radiance of intellect had come into being, a radiance and splendour went forth from it. From this the nature of the rational soul came into being.[11]

As shown by S.M. Stern, the above is in accordance with the doctrine of emanation as found in the so-called *Ibn Hasday's Neoplatonist*.[12] The author of this treatise as well as Isaac Israeli discuss the degrees of emanation and particularly the gradation of the intensity of light in the process of emanation. Concerning this, Isaac Israeli says: "Regarding the quality of emanation of the light from the power and the will, we have already made it clear that its beginning is different from its end, and the middle from both extremes, and this for the following reason: when its beginning emanated from the power and the will, it met no shade or darkness to make it dim or coarse."[13]

We have placed Ibn Giat's verses into the framework of ideas concerning the theory of emanation. We may attempt to paraphrase them as follows:

> God split apart loftly Wisdom; its fountains swelled and did not diminish; a wave of the springs of Intellect emanated from Him and this was the beginning of God's works.[14]

11 A. Altmann and S.M. Stern, *Isaac Israeli: A Neoplatonic Philosopher of the Early Tenth Century* (Oxford: Oxford University Press, 1958), p. 119.

12 *Op. cit.*, p. 98.

13 *Op. cit.*, p. 88 and see also p. 102.

14 The scriptural verses which are reflected in this passage are the following: Psalms 136:13, Genesis 7:19-20; Genesis 47:13; Job 40:19. The use of the plural in חכמות גבהו has a parallel in one of Saadia Gaon's poems where we read: תבונותיך גבהו. This was pointed out by M. Zulay in

The second quotation may be rendered as follows:

> Your deeds are: At the beginning You created the splendors of Wisdom. Their nature is beyond comprehension and those who ponder it say: how mighty are Your deeds.
>
> Your deeds are: from the light of wisdom You brought into existence the element of Intellect, which is like the radiance of fire...
>
> Your deeds are: from the radiance of the Intellect You brought forth the Soul...

The similarity with Isaac Israeli's text and with *Ibn Hasday's Neoplatonist* is evident, and it is safe to assume that all three were using a common source, probably an Arabic treatise, as Stern indeed had proposed in connection with Israeli and the *Neoplatonist*.[15]

Let us now return to the quotation found in *The Exalted Faith*. What is the exact meaning of the root גזר in בגזרי חכמות גבהו גזר? What did Abraham ibn Daud intend to prove with Ibn Giat's verses?

Solomon ibn Gabirol in his *Royal Crown*, when describing creation, says: וְקָרָא אֶל הָאַיִן וְנִבְקַע (and He called out to nothingness and it was split).[16] The Hebrew root גזר is synonymous with the Hebrew root בקע. Accordingly, we may consider Ibn Giat's passage as parallel to Ibn Gabirol's. In both, the process of creation, at its very beginning, is described with the help of a verb that means: to split. Shlomo Pines proved that the verb בקע in Ibn Gabirol resembles a usage found in a passage occurring in a treatise by Avicenna. Pines also places the use of the Arabic equivalent, the root *falaḳa*, in the context of writings which present the reader with an image of the created universe in its various gradations.[17] This is, of course, also the context of the *Royal Crown*, as pointed out by Pines. We may now add Ibn Giat's poem to this group. This long poem, which consists of many parts, also has as its subject the presentation of the

his *Ha-Askola ha-Paytanit shel Rav Sa'adya Gaon* (Jerusalem: The Schocken Institute, 1964), p. 105. The meaning of the phrase is as in the singular and it was translated accordingly, to avoid using the awkward "Wisdoms."

15 *Op. cit.*, p. 96.

16 Section 9; See *Keter Malkhut*, ed. by Y.A. Seidman (Jerusalem: Mossad Harav Kook, 1950), p. 24.

17 Shlomo Pines, "'And He called out to nothingness and it was split'—A Note on a Passage in Ibn Gabirol's *Keter Malkhut*," in *Tarbiz*, vol. 50 (1980-1981), pp. 339-347.

created world as one of gradation, beginning with the loftiest emanation, namely that of Wisdom and descending through various stages to the material world. For the earliest stage of emanation (for the moment at which it begins), Ibn Gabirol and Ibn Giat use the word: to split, בקע or the synonymous גזר. Both words are used in the Bible for the splitting of waters, e.g. in Genesis 7:11, Exodus 14:21, Psalms 136:13, etc. In Isaiah 58:8, the passive of *baka*ʻ occurs in connection with the spreading of light. Both poets, indeed, employ metaphors of light and water in describing the process of emanation. In Ibn Gabirol we read: וְהַחָכְמָה מְקוֹר חַיִּים מִמְּךָ נוֹבַעַת... וְשׁוֹאֵב מִמְּקוֹר הָאוֹר מִבְּלִי דְלִי... וְקָרָא אֶל הָאַיִן וְנִבְקַע, (and Wisdom is the fountain of life and from You it streams forth... without bucket from the fountain of light it draws... and He called out to nothingness and it was split),[18] while Ibn Giat says: גזרי חכמות גבהו גזר ומקוריהם גברו... גל עינות שכל (God split apart lofty Wisdom; its fountains swelled; a wave of the springs of Intellect), and in the second passage: זהרי חכמה (splendours of Wisdom). It seems, therefore, plausible to suggest that in order to convey the idea of Wisdom emanating from God which bears in itself the diversity of subsequent creation, writers in the Arabic tradition as well as in Hebrew poetry employ the word "to split," implying by this the unity of a first substance "which... is the substratum of diversity."[19] "To split" is, then, the beginning of the process of emanation, which is further described through metaphors of sources of light and fountains of water.[20]

If we now return to Abraham ibn Daud, we can clearly see the purpose of his quoting this passage by Ibn Giat. Ibn Daud's chapter, in which this quotation is used to support his thesis (called כתובים מעידים, "what scriptural verses testify about the above") deals with the order of the universe and especially with the philosophical problem of "what is called the 'Many from the One'."[21] Ibn Daud recalls this passage from Ibn Giat to prove that there is a chain of intermediaries between the One (God) and the Many (the diversity of the created universe).

The second quotation from one of Ibn Giat's poems occurs in the same chapter of *The Exalted Faith*. It reads:

18 *Keter Malkhut*, section 9, ed. Seidman (see above note 16), pp. 20-24.

19 Altmann and Stern, *op. cit.*, p. 119.

20 [See now: Adena Tanenbaum, *The Contemplative Soul; Hebrew Poetry and Philosophical Theory in Medieval Spain* (Leiden, Brill, 2002), pp. 106-107.]

21 *The Exalted Faith* (see above note 1), p. 169.

ובאשר הראשון יתברך לא יקיף בו מקום ובאשר מדרגת קדושתו למעלה ממדרגת אלה הנקראים שכליים יאמרו קצת נכבדינו: צָרוּ מְקוֹמוֹת מֵהֲכִילֶךָ/ וְשַׁחוּ מְרוֹמוֹת מִסְּבוֹל גָּדְלֶךָ/ וְתֵכּוּ אֲדָמוֹת לְפַעֲמֵי רַגְלֶיךָ/ וְעַל גַּב חָכְמוֹת נִתְקְעוּ אָהֳלֶיךָ/ כִּי אֵין מַחֲנֶיךָ אֹהֶל וְאוּלָם.

> Concerning [the claims that the First, may He be blessed, is not encircled by a place and that the grade of His holiness is above the grades of these [entities] that are called "intellects," some of our venerable people said, Places are narrow from encompassing You and heights are bent down from bearing Your greatness. Lands melt at Your footsteps, and upon Wisdom is Your tent thrust, because Your camp is not in a tent or a hall.[22]

This passage is much simpler than the previous one. In it, Ibn Giat expresses the old Rabbinic doctrine, based on biblical antecedents, according to which the world is not the place of God but God is the place of the world.[23] This idea is found frequently in the poems of the classic Golden Age poets, and as shown by Aron Mirsky, its frequent use is caused by the connection between these poems and the basic philosophic-theological work by Baḥya ibn Pakuda, *Duties of the Heart*.[24] It is the cardinal belief in the incorporeality of God and, for that reason, finds its place in many liturgical poems of the Spanish school. Mirsky collected a number of such passages from the poems of Ibn Gabirol and Judah Halevi.[25] Ibn Giat's words, as quoted by Ibn Daud, may now be added to them.

22 *Ibid.*, Hebrew section, p. 323 (162b, 11.5-9); English section, p. 180. The quotation is from a poem beginning: "שירו לאלהים" see Davidson, *op. cit.*, letter shin (supplements in vol. 4), number 54. The best text of this poem is the one published by Joseph Marcus in *Sinai*, vol. 56 (1965), pp. 22-23. See also: David, *op. cit.*, pp. 474-475. In Ibn Daud's text the word צרו became corrupted into סרו, therefore the mistranslation: "Place turn aside." The translation of תכו as "melted" was left intact for lack of a better one.

23 See A. Marmorstein, *The Old Rabbinic Doctrine of God* (London, 1927), pp. 92-93 and Altmann and Stern, *op. cit.*, p. 126, note 1.

24 A. Mirsky, "Hebrew Poems from Spain Based on the Second Gate (*Sha'ar Ha-Behina*) of R. Bahya Ibn Paquda's *Hovot Ha-Levavot*," in *Tarbiz*, vol. 50 (1980-1981), pp. 303-338 and his article on the same subject in *Hebrew Language Studies Presented to Professor Zeev Ben-Hayyim* (Jerusalem: The Magnes Press, 1983), pp. 383-406.

25 Mirsky, in *Tarbiz, ibid.*, pp. 333-334.

The Poems in the *Barcelona Haggadah*
A Literary Study

Since the *Haggadah* itself is a book intended uniquely for the home, it might seem strange that texts for the public service in the synagogue are appended to it. Yet a number of Sephardi illuminated *Haggadoth* of the fourteenth and fifteenth centuries contain, in addition to the *Haggadah* proper, a group of *piyyutim*, "liturgical poems," written specifically for the festival days and intermediate Sabbath of Passover, as well as for the Sabbath preceding the festival (*shabbath ha-gadol*).

Most of these poems, by some of the finest of medieval Hebrew poets, have no direct connection with the home ceremony of Passover. There are, however, exceptions. It is logical that a book for home use would include *'azharoth*—rhymed summaries of the religious regulations concerning Passover and the Passover home ceremony, the *Seder*—since, although *'azharoth* are routinely recited on the Sabbath preceding Passover, it made good sense to include them in the *Haggadah* as useful guides for the complicated preparations for and procedures during the *Seder*. One could equally explain the appearance of poem 5,[*] "A watch-night this," [*Lel Shimmurim*] since the poem is for the eve of Passover, and the owners of these volumes may have wished to have the entire liturgy for the evening, both at synagogue and in the home, available in one book. Yet this factor does not explain why texts belonging to the public services for other days of the festival were added to *Haggadah* manuscripts. It is conceivable that the custom harks back to before the thirteenth century, when the *Haggadah* was not yet regarded as a separate book, and was presented as part of larger prayerbooks containing all the Passover texts, or even those for other festivals too.[1]

* The Poem numbers refer to the translation of texts in the *Commentary* volume of the facsimile edition of *The Barcelona Haggadah* (London, 1992), pp. 75-171

1 See Bezalel Narkiss, *The Golden Haggadah* (London, 1970), pp. 10-11.

The present manuscript is one of a group of similar books, each containing a selection of liturgical poems (*piyyutim*) besides the *Haggadah* proper. Interestingly, most such volumes do not contain the full text of the standard prayers, which were probably considered familiar enough to bear omitting, but only the poetic ones specific to Passover. Just one *Haggadah* manuscript, British Library MS Or. 1404, includes the complete texts of standard prayers as well as the liturgical poems.

The most important manuscripts in this group, besides the present one, are the *Sarajevo*, *Golden* and *Rylands Haggadoth* as well as British Library Or. 1404 mentioned above. The first three have already appeared in facsimile, and their *piyyutim* described and analyzed.[2] A number of hitherto unpublished poems have appeared in print for the first time as a result,[3] and translations have occasionally also been included. Selected poems were rendered into German in the *Sarajevo Haggadah*, while all the poems in the *Rylands Haggadah* were translated into English by Raphael Loewe,[4] who has performed the same invaluable service in the present publication. The selection of the poetic texts is similar in each manuscript, yet no one version of any *piyyut* can be regarded as definitive without comparing it with all the manuscript and printed versions available. Indeed, juxtaposing the poems appearing in the present manuscript with their counterparts in the *Rylands Haggadah* (as Raphael Loewe has done for this edition) and with other sources, reveals some significant variants. To facilitate the collation of texts, Loewe, in the bibliography of the poems appearing in the *Rylands Haggadah*, provides references to other *Haggadah* manuscripts as well as to manuscripts of the former Sassoon Collection.[5] These references may be augmented by others.

Liturgical poems similar to the ones in these *Haggadoth* appear also in the Passover sections of various manuscript festival prayerbooks (*mahzorim*) ascribed to the Sephardi rite or to its close relatives, the Provençal and North African rites. The *mahzor* manuscripts that show

2 Dav. Heinr. Mueller and Julius v. Schlosser, Die *Haggadah von Sarajevo* (Vienna, 1898), pp. 54-92; Narkiss (see n. 1), pp. 11-16; Raphael Loewe (ed.), *The Rylands Haggadah* (London and New York, 1988), 17-20, pp. 23-4.

3 Mueller and Schlosser (see n. 2), pp. 78-80, and e.g. the poems 7 and 4 in the present volume, fols. 99b and 8a.

4 Mueller and Schlosser (see n. 2), pp. 81-92; Loewe (see n. 2), pp. 25-31, 37-66.

5 Loewe (see n. 2), pp. 23-4.

great affinity to this group of *Haggadoth* include: Copenhagen, Royal Library, MS Hebr. 30;[6] Paris, Biblotheque Nationale, MS Hebr. 658; London Jews' College, MS Montefiore 203; Moscow, Lenin Library, MS Gunzburg 198,[7] the Moscow manuscript containing a colophon explicitly stating that it was written in Barcelona in 1264-5.[8] Further localization is difficult to detect within this group, since contacts between communities were close. The present manuscript displays features which characterize the rites of the Sephardi as well as the related Provençal and North African liturgies. Indeed, the poetic components of these liturgies are so similar that it is almost impossible to tell them apart. Leopold Zunz long ago called attention to this commonality, but also discerned some subtle differences between them.[9] Zunz, in including the present manuscript in his study, characterizes it as belonging to the Provence tradition.[10] This designation was based on the fact that it includes the Aramaic translation of biblical readings, called the "Jerusalem Targum," as well as Aramaic poems for the Seventh Day of Passover and the First Day of Pentecost. The use of this *Targum* and of Aramaic *piyyutim*, while customary in Provence, was unknown in Spain.

This distinction is of help in determining the rite of our *Haggadah*, and lends support to the conclusion reached by Malachi Beit-Arié, in a paper in the present volume, in which he argues, on the basis of codicological and paleographical considerations,[11] that the present manuscript is a composite one. He points out that its original part (fols. 9-151) contains texts according to the Spanish rite, while its additional and minor parts (fols. 1-8 and 152-61) incorporate material according to the Provençal rite.

6 Many poems were published for the first time from this manuscript, see e.g. J. Schirmann, "Poets Contemporary with Mose ibn Ezra and Jehuda hallevi," *Studies of the Research Institute for Hebrew Poetry* II (1936), pp. 170, 182, 190; H. Brody, "Hitherto Unpublished Poems by Abraham ibn Ezra," *ibid.* VI (1945), pp. 5-6, 12-13; A.M. Habermann, *Athereth Renanim* (Jerusalem, 1967), p. 234; Yonah David, *The Poems of Rabbi Isaac ibn Ghiyyat* (A Tentative Edition, Jerusalem, 1987), p. 505; see note 27 below.

7 See A.I. Katsh, *Yiggal Hazon* (Jerusalem, 1964). The manuscript number is mistakenly given as 108 on p. 11.

8 Katsh (see n. 7), p. 12.

9 Leopold Zunz, *Die Ritus des synagogalen Gottesdienstes* (Berlin, 1859), pp. 45-50. See also his "Ritus der Synagoge von Avignon," *Allgemeine Zeitung des Judenthums* III (1839), pp. 78-9, 470.

10 Zunz (see n. 9), p. 46.

11 See his description of the manuscript in *The Barcelona Haggadah; Commentary*, pp. 14-23.

In the main part, on fols. 105-19, we find the Torah readings for all the days of Passover, which, in accordance with the Spanish rite, are not accompanied by the Aramaic translation. On the other hand, on fols. 152-55, we find the Aramaic Jerusalem *Targum* to the reading of the Seventh Day of Passover, appearing there without the original Hebrew, an Aramaic poem illustrating the theme of the same reading; the reading for the First Day of Pentecost accompanied by the Jerusalem *Targum* (the Hebrew and Aramaic in alternating verses); and an Aramaic poem. The inclusion of these texts reflects the usage of Provençal Jews.

Other textual peculiarities likewise suggest that the manuscript falls into distinct parts that reflect two different liturgical traditions. Such a conclusion fully explains the appearance in the manuscript of two different versified versions of the laws of Passover (*'azharoth*): on fols. 99b-104a one finds the *'azharoth* by Abraham Ṣebi ben Isaac Halevi of Tamakh (poem 7) and by Zeraḥyah Halevi (poem 9), while on fols. 2a-6b we find these duplicated by Kalonymus Nasi (poem 1), a Provençal poet who lived in the thirteenth century.[12] Kalonymus' *'azharoth* are characteristic of the Provençal rite,[13] while the former are found in liturgical books which follow the Spanish usage.

The situation is identical with respect to the prayer for dew, of which, again, the manuscript contains two sets of poems. On fols. 147a-148b, the poems for dew are by Solomon Ibn Gabirol and an anonymous poet (poems 45-8), while on fols. 7b-8b, the corresponding texts are by Abraham Ibn Ezra, and a different, more archaic, anonymous poet (poems 3-4). The latter group is documented in Provençal prayerbooks, while the former appears in Spanish ones.

Three additional poems (poem 56, fol. 153b; poem 58, fol. 156a; poem 59, fol. 158a) are not only characteristic of the Provençal rite, but the second and third are the work of the Provençal poet, Joseph ben Ḥanan Ezobi.

On the basis of all of the above, there is no doubt that the present manuscript represents two liturgical traditions:

12 Zunz, "Ritus der Synagoge von Avignon" (see n. 9), p. 679 and Zunz (see n. 28), p. 479. See also *Encyclopaedia Judaica* IX (Berlin, 1932), pp. 845-6.

13 Cf., however, MS Sassoon 514, fol. 36ff. which in its Spanish part contains the *'azharoth* by Kalonymus (fol. 36ff). About this manuscript, see further below.

1. fols. 9-151: the main body of the manuscript, with poems according to the Spanish rite;
2. fols. 1-8 and 152-61: supplementary sections, containing poems according to the Provençal rite.

As pointed out above, the supplementary parts do not merely expand the Passover repertoire, but duplicate it, and include poems for Pentecost, a festival that falls seven weeks after Passover. Their presence in particular demands an explanation. Malachi Beit-Arié suggests two possible explanations for this apparent anomaly. First, he considers it possible that the additional leaves "were dismantled from a larger copy of Provençal *piyyutim* and bound together" with the original part.[14] Second, he thinks it conceivable, on the basis of codicological evidence, that "the additional first and last quires were originally prepared as a Provençal-rite supplement to the original Catalan manuscript."[15]

This second suggestion is supported by further evidence of a textual nature. The arrangement of the texts on the leaves added at the end (fols. 152a-160a) indicates that they were written intentionally to supplement the main body of the manuscript. These leaves contain two types of text for the Seventh Day of Passover and the First Day of Pentecost: on the one hand, Aramaic *Targum* and Aramaic poems, and on the other hand, poems of the *zulath* type. If these pages had ever formed part of a larger prayerbook, one would expect the order for Passover to have been concluded before that of Pentecost was begun, and that the selection would include other texts as well, and not only *Targum* and *zulatoth*. Here, however, the Aramaic *Targum* texts and the poems for Passover and Pentecost are copied without interruption, followed by the two *zulatoth*, one for the Seventh Day of Passover (poem 58), and another, immediately following it, for the First Day of Pentecost (poem 59). The poem that precedes them, *yevussar 'am 'evyon* (poem 56), a *pizmon* for the prayer for dew, on fol. 153b, was clearly copied for one purpose only: to fill the blank space left at the end of the previous section. Furthermore, the *Targum* for the Seventh Day of Passover, that appears without the text of the original Hebrew Torah reading, seems inconsistent with the presentation of the *Targum* for the First Day of Pentecost, that is copied together with the

14 *The Barcelona Haggadah; Commentary*, p. 16

15 *ibid.*

Hebrew, in alternating verses. The most obvious explanation is that the scribe of the additional leaves was fully aware that the Torah reading for the Seventh Day of Passover had already appeared in Hebrew in the original part of the manuscript (fols. 115a-18b) and therefore did not need to be repeated. However, since the Torah reading for Pentecost did not feature in the original *Haggadah*, the scribe of the supplement naturally supplied the Hebrew text together with the Aramaic one.

In view of these factors, there can be no doubt that the additional leaves were intentionally prepared as a separate unit, in order to augment the original part of the *Haggadah*.

We find a similar situation in Manuscript Sassoon 514, which is also a *Haggadah* according to the Spanish rite, with a supplement written 'by a later sq[uare] Avignon hand.' The Avignon part (fols. 253-79) has the Jerusalem *Targum* to the Torah readings for the Seventh Day of Passover and for the First Day of Pentecost, accompanied by Aramaic poems,[16] exactly as is the case in the manuscript described here. In both cases the Aramaic poems appear with cantillation marks, a phenomenon not known from other sources.[17]

These two manuscripts now enable us to document the addition of specifically Provençal liturgical pieces to Spanish *Haggadoth*. The supplementary parts were probably commissioned by the Provençal purchasers of exquisite Spanish *Haggadoth*, who felt the need to augment them with favorite liturgical pieces found to be lacking in the Spanish part. The new leaves were designed and written to resemble the original, probably not much after the completion of the originals.[18] It is interesting to note that the supplementary parts in both manuscripts lack illuminations or illustrations. Nevertheless, it remains unclear why liturgical texts for Pentecost were included in these *Haggadah* manuscripts devoted otherwise entirely to Passover. One could perhaps advance the following suggestion: the similarity between the general themes and biblical readings for the Seventh Day of Passover and the First Day of Pentecost made it natural to express the link formally. Both feature Torah readings which deal with dramatic events in biblical history: the crossing

16 David Solomon Sassoon, *Ohel Dawid; Descriptive Catalogue of the Hebrew and Samaritan Manuscripts in the Sassoon Library* (London, 1932), pp. 303-4.

17 See Hebrew Section, p. 1, note 1.

18 See Beit-Arié, *The Barcelona Haggadah; Commentary*, p. 16.

of the Red Sea and the giving of the Law on Mount Sinai, respectively. It was apparently felt in Provence that such themes call for special liturgical embellishment, and this was provided by the Jerusalem *Targum* portions, the Aramaic poems and the *zulatoth*, which contain epic retelling of the biblical events, enriched by legendary details and presented as lively dialogue. Since the Seventh Day of Passover and the First Day of Pentecost shared these features, and were thus treated liturgically in a similar manner, the copyists and owners of codices were inclined to present the special liturgies of the two days side by side.

A third dramatic biblical event, the death of Moses, which is the subject of the synagogue reading on the festival of *Simḥath Torah*, received similar attention in the Provençal rite, at least as far as the *zulath* is concerned.[19] Yet since *Simḥath Torah* occurs some six months after Passover, while Pentecost not only follows Passover after a relatively short interval, but also is connected with it biblically (cf. *Exodus* 23, 15ff. and *Deuteronomy* 16, 9ff.), it made sense to include only the Passover and the Pentecost texts.

To summarize: in the present manuscript we find the *Haggadah, piyyutim* and Torah readings according to the Spanish rite (fols. 9-151); and poems, Aramaic *Targumim* and Aramaic *piyyutim* according to the Provençal custom (fols. 1-8 and 152-61). In the main part (fols. 9b-16b, 99b-104a, 136b-151a) there are 46 poems; while in the supplementary part their number is 9, with one poem (poem 6, fol. 85a) appearing within the *Haggadah* proper.

Most of the *piyyutim* found in *Haggadoth* of this type belong to the genre called *yoṣeroth*, or poems accompanying the *yoṣer* blessing, recited each morning, in which God is praised as creator of the world. This poetic genre developed in the Holy Land towards the end of the Byzantine period, and served as a vehicle for liturgical change and creativity, providing poetic embellishment to the morning service, and relieving the monotony of the standard prayers. Originally, the poetic *yoṣer* would have served as a substitute for the standard text, and would have retained only a few statutorily required liturgical formulae, while offering a wealth of poetic variations on the basic themes of the service. Complex *yoṣer* compositions used to encompass the entire prayer-sequence, from the call

19 See Leon J. Weinberger, "*Me-rosh mi-kadmei erez nesukha—zulath al petirath moshe l-r. Yehoseph Ezobi,*" *Hebrew Union College Annual* XXXVII (1966), pp. 1-11 (Hebrew section).

to prayer, to the *shema'* and to the last of the three blessings surrounding it. A *yoṣer* of the classic period of the *piyyut* was a many-tiered but integrated work, consisting of a series of closely linked components. The opening poem in such a cycle was attached to the first extended blessing, that praises God as the *yoṣer 'or*, 'maker of light,' the first word of which gave its name to the genre. Subsequent components received their names from key words appearing at significant junctures later in the same service. Each element offered an elaboration, usually brief and fairly simple, on the themes suggested by the three main blessings (creation, Israel's chosenness, redemption) and by the *kedushah de-yoṣer*, 'sanctification,' a sequence based on *Isaiah* 6, 3 and *Ezekiel* 3, 12.

Many generations of poets, spanning several centuries, practiced their skills by composing such *yoṣeroth*. No wonder, therefore, that in time, both the content and the form of this genre grew stale and lacking in creativity. The genre was ripe for major change around the time that Hebrew poetry began to blossom in Spain in the tenth-eleventh centuries.

The long history of the *yoṣer*, and the various stages in its development, have been thoroughly documented in a monumental study by Ezra Fleischer, who, on the basis of hitherto unknown manuscript materials, mainly from the Cairo Genizah, details the various stages in the origin, development, decline and transformation of the *yoṣer*.[20]

In Spain, a new school of Hebrew poetry, which broke with older traditions in a revolutionary manner, brought forth a revitalized and restructured kind of *yoṣer* poem. The complex cycles which used to embellish all the main components of the morning service disappeared. Instead, poets now focused on one component or another without necessarily providing compositions for the other significant points in the service.[21] Furthermore, the Andalusian poets wrote in poetic metres borrowed from Arabic literature and in a strophic system influenced by Andalusian models, liberally sprinkling their liturgical compositions with motifs taken from secular Arabic poetry. An analysis of some characteristics of Hebrew religious poetry in Golden Age Spain, with a selection of poems in the original and translation, has been published by Raymond P. Scheindlin.[22]

20 Ezra Fleischer, *The Yozer: Its Emergence and Development* (Jerusalem, 1984).

21 Fleischer (see n. 18), pp. 475-604.

22 Raymond P. Scheindlin, *The Gazelle; Medieval Hebrew Poems on God, Israel and the Soul* (Philadelphia, 1991).

As a result of this transformation, the *yoṣeroth* of the Spanish school tended to take the form of short, free-standing, lyrical poems, reflecting the philosophical, theological and religious concerns of their authors. God, ways of knowing Him, proofs of his existence, his attributes, his transcendence and immanence, the creation of both the macrocosm and of the microcosm, man's relationship with God, the body and soul, and the frailty of life, are among the themes addressed by these great Spanish Hebrew poets. The close affinity between the ideas expressed in philosophical-theological works and poems of the period has been demonstrated recently by Aharon Mirsky.[23] Another central theme is the nature of Jewish nationhood. Many poems explore the nature of Israel, its chosenness, its sufferings in the Diaspora, its relationship to other nations and its invincible trust in ultimate redemption. In all these kinds of poetry, the voice of the individual is clearly audible, but, at the same time, one cannot escape the impression that the poet speaks not only for himself, but also for the entire community. This intermingling of voices, the communal and the personal, is one of the major characteristics of the Hebrew poetry of the Spanish Golden Age.

The prayerbooks according to the Sephardi and related rites absorbed just some of the religious poems of the Spanish Hebrew poets; in a sense they can be looked on as selective anthologies. Unfortunately, however, we do not possess prayerbooks written in the eleventh-twelfth centuries, which might show us the liturgical application of these poems in the period in which they were written. Our sources are centuries younger, and we know neither the original settings of many of these poems, nor the poets' intentions concerning their liturgical use.

This uncertainty applies particularly to the *yoṣer* poems found in the fourteenth- and fifteenth-century manuscripts, in which they are assigned to different days of the festival in various sources: a certain poem may be allocated to the liturgy of a particular day in one document, and to an entirely different one in another. The scribe of the present manuscript went so far as to omit particularly all designations to days of the festival, and preferred to group the poems by genre, apparently leaving it to the

23 [See now: Aharon Mirsky, *From Duties of the Heart to Songs of the Heart; Jewish Philosophy and Ethnics and Their Influence on Hebrew Poetry in Medieval Spain* (Jerusalem, 1992; in Hebrew); See now also: Adena Tanenbaum, *The Contemplative Soul; Hebrew Poetry and Philosophical Theory in Medieval Spain* (Leiden, 2002).]

prayer leader to select texts according to taste. There are only two exceptions to this: poem 30 (fol. 141b) is identified as being for the Intermediate Sabbath of the festival, while poem 53 (fol. 150b) is designated for "The Day of the Song," the Seventh Day of Passover.

In sum, these *yoṣer* poems are "neutral" compositions, rarely referring to a specific festival or ritual, and, as a result, were used on various occasions. Their appeal was so general, on account of their aesthetic and thematic qualities, that in many instances they could be regarded as independent, lyrical religious compositions and not as texts that fulfill a specific liturgical function. This universal spirituality enables most of them to speak to the heart and mind of even modern readers.

Several other genres, besides the *yoṣer* poems, appear in this group of Spanish *Haggadoth*. The versified Passover rules (*'azharoth*), that have already been mentioned, might seem difficult to appreciate unless it is understood that Jewish tradition regards study as little less important than the implementation of the ceremony itself. In these poems, like in many of the others, a close knowledge of the Hebrew Bible is assumed, and the poet, reapplying quotations in unfamiliar contexts, creates a literary texture of rare brilliance.

In the service for the First Day of Passover, one finds poems related to the prayer for dew. These fall into a category known as *kerovah*, poetic compositions attached to the '*amidah*, the statutory sequence of blessings that forms the core of each service. They focus on the themes of water and fertility.

In addition to the poetic compositions, the *Haggadoth* contain the Torah readings and *Haftaroth*, 'readings from the Prophets,' for Passover. The *Haftaroth* appear with their Aramaic translation, in alternating verses. As discussed above, the supplementary part of the manuscript incorporates a number of unusual features: poetic texts; Torah readings; Aramaic translations; and Aramaic poems on the crossing of the Red Sea and on the giving of the Law on Mount Sinai, for the Seventh Day of Passover and the First Day of Pentecost, respectively.

These are the poetic genres found in the *Barcelona Haggadah*:

'Azharoth and *pizmon* (rhymed summary of the laws for Passover and the home ceremony):

1 and 2, 7 and 8, 9 and 10

Reshuth (introductory poem to the *nishmath* prayer): 11, 12, 13, 14, 15, 16, 17

Muharrakh (introductory poem to the *nishmath* prayer): 18
Nishmath (poem attached to the *nishmath* prayer): 19, 20
Kaddeesh (introductory poem to *Kaddeesh)*: 21
yoṣer (poem attached to the *yoṣer 'or* blessing): 22
'Ofan (poem attached to the *ve-ha 'ofanim* section): 23, 24, 25, 26, 27
Me'orah (poem attached to the *yoṣer ha-me'oroth* blessing): 28, 29, 30, 31
Ahavah (poem attached to the *'ahavah* blessing): 32, 33, 34, 35, 36, 37
Zulath (poem attached to the section: *'ein 'elohim zulathekha*): 38, 39
Ge'ullah (poem attached to the *ge'ullah* blessing): 40, 41, 42
Mi kamokha (poem attached to the *mi kamokha* section): 43, 44

Following this main group of poems, we find a series of prayers for dew (poems 45-9, fols. 147a-149a), which is followed by one poem each of the *me'orah*, *'ahavah*, *mi kamokha*, *'ofan* and *sim shalom* types (poems 50-4, fols. 149a-151a). Since these poems appear immediately after the prayer for dew to be read on the First Day of Passover, one might think that they were intended to follow it on the same day. But in fact they precede it. In addition, one of the poems in the group (poem 53, fol. 150b) is clearly designated for the Seventh Day of Passover, the "Day of the Song." It is clear, therefore, that the location of these texts is not chronological, and that no designation for any particular day was intended by the scribe.

In the supplementary sections there are an example of *'azharoth*, and its hymnic sequel (poems 1, 2), poems for the prayer for dew (poems 3, 4, 56), two Aramaic poems (55, 57) and two *zulatoth* (poems 58-9).

The names of the authors of the poems are only occasionally indicated in the manuscript. Such indications are found on fol. 99b (Abraham Ṣebi ben Isaac Halevi, poem 7); fol. 101b (Zeraḥyah Halevi, poem 9); fol. 140b (Moses ben Naḥman, poem 27); fol. 149b (Isaac of Castellon, poem 51); fols. 150b and 151a (Judah Halevi, poems 53-4). Other attributions appear in acrostics.

There follows an alphabetical Hebrew list of the poems found in the manuscript, preceded by the sequentially numbered translation numeration.[23a] Those from the supplementary section are marked with an asterisk. The opening words of each poem are given, followed by the folio on which it appears in the manuscript. In each entry there is a reference to

23a See above, p. 239*, note *.

Israel Davidson, *Thesaurus of Medieval Hebrew Poetry* (New York, 1924-38, reprinted 1970), identified by ד. The manuscript shares 31 poems with the *Rylands Haggadah*, in which case reference is made to Raphael Loewe (ed.), the *Rylands Haggadah* (London, 1988), identified by ל. All variant readings between the present manuscript and the *Rylands Haggadah* are identified by Raphael Loewe in the notes to his translations in the present volume.[24]

22 אביעה רננות (ב138) ד.א. 245

*59 אגיד חסדי אל (א158) ד.א. 431

38 אזי בהגלותך (ב144) ד.א. 2202; ל # 13

7 אזכור מקור חיי (ב99) ד.א. 2226

*55 אזל משה (ב152) ד.א. 2306

17 אכסוף לימים (א137) ד.א. 3286

21 אל ראשון בלי סבה (שיר יחודש במקדש) (א138) ד.א. 4007; ל # 59

* 3 אמון מנעוריו (ב7) ד.א. 5584

9 אמרת ה׳ צרופה (ב101) ד.א. 5950; ל # 3

*58 ארומם אל רם (א156) ד.א. 7054

*57 ארעא רקדא (ב154) ד.א. 7669

* 4 אשיחה נפלאות (יערף כמטר) (א8) ד.א. 7907

28 את מחזה הוד אל (א141) ד.א. 8559; ל # 75

בטל אצור ר׳ שזופת שמש

* 1 [בנים שמעו לי] (ב2) ד.ב. 1042

13 גלילי זבול (ב136) ד.ג. 159; ל # 33

10 זמרה עם נכאה (ב103) ד.ז. 263; ל # 4

33 חשק לבבי (ב142) ד.ח. 548

*56 יבושר עם אביון (ב153) ד.י. 136

15 יבש בעצר (א137) ד.י. 177; ל # 67

51 ידע לבבי כי בלי ידע (ב149) ד.י. 645

37 יה למיחלים (א144) ד.י. 945; ל # 43

16 יה למתי בבית שבי (א137) ד.י. 947

25 יה שכינתך (א140) ד.י. 1136; ל # 72

49 יום הפילי תחנתי (ב148) ד.י. 1682; ל # 22

42 יום ליבשה (א146) ד.י. 1814

39 יום נפלא (א145) ד.י. 1865; ל # 64

24 On the various genres see Loewe (n. 2), pp. 17-19; T. Carmi (ed.), *The Penguin Book of Hebrew Verse* (1981), pp. 51-5; and the footnotes of poems in the translation included in this volume.

40 יום פדותי (145א) ד.י. 1887; ל # 14
29 יום תאוה (141ב) ד.י. 1954; ל # 74
11 יונה מעונה מה תען בשיחיה (136ב) ד.י. 2044; ל # 6
35 יונה נכספה (143ב) ד.י. 2052; ל # 12
30 יושבה בגנים (141ב) ד.י. 2367; ל # 10
31 יזכרו פלאיך (142א) ד.י. 2413; ל # 61
23 יחיד מקדם (139ב) ד.י. 2577; ל # 9
44 יחיד מקים כושל ר׳ מי כמוך יחיד מקים כושל
34 ימי קדם (143א) ד.י. 2938
41 ימים רבואות (145ב) ד.י. 2954; ל # 65
2* ימינך אל נגלית (6ב) ד.י. 2974
50 יעלת אהבים שמחי (149א) ד.י. 3198; ל # 28
53 יענה את מהלל (150ב) ד.י. 3233
יערף כמטר ר׳ אשיחה נפלאות
32 יפה נוף רדוי נוף (142ב) ד.י. 3356; ל # 62
24 יקרו להלל (139ב) ד.י. 3668; ל # 26
26 ישעך יזכירו (140ב) ד.י. 4188
18 כיום ולחי (137ב) ד.כ. 229; ל # 7
5 ליל שמורים אותו אל חצה (9ב) ד.ל. 726; ל # 5
48 מבטח כל היצור (147ב) ד.מ. 145; ל # 18
52 מי אשש בלתך (150א) ד.מ. 994
36 מי יתנני (143ב) ד.מ. 1132; ל # 63
44 מי כמוך יחיד מקים כושל (146ב) ד.מ. 1178
43 מי כמוך שחקים רקע (146א) ד.מ. 1201
27 מידך יה כבודך (140ב) ד.מ. 1289
20 נשמת יוצאים לאורות (138א) ד.נ. 732; ל # 58
19 נשמת ישראל עמך (137ב) ד.נ. 766; ל # 8
6 פסח [מצרים] אסירי יצאו חפשים (85א) ד.פ. 144; ל # 1
14 צור לבבי (136ב) ד.צ. 205
54 קוראים בלבב שלם (151א) ד.ק. 244
45-7 שזופת שמש (שלח רוחך, בטל אצור) (147א) ד.ש. 776; ל # 15-17
43 שחקים רקע ר׳ מי כמוך שחקים רקע
21 שיר יחודש במקדש ר׳ אל ראשון בלי סבה
46 שלח רוחך ר׳ שזופת שמש
12 שרש בנו ישי (136ב) ד.ש. 2214; ל # 66

The authorship of some poems remains doubtful. When the acrostic yields a commonplace name, such as Isaac, without further identification, it may be difficult or impossible to discover the identity of the poet. Unsurprisingly, some poems signed 'Isaac' are attributed variously to Isaac Ibn Ghayyat of the eleventh century or to Isaac ben Zeraḥyah Gerondi of the thirteenth. In the present state of our knowledge, we have little alternative but to follow commonly accepted attributions, without examining anew their accuracy.

Abraham Ibn Ezra 3, 17(?), 36 [25]
Abraham Ṣebi ben Isaac Halevi of Tamakh 7[26]
Ezobi, Joseph ben Hanan 58, 59[27]
Hasan 33[28]
Isaac 20, 56[29]
Isaac ben Zeraḥyah Gerondi 49[30]
Isaac Ibn Ghayyat 11, 15, 18, 23, 24, 28, 29, 30, 32, 34, 41[31]

25 See Israel Levin (ed.), *The Religious Poems of Abraham ibn Ezra* (Jerusalem, 1975-80), I, pp. 46-7, II, pp. 206-7, I, pp. 191-3. Our manuscript is not mentioned among the sources listed by Levin. According to Ezra Fleischer, poem 17 is by Abraham of Cordova and not by Abraham ibn Ezra, see his review of Levin's book, *Kiryat Sefer* 51 (1976), p. 666.

26 Published from our manuscript by Leon Feldman, "Piyut to the Seder of Passover by Rabbi Abraham Tamach," *Hadarom* 31 (5730), pp. 217-22.

27 Poem 58 was published by Benjamin Bar-Tikva in *Sefer Aviad: kovetz ma'amarim u-mehkarim le-zekher Dr. Yeshayahu Aviad-Wolfsberg* (Jerusalem, 1986), pp. 185-194. Bar-Tikva used manuscript Copenhagen 30 as well as the present manuscript for his critical edition. Poem 59 was published by Hayyim Schirmann, *Hashirah ha-ivrith bi-sefarad u-be-provence* (Jerusalem-Tel Aviv, 1961, 2nd ed.), pp. 344-8 on the basis of manuscript Copenhagen 30 (see n. 6).

28 The poem has not previously been published, in the original or in translation. Leopold Zunz, *Literaturgeschichte der synagogalen Poesie* (Berlin, 1865), p. 490, mentions that the poem is found in a thirteenth-century Catalan *Mahzor*. The poem is also found in the following manuscripts: Lenin Library, Moscow, Manuscript Gunzburg 198, no. 107; Jews' College, London, Manuscript Montefiore 203; Bibliotheque Nationale, Paris, MS Hebr. 658 fol. 29a; Oxford, Bodleian Library, 2712/6; Cambridge, University Library, T.S.N.S. 242.22. I am grateful to Professor Ezra Fleischer of the Hebrew University of Jerusalem for providing me with the list of these sources, as well as the sources for poems 14 and 51. The poem is also mentioned in Fleischer (see n. 20), p. 536. In the Montefiore manuscript, at the end of the poem, the verse from *Hosea* 11, 1 is added.

29 Poem 20 was published by Katsh (see n. 7), pp. 43-4 and by Dov Jarden, *Heruth* (newspaper), 14 Nissan 5724 (1964).

30 Some scholars also attribute to him poems 23, 24, 28 and 29 (listed here under Isaac Ibn Ghayyat); see their respective entries in Davidson.

31 See Yonah David (ed.), *The Poems of Rabbi Isaac Ibn Ghayyat; a tentative edition* (Jerusalem, 1987), pp. 188-9, 231, 307-8, 322, 329, 348-9, 371-2, 424. See n. 30.

Isaac of Castellon 51[32]
Joseph 40, 35, 50
Joseph Ibn Abitur 19
Judah Halevi 13, 16, 26, 31, 37, 39, 42, 44, 52, 53, 54[33]
Kalonymus Nasi 1, 2[34]
Me'ir ben Isaac *Sheliaḥ Ṣibbur* 5, 57[35]
Menaḥem 22[36]
Moses Ibn Ezra 25
Moses ben Naḥman 27[37]
Solomon Ibn Gabirol 12, 43, 45, 46, 47[38]
Tam, Jacob ben Me'ir 21
Zeraḥyah Halevi Gerondi 9, 10[39]
Anonymous 4, 6, 14, 38, 48, 55[40]

32 This poem has not previously been published in the original or in translation. Zunz (see n. 28), p. 558, lists it on the basis of the present manuscript ("Harl.14761," where "Harl." is an error). According to Zunz, ibid. and note 1, דקשטיון stands for "de Capestan." The poem is also found in Cambridge, University Library, T.S.N.S. 149.3 (see n. 28).

33 See Dov Jarden (ed.), *The Liturgical Poetry of Rabbi Yehuda Halevi* (Jerusalem, 1978-86), pp. 325, 350-1, 169 (for the festival of Succoth); pp. 404-5, 392-5, 345-7, 373-5, 341-3, 382-7, 332-4, 406-7.

34 See above n. 12 and n. 13. The beginning of poem 1 is missing, because the quire on which this text is copied is not complete, see Beit-Arié, in the present work, pp. 243*-244*.

35 For poem 57 see Hebrew section, pp. 23-32, 81.

36 This poem has not previously been published in the original or in translation. The poem is also found in Manuscript Montefiore 203, fol. 52b.

37 See H.D. Chavel, *Kitvei Rabbenu Moshe ben Naḥman* I (Jerusalem, 1963), pp. 394-395.

38 See Dov Jarden (ed.), *The Liturgical Poetry of Rabbi Solomon Ibn Gabirol* (Jerusalem, 1971-3), 347-9, 337-41, 334. Poems 45-7 are Gabirol's composition for the prayer for dew. Poem 47, beginning *be-ṭal aṣur* is interrupted (after the letter *ḥeth*), in our manuscript as well as in the *Rylands Haggadah* (fols. 39b-40a), by poem 48, *mivtah kol ha-yeṣur*. After the completion of *mivtah*, without any indication in the manuscript, *be-ṭal aṣur* is resumed, as is the case in some printed editions (see its entry in Davidson). In the *Rylands Haggadah*, the text extends only to letter *lamed.*

39 See Isaac Meiseles (ed.), *Shirath Ha-Ma'or; Piyyuṭei Rabbi Zerahya Ha-Levi* (Jerusalem, 1984), pp. 85-96, 97-8. Meiseles used the present manuscript for establishing the text of these poems.

40 Poem 4 was published by Dov Jarden on the basis of three manuscripts, including the present one, in *Sinai* LXIX (1971), pp. 16-21 and *Sinai* LXX (1972), p. 120; on poem 6 see E.D. Goldschmidt, *The Passover Haggadah; Its Sources and History* (Jerusalem, 1960), pp. 99-101; poem 14 is hitherto unpublished in the original or in translation; the text is also found in Manuscript Gunzburg 197, where it is attributed to Rabbi Yonah, and in Manuscript London, British Library, Or. 1424 (see n. 28); poem 38 was published by Habermann (see n. 6), p. 141; on poem 55 see Joseph Yahalom, "*Ezel Moshe*, according to the Berlin Papyrus," *Tarbiz* XLVII (1978), pp. 173-84. [See now: Michael Sokoloff and Joseph Yahalom, *Jewish Palestinian Arameic Poetry from Late Antiquity* (Jerusalem, 1999), pp. 82-86.]

The Liturgy of the *Rothschild Mahzor*

The *Rothschild Mahzor* contains the order of prayer for the entire year according to the rite of the Jews of Italy. Taking its name from the oldest and most important Jewish community in Italy, this rite is commonly called the Roman rite. It is one of the oldest, if not the oldest, order of liturgy in virtually continuous use outside the ancient lands of Babylonia and Israel.

The Roman *mahzor* has survived in a large number of medieval and later manuscripts and was published frequently since its first printed edition in 1486 (six years before the *Rothschild Mahzor* was written). Still, it had been practically unknown outside of the Italian Jewish communities until the nineteenth century. Samuel David Luzzatto (1800-1865), the great Italian-Jewish pioneer of modern Jewish scholarship, in a letter of 1838 to Leopold Zunz (1794-1886), one of the founding fathers of the "Science of Judaism," expressed his astonishment over the fact that Zunz was unfamiliar with the contents of the Roman *mahzor*. Luzzatto then proceeded with a detailed description of its main features.[1] Since then, however, the Roman prayer book among all other prayer books may have received the most scholarly attention. Luzzatto himself returned to the subject and, in 1856, published in Hebrew his historical and descriptive study of the liturgy of the Italian Jews, as an introduction to his edition of the Roman *mahzor*.[2] Three years later Zunz provided the first characterization of this rite in a European language.[3] More than a century later, in 1966, one of the most prominent scholars of Jewish liturgy in our times, E.D. Goldschmidt, republished Luzzatto's introduction, with a detailed commentary in which he presented the latest results of

1 *Iggerot Shedal*, vol. I (Przemysl, 1882, reprint: Jerusalem, 1967), pp. 433-476 (Letter number 201).

2 Two volumes, Leghorn, 1856.

3 L. Zunz, *Die Ritus des synagogalen Gottesdienstes* (Berlin, 1859), pp. 76-79.

scholarly research relating to the history and development of the Roman rite. As an appendix to Goldschmidt's edition of Luzzatto's introduction there appears a bibliography of the printed editions of the Roman *mahzor* prepared by J.J. Cohen.[4]

Thus, the prayer book of Italian Jewry is among the few of the various Jewish rites that received comprehensive and competent scholarly scrutiny. Still, much remains to be done in this area. A thorough, comparative study of the large number of medieval manuscripts of the Roman *mahzor* is a *desideratum*. Such a study may reveal many local variants and could help in establishing the chronology of changes and transformations that influenced the shaping of this rite.[5]

The present brief essay on the liturgy of the *Rothschild Mahzor* is an attempt to provide what is probably the first English treatment of the subject.

The *Rothschild Mahzor* is a good representative of a group of manuscripts and of the first printed editions that contain the full order of prayers for both the community and the individual, as well as detailed instructions regulating conduct in the synagogue and the home.[6] The public prayer service for weekdays, New Moon, special Sabbaths, major and minor holidays, the Days of Awe (*Rosh Ha-Shanah* and Day of Atonement and the days between them), and regular and special fast days takes up, of course, the largest part of the manuscript. This public order of prayer may be divided into two components: the standard prayers and the liturgical embellishments (*piyyutim*) added to them on special days of the Jewish calendar. Needless to say, the standard prayers are the ones that are closest in text and in arrangement to the prayers of other rites, and indeed, the differences between the Italian rite and that of the Ashkenazi or Sephardi communities, for example, are not too many or too radical. The order and sometimes the wording of the preliminary morning prayers (the *birkhot ha-shahar*, *birkhot ha-Torah*, and *pesukei de-zimra*) display variations when compared to other

4 Samuel David Luzzatto, *Introduzione al Formulario delle Orazioni di rito italiano, pubblicata in ebraico, a Livorno nel 1856, con annotazioni e un saggio sul rito italiano di E.D. Goldschmidt e una bibliografia di J.J. Cohen del Machzor e Sidur Tefila italiani* (Tel Aviv, 1966) (in Hebrew).

5 For a tentative list of Roman *mahzor* manuscripts see A. Freimann, *Union Catalog of Hebrew Manuscripts and Their Location*, vol. 2 (New York, 1964), numbers 5264, 1-8, and 5290, 1-6. See also Metzger's article cited in the following note, pp. 192-195 [see also below p. 000].

6 For example, the manuscript described in detail by Mendel Metzger in his article "Un Mahzor

rites and even within the manuscript tradition of the Roman rite itself. The blessings surrounding the *Shema* and the text of the *Amidah* are basically identical with those found in other prayer books. The version of the *Kedushah* for all services (*Shaharit*, *Musaf*, and *Minhah*) is the one that begins with the word *keter*. The supplications (*Tahanun*) for Mondays and Thursdays contain verses and litanies different from those appearing in the Ashkenazi rite. A major deviation, stemming from ancient times, is reflected in the Friday night service. The middle sections of the benedictions surrounding the recitation of the *Shema* which are always the same in *all* evening services in other prayer books are different for the Sabbath in Italy. For example, instead of the words *emet ve-emunah kol zot...* the text in the Roman *mahzor* reads *emet ve-emunah ba-shevi'i kiyyamta gazarta...* Other differences occur in the Grace after Meals where a part of the Sabbath version is again unlike the one for weekdays. The *nishmat* hymn, the verses for the taking out of the Torah from the Ark, the announcing of the new moon, the *havdalah* for the conclusion of Sabbath, the form for the counting of the *omer (she-ha-yom la-omer yom ehad...)*, the conclusion of *al ha-nissim* for Hannukah and Purim (*u-ke-shem she-asita immahem nes...*), the Torah reading for the fast day of the Seventeenth of Tammuz (Exodus 32:11 ff. without omissions), the blessing for *rahem* (=*nahem*) for the Ninth of Av (*menahem ziyyon iro ve-avelei ammo be-vinyan yerushalayim*), the Hebrew *Kol nedarim* instead of the Aramaic *Kol nidrei* for the eve of the Day of Atonement display some special features of the standard liturgy of the Italian Jews.[7]

The situation regarding the liturgical embellishments, *piyyutim*, for holiday, fast day, and special Sabbath services is entirely different. In the words of Shalom Spiegel: "These additions, called *piyyut*, or poetry, constitute—in contrast to the stable and stationary standard prayers—an ever-changing and restless element in the Jewish liturgy. They enliven with

italien enluminé du XVe siècle," in *Mitteilungen des kunsthistorischen Institutes in Florenz*, vol. 20, 1976. pp. 159-196, and manuscripts in the British Library (e.g., numbers 626-627 in Catalogue Margoliout, cf. also JQR, O.S., vol. 16, 1904, pp. 73-97), in the Bodleian Library (Neubauer Catalogue, numbers 1057-1058), in the Sassoon collection (Catalogue, number 23), and several manuscripts at the Library of the Jewish Theological Seminary (numbers 4457 and 4653) and others.

7 For a detailed treatment of the peculiarities of the standard liturgy of the Roman *mahzor* see Goldschmidt's study in the work cited above in note 4, pp. 79-98.

personal accent or local color the established and universal order of services and, unlike the latter, frankly bespeak the soil and sun, season or situation, which nurtured or ripened them."[8] This poetry, dedicated to the major themes of each holiday or fast day, sings of the wonders of creation, the anguish of exile, the hope for redemption. Its language and substance recreate in the poetic manner of each locality and each generation the teachings and legends of the Bible and of the Rabbis. The *Rothschild Mahzor* is rich in *piyyutim*. It is a veritable anthology containing poems drawn from the classical heritage of the Land of Israel, such as the poems of Eleazar Kallir (probably sixth century) and among them major compositions for the Ninth of Av that are not in other rituals and that have not yet been published.[9] Works of Ashkenazi as well as Sephardi poets, such as Meir bar Isaac of Worms (eleventh century), Solomon ibn Gabirol (ca.1021/22-1053/58), and Judah Halevi (ca. 1075-1141), also entered the Roman *mahzor*. The local flavor, however, is added by the inclusion into the prayer book of liturgical poems by Italian Hebrew poets, for example, Jehiel ben Abraham of Rome (tenth-eleventh century), Judah ben Menahem of Rome (twelfth century), Joab ben Benjamin (thirteenth-fourteenth century), Judah Messer Leon (fifteenth century), and many others.[10] Most of the liturgical poems in the *Rothschild Mahzor* are available in the various printed Italian prayer books. There are, however, quite a number of them which for one reason or another were never published. It is one of the characteristics of the manuscript tradition of the *mahzorim* that they display a larger variety of *piyyutim* then their printed counterparts, and the *Rothschild Mahzor* together with other similar manuscripts provide an excellent source for hitherto unpublished *piyyutim*.[11] The *Rothschild Mahzor*, in addition to the standard prayers and special liturgical hymns for the public prayer service, contains psalms and prayers for the pious individual for his private devotion. Such a text is

8 Shalom Spiegel, "On Medieval Hebrew Poetry," in *The Jews; Their History, Culture, and Religion*, ed. Louis Finkelstein, 3rd ed. vol. 1 (New York, 1960), p. 866.

9 See the poems on fol. 212v and fol. 214r, listed in Israel Davidson's *Thesaurus of Medieval Hebrew Poetry*, vol. 1 (New York, 1924; reprint: New York, 1970), *aleph* 8645 and 198. Other, similar *piyyutim* were published recently by Ezra Fleischer; see *Hasifrut*, vol. 2, 1970, pp. 230-236, and *HUCA*, vol. 45, 1974, pp. 21-23.

10 The *piyyutim* and their authors are enumerated and discussed by Luzzatto in the work cited above in note 4, pp. 42-77.

11 *Ibid.*, pp. 99-102.

the great hymn *Keter Malkhut* (*The Royal Crown*) by Solomon ibn Gabirol, which is the opening prayer in our manuscript; a philosophical meditation by Moses Rieti (1388-ca. 1460), an Italian rabbi who in his work endeavored to imitate Dante;[12] and the prayer by Judah ben Jehiel Messer Leon, an Italian Jewish scholar and physician of the fifteenth century, who was the only Jewish physician of the Renaissance allowed to treat both Jewish and Gentile patients, by special decree of the Holy Roman Emperor, Frederic III.[13]

For illness, other disasters, or persecutions, extraordinary fast day rituals were instituted.[14] Also, selections of psalms for penitents and for times of anguish were included. A group of psalms in the *Rothschild Mahzor* bears the heading in Hebrew letters *mizmorim penitenziali* (penitential psalms). This is quite strange in a Hebrew prayer book, especially because the very selection of seven penitential psalms is found in Christian prayer books. For the time being, no other Jewish prayer book containing a similar group of psalms, designated as penitentials, could be located. This puzzling phenomenon betrays an additional aspect of Christian influences on the Jews of Italy.[15]

The last major section of the contents of the *Rothschild Mahzor* consists of liturgical and other instructions and regulations dealing with various facets of Jewish life, both public and private. It is not unusual to find such texts in a prayer book. The famous German-French *Mahzor Vitry* (twelfth century)[16]

12 *Iggeret yaar ha-levanon* (fols. 463r-466v). This work appears in many manuscripts; see Freimann, op. cit., vol. 2, numbers 352 and 3695. On Rieti and his "Dantesque imitation," the *Mikdash me'at*, see Cecil Roth, *The Jews in the Renaissance* (Philadelphia, 1959), pp. 103-105. [See now: *Miqdash Me'at by Moses de Rieti*, the special issue of *Prooftexts*, 23.1.2003.]

13 *Adonai elohei ha-zevaot ka-asher nishkafti...* (fols. 467r-468r). As far as it can be determined, this prayer is unknown and unpublished. On Messer Leon's life and activities as physician, see the article by Daniel Carpi, "R. Jehudà Messer Leon a la sua attività come medico," in Michael, vol. 1, 1972, pp. 277-301 (in Hebrew), and esp. p. 283, note 34, where the sources referring to Messer Leon as "de Monticulo" are discussed, a designation that also appears in our manuscript, fol. 467r. See now also *The Book of the Honeycomb's Flow; Sepher Nopheth Suphim by Judah Messer Leon*, a critical addition and translation by Isaac Rabinowitz (Ithaca and London, 1983), pp. XVIII-XLVI, and esp. note 11.

14 Fols. 401r-410v. On the fast day ritual in the prayer book of Italian Jews, see E.D. Goldschmidt, *On Jewish Liturgy* (Jerusalem, 1978), pp. 177-186 (in Hebrew).

15 The heading and the psalms are on fols. 459r-460r. On these psalms in Christian worship, see *New Catholic Encyclopedia*, vol. 11 (New York, 1967), pp. 85-86. On Christian influences on the Jews in Renaissance Italy in general, see Roth, op. cit., passim.

16 Second ed. (Nuremberg, 1923).

similarly includes legal and religious texts side by side with liturgy. Such large compendia served as one-volume handbooks guiding the Jews through the intricacies of day-to-day religious observance. It is therefore no wonder that in the *Rothschild Mahzor* we find, in addition to the rubrics preceding the prayer service for each occasion, detailed instructions for the preparations for the holidays, particularly Passover and *Sukkot*. Furthermore, rather extensive summaries of the laws and ceremonies concerning circumcision, the redemption of the first born, weddings, funerals, the duties incumbent upon the father in the education of his children, the preparation of *zizit* and *tefillin* as well as of *mezzuzah*, blessings on wine, beverages, and food, some laws of *kashrut*, and the reading of the Torah and the *Haftarot* (the latter with a series of mnemonic rhymes) follow the liturgical sections. Also, a legal formulary for various types of family and business documents, directions for forecasting storms, medical advice, especially about blood-letting (phlebotomy), and rules for the calculation of the Jewish as well as the Christian calendar[17] are part of the *Rothschild Mahzor*. Most of these texts are also found in other *mahzor* manuscripts or in legal compendia. The liturgical instructions and laws in the *Rothschild Mahzor* conform largely to the text of the standard Italian-Jewish code, the *Shibbolei ha-leket* by Zedekiah ben Abraham min ha-anavim of Rome (thirteenth century).[18]

The richness of the *Rothschild Mahzor* in form and in content bears testimony to the fullness of the religious and esthetic life of the Jews in Renaissance Italy. Further study of this *mahzor* in the context of other medieval *mahzorim* from Italy will undoubtedly continue to enhance our knowledge of this glorious and intriguing period in Jewish history.

17 The texts mentioned are found on fols. 414r-456r. The calculations for the Christian calendar that use Italian names for the months as well as for the Zodiac, all in Hebrew letters, appear on fols. 450v-453r. On fol. 451r, the Italian "anno bisestile" (leap year) is transliterated into Hebrew letters. A few other Italian words occur in the text of the instructions, fols. 31r, 91r, 419r. A mnemotechnic rhyme, also in Italian in Hebrew letters, deals with the number of days in the Christian months, see fol. 451r.

18 This important code does not yet have a complete, critical edition. When such is prepared, the long excerpts in the various manuscripts of the Roman *mahzor* should be taken into consideration. For the best available editions now, see ed. Buber (Vilna, 1886), and ed. Mirsky (New York, 1966). [See now also: *Shibbolei ha-leket*; Part Two. Edited by Simcha Chasida (Jerusalem, 1988).]

Alexander Marx

MARX, Alexander (29 Jan. 1878–26 Dec. 1953), historian and librarian, was born in Elberfeld, Germany, the son of George Marx, a merchant and banker, and Gertrude Simon. The family moved to Konigsberg when Alexander was seven, and he received an intensive secular and Jewish religious education. After graduating from the Gymnasium, he spent a year in Halberstadt engaged in rabbinic studies under the tutelage of the renowned Rabbi Joseph Nobel. Between 1896 and 1903 Marx studied at the universities of Berlin and Konigsberg and at the Orthodox Rabbinical Seminary in Berlin. He received his Ph.D. from the University of Konigsberg in 1903.

During his student years in Berlin, Marx attended lectures offered by Moritz Steinschneider at a private institution, the Veitel-Heine Ephraim Institute. Steinschneider was considered one of the founders of modern Jewish scholarship and the father of scholarly Hebrew bibliography. Marx became his favorite student, and a deep friendship developed between the two men. Marx was influenced by Steinschneider to such an extent that A.S.W. Rosenbach, the great American book dealer and bibliophile, remarked many years later: "Europe had its Steinschneider, America now has its Marx."

Although Steinschneider exerted the most profound influence on Marx's scholarly work and on his contributions as a librarian, Marx was also indebted to his other teachers, prominent historian Abraham Berliner, philologist Jacob Barth, and rabbinic scholar David Hoffmann, rector of the Orthodox Rabbinical Seminary in Berlin. In 1905 Marx married Hoffmann's daughter, Hanna; they had two children.

In 1898 Marx traveled to England in order to study Hebrew manuscripts in connection with his work on a critical edition of an ancient Hebrew work of chronology, the *Seder Olam*. While in England, he visited Solomon Schechter in Cambridge. When Schechter assumed the presidency of the Jewish Theological Seminary of America in New York

City in 1902, his first concern was to assemble an outstanding faculty. Young Marx had made a great impression on Schechter, and he invited Marx to become a professor of history and librarian at the newly reorganized institution. Marx arrived in New York City in 1903 and for the following half century served the seminary in his dual capacity. He also played a leading role in various American Jewish academic and cultural organizations, including the Jewish Publication Society, the American Academy for Jewish Research (president, 1931-1933) and the American Jewish Historical Society.

Marx's contributions as historian and as librarian are thoroughly intertwined. During his tenure as librarian at the seminary, his main goal was to amass an extensive collection of primary sources, medieval manuscripts, archival documents, and early printed books. Much of his own historical research made use of such primary sources. Under his direction, the seminary library grew into one of the largest and finest depositories of Jewish manuscripts and books in the world. In addition to collecting books, manuscripts, and documents, Marx was also concerned with the preservation of Jewish art and ceremonial objects. The Jewish Museum in New York City had its origins at the library and was under Marx's direction until the 1940s. Authors of many important works in Jewish studies acknowledge their reliance on the rich resources of the seminary library and Marx's help. His annual reports about new acquisitions and library activities contain a wealth of original bibliographical and historical information about rare Hebrew books and manuscripts. These reports were collected and published in 1977 in *Bibliographical Studies and Notes on Rare Books and Manuscripts in the Library of the Jewish Theological Seminary of America*. Marx was the author of many other bibliographical studies, some concerning the discovery and description of hitherto unknown books and others embracing wider topics, such as "Illustrated Haggadahs," "The Literature of Hebrew Incunabula," "Notes on the Use of Hebrew Type in Non-Hebrew Books, 1475-1520," and "The Choice of Books by the Printers of Incunabula."

As a historian, Marx studied ancient, medieval, and early modern Jewish history; he was interested in the literary, cultural, social, political, and economic aspects of the history of the Jews. One of his first publications, a 1903 edition of chapters 1-10 of the ancient Hebrew *Seder*

Olam, is a model of a text-critical edition. In numerous articles, Marx published and analyzed texts relating to Jewish history in Spain, Italy, Germany, Bohemia, and Moravia, among other places. His most notable contributions include "Untersuchungen zum Siddur des Gaon R. Amram; I. Die handschriftliche Überlieferung," "The Expulsion of the Jews from Spain," "Maimonides and the Scholars of Southern France," "Astrology among the Jews in the Twelfth and Thirteenth Centuries," "A Jewish Cause Celebre in Sixteenth Century Italy," and "A Contribution to the History of the Jews in Cochin."

Marx summarized his views on Jewish history in "Aims and Tasks in Jewish Historiography." He rejects the concentration on the "monotonous description" of agonies suffered by Jews in the Middle Ages (the "lachrymose" conception of Jewish history) and also wants to limit the preoccupation with literary history. He advocates a balanced treatment in which "constitutional, social and economic history" takes its rightful place. He also demands that Jewish history be placed in the framework of general history of all the countries where Jews had lived, believing that it must become an "organic part of the history of the world."

Besides his bibliographical and historical studies, Marx wrote numerous biographies of medieval and modern Jewish personalities, such as Saadia Gaon, Rashi, Maimonides, Moritz Steinschneider, David Hoffmann, Mayer Sulzberger, and Solomon Schechter. These concise biographies are based on primary and secondary sources and, in the case of modern subjects, on personal acquaintance.

The crowning achievement of Marx's work as a historian is his one-volume *History of the Jewish People* (coauthored with Max L. Margolis [1927]). Avoiding a preoccupation with literary history, it is, rather, "a history of the entire people, of the mass," focusing primarily on economic and social concerns. Within a relatively limited space, this work has come to be a very frequently consulted reference book because of the reliability of its information, which it presents in a continuous narrative.

Marx saw himself as a link between the Old and the New Worlds. He helped to develop centers of Jewish scholarship in the United States, utilizing the knowledge he had acquired as a student of outstanding European scholars. He took advantage of his many personal and family connections with the Jewish scholarly establishment in Western and Central Europe in order to facilitate the transfer of ideas, people, and books from the threatened and disintegrating centers of European Jewish learning to the United States. As a teacher, as a scholar, and particularly as the man who almost single-handedly was responsible for making the library of the Jewish Theological Seminary of America into one of the most important collections of Hebraica and Judaica in the world, Marx was one of the most significant scholars in Jewish studies in the United States in the first half of the twentieth century.

Marx died in New York City. His brother, Moses, was a bibliographer and librarian, and his sister, Esther, was married to Nobel Prize-winning Israeli novelist S.Y. Agnon.

Alexander Marx's papers, including his extensive correspondence, are in the library of the Jewish Theological Seminary. Many of Marx's bibliographical studies, essays, and biographies are included in his *Studies in Jewish History and Booklore* (1944) and *Essays in Jewish Biography* (1947). During his lifetime, two Festschriften were published in his honor: David Frankel, ed., *Sefer Ha-Yovel: A Tribute to Professor Alexander Marx... on Completing Forty Years of Distinguished Service as Librarian of the Jewish Theological Seminary of America* (1943) and *Alexander Marx Jubilee Volume on the Occasion of His Seventieth Birthday* (2 vols., 1950), which includes a bibliography of his writings compiled by Boaz Cohen and biographical appreciations by Rebekah Kohut and Solomon Goldman. Abraham S. Halkin's article, "Alexander Marx," in *American Jewish Year Book,* vol. 56 (1955), assesses his importance as a historian. See also Menahem Schmelzer, "Alexander Marx (On the Occasion of the 100th Anniversary of His Birth)," in *Jewish Book Annual*, vol. 35 (1977-1978), pp. 123-27. His role in the growth of the library of the Jewish Theological Seminary is discussed in detail in Herman Dicker *Of Learning and Libraries: The Seminary Library at One Hundred* (1983). See also Dicker, ed., *The Mayer Sulzberger-Alexander Marx Correspondence, 1904-1923* (1990). Obituaries include Adolf Kober, *Historia Judaica* 16 (1954); Louis Finkelstein, *Proceedings of the Rabbinical Assembly of America* 18 (1954); and H.A. Wolfson et al., *Speculum* 29 (1954).

Scheiber's Beloved Books

Alexander Scheiber had three loves: books, people, and learning. This combination is not as common as it seems. Many scholars are recluses, and many bibliophiles are familiar only with the externals of their prized books. Scheiber had the rare talent of combining his various loves into one harmonious blend. He was thoroughly familiar with the content of his books; his memory of what was contained in them was phenomenal and legendary. Not only did he know exactly what books were in his library and where they were located (often the books were shelved in double rows), he was able to quote references by heart, giving page and even footnote numbers. He also possessed a tremendous storehouse of oral lore concerning *Gelehrtengeschichte*, biographies of scholars, their masters, colleagues or disciples, their bibliographies and countless anecdotes about them. And what a gifted recounter he was! The mixture of exact and encyclopedic knowledge, an almost total recall of even the tiniest details, the many humorous, lively and sometimes spicy tidbits kept his audience spellbound.

For Scheiber, these feats of memory and the entertaining telling of stories served to promote and spread learning and knowledge. The pursuit of scholarship and research by themselves were not, however, the ultimate goals of his activity. Although it is true that his scholarship was as objective, critical and without prejudice as is humanly possible, his was also a deep and unwavering belief in the moral and ethical force of the great heritage of the past. He had an imperative inner need to help transmit the wisdom and tradition of the ages to generations to come. He knew that only through the values preserved in the teachings of the traditions of the past could the community and the individual be sustained and guided. In the most difficult times, Scheiber worked hard, and in a very subtle and clever way, sometimes even at considerable danger to

* My grateful thanks to Evelyn Cohen for her most helpful stylistic suggestions.

himself, to keep these messages alive and to convey them to his listeners and students. At a time when one-sided indoctrination was the order of the day, Scheiber managed to keep the doors open a crack for a fresh and revitalizing breeze from different ideologies and philosophies. One of the ways in which this was achieved was by Scheiber's ongoing effort to obtain and discuss books and articles that were published abroad. The arcane and abstract nature of many of these publications served Scheiber's purpose excellently; as these works were not suspected of being subversive, he could talk and write about them innocently. The result was that he succeeded in keeping alive the awareness of interconnectedness with the outside world, despite sharp and hostile political divisions. In order to fulfill these goals, Scheiber pursued with uncommon avidity and alacrity the expansion of his library. He maintained contact with scholars of Judaic and Oriental studies all over the world and was able to obtain important publications from the United States, Israel and elsewhere. Accordingly, in the post-Second World War period, when other libraries in Hungary were either uninterested or unwilling to acquire books in the field of Jewish studies, Scheiber's library continued to grow and become a most important and unique resource.

Scheiber loved his books not only for their contents; he had an almost sensual enjoyment when holding a book in his hands. It mattered greatly to him how a book looked, how it felt when one touched it, even how it smelled. Still, the library functioned mainly as an instrument of his virtuosity in scholarship and teaching. Working late hours at his book-crammed study, he used the library for all the rich results that he produced as quintessential Jewish scholar both in his written and oral teachings. Indeed, Scheiber's multifaceted personality is mirrored in his highly important library.

In the present context, writing about him and his books, at the time when the collection becomes available for use to the scholarly public at large [at the library of the Hungarian Academy of Sciences], it seems that it is fitting to single out Scheiber's preoccupation with Jewish booklore and bibliography. This great interest found expression in his scholarly writings as well as in his private library.

We find many contributions to these areas in his bibliography which

1 See: Robert Dan, *Scheiber Sandor irodalmi munkassaganak bibliografiaja*. In: S. Scheiber, *Folklor es targytortenet*, Masodik, bovitett kiadas, volume 2 (Budapest, 1977), pp. 507-573 and

contains close to 1600 entries.[1] Scheiber also wrote a large number of reviews, not only of individual books, but comprehensive surveys of then current publications.[2] He compiled or supplemented bibliographies of leading scholars (L. Blau, I. Goldziher, M. Guttmann, B. Heller, S. Klein, I. Loew, A. Loewinger, J. Wellesz).[3] He published a bibliography of Maimonidean scholarship in Hungary.[4] The history of the Jewish book, from ancient to modern times, was a topic with which he dealt frequently. Immediately after the discovery of the Dead Sea Scrolls, Scheiber published a series of articles about them.[5] Among the various depositories of *Genizah* fragments, he searched for, discovered and subsequently published medieval Hebrew booklists and information regarding the work of medieval copyists of Hebrew books.[6] His interest also extended to Hebrew booklists originating from later periods.[7] He wrote on subjects that have bearing on the history of the early Hebrew printed book,[8] particularly the appearance of the earliest illustrated printed *Haggadah*.[9]

Scheiber perused catalogs and bibliographies with the kind of excitement that other people experience when they read mystery novels. The fact that he regarded them as the most essential tools of scholarship is manifested in the large number of review articles which he devoted to them.[10] He was also attracted to the great Jewish bookmen and librarians. Accordingly, we have from his pen admiring portraits of Alexander Marx, Elkan Nathan Adler, Solomon Schiller-Szinessy and Salman Schocken.[11] Hungarian Judaica and Hebraica were, of course, a special concern to him. He wrote about the fate and state of Jewish libraries in Hungary[12] and contributed to the bibliography of Hungarian Jewish periodical

vol. 3 (Budapest, 1984), pp. 587-608.

2 *ibid.*, nos. 38, 48, 168, 171, 205, 208, 350, 377, 409, 423, 446, 763, etc.

3 *ibid.*, nos. 23, 199 and 517, 113, 55 and 56, 397 and 460, 158, 462, 955.

4 *ibid.*, number 114.

5 *ibid.*, nos. 224, 288, 302, 348, 352.

6 *ibid.*, nos. 323, 948, 991, 1030, 1035, 1083, 1188, 1388, 1428.

7 *ibid.*, nos. 1234, 1258.

8 *ibid.*, nos. 112, 748, 997.

9 *ibid.*, nos. 776, 1481.

10 *ibid.*, nos. 13, 849, 1171-1174, 1316-1317, 1349, 1357, 1351-1352, 1359, 1400-1401, 1439-1440, 1476, etc.

11 *ibid.*, nos. 426, 291, 585, 940.

12 *ibid.*, nos. 165, 235, 1009, 1127, 1168, 1263.

13 *ibid.*, nos. 389, 491, 597, 660, 772.

liturature.[13] His lifelong interest in the recovery of Hebrew manuscripts and manuscript fragments in Hungarian libraries and archives is attested to in a long series of articles and culminated in his well-known and often-consulted book on the subject.[14]

Finally, mention should be made of Scheiber's widely quoted contributions on illuminated Hebrew manuscripts, especially his work on the *Kaufmann Haggadah*[15] and on the Jewish scribe-illuminators of the eighteenth century.[16]

Alexander Scheiber's library, his scholarship, his leadership, and his teachings were inseparably intertwined. Undoubtedly, his great library will continue to serve generations of eager students and scholars. Thus, together with the rich scholarly and literary heritage that he left behind, the library will be a living memorial to a towering scholar, inspiring teacher, courageous leader, and a great lover of books and people.[17]

14 *ibid.*, nos. 263, 289, 310-311, 427, 429, 448, 452, 501, 590, 665, 945 (his book), 1383.

15 *ibid.*, number 487.

16 See: *Occident and Orient: A Tribute to the Memory of Alexander Scheiber*, edited by Robert Dan (Budapest-Leiden: Akademiai Kiado and E.J. Brill, 1988), p. 331, note 2.

17 [See also in the Hebrew section, pp. 000.]

Indexes

Index of Sources

* The indexes were prepared by Mr. David Kerschen.

Index of Names

For list of additional names see pp. 78*-82*, 252*-253*

Index of Places

For list of additional places see p. 77*

Index of Manuscripts and Poems

For list of additional manuscripts see pp. 81*-82*

For list of addional poems see pp. 250*-251*

Index of Books

For list of additional books see pp. 59*-76*, 92*-95*

List of Books and Periodicals in which these Articles were Previously Published

"Personal Recollections", Reprinted from L. Braham and S. Miller's *The Nazis' Last Victims: The Holocaust in Hungary*, pp. 177-184, by Wayne State University Press ©1998.

"The Hebrew Manuscript as Source for the Study of History and Literature", in *A Sign and a Witness: 2,000 Years of Hebrew Books and Illuminated Manuscripts*, ©1988 by The New York Public Library Astor, Lenox and Tilden Foundations.

"Hebrew Manuscripts and Printed Books among the Sephardim Before and After the Expulsion", from *Crisis and Creativity in the Sephardic World, 1391-1648*, edited by Benjamin Gampel. ©1997 Columbia University Press. Reprinted with permission of the publisher.

"Hebrew Incunabula: An Agenda for Research", *Judaica Libarianship*, vol.2 ©1985. Association of Jewish Libraries.

"Hebrew Printing and Publishing in Germany 1650-1750. On Jewish Book Culture and the Emergence of Modern Jewry", published in the *Leo Baeck Institute Year Book* vol. XXXIII (1988) pp. 369-383.

"Decorated Hebrew Manuscripts of the Eighteenth Century in the Library of the Jewish Theological Seminary of America", appearing in *Occident and Orient: A Tribute to the Memory of Alexander Schreiber*, ©1988 by Magyar Tudomanyos Akademia.

"A Fifteenth Century Hebrew Book List", *Studies in Bibliography and Booklore*, vol. 20, ©1998 Library of Hebrew Union College-Jewish Institute of Religion.

"Rashi's Commentary on the Pentateuch and on the Five Scrolls, Venice, Bomberg, 1538", appearing in *Studies in Jewish Bibliography, History and Literature in Honor of I. Edward Kiev*, edited by Charles Berlin, ©1971 by Ktav Publishing.

"Guides to the Perplexed in the Wilderness of Hebraica: From Historical to Contemporary Bibliographies and Catalogs of Hebraica", first appeared in the *Harvard Library Bulletin*, n.s. 6, no. 2 (1995), 9-23, reprinted by Harvard College Library in 1996.

"On Judaica Research Services", *Judaica Librarianship*, vol. 4. ©1988-89 Association of Jewish Libraries.

"One Hundred Years of Genizah Discovery: The American Share", *Myer and Rosaline Feinstein Foundation Lecture* No. 2. Published and copyrighted by The National Foundation for Jewish Culture/Council of Archives and Research Libraries in Jewish Studies, 1998

"Building a Great Judaica Library – At What Price?". Published in *Tradition Renewed: A History of the Jewish Theological Seminary*, ed. by Jack Wertheimer, New York, The Jewish Theological Seminary, 1997.

"The New Jewish Theological Seminary Library", published in the *Jewish Book Annual*, Vol. 42, ©1984-85 Jewish Book Council.

"The Contribution of the Genizah to the Study of Liturgy and Poetry", *The Proceedings of the American Academy for Jewish Research*, vol. 63 ©1997-2001.

"Some Examples of Poetic Reformulations of Biblical and Midrashic Passages in Liturgy and Piyyut", appearing in *Porat Yosef: Studies Presented to Rabbi Dr. Joseph Safran*, ed. by Bezalel Safran and Eliyahu Safran, ©1992 by Ktav Publishing.

"How was the High Priest Kept Awake on the Night of Yom Ha-Kippurim?", published in *Saul Liieberman (1898-1983), Talmudic Scholar*, ed. by Meir Lubetski, *Jewish Studies*, vol. 23. The Edwin Mellen Press, 2002.

"Penitence, Prayer and (Charity?)", *Journal for the Study of the Old Testament*. Supplement Series, 154. *Minhah le-Nahum: Biblical and Other Studies Presented to Nahum M. Sarna in Honour of his 70th Birthday*. edited by Marc Brettler and Michael Fishbane. ©1993 Sheffield Academic Press.

"*Sefer Or Zarua* and the Legend of Rabbi Amnon", *Biblotheca Rosenthaliana: Treasures of Jewish Booklore*, ed. by Adri K. Offenberg and others, Amsterdam University Press, 1994.

"Two Philosophical Passages in the Liturgical Poetry of Rabbi Isaac Ibn Giat", *Of Scholars, Savants, and their Texts: Studies in Philosophy and Religious*

Thought. Essays in Honor of Arthur Hyman, ed. by Ruth Link Salinger. ©1989. Peter Lang Publishers.

"The Poems in the *The Barcelona Haggadah*: A Literary Study, *The Barcelona Haggadah*, edited by J. Schonfield, ©1992 by Facsimile Editions.

"The liturgy of the *Rothschild Mahzor*, *The Rothschild Mahzor, Florence 1492*". New York, The Library of the Jewish Theological Seminary, 1983.

"Alexander Marx", an essay appearing in *American National Biography*, ©1999 by the American Council of Learned Societies. Published by permission of Oxford University Press, Inc.

"Scheiber's Beloved Books", *Catalogue of the Scheiber Library*, ©1992 Library of the Hungarian Academy of Sciences.

We are grateful to the publishers for their kind permission to reprint the articles included here.

www.ingramcontent.com/pod-product-compliance
Lightning Source LLC
Chambersburg PA
CBHW030939150426
42812CB00064B/3048/J

* 9 7 8 9 6 5 4 5 6 0 4 3 6 *

מחקרים בביבליוגרפיה יהודית
ובפיוטי ימי הביניים

מנחם חיים שמלצר

מחקרים בביבליוגרפיה יהודית ובפיוטי ימי הביניים

קובץ מאמרים

בית המדרש לרבנים באמריקה
ניו יורק וירושלים תשס"ו

ISBN 965-456-043-7

להוצאת בית המדרש לרבנים באמריקה
תשס״ו

Printed in Israel
סדר ועימוד: שולמית ירושלמי, ירושלים
לוחות והדפסה: אופסט, שלמה נתן בע״מ, ירושלים

תוכן העניינים

דברי פתיחה

כרך נאה זה, המאסף מסות ומחקרים פרי עטו של פרופסור מנחם שמלצר, שראו אור באכסניות רבות ושונות, הוא מחוות תודה עמוקה למחברם, על פועלו המסור וארוך השנים בשירות בית המדרש לרבנים באמריקה ובלימודי היהדות בכלל. ר׳ לוי יצחק מברדיטשב היה אומר שיראת השם מתגלה בשתי דרכים: הדרך האחת מתגלה במי שמקדישים ימיהם, בדבקות ובמסירות, לעבודת השם, אך אינם משקיעים שום תועפות כוח בקירוב רחוקים אל בוראם — לא בהחזרת אלה שנתרחקו מעל אלוהיהם ולא בקירוב אלה שניטַפשו בחטאם. הדרך השנייה מתגלה במי שמבקשים לחלוק את אהבת האל שלהם עם אחרים. אם נוח הוא דוגמה לטיפוס הראשון, אברהם מייצג את השני; עליו אפשר לומר במילות המשנה, ״שרוח המקום ורוח הבריות נוחה הימנו״.

תלמידי חכמים, כמוהם כיראי שמים אמיתיים, מחסרים כל ימיהם טובה מעצמם, אך יש בהם רק מעטים שבמסירותם להרחבת יריעות אוהלם העיוני מוצאים זמן להקל על מלאכתם של אחרים. ואכן, על פרופסור שמלצר אפשר לומר שהועיל כל כך לתחום המחקרי שעסק בו, בדיוק מפני שהקדיש כה הרבה משל עצמו לסייע לעבודת עמיתיו. נדיבות רוחו שקולה בעוצמתה לרוחב דעתו. משנת 1964 עד שנת 1987, בעת ששימש ספרן בית המדרש לרבנים וערך את ״קטלוג כתבי היד העבריים ומיקומם״ (*Union Catalogue of Hebrew Manuscripts and Their Location*) של אהרן פריימן, ואת ״מחקרים ביבליוגרפיים ורשימות על ספרים וכתבי יד נדירים בספריית בית המדרש לרבנים באמריקה״ (*Bibliographical Studies and Notes on Rare Books and Manuscripts in the Library of the Jewish Theological Seminary of America*) מאת אלכסנדר מרכס, משך ידיו מעבודת המחקר שלו עצמו כדי להביא לגמר את פרי עמלם של חוקרים אחרים, חיים כמתים.

העריכה המופלאה של שמלצר את ספרו של שלום שפיגל ״אבות הפיוט״, מזכירה את התפקיד שמילא בשעתו צונץ, כשהביא לדפוס בשנת 1851 את כתב היד הלא־גמור של ספרו של רנ״ק, ״מורה נבוכי הזמן״. שני המפעלות הצריכו מאמץ כביר של לימוד נרחב ושל ביטול עצמי מוחלט כדי להציל מתהום הנשייה מפעל חיים שלא הושלם. לאמיתו של דבר, דומה לי שאי־הסדר והמצב הגולמי ששררו בניירות של שפיגל תבעו מפרופסור שמלצר דמיון, תושייה וסתם עבודה קשה, במידה גדולה יותר מזו שכתב היד של קרוכמל, השלם והמאורגן יותר, דרש מצונץ. ולא יכול להיות ספק באשר לעליונותו של המוצר המוגמר ששמלצר הוציא מתחת ידיו, מבחינת יופיו החיצוני ומיעוט השגיאות בו. האיכות הגבוהה והטעם הטוב, הניכרים בַּפרסום לכל אורכו, הם יד ושם לגדולת מחברו ולאנושיות עורכו.

שנה לאחר שאנו מציינים מאה וחמישים שנה לייסוד בית המדרש לרבנים בברסלאו, בשנת 1854, פרופסור שמלצר הוא מעין גשר חי אל בית המדרש, שהיה מאבני השתייה של "חכמת ישראל". פרופסור שמלצר, שנולד בהונגריה ועזב אותה בשנת 1956, עוד הספיק לפני צאתו ללמוד בבית המדרש היהודי התיאולוגי של בודפשט, שנוסד בשנת 1877 והיה צאצא ישיר של המוסד מברסלאו — כמה מבוגרי ברסלאו נמנו עם המייסדים בבודפשט. מי שהשפיע על פרופסור שמלצר בצעירותו יותר מכל היה פרופסור אלכסנדר שייבר, האחרון שגילם בדמותו את הרוח הנפלאה שפיעמה ביהדות הונגריה, והמשיך לקיים, בעצמו וללא עזרה, את בית המדרש, שנתמעט כל כך, לאורך ליל הבלהות של השואה ותקופת הדיכוי הקומוניסטי שבאה אחריו. בנסיבות אלה של קדרות ובדידות למד פרופסור שמלצר את ערכן של אבני הבניין ששימשו בשעתן את "חכמת ישראל": שליטה מעמיקה בתנ"ך ובתלמוד, ידיעת שפות זרות, בקיאות בפילולוגיה ובפליאוגרפיה, היסמכות על הארכיונים בחיפוש אחר אוצרות מורשת לא נודעים, ויישום של פרספקטיבה היסטורית. מעל לכל התענג פרופסור שמלצר על הריגוש שבגילוי, זה הריגוש שאפיין את חלוצי "חכמת ישראל", שעינם שזפה ראשונה את הנוף רחב הידיים של העָבר היהודי, בימים שזה נסתר עדיין מדמיונם של רוב החוקרים.

מחקריו של פרופסור שמלצר עצמו, בדומה לידע רחב הפּארות של אותם חלוצים, משתרעים על פני שטח עצום של יצירתיות ספרותית יהודית, מספרות ימי הביניים לענפיה השונים ועד תולדות הדפוס העברי במאה הי"ח; ועתים רבות נצפה הוא מבעד לעדשת הפיוט. כינוס היבול העשיר הזה למקום אחד יש בו מן הפיצוי, והוא ינציח מקור בלתי נדלה של רוחב דעת.

יצחק (איסמר) שורש
ניו יורק תשס"ה

* תורגם מאנגלית על ידי הגב' עדה פלדור.

פתח דבר

המאמרים הרואים אור בכרך זה הם פרי התעניינותי זה למעלה מארבעה עשורים בשני תחומי לימוד: השירה העברית בימי הביניים וביבליוגרפיה יהודית. המאמרים מופיעים כאן בגירסתם המקורית, בשינויי עריכה מועטים ובתוספת אי־אלו נתונים ביבליוגרפיים חיוניים.

בשנות השישים של המאה הקודמת, כתבתי את עבודת הדוקטור שלי על יצירתו הפיוטית של החכם הספרדי הדגול ר׳ יצחק אבן גיאת, שחי בלוסנה שבספרד במאה האחת עשרה, שיצירתו הליטורגית השפיעה מאוד על הדורות הבאים של המשוררים העברים בספרד, בעיקר על משה אבן עזרא. תוכניתי המקורית היתה להכין מהדורה ביקורתית שתכלול את כל שירי רי״צ גיאת, אך למרבה הצער, ומסיבות שונות, לא עלה בידי לממש את כוונתי. בכל זאת, פרסמתי כמה מאמרים על רי״צ גיאת, ואלה כללו גם כמה שירים שלו, שלא נדפסו עד אז בשום אכסניה.

מאמצע שנות השישים ועד אמצע שנות השמונים היה עיקר מעייני נתון לעבודתי בתור ספרן בית המדרש לרבנים בניו יורק. בשנים ההן הייתי פעיל גם בארגון המקצועי של ספרני היודאיקה בארצות הברית: הרציתי כמה הרצאות וכתבתי כמה מאמרים על תולדותיה של ספריית בית המדרש ועל נושאים שונים בביבליוגרפיה יהודית. שפר חלקי ונתאפשרה לי גישה למכמני הספריה בבית המדרש, וכמובן גם לאוצרות של מוסדות אחרים — זכות שהניבה מספר מחקרים על כתבי יד עבריים ועל ספרים נדירים.

מאוחר יותר, משנות התשעים ואילך, גבר ענייני בשירה העברית של ימי הביניים באשכנז. שמחתי לגלות שרבנים אשכנזים בימי הביניים היו גם מחברים פוריים של שירים לעת מצוא, בדרך כלל שירי חתונה — עובדה זו עמדה בניגוד מסוים לרושם הסטראוטיפי כאילו רבנים אלו חיברו רק שירים שטופי דמע, לרגל מאורעות טרגיים. כמה ממאמרי היותר מאוחרים עוסקים בפיוטי אשכנז.

לבסוף פרסמתי כמה סקירות ביבליוגרפיות. אלה הוקדשו לתלמידי החכמים הדגולים של בית המדרש בניו יורק — אלכסנדר מרקס ואליעזר אריה (לואיס) פינקלשטין, שהיו נערצים עלי — ולמורי ורבי אלכסנדר שייבר מבודפשט, שעודד אותי לצאת לדרך העיסוק במדעי היהדות.

המאמרים שנקבצו בכרך זה משקפים את הנושאים ותחומי העניין האלה.

חובה נעימה לי להביע את תודותי לאלה שאפשרו את עבודתי במהלך השנים ולאלה שסייעו בהוצאת הכרך הזה לאור. יעמדו על הברכה פרופ׳ שמואל גליק ומר ישראל חזני ממכון שוקן בירושלים על מאמציהם המיומנים ועל התבונה שגילו בהכנת המאמרים

לפרסום מחודש, במהדורת־מאסף נאה — אלמלא עמלם, לא היה הספר יכול לראות אור; אני מודה גם למר דוד קירשן על הכנת המפתחות, בעברית ובאנגלית. פרופ׳ ג׳ק ורטהיימר, פרובוסט בית המדרש לרבנים באמריקה, ופרופ׳ אלן קופר, יושב ראש ועדת הפרסומים שלו, תמכו במיזם מראשית ועד אחרית. בית המדרש וספרייתו היו לי בית מקצועי ואקדמי במשך ארבעים וחמש שנים, והריני מכיר תודה לכל מנהליו בשנים האלה. היתה לי הזכות לשרת בתקופת כהונתם של שלושה נגידים — פרופ׳ א״א פינקלשטין ופרופ׳ גרשון ד׳ כהן, זכרם לברכה, ופרופ׳ יצחק שורש, ייבדל לחיים ארוכים — ואני אסיר תודה להם על האמון שנתנו בי, על התמיכה שהעניקו לי ועל מחוות טוב רבות שהרעיפו עלי.

אך כמובן, את התודות העמוקות ביותר אני חב למשפחתי: לאשתי רות, על סבלנותה, הבנתה ואהבתה, ולילדינו נעמי ואלי סטילמן, שי שמלצר וליזה רוטמיל ובקי ומרק בניס, שמילאו את לבנו גאווה בהישגיהם. ואחרונים אחרונים חביבים: נכדינו — אבינועם, לידיה ואלכסנדר — הם לי מקור נחת ושמחה, ואני מתפלל בכל יום לשלומם ולאושרם.

מנחם ח׳ שמלצר
ניו יורק תשס״ו

* תורגם מאנגלית על ידי הגב׳ עדה פלדור.

פירוש אלפביטין על י״ג פיוטים ארמיים
מבוא

הטכסט המתפרסם כאן בפעם הראשונה הוא פירוש מאחד מרבותינו הראשונים על י״ג פיוטים ארמיים לחג השבועות. פיוטים אחרים בארמית שנועדו לחג השבועות וגם לשאר החגים כלולים בכתבי יד מימי הביניים של מחזורים רבים לפי מנהגי צרפת, אשכנז ואיטליה.[1] הפיוטים הארמיים נאמרו דרך כלל כהוספות לתרגומי פרשת היום ולתרגום הפטרתה, במיוחד בימים שנקראו בהם פרשיות דרמטיות כגון בשביעי של פסח, ביום א׳ דשבועות ובשמחת תורה. ביום א׳ דשבועות קישטו פיוטים ארמיים, שנקראו בכמה מקורות על פי צורתם האלפביתית בשם ״אלפביטין״, את פרשת מתן תורה ואת עשרת הדיברות. סדר אמירתם היה קבוע ולכל דיבר ודיבר נועד פיוט ארמי אחד ולפעמים אף יותר. במשך הזמן הושמטו רובם של הפיוטים הארמיים מהמחזורים, בלי שום ספק בגלל הטורח שנגרם לציבור על ידי הארכת סדר התפלה באמירת פיוטים רבים שלשונם ועניינם היו קשים. בכתבי יד משלהי ימי הביניים מוצאים אנחנו שמספר הפיוטים הארמיים מתמעט וברוב המחזורים אין למצוא פיוט לדיבר התשיעי והעשירי בכלל. בתקופת הדפוס, מסוף המאה הט״ו ואילך, נָשרו כמעט כולם מהמחזורים הנדפסים לפי מנהג אשכנז ואיטליה ונשארו רק בודדים מהם והנפוץ והידוע ביניהם הוא הפיוט, ״אקדמות מילין״, שעד ימינו נוהגים לאומרו בבתי הכנסיות של האשכנזים ביום ראשון של שבועות.[2]

מובן מאליו שהפיוטים הארמיים היו זקוקים לפירושים אולי עוד יותר משאר הפיוטים ואמנם נשתמרו בכתבי יד כמה פירושים מהראשונים. הקדומים שבפירושים אלה יצאו בלי שום ספק מבית מדרשו של רש״י.[3]

1 בספריית בית המדרש שלנו לבד נמצאים כעשרה כתבי יד המכילים פיוטים ארמיים. באחד מהם מלווים הפיוטים הארמיים לשבועות בציורים מעניינים. >ראה על כתב יד זה בצלאל נרקיס, ״ציורים לעשרת הדיברות במחזור אשכנזי זעיר בן המאה השלש־עשרה״, עשרת הדיברות בראי הדורות, בעריכת בן ציון סגל, ירושלים תשמ״ו, עמ׳ 389-407.< מענין גם שבכ״י ששון, מס׳ 514 (אהל דוד, עמ׳ 303-304) נמצא הפיוט ארכין (להלן בנספח, מס׳ א׳) בליווי טעמי המקרא.

2 על הפיוטים הארמיים בכלל ראה לאחרונה, עזרא פליישר, שירת הקודש העברית בימי הביניים, ירושלים 1975, עמ׳ 46 ועמ׳ 271-472; וראה בספרות המצוינת להלן בהערות 4-9; וראה גם חיים שירמן, ״פיוט ארמי לפייטן איטלקי קדמון״, לשוננו כא (1956-1957), עמ׳ 212-218. וראה בהערותיו של ש׳ אברמסון, שם, כה (1960-61), עמ׳ 31-34. >ראה יוסף יהלום ומיכאל סוקולוף, שירת בני מערבא — שירים ארמיים של יהודי ארץ־ישראל בתקופה הביזנטית, ירושלים תשנ״ט.<

3 ראה להלן עמ׳ 3.

כאמור, נשכחו הפיוטים הארמיים במשך הדורות וגם פירושיהם נשארו טמונים בכתבי יד. רק בתחילת ימיה של חכמת ישראל, ובעיקר על ידי עבודתו של יום טוב ליפמן צונץ, שב זכרם לספרות המדעית. צונץ רשם, על פי כתבי יד הרבים של המחזורים שבדק, את כל הפיוטים הארמיים שהיו ידועים לו ותיאר את מבניהם השיריים ואת תוכניהם האגדיים. הוא זיהה את מחבריהם, הבחין בגיליהם ובמקומות מוצאם השונים ועמד על הקשר ההדוק הקיים בין סוג ספרותי זה ובין הספרות התרגומית מצד אחד, ובין הספרות המדרשית מצד שני.[4]

רק אחרי עבור שנים מאז הופעת ספריו של צונץ החלו המלומדים בהוצאתם לאור של הטכסטים. בז בכר היה הראשון שפירסם כמה פיוטים ארמיים ואף הביע את דעתו עליהם שהם קדומים מאד. לפי בכר יוסדו פיוטים אלה בתקופה שהטכסטים התרגומיים עדיין לא הגיעו לשלב הקאנוניזאציה ושבה היתה פעולת המתורגמנים חיה וערה.[5]

קבוצה גדולה של פיוטים ארמיים הופיעה בדפוס אגב הוצאתו לאור של מחזור ויטְרי על ידי שמעון הלוי הורוויץ בשנת תרנ״ג. בחיבור זה כלול גם פירוש רחב על הפיוטים ועד ימינו הוא הפירוש היחידי מסוג זה שנמצא בדפוס.[6]

משה גינזבורגר, בשני מאמרים שהוקדשו לנושא זה, הוציא לאור את רובם של הפיוטים שנרשמו ע״י צונץ ושלא היו כלולים במחזור ויטרי.[7]

אע״פ שהפירסומים הנ״ל, ובמיוחד אלה של גינזבורגר, חשובים הם כשלעצמם, מוגבלים הם מחמת היותם מיוסדים רק על מספר קטן של כתבי יד ומשום שחסר בהם מנגנון ביקורתי וניתוח ספרותי ולשוני.

בשנים האחרונות חל מפנה בחקר הפיוט הארמי עם הופעתן של שתי עבודות חשובות. אברהם טל, בחיבורו ״הפיוטים הארמיים לשבועות; בחינתם הדיאלקטית ותרומתם למילון הארמי״ (להלן: טל), הכין טכסט מתוקן של עשרה פיוטים על פי שמונה כתבי יד מהבריטיש מוזיאום ומפַּרמַה והוסיף עליהם תרגום עברי, חילופי נוסחאות ופירוש מפורט. אמנם עיקר תרומתו של טל היא בזה שהוא בדק את המסורת הלשונית המשתקפת בפיוטים הנ״ל. על יסוד בדיקה פילולוגית יסודית של לשון הפיוטים עלה בידי טל להגיע למיונם של עשרת הפיוטים שדן בהם. הוא קבע שהחומר הזה מייצג שלש קבוצות מבחינה לשונית: קבוצה אחת של הפיוטים שייכת למסורת לשונית שהיא תלוייה בלשונו

4 בעיקר בספר *Literaturgeschichte der synagogalen Poesie*, ברלין 1865, עמ׳ 74-80 (רשימת הפיוטים הארמיים האנונימיים); וראה גם עמ׳ 150-151 (על הפיוטים הארמיים שייסד ר׳ מאיר ב״ר יצחק שליח צבור) ועוד. ראה גם בספרו, הדרשות בישראל, נערך והושלם על ידי חנוך אלבק, ירושלים תשי״ד, עמ׳ 194 ובהערות שם, עמ׳ 512.

5 "Alte aramäische Poesien zum Vortrage des Haphtara–Targum", *MGWJ* 22 (1873), עמ׳ 220-228.

6 מחזור ויטרי, מהד׳ הורוויץ, ברלין תרנ״ג; מהד׳ ב׳, נירנברג תרפ״ג, עמ׳ 305-309; 335-344; והפירוש, שם, עמ׳ 310-334.

7 "Aramäische Introduktionen zum Targumvortrag an Festtagen", *ZDMG* 54 (1900), עמ׳ 113-124; "Les introductions araméenes a la lecture du Targoum", *REJ 73* (1921), עמ׳ 14-26 ועמ׳ 186-194.

של התלמוד בבלי, קבוצה שניה כוללת בתוכה פיוטים שנתחברו בלשונה הארמית של ארץ ישראל והקבוצה השלישית יש בה פיוטים שלשונם מעורבת מארמית מזרחית ומארמית מערבית.[8]

המחקר השני החשוב הוא מאמרו של יוסף היינימן, ״שרידים מיצירתם הפיוטית של המתורגמנים הקדומים״ (להלן: היינימן, שרידים). במאמר זה היינימן מנתח שבעה פיוטים ארמיים מבחינת מתכונתם התבניתית ומבחינת החומר האגדי הטמון בהם. בדיונו על אופיים הלשוני של הפיוטים היינימן מסתמך בעיקר על מסקנותיו של טל. תוצאות מחקרו של היינימן מאשרות את ההנחה על קדמותם של הפיוטים שהם לפי דבריו מראשית היצירה של הספרות הפייטנית ונשתמר בהם הֵד לשירה עממית שבעל־פה שהכילה בקרבה גם אלמנטים אֶפִּיים.[9]

שני החוקרים הנ״ל הניחו יסוד למחקר לשוני וספרותי נוסף בנושא זה. אולם מחקר כזה יצטרך לכלול את כל היצירה הפיוטית הארמית, הן את הקדומה והן את המאוחרת, דהיינו גם את פיוטיהם של פייטני אשכנז, צרפת ואיטליה מהמאות הי״א והי״ב.[9א]

הפירושים על הפיוטים הארמיים מכילים ידיעות חשובות מאד להבנת הטכסטים. אבל יתר על כך, יש להם ערך עצמאי כמקורות לתורתם של הראשונים. כאמור לעיל, רק פירוש אחד מסוג זה נדפס עד עתה, הוא הפירוש שבתוך מחזור ויטרי.[10] פירושים נוספים נמצאים בכתבי יד, לרוב על גליונות של מחזורים שונים.[11] בזמננו יהיה הרבה יותר קל לעמוד על זהות מחבריהם או מלקטיהם של פירושים אלה בעזרת המבוא הגדול על תולדות מפרשי הפיוט שצירף א״א אורבך למהדורתו של ס׳ ערוגת הבושם.[12]

אחד הטכסטים המעיינים בשטח זה הוא הפירוש לארבעה פיוטים לעשרת הדיברות לר׳ יעקב ב״ר שמשון, מבית מדרשו של רש״י.[13] מעניין שר׳ יעקב ב״ר שמשון חיבר לא רק פירוש לפיוטים ארמיים, אלא גם ייסד פיוט ארמי אחד,[14] הוא הפיוט ל״לא תחמוד״, שהוא

8 חיבורו של טל לא הופיע בדפוס. הוא הוגש כעבודת גמר לאוניברסיטה העברית בשנת תשכ״ו. אני מודה לד״ר טל על ששלח לי טופס מעבודתו. פיוט אחד, מס׳ 3 בעבודתו, י״ל על ידו במהדורה ביקורתית בלשוננו לח (תשל״ד), עמ׳ 257-268. הפיוט מיוחס ע״י צונץ (*Literaturgeshichte*, עמ׳ 286) לר׳ יום טוב ב״ר יצחק מ־Joigny, בן המאה הי״ב, ראה טל, שם, עמ׳ 258.

9 הספרות ד (1974), עמ׳ 362-375, וסיכום אנגלי, שם, עמ׳ XIX-XVIII, עם ביבליוגרפיה מפורטת בסוף המאמר.

9א <ראה בסוף הע׳ 2.>

10 עמ׳ 310-334. <ראה ישראל תא־שמע, ״על הפירוש לפיוטים הארמיים שבמחזור ויטרי״, קרית ספר נז (תשמ״ב), עמ׳ 101-108.>

11 למשל בכתב יד ברלין מס׳ 177 שהעתק ממנו נמצא בספריית שוקן בירושלים; אני מביע את תודתי לידידי ד״ר יעקב קצנשטיין על שהמציא לי צילומו של פירוש זה; כ״י המבורג 152; כ״י בית המדרש שלנו, מס׳ 4460 ומס׳ 4466 ועוד.

12 ירושלים תשכ״ג.

13 כ״י פרמה 159, דף 121 ואילך; ראה צונץ, *Literaturgeschichte*, עמ׳ 458; על ר׳ יעקב ב״ר שמשון ראה אביגדור אפטוביצר, מבוא לס׳ ראבי״ה, ירושלים תרצ״ח, עמ׳ 366-367 ולאחרונה, ישראל שציפנסקי, רבינו אפרים, ירושלים תשל״ו, עמ׳ 97 ואילך.

14 י״ל ע״י גינזבורגר, *REJ* (לעיל, הערה 7), עמ׳ 188-189. <ראה אברהם גרוסמן, חכמי צרפת הראשונים, ירושלים תשנ״ה, עמ׳ 425-533.>

בעצמו פירש. דברי ר׳ יעקב נמצאים בכ״י פרמה 159 יחד עם חומר חשוב המכיל ידיעות על אודות המנהגים השונים של דרך אמירתם של התרגומים ושל הפיוטים ביום א׳ דשבועות.

החיבור הנדפס להלן נזכר בפעם הראשונה בשנת 1857 ע״י י״ל דוקעס.[15] דוקעס מצא בכתב יד אחד שבבית המדרש בלונדון (היום מספרו: 6)[16] את הפירוש שלנו, וזיהה אותו על פי שמות החכמים הנזכרים בו, כמעשה ידיו של ר׳ צדקיה בן ר׳ אברהם מן הענוים, בעל שבלי הלקט. שטיינשניידר רשם את החיבור כחיבורו של בעל שבלי הלקט על פי עדותו של דוקעס,[17] אבל אחרי שצונץ[18] וגם ילינק[19] קבעו שבאמת הפירוש הוא לאחיו של בעל שבלי הלקט, ר׳ בנימין, קיבל שטיינשניידר את דעתם.[20] וכך סברו גם חכמים אחרים, כגון, ההיסטוריונים פוגלשטיין וריגר[21] ואחריהם מ״ד קאסוטו.[22] מעניין שש״ז שכטר חשב בתחילה שהפירוש הוא לר׳ צדקיה,[23] אולם לאחר זמן כנראה הגיע למסקנה שבאמת הוא לר׳ בנימין.[24] ילינק גם רצה להוציא לאור חלק של הפירוש אבל הדבר לא יצא לפועל.[25] התיאור המפורט ביותר של החיבור ניתן על ידי שלמה בובר במאמר שלם שהקדיש לו.[26] גם בובר הודיע על רצונו לפרסם את הטכסט. הרבה שנים אחריו דן י״ל מיימון בקיצור בפירוש שלפנינו, וכמו בובר לפניו כך גם הוא הכריז על כוונתו להדפיס אותו;[27] מסבות שאינן ידועות לי לא איסתייע מילתא ונשאר החיבור בכתב יד עד ימינו. אולם, ממה שכתבו בובר ומיימון על אודות הפירוש ברור שהם ייחסו אותו לר׳ צדקיה בוודאות. ואמנם אפשר להבין בהחלט מה גרם לחילוקי הדעות בין החכמים בענין זהותו של המחבר.

15 במאסף אוצר נחמד, מחברת שניה, וינה תרי״ז, עמ׳ 199.

16 ראה Add. Neubauer, *Catalogue of the Hebrew manuscripts in the Jews' College, London*, אוקספורד 1886, עמ׳ 2-3. <כתב היד נמכר במכירה פומבית, על ידי Christie's, ב־23 ביוני 1999, מס׳ 8.>

17 *Catalogus librorum hebraeorum in Bibliotheca Bodleiana*, ברלין 1852-1860, עמ׳ 2767-2769.

18 *Die Ritus des synagogalen Gottesdienstes*, ברלין 1859, עמ׳ 195.

19 קונטרס המגיד, וינה תרל״ח, עמ׳ 29.

20 המזכיר 18 (1878), עמ׳ 3.

21 ראה *Geschichte der Juden in Rom*, א, ברלין 1896, עמ׳ 381-382.

22 במאמרו על בנימין בן אברהם מן הענוים, *Encyclopaedia Judaica* (בגרמנית), 2, עמ׳ 798-799.

23 במבוא לאבות דרבי נתן, וינה 1887, עמ׳ XI. שם הוא מזכיר את הפירוש שלנו ואת ההבאות מאדר״נ הנמצאות בו.

24 פוגלשטיין וריגר (לעיל, הערה 21), עמ׳ 381, הערה 8: "nach Schechters brieflich ausgesprochener Meinung ist Jellineks Ansicht die richtige".

25 קונטרס המגיד, שם.

26 ״בקורת כתב יד אחד״, ברכת אברהם, החלק העברי של ס׳ היובל לכבודו של אברהם ברלינר, ברלין תרס״ג, עמ׳ 1-6. במאמר זה רושם בובר את שמות הספרים, את שמות החכמים ואת המלים הלועזיות שבפירושנו.

27 ״שירים ופיוטים ארמיים״ (יחד עם פירושו של בעל ״שבלי הלקט״ לכמה פיוטים ארמיים לשבועות מתוך כתב־יד), סיני טו (תש״ד-תש״ה), עמ׳ ל-לו. בסוף המאמר כתוב: ״...כמה פיוטים ארמיים וכו׳ ואשר אני מפרסם עכשיו עם פירוש מתוך כתב יד שנתחבר לפני שבע מאות שנה בערך מאת רבנו צדקיה ברבי אברהם הרופא ז״ל בעל שבלי הלקט״. אמנם כאמור, הפירוש לא יצא לאור. ראה גם בביבליוגרפיה של כתבי הרב מיימון שהוכנה ע״י נפתלי בן־מנחם, ״מנחה לר׳ יהודה לייב הכהן מיימון בגבורות״, בעריכת ל׳ קופרשטיין, תל אביב תשט״ז, עמ׳ 99, מס׳ 354: ״המאמר לא נשלם״.

במשפחת מן הענוים במאה הי״ג חוזרים שמות זהים לרוב, וכשבעל שבלי הלקט מדבר על בני המשפחה הוא משתמש בכינויים ״אחי״ ו״אחי שני״ ולא תמיד ברור אם הכוונה לאח ממש או לבן־דוד. כך הוא מזכיר פעם אחת ״ואחי ר׳ צדקיה בר׳ בנימין נר״ו״[28] ושם אין שום ספק שהכוונה לבן־דודו, כי שם אביו של צדקיה, בעל שה״ל היה ר׳ אברהם ולר׳ אברהם זה היה אח בשם ר׳ בנימין. כדי לעמוד על היחס המשפחתי אעתיק כאן את החלק הנוגע לענייננו מתוך אילן־היחס שהכין קאסוטו:[29]

בפירוש שלנו מזכיר המחבר כמה פעמים את אחיו ר׳ צדקיה ואת אחיו ר׳ משה ואת אחיו השני ר׳ יהודה. נראה לי שעל פי פשוטם של דברים[29א] מתחייב לומר שהמחבר היה אחד מבני אברהם, או בנימין או יחיאל. אולם, על יחיאל אין לנו ידיעות כמחבר בשעה שר׳ בנימין חיבר כמה חיבורים ודבריו על סדרי התפלה וגם פירושיו על התפלות מובאים לעתים קרובות מאד בספרו של אחיו, בס׳ שבלי הלקט.[30] על יסוד זה יש לקבל את הזיהוי של צונץ, ילינק, שטיינשניידר, שכטר, פוגלשטיין, ריגר וקאסוטו, ולהכיר בר׳ בנימין בן ר׳ אברהם מן הענוים, אחיו של ר׳ צדקיה כמחברו של הפירוש.

בכ״י נקרא הפירוש בשם ״פירוש אלפביטין״. ואמנם, מיד בתחילת הפירוש מבאר המחבר את מובן הביטוי ״אלפביטין״. אחרי הערה כללית זו ניגש המחבר לפירוש הקטעים מהתרגום הבאים לפני הפיוט ומעיר גם על סדר אמירתם: ״נהגו לתרגמו תחילה בתרגומו של אונקלוס ואחר כך מתרג׳ אותו בירושלמי, וכל כל פסוק ופסוק כסדר הכתוב במחזור״.[31] דרכו בפירוש הפיוטים היא כך: דרך כלל, אחרי הבאת דיבור המתחיל מהפיוטים הוא מפרש את מובנה של כל היחידה ומביא סמוכין לרעיון המתבטא בה מהספרות התלמודית והמדרשית. אחר כך הוא מבאר את המלים הקשות בעזרת מקורות חז״ל, ובמקרים בודדים על יסוד כתבי הראשונים. אם יש צורך, המחבר מסביר מלים קשות גם בעזרת לעזים

28 ראה שבלי הלקט, חלק שני; י״ל ע״י הרב מנחם זאב חסידה, מהד׳ צילום מתוך ירחון ״הסגולה״, תרצ״ד־תרצ״ז, ירושלים תשכ״ט, עמ׳ קו.

29 *Encyclopedia Judaica* (בגרמנית), 2, עמ׳ 791-792.

29א בובר, הקדמה לס׳ שבלי הלקט, עמ׳ 6 ועמ׳ 7, אות לב ואות לה, סובר שלפעמים ״אחי״ פירושו ״אחי שני״ וראה לעיל הערה 28. אמנם לרוב יש לפרש את הכינויים כפשוטם.

30 ראה בהקדמה לס׳ שבלי הלקט, עמ׳ 6 ועמ׳ 10 וראה במבוא לספר הנ״ל, מהד׳ רש״ק מירסקי, ניו יורק תשכ״ו, עמ׳ 37-39. <ראה שבלי הלקט, החלק השני... [י״ל] בידי שמחה... חסידה, ירושלים תשמ״ח, עמ׳ 37-41. וראה לאחרונה על כתב היד ועל זהותו של מחבר הפירוש במאמרו המפורט של ישראל מרדכי פלס, ״פירוש פיוטי האלפביטין המיוחס למשפחת שבלי הלקט ורבינו משה ב״ר מאיר מפירירה״, זכור לאברהם, קובץ תורני, חולון תשס״ב־תשס״ג.>

31 להלן, עמ׳ 1. (המספרים כאן ולהלן, וכן במפתחות, הם המספרים שבמהדורת המקורית, והם מצוינים בגליונות האלפביטין.)

32 לפי ילינק (לעיל, הערה 19), המחבר ידע והבין לשון יוונית, וכך כותב גם בובר בס׳ היובל לברלינר הנ״ל (לעיל, הערה 26), עמ׳ 5. אמנם נכון שהמחבר משתמש כמה פעמים במלים יווניות כדי להסביר

שהכוונה בהן לשפה האיטלקית.[32] לעתים קרובות מזכיר המפרש גירסאות שונות שבטכסטי הפיוטים לפי המחזורים השונים,[33] כמו כן הוא מראה לפעמים שיש פירושים שונים על מקומות מסויימים שבפיוטים. בדרך כלל הוא מחליט בין הגירסאות והפירושים, בוחר במה שנכון לדעתו, אחרי הנמקת הבחירה, ודוחה את הפירושים שאינם מתקבלים על דעתו.[34]

כפי שיש לראות מההערות על גוף הפירוש, נוסח ההבאות מספרות חז״ל בפירוש שונה הרבה פעמים מהנוסחאות המקובלות בטכסטים שלפנינו, ויש ששינויים אלה מראים על נוסח אחר לגמרי של הטכסטים הנדונים.[35] נמצאים בפירוש גם מאמרי אגדה שאינם ידועים לנו ממקור אחר.[36] מובן מאליו שהמפרש מציע כמה פעמים הסברים מקוריים מדעתו שאין למצוא להם מקבילים במקום אחר.[37]

כאמור, הפירוש שלנו נשתמר בכתב יד שבבית המדרש בלונדון, מס׳ 6.[38] עד כמה שידוע לי זה כתב היד היחידי המכיל את פירושנו.[38א] כתב היד הוא על קלף, נכתב בכתיבה איטלקית רבנית טיפוסית של המאה הי״ד. על מאה זו מעידה גם חתימת בעלים מחודש נובמבר שנת קנ״ב הנמצאת בכ״י.[39] כמה פעמים נזכרים שמות חכמים בחיבור בצירוף ברכה לחיים,[40] אמנם אין מזה ראיה שכתב היד נכתב בחיי חכמים אלה, כי יכול להיות שברכות אלה מועתקות הן ממקור יותר קדום.

מלים קשות, אבל אין ראיה מזה שהוא באמת ידע יוונית. קרוב לוודאי שהוא שאב את ידיעותיו בעניין זה ממקורות עבריים שקדמו לו. רק פעם אחת הוא מביא מלה יוונית (איתוניבא, בסוף הפירוש לפיוט י״ב) שלא יכולתי למצוא את פתרונה ושהיא אינה רשומה במלונים התלמודיים והתרגומיים הרגילים. והנה רשימת המלים היווניות: אלפביטא (אלפא ביטא גמא) 1; קיריס 6, 7, 37, 46, 69; אורנוס 7; גינוס 7; אירימון 27; תיאור 28; מיסטר 33; איליאוס 41; קוזמוס 46; דולוסי 50; פיילי 51-52; תנסיא 62; מרוס 64; איתוניבא 66. פעם אחת הוא מביא מלה ערבית (ביזיאה, ראה ג׳, הערה 105). רבינו מפרש כמה פעמים מלים על פי ״לעז גרמטקה״. לפי בובר הכוונה בביטוי זה ליוונית. פוגלשטיין וריגר (לעיל, הערה 21) עמ׳ 381-382 מפרשים אותו כציון ללשון רומית וכך אמר לי פרופ׳ דניאל קרפי שבמקורות איטלקיים מימי הביניים היה שכיח ביטוי זה לציון הרומית. להלן רשימת המלים ב״לעז גרמטקה״: אירימון בוסקו 27; דולורסי 50; זונא 51. ואלה הן המלים הלועזיות שלא פוענחו: יקווינטור, עמ׳ 11; פנטי, עמ׳ 13; גונדא, עמ׳ 56.

33 עמ׳ 2; 3; 12; 14; 17; 19; 21; 25; 28; 36; 51; 58; 66; 70.

34 עמ׳ 2; 4; 8; 9; 14; 15; 21; 29; 32; 33; 4.

35 עמ׳ 4 והע׳ 30 שם; 14 והע׳ 68-69 שם; 16 והע׳ 95 והע׳ 98 שם; 17 והע׳ 100 והע׳ 102 שם; 24 והע׳ 55-56 שם; 27 והע׳ 4 שם; 28 והע׳ 18 שם; 29 והע׳ 38 שם; 30 והע׳ 45 שם; 32 והע׳ 21 שם; 33 והע׳ 30 שם; 35 והע׳ 55 שם; 38 והע׳ 81 שם; 39 והע׳ 6 שם; 40 והע׳ 9 שם; 45 והע׳ 4 שם; 47 והע׳ 21 שם; 49 והע׳ 6 שם; 53 והע׳ 9 שם; 55 והע׳ 35 שם; 56 והע׳ 43 שם; 61 והע׳ 95 שם; 73 והע׳ 93 שם.

36 עמ׳ 4 והע׳ 27 שם; 5 והע׳ 36 שם; 6 והע׳ 50 שם; 10 והע׳ 10 שם; 16 והע׳ 97 שם; 26-27 והע׳ 85 והע׳ 88 שם; 50 והע׳ 16 שם; 52 והע׳ 3 שם.

37 עמ׳ 3 והע׳ 19 שם; 39 והע׳ 5 שם; 40 והע׳ 17 שם; 43 והע׳ 51 שם; 63 והע׳ 23 שם; 66 והע׳ 71 שם.

38 ראה לעיל, הערה 16.

38א אחרי מסירת המאמר לדפוס מצאתי בכ״י של מחזור איטלקי בבית המדרש שלנו (מס׳ 4814) על גליון דף 124 ע״ב את התחלת הפירוש שלפנינו. הקטע נגמר שם במלים ״במקום טהרה וקדושה״. ראה להלן עמ׳ 4, ד״ה יה יהב רשו.

39 מועתקת מהקטלוג הנזכר בהערה 16, עמ׳ 3.

הטכסט הוא בדרך כלל מדוייק, לפעמים יש תיקונים מעל לשורה ועל הגליון וטעויות סופר אינן מרובות.[41] במקרים אחדים ציון הפרקים שבמקורות חז״ל אינו מתאים למה שנמצא בטקסטים שלפנינו.[41א]

להלן שלוש רשימות: רשימה של שמות החכמים הנזכרים בפירוש; מפתח של המקורות ורשימת הלעזים (לרשימה על פי דפי הספר ראה להלן במפתחות).

רשימת שמות החכמים

בנימין בן משה[42] [38; 39; 43].

גרשום[43] [46].

דניאל[44] [19; 26; 33; 34; 38; 39; 42; 43; 44].

יהודה[45] [25; 26; 41].

יואב[46] [14].

מנחם בן סרוק [64].

מרדכי בי״ר בנימין[47] [56].

משה[48] [36; 69].

נתן[49] [10].

סעדיה גאון [63].

40 ר׳ דניאל נר״ו 19; ר׳ יהודה נר״ו 25, 26; ר׳ יואב נר״ו 14; ר׳ משה נר״ו 69; ר׳ צדקיה נר״ו 15, 33, 51.

41 עמ׳ 3 והע׳ 22 שם; 9 והע׳ 23 שם; 35 והע׳ 54 שם; 43 והע׳ 49 שם.

41א עמ׳ 6 והע׳ 51 שם; 37 והע׳ 71 שם; 49 והע׳ 6 שם; 53 והע׳ 9 והע׳ 14 שם; 57 והע׳ 46 שם; 68 והע׳ 29 שם; 58 והע׳ 66 שם.

42 אין לנו ידיעות נוספות עליו. לפי פוגלשטייטן וריגר (לעיל, הערה 21) עמ׳ 375, הערה 3, אולי היה אחיו של ליאונטי (יהודה) בן משה, שנפטר בשנת 1216 (ראה הנ״ל, עמ׳ 372). השערה זו מתקבלת על הדעת כי דברי ר׳ בנימין ב״ר משה זה נמסרים בפירושנו על ידי ר׳ דניאל שהיה אחד מרבותיו של רבינו. אם כן חי קרוב לודאי דור אחד לפניו.

43 הכוונה לרבינו גרשום מאור הגולה.

44 היה אחד מרבותיו ויש שמזכירו בצירוף ברכה לחיים (עמ׳ 19) ויש ששמו בא בצירוף ברכה למתים (עמ׳ 33). ראה פוגלשטיין וריגר (לעיל, הערה 21) עמ׳ 375, הערה 4, ושם נזכרת השערתו של שטיינשניידר שאולי הוא היה זקנו של יהודה רומאנו, בן המאה הי״ד.

45 מזכיר אותו בכינוי ״אחי שני״. גם בעל שבלי הלקט, אחיו של מחברנו, מביא את דבריו כמה פעמים, ראה בהקדמתו של בובר לס׳ שבלי הלקט, עמ׳ 6 ועמ׳ 11, ומירסקי, במהדורה של הספר הנ״ל, מבוא, עמ׳ 34-35. ר׳ יהודה זה היה בנו של ר׳ בנימין, דודו של מחברנו.

46 מרבותיו של רבינו. ראה פוגלשטיין וריגר (לעיל, הערה 21) עמ׳ 375, הערה 5. לפיהם אולי היתה פאולה בת ר׳ אברהם מן הענוים נכדתו, על פאולה ראה ב־*Encyclopaedia Judaica* (בגרמנית), 2, עמ׳ 797.

47 אין לנו ידיעות נוספות עליו. ראה פוגלשטיין וריגר, שם, עמ׳ 375.

48 אחיו של מחברנו (״ופירש ר׳ משה אחי זצ״ל״, להלן עמ׳ 36; ״ור׳ משה אחי נר״ו״, עמ׳ 69), וכך סבורים גם פוגלשטיין וריגר, שם, עמ׳ 376 והערה 7 שם, וקאסוטו, באילן היחס של משפחת מן הענוים, *Encyclopaedia Judaica* (בגרמנית), 2, עמ׳ 791-792. אולם לפי בובר, הקדמה לס׳ שבלי הלקט, עמ׳ 7, אות לה, הוא היה בן דודו של רבינו. ראה לעיל הערה 29א.

49 מרבותיו של רבינו. אולי זהה עם ר׳ נתן בן מנחם שהיה רבו של בעל שבלי הלקט, ראה פוגלשטיין וריגר, שם, עמ׳ 375, הערה 7 ובובר, שם, עמ׳ 7, אות לז.

צדקיה[50] [15 ; 33 ; 51].
צרפתים [29].
רבותיי [41].
שלמה (רש"י) [19 ; 41].
שמואל[51] [49].

מפתח המקורות

אבות דר' נתן[52]

נו"א לג עמ' 97 [7]; נו"ב לח עמ' 98 [72]; נו"ב מב עמ' 117 [71].

איכה רבה[53]

א יב עמ' 50 [57].

אלף המגן[54]

בראשית רבה[55]

א ד עמ' 7 [4]; ב ב עמ' 15 [61]; ב ג עמ' 15-16 [20]; ג ב עמ' 19 [25-26]; ג ז עמ' 23]40]; ח י עמ' 63-64 [28]; י ט עמ' 85 [40]; יא ג-ד עמ' 90 [42-43]; יב א עמ' 97-99 [26]; יב ח 106-107 [24]; טז ג עמ' 144 [61]; טז ד עמ' 147 [27]; יח ו עמ' 168 [68]; יט א עמ' 170-171 [68]; יט ב עמ' 171 [70]; יט ד עמ' 172-173 [69]; כ ב עמ' 183 [69-70]; כ ה עמ' 186-187 [70-71]; כו ה עמ' 248-249 [49]; לג ב עמ' 304 [54]; לח יג עמ' 361-364 [2-3]; מא ז עמ' 394 [25]; נא ה עמ' 536 [47]; נו ה עמ' 600-601 [45-47]; סה א עמ' 713 [56]; סח יב עמ' 786 [15]; עמ' 788 [5-6]; פ ז עמ' 960 [11-12]; פה ד עמ' 1037 [50]; פז א עמ' 1061 [71]; צג י עמ' 1160 [11 ; 27-28]; צט ז עמ' 1278 [34].

בראשית רבתי[56]

עמ' 90 [45-46].

דברים רבה[57]

ג ז [11]; ז ט [3].

ויקרא רבה[58]

א יא עמ' כו [65]; ו ג עמ' קל-קלה [32-33 ; 36]; ו ה עמ' קלט [32]; ו ח

50 הוא אחיו, מחברו של הספר שבלי הלקט.
51 הוא מחברו של הספר אלף המגן, ראה להלן עמ' 57, הערה 4.
52 מהד' ש"ז שכטר, ווינה 1887.
53 מהד' ש' בובר, וילנא תרנ"ט.
54 ראה לעיל, הערה 51.
55 מהד' י' תיאודור וח' אלבק, הדפסה שניה, ירושלים תשכ"ה.
56 מהד' ח' אלבק, ירושלים ת"ש.
57 דפוס ראם, וילנא.
58 מהד' מ' מרגליות, ירושלים תשי"ג-תש"ך.

עמ׳ קמ-קמא [37]; יא ז עמ׳ רלו [34-35]; יא ט עמ׳ רמא-רמב [62]; יב א עמ׳ רמט-רנ [66]; יט ו עמ׳ תלב ואילך [36-37]; כג יב עמ׳ תקמו [21]; לג א עמ׳ תשנו [33]; לג ו עמ׳ תשסז [25].

מדרש אגדה

מדרש השכם (והזהיר)[59]

יתרו עמ׳ 48 [21]; יתרו עמ׳ 49 [26].

מדרש שמואל[60]

כג ג עמ׳ 112 [25].

מילי דשבועות[61]

[6; 9].

מכילתא דר׳ ישמעאל[62]

ויסע ג עמ׳ 162 [43]; ויסע ד עמ׳ 168 [43]; בחדש ח עמ׳ 232-233 [52-53].

מסכת סופרים[63]

טז ה [29].

משנה

שבת

א א [42].

עירובין

ח ט [54].

פסחים

ט ו [46]; י ט [46].

שקלים

ג א [17]; ג ב [1]; ה ו [59].

תענית

ד ח [9; 10].

סוטה

א ח [54-55].

בבא בתרא

ט ה [57].

סנהדרין

ד ג [18]; ד ה [61]; ז ג [60]; ט ו [59-60]; י ב [73].

59 מהד׳ י״מ פריימן, לייפציג תרל״ג.
60 מהד׳ ש׳ בובר, קראקא תרנ״ג.
61 ראה להלן א׳, הערה 50.
62 מהד׳ ח״ש הארוויטץ וי״א רבין, מהד׳ שניה, ירושלים תש״ך.
63 מהד׳ מ׳ היגר, ניוארק תרצ״ז.

עבודה זרה

ג ח [36].

אבות

א ג [51]; ד ד [35]; ה א [39]; ה ח [52]; ה ט [48]; ו ה [61]; ו י [60].

ערכין

ג ד-ה [72].

נדה

ט ו [63].

סדר עולם רבה[64]

יא עמ׳ 47-48 [34].

סידורים

[14; 17; 18; 20; 28; 32; 36; 58; 70].

ספרי במדבר[65]

בהעלותך עז עמ׳ 71 [42].

ספרי דברים[66]

כד עמ׳ 34 [40]; רעג עמ׳ 293 [60]; שמה עמ׳ 402 [8].

ספרים

[2; 3; 8; 12; 15; 21; 29; 34; 66].

ערוך[67]

ערך אלייסטון [41]; בארג [41]; לפרא [41].

פלוגתא דקראי[68]

[5].

פסיקתא דרב כהנא[69]

א עמ׳ 3-4 [17]; א עמ׳ 9 [17]; ג עמ׳ 40 [17-18]; ד עמ׳ 58 [67]; ד עמ׳ 58-59 [73]; ט עמ׳ 147 [53]; יב עמ׳ 209 [10]; יב עמ׳ 213 [3]; יג עמ׳ 236 [27]; יד עמ׳ 246 [64]; כא עמ׳ 323 [16]; כג עמ׳ 334 [39-40].

פסיקתא רבתי[70]

ה כא ע״א-ע״ב [17]; כא ק ע״א [10]; מו קפז ע״ב-קפח ע״ב [39-40].

64 מהד׳ ד״ב רטנר, דפוס צלום ניו יורק תשכ״ו.

65 מהד׳ ח״ש הארוויטץ, לייפציג תרע״ז.

66 מהד׳ א״א פינקלשטיין, הוצאה שניה, ניו יורק תשכ״ט.

67 מהד׳ ח״י קאהוט, וינה וניו יורק תרל״ח-תרנ״ב.

68 ראה להלן א׳, הערה 36.

69 מהד׳ ד׳ מנדלבוים, ניוארק תשכ״ב.

70 מהד׳ מ׳ איש שלום, וינה תר״מ.

פרקי דר׳ אליעזר[71]

לא [46]; מו [6].

רות רבה[72]

ב ב [73].

שיר השירים רבה[73]

א ב [16]; א יב [14]; ד ח [28]; ד יא [15]; ד יג [13-14]; ה א [16]; ז ד [19].

תוספתא[74]

שבת

א א [42]; א ד [42].

סוטה

ז ג [32-33].

בבא קמא

ז ב [53]; ז ח [56]; ז י-יג [56-59; 61; 63].

תורת כהנים[75]

יב י [54].

תלמוד בבלי

ברכות

ו ע״א [19]; ט ע״ב [22]; יט ע״א [14]; כד ע״א [65]; כח ע״א [7]; כט ע״ב [8]; מ ע״א [21]; מז ע״א [57]; נד ע״ב [5; 71]; נה ע״א [59].

שבת

כ ע״ב [42]; כה עב [41]; לד ע״ב [42]; לה ע״א [53]; מד ע״א [44]; נד ע״ב [19]; נז ע״ב [63]; עג ע״ב [55]; עו ע״ב [21]; פו ע״ב [40]; פח ע״א [13]; צ ע״א [15]; צב ע״א [55]; קב ע״ב [58]; קט ע״ב [71]; קיג ע״א-ע״ב [43-44]; קיז ע״ב [41-42]; קיט ע״א [41; 43; 55-56]; קכט ע״א [52]; קנ ע״א-ע״ב [44]; קנב ע״א [59]; קנז ע״א [44];

עירובין

כא ע״ב [15; 25]; צו ע״א [15].

פסחים

ז ע״ב [46]; ח ע״ב [64]; עד ע״ב [21]; פט ע״ב [57]; קו ע״א [44]; קיב ע״א [62; 72]; קיג ע״ב [43]; קיח ע״א-ע״ב [30].

71 דפוס ווארשא, עם ביאור הרד״ל.

72 דפוס ראם, ווילנא.

73 כנ״ל.

74 מהד׳ ש׳ ליברמן, ניוארק תשכ״ב (סדר מועד); שם תשל״ג (סדר נשים; סוטה וכו׳); מהד׳ מ״ש צוקרמאנדל, הדפסה שלישית, ירושלים תשכ״ג.

75 מהדורת רא״ה וייס, וינה תרכ״ב, מהדורת צילום נ״י תש״ז.

יומא

כ ע״ב [20]; נד ע״א [18]; פג ע״א [66].

ביצה

טו ע״ב [42]; טז ע״א [42]; כא ע״א [41].

ראש השנה

ט ע״א [42]; לב ע״א [39]; לג ע״ב [28-29].

תענית

ז ע״א [15]; ח ע״א [15]; יד ע״ב [14]; יט ע״ב [54]; כ ע״ב [62]; כג ע״א [58].

מגילה

ב ע״ב [18]; ה ע״ב [28]; ט ע״ב [1]; יא ע״א [44; 49]; יד ע״א [51]; לא ע״ב [32; 71].

מועד קטן

ד ע״ב [18-19]; ח ע״ב [62]; יז ע״א [32]; כה ע״ב [28].

חגיגה

יב ע״א [39].

יבמות

קיז ע״א [59].

כתובות

ל ע״א-ע״ב [48]; מו ע״א [73]; סו ע״ב [47].

נדרים

כב ע״ב [41]; צא ע״ב [59].

סוטה

ט ע״ב [68]; יד ע״א [10-11; 26]; כב ע״ב [55]; לה ע״א [71]; מז ע״א [36].

גיטין

לה ע״א [36]; נה ע״ב [14]; סח ע״ב [27]; ע ע״א [63].

קידושין

ע ע״ב [68].

בבא קמא

נו ע״ב [66].

בבא מציעא

מג ע״א [63]; נז ע״ב [57; 63]; סו ע״ב [62]; קו ע״א [38]; קיט ע״א [12].

בבא בתרא

סא ע״ב [58].

סנהדרין

כב ע״א [25]; כט ע״א [69-70]; לז ע״א [35; 63]; לח ע״א-ע״ב [24]; מג ע״ב-מד ע״א [35; 66]; מט ע״א [48]; נב ע״א [25]; סט ע״ב [73]; עד ע״ב [61-62]; פא ע״ב [59-60]; צג ע״א [27].

שבועות

מז ע״ב [63].

עבודה זרה

ב ע״ב [5]; י ע״ב [49]; כח ע״ב [32]; לה ע״א [29].

הוריות

יג ע״ב [54].

מנחות

מג ע״א [13]; קא ע״א [46].

חולין

יח ע״א [35; 54]; לא ע״ב [6]; נט ע״ב [63]; קיב ע״א [15].

בכורות

מג ע״ב [19]; נ ע״ב [71].

ערכין

טז ע״א [35].

נדה

ל ע״ב [34]; מז ע״א [49].

תלמוד ירושלמי

ברכות

פ״ט ה״ז (יד ע״ב) [55].

שבת

פ״ו ה״ד (ח ע״ב) [13].

סוטה

פ״ה ה״ז (כ ע״ג) [55].

תנחומא הישן

נח א [68]; וירא כג [46]; תולדות ב [46-47]; וישב ב [32]; וישב ה [52]; כי תשא טז [8]; ויקרא ז [37-38]; צו יג [46]; נשא כח [34]; נצבים ג [22].

תנחומא בובר[76]

ואתחנן א [37].

תרגום אונקלוס

בראשית

א כ [71]; ב א [40]; ב כא [12; 51]; ג ו [69]; ד ב [63]; טו יז [20]; כד סו [14; 67]; כז יא [18]; לב טז [44]; לד יד [35]; לה ד [22; 55]; לז כה [50]; מ א [37]; מב ט [71]; מב כה [41; 73]; מג כג [34]; מג לא [11]; מד ז [29]; מז לא [51].

שמות

ב י [68]; ג ט [72]; ה יב [69]; ט י [3]; י כב [22; 34]; יב ח [36]; יד כב [34];

76 מהד׳ ש׳ בובר, וילנא תרמ״ה.

יד כד [67]; יד כז [60]; טז יח [68]; טז לא [42]; יט כה [1]; כ ה [54]; כ ז [31]; כב ב [64]; כב טו [69; 72]; כג ח [65]; כג כט [27]; כד יב [54]; כה כג [43]; כו ה [55]; כח טז [64]; כח יח [12]; כח כ [13]; לב כה [65].

ויקרא

א טז [28]; ו ה [37]; יא ג [56]; יג ג [70]; יג ט [32]; טז יב [3; 67]; יח ג [37; 60]; יט טז [30]; כה יח [28].

במדבר

ד טו [60]; יט ב [63]; כא ו [53]; כג ז [67]; כד יד [23]; לב לו [48].

דברים

א ז [36]; ג כה [19]; ו ז [66]; יג ו [60]; יט יא [53]; כב י [50]; כב כג [71]; כד ז [60]; כז ט [70]; כח נו [41]; לב א [36; 41; 67]; לב כה [12]; לב מב [67].

תרגום ירושלמי[77]

בראשית

א ב [20]; ב ב [8]; יג טו [22]; כב ג [14; 46]; לד יב [12]; לז ט [18]; מד ל [28].

שמות

יד לא [9]; ב ב [9]; ב יג [48]; כא כח [4; 7]; כד י [6].

ויקרא

א ט [50]; א טו [29].

במדבר

יג כד [18]; יג כו [69].

דברים

ד כד [24]; לג ד [11].

תרגום לנביאים ולכתובים

יהושע

יג ג [4].

שופטים

ג יא [41]; ג טז [40].

שמואל א

כא ח [72-73].

שמואל ב

יח יד [55]; כא יט [73].

מלכים ב

ו ו [42]; כג ז [68].

ישעיה

ה כו [68]; י כה [38]; יז ז [65]; מא יט [14]; נח א [30]; נט ה [65].

77 בדפוסים הרגילים וגם לפי מהד׳ של ד׳ רידר, ירושלים 1974.

ירמיה

ב ה [20].

עמוס

ו ו [51].

תהלים

יח י [1]; יט יא [11]; קכ ד [67].

משלי

א טז [57]; ה כב [55]; יד כא [43]; כה יא [18].

איוב

ג ד [22]; טו טו [7]; לג יד [68]; לג כ [66]; לח כב [62]; מ יז [63].

שיר השירים

ב ח [12]; ז ט [27]; ח יד [66].

איכה

ב י [54]; ג יב [6].

רשימת הלעזים

angeli [7]
avvocato [6]
dolosi [50]
domino [28]
ecclesia [21; 24]
fabbricato [21]
grazia [12]
infranto [59]
miele [41]
pajola [51]
porpora [3]
ripa [37]
segmenti [51]
smeraldo [12]
treccia [18]
zappa [58]
zona [51]

תודתי נתונה למנהלי Jews' College בלונדון על שהמציאו לי צילום של כתב היד של הפירוש ועל טובם בנתינת הרשות לפרסמו; לד״ר אברהם טל (רוזנטל) על שהרשה לי להדפיס כאן את הפיוטים מס׳ א׳, ב׳, ו׳, ח׳, י׳, י״א וי״ג (ראה נספח) על פי הטכסט המתוקן שהוא הכין לעבודת הגמר שלו ולגברת סנדרה סטו (Stow) ולפרופסור דניאל קרפי על עזרתם בתעתיק הלעזים האיטלקיים.

תודה כפולה ומכופלת חייב אני לידידי הפרופ׳ ר׳ חיים זלמן דימיטרובסקי על ששידלני ועודדני להכין ולגמור עבודה זו לדפוס; בלי התעניינותו התמידית ועזרתו המרובה חיבור זה לא היה יוצא לאור בזמן הזה ובצורתו הנוכחית. פרופ׳ דימיטרובסקי גם הואיל בטובו להעיר הרבה הערות חשובות לטכסט והן מובאות להלן בהערות בתוך סוגריים מרובעים.

א פירוש אלפביטין

[1] תחלת הדבר אנו צריכין לפרש למה נקראו **אלפביטין**,[1] לפי שהן מסודרין באלף בית והוא לשון יוון אלפביטא, כדאיתא במשנת שקלים לעניין שלש קופות שבהן תורמין הלשכה וכתוב עליהן אלף בית גימל, ר׳ יוסי אומ׳ יוונית כתוב עליהן אלפא ביטא גמא.[2] ומהו עילוייו של לשון יוון יותר מכל שאר לשונות, לפי מה שאמ׳ חכמ׳ ז״ל יפת אלהים ליפת וישכ׳ באהלי שם יפיותו של יפת ישכן באהלי שם, וזהו לש׳ יוונית, ועיקרו במגילה.[3] **ויירד משה ונחת משה כו׳**, נהגו לתרגמו תחילה בתרגומו של אונקלוס ואחר כן מתרג׳ אותו בירושלמי, וכן כל פסוק ופסוק כסדר הכת׳ במחזור.[4]

אלפביטא

ארכין ה׳ שמייא לסיני כול׳,[5] ייסד התורגמן על דרך המקרא ויט שמים, ופת׳ **ארכין** הטה.
[2] וכן תרג׳ ויט שמים, וארכין שמייא. [6]**מהימני**, על דרך המקרא בכל ביתי נאמן הוא. [7]**תא**
סוק, בוא עלה. כמ׳ שנ׳, ואל משה אמר עלה וגו׳,[8] וזהו מיוסד על עליית משה בענן,

1 המונח אלפביטין לציון פיוטים שהם מסודרים על פי א״ב נמצא כבר במדרש. ראה למשל שהש״ר א א ז: ״הדין פייטנא כד עביד אלפא ביתא״ וכו׳: השווה מה שכתב על המונח הזה שירמן, *JQR*, ס״ח, 44 (1953), עמ׳ 131-132.

2 משנה שקלים פ״ג מ״ב; במשנה שלפנינו בעל המאמר הוא ר׳ ישמעאל ובכ״י מינכן: ר׳ שמעון (ראה ד״ס, שקלים, עמ׳ 23 וראה שם גם על צורות הכתיב השונות של אלפא ביטא גמא) אבל בבבלי יומא סב ע״א ובמקבילות: ״אילימא ר׳ יוסי דקופות״ וכו׳. ראה ד״ס, יומא, עמ׳ 172, אות ע; הנ״ל, מגילה, עמ׳ 117, אות ו.

3 מגילה ט ע״ב.

4 שמות יט כה, ותרגומים שם. בפסח ובשבועות נהגו לקרוא את פסוקי פרשת היום ולתרגמם בשני התרגומים ואח״כ החלו לאמור את הפיוטים הארמיים. ראה מ״ו, עמ׳ 336 וראה להלן ו, הערה 2. על קריאת התרגומים בצבור בשבתות מיוחדות ובחגים גם אחרי שפסק המנהג של קריאת התרגום בכל שבת ראה צונץ, הדרשות, עמ׳ 194 ועמ׳ 512 (שם נזכרים גם כ״י של מחזורים שכלולים בהם התרגומים לפרשיות מיוחדות), ראה גם היינימן, שרידים, עמ׳ 364.

5 דווידזון, א, 7648. ראה היינימן, שרידים, עמ׳ 363-364, הנוסח הארמי בצירוף תרגום עברי, טל (לעיל במבוא, הערה 8), עמ׳ 86-93 (הנוסח הארמי, תרגום עברי ופירוש).

6 תהלים יח י, ות״י שם.

7 במדבר יב ז.

8 שמות כד א.

שהטה שמים על הר סיני ועלה, כמ' דתימר ומשה ניגש אל הערפל אשר שם הר האלהים.[9] ויש ספרים שכתוב בהן **תסוק** ופת' תעלה, והראשון צח. **בני פלטין לא יבהלונך כו'**, לפי שהיה משה מפחד שלא יעמדו המלאכים להזיקו, בישרו שלא יוכלו להזיק לו. לכך ייסד המתורגמן בני פלטין שלמעלה לא יוכלו להבהילך שכבר כבש אותם אברהם זקינך מתחילה שהאכילם והשחידם, בפרשת וירא אליו.[10] ע"א, מיוסד על יעקב אבינו, דכת' ויאבק איש עמו וירא כי לא יכול לו, וכת' כי שרית עם אלהים.[11] **גומרין דאתון כו'**, ואם תאמר, היאך אעלה במקום שכולו אש לוהט, כבר עשיתי כזאת לאברהם זקינך שהפילו נמרוד לכבשן האש ולא הזיק לו. והמעשה מפורש בבראשית רבא שלהי פרשת נח, ר' חייא בריה דר' אדא דמן יפו אמ', תרח מוכר צלמים היה, חד זמן נפק לאתר חד כיון שיצא הושיב אברהם בנו למכור תחתיו. כי הוה אתי בר נש ובעי מיזבון הוה אמ' ליה, בר כמה שנין את. אמ' ליה, בר נ' או בר ס'. אמ' ליה, בר נ' בעי למיסגד לבר יומא, והוה מתבייש ואזיל ליה. חד זמן אתא חד' איתתא טעינא חד פינך, פי' קערה, דסלת ואמרת ליה, הא לך קרוב קדמיהון. קם נסב בקולסא, פי' פטיש, ותברינון ויהב ההוא בוקלסא[11א] בידיה דרבה דהוה ביניהון. כיון דאתא אבוהא אמ', מאן עבד להון כדין. אמ' ליה, מה נכפור מינך, איתתא חדא אייתת חד פינך דסלת ואמרת לי הא לך קרוב קדמיהון, דין הוה אמ' אנא איכול קדמאי ודין הוה אמ' אנא אכיל קדמאי, קם הדין רבה דביניהון ותברינון. אמ' ליה, מה את מפלי בי, פי' מלעיג, וידעין אינון כלום. אמ' ליה, לא ישמעו אזניך מה שפיך אומרת. נסביה ומסריה לנמרוד. אמ' ליה נמרוד, נסגוד לנורא, אמ' ליה, נסגוד למיא דמטפי לנורא. הדר אמ' ליה, ניסגוד למיא. אמ' ליה, ניסגוד לרוחא דמבדר עננא. הדר אמ', ניסגוד לרוחא. אמ' ליה, ניסגוד לבר נשא דסביל רוחא. אמ' ליה, מילין את משתעי, אני איני משתחוה אלא לאור, הריני משליכך בתוכו ויבוא אלוה שאתה משתחוה לו ויציל אותך ממנו. כיון שירד אברהם לכבשן האש נגלה הק' בכבודו והצילו, הה"ד אני ה' אשר [3]
הוצאתיך מאור כשדים.[12] לכך ייסד המתורגמן **גומרין דאתון אדליק נמרוד. גומרין** תרג' גחלי אש.[13] **אתון** תרג' פיח כבשן.[14] **למיכוי** לש' כויה. **דבק לית הוא כו'**, ואם תאמר, אני ירא מאשן שלמלאכים שהוא קשה יותר מאשו שלהדיוט. גם מזה אל תירא, שאינו דבק בך, לפי שעמך שכינתי, אש אוכלת אש. על שם כי ה' אלהיך אש אוכלה הוא.[15] **הא אנא**

9 שמות כ כא (בפסוק: "אשר שם האלקים"); על עליית משה בענן בשעת מתן תורה ראה מכילתא, בחדש ט, עמ' 238-239.

10 השווה שמות רבה כח א: "באותה שעה בקשו מלאכי השרת לפגוע במשה, עשה בו הקב"ה קלסטירין של פניו של משה דומה לאברהם" וכו'.

11 בראשית לב כה-כו, כט. כלומר, "דכבש יתהון סבך" וכו' אינו מוסב על אברהם אלא על יעקב.

11א כך הוא בכ"י.

12 ב"ר לח יג, עמ' 361-364 וראה בש"נ ובמ"י שם.

13 למשל ויקרא טז יב, ות"א שם.

14 שמות ט י ות"א שם.

15 דברים ד כד; ראה יומא כא ע"ב; השווה פס"ר כ, צו ע"א ואילך: "בשעה שעלה משה למרום... פגע בו קמואל המלאך... גער במשה... ילוד אשה מהלך במקום אש... עד שהגיע למקום הדרניאל... באותה שעה נתגלגלו רחמיו של הקב"ה ויצתה בת קול ואמרה לו להדרניאל... ולא עזבתם אותי עד ששרפתי מכם כתות באש" וכו'. ראה רמא"ש שם.

מלבש לך, ועוד אין לך לירא מן המלאכים כי הנני מלבישך מזיו יקרי שיש בו גבורה
שיפחדו המלאכים מליקרב אליך,[16] זהו פתרון **דאית ביה גברו דלא ליקרוב לותך**. **פורפורן**,
לש׳ לעז פורפור׳[17] והוא בגד יקר, והוא מיוסד על שם כי קרן עור פני משה,[18] כמה
שמפרש והולך. ע״א. **פורפרן**, בגימטריא תרי״ג, **נתייתרו ג׳**[19] על שם הלא כתבתי לך
שלישים,[20] וכל מעשה אותו היום היה משולש כמפורש בפסיקתא דשבועות.[21] והוא
מיוסד על לש׳ האגדה, בני אם תקח אמרי, אמ׳ ר׳ יהודה בר שלום אימתי אתה נקרא בני
כשתקח אמרי, למה הדבר דומה, למל׳ שאמ׳ לו בנו אבא סמניני בתוך המדינה כדי שידעו
הכל שאתה[22] בנך. אמ׳ לו אביו, תרצה שידעו הכל כי אתה בני לבוש פורפורא שלי ושים
עטרה שלי בראשך וידעו הכל שאתה בני. כך אמ׳ הק׳ לישראל, תרצו שידעו הכל שאתם
בניי עסקו בתורה.[23] ועל לשון האגדה הזאת ייסד **הא אנא מלבש לך פורפירן דידי**. ויש
ספרים שכת׳ בהן **דלית גבר דיקרוב לותך**, והמלאכים מצינו שנקראו אישים.[24] **וקבעית קרני** [4]
כול׳, קרני הודא, על שם כי קרן עור פניו.[25] **תנגשיניה בהון**, כי יגח שור תרג׳ ירושלמ׳
ארום יגש.[26] **זעירא לא תיהוי כו׳**, **חי אנא וקיים כו׳**, ואל תהיה קטן בעיניך, כי חי אני
שבראתי צורתך עד שלא בראתי רום ועומק, היינו שמים וארץ. **איקוניך**, פי׳ צורתך.[27]
שהרי התורה קדמה לעולם, שנ׳ קדם מפעליו מאז. וכת׳ בה כמה פעמ׳ וידבר ה׳ אל משה
לאמר ודבר זה רמוז בתחילת התורה בראשית ברא אלהים את השמים ואת הארץ אל
תיקרי את השמים אלא השם ים את הארץ, שעשה הים יבשה והעביר ישׂ׳ בתוכו.[28]
ובבראשית רבא, אמ׳ ר׳ בנייה העולם לא נברא אלא בזכות התורה שנ׳ ה׳ בחכמ׳ יסד ארץ,
ר׳ ברכיה אמ׳ בזכות משה שנ׳ וירא ראשית לו.[29] **טירוני מרומא כו׳**, **יה יהב רשו לבישרא**
כו׳, כשעלה משה למרום התחילו המלאכים תמיהין ואומ׳ זה לזה מאיין בא זה האכסניי
ואם הק׳ נתן רשות לבשר ודם שיעלה לרקיע מעתה אנו נפסדין ומיטמאין בהן כמ׳ עזה

16 שבת פח ע״ב; פס״ר כ, צח ע״א. [וראה דב״ר פי״א אות ג. ״גברו״ על משקל ״פלגו״, ראה ד״ס לב״ק טו ע״א אות ת ופי׳ ר׳ יונתן לב״ק שם.]

17 porpora באיטלקית.

18 שמות לד לה.

19 לא מצאתי מקור אחר לגימטריא זו; על צורות הכתיב השונות של פורפרין ראה במ״י לב״ר עד טו, עמ׳ 873. בכ״י יש רווח בין הפ״י ובין הרי״ש אבל ברור שאי־אפשר להוסיף ביניהן אות כי רק בלי אות נוספת עולה 616 ועל זה אומר ״נתייתרו ג׳״.

20 משלי כב כ.

21 פסדר״כ, יב, עמ׳ 213.

22 צ״ל ״שאני״, וכך תוקן על הגליון: ״י״ג שאני״.

23 דב״ר ז ט; דב״ר, מהד׳ הגר״ש ליברמן, עמ׳ 111-112, בשינויים קטנים.

24 ראה רמב״ם, הלכות יסודי התורה, פ״ב ה״ז ועוד.

25 שמות לד כט.

26 שמות כא כח, ות״י שם (כן בניאופיטי, אבל בנדפס ובמהד׳ רידר: וארום ינגש).

27 לא מצאתי מקור לאגדה שצורתו של משה נבראה לפני בריאת העולם. ראה גם היינימן, שרידים, עמ׳ 370, ומהלשון נראה שהמפרש מוכיח דבר זה מדעתו.

28 משלי ח כב; על פסוק זה מיוסדת הדרשה המפורסמת שהתורה קדמה לבריאת העולם (ב״ר א ד, עמ׳ 6) ובדומה לזה מפרש רבינו מדעתו. וראה בהערה הקודמת.

29 ב״ר א ד, עמ׳ 7.

ועזאל.[30] **טירוני**, לש׳ שררה, סרני פלשתים תרג׳ טורני פלשתאי.[31] **אנפריסין**, עיקרו מלשון
אנפרות והוא לש׳ הפסד וחסרון.[32] והאומרין **אנן אינפריפסין** איני יודע מה אומרין. ויש
לפרשו כלפי למעלה, והיא תשובת המקום למלאכים וכה פת׳ **יה יהבי רשות לבישרא**,
כלומ׳ אני נתתי רשות לבשר ודם לעלות הנה במקום טהרה וקדושה ומעתה אני הוא
המליץ שלהן, לפי שכשחטא אדם הראשון ודור אנוש ודור המבול ודור הפלגה היה
למלאכים פתחון פה על מה שאמרו בתחילת ברייתו שלאדם, מה אנוש כי תזכרנו ובן אדם
כי תפקדנו,[33] מה אדם ותדעהו,[34] ועתה במתן תורה היה להק׳ פתחון פה כנגדן.[35] ומצאתי
אגדה, אמ׳ ר׳ אלעזר בוא וראה כמה חיבתן שלישראל לפני המקום, מלך בשר ודם עבדו [5]
מכעיס אותו מלקה אותו ואחר כך רוצה לרפאותו, אבל הק׳ אינו כן אלא מקדים רפואה
למכה ליש׳ שנ׳ ברופאי ליש׳ ונגלה עון אפרים, למה הדבר דומה למלך שהיה לו בן אחד
והיה יודע המלך שהוא יחטא לפניו והוא מלקה אותו לפיכך עשה לו המלך אפירופסין
הרבה שכל כעס וכעס שהוא כועס הן עומדין ומפייסין את המלך על אותו הכעס כו׳, ופת׳
מליץ והוא למד מעניינו, והאגדה הזאת בפלוגתא דקראי הוא.[36] **כד חמון מלאכ׳ כו׳**,
לענותנא איתקרי משה כו׳, **מכון שמייא כו׳**, **נזעו מלאכייא כו׳**, כל אילו ארבע שיטות הן
מוכיחות זו על זו ותלויות זו בזו. וכה פירושן, כשבאו המלאכים שהיה הק׳ משיב להם על
התימה שהיו תמיהין ואומ׳ **דין אכסנא הבא מאן הוא** והיה הק׳ משיבן **אנא מהודע לכון מי
הוא האכסניי**. **לענוותנא איתקרי משה**, כלומ׳ לשם ענוותו נקרא משה כמ׳ דתימ׳ והאיש
משה עניו מאד,[37] רועה שלבניי ונאמן ביתי[38] ובזכותו **מכון שמייא** על סיני, לשון שפלות,
כדאמ׳ דהוה ממכיך טורי מקמיהו, בברכות פרק הרואה.[39] **ורמת ארעא**, היינו הר סיני

30 פס״ר כ, צו ע״ב, אבל שם אין זכר לענין של עזה ועזאל; על שהמלאכים הנ״ל נטמאו ונפסדו כשבאו במגע עם בנות האדם ראה אגדות היהודים, ה, עמ׳ 153.

31 יהושע יג ג, ות״י שם.

32 במחזור היידנהיים הגירסא ״אנפרטין״; היינמן, שרידים, עמ׳ 364 גורס ״אנפריטין״ ומתרגם ״משרת״ (?); רבינו מפרש מלשון אנפרות, ראה ערוך ערך אנפרות.

33 תהלים ח ה.

34 שם קמד ג.

35 השווה למשל מדרש תהלים, עמ׳ לז-לח, על תהלים ח׳ ה׳ הנ״ל; תהלים קמ״ד ג׳ הנ״ל מובא בפרקי דר׳ אליעזר, ראש פרק י״ג, בקשר לטענות המלאכים נגד בריאת העולם; על התנגדותם של המלאכים לבריאת האדם ראה אגדות היהודים, ה, עמ׳ 69-70.

36 את האגדה בשם ר׳ אלעזר לא מצאתי וראה מגילה יג ע״ב. כמו כן לא יכולתי לקבוע לאיזה מדרש מתכוון רבינו בשם ״פלוגתא דקראי״; אולם מסתבר שהיה לפניו מדרש על שני כתובים המכחישים זה את זה. השווה גנזי שכטר, א, עמ׳ 216 ואילך ובמיוחד עמ׳ 227-229, ששם עוסק בעל המדרש בענין שהקב״ה מקדים רפואה למכה; ראה גם ורטהימר, בתי מדרשות, א, עמ׳ רמז ואילך; ראה גם את ההוספה בפיסקא מ״ב, ספרי, נשא. אני מודה לפרופ׳ רא״ש רוזנטל על שהואיל בטובו להעיר לי על המקורות הנ״ל [ואע״פ שרבינו למד פירושו מעניינו ברור שהמלה ״אפירופסין״ פירושה ״מגן ונציג״, ועי״פ זה ברור שאין קאהוט בערך איפרפוס צודק וראה גם בערך פרפסט].

37 במדבר יב ג.

38 שם ח.

39 ברכות נד ע״ב.

שנתלש ונכפה כגיגית על ישׂ׳ כדאית׳ בראש מסכת ע״ז,[40] ונמצא עומד בין החיות
והאופנים, מיד נזעו המלאכים, נכנס רתת וזיע בלבם שהיו רואין משה עומד בערפל
ומתגבר כנגדם.[41] **סערות גופיה כו׳, עול וקריב לך כו׳, פסל לך לוחין כו׳, סערות**, בסמך,
פי׳ לשון חימה וכעס וסער.[42] כלומ׳, כל סערות לבו עמדות ונשתככו יחד לאחר שראה
[6] צורת יעקב אבינו חקוקה בכסא הכבוד[43] ומעוררת לפניו וסמך ונשען על זכותו, לפי שהיה
יעקב קורא לו וצווח מכסא הכבוד ואומ׳ למשה **עול וקריב לך כו׳**.[44] **פסל לך לוחין מן
סנפירינון**, תרג׳ ירושלמי שלספיר הוא סנפירינון.[45] **כסא** תרג׳ כורסא. ומפרש בברייתׄ דר׳
אליעזר, ר׳ יוחנא אומ׳ הלוחות לא נבראו מן הארץ אלא מן השמים מעשה ידי הק׳ שנ׳
והלוחות מעשה אלהים המה הלוחות שהיו מקדם.[46] ויש לפרש **שערות גופיה**, כאדם
שעומדין שערותיו כשרואה פתאום דבר שהוא נבהל עליו, אבל אחר שנתיישב דעתו **צהיל
הוה ליביה כו׳. אפולוגוס**, פי׳ מליץ יושר, אבוקטו בלע״ז.[47] פ״א, **אפולוגוס**, שומר.
כמטרה לחץ תרג׳ כפלגיסא לגיירא ותרג׳ שומר נטר.[48] **קרבו מלאכייא כו׳, קיריס**, לש׳ יוון
אדון.[49] **רישא וכיפא כו׳**, כיון שנתן הק׳ רשות למשה וחיזקו לעמוד כנגד המלאכים מיד
אחז בכסא הכבוד והיה מקנתרן כדאית׳ במילי׳ דשבועות, מיד הלכו המלאכים לפני הק׳
ואמ׳ לפניו רבונו של עולם מי יצילנו מידי וכול׳.[50] **רישא וכיפא**, על בקיעת הים ייסדו

40 ע״ז ב ע״ב, ושם לא נזכר שההר נתלש ממקומו, אבל ראה מכילתא, בחדש ג, עמ׳ 214: ״בתחתית ההר, מלמד שנתלש ההר ממקומו״, וראה שם הערה 17 וראה פרקי דר׳ אליעזר, ראש פרק מ״א ומה שכתב הרד״ל שם, אות ד.

41 השווה פרקי דר׳ אליעזר, הנ״ל: ״וממקומו נתלש הר סיני ונפתחו השמים ונכנס ראש ההר בשמים וערפל מכסה את ההר״ וכו׳.

42 השווה ירמיה כג יט.

43 ב״ר סח יב, עמ׳ 788. ״ונשתככו״ — על־פי אסתר ז י.

44 לא מצאתי מקור לזה במדרשים; ואולי מיוסד על האגדה המספרת שבשעה שהתנפלו המלאכים על משה כשהוא עלה למרום לקבל את התורה אחז משה בכסא הכבוד (שחקוק בו איקונין של יעקב, ראה בהערה הקודמת) ואז התגבר משה והשיב למלאכים וכו׳, השווה פס״ר כ, צח ע״א ומקבילות.

45 שמות כד י, ות״י שם.

46 פדר״א פמ״ו ועיין רד״ל שם, אות כא; ראה ספרי, בהעלותך, קא, עמ׳ 99-100: ״מצינו שהספיר של לוחות של משה היה וכו׳ ובמקום אחר הוא אומר והלוחות מעשה אלקים המה (שמות לב טז) ואומר ויראו אלקי ישראל ותחת רגליו כמעשה לבנת הספיר (שם כד י), מקיש מעשה למעשה, מה מעשה האמור להלן של ספיר אף מעשה האמור כאן של ספיר״. ואפשר לפרש שגם הלוחות הראשונים של ספיר היו אלא שהם נפסלו מן הספיר שמתחת לכסא הכבוד והלוחות השניים נפסלו מספיר שהיה של משה; אולם את העניין שמשה בעצמו פסל את הלוחות הראשונים לא מצאתי במקום אחר (ראה היינימן, שרידים, עמ׳ 370) [ואי־אפשר לפרש כן לפי דברי רבינו עצמו, שהרי בפירוש נאמר בפדר״א ״מעשה ידי הק׳״. על כן נר׳ ש״פסל לך״ אינו צווי אלא עבר, כלומר, יעקב צווח: דמלכא חייא פסל לך וכו׳, כלומר כבר פָּסַל לך לוחות מן...].

47 avvocato באיטלקית.

48 איכה ג יב, ותרגום שם, השווה ערוך ערך פלגס, וראה בס׳ השרשים בערך נטר.

49 על השמוש במלה זו ראה היינימן, הנ״ל, עמ׳ 368.

50 השווה פס״ר כ, צח ע״א; אבל לא מצאתי את הלשון ״מיד הלכו המלאכים״ וכו׳. ״מילי דשבועות״ הנזכרות כאן ולהלן בראש הפירוש לדיבר ראשון, פיוט ג׳, כנראה כללו מדרש הנועד לחג השבועות ובו אגדות על מעשה מתן תורה בדומה לפרשיות כ׳ ואילך שבפס״ר. ראה הערת רמא״ש, שם, צד ע״ב אות ב.

המתורגמן כדאמ׳ בחולין פ״ק, מטבילין בראשין ואין מטבילין בכיפין,[51] ופת׳ גל הים, זה נראה לי עיקר. וברוב הספרים כתוב **רישא דכיפא בחוטרא הוא תבר**, אבל קשה בעיניי לפרשו על עניין הסלע לפי שלא היה המעשה עד סוף מ׳ שנה. ועוד יש לפרשו על הים [7] כדאית׳ באבות דר׳ נתן, אמרו יש׳ אין אנו יכולין לעבור עד ייעשה הים סלעים, נטל מטהו והטילה על הים ונעשה סלעים סלעים, אמרו אין אנו יכולין לעבור כו׳.[52] או יש לפרשו על הכותו בצור בחורב כשבאו לרפידים כמ׳ שנ׳, הנני עומד לפניך שם על הצור בחורב והכית בצור ויצאו ממנו מים וגו׳,[53] וזה היה קודם מתן תורה והוא מפורש בסוף פרש׳ ויהי בשלח. **למנגשא**, וכי יגח שור תרג׳ ירושלמ׳ וארום יגש תורא.[54] **תיסב אורייתי כול׳.**

ב ויִדבר אלהים כול׳

אלפא ביטא

אנגלי מרומא כו׳,[1] פי׳ **אנגלי**, מלאכים והוא ממש לשון לעז אנגילי,[2] ושמים לא זכו בעיניו תרג׳ ואנגלי שמייא,[3] **בכון אנא צוח כו׳**, **אורנוס**, שמים בלשון יוון.[4] **קיריס**, אדון.[5] **גבר אנא מן גינוס כו׳**, פי׳ **גינוס**, ייחוס ופת׳ מיוחס בלשון יוון.[6] **גיברי חילא כו׳**, **גלי**, פי׳ שערים כמ׳ טרוקו גלי דאי אתון כו׳.[7]

וסליק משה לרקיעא ואמ׳ למלאכייא לית אנא נחית,[8] כלפי שאמרו המלאכים **דאי את סליק סופך למינחת**[9] השיבן משה ואמ׳ **לית אנא נחית עד אורייתי אסב**, לפי שהמלאכים

51 חולין לא ע״ב (וזה בפרק ב׳ ולא בפרק קמא).

52 אדר״נ, נו״א, פל״ג, עמ׳ 97.

53 שמות יז ו.

54 שמות כא כח, וראה לעיל הערה 26.

1 דוידזון, א, 6374 (וראה להלן הערה 8): ראה היינימן, שרידים, עמ׳ 365 (החלק הראשון של הפיוט בצירוף תרגום עברי): טל, עמ׳ 103-109 (הנוסח הארמי, תרגום עברי ופירוש).

2 angeli באיטלקית.

3 איוב טו טו, ובתרגום שם (הנוסח בתרגום, ״ואנגלי מרומא״, כהתחלת הפיוט כאן, ולא אנגלי שמייא – הנוסח המובא ע״י המפרש).

4 על השימוש במלה זו בפיוטים ראה צונץ, ס״פ, עמ׳ 118 הערה d.

5 ראה לעיל א, הערה 49.

6 ראה ערוך ערך גנס.

7 ברכות כח ע״א. [וכנראה שגרס בגמרא ״דאי אתון עברי ר״ג מצערי״.]

8 כאן מתחיל חלק חדש של הפיוט וכבר ראה צונץ (ליטג׳, עמ׳ 75) שהפיוט שלפנינו מורכב משני חלקים: ראה גם דוידזון, א, 6374, והיינימן, שרידים, עמ׳ 367, הערה 20. המלים ״וסליק משה״ כתובות בכ״י באותיות גדולות, כעין כותרת, כדי לציין התחלת חטיבה חדשה.

9 הוא הטור האחרון של החלק הראשון של הפיוט.

היו מבקשין אותה כמ׳ דתימ׳, מה אדיר שמך בכל הארץ אשר תנה הודך על השמים.[10] **עד**
[8] **אצבע גבורה תכתב**, על שם כתובים באצבע אלהים[11]. וברוב הספרים כתוב **באצבע**,
והבי״ת היא יתירה ואינה צריכה להיות. והקורא טעות בידו, דהא אתי באל״ף בי״ת
והבי״ת לפנינו, ועוד, **תכתב** מוסב על האצבע ואם תקרא **באצבע** בבי״ת יסוד על התורה
וצריך לומ׳ **תיכתב. כלתי**, חמודתי, ויכל אלהים תרג׳ ירוש׳ וחמיד.[12] ויש לפרשו לש׳ כלה
ממש דכת׳ מורשה קהילת יעקב אל תיקרי מורשה אלא מאורסה.[13] ובמדרש, ויתן אל משה
ככלותו, ככלתו כת׳.[14] ודמיון שני חיתונים היו במתן תורה, האחד, נדמה הק׳ לחתן ויש׳
לכלה והתורה קידושין ומתן סיבלונות, השני, נדמה יש׳ לחתן והתורה לכלה ומשה
סרסור[15]... **עד בריוני נחמה**, בריוני, פי׳ בוראי. **עד בלוחות נדמה**, פי׳ **נדמה**, לשון שתיקה
כמ׳ לך דומיה תהילה.[16] כלומ׳, עד שנקבל הלוחות ואחר כך אלך לי ונשתתק. שלא יהיו עוד
בינינו טענות ותיגר. ע״א. נדמה, נשתכר, לשון דמים.[17] ועוד יש לפרשו לש׳ אורה, כי נר
מצוה ותורה אור,[17א] מלשון עם דמדומי חמה.[18] **עד השופרין תוקעין**, זה ייסד המתורגמן על
העלייה שעלה משה בהר ונתקדש בענן קודם מתן תורה. כלומ׳, לא ארד עד שיתקדש העם
ויעמוד סביבות הר סיני לקבל התורה ואשמע קול השופרין שמתחילין לתקוע אז ארד לי,
שכך ציוה לו הק׳ שירד שלא יאמרו ישראל משה עומד בהר וקורא אנכי ה׳ אלהיך.[19]
[9] **עד אמון בי**, על שם ואהיה אצלו אמון,[20] שאוליך אותה למבקשיה. פ״א. **עד המון בי**

10 תהלים ח ב, וראה מה שנדרש עליו במדרש תהלים, עמ׳ 74: ״אמרו (המלאכים) לפניו: רבונו של עולם, נאה הוא לך שתתן תורה בשמים״ וכו׳.

11 שמות לא יח.

12 בראשית ב ב. נוסח התרגום המובא כאן איננו בתרגומים שלפנינו, אולם הראשונים מביאים אותו עפ״י הספרים של התרגום הירושלמי שהיו לפניהם. ראה תורה שלימה, ח״ב, עמ׳ קפו הערה כו; ראה גם בחיבורו של אחיו של המפרש, בשבלי הלקט, ח״א, סימן עו (מהד׳ בובר, עמ׳ 56; מהד׳ מירסקי, עמ׳ 299-300 והערות שם): ״יש מפרשים שנקרא שבת חמדת ימים דכתיב ויכל אלקים ביום השביעי, אין ויכל אלא לשון חמדה״ וכו׳.

13 ספרי דברים, פיסקא שמה, עמ׳ 402 ומקבילות.

14 תנחומא הישן, כי תשא, פיסקא טז.

15 ראה על עניין זה אגדות היהודים, ו, עמ׳ 36, הערה 200. <ראה גם רבי אלעזר בירבי קליר, קדושתאות ליום מתן תורה, ההדירה... שולמית אליצור, ירושלים תש״ס, עמ׳ 17-18.> על משה כסרסור ראה להלן ג׳, עמ׳ 12, ד״ה מלאכייא שושבינין; השווה שמות רבה ג ה; שם מג א.

16 תהלים סה ב.

17 הנוסח אצל טל ״נרמה״, ברי״ש, ולפי זה הוא מתרגם ״עד לוחות אזרוק״, ומביא את הפסוק משמות ל״ב י״ט בסמוכין (ראה טל, עמ׳ 103-104, טור 12 ועמ׳ 108). [וקשה לומר שמשה רומז לשבירת הלוחות. ע״כ נראה שצריך לקרוא ״נשתכר״, ובשי״ן שמאלית, כלומר נקבל שכר ועל זה הוא אומר ״לשון דמים״. ובדיקה נוספת בכ״י מאשרת את הנ״ל ולפי זה לא יפסיק פירוש זה את העניין (ראה בהערה הבאה). ובפיוט גרס רבינו ״נדמה״ והשווה לזה ״נהוג נשיאותך ברמים״ (כתובות קג ע״ב ואוצה״ג שם). וההמשך ״זרוק מרה״ וכו׳ אפשר שהוא פירוש לברמים.]

17א משלי ו כג.

18 ברכות כט ע״ב ועוד. ״ועוד יש לפרשו״ וכו׳ חוזר לנוסח ראשון.

19 השווה שמות רבה כח ג: ״אני גולה להם את הרקיע ואומר אנכי ה׳ אלקיך, הם אומרים: מי אמר, הקב״ה או משה, אלא ירד משה ואח״כ אני אומר אנכי״ וכו׳.

20 משלי ח ל.

תובעין, על שם דבר אתה עמנו ונשמעה,[21] וזה הלשון נראה לי עיקר. **עד ונוריד יקרה,** התור׳ נקראת יקרה על שם יקרה היא מפנינים.[22] **עד זהוא נזהא בעננא,** פי זהוא, לשון גבוה.[22א] **עד חכמה נחמ[ה]**[23] **עין בעין,** וירא ישראל תרג׳ ירושל׳ וחמון.[24] **עד טבעת נחזה,** פי׳ לפי שדרך בני העולם לקדש ולארס בטבעת ומתן תורה נדמה ליום חתונה כדאמ׳ ביום חתונתו זו מתן תורה,[25] לפיכך דימה המתרגם התורה שהיא היתה הקידושין שליש׳ לטבעת. **חקוקה מזה ומזה,** על שם מזה ומזה הם כתובים.[26]

ג אנכי ה׳ אלהיך

דבירא קדמאה כו;[1] הכל הוא מפורש במילי׳ דשבועות.[2] **זיקין,** כמו קורות ועמודים שלאש, מלשון מאזרי זיקות,[3] **זיקין,** כמ׳ זיקוקין. **נור ואשא חדא מילתא הוא.**[4]

אלפא ביט׳

ארעא רקדא כו׳,[5] ייסד המתורגמן על יסוד ארץ רעשה אף שמים נטפו,[6] שבמתן תורה היה
תחילה רעש ורעד ולבסוף שמחה כדכת׳ ארץ יראה ושקטה,[7] בתחילה יראה ולבסוף שקטה,
בתחילה יראה שכבר התנה הקב״ה עם בריית העולם שאם לא יקבלו יש׳ את התורה יחזירם
לתהו ובוהו והיה העולם ירא שמא יהו יש׳ ממאנין לקבלה כמו שמיאנו שאר אומות, [10]
ולבסוף שקטה לאחר שקיבלו את התורה הה״ד נמוגים ארץ וכל יושביה אנכי תיכנתי עמודיה
סלה,[8] בזכות אנכי תיכנתי עמודיה,[9] והיתה אז שמחה לפני המקום יותר מבריאת העולם.[10]

21 שמות כ יט.
22 משלי ג טז.
22א [ראה ערוך ערך זה ג׳.]
23 בגוף כה״י: ״נראה״; על הגליון: ״נחמ[ה]״.
24 שמות יד לא.
25 משנה תענית פ״ד מ״ח; פסדר״כ, כו, עמ׳ 397 ומקבילות.
26 שמות לב טו.

1 ת״י לשמות כ ב; מחזור ויטרי, עמ׳ 337.
2 ראה לעיל א, הערה 50.
3 ישעיה ג יא.
4 זה בניגוד לפירוש שבמחזור ויטרי, עמ׳ 319: ״אש ונור מופלגים זה מזה בלשונם״ וכו׳.
5 דוידזון, א, 7669: מפורש במחזור ויטרי, עמ׳ 311 ואילך.
6 תהלים סח ט.
7 שם עו ט.
8 שם עה ד.
9 פס״ר כא, ק ע״א וראה שבת פח ע״א.
10 לא מצאתי מקור לזה. [וראה תנחומא, שמיני, אות ב; זוהר ח״א, קטו ע״א, ומדרש תהלים, עה, אות א, ב. ואולי צירף לכאן את הדרשה בתענית כו עב.]

ופת׳ נטפו זימרו[11] כמ׳ אל תטיפו יטיפון[12] והוא לש׳ דיבור וכן והטף אל דרום.[13] **כד אריס**
קיריס, כשאירס הק׳ כנסת יש׳ לאחר יציאתה ממצרים, והוא כמ׳ שפירשנו למעלה, ביום
חתונתו זו מתן תורה.[14] **באצבעתיה יהב לה כו׳**, **באצבעתיה**, פי׳ שבא תחת הבי״ת השנית
והעי״ן קמוצה[15] שהוא כמ׳ אצבעותיו, שאם תאמר שהוא לשון אצבע מיוחד היה
באצבעיה,[16] והוא על יסוד כתובים באצבע אלהים.[17] וכה פתרונו בעת שאירס הק׳ כנסת יש׳,
מידיו נתן לה חמש עזקין, הם חמשה חומשי תורה.[18] ועוד יש לומ׳ **באצבעתה**, תי״ו קמוצה
לש׳ נקיבה ומוסב על כנסת יש׳ ופת׳ כשאירס הק׳ כנסת יש׳ נתן באצבעותיה ה׳ טבעות, ותפש
המתרגם זה הלשון לפי שדרך העולם לקדש בטבעות, וזה עיקר. **נהירו**, כמ׳ נהירו ושוכלתנו,[20]
לש׳ חכמה. ויש לפרשו לש׳ נהורה.[21] **ועל כל עיזקא ארבע טבעין**, לש׳ טבע.[22] **בבהירו**, לש׳
בהיר הוא בשחקים,[23] כמ׳ בירור, ומה הם אילו ארבעה החותמות הטבועין בהם, **צדקא**, **דינא**,
חסדא, **חוסנא**,[24] מפי מורי ר׳ נתן זצ״ל.[24א] **גבילן בצדקא**, לש׳ גבול. **חתימן בדינא**, שהתור׳
משפטים לפניה ולאחריה, לפניה שם שם לו חק ומשפט, לאחריה ואלה המשפטים.[25] **נקישן**,
לש׳ מקשה, לש׳ נופל על מעשה הטבעות. **בחסדא**, כדדרש ר׳ שמלאי תורה תחילתה גמילות
חסדים וסופה גמילות חסדים כול׳.[26] **טביען בחוסנא**, לשון טבע, **בחוסנא**, מגזירת חוסה ה׳ על
[11] עמך,[27] ולש׳ רחמים הוא. אמ׳ הק׳ ליש׳, עשו אתם צדק ומשפט ואני אתן לכם חסד
ורחמים,[28] לכך לא נוכל לפרשו לש׳ חוסן. ולש׳ המקרא הוא ואירשתיך לי באמונה
ואירשתיך לי בצדק ובמשפט ובחסד וברחמים.[29] פ״א. **בחוסנא**, לש׳ חוסן ממש כמ׳ דכת׳,
המון מעיך ורחמיך אלי התאפקו,[30] ויצא ויתאפק מתרגמינן ואתחסן.[31] **דהב אובריזא**, פי׳,

11 מוסב על לשון הפיוט: ״ארעא רקדא שמיא זמרו״; ומפרש את המלה ״נטפו״ (תהלים סח ט) במובן זמרו.
12 מיכה ב ו.
13 יחזקאל כא ב.
14 ראה לעיל ב׳, הערה 25.
15 באצבעָתיה.
16 באצבעֵיה.
17 שמות לא יח.
18 כך גם בפירוש שבמחזור ויטרי, עמ׳ 311.
19 באצבעתָה. ומה שאומר אח״כ ״באצבעותיה״ כוונתו בכל אחד מאצבעותיה.
20 דניאל ה יד.
21 לשון אור.
22 לשון לקבוע צורה.
23 איוב לז כא.
24 במחזור ויטרי, עמ׳ 311: ״ומה הן הטבעות: צדק ומשפט חסד ורחמים״, כאשר מפרש והולך.
24א ראה במבוא, עמ׳ 7.
25 פסדר״כ יב, עמ׳ 209 ובמקבילות, ובכולם הגירסא ״דינים מלפניה״ וכו׳.
26 סוטה יד ע״א.
27 יואל ב יז.
28 דב״ר, ג ז, וראה רש״י על הושע ב כא.
29 הושע ב כא.
30 ישעיה סג טו.
31 בראשית מג לא ות״א שם; ראה גם בפירוש שבמחזור ויטרי, עמ׳ 312.

מפז רב תרג׳ אובריזין.[32] ואותם הטבעות שנתן לה היו מזהב מופז,[33] ומה הם הטבעות,
חמשה חומשי תורה.[34] **אחסנא**, לש׳ חוסן, אינמי לש׳ אחסנא על שם מורשה קהילת
יעקב.[35] **מטרונא**, גברת, פי׳, כדאמ׳ בבראשית רבא, וישימני לאב לפרעה, לפטרון, הכי נמי
לאשה, מטרונא.[36] כמ׳, שקמתי אם בישראל.[37] **הוא יהב בידא עשר יקינטנייא**, על שם
עשרת הדיברות, והמשיל התורה באבנים יקרות על שם לא תסולה בכתם אופיר,[38]
יקווינטו בלע״ז.[39] **ותלת מאוון כו׳**, המוהר הראשון היה עשרת הדיברות, כי בששה בסיון
במעמד הר סיני לא נצטוו רק עשרת הדיברות בלבד,[40] אבל המוהר השני דהיינו תוספת
כתובה גדול במאד מאד, הם תרי״ג מצות, רמ״ח בעשה ושס״ה בלא תעשה. **אפריפריא**,
יש מפרשין מלשון אפריפרין לכלה והוא מלשון אפריון,[41] ויתכן לפרשו באהל מועד.[42]
ואנן סבירא לן **אפריפריא** תוספת כתובה כדאמ׳ בבראשית רבא פ״א, הרבו עלי מוהר,
מוהר פורנון, מתן פראפורנון.[43] ובירושלמי מתרגם ליה, פרן וכתובה.[43א] **ועוד נראה** [12]
לפרשו מלשון הבו ליה אפריה לר׳ שמעון, בסוף בבא מציעא,[44] והוא לש׳ **לעז גרציאה**.[44א]
ובמקצת ספרים כתוב **באפרי א(?)פרייא**[45] והכל אחד הוא. **זמרגדין ארבעין ותמנייא**, תרג׳
נופך אזמרגדין ובלע״ז איזמרגדו,[46] תלויות על צואר הכלה וקבועות בשפתות מלבושיה
כמ׳ שפה יהיה לפיו סביב.[47] **חטף לארוסתיה**, פי׳, חטף הק׳ את כנסת ישראל בחלקו
להיותה ארוסתו מבין הבתרים.[48] ע״א. חטף הק׳ מעל ארוסתו ממה שגזר עליה בין
הבתרים ק״צ שנה כשדפק על פתחה במצרים והיא היתה ישינה מן הגאולה כי היתה

32 תהלים יט יא ותרגום שם.
33 השווה מלכים א י יח.
34 ראה לעיל הערה 18.
35 דברים לג ד, ותרגום ירושלמי שם, וכן בפירוש שבמחזור ויטרי, עמ׳ 312.
36 ב״ר צג י, עמ׳ 1160. והראיה היא — פטרון לזכר, מטרונה לנקבה. וראה להלן ה׳, הערה 9.
37 שופטים ה ז.
38 איוב כח טז.
39 לא זוהה.
40 ראה מכילתא, בחדש ט, עמ׳ 237.
41 ראה משנה בבא מציעא פ״ו מ״א: ״פריפרין וחלילים לכלה״; ופירוש רש״י שם: ״עצים משופים ונאים לעשות לו אפריון״ (עה ע״ב).
42 השווה שמות רבה ג ט: ״אפריון עשה לו. ר׳ עזריה בשם ר׳ יהודה בר׳ סימון פתר קרייה במשכן, אפריון, זה משכן״ וכו׳; פסדר״כ, א, עמ׳ 3: ״אפריון, זה אהל מועד״.
43 ב״ר פ ז, עמ׳ 960 ובח״נ ובמ״י שם.
43א בראשית לד יב, ותרגום ירושלמי שם.
44 בבא מציעא קיט ע״א; השווה ערוך ערך אפרייא א׳.
44א grazia באיטלקית. וראה רש״י לב״מ הנ״ל: ״אפריון חן שלנו״.
45 במחזור ויטרי, עמ׳ 336: ״באפרי אפרייא״.
46 שמות כח יח, ובתרגומים שם; צורה עתיקה של המלה האיטלקית smeraldo.
47 שמות כח לב.
48 היינו שכנסת ישראל נבחרה להיות ארוסתו של הקב״ה משעת ברית בין הבתרים. ואולי היתה לפני המפרש דרשה בה דרשו את הפסוק ״והאמין בה׳ ויחשבה לו צדקה״ (בראשית טו ו) בקשר לפסוק ״וארשתיך לי באמונה״ (הושע ב כב) לענין זה; ודרשות דומות נמצאות במכילתא, ויהי ו, עמ׳ 115-114 ובמקבילות.

סבורה להשלים ת׳ שנה ולא ישבה שם אלא רד״ו שנה, וכן תרגם רב יוסף בפסוק אני
ישינה.[49] **ארתיק**, דפק. **דמכא**, ישינה, ויישן תרג׳ ודמוך.[50] **בתוון**, בחדר, תרג׳ ומחדרים
ומתווניא.[51] **טען יתה כו׳**, פי׳, על שם ואשא אתכם על כנפי נשרים,[52] ורבותינו דרשו ז״ל,
בליל שעשו פסח מצרים נעשה להם נס ועפו לארץ יש׳ ואכלו את הפסח לפי שאסור לאכל
קדשים בחוצה לארץ ובו בלילה שבו למצרים.[53] **שלווא**, שליו. **אורתא**, ערב, על שם בתת
ה׳ לכם בערב בשר לאכול ולחם בבקר לשבוע.[54] **ימא בזע לה כו׳**, היינו קריעת הים. **גנון**,
כילת חתנים.[55] **קטר**, קשר. **זיהורין**, ענני כבוד והוא לש׳ זוהר. משמע במתן תורה לש׳ שני
חיתונין כמ׳ שפירשתי,[55א] האחד הק׳ כחתן וכנסת יש׳ ככלה, השיני כחתן
והתורה ככלה, על כן ייסד המתורגמן **מלאכייא שושבינין** ומשה היה סרסור [13]
בר גנון, בן אותה הכילה והחופה.[56] **פנטירין**, פנטי בלע״ז.[57] ויש מפרש׳ מלש׳ כרום ימא
ובורלא ופנטרי[58] ומפרשו על הגנון שהיתה עשוייה באבנים טובות ומרגליות,[59] והכל הוא
משל על מתן תורה. **כליל מלכו כו׳**, אמרו רבותינו ז״ל כשאמרו ישראל נעשה ונשמע ירדו
מלאכי השרת וקשרו לכל אחד ואחד מיש׳ שני כתרים, אחד כנגד נעשה ואחד כנגד
נשמע.[60] ועל ידיה שני צמידים על שם הלוחות שניתנו מיד ליד, **שירין**, תרג׳ צמידים.[61]
עגילים, כמ׳ עגיל וכומז והוא תכשיט האזן על שם ששמעו קול הדיבור.[62] **טבע אנחירין**,
כמ׳ נזמי האף בישעיה.[63] **לבוש דרקמא**, על שם ואלבישך רקמה ואנעלך תחש.[64] **בוץ שזיר**
תכלא וארגוונא, על עניין מעשה המשכן, שש משזר תכלת וארגמן. **פרזומא**, כדאמ׳
בהתכלת, רמא תכלתא לפרזומא דאינשי בייתיה,[66] ובירושלמ׳ פרק במה אשה בשבת,

49 פסדר״כ, ה, עמ׳ 87-88 ובמקבילות; ובתרגום לשיר השירים ה׳ ב׳ אין דרשה כזו, אולם היא נמצאת בתרגום לשיר השירים ב׳ ח׳; התרגום לכתובים נקרא על שם רב יוסף, ראה צונץ, דרשות, עמ׳ 36 ועמ׳ 253 הערה 21.

50 בראשית ב כא, ובתרגומים שם.

51 דברים לב כה, ובת״א שם.

52 שמות יט ד.

53 תרגום יונתן שם: ״ואובילית יתכון לאתר בית מוקדשא למעבר תמן פיסחא״ וכו׳. וראה מכילתא, בחדש ב, עמ׳ 207 ובהערות לשורה 15 שם.

54 שמות טז ח.

55 כך גם במחזור ויטרי, עמ׳ 314: ״גנון כילת חופת חתנים״. וראה להלן אות פ.

55א ראה לעיל ב, הערה 15.

56 מחזור ויטרי הנ״ל: ״בר גנון הוא בן החופה הוא המוציא והמביא והמכניס כלה לאפריון״.

57 לא זוהה.

58 ת״א לשמות כח כ.

59 על חופה העשויה מאבנים טובות ומרגליות ראה למשל ב״ר, יח א, עמ׳ 162.

60 שבת פח ע״א.

61 בראשית כד כב, ובתרגומים שם. וראה בשיה״ש רבא המובא להלן בהערה 68.

62 במדבר לא נ; ראה פס״ר, לג, קנה ע״א: ״ועגילים על אזניך (יחזקאל טז יב) א״ר ברכיה הכהן ברבי אילו הדברות״. ובשה״ש רבא הנ״ל נדרש באופן אחר.

63 ישעיה ג כא.

64 יחזקאל טז י.

65 שמות כו א.

66 מנחות מג ע״א.

המחלצות פרזומטא,[67] והוא מיוסד על לש׳ האגדה במדרש חזית, שלחיך פרדס רמונים. לשון בני אדם הוא מה שלח פלן לארוסתיה, ר׳ חננא בר פפא ור׳ סימון, ר׳ חננא אמ׳ היא הכניסה לו שלשה עשר דבר כמו שמפורש באלה שמות וזאת התרומה אשר תקחו וגו׳. ר׳ סימון אמ׳ והוא הכניס לה י״ג דבר כמ׳ שמפורש ביחזקאל ואלבישך רקמה וגו׳, ר׳ סימיי אמ׳ פורפירון, תירגם עקילס פילקטון, ואנעלך תחש תחת עורות תחשים, ואחבשך בשש תחת שש ועזים, ואכסך משי, ר׳ אייבו ור׳ יהודה ביר׳ סימון, ר׳ אייבו אמ׳ עשאן ממש בעולם, ור׳ יהודה אמ׳ הקיפן ענני כבוד המד״א לא ימוש עמוד הענן, ואעדך עדי, תני ר׳ שמעון בן יוחיי זיין היה ליש׳ בסיני והיה שם המפורש חקוק עליו וכשחטאו נוטל מהם, ואתנה צמידים על ידיך אילו שני לוחות הברית, ורביד על גרונך זו תורה המד״א ענדם על גרגרתיך וגו׳, ועטרת תפארת בראשך זו השכינ׳ כמ׳ דתימ׳ ויעבר מלכם לפניהם וה׳ בראשם, וזהו פי׳ **כליל מלכו ברישה**, ואילין אינון חמשתי אחרנייתא, ותעדי זהב וכסף ומלבושך שש ומשי ורקמה.[68] **מן ביתא דאבוהא כו׳**, באגדת חזית, כת׳ ויסע ישר׳ וכל אשר [14] לו ויבא בארה שבע, לאיכן הלך, לקוץ ארזים שנטע אברהם זקינו בבאר שבע הה״ד ויטע אשל בבאר שבע. כת׳ והבריח התיכון אמ׳ ר׳ לוי הבריח התיכון שלשים אמה היה בו ומהיכן נמצא בידם לשעה אלא מלמד שהיו מוצנעים אצלם עד שאבינו יעקב קיים הה״ד וכל איש אשר נמצא אתו.[69] **תרעין**, שערים. **דקס מרין**, שני מלות הן ופירושו עצי ארזים, עצי עולה דאברהם תרג׳ ירושלמ׳ קיסין,[70] תהדר[71] ותאשור תרג׳ מורנין ואשכרועין.[72] והאומר **אעלת לארוסתיה** טעות הוא כי פי׳ **ארוסתיה** ארוסתו ואין הלשון מוכיח כן, שהוא מדבר על כנסת ישראל שהיא הביאה לארוסה כך וכך. והנכון כמ׳ שפירשתי **אעלת לארוסה**. ובסידורין המצויין אצלנו כתוב **דקסמרין** מלה אחת. ובמקצת סידורים כת׳ **לקסמרין** ודבר למד מעניינו להיותו ממיני ארזים, ומפי מורי ר׳ יואב נר״ו[73] שמעתי **לקסמרין**, לבנים, ואין לי ראייה, ושמא עיקרו כדאמרינן ב...ה.[74] והנראה בעיני שהן שתי מילות כמ׳ שפירשתי. **למרפק**, כמ׳ מתרפקת על דודה והוא לשון דיבוק וחיבור.[75] **נעשה ונשמע משתעין בתריהון כו׳**, מספרין, ויספר תרג׳ ואשתעי,[76] לקיים שניהן ולא לזלזל בהן ויהיו מתפרשין לפני החתן וישמח, וגם הכלה תשמח בכסא אפריונה. **בתריהון**, חיריק תחת הבי״ת כמ׳ בתרוויהון, ופירושו בשניהם. **לפקפק**, כמ׳ שפקפק בנטילת ידים[77] ופת׳ לש׳

67 ירושלמי שבת פ״ו ה״ד (ח ע״ב): ״המחלצות (ישעיה ג כב) פירזומטא״. וראה הירושלמי כפשוטו להגר״ש ליברמן, עמ׳ 108.

68 שיה״ש רבה ד יג בשינויים. וראה גם לעיל הערות 61-62.

69 שם א יב בשינויים.

70 בראשית כב ג, ות״י שם.

71 צ״ל ״תדהר״.

72 ישעיה מא יט, ות״י שם.

73 ראה במבוא, עמ׳ 7.

74 אינני יכול לכוונו.

75 שיה״ש ח ה. וראה רש״י וראב״ע שם, וכך מפרש גם במחזור ויטרי, עמ׳ 315.

76 בראשית כד סו ובת״א שם.

77 ברכות יט ע״א.

זילזול. **יתפרשון**, בין בשי״ן בין בסי״ן יתכן פירושו.[77א] **דייספק**, כסא, כמ׳ אשקא דדייספק
חרוב ביתר, בגיטין פרק הניזקין.[78] **סלים אתקבע לה כו׳**, פי׳ סולם קבע לה לעלות לבית
חופתה מצורת[78א] בית אביה לכסא החתן, והוא דרך משל ודמיון על מתן תורה ועל מעשה
אהל מועד, כחתן הבונה בית חתנות לבנו,[79] וזה הסולם מדבר על סיני שעלה שם משה
[15] לקבל התורה. ולש׳ האגדה בבראשית רבא, ויחלם והנה סלם וג׳, רבנין פתרין קרייה בסיני,
אמ׳ סלם בגימט׳ סיני, מוצב ארצה ויתייצבו בתחתית ההר, וראשו מגיע השמימה וההר
בוער באש עד לב השמים, והנה מלאכי אלהים זה משה ואהרן, עולים ומשה עלה, ויורדים
בו וירד משה,[80] ובסיני הראה לו כל מלאכת המשכן כמ׳ דתימ׳ כאשר הראית בהר.[81]
דתיסק לגנונא, לרקיע כמ׳ דתימ׳ ומשה עלה אל האלהים.[82] **עדרין בה שבעין כול׳**, פי׳
ומתקבצין בו שבעים. כמ׳ דתימ׳, ואל הזקנים אמר שבו לנו בזה,[83] והם כנגד הסנהדרין
היושבין בלשכת הגזית לפרש שם סתומותיה שלתורה ולהיותם נוחים זה לזה בהלכה[84]
כדבש וחלב כדי להתחדד זה מזה.[85] **עדרין**, פי׳ לש׳ עדר. **בתולן**, למ״ד רפי ופת׳
סתומותיהן כמ׳ בתולת הוורד[86] ועיקרו מלשון בתולה. ויש לפרש **בתולן**, למ״ד דגושה
והבי״ת אינה יסוד והוא כמ׳ תילי תילים.[87] **לשננא**, כמ׳ ושננתם לבניך.[88] ועוד יש לפרש
דליהוון היך חלבא על דובשא כו׳, שיהיו דברי תורה מיושבין בלי קושיא וספק ויהיו
עריבין ללומדיהן כדבש וחלב על שם דבש וחלב תחת לשונך,[89] וזה נראה לי עיקר.
לאיתלבנא, כמ׳ מחשף הלבן,[90] על שם צחורות,[91] והוא לש׳ צח ונקי. והרבה יש בתלמוד,
מחוורתא כדשניין מעיקרא.[92] ויש לפרשו מלשון זריז ומלובן ופת׳ מחודד. ובמקצת ספרים
כתוב **דליהוון חכמכמא כחלבא על דובשא** ואיני יודע מה הוא. ואחי ר׳ צדקיה נר״ו[93]

77א ראה להלן או פ׳ (פרס).

78 גטין נה ע״ב, כגירסת הערוך, ראה ערך דיספק.

78א [ואולי צ״ל בפיוט ״מדירתא״ וכאן ״מדירת.]

79 תענית יד ע״ב ועוד; ״כחתן״ השתרבבה לכאן בטעות.

80 ב״ר סח יב, עמ׳ 786.

81 שמות כו ל (לשון הפסוק: ״אשר הראית בהר״; ובשמות כז ח: ״כאשר הראה אותך בהר״).

82 שם יט ג.

83 שם כד יד.

84 תענית ח ע״א.

85 ראה תענית ז ע״א: ״ברזל בברזל יחד, לומר לך מה זה אחד מחדד את חבירו אף שני תלמידי חכמים מחדדין זה את זה בהלכה״ [ועל כן אם לא יהיו נוחים זה לזה לא ישבו בצוותא ולא יוכלו לחדד זה את זה].

86 שבת צ ע״א.

87 עירובין כא ע״ב.

88 דברים ו ז.

89 שיה״ש רבה ד יא: ״רבנן אמרי כל מי שאומר דברי תורה ברבים ואינן עריבין על שומעיהן כדבש וחלב המעורבין זה בזה״ וכו׳.

90 בראשית ל לז.

91 שופטים ה י.

92 עירובין צו ע״א.

93 ראה במבוא, עמ׳ 8.

דיקדק בלשון הזה ופירש, **דליהוון היככמכא דחלבא**, כדאיתא בחולין, ההוא בר יונה דנפל
לכדא דכמכא,[94] ולשון הראשון נראה עיקר בעיניי. ומה שאמ׳ **כחלבא על דובשא** לפי לשון [16]
האגדה הנדרשת באגדת חזית, כי טובים דודיך מיין, נמשלו דברי תורה ביין, במים, בשמן,
בדבש, בחלב. במים, הוי כל צמא לכו למים, מה המים חנם בעולם כו׳, אמ׳ ר׳ חמא בר
עוקבא מה המים מגדלין את הצמחים כך דברי תורה מגדלין כל מי שלומד בהן כל צורכן,
אי מה המים מבאישין בקנקן יכול אף דברי תורה כן ת״ל יין, מה היין כל מה שהוא
מתיישן בקנקן הוא משתבח והולך כך כל מה שדברי תורה מתיישנים בגופו שלאדם הן
משתבחין והולכין, אי מה המים אין ניכרין בגוף יכול אף דברי תורה כן ת״ל יין, מה היין
ניכר בגוף כך כל מי שיש בו דברי תורה מראין עליו באצבע, אי מה מים אין משמחין את
הלב יכול אף דברי תור׳ כן ת״ל יין, מה יין משמח את הלב כך דברי תורה משמחין את
הלב שנ׳ פקודי ה׳ ישרים משמחי לב, אי מה היין מחרף את הגוף יכול אף דברי תורה כן
ת״ל שמן, מה השמן מעדן את הגוף כך דברי תורה מעדנין את הגוף, מה השמן מביא אורה
לעולם כך דברי תורה מביאין אורה לעולם שנ׳ נר לרגלי דבריך ואור לנתיבתי, אי מה
השמן מר יכול אף דברי תורה כן ת״ל דבש, מהו הדבש מתוק אף דברי תורה כן, אי מה
הדבש יש בו קצרים, פי׳ קצף וחלאה, יכול אף דברי תורה כן ת״ל חלב, מה חלב נקי אף
דברי תורה נקיים, אי מה חלב תפל יכול אף דברי תורה כן ת״ל דבש וחלב, מה דבש וחלב
כל זמן שהן מעורבין זה בזה אין מזיקין את הגוף אלא מעדנין את הגוף אף דברי תורה כן
שנ׳ כי חיים הם למוצאיהם ואומ׳ רפאות תהי לשרך.[95] **פרס למקטור כו׳**, פי׳ ציוה הק׳
לפרוש ולקשור במדבר אהל מועד שממנו אורה יוצאה לעולם, וכן מצינו בחלוני בית
המקדש שקופים אטומים, שהיו צרין מבפנים ורחבים מבחוץ.[96] **לארוסתא**, באל״ף ולא
בה״א והוא כמ׳ ארוסה בלא מפק ה״א. **גנון לגו מן גנון**, חופה לתוך חופה, על שם המשכן
שהיה בתוך אהל מועד לתוספת צניעות לדוגמת חתן וכלה שעושין להן כילה בתוך כילה
לצניעות,[97] ובאגדת חזית, באתי לגני, לגנוני.[98] **בשביסתא**, בתכשיטים, מלש׳ השביסים
דישעיה.[99] ולשון האגדה בפסיקתא דויהי ביום כלות, אמ׳ ר׳ יהודה ביר׳ אילעאי משל [17]
למלך בשר ודם שהיתה לו בת קטנה עד שלא הגדילה ובאת לידי סימנין היה רואה אותה
בשוק ומדבר עמה, במבואות ומדבר עמה, כיוון שהגדילה ובאת לידי סימנין אמ׳ המלך

94 חולין קיב ע״א וראה ד״ס, קנ״ב ע״ב, אות ר; ר׳ צדקיה מפרש את המלה ״היככמכא״ כשתי מלים — ״היך כמכא״ — וגורס במקום כחלבא: ״דחלבא״.

95 שיה״ש רבא א ב׳, בשינויים; השווה ספרי דברים פיסקה מח, עמ׳ 110-111 ומקבילות; דברים רבה, מהד׳ הגר״ש ליברמן, עמ׳ 109 הערה 1; א׳ מירסקי, ידיעות המכון לחקר השירה העברית, ז, עמ׳ 15-17.

96 פסדר״כ, כא, עמ׳ 323 ומקבילות.

97 מחזור ויטרי, עמ׳ 316-317: ״ועל זה כיון המשורר דלהוו צנועים בשביסתא, ר׳ יוסי אומר חדר. ולשון מדרש הוא באלה שמות, ויסב את העם, הסיבן בשביסתין, משל לכלה שתיקן לה אביה חדר בתוך חדר כדי שתהא צנועה ביותר״. וראה הערה ס׳ שם: ״ליתא במדרש שלפנינו״.

98 שיה״ש רבא ה א, ונמצא גם בפסדר״כ, א, עמ׳ ו בפיסקא שממנה מביא המפרש מאמר ארוך בסמוך. ואולי בפסיקתא שלפניו המאמר ״באתי לגני, לגנוני״ היה חסר ולכן הביאו מאגדת חזית.

99 ישעיה ג יח.

אין כבודה שלבתי שאהא מדבר עמה בפרהסיא אלא עשו לה פאפיליין ונדבר עמה מתוך פאפיליון, כך בתחילה כי נער ישראל ואוהבהו היה מדבר עם ברייותיו בפרהסיא, במצרים סיפר עמהם בפרהסיא שנ׳ ועברתי בארץ מצרים, בים ראו אותו שנ׳ וירא ישראל, בסיני ראו אותו שנ׳ פנים בפנים דיבר ה׳ עמהם וגו׳. וכיון שקיבלו את התורה נעשו לו לאומה שלימה, אמ׳ אין כבודן שלבניי שאהא מדבר עמהם בפרהסיא אלא יעשו לי משכן ואהא מדבר עמהם מתוך משכן.[100] אינמי **גנון לגו מן גנון**, המשכן בתוך חופת ענני כבוד.[101] ויש סידורים שכתוב בהן **פרס למקטור במדברא גנון חורן לארוסתא**, ופת׳ כילה אחרת, הגנון הראשון מעמד סיני והגנון האחר אהל מועד שהוא **גנון לגו מן גנון**, כמ׳ שפירשנו המשכן בתוך אהל מועד. והוא מיוסד על לשון האגדה, ויהי ביום כלות משה, כלת כת׳, יומא דעלת כלתא לגנונא, מה כת׳ למעלה מן העניין ברכת כהנים, יברכך, יאר, וישא, אמ׳ ר׳ יהושע דסכנין בשם ר׳ לוי למה הדבר דומה למלך שקידש את בתו ועשה לה קידושין גדולים ושלטה בהן עין הרע וכיון שבא המלך להשיא את בתו מה עשה נתן לה קמיע ואמ׳ לה יהא הקמיע הזה עליך שלא ישלוט בך עוד עין הרע. כך כשבא הק׳ ליתן תורה ליש׳ עשה להן פומפון גדולה כמ׳ דתימ׳ וכל העם רואים את הקולות ולא היו אלא קידושין כמ׳ דתימ׳ לך אל העם וקידשתם ושלטה בהן עין הרע ונשתברו הלוחות. אחר כך לא עשה כן אלא כיון שבאו ועשו את המשכן נתן להם הק׳ הברכות תחילה כדי שלא תשלוט בהן עין הרע, לפיכך כת׳ יברכך ואחר כך ויהי ביום כלות.[102] ועוד יש לפרש **פרס למקטור במדברא**, תכיפה, תכף לקשור במדבר. כמ׳ בפרס הפסח, בפרס העצר׳, בפרס החג.[103] **צווא למדמוך כו׳**, **צווא**, פי׳ נתחבר, לש׳ צוותא, והוא מיוסד על שם בין שדי ילין.[104] **למידמוך**, לישן. [18] **ביזייתא**, שדיים, בלשון ערבי ביזיאה. ובפסיקתא דזכור, ליטין ביזיא דהכדין אנקון.[105] על יסוד בדי ארון שהיו בולטין ויוצאין כשני דדי אשה.[106] **וקווצתא דרססן**, על שם קווצותיי רסיסי לילה.[107] **אפותא**, מצח. ובמקצת סידורים כתוב **צבא למידמוך**, ופת׳ לשון רצון, כמ׳ די הוה צבא הוה מחי.[108] **קומתה כתמרא**, על שם זאת קומתך דמתה לתמר ושדיך לאשכולות.[109] **סגולין**, אשכולות, נחל אשכול תרג׳ ירושלמ׳ נחלא דסגולא,[110] ועל כן שלש נקודות שלפתח קטן נקראין סגול שהן עשויין כאשכול.[111] **תדייא**, שדיים. **ריחא דנחירא**, על

100 פסדר״כ, א, עמ׳ 3-4, בשינויים.

101 שמות מ לד, ועוד.

102 לפנינו צירוף שני מאמרים, האחד מפסדר״כ, א, עמ׳ 9 שו׳ 17, והשני מפס״ר, ה, כא ע״א-ע״ב: ״דבר אחר [ויהי ביום כלות משה וגו׳] מה כתב למעלה מן העניין״ וכו׳. והשווה הערת רמא״ש, שם, יח ע״א, אות ס.

103 שקלים פ״ג מ״א; על פירוש פרוס במובן תכיפה ראה בתוספתא כפשוטה, מועד, עמ׳ 674, ולהלן מפרש את המלה במובן פרוסה, ראה ד׳, הערה 65.

104 שיה״ש א יג. וראה להלן הערה 106.

105 פסדר״כ, ג, עמ׳ 40. בערוך ערך בז א׳ לשון יון. וראה מה שכתב קאהוט שם.

106 יומא נד ע״א.

107 שיה״ש ה ב.

108 דניאל ה יט.

109 שיה״ש ז ח.

110 במדבר יג כד, ובתרגום ירושלמי שם.

111 ראה ס׳ דקדוקי הטעמים, מהד׳ א׳ דותן, תשכ״ד, ח״ב, עמ׳ 159.

שם וריח אפך כתפוחים.[112] תפוחי זהב חזורין דדהב.[113] **ראשה ככרמלא כו׳**, על שם ראשך עליך ככרמל ודלת ראשך כארגמן.[114] קליעתה, טריצא בלע״ז.[115] **צוארה שעיע**, על שם צוארך כמגדל השן.[116] שעיע, תרג׳ ואנכי איש חלק, שעיע.[117] שן ופיל אחד הוא.[117א] **שררה כאידרא דזיהרא כו׳**, על שם שררך אגן הסהר.[118] **זיהרא**, כמ׳ סיהרא, והנה השמש והירח תרג׳ ירושלמ׳ זיהרא.[119] **ולש׳ אידרא**, על שם סנהדרין היתה כחצי גורן עגולה.[120] **גווה ערמת חנטין**, על שם בטנך ערימת חטים סוגה בשושנים.[121] מקפא, כמ׳ מוקפת חומה.[122] **חניטין**, לש׳ חנטה ופריחה. ובסידורים המצויין אצלינו כתוב **כאידרא דזיתא** ואיני יודע ליישבו על הנכון. **תקוף עינהא כו׳**, על שם עינך בריכות בחשבון.[123] ופי׳ **בדין** כמו אילו הן עוגיות בדידין שבעיקרי גפנים דמועד קטן, שהן כמו בריכות, ומלשון [19] בית הבד שהוא בניין עשוי כבריכה לזתים.[124] **דחטבין**, לש׳ חטיבה אחת[125] והוא לש׳ צורה, וכה פת׳ עינייך בריכות ונאות בצורתן על מילואתן. ומרי ר׳ דניאל נר״ו[126] היה אומ׳ **כתרין בריכן דחשבון קשיטין**, על שם הפסוק עינייך בריכות בחשבון.[127] **ונחירא זקוף**, על שם אפך כמגדל הלבנון צופה פני דמשק,[128] פי׳ אפה זקוף ומיושר כמגדל הלבנון צופה פני דמשק, שלא כדברי רבינו שלמה זצ״ל שפירש אפך לשון פנים ואמ׳ שאין שבח האדם והאשה בהיות חוטמם גדול כמגדל.[129] ואין כן פירושו ולא יתכן לפרש אפך לשון פנים כמ׳ אפים שאינו ביו״ד, אלא עיקר פירושו כמ׳ ונזמי האף[130] והוא החוטם, ופת׳ אפך אינו שקוע, כמו שאנו מפרשין או חרום או שרוע, חרום זה שחוטמו שוקע בין עיניו,[131] אלא זקוף ומיושר כמגדל הלבנון שהוא עומד וצופה ביושר נגד פני דמשק. פי׳ מגדל הלבנון, זה בית המקדש כמ׳ דתימ׳ ההר הטוב הזה והלבנון ותרג׳ בית מקדשא שהוא עתיד

112 שיה״ש ז ט.

113 משלי כה יא, ובתרגום שם.

114 שיה״ש ז ו.

115 treccia באיטלקית.

116 שיה״ש ז ה.

117 בראשית כז יא ובתרגומים שם.

117א [כנראה שלפניו היה ״ופילייא״ ופי׳ שגם פיל מובנו שן הפיל. ראה למשל וי״ר ה ב, עמ׳ קה בח״ג.]

118 שיה״ש ז ג; ובשיה״ש רבא על הפסוק ״אגן הסהר״: ״אדרא דאזהרא״.

119 בראשית לז ט; ובתרגום ניאופיטי: ״זהרא״; ובשיה״ש רבא הנ״ל: ״אית אתרין דקריין וצווחין לזהרא סהרא״.

120 סנהדרין פ״ד מ״ג והשווה בשיה״ש רבא הנ״ל.

121 שיה״ש ז ג.

122 מגילה ב ע״ב.

123 שיה״ש ז ה.

124 מו״ק ד ע״ב.

125 ברכות ו ע״א ועוד.

126 ראה מבוא, עמ׳ 7.

127 שיה״ש ז ה; במחזור ויטרי, עמ׳ 337 הנוסח כמו הנוסח המובא בשם ר׳ דניאל.

128 שיה״ש שם.

129 ראה רש״י על הפסוק הנ״ל.

130 ישעיה ג כא.

131 ויקרא כא יח ופרש״י שם, ומחזור ויטרי, עמ׳ 318 וזה עפ״י בכורות מג ע״ב.

להתרחב עד דמשק, כמ׳ דתימ׳ ודמשק מנוחתו.[132] **כצפותא דדרמשיק**, כמצפה דמשק, ומצפה הוא המגדל על שם שהצופה עומד עליו ורואה למרחוק. **דרמשיק**, תרג׳ ירושלמ׳ שלדמשק.[133] **ולא מחמטין**, מלשון כי היכי דלא ליחמטן אליתייהו דפרק במה בהמה יוצאה דשבת, ופירושו לשון גירוד וחיבול, ובחורי ישראל הכריע תרג׳ אחמיט.[134]

[20] ד לא יהיה לך

מתרגמ׳ אותו בתרג׳ אונקלוס ובתרג׳ ירושלמי[1]

אלפא ביט

אמין שתין לרומא כו׳,[2] תפש המתורגמן לייסד **אמין שתין לרומא** על הדרך הכת׳ בנבוכדנצר הרשע כשהקים הצלם בבקעת דורא, דכת׳ ביה רומיה אמין שתין.[3] וכה פת׳, אפי׳ אם יהיה אורך הצלם ששים אמות ויותר, כולו בושה וכלימה. לפי שאין בו תועלת ונחשב הבל וריק כאילו אינו כלום שאין ממשות באלהותו. **חשיב למה**, תהו ובהו תרג׳ ירוש׳ למא,[4] וילכו אחרי ההבל ויהבלו תרג׳ והוו ללמא,[5] בראשית רבא, והארץ היתה תהו ובהו. למא ולא כלום.[6] ובמקצת סידורים כתוב **חשיב לא מה**, שתי תיבות. כלומ׳, אינו חשוב כלום. ונראה לפרש **לא מה** כמ׳ וכל דיירי ארעא כלא חשיבין, נסירת השמש ברקיע נקרא שמו לא, כמפורש פ״ק דיומא.[7] **בתנון קוטרא כו׳**, הנה בא להודיעך שאין בו ממש על ידי שהוא עשוי בידי ברייה ואין כח בברייה לבראות ברייה אחרת שיהא בה ממש שהרי מותר האדם מן הבהמה איין כי הכל הבל,[8] ובא להזכיר תחילת עסקו מלאכותיו על ידי אש ועשן. תרג׳ עשן תנן.[9] **קוטרא**, כמ׳ כן עשן, כמ׳ כקיטור הכבשן.[10] **וקל זני זמרא**, קול מיני

132 שיר השירים רבא ז ד, ות״א לדברים ג כה.
133 בראשית יד טו, ראה ערוך, ערך דרמשק.
134 שבת נד ע״ב; ראה פסקי הרי״ד, מהד׳ רא״י וורטהיימר ור״א ליס, ירושלים תשכ״ד, טור שג: ״פי׳ שאליותיהן גדולות ושמינות יישברו אם יגרדו אותן על גבי קרקע, ובחורי ישראל הכריע (תהלים עח לא), תרג׳ אחמט״; וכן בת״י שלפנינו.

1 ראה לעיל א׳, הערה 4.
2 דוידזון, א, 5697.
3 דניאל ג א.
4 בראשית א ב. ומה שמביא מהתרגום ירושלמי אינו בתרגומים שלפנינו לבראשית הנ״ל, אולם נמצא בכמה מקומות אחרים וראה מ״י לב״ר המובא בהערה 6.
5 מלכים ב יז טו וירמיה ב ה ות״י שם.
6 ב״ר ב ג, עמ׳ 15-16.
7 דניאל ד לב, ונדרש ביומא כ ע״ב. [והוא פירוש שני: נחשבים כלא (כמו ביומא) מה הם חשובים (ישעיה ב כב).]
8 קהלת ג יט.
9 בראשית טו יז, ות״א שם ועוד.

זמר, כמעשה שהיה בצלם נבוכדנצר הרשע, בעידן די תשמעון קל קרנא משרוקיתא קתרוס
סבכא פסנתרין וסומפונייא וכל זני זמרא וג׳.[11] **אתון למקטרא**, באין לקטר לפניו, מלש׳
קטרת. **ומנפח הוא בכורא**, כבשן, כמ׳ כור הברזל.[12] פ״א. **למקטרא**, לש׳ ציור דמות וצורה [21]
כדאמ׳ בויקרא רבא סוף פרש׳ אחרי מות, הריני צר כל קטירין שלו בדמות הנואף,[13] ופת׳
דמותו וקשרי איבריו. **גביל כמה דבלישא כו׳**, והפסל הוא מגובל כדרך אשר[13א] גיבול
העיסה כדרך ששופך המים בעיסה בדקדוק, כך מדקדקין בהיתוך הכסף. **דלייש עיסה**,
הלש את העיסה. ס״א. **גביל כמה דבליסא שפיך כלייש עיסה**, פי׳ הפסל הוא מגובל מכמה
תערובות מיני מתכות מעורבין זה בזה כמ׳ עיסה בלוסה, מעורבת הקמח עם הסובין
והמורסן,[14] ומתיכין אותו כלישת העיסה, ועיקר. והוא מורקע ומרודד מכסף חיל העם
ומתוקן בפטיש. **גבילי**, פי׳ כמ׳ גביל לתורי,[15] והוא לש׳ לישה. **דיב**, כמ׳ מידב דייב.[16]
מורקע, מרודד כמ׳ וירקעו את פחי הזהב.[17] **אוכלוסא**, פי׳ המון עם, ובלע״ז קורין להמון
עם איכליסיאה וכן למקום כניסייתם.[18] **ומנפח בקורנסא**, אין לפרשו לש׳ נפיחה כמ׳ נופח
באש פחם,[19] שאין נופל לש׳ נפיחה בפטיש אלא לש׳ נפח, כלומ׳ האומן נקרא נפח, מנפח
ומכה בפטיש על הסדן, פאבריקטו.[20] קורנסא, פטיש. **דהוא סייף וחסיל**, והפסל יש לו
אחרית ותכלה, שכל מי שיש לו ראשית יש לו אחרית, והוא כלה ומשתנה וסופו להיחלף
ולהיפסל, כמו המטבע שמעבירה המלכות בכל עת כרצונו. כך כל אומה לאחר שהיא
יגיעה ונבאשת באליליה שאין בם תועלת ועזרה פוסלת אותם ועובדת לאלילים אחרים,
ומאחר שסופם להעבירם מה יועיל להם, אתמהא. פ״א. **מתחליף**, במדרש השכם, למה
נקראו אלהים אחרים, ר׳ אליעזר אומ׳ מחדשין להן אלוהות הרבה בכל יום, כיצד, היה לו
שלזהב נצרך לו עשאו שלכסף, נצרך לו עשאו שלנחשת, נצרך לו עשאו שלברזל, נצרך לו
עשאו שלעופרת.[21] **סייף**, מלש׳ סוף. **וחסיל**, כמ׳ כי יחסלנו הארבה,[22] ושפה אחת
לכולם.[23] **שניי**, שמשתנה דמותו ומתבער לאחר שהוא בלה. **הוא בוטמי מתקליל כו׳**,

10 בראשית יט כח.

11 דניאל ג ה.

12 דברים ד כ.

13 וי״ר כג יב, עמ׳ תקמו וח״נ שם.

13א המלה באה בסוף השורה ואין לה מובן והאות האחרונה יכולה להיות גם דלי״ת.

14 שבת עו ע״ב ורש״י שם ד״ה בלוסה: ״מעורבת בסובנה ובמורסנה״.

15 ברכות מ ע״א.

16 פסחים עד ע״ב. [נראה שמפרש גירסא אחרת שגרסה בפיוט ״דיב לישא״.]

17 שמות לט ג.

18 ecclesia באיטלקית. וראה להלן הערה 49 ושם כתובה המלה בקו״ף.

19 ישעיה נד טז.

20 fabbricato באיטלקית.

21 ס׳ והזהיר, יתרו, עמ׳ 48 (מן המכילתא, בחדש ו, עמ׳ 224); על מדרש השכם ויחסו לס׳ והזהיר ראה אלבק בהערות לצונץ, הדרשות בישראל, עמ׳ 428-429.

22 דברים כח לח.

23 מליצה עפ״י בראשית י״א א׳. ור״ל שפירוש סייף וחסיל אחד הוא ומשתמש כמליצה זו גם להלן, ראה הערה 48.

[22] והפסל עשוי מאשירה קלה ונבזה, ואם הוא יקר תחילה בעיני עובדיו סופו להיות נקלה וזולל ביניהם לאחר שיצעקו ואין עונה.[24] תחת האלה תרג׳ תחות בוטמא.[25] **דיוקנין מחליל**, והוא מחלל את צורתו ומבזה אותה אחר שאין בו תועלת ואומ׳, מה בצע ביופייתה. פ״א. **דיוקנין מחליל**, צורה חלולה שהרי אין בו רוח. **ופום ליה ולא ממליל**, על שם פה להם ולא ידברו.[26] **ובנורא מתרמי כו׳**, והפסל משליכין אותו באש, ואינו מתגבר ואינו חושב לצאת מתוכו. והוא פיקח, שיש לו פיתוח[26א] עינים, ואינו רואה. על שם עיניים להם ולא יראו.[27] **וסמי**, עיוור, כמ׳ סומא. **חמי**, רואה תרג׳ ירושלמ׳.[28] **זהום ומטונן כו׳**, והפסל הוא מזוהם ומלוכלך בטבעו. **ומוקבע**, בתחילתו. **בכור**, הוא כבשן, כמ׳ כור הברזל.[29] **ויי ליה לשמע**, אוי לו לאדם השומע ומשתחווה לפסל שאינו שומע, על שם אזנים להם ולא ישמעו.[30] **זהום**, לש׳ זוהמא. **ומטונן**, משוקץ ומגואל, כמ׳ יגאלוהו חושך וצלמות תרג׳ יטננון.[31] **וסגיד**, משתחווה. **חביש בקבלא וסריח כו׳**, והפסל הוא חבוש בבית האסורין, במקום חושך וסרחון, כדי להבריחו מן הגנבים שהרי אין בו כח להציל עצמו. ומפורש בתנחומא, ותראו את שיקוציהם עץ ואבן, בוא וראה מעשה אומות העולם, אם היתה יראתו שלעץ או שלאבן היתה מונחת בחוץ נוהג בה הפקר, שנ׳ ותראו את שיקוציהם עץ ואבן. היתה שלכסף ושלזהב מכניסה בחדרי חדרים ויזהר בה וישמרוה מן הגנבים שלא יגנבוה בני אדם, שנ׳ כסף וזהב אשר עמהם,[32] וכל זה אינם מכירין מרוב יתרון טפשותם. והפסל עצמו אינו חושש על הסרחון למה, **דנחיר ליה ולא מריח**, על שם אף להם ולא יריחון.[33] **חביש**, כמ׳ מי שהיה חבוש בבית האסורין.[34] **קבלא**, תרג׳ אפילה.[35] **סריח**, הראשון לש׳ סרחון ובאשה, **סריח** אחרון לש׳ ריבוי ועודף כמ׳ וסרח העודף,[36] או
[23] יש לפרשו לש׳ סרחון ממש, שמא תאמר נפשו שלפסל נקיטה עליו שהוא מיטפש[37] ומשתטה על ריח הסרחון הרע, אינו יכול לחוש בזה שהרי אף להם ולא יריחון.[38] **טובעיה אין מיתפש כו׳**, והפסל כל כמה שהוא גדול בטבע גולמו כוחו קטן כי יכבד ויפול על פניו ומתלכלך, ואם תאמר מה אנו חוששין בנפילתו והלא הנופל סופו לעמוד, אינו כן שהרי

24 עפ״י ס׳ והזהיר המובא לעיל בהערה 21 (ראה מכילתא, הנ״ל, עמ׳ 223).
25 בראשית לה ד, ות״א שם.
26 תהלים קטו ה.
26א [נראה שרבינו מפרש גירסא שגרסה בפיוט ״פתיח הוא וסמי״.]
27 שם.
28 למשל בראשית יג טו.
29 דברים ד כ, ועוד.
30 תהלים קטו ו.
31 איוב ג ד, ות״י שם.
32 תנחומא הישן, נצבים, פיסקא ג.
33 תהלים קטו ו.
34 ברכות ט ע״ב ועוד.
35 שמות י כב, ועוד.
36 שמות כו יב.
37 כנראה שבנוסח שהיה לפניו היה כתוב ״מיטפש״, ולא כמו במחזור ויטרי, עמ׳ 339, ״מתעפיש״.
38 תהלים קטו ו.

היאך יקום מאחר שאין רוח בקרבו, גם ידיו אין בהם כח להישען עליהם ולקום, על שם ידיהם ולא ימישון.[39] **טובעיה**, טבע גולמו. **מיתפש**, לש׳ ריבוי וגודל. **מתרפש**, לש׳ רפש וטיט.[39א] **יתיב שמין כו׳**, והפסל יושב שמן ועב בצורתו ואינו נמלך לא עם נביא ולא עם חוזה, גם אינו יודע מי יהיה עבד או מלך בעולם. ואם צריך לצאת לגדולים או לקטנים מתלכלך על ברכיו, למה, לפי שאינו יכול להלך, על שם רגליהם ולא יהלכו,[40] ולש׳ גניי בע״ז הוא[41] כמ׳ דתימ׳, כרע בל קורס נבו. וכן, גרעו קרסו יחדו ולא יכלו מלט משא, נתלכלכו ולא יכלו מלט משא וג׳, נתלכלכו ולא יכלו להוציא משא הריעי שלהן.[42] ויש מפרשין **ולא ידע מאן עבד ומאן מליך**, מה יעשה ומה יחשוב, כלומ׳ שאין בו ממש כלל, ולש׳ **מליך ומתמליך**, עצה. כמ׳, להן מלכא מלכי ישפר עלך.[43] לכה איעצך תרג׳ אימלכינך.[44] **כפין וצהי**, והפסל הוא רעב וצמא והוא תועה ומטעה, גם את ידיו שהן עומדות פשוטות כאילו מבקש שום דבר והוא אינו מבקש כלום לפי שאינו מדבר. **לא פשוט ידוי כו׳**, לפי שאמרנו **וידוי מטעי** שעומד בידים פשוטות ואינו לוקח בהן כלום בא לומ׳ שאם לא עשאו האומן מתחילה בידים פשוטות הוא אינו יכול לפושטם ואינו מטלטל עגבותיו[45] ממקום למקום, ולש׳ גניי בע״ז הוא, ואינו מודיע מעשיו בעולם, כמוהו יהיו כל עובדיו, על שם כמוהם יהיו עושיהם.[45] **יסודוי**, עגבותיו, כמ׳ עד שתותיהם,[47] יסודות ושתות שפה אחת לכולם.[48] **מן כורא לקלס עבר כו׳**, והפסל מן הכור והכבשן שלאומן לקילוס העם מעבירין אותו היום. כלומ׳ בעוד שהוא חדש ויוצא מתחת ידי [24]
האומן מקלסין אותו, אבל למחר מניחין אותו ושוברין אותו שאין ממש בעבודתו. או יש לפרש **לקלס**, בית כנסייה שלהן, והוא לשון לע״ז איקליסיאה.[49] השוטים שעובדים אלוהות כיוצא באילו שאין בהן תקנה, היאך אומ׳ שהק׳ יש לו בן, חלילה לאל מרשע ושדי מעול[50] וחלילה ליראי השם לענות זאת, אך זה יש להאמין כי אלהינו ה׳ אחד ואין אחר להתחבר אליו. לפי שאחדותו אינו כשאר האחדים, לפי ששאר האחדים יתחבר אחד עם אחד, אחר כמוהו, ויהיו שנים, וכן יתחבר אחד אל אחד עד שיתרבה החשבון עד אין מספר, אבל אחודתו[50א]

39 שם ז. [אין = אם, כלומר, אם יגדל וירבה.]

39א ישעיה נז כ.

40 תהלים שם.

41 מלה זאת נמחקה ע״י הצנזור ונראה שצ״ל ״בע״ז״.

42 ישעיה מו א-ב, ופרש״י שם. וראה גם מגילה כה ע״ב. [ואין ספק שלפני רבינו היתה הגירסא ״בכורעתיה מתהליך״, כלומר, בכרעיו מתהלך (עושה צרכיו).]

43 דניאל ד כד.

44 במדבר כד יד, ובתרגומים שם.

45 ראה לעיל הערה 42.

46 תהלים קטו ח.

47 שמואל ב י ד.

48 ראה לעיל הערה 23.

49 ecclesia באיטלקית; וראה לעיל הערה 18 ומפרשו על פסלי אותו האיש, שמעמידים באיקליסיאות שלהם.

50 איוב לד י.

50א כך הוא בכ״י.

שלמקום ב״ה, הוא אחד מיוחד שאין אחד אחר כמוהו להתחבר עמו.[51] **נפחית באדם קדמאי**, והק׳ ישתבח שמו, מתפאר ומשתבח במעשיו, כשנפחתי באדם הראשון נשמת רוח חיים דקדקתי לבראותו אחר כל מעשה בראש׳, שלא יאמרו שבראתי עמו את העולם וסייעני במעשה בראשית,[52] והדל״ת **דבראי** נקודה בחירק ואינינה[52א] יסוד. פ״א. **דלא יימרון עימיה דבראי**, שלא יאמרו שיש מנהיג אחר בעולם זולתי. לפי שתחילה נאמ׳ נעשה אדם, יכול שתי רשוייות יש ת״ל ויעש אלהים את האדם, ויפח באפיו נשמת חיים.[53] ולזה הלשון הדל״ת פתוחה והיא יסוד, והוא מלשון מדברנא דאומתיה[54] ופת׳ מנהיג. **נשמתא מן שמאי**, מן השמים כמ׳ דאת אמ׳ ויפח באפיו נשמת חיים, בראשית רבא.[55] **סביל אנא בכורסי נורא**, עוד משתבח הק׳ ואומ׳, אני סובל בכחי כסא כבודי שהוא מאש.[56] **וקדמיי נהר נורא**, כמ׳ דתימ׳ נהר דינור נגד ונפק מן קדמוהי וגו׳,[57] הסטים והשוטים איך הם באין לדמות ולהמשיל הפסילים שאין בהם ממש לכוחי וגבורתי שאני אש אוכלת אש.[58] **לייחרא**, כמו מתחרה
[25] בארז,[59] ואיך תתחרה את הסוסים.[60] (ומה ש).[61] **עוד כל מליך פריס**, עוד הק׳ משתבח ואומ׳, עוד אני במלכותי משבר כל מלכיות שבעולם, ואני פוסע כל העולם כולו שהוא מהלך ת״ק שנה בקפיצה אחת ובדריסת רגל אחת, אבל אילו הפסילים[62] שלכם כלום יש בהם כח לקפוץ ברגליהם אפי׳ כדריסת תינוק המוטל בעריסה. באגדה דשמואל, ר׳ אבין בשם ר׳ שמעון בן יוחיי אמ׳ מצינו שהילך הק׳ מהלך חמש מאות שנה בשביל ליטול לו שם טוב דכת׳ אשר הלכו אלהים לפדות לו לעם.[63] **פריס**, כמ׳ פריסת מלכותך,[64] פרוסה.[65] **מהגון**, תינוק, כמ׳ נפישי משכי דהוגני,[66] מפי ר׳ יהודה אחי שני נר״ו.[67] **פרין טפשי קהליי**

51 השווה רמב״ם, הלכות יסודי התורה, פ״א ה״ז.

52 סנהדרין לח ע״א.

52א כך הוא בכ״י.

53 שם ע״ב וראה ב״ר ח ט, עמ׳ 62-63 ובמ״י שם; ״ויעש אלקים״ וכו׳, לפנינו ״ויברא אלקים״ וכו׳ (בראשית א כז); הפסוק ״ויפח באפיו״ וכו׳ (שם ב ז) אינו מובא במקורות הנ״ל בקשר לדרשה זו, ואולי נשגר מלהלן.

54 כתובות יז ע״א ועוד.

55 לא מצאתי ממש כלשון זו, אבל ראה ב״ר יב ח, עמ׳ 106-107; ״ויפח באפיו נשמת חיים, מן העליונים״.

56 לא מצאתי מאמר כזה, אבל יש להשוות את המאמר הידוע שהקב״ה סובל את עולמו בזרועו. ראה תרגום יונתן לדברים ל״ג כ״ז; וראה ברשימתו של צונץ, ס״פ עמ׳ 509-511; על שכסא כבודו של הקב״ה הוא מאש ראה דניאל ז ט. [ראה פדר״א, פ״ד, והגהות הרד״ל אות טז.]

57 דניאל ז י, בכ״י ט״ס: ״קדמוהו״.

58 דברים ד כד, ות״י שם.

59 ירמיה כב טו.

60 שם יב ה.

61 צריך למחוק.

62 ״הפסילים״ נמחק ע״י הצנזור.

63 מדרש שמואל, פכ״ג ג, עמ׳ 112.

64 סנהדרין כב ע״א.

65 כאן מפרש פרס מלשון פרוסה ולא כמו לעיל. ראה ג׳ הערה 103.

66 סנהדרין נב סע״א. [נראה שגרס במקום ״דליהוו״, מהגון.]

67 ראה מבוא, עמ׳ 7.

כו׳, עוד משתבח הק׳ ואומ׳, כמה הם זונים אחרי לבבם ואחרי עיניהם השוטים שהיו בקהלי והיו מוציאין דיבה ואומ׳ ששתי רשויות יש.[68] **פרין או פרון טפשי קהליי,** פת׳ הזנו, כדאיתא בבראשית רבא פרשת מ״א, באיניש דבחר פורנא דאימיה,[69] ובויקרא רבא פרש׳ אחרי מות, ואמר לבלה ניאופים תרג׳ עקילס פליאה פורני דהוות מבלייה גיירייא.[70] **ואמרין לחגיי,** פת׳ וקוראין שם חגיהן ואידיהן על שם הבן.[71] פ״א. **ואמרין לחגיי, בה״א ולא בחי״ת,** ופת׳ כמ׳ לועגיי כמ׳ ולהג הרבה יגיעת בשר. ומפורש בעירובין, כל המלעיג על דברי תורה נידון ביגיעת בשר.[72] וכלפי אמנה שלנוצרים הוא מיוסד, שאומ׳ אב ובן ורוח הקודש.[73] **צורתיה דאדם ציירית כו׳,**[74] עוד משתבח הק׳ ואומ׳, אני בראתי כל מעשה בראשית וציירתי צורת אדם בלי טורח ועצב. בבראשית רבא פ״ג, ר׳ ברכיה בשם ר׳ יודהביר׳ סימון פתח, בדבר ה׳ שמים נעשו, לא בעמל ולא ביגיעה ברא הק׳ את עולמו אלא בדברו.[75] [26] **בורייתיה ברייה,** ברייתו בראתי. **ולא אתכריית,** לא נבהלתי ולא נשתוממתי בבריאתו, כמ׳ אתכריית רוחי דדניאל.[76] **קנאי אנא בנאי כו׳,** עוד משתבח הק׳ ואומ׳, היזהר במוראי כי אני אל קנא, כמ׳ שנ׳ כי אנכי ה׳ אלהיך אל קנא.[77] **בנאי,** מפואר. שבניתי העולם ואין בו שום חסרון, שמא שמעת מימיך אדם אומ׳ העולם חסר כך וכך, אתמהא.[78] **לא אתקניתי,** במדרש השכם, אני שליט בקנאה ואין הקנאה שולטת בי,[79] כלומר אין מי יתקנא לי ולאלהותי ולמעשה ידיי שייבנה עולם אחר כנגדי, על כן להטביע טבע[79א] אחר כנגדי וצורה אחרת לשם אלהות לא תחליפוני בכך כי כולם הבל. **ריחמתיך ברישיך,** זאת היא בשורת הק׳ שמבשר כנסת יש׳ על שהיא סובלת צרות בגלותה על ייחוד השם ואמ׳ לה אהבתיך מתחילת גלותך ועוד אני אוהבך כמאז, אך יש לך לסבול האכסנייא[80] והגלות ועלי **לנחומי עקתיך.** ור׳ יהודה אחי שני נר״ו[81] פירש שאומ׳ הק׳ לכנסת יש׳ אין לך לעבוד אלוה בעולם זולתי שכבר הוריתי לך תורה שהיא גמילות חסדים ורחמים ראשה וסופה, ראשה, **סביל אכסנייא,** לרחם על העניים, להלביש ערומים, וסופה, **לנחומי עקתיך,** לנחם אבלים,

68 ראה המקורות המובאים בהערה 53.

69 ב״ר מא (מ) ז, עמ׳ 394.

70 וי״ר לג ו, עמ׳ תשסז ובח״נ ובהערות שם.

71 כנראה הכוונה לחג המולד. [ונראה שגרס ״ואמרין לחגיי (להגיי)״ במקום ״דאמרי לדחלי״.]

72 עירובין כא ע״ב וראה בד״ס שם, עמ׳ 75 אות א.

73 במחזור ויטרי, עמ׳ 339, נמחק מנוסח הפיוט החלק המדבר נגד הנוצרים, ראה שם הערה א׳.

74 מכאן עד סוף הפיוט מפורש במחזור ויטרי עמ׳ 322-333, וגם שם נמחקו הדברים הפולמוסיים, ראה שם.

75 ב״ר ג ב, עמ׳ 19.

76 דניאל ז טו.

77 שמות כ ה.

78 ב״ר יב א, עמ׳ 97-99, ושם מדובר על שלמות הבריאה. [ומפרש ״בנאי״ כמו בנוי, כלומר, בפאר של בניני.]

79 ס׳ והזהיר, יתרו, עמ׳ 49 [מן המכילתא, בחדש ו, עמ׳ 226]; וראה לעיל הערה 21.

79א [אולי גרס ״טבע לקיבלי״.]

80 כאן כמובן מקום זר ומקביל לגלות.

81 ראה מבוא, עמ׳ 7.

כדדרש ר׳ שמלאי, תורה תחילתה גמילות חסדים וסופה גמילות חסדים, תחילת׳ גמילות
חסדים ויעש ה׳ אלהים לאדם ולאשתו וג׳ וסופה גמילות חסדים ויקבר אותו בגיא.[82] **שמעי**
חדותי, גם אילו דברי הק׳ ליש׳, **שמעי חדותי** וכה פת׳, שמעי אלי כנסת ישראל שאת ראש
שמחתי, על שם כי ישוב ה׳ לשוש עליך לטוב.[83] ואת קרויה בתי כמ׳ דתימ׳, שמעי בת
וראי.[84] פ״א. **חדותי**, מיוחדת שלי, תרג׳ אחר חדא תרג׳ אחת חדתא.[85] על שם אחת היא
יונתי תמתי.[86] ומורי ר׳ דניאל[87] פירש **שמעי חדותי**, כלתי. ואמ׳ שנמצא באגדה שכן קורין
[27] בכרכי הים כלתי חדותי.[88] ואיתא בגיטין במעשה דאשמדאי, חזו לההוא חדותא דהוו חדו
לה.[89] **תתיהב למאן דיהוי ליך**, זה מוסב על התורה שהזכרנו וכה פת׳. לזאת אני אומר לך
שתקבלי תורתי שהיא נתונה לך למלאות כל דבר הצריך והראוי להיות. **לך**, כלומ׳ שכל
חסרונייך יתמלאו בה. **אך אלה אוחרן לא יהוי ליך**, שלא תפני לבך מיראתי.

ה אלפא ביט אוחרן[1]

איתו כרועו לצלמי, ייסד המתורגמן כדי להזכיר הנסים והנפלאות שהפליא הק׳ לחננייה מישאל ועזריה, שמסרו עצמן לכבשן האש ולא רצו לעבוד ע״ז. **איתו כרועו לצלמי לולבי דתמר**, לחננייה מישאל ועזריה קורא **לולבי דתמר**, וכן הוא בתרגום שיר השירים בפסוק אמרתי אעלה בתמר על הניסיון שנתנסו חננייה מישאל ועזריה,[2] ובסנהדרין פרק חלק, אמרתי אעלה בתמר אחזה בסנסניו, ולא עלה בידי אלא סנסן אחד שלחננייה מישאל ועזריה.[3] **אמ׳ להון ננסא**, זהו נבוכדנצר שהיה ננס כדאמ׳ הוא אמה וזקנו אמה ועל כן אמ׳ ושפל אנשים יקים עלה.[4] **ארמיית שממה**, כה פת׳, הזכרו[4א] כי השלכתי שממה בבית

82 סוטה יד ע״א.
83 דברים ל ט.
84 תהלים מה יא.
85 לא מצאתי מקור לזה.
86 שיה״ש ו ט.
87 ראה מבוא, עמ׳ 7.
88 לא מצאתי מקור לזה.
89 גטין סח ע״ב.

1 הוא הפיוט המתחיל ״חנניה מישאל ועזריה״ (דוידזון, ח, 421) ומצורף אליו הפיוט ״בה שעתא״ (שם, ב, 166; וראה להלן הערה 34) ושניהם מפורשים במחזור ויטרי, עמ׳ 320-323.
2 שיה״ש ז ט, ותרגום שם.
3 סנהדרין צג ע״א.
4 ב״ר טז ד, עמ׳ 147 ובמ״י שם; האגדה מספרת על פרעה ועל נבוכדנצר שהיו ננסים ולומדים את הענין מהפסוק ״ושפל״ וכו׳ (דניאל ד יד) הן ביחס לפרעה (מו״ק יח ע״א) והן ביחס לנבוכדנצר (ילקוט שמעוני, ח״ב, רמז תתרסב, ומובא במ״י הנ״ל), אולם המאמר ״הוא אמה וזקנו אמה״ נאמר רק על פרעה (מו״ק הנ״ל).
4א כך הוא בכ״י ואולי צ״ל ״תזכרו״.

חופתו שלהק׳ והוא בית המקדש. פ״א. **ארמיית**, לש׳ שממה וצדו[5] כדאיתא בפסיקתא
דדברי ירמיהו, למה נקרא שמו ירמיהו שנעשה בית המקדש אירימון בימיו[6] והוא לשון
יוון. ובלע״ז[7] גרמטקא, אירימון בוסקו[8] ופת׳ יער. **אית לן פטרון**, זו היא עניית חננייה
מישאל ועזריה, ופת׳ פטרון כדאיתה[8א] בבראשית רבא. וישימני לאב לפרעה, לפטרון.[9] [28]
שמיה לא ינום, על שם לא ינום ולא יישן שומר ישראל.[10] **באבונן דלעיל רוחצין**, בטחונינו.
לבטח תרג׳ לרוחצן.[11] **טליותן**, נערותינו. כדאמ׳, ר׳ יוחנן אמ׳ כד הוינא טלייא אמרנא
מילייא ושאלנא לסבייא ואשתכח כוותנא.[12] והנער איננו אתנו, תרג׳ ירושלמ׳ וטלייא.[13]
גרמין אתון גרמיכון, גורמין אתם לעצמיכם לישרף. **קטם**, תרג׳ דשן.[14] **דימניס**, אדנות
כדאמ׳ בבראשית רבא פ״ח, משל למלך ואיפרכוס שהיו נכנסין במדינה והיו בני המדינה
מבקשין לומ׳ למלך דומינו,[15] והוא לש׳ לע״ז ממש. דומינו,[16] אדון. ובמקצת סידורים
מצאתי כתוב **גבורה ודינמיס**,[17] ולפי משמעו הוא לש׳ כח ואיילות, באגדת חזית, אכן אתה
אל מסתתר. אמ׳ ישעיה, אכן יש בך דינמיס לעשות, אלא שאתה מסתתר. אמ׳ לו, אלהי
ישראל מושיע, חוזר אני ומתנקם.[18] ולפי משמעו אך בך אל,[19] אך בך כח ואיילות כמ׳ יש
לאל ידי.[20] **דחילתא דצלמך כו׳**, **תיאורו יתן**, תואר שכינתו יהיה עמנו להצילנו. ס״א.
תיאורון דידן, כלומ׳ הוא התואר והבטחון שלנו. פ״א. **דע דפטרונן תיאורו יתן**, התי״ו רפי
והכל נקוד בחולם ופתרונו, אלהותו עמנו שכן תיאור לש׳ יוון אלוה.[21] **היך כפרתון כו׳**,
אנדרטי, צלם שלי והיא צורת אדם כמ׳ איתשעו כל אנדרטיא דסוף מועד קטן.[22] **האידנא**,
עתה כמ׳ בהא עידנא.[23] **דלא בטיבותכון**, שאין עליכם בזה טובת הנאה אחרי שתשתחוו
בעל כרחכם. **ומה אנן אמרין לדר בשמיא**, כלומ׳ אם נשתחווה לצלם איך יהיה לנו פתחון
פה לפניו ואם תאמר נשתחווה בלילה או בסתר, הלא הוא **גלה עמיקת׳ ומסתרתא**. **זריק**

5 שמות כג כט, ות״א שם ועוד.
6 פסדר״כ, יג, עמ׳ 236.
7 ״ובלעז״ נמחק.
8 לא זוהה. על המונח ״בלעז גרמטיקא״ ראה מבוא, עמ׳ 5-6.
8א כך הוא בכ״י.
9 ב״ר צג י, עמ׳ 1160, וראה לעיל ג׳, הערה 36.
10 תהלים קכא ד.
11 ויקרא כה יח, ובתרגומים שם ועוד.
12 מגילה ה ע״ב.
13 בראשית מד ל, ות״י שם.
14 ויקרא א טז ועוד.
15 ב״ר ח י, עמ׳ 63-64.
16 domino באיטלקית.
17 במחזור ויטרי, עמ׳ 337: ״גבורה ודינמיט״.
18 שיה״ש רבא ד ח, בשינויים.
19 ישעיה מה יד; וראה שיה״ש רבא הנ״ל.
20 בראשית לא כט.
21 צ״ל תיאום.
22 מו״ק כה ע״ב, בד״ס שם, אות פ.
23 ראה לעף בשנתון של צינציניטי [*HUCA*] ב, עמ׳ 194.

אנא לכון, מכפתין, קשורין כמו כפיתו בסרבילהון.[24] **זעיף**, לש׳ רוגז כמ׳ והנם זועפים.[25]
מיללא, כמ׳ ילולי ייליל,[36] לש׳ יללה והיא תרועה. **חי וקיים הוא פטרון דידן, חבל**, לש׳ [29]
אוי. **חס לן**, חלילה לעבדיך, תרג׳ חס לעבדך.[27] **טבחית ונכסית גוזלייא בציון**, לפי שכנסת
יש׳ קרוייה יונה.[28] **טייס ונהים הוינא**, כלומ׳ הייתי קל לפרוח כנשר ונוהם כאריה בבית
המקדש להחריבו. **טלקית רישי מיינקיכון**, ומלק את ראשו תרגום ירוש׳ ויטלק.[29] **רישי**
מיינקיכון, על שם בת בבל השדודה אשרי שישלם לך וג׳ אשרי ונפץ את עלליך אל
הסלע.[30] **יווי עלך ננסא**, פי׳ יווי לש׳ ווי. **תיאורו יתן**, כמ׳ שפירשנו. והצרפתים אומרים
תיאורו יתך[31] ומפרשין יארר אותך, וקשה לי לפרש כן לפי שהתי״ו נראית יסוד והנכון כמ׳
שפירשתי. **כל יתבי ארעא, כל סגריטין דידי**, ס״א סנקליטין, פי׳ בתי דינין.[32] **לא חשחין**
אנחנא, חישוק לש׳ חשק. ויש לפרשו לש׳ דיבוק כמ׳ חשוק שפתותיך זו בזו, בעבודה זרה
פרק אין מעמידין.[33] **בה שעתא**[34] כו׳, **חד שבעה ארבעין ותשעה**.[35] פי׳, הפסוק כך הוא, **חד**
שבעה על די חזי למזייה,[36] ארבעין ותשעה הוא הפירוש. וכה פת׳ הפסוק, על מה שהיה
ראוי להדליקו, הדליקו שבעה פעמ׳ שבעה הרי מ״ט פעמים,[37] וכן מזוקק שבעתיים מ״ט
פנים, במסכת סופרים.[38] **למזייה**, לש׳ דליקה. **כפיתין**, קשורין. **אסתכי מלכא מפלטוריה**,
הבית המלך מחצר מלכותו. **הדברי מלכא**, שרים ומנהיגי המלך. **די אכלו קרציהון**, שסיפרו
רכילותם, קרא בגרון תרג׳ אכלי,[39] רכיל תרג׳ קורצין.[40] **לבר אלהין**, מלאך, וסופו מוכיח, [30]

24 דניאל ג כא.

25 בראשית מ ו.

26 ר״ה לג ע״ב.

27 בראשית מד ז, ותרגומים שם.

28 ברכות נג ע״ב.

29 ויקרא א טו, שם ה ח. [בתרגום אונקלוס: ״וימלוק״ (ואינה בשימוש בארמית וייתכן שגרס ויטלק וצ״ל ״בתרגום״, וראה בת״י לפסוק ט״ז שם).]

30 תהלים קלז ח-ט, בכ״י חסרה המלה ״שיאחז״.

31 כך הגירסה במחזור ויטרי, עמ׳ 337, וראה לעיל, ד״ה דחילתא וכו׳.

32 עפ״י ב״ר ח ג, עמ׳ 59: ״משל למלך שהיה לו שני סינקליטין״ וכו׳. ובמחזור ויטרי עמ׳ 321, מפרש: ״בבר׳ רב׳ סנקליטין, יועצים ושרים״. ונראה שגרס במקום ״כולא אנא״ — ״כל יתבי ארעא אנא״.

33 ע״ז לה ע״א. [וברור שנפל כאן שיבוש שהרי מה שייך לפרש חשחין — חישוק, לשון חשק! יתר על כן, על זה ודאי היה מביא הפסוק בדניאל ג׳ ט״ז (כמו במחזור ויטרי). ועוד, הפירוש לשון דיבוק אין לו שום מובן לגירסא.]

34 כאן מתחיל טקסט חדש שצורף לראשון. ראה לעיל הערה 1.

35 בכ״י בטעות: ״ושבעה״.

36 דניאל ג יט; כלומר, הפסוק בדניאל הוא ״חד... למזיא״. ״ארבעין״ וכו׳ הוא הפירוש של המתרגם.

37 מדרש תהלים כח, עמ׳ 229.

38 מסכת סופרים פט״ז ה״ה, מהד׳ היגר עמ׳ 287-288. בנוסח שלפנינו הפסוק ״מזוקק שבעתיים״ (תהלים יב ז) אינו נזכר, אולם במדרש תהלים, יב, עמ׳ 107-108, מסדר את המאמר על הפסוק הנ״ל והפסוק מובא בסוף המאמר בירושלמי סנהדרין פ״ד ה״ב (כ״ב ע״א). כנראה שבנוסח של מסכת סופרים שהיה לפני המפרש, הוזכר הפסוק בדומה למקורות הנ״ל.

39 ישעיה נח א, ות״י שם.

40 ויקרא יט טז, ות״א שם.

די שלח מלאכיה.[41] **אדרגזרייא גדברייא דתברייא תפתייא**, לש׳ שררה במלכות, כל אחד לפי מעלתו. **הדמין יתעבד**, יהרג לפי חרב. **הללו את ה׳ כל גוים כול׳**,[42] בפרק ערב פסחים מפרש כי חננייה מישאל ועזריה אמרו זה המזמור כשיצאו מתוך כבשן האש,[43] שאז נשתבח המקום ב״ה על הנס שעשה ליש׳, שהרי נבוכדנצר שלח שלוחים בכל העולם להודיע הנס כמ׳ דתימ׳ נבוכדנצר מלכא לכל עממייא אומייא וגו׳ אתייא ותמהיא די עבד עמי אלהא עילאה וגו׳.[44] **ואמת ה׳ לעולם אמ׳ גבריאל**, גם זה מפורש שם בפרק ערב פסחים, אמ׳ ר׳ יוחנן בשעה שהפיל נמרוד הרשע את אברהם אבינו לתוך כבשן האש אמ׳ גבריאל לפני הק׳ ארד ואציל צדיק זה מתוך כבשן האש, אמ׳ לו הק׳ אני יחיד בעולמי ואברהם יחיד בעולמו, נאה ליחיד להציל ליחיד. ולפי שאין הק׳ מקפח שכר כל ברייה אמ׳ לו, תזכה ותציל ג׳ מבני בניו כדדרש ר׳ שמעון הצידוני, בשעה שהפיל נ״נ הרשע חננייה מישאל ועזריה לתוך כבשן האש אמ׳ יורקמי שר הברד לפני הק׳ ארד ואצנן את הכבשן ואציל את הצדיקי׳, אמ׳ לו גבריאל אין גדולתו של הק׳ בכך אלא אני שר שלאש ארד ואקרר מבפנים ואקדיר מבחוץ ואעשה נס בתוך נס, אמ׳ לו הק׳ רד והצל, באותה שעה פתח גבריאל ואמ׳ ואמת ה׳ לעולם,[45] שהקים לי אמונתו.[46]

ו לא תשא [31]

מתרגמנן אותו בתרג׳ אונקלוס ובירושלמ׳.[1]

עמי בני ישראל, לא ישתבע כו׳, ולמה לא מתרג׳ דבירא תליתאה, דבירא רביעאה,[2] לפי שאנכי ולא יהיה לך לבד נאמרו מפי [הק׳],[3] דכת׳ וירא העם וינועו ויאמרו אל משה דבר אתה עמנו ונשמעה וגו׳.[4] וזה היה אחרי שנאמ׳ אנכי ולא יהיה לך. ולש׳ המקראות מוכיחין, אנכי ה׳ אלהיך, לא יהיה לך אלהים אחרים על פני, הרי הקודש[4א] מדבר בעצמו,

41 דניאל ג כה, כח.
42 תהלים קיז א.
43 פסחים קיח ע״א; וראה בד״ס שם, עמ׳ 373-374 [וראה עוד שם, עמ׳ 306 אות א], וראה להלן ז׳, הערה 62א, וראה ג״ב צרפתי, לשוננו מא (1976), עמ׳ 21-28.
44 דניאל ג לא-לב.
45 פסחים קיח ע״א-ע״ב בשינויים.
46 וכן בפירוש רש״י שם (קיח רע״ב): ״שקיים לי דברו ושמר לי הבטחתו״ וכו׳.

1 ראה לעיל א׳, הערה 4.
2 ראה לעיל בראש פיוט ג׳: בת״י ובתרגום ניאופיטי לעשרת הדיברות מקדים ״ויקרא קדמאה כך הוא נפיק״ וכו׳ רק לשני הדיברות הראשונים ובשאר הדיברות מתחיל במלים ״עמי בני ישראל״ וכו׳, אולם במחזור ויטרי, עמ׳ 337 ואילך, נמצא לפני כל דיבר ״דיברא תליתאה כד הוה נפיק, דיברא רביעאה כד הוה נפיק״ וכו׳; וראה יהודה קומלוש, המקרא באור התרגום, עמ׳ 261.
3 בכ״י, בטעות: ״משה״.
4 שמות כ יח-יט.
4א כך הוא בכ״י.

מיכן ואילך על ידי סרסור, לא תשא את שם ה׳ אלהיך לשוא ולא נאמ׳ לא תשא את שמי לשוא וכן כולם.[5]

אלפא ביט

אמגן מומי לא תשתבע כול׳,[6] לא תשא את שם ה׳ אלהיך לשוא, תרג׳ לא תימי בשמא דה׳ אלהך למגנא.[7] וכה פת׳, על שוא ושקר לא תהיה נשבע כדי שלא **ת[זע] זע דמסתביל ארבע**, ר׳ דניאל נ״ע[8] פירש שלא יזעזע הק׳ על כסאו שהוא חונה על ארבע חיות הקודש. ויש מפרשין, על ארבע רוחות העולם. והנראה בעיני לפרש, שלא תזעזע העולם המיוסד בארבע אימות, אש ומים ורוח ועפר.[9] לפי שעל שבועת שוא נענש כל העולם כולו כמ׳ דתימ׳, על כן אלה[10] אכלה ארץ ויאשמו יושבי בה,[11] ולא תגרום להביא צרעת על בשרך [32] לפי שהשבועה והאלה היא נוקבת כקוץ המוציאה דם.[12] **סגירו**, צרעת, תרג׳.[13] ששבועת שוא מדמת[13א] צרעת על האדם כמפורש לפנינו באות פ״ה על גיחזי.[14] **הרזא**, נוקבת כמ׳ דהרזיה בסילווא,[15] וסילווא היא קוץ. **גופך לא תחייב במימרין דמומי לטו חתייא גומרין כול׳**, פי׳ אל תרשיע גופך בדברי פיך. על שם, אל תתן את פיך לחטיא את בשרך.[16] כלומ׳, אל תהיה שבועת שוא קלה בעיניך לפי שאין לך בה הפסד ממון, לפי שהשבועה היא אלה כדכת׳ בשבועת האלה.[17] ובמקצת סידורים כתוב **דמומי ולטו**, והוי״ו יתירה לפי שלטו הוא פירוש מומי. **חתיא גומרין**. כלומ׳, השבועה היא חרם וקללה אוכלת כגחלי אש, תרג׳ גחלים גומרין,[18] והיא נדבקת ונכנסת ברמ״ח איברים שכן מנין האותיות חר״ם רמ״ח.[19] ומצאתי בתנחומא פרש׳ וישב יעקב, אמ׳ ר׳ עקיבה החרם היא השבועה והשבועה היא

5 פס״ר, כב, קיא ע״א ומקבילות. והשווה לשון הרמב״ן בפירושו לשמות כ׳ ז׳: ״והנה לשון הכתוב הזה את שם ה׳ אלקיך כאלו משה ידבר וכן בכל הדברות אחרי כן ובשנים הפסוקים הראשונים השם ידבר״ וכו׳.

6 דוידזון, א, 5566; טל עמ׳ 51-59 (הנוסח הארמי, תרגום עברי ופירוש).

7 שמות כ ז, ות״א שם.

8 ראה מבוא, עמ׳ 7.

9 ראה אוצר המונחים לקלצקין, בערך אם.

10 תיבת ״אלה״ נכפלה בטעות בכ״י.

11 ישעיה מד ו. וראה תרגום שם.

12 טל, עמ׳ 53, מעיר על ב״ב קנא ע״ב וכתובות צא ע״א: ״סילווא דלא מבע דמא״; ורש״י בכתובות שם: ״קוץ שאינו מוציא דם בנוקבו בבשר כלומר שמתא ונידוי״; וראה גם במאמר המובא להלן, הערה 20.

13 ויקרא יג ט, ועוד. כרגיל סדר המלים הפוך!

14 ראה להלן ד״ה פום ממליל וכו׳.

15 ע״ז כח ע״ב; ״חרזיה״ בחי״ת וכן בערוך, ערך חרז א׳ אבל כאן פעמיים ״הרזא״, ״הרזיה״, בה״א; וכן אצל טל, ״הרזא״, ראה הערתו שם, עמ׳ 53.

16 קהלת ה ה.

17 במדבר ה כא, וראה להלן הערה 21.

18 ויקרא טז יב ועוד.

19 מו״ק יז ע״א.

החרם, למד מיהושע שהחרים את יריחו כול׳, ובפילגש בגבעה כת׳ השבועה הגדולה היתה לאשר לא יעלה אל ה׳ המצפה, וכי שבועה היתה שם אלא ללמדך שהחרם היא השבועה, ועוד למד משאול בן קיש דכת׳ ארור האיש אשר יאכל לחם עד הערב וג׳, וכת׳ ויונתן לא שמע בהשביע אביו את העם וגו׳,[20] ובמקום אחר בתנחומא, והשבועה היא החרם כמ׳ דתימ׳ והשביע הכהן את האשה בשבועת האלה.[21] **הלין מומתא**, אילו השבועות והאלות מכלין דבר שאפי׳ האש אין בו כח לכלותו, כדכת׳ ובאה אל בית הגנב ואל בית הנשבעים בשמי לשקר וכלתו ואת עציו ואת אבניו, שהאש אוכלת עצים ולא אבנים אבל החרם מכלה הכל.[22] **סתרא**, כמ׳ בניין נערים סתירה.[23] **זכריה חמי לה טייסא**, פי׳ זכריה הנביא ראה בחזון מגילה עפה. ויקרא רבא, מהו עפה, טייסא.[24] כפתח[24א] ההיכל [33] מידתה פרושה,[25] כדכ׳ ויאמר אלי מה אתה רואה ואומר אני רואה מגילה עפה ארכה עשרים באמה ורחבה עשר באמה,[26] והיא כתובה פנים ואחור קינים והגה והי.[27] **חריתי בה מיני קנסא**, קינים והגה והי לנשבע לשוא ולמי שמשביע חבירו לשקר, כמ׳ דתימ׳ הוצאתיה ובאה אל בית הגנב ואל בית הנשבעים בשמי לשקר וגו׳.[28] **למימי**, לנשבע. והאומ׳ **למומי** טעות בידו, כי מומי שם דבר ופת׳ שבועה ואינו שם הפועל. והנכון **למימי**, כמ׳ שפירשתי. **רוכסא**, מלש׳ והיה העקוב למישור והרכסים לבקעה.[29] כלומ׳, משביעו בעקובה וחמס, והכי איתא בויקרא רבא פרש׳ ו׳, הוצאתיה ובאה אל בית הגנב, זה הגונב דעתן שלבריות, טעין ליה טענתא דמגן ומייתי להון לידי מומתא.[30] ור׳ דניאל נ״ע[31] פירש **ברוכסא**, לש׳ חיבור מלשון וירכסו את החשן.[32] ותימה, שאם משביעו על האמת למה ייענש. **טובהון דלנפשהון מגמרין כו׳**, פי׳ אשריהם הצדיקים שמלמדין ומרגילין את עצמן שלא להישבע אפי׳ באמת וכל שכן על שקר.[33] וטוב להם לשמור פיהם, כדכת׳ שומר פיו ולשונו שומר מצרות נפשו,[34] לפי שהחיים והמות ביד לשון כדאיתא בויקרא רבא פרש׳

20 תנחומא הישן, וישב, פיסקא ב.

21 לא מצאתי בתנחומא אבל ראה וי״ר ו ה, עמ׳ קלט ובמקבילות.

22 תוספתא, סוטה, פ״ז ה״ג וראה בתוספתא כפשוטה, עמ׳ 677 ד״ה בא וראה.

23 מגלה לא ע״ב.

24 וי״ר ו ג, עמ׳ קל.

24א צ״ל ״בפתח״.

25 זה תרגום עברי של הטור הארמי המקורי: ״בפיתחא דהיכלא משחתא פריסא״ (טל, עמ׳ 51).

26 זכריה ה ב. וראה בוי״ר הנ״ל, עמ׳ קלא.

27 יחזקאל ב י והשווה עירובין כא ע״א: ״אמרו יחזקאל ולא פירשו וכו׳ עד שבא זכריה בן עדו ופירשו״ וכו׳.

28 תוספתא (הערה 22 לעיל) וראה תוספתא כפשוטה, שם, עמ׳ 677 ד״ה ובאה.

29 ישעיה מ ד.

30 ראה את הנוסח המובא בח״נ, וי״ר ו ג, עמ׳ קלה (לשורה 4) ובהערות שם.

31 ראה מבוא, עמ׳ 7.

32 שמות כח כח. [רבינו לא הסביר את פירושו של ר׳ דניאל. ונראה שכוונתו לגלגול שבועה, כלומר, בדבר שמן התורה הוא פטור משבועה והוא מחבר לו שבועה ע״י גלגול, ואולי משום כך סובר ר״ד שהוא נענש.]

33 וי״ר ו ג, עמ׳ קלב ומקבילות.

34 משלי כא כג.

ל״ג, מות וחיים ביד לשון, תירגם עקילס מיסטר ומכירין, מות מיכן וחיים מיכן.[35] פי׳, והם
כלי זיין בלש׳ יוון. כלומ׳, מגן וחרב, מגן הם חיים, וחרב הוא מות.[36] זה הלשון **מיסטר** לא
נתברר לנו על הנכון מה הוא בלש׳ יוון, ומשיקול הדעת פירשנוהו כן. על כן נראה לי עיקר
פירושו כמ׳ שפירש אחי ר׳ צדקיה נר״ו[37] שפירש **מיסטר ומכירין**, הכאות וחבלות, **מיסטר**, [34]
הכאת לחי, כמ׳ בא מלאך וסטרו על פיו,[38] **מכירין**, חבלה בסכין או בחרב והוא לש׳ יוון
חרב, מכירא. וכן יש מפרשין כלי חמס מכירותיהם, שמעון ולוי שנתגאו בחרבם על שכם
חמס הוא בידם, שהרי לא להם נאמ׳ ועל חרבך תחיה.[39] ור׳ דניאל נ״ע[37] פירש **מיסתר**
בתי״ו, לש׳ סתירה. אך אני מצאתיו כתוב בטי״ת וכן נראה לי עיקר כמ׳ שפירשנו. **כד
איתכבישת קרתא דדיקלי**, פי׳, כשכבש יהוש׳ יריחו עיר התמרים[40] ביום השבת נפלה
חומת העיר תחתיה ונכבשה, על כן החרימה יהושע והחרים כל שללה לפי שמעשה שבת
אסורין בהנאה.[41] ובשבת היה דכת׳ ויהי ביום השביעי וישכימו כעלות השחר ויסבו את
העיר וג׳ ויאמר יהושע אל העם הריעו כי ה׳ נתן לכם את העיר,[42] ותפל החומה תחתיה
וגו׳.[43] וכן מפורש בסדר עולם, ויהי ביום השביעי, ר׳ יוסי אומ׳ שבת היה.[44] ובתנחומ׳
פרש׳ נשא, אם יאמר לך אדם למה חילל יהושע את השבת ביריחו אמור לו על פי הגבורה
עשה שנ׳ ויאמר ה׳ אל יהושע ראה נתתי בידך את יריחו ואת מלכה גיבורי החיל וסבותם
את העיר כל אנשי המלחמה הקף את העיר פעם אחת כה תעשה ששת ימים ושבעה כהנים
ישאו שבעה שופרות היובלים לפני הארון וביום השביעי תסובו את העיר שבע פעמים,
ומניין שהיה שבת, שאין שבעה ימים בלא שבת. ועוד דבר אחד עשה יהושע מדעתו מה
שלא נאמר לו, כיון שנכבשה יריחו שבת היתה, אמ׳ יהושע השבת כולה קודש וכל מה
שכבשנו בשבת יהא קודש לה׳ שנ׳ וכל כסף וזהב וכלי נחשת וברזל קודש הוא לה׳ אוצר
ה׳ יבוא.[45] **איטמור**, לש׳ הטמנה. **שורהא**, חומותיה, תרג׳ חומה שורא.[46] **קיבלי**, חשך
אפילה, תרג׳ חושך קבל.[47] **סימא**, תרג׳ מטמון.[48] **מגני שבטיה בחיסודא דכאיר**, ס״א
דאכאיר, פי׳, עכן גינה שבטו בחרפת כיעורו, שמעל בחרם וחמד הנכסים והממון שראה

35 וי״ר לג א, עמ׳ תשנו וח״נ שם.

36 פירוש זה שונה מהפירוש הניתן בערוך, ערך מצטרא, ראה בעה״ש שם.

37 ראה מבוא, עמ׳ 8.

38 נדה ל ע״ב.

39 ב״ר צט ז, עמ׳ 1278.

40 דברים לד ג.

41 בכתובות לד ע״א: ״או מה קודש אסור בהנאה אף מעשה שבת אסור בהנאה ת״ל לכם שלכם יהא״. ועיין להלן והערה 45.

42 יהושע ו טו-טז.

43 שם כ.

44 סדר עולם רבה, פי״א, מהד׳ רטנר עמ׳ 47-48.

45 תנחומא הישן, נשא, פיסקא כח. [ועיין עוד שם, מסעי אות ה, ובמ״ר כג ו.]

46 שמות יד כב.

47 שמות י כב.

48 בראשית מג כג.

בביזה. וגרם לו ליהושע, שהיה מנהיגן שלישראל, ליפול על פניו.[49] וגרם שנהרג יאיר, שהיה שקול כרובו שלסנהדרין[50] שיושבין בלשכת הגזית, שהוא טיבורו שלעול׳.[51] **מגני**, [35]
פי׳ לש׳ גניי. **חיסודא**, תרג׳ חרפה.[52] **כאיר**, לש׳ כיעור. **דסאיר**, ראה, כמ׳, האי טבחא דלא סר סכיניה,[53] פת׳ לש׳ הראה. **איתקטיל יאיר**, כשהלכו על עי, דכת׳ ויכו מהם אנשי העי כשלשים וששה איש, שלשים וששה לא נאמר אלא כשלשים וששה, זה יאיר שהיה שקול כרובה שלסנהדר׳,[50] דהיינו שלשים וששה איש, שסנהדרין כולה שבעים ואחד, נמצא רובה שלשים וששה. **סהדא רבא פרסם קדמין**, פי׳, הק׳ שהוא העד הגדול והנאמן, כמ׳ דתימ׳ והייתי עד ממהר במכשפים ובמנאפים ובנשבעים לשקר וגו׳,[54] גילה הדבר ליהושע ואמ׳ לו, חטא ישראל וגם לקחו מן החרם וגם עברו את בריתי וגם גנבו וגם כחשו וגם שמו בכליהם. ה׳ פעמים כת׳ גם, על שמעל בה׳ חרמים, כמפורש בסנהד׳ פרק נגמר הדין, ד׳ בימי משה, האחד במלך ערד דכת׳ אם נתן תתן את העם בידי והחרמתי את עריהם, השני במדין שנהנה מן המלקוח קודם הרמת תרומתה דהוי כאיסור חרם, והשלישי והרביעי בסיחון ועוג דכת׳ ונחרם את כל עיר מתים הנשים והטף, והחמישי בימי יהושע, זה שנכשל בו.[55] ואע״פ שהוא מעל בסתר הק׳ גילה הדבר כמ׳ ששנינו, המחלל שם שמים בסתר נפרעין ממנו בגלוי.[56] וזהו פי׳ **פרסם קדמין**, גולה הראשונות שלא היו ידועין, הד׳ חרמין שמעל בימי משה שלא נתגלו לישראל עד עתה בימי יהושע כשמעל בזה. פ״א **בחמש דשקר**, שמעל בחמשה חומשי תורה, כדאיתא התם פרק נגמר הדין.[57] **עדבא כבשיה**, הגורל לכד אותו, כדכת׳ וילכד עכן בן כרמי.[58] **פום ממליל שחיתא וכדבין**, פי׳, הפה שדיבר שקר וכזב, הוא גיחזי שנשבע לנעמן, כמ׳ שנ׳ הואל וקח ככרים, שלא היה מאמינו בלא שבועה, שאין הואל אלא לש׳ אלה.[59] **חריטין**, כדכת׳ ויצר שני ככרים כסף בשני חריטים ושני [36]
חליפות בגדים וכו׳.[60] ופת׳ חריטים, סדינים כמ׳ והחריטים דישעי׳.[61] **צת רביה**, האזינו תרג׳ אציתו,[62] האזין אלישע רבו ברוח הקודש וקיללו בכאב הצרעת, דכת׳ וצרעת נעמן

49 יהושע ז ו, י.

50 וי״ר יא ז, עמ׳ רלז.

51 סנהדרין לז ע״א ועוד.

52 בראשית לד יד.

53 חולין יח ע״א.

54 בפנים ״ובמנאפים ובמכחשים״ ותוקן על הגליון; מלאכי ג ה.

55 סנהדרין מג ע״ב-מד ע״א, אבל ה׳ החרמים אינם נמנים שם. אולם, מנינם נמצא בירושלמי סנהדרין פ״ו ה״ג (כג ע״ב). הפסוק ביהושע ז׳ י״א שכתוב בו ה׳ פעמים גם נדרש בבבלי הנ״ל באופן אחר; וראה רבינו חננאל, סנהדרין מג ע״ב; וראה ב״ר פה יד, עמ׳ 1049 ובמ״י שם.

56 פרקי אבות פ״ד מ״ד.

57 סנהדרין מד ע״א.

58 יהושע ז יח.

59 ראה ערכין טז ע״א ומה שצויין שם על הגליון בשם השאילתות. ראה שאילתות, מצורע, שאילתא פח (מהד׳ מירסקי, שאילתא קד, עמ׳ קכג) ומה שכתב הנצי״ב שם, אות כח [וראה נדרים סה ע״א].

60 מלכים ב ה כג.

61 ישעיה ג כב [ומפני שבפסוק הבא בישעיה נזכרו הסדינים צריך לפרש שכוונת הפירוש היא סודרין; וראה פי׳ רש״י למלכים שם וס׳ השרשים לאבן ג׳אנח, ערך חרט].

62 דברים לב א, ות״א שם.

תדבק בו ובזרעו עד עולם, ונצטרע הוא ובניו על אותו החט׳.[63] **שחיתא**, כמ׳ וכל עילא ושחיתא לא השתכחת ביה.[64] ובמקצת סידורים כתוב **ולטייה כאובין**, ופירש ר׳ משה אחי זצ״ל[65] שהוא לשון בינה כמ׳ כשהבין, כלומר כשהסכית אלישע רבו ברוח הקוד׳ והבין מה שעשה גיחזי קיללו בצרעת, ובלש׳ משנה, אני אהיה אובין לפניך.[66] **קושטא אישתבע דמגורתהּ אפיא גבה**. פי׳, אמת נשבעה אותה האשה שלשה שכינתה אצלה כשנתגבלו המעות בתוך העיסה ואפת הפת בתנור ולא ידעה במעות עד אשר שיברה הלחם, ואעפ״כ נענשה לפי שנהנית עיסה כשיעור מקום המעות. והמעשה הזה מפורש בויקרא רבא פרש׳ ו׳ ובגיטין פרק השולח, עובדא הוה בחדא איתתא דעלת מילש גבי מגירתהּ והוו צייריו בשושיפה תלתא דינרין, יהבת יתהון על סודרא אתגבלון בלישה, אפת פיתא ואזלא לה, אמ׳ לה בעלה הב לי תלת דינרייא, אזלת בעיא להון גבי מגירתהּ, אמרה לה דילמא חמית לי הלין תלת דינריא, הוו לההיא מגירתהּ תלת בנין, אמרה ההיא איתתא תקבור ברה אין היא ידעת בהון, גרמין חובהא וקברתיה, אמרה אילולי דהיא חשידא לא הוות קברה ליה, אזלת ואמרה ליה דילמא חמית לי הלין דינרייא, אמרה תקבריה ההיא איתתא לאידך ברה אין היא ידעה בהון, גרמין חובהא וקברתה לברה אחרינא, זימנא אחרינא אמרה לה דילמא אשכחת הלין דינריא, אמרה תיקבריה ברא תליתאה אין היא ידעה בהון, גרמין חובהא וקברתה, אמ׳ לה בעלה לית אנת אזלא מנחמא להדא מגירתיך, נסיבת תרין עיגולין ואזלא מנחמא לה, כיון דקצון עיגולא נפלין הלין תלת דינרייא מיניה, הדא היא דברייתא אמרין בין זכיי בין חייב למומי לא תיעול.[67] **מגירתהּ**, שכינתה. ואל כל שכיניו, תרג׳ ולכל מגירוהי.[68] **למיטווא**, לש׳ אפייה. צלי אש, תרג׳ טוי נור.[69] **ריפי דאנטוכיא**, בויקרא רבא
[37] פרש׳ י״ט, אמרו כיון שעלה נבוכדנצר להחריב את ירושלים בא וישב לו בריפי שלאנטוכיא, ירדו סנהדרין לקראתו. אמרו לו הגיע זמנו של בית זה ליחרב, אמ׳ להן לאו, אלא יהויקים מלך יהודה מרד בי תנו אותו לי, נתנוהו כול׳, חזר וישב לו בריפי שלאנטוכיא, ירדו סנהדרין לקראתו. אמרו לו הגיע זמנו של בית זה ליחרב, אמ׳ להן לאו, אלא תנו לי יהויכין ואני הולך, נתנוהו לו[70] והמליך עליה׳ צדקיהו שהיה שמו מתניה והוא הסיב שמו וקראו צדקיהו, כמפורש בספר ירמיהו,[71] והשביעו שלא ימרוד בו. וחילל שבועתו, דכת׳ וגם במלך בבל מרד אשר השביעו באלהים וגו׳.[72] ונענש על כך שנשחטו בניו לפניו והוא נתעוור, כדכת׳ ואת עיני צדקיהו עיוור.[73] ומפורש בויקרא רבא פרש׳ ו׳,

63 סוטה מז ע״א. [ונראה שגרס בכאבין או כאבין.]

64 דניאל ו ה. הפירוש הזה שייך לאות פ׳.

65 ראה מבוא, עמ׳ 7.

66 ע״ז פ״ג מ״ח וראה אפשטיין, מבוא לנוסח המשנה, עמ׳ 89.

67 וי״ר ו ג, עמ׳ קלב-קלה וח״נ והערות שם; גטין לה ע״א.

68 דברים א ז, ות״א שם.

69 שמות יב ח, ובתרגומים שם.

70 וי״ר יט ו, עמ׳ תלב ואילך, עמ׳ תלו ואילך ובח״נ ובהערות שם.

71 זה אינו בירמיה אלא במלכים ב כד יז.

72 דברי הימים ב לו יג (בפסוק ״וגם במלך נבוכדנאצר״ וכו׳).

73 מלכים ב כה ז.

והבאתי עליכם חרב נקמת נקם ברית, נקם בברית ונקם שלא בברית, זה סימוי עיניים
שסימא עיני צדקיהו מלך יהודה, הה״ד אם לא באלתי אשר בזה ובריתי אשר הפר, אם לא
באלתי אשר בזה זו שבועה שנשבע לו, ובריתי אשר הפר זו בריתי שלסיני. ונתתיו בראשו,
ר׳ הונא ור׳ אחא בשם ר׳ יוחנן זה סימוי עינים שהוא תלוי בראשו.[74] פי׳ **ריפי** מחוז ולש׳
לע״ז הוא ריפא.[75] **קיריס**, אדון לש׳ יוון.[76] **אמטייה**, ל׳ הוליכו להמליכו. **כורסא**, כסא
מלכות. **טפש וסרח**, חטאו משקה תרג׳ סרחו.[77] **בנימוסה**, ובחקתיהם לא תלכו תרג׳
ובנימוסיהון לא תהכון.[78] **טבחון פרחוי**, לפי שהיו עיניו דומות לעיני אדם הראש׳ ולא היו
יודעין מהיכן יעוורוהו עד ששחטו בניו לפניו וראו מהיכן זלגו עיניו דמעות ועיורוהו.[79]
טפון ליה פנסא, כיבו לו המאורות, לא תכבה תרג׳ לא תטפי.[80] **פנס**, היא אבוקה. כלומ׳,
עיוורו עיניו והוא כיבוי נרותיו. **שרי ציבחר למימי במילין**, מותר הוא מעט לישבע בדברים,
ואימתי כשיגרום מזלו שלאדם בחמלת ה׳ עליו להיותו שקול כאחד מהצדיקים הקרואים
יראי ה׳, שנתנסו לבוראן ולא נמצא בהן דופי אפי׳ בשגגה. ומפורש בתנחומ׳ פרש׳ ויקרא,
את ה׳ אלהיך תירא וגו׳, שתהיה שקול כאותן שלשה שכת׳ בהן יראי ה׳, [ביוסף][80א] כת׳ [38]
בו את האלהים אני ירא, באברהם כת׳ בו כי עתה ידעתי כי ירא אלהים אתה, ובאיוב כת׳
ביה תם וישר וירא אלהים וסר מרע. ואותו תעבוד, שתהא עוסק בתורה ובמצוות. ובו
תדבק, שתכבד תלמידי חכמ׳ ותהנה אותם מנכסיך. ובשמו תשבע, אמ׳ להן משה לא תהיו
סבורים שמא התרתי לכם להישבע בשמו אפי׳ באמת אלא אם יש לכם כל המידות האילו
אחר כך אתה רשאי להישבע בשמו באמת כמ׳ דתימ׳ את ה׳ אלהיך תירא ואותו תעבד ובו
תדבק ואחר כך ובשמו תשבע.[81] **ציבחר**, תרג׳ מעט מזער.[82] **לותיה**, מזלו כמפורש בבא
מציעא פרק המקבל, דאמ׳ ליה משום לתך הוא.[83] ור׳ דניאל נ״ע פירש בשם הר׳ בנימן בן
הר׳ משה זצ״ל,[84] אם גרם המזל שלאדם מרוב חמתו וכעסו להיכשל באילו העבירות
הגדולות והנוראות שנאנסו[85] עושיהן ולא נידונו כשוגגין אלא כמזידין. עוד פירש משמו

74 וי״ר ו ח, עמ׳ קמ-קמא וח״נ והערות שם.

75 ripa באיטלקית.

76 ראה לעיל א, הערה 49.

77 בראשית מ א, ותרגומים שם.

78 ויקרא יח ג, ותרגומים שם.

79 תנחומא בובר, ואתחנן, פיסקא א, עמ׳ 8; ילקוט שמעוני, סוף מלכים ב; וראה אגדות היהודים, ו, עמ׳ 383 הערה 7.

80 ויקרא ו ה, ותרגומים שם.

80א בכ״י בטעות: ״באברהם״.

81 תנחומא הישן, ויקרא, פיסקא ז, בשינויים.

82 ישעיה י כה, ובת״י שם ועוד.

83 ב״מ קו ע״א. וראה בד״ס שם, עמ׳ 310, אות ט; וראה טל, עמ׳ 58, הערה 2.

84 ראה מבוא, עמ׳ 7.

85 [ברור שהוא מפרש ״שרי״ התחיל. כלומר, התחיל להשבע מעט... מי שגרם לו מזלו שבשעת חמתו נתקל באחת מן העברות הנוראות שהן מנוסות שעושיהן אינם יוצאים ריקם (= ״לבר״) מן העונש. והענין חוזר למעשי האשה וצדקיה, שהובאו לעיל, שהם נשבעו בשעת חמתם (השווה הלשון חגיגה י ע״א) והרי שבועתם כשבועת אונסין ומכל מקום נענשו (וראה נדרים כח ע״א ושבועות כו ע״א תוספות ד״ה את.]

דאיתנסו לבר לברייהון, דבר זה מנוסה לעושיהם שלא יצאו ריקם אלא יענשו. **בחמלין**, פירש שתי מילות, בחם לין, כלומ׳ בחמתן וכעסן, כמ׳ בשלם הבשר,[86] בישל להם. **תדיר יאי לקיומי אסר וקיימי**, ואע״פ שאנו אומ׳ שאסור לישבע אפי׳ על האמת מותר לאדם להישבע יום יום ללמוד תורה ולקיים את המצות, כדכת׳ נשבעתי ואקיימה לשמור משפטי צדקך,[87] ואז בעשותך זאת הקב״ה יהיה בעזרך. **ובשופריה לך יתחמי**, על שם מלך ביופייו תחזינה עיניך,[88] ונתן לך רחמים ורחמך והרבך.[89]

ז זכור

מתרג׳ אותו באונקלוס ובירושלמ׳.[1]

אלפא ביט

ארעא ורקיעא ודי בהון ושבימי,[2] פי׳ ארץ ושמים וכל אשר בהם הכל יסדה ידי בששה ימים, כמ׳ דתימ׳ אף ידי יסדה ארץ וגו׳.[3] **שכללה**, יסדה, כמ׳ ושורייא שכלילו ואושייא יחיטו דעזרא.[4] **בעשרה פתגמי**, בעשרה מאמרות, הן ט׳ ויאמר ויאמר, הכתובים עד ויכלו השמים, ובראשית חשוב מאמר שנ׳ בדבר ה׳ שמים נעשו. ולמה אין כת׳ בו מאמר, לפי שבו נברא שמים וארץ. ועל כן מאמר זה סתום. שאין רשות לשואל לשאל מה היה קודם בריאת העולם. כלומ׳, בכל הכתוב בו ויאמר יש לך רשות לישא וליתן ולדרוש, אבל בבריית שמים וארץ אין כתוב ויאמר, שאסור לדרוש בהן.[5] פ״א, **בעשרה פתגמי**, בי׳ מידות שבהן נברא העולם ואילו הן, בחכמה ובתבונה דכת׳ ה׳ בחכמה יסד ארץ כונן שמים בתבונה, בדעת שנ׳ בדעתו תהומות נבקעו, בחסד ואמת צדק ושלום שנ׳ חסד ואמת נפגשו צדק ושלום נשקו, בגערה דכת׳ ויתמהו מגערתו, בגבורה דכת׳ נאזר בגבורה, רחמים דכת׳ זכור רחמיך ה׳ וחסדיך כי מעולם המה, בחגיגה פרק אין דורשין.[6] **גמירא דכולא שבתא**,

86 מלכים א יט כא. לין = להם.
87 תהלים קיט קו; ונדרש בחגיגה י ע״א על הנשבעין לקיים את המצוה.
88 ישעיה לג יז.
89 דברים יג יח. וראה את הטור האחרון של הפיוט: ״ויפשינך ויסגינך ויתן לך רחמי״.

1 ראה לעיל א׳, הערה 4.
2 דוידזון, א, 7708 (שם: ״ארקא ורקיע״); מפורש במחזור ויטרי, עמ׳ 328 ואילך.
3 ישעיה מח יג.
4 עזרא ד יב.
5 אבות פ״ה מ״א; ר״ה לב ע״א ועוד. כוונת המפרש שבכל מקום שכתוב במעשה בראשית מלת ״ויאמר״ מותר לדרוש במעשה אותו היום אבל אין דורשין בבריית שמים וארץ כי אין כתוב בה ״ויאמר״. לא מצאתי כפירושו זה של רבינו והעניין נדרש מפסוקים אחרים במקורות, ראה חגיגה יא ע״ב וראה תוספתא כפשוטה, חגיגה, עמ׳ 1295-1296, ד״ה יכול קודם למעשה בראשית [ונראה שכוונתו לב״ר א י, עמ׳ 8: ״מה ב׳ זה סתום מצדדיו״ וכו׳. והשווה גם זוהר בראשית טז ע״ב).
6 חגיגה יב ע״א, בשינויים.

תכלית כל מלאכתי, חפצתי בשבת ורציתי בו. כמ׳ שנ׳, ימים יוצרו ולא אחד בהם,[7] זה פירש ר׳ דניאל בשם הר׳ בנימן נ״ע.[8] פ״א, **גמירא דכולא שבתא**, מצאתי אגדה, ויכל אלהים ביום השביעי, אתה מוצא כשברא הק׳ את עולמו היה בורא בכל יום שלש בריות, בערב שבת היה כל היום עסוק במלאכת האדם, שעה א׳ עלה במחשבה, ב׳ נמלך במלאכי [40]
השרת, ג׳ כינס עפרו, ד׳ גיבלו, ה׳ ריקמו וציירו, ו׳ העמידו על רגליו, ז׳ נפח בו נשמה, ה׳ הכניסו לגן עדן, ט׳ ציוה אותו, י׳ חטא, י״א ישב עליו בדין, י״ב בא ליתן אפופסין, נכנסה שבת והגינה בעדו ונטל דימוס, התחיל אדם מקלס מזמור שיר ליום השבת, אמר לו אני ואתה נקלס להק׳ שכך נתן בי כח, טוב להודות לה׳, עד שלא נכנסה שבת היה הק׳ כביכול יושב ומצטער בעולמו, כל מה שבראתי בעד אדם ועכשיו הוא אפופסין והוא ביטל כל המלאכה שעשיתי והוא חוזר[8א] העולם לתהו ובהו שאין עוד אדם בעולם וכן ירמיה אמ׳ ראיתי את הארץ והנה תהו וגו׳, אמ׳ הק׳ הרי לכל מה שבראתי אבידין, מה הועלתי כותב מלאכת יום אחד, יום שני, יום שלישי, רביעי, חמישי, ששי, איכן הוא מעשה מלאכתי, עכשיו נוטל אדם אפופסין וכל מלאכתי בטילה, עד שהמקום מיצר על עולמו נכנסה שבת ונטל דימוס, אמ׳ הק׳ כל מלאכה שעשיתי השבת כילה לכך נאמ׳ ויכל אלהים ביום השביעי,[9] וזהו פת׳ **גמירא דכולא שבתא**, פ״א. **גמירא דכולא**, עיקר תשלום כל יצירת בראשית מה היה, שבת. בראשית רבה פרש׳ י׳, משל למלך שעשה לו חופה, ציירה, סיידה וכיירה, מה היתה חסירה, כלה שתיכנס לחופה, כך מה היה העולם חסר, שבת.[10] לפי שהיה הק׳ בורא עולמות ומחריבן[11] והיו כל יצירות בראשית תוהין ובוהין תאמר שמא יחזירנו לתהו ובהו, לאחר שבא שבת נתבסס העולם, שנ׳ ויכלו השמים והארץ וג׳ ותרג׳ ואשתכללו שמיא וארעא.[12] אימתי נגמר שכלולו, ויכל אלהים ביום השביעי.[13] **גזירת אורייתי לאלפא לרחומיי**, שבשבת ניתנה התורה ליש׳,[14] שהן אהובים למקום כמ׳ דתימ׳ אהבתי אתכם וג׳.[15] **לשעורי גרמידי דתחומיי**, אמות התחום שהן אלפיים אמה. גומד ארכה תרג׳ גרמידא.[16] **דליקלעון בנייח שדכא**, שיכנסו למנוחת שקט מקבלי תורתי. כלומ׳, לכך נתתי להם התורה בשבת שיזכו בה מקיימיה לעולם שכולו שבת.[17] **דליקלעון**, כמ׳ דמיקלע [41]

7 תהלים קלט טז. ונדרש לעניין זה בפס״ר, כג, קטו ע״א, וראה בהערות רמא״ש שם.

8 ראה מבוא, עמ׳ 7.

8א והוא חוזר, כלומר עושה שהעולם חוזר.

9 פס״ר, מו, קפז ע״ב-קפח ע״ב; פסדר״כ, כג, עמ׳ 334 ומקבילות. הנוסח שלפנינו כנראה שלם ואחיד הוא, ראה בהערות רמא״ש לפס״ר הנ״ל, אות לו, לז. ראה לאחרונה בלוח הנוסחאות של אגדה זו בספרו האנגלי של A. J. Saldarini על אדר״נ נו״ב, 1975, עמ׳ 303-305.

10 ב״ר י ט, עמ׳ 85.

11 ב״ר ג ז, עמ׳ 23.

12 בראשית ב א, ות״א שם.

13 פס״ר, מו, קפח ע״א (סוף הדרשה המובאת בהערה 9 לעיל).

14 שבת פו ע״ב.

15 ספרי דברים, פיסקא כד, עמ׳ 34; שמות רבה א א ועוד.

16 שופטים ג טז, ות״י שם.

17 לא מצאתי מקור לזה.

ליה ענייא,[18] זיל לקילעך.[19] **שדכא**, לש׳ שקט, ותשקט הארץ תרג׳ ושדוכת.[20] **צייתי פתגמיי**, תרג׳ האזינו אציתו.[21] **הייא ואשור מזרזא**, רבינו שלמה זצ״ל פירש בפרק כל כתבי הקודש אשור הייא, התחזקו והתאשרו באומנותכם למהר ולטרוח בצרכי שבת.[22] ולשון רבותיי אשוור הייא, והוא לש׳ קפיצה ודילוג, שהיה ממהר בהליכתו, הייא לש׳ מהירות, כלומ׳ שצריך אדם להקדיש ולמהר בצרכי שבת.[23] **תפנוק**, תענוגים, הרכה בך והענוגה תרג׳ דמפנקא.[24] **הלייסטון**, מפורש בערוך, יין הנעשה בשמש שהוא מתוק, שיש בלש׳ יוון איליאוס.[25] **בארג**, יין מבושל ועומד על שלישו והוא לש׳ פרסי, בערוך.[26] ויש מפרשין יין ממותק בעשבים טובים.[27] **כוורי**, דגים. **לפדא**, בערוך, תבשיל שלתאנים.[28] **אינומילי**, יין ודבש ופלפלין,[29] דבש לש׳ לע״ז מילי.[30] **ולתלותיה שירותיה**, ולהשליש סעודתו, פי׳ על שם שלש סעודות. **ולמבצע המוציא**, על שתי ככרות משום לחם משנה. **ובגלימא ובכסו ליקוריה**, ובטליתות ובגדים נאים לכבדו. **מעידן מיעליה**, מעת כניסתו, כמ׳ ועד מיעלי שמשא דדניאל,[31] כמעשה דר׳ יהודה ביר׳ אילעאי שהיה רוחץ בערב שבת פניו ידיו ורגליו בחמין ומתעטף בסדין המצוייץ ודומה למלאך ה׳ צבאות,[32] וכדאמ׳ פרק כל כתבי הקודש, ר׳ חנינא מיעטף וקאי אפנייא דמעלי שבתא.[33] **זוודתיה מדאנהר**, פי׳ מזונותיו, צדה לדרך תרג׳ זוודין.[34] **מדאנהר**, מבעוד יום לבשל ולהטמין ולאופות.[34א] ור׳ יהודה אחי שני זצוק״ל[34ב] פירש, שצריך להשכים ערב שבת בשחרית. כדאמ׳ ר׳ חסדא לעולם ישכים אדם
להוצאת שבת שנ׳ ויהי ביום השישי והכינו לאלתר.[35] **זיפתא ופסיל פתילתא**, זפת ושאר [42]
פסולי פתילות ושמנים שאינן צפין להימשך אחר פתילה שלא להדליק בהן,[36] ויצף הברזל תרג׳ וקפא ברזלא.[37] פ״א. **דלא לאקפויי**, אפתילת׳ קאי, כלומ׳ כשאינו להקפות את

18 ביצה כא ע״א.

19 נדרים כב ע״ב.

20 שופטים ג יא, ות״י שם ועוד.

21 דברים לב א, ות״א שם.

22 שבת קיט ע״א, ורש״י שם ד״ה ומשלים להו.

23 ראה ערוך, ערך שוור [וראה עוד מה שכתב קאהוט בערך אשר ג׳].

24 דברים כח נו, ות״א שם.

25 עה״ש, ערך אלייסטון.

26 עה״ש, ערך בארג.

27 עה״ש, בערך הנ״ל.

28 עה״ש, ערך לפדא.

29 שבת קמ ע״א.

30 miele באיטלקית ומלת ״לע״ז״ נמחקה.

31 דניאל ו טו. נראה שלפניו היה החרוז בסדר הפוך.

32 שבת כה ע״ב.

33 שם קיט ע״א.

34 בראשית מב כה, ובתרגומים שם.

34א כך הוא בכ״י.

34ב ראה מבוא, עמ׳ 7.

35 שבת קיז ע״ב.

36 שבת כ ע״ב.

37 מלכים ב ו ו, ובת״י שם; ומובא גם ברש״י שבת כא ע״א, ד״ה לא להקפות.

הפתילה אז הוא אסור, ופי' להקפות לעבות.[38] **חומריה לפלפולי**, חומר דיקדוקי איסוריו שלשבת לדקדק כראוי ושלא להטמין ברמץ גזירה שמא יחתה בגחלים,[39] וצריך להוסיף מחול על קודש כדילפינן מתשבתו שבתכם.[40] **טובא חדויי**, להרבות שמחה. ומצינו לש'[בת] שמחה, דכת' וביום שמחתכם ואמ' מר זה שבת.[41] **טירדא וטירחא למבטל**, **טעים רישוותיה**, טעם רשויותיו לדעת שהן שמונה. ר' דניאל נ"ע[42] פירש על שם שתים שהן ארבע בפנים ושתים שהן ארבע בחוץ.[43] ולי נראה לפרש על מה ששנינו בראש תוספת שבת, ד' רשוייות לשבת, רשות היחיד ורשות הרבים, כרמלית ומקום פטור, הרי ארבע,[44] ובסופה דההיא תני, אבל ים ובקעה וכרמלית דהיינו קרן זוית ואצטוונית אינן לא כרשות הרבי' ולא כרשות היחיד,[45] הרי ד' רשוייות אחרות, נמצאו כולם ח'. **יזופתא למיזף**, ואם אין לאדם מה להוציא יקח בהלוואה כדי להרבות בתפנוקי שבת לפי שאני מוכן לפרוע יותר ויותר כדאיתה בביצה, בניי לוו עלי ואני פורע.[46] **אסקריטי**, תרג' צפחית בדבש.[47] **ריחני**, תבשילין מבושמים. **טופנא**, לש' ריבוי מלש' טפי. כדאיתא במסכת ביצה, כל מזונותיו שלאדם קצובין לו מראש השנה עד ראש השנה חוץ מהוצאת שבתות וימים טובים שאם הוסיף מוסיפין לו ואם פיחת פוחתין לו,[48] ובבראשית רבא, ויברך אלהים את יום השביעי, בירכו בהוצאה, ר' לוי בש' ר' חמא ביר' חנינא אמ' כל יום שיש בו חסרון כתוב בו ברכה ואינו חסר כלום, בחמישי נבראו עופות ודגים ובני אדם שוחטין עופות [43] ואוכלי' ואינן חסירין כלום, בשישי נברא אדם ובני אדם מתין וכת' בו ברכה ואינן חסירין כלום, בשביעי מה אית לך למימר, [ר' חמא ביר' חנינא אמ' מפני ההוצאה, ר' אלעזר בשם ר' יוסי בן זימרא][49] ר' לוי בשם ר' יוסף בן זימרא אמ' מפני האיסטניסים,[50] וסימן זה יהא בידך תחילת המסכתא יציאות השבת שתים שהן ארבע, כלומ' הוצאות שבת נכפלין שתים לארבע שכן מצינו עומרה כפול שני, שני העומר לאחד.[51] **כלדאי בדקו על יוסף מוקרי שבי**, פי' **כלדאי**, חוזי בכוכבים, כמ' מניין שאין שואלים בכלדיים שנ' תמים תהיה.[52] ומעשה דיוסף מוקיר שבי מפורש פרק כל כתבי הקודש, יוסף מוקיר שבי הוה ההוא גוי

38 שבת שם, וראה בר"ח ובערא"ש שם.

39 שם לד ע"ב.

40 ר"ה ט ע"א.

41 [אע"פ שכרגיל הקיצור "לש'" מובנו "לשון" נראה שכאן פתרונו "לשבת", כלומר, לשון שמחה נופלת גם על שבת ולא רק על חגים.] ראה ספרי דברים, פיסקא עז, עמ' 71.

42 ראה מבוא, עמ' 7.

43 שבת פ"א מ"א.

44 תוספתא שבת פ"א ה"א ובש"נ שם.

45 שם ה"ד. [הוא חושב קרן זוית ואצטוונית לשתים, היינו כתירוץ הגמרא בשבת ז ע"א. ופלא שהביאו מן התוספתא. וראה תוספתא כפשוטה, עמ' 4 ד"ה והאסקופה.]

46 ביצה טו ע"ב.

47 שמות טז לא, ות"א שם.

48 ביצה טז ע"א, ובד"ס שם, עמ' 34.

49 המלים שבתוך הסוגריים נכתבו בין השורות.

50 ב"ר יא ג-ד, עמ' 90 ובח"נ ובמ"י שם.

51 מכילתא, ויסע ב, עמ' 162; שם ד, עמ' 168, אבל נתינת הסימן כנראה חידושו של המפרש הוא.

52 פסחים קיג ע"ב.

בשיבבותיה דהוו נפישי נכסיה טובא, אמ׳ ליה כלדאי יוסף מוקיר שבי אכיל להו לנכסיה
דההוא גברא, אזל זבן בהו מרגינתא אותבינהו בסדיניה, אתא זיקא אפרחיה לסדיניה במיא
ואתא כוורא ובלעיה, אסקוה לההוא גברא כוורא אפנייא דמעלי שבתא, אמרו מאן זבין כי
השתא, יוסף מוקיר שבא, אמטייוה ניהליה זבנוה ואשכח בהו מרגניתא זבנינהו בתליסר
אלפי עיליתא דדינרי.[53] ופי׳ **כייל ואכיל**,[53א] מכלה ואוכל, ור׳ דניאל פירש בשם הר׳ בנימן
נ״ע,[54] מודד ואוכל, כלומ׳ מקבץ ואוכל. **לודיקי דמברר**, אדם אחד מלדוקייא שהיה מברר
מנה טובה לשבת אשריו שזיכהו הקב״ה לעושר גדול שהיה אוכל על שולחנות וקערות
שלזהב וכסף.[55] אשריו תרג׳ **טוביה**.[56] שולחן תרג׳ **פתורא**.[57] **צעי**, פי׳ קערות. ומעשה
הלודיקי מפורש בפרק כל כתבי הקודש, אמ׳ ר׳ חייא בר אבא פעם אחת נתארחתי אצל
בעל הבית בלדוקייא והביאו לפניו שולחן שלזהב משאוי י״ו בני אדם וי״ו שלשלאות כסף
קבועות בו וקערות וכוסות וקיתונות וצלוחיות שלכסף קבועות בו ועליו כל מיני מאכל וכל
מיני מגדים, כשהן מניחין אותו אומ׳ לה׳ הארץ ומלואה וכשהן מסלקין אותו אומ׳ השמים
שמים לה׳ והארץ נתן לבני אדם, אמרתי לו בני, מפני מה זכית לכך, אמ׳ לי ר׳, קצב הייתי
וכל בהמה נאה שבאה לידי אמרתי זה לכבוד שבת, אמרתי לו ברוך המקום שזיכך לכך.[55]
ממלל אסיר ורעיוני שרי, פי׳ דיבור אסור שאסור לאדם לדבר מענייני חפציו בשבת אבל
הירהור דדיבור מותר דכת׳ ודבר דבר, דיבור אסור הרהור מותר.[58] **נשי וגברי**, הנשים [44]
והאנשים חייב׳ בשמירתו, כמ׳ דתימ׳ אתה ובנך ובתך.[59] **סכום דאתי איתסר**, חשבונות
שלהבא שצריכין אסור לחשבן בשבת והטעם מפורש פרק שואל, גזירה שמא יכתוב,
ושעברו מותר אך שלא יהיה צורך בהן.[60] **ענייני מצוה**, חשבונות שלמצוה כגון תקופות
ומולדות ושאר חשבונות שלמצוה מותרין.[61] **פנסא דטפי כול׳**, נר שהדליקו בה באותה
שבת אע״פ שכבתה אסור לטלטלה, שהרי היא מוקצה מחמת איסור, כל שכן שאסור

53 שבת קיט ע״א, וראה בד״ס שם, עמ׳ 267.

53א ונראה שגרס כך במקום אכלינהו.

54 ראה מבוא, עמ׳ 7.

55 שבת קיט ע״א, וראה בד״ס שם, עמ׳ 267-268.

56 משלי יד כא, ועוד; ובת״י שם ״טובוהי״, וגירסתו שונה משלנו בפיוט.

57 שמות כה כג, ותרגומים שם ועוד.

58 שבת קיג ע״א-ע״ב. על הרהור כדיבור ראה פסקי רי״ד, מהד׳ וורטהיימר וליס, עמ׳ תקלה.

59 שמות כ י.

60 שבת קנ ע״א-ע״ב. אולם הטעם אינו מפורש שם והוא ניתן ברמב״ם, הלכות שבת פכ״ג הי״ח; וראה מה שכתב על עניין זה רמ״מ כשר, תורה שלימה, לבראשית ל״ט י״א, עמ׳ 1501. [ודברי המתורגמן מופלאים שהרי אין הבדל בין להבא ולשעבר. ודברי המפרש רחוקים מאד שהרי אם גרס בפיוט ״לגמרי״ ודאי שאין פירושו מתקבל. אבל אפילו אם לא גרס מה מועיל ״אך שלא יהא צורך בהן״ שהרי גם להבא לא אסור אלא אם יש לו צורך בהם. ראה רמב״ם שם ותוספתא שבת פי״ז (י״ח) ה״ט. וקרוב שגרס בברייתא חשבונות שעברו [מותר] ושעתידין להיות אסור. ופירש את קושיית ורמינהי על הסיפא ״ושעתידין להיות אסורין״ והרי בברייתא השניה חלקו בין צריכין לשאין צריכין. ועל זה משיב ״ולטעמיך״, שאתה סובר לעתיד אסורין מכל מקום תיקשי לך היא גופא, למה חשבונות של מה בכך אסורין בכל אופן.]

61 שם קנ ע״א [ומקור למה שאומר על חשבון התקופות והמולדות ראה שבת עה ע״א].

לטלטלה כשהיא דולקת, גזירה שמא יכבה.[62] **צפרא ופנייא**, בוקר וערב ראוי לקדשו על הכוס כדאמ' פרק ערב פסחים,[62א] זכור, זכריהו על היין בכניסתו. אין לי אלא בערב, פי', לפי שעתה צריך זכירה שעדיין אין אנו עסוקין בשבת כלל, ביום מניין, ת"ל את יום.[63] **צפרא**, בקר. **פנייא**, ערב. **קשיש ציבי**, המקושש עצים שחיללו העלה עליו אף וחימה וסקלוהו.[64] **אחליה**, חילל אותו, ור' דניאל נ"ע[65] פירש **אח ליה**, שתי מלות, כמ' כל הזוכרו אומר אח לראשו דמגילה,[66] ופת' אוי לו. **ציבי**, פי' עצים. **שבייא דילי כו'**, על שם למען ינוח שורך וחמורך וינפש בן אמתך והגר.[67] **עיירים** עשרה תרג' **עילי** עשרא.[68]

ח כבד את אביך [45]

מתרג' אותו בתרג' אונקלוס ובתרג' ירושלמי.[1]
עמי בני ישראל כול'.[1א]

אלפא ביט

אמר יצחק לאברהם אבוהי מה נאה מדבחא די בניית לי אבא,[2] פי', יצחק לא עמד לבנות את המזבח עם אביו שכן הוא אומר, ויבן שם אברהם את המזבח.[2א] ומצאנו אגדה, ויצחק היכן היה, מלמד שנטלו אביו והצניעו שלא יזרוק בו סמאל אבן ויפסל מן הקרבן.[3] **בפריע פשוט ידך כו'**, **בפריע**, פי' מהרה. **עד דאנא מצלי**, וכי מה תפילה התפלל על המזבח והיכן מצינו שהתפלל, אלא כשעקד אברהם אבינו את יצחק בנו על גבי המזבח התפלל יצחק ואמ', רבונו של עולם גלוי וידוע לפניך שאם אני רוצה, שאין אבי יכול לשוחטי. אלא כשם שאני כובש

62 שם מד ע"א, קנז ע"א.
62א ראה ד"ס פסחים, עמ' 306, אות א, וראה לעיל ה', הערה 43.
63 פסחים קו ע"א.
64 במדבר טו לב-לו.
65 ראה מבוא, עמ' 7.
66 מגלה יא ע"א וראה גם להלן ט', הערה 14.
67 שמות כג יב.
68 בראשית לב טז, ות"א שם (בנדפס "ועירי" אבל במהדורת ברלינר "ועילי").

1 ראה לעיל א', הערה 4.
1א ראה לעיל ו', הערה 2.
2 דוידזון, א, 5812; ראה היינימן, שרידים, עמ' 366-367 (המקור הארמי בצירוף תרגום עברי); טל, עמ' 80-85 (הנוסח הארמי, תרגום עברי ופירוש); ומפורש גם במחזור ויטרי, עמ' 330-331.
2א בראשית כב ט.
3 ב"ר נו ה, עמ' 600 (שם, במקום "סמאל", "ההוא דייגער ביה והוא סמאל", ראה שם עמ' 598-599); ראה שפיגל, מאגדות העקדה, ס' היובל לכבוד אלכסנדר מארכס, עמ' תקכב.

את יצרי להישחט לפניך כן יכבשו רחמיך את כעסך ואהיה מקובל לפניך כרצון ונדבה.[4] **גלי**
אדרעך, פי׳ זרועך. **ואסור חרצך**, קשור מתניך. **היך גבר דעביד שירותא דברייה**, פי׳, כמי
שרוצה לעשות עבודת בוראו. **שירותא**, פי׳, לש׳ שירות כמ׳ משרת משה.[5] פ״א. **היך גבר**
דעביד שירותא דברייה, כמי שעושה סעודת חופת[6] בנו. **שירותא**, פי׳ סעודה, וזה הלשון
עיקר. **דין הוא יומא כול׳**, **היך תיזיל ותימור לשרה אמי כו׳**, **ונשיק יצחק כו׳**, **זרוק דמי על גבי**
מדבחא וכנוש קטמי, פי׳, אסוף אפרי והולך אותו לשרה אמי. באגדה, ר׳ יוסי אומ׳ אמ׳ יצחק
לאביו, אבא, קשור ידיי ורגליי שלא אבעוט בך ונמצאתי מחלל מצות כבד ונמצאתי
[46] מתחייב שתי מיתות לשמים, אבא, מהר עשה רצון יוצרך וגלול בגדיך וחגור מתניך זרוק
דמי ושרוף חלבי ואיבריי וקח אפר שלי והוליכהו לאמי ותניחהו באוצרה שכל זמן שתראני
תאמר זהו בני, ועכשיו תשחטני ותיבדל ממני, איך תאמר לשרה ומה תעשו עלי לזקנתכם,
אמ׳ לו, בני, יודע אני שמיתתנו קרובה, מי שניחמני עד כאן הוא ינחמנו עד יום מיתה.[7] **חיי**
ומותי כולא בידיה כול׳, **ולא תסאיבני**, פי׳ לש׳ טומאה. כלומ׳, אל תפגל קרבנך שלא
תחשוב בי מחשבה אחרת הפוסלת ומפגלת את השחיטה, ומצינו שהפיגול נקרא טמא
כדתנן הפיגול והנותר מטמאין את הידים.[8] פ״א. היזהר שלא תטיל בי מום ואיפסל לקרבן,
כמ׳ דתימ׳ ירעה עד שיסתאב,[9] ופירש רבינו גרשום זצ״ל עד שיפול בו מום,[10] כדכ׳ בפרש׳
ערכין ואם בבהמה הטמא׳ ופירשו חכמ׳ ז״ל בבעל מום הכת׳ מדבר.[11] ולש׳ האגדה
בתנחומא, ויעקד את יצחק, כשבא לשחוט אמ׳ לו, אבא, אוסריני שהנפש חצופה היא שלא
נראה[11א] את המאכלת ואזדעזע ויפסל הקרבן. בבקשה ממך אל תעש בי מום, מיד וישלח
אברהם את ידו.[12] **לא תהוי בכי דלא אעכבך אבא כו׳**, **טובי**, אשריי. **קיריס**, אדון בלשון יוון.[13]
קוזמוס, עולם בלשון יוון.[14] **ניחא רוחא דאמי שרה**, נחת רוח הוא לשרה אמינו מה שיצאנו
שנינו אנחנו בלב שלם.[15] **סכינך אבא כול׳**, **ואמושיניה**, פי׳ ואבדוק אותו משום פגם.[16] ולפי
שהיה שמח במצוות הבורא היה אומ׳ כן דרך שמחה, והוא מלש׳ אולי ימושיני אבי.[17] **עיניי**

4 ראה מחזור ויטרי, עמ׳ 330: ״ומה היה [יצחק] מתפלל: רבונו של עולם יהי רצון מלפניך שיחשב חלבי ודמי וכו׳ כך אמר לי ר׳ שמצא אגדה זו, ע״כ״; ראה שפיגל, שם, עמ׳ תקמו, הערה לשורות 91-90, ומה שכותב שם שבכל המקורות הישנים מתפלל אברהם בלבדו אבל בבראשית רבתי, עמ׳ 91, נמצא שגם יצחק התפלל; אולם לא מצאתי מקביל ללשון התפלה כמו שהיא לפנינו.

5 במדבר יא כח.

6 בכ״י: ״חופתו״; ולעצם העניין השווה שפיגל, שם, עמ׳ תקלו.

7 בראשית רבתי, עמ׳ 90 ומקבילות; ראה שפיגל, שם, עמ׳ תקמב, הערה לשורה 41.

8 פסחים פ״י מ״ט.

9 שם פ״ט מ״ו ועוד.

10 ראה בפירושו למנחות קח ע״א.

11 מנחות קא ע״א.

11א כך הוא בכ״י.

12 תנחומא הישן, וירא, פיסקא כג. וראה גם לעיל, הערה 7.

13 ראה לעיל א, הערה 49.

14 ראה הערתו של טל, עמ׳ 84.

15 ת״י לבראשית כ״ב ח׳: ״ואזלו תרויהום בלב שלים כחדא״ (מובא ע״י טל, עמ׳ 84).

16 תנחומא הישן, צו, פיסקא יג: ״שנתעכב אברהם לבדוק הסכין״ וכו׳.

17 בראשית כז יב.

חמון קיסין מסודרין, פי׳, ענייי ראו עצי המערכה והאש דולקת עליהם ביום קרבני,[18] **עצי העולה** תרג׳ ירוש׳ קיסין.[19] **פתח פומך ובריך אבא כו׳**, לפי שהיה לו לברך ברכת הזבח קודם שחיטה שכל המצוות כולן מברך עליהן קודם עשייתן.[20] **צוארי פשוט לך אבא, קמו מלאכייא ומפייסין למריהון**, מצאתי במדרש אגדה, אמ׳ ר׳ ישמעאל באותה שעה נכנסו מלאכי שרת [47]
והיו מציצין באברהם שהיה זקן ויצחק שהוא נער והיה כפות כרחל לשחיטה והיו מתאנחים ובוכים כנגדן שנ׳ הן אראלם צעקו חוצה וגו׳, חוצה היא בידיה למיכוס ית בריה. נשמו מסילות, אין אברהם מקבל את העוברים ואת השבים. שבת עובר אורח, כמ׳ דתימ׳ חדל להיות לשרה אורח כנשים. הפר ברית, ואת בריתי אקים את יצחק. מאס עדים, וישב בין קדש ובין שור, לא חשב אנוש, לא עמדה זכות לאברהם. ומניין שמלאכי שרת היו שם, נאמ׳ כאן ממעל לעצים ונאמ׳ להלן שרפים עומדים ממעל לו, אמ׳ להם הקב״ה כל מה שעשיתי ושבראתי לא עשיתי ולא בראתי אלא בשביל אברהם, ואם אני מאבדו צבאות שמים וארץ על מי הם עומדים, שנ׳ אם לא בריתי יומם ולילה וג׳, ואין בריתי אלא יצחק שנ׳ ואת בריתי אקים את יצחק. וכיון שראו מלאכי השרת שכך השיבם הק׳, מיד נתנו הודאה למקום שנ׳ ה׳ אדונינו מה אדיר שמך בכל הארץ.[21] **רחמוי דאבוי אנן משאבין**, פי׳ המלאכים היו אומ׳ אנן מתמלאין רחמים על אביו, שהוא גומל חסד, וכבר גמל עמנו חסד בעת מילתו,[22] ולמה הזכיר **מלח**, לפי שהמלח סימן טוב לכל גומלי חסדים כדאמ׳ מלח ממון חסד[23] וכל ברית שאין לה קצבה קרוייה ברית מלח, כמ׳ דתימ׳ ברית מלח עולם היא.[24] וגם על הקרבנות כת׳ לא תשבית מלח.[25] וגם כי באותו הזמן אותן המלאכים עצמן הלכו להציל את לוט, ופשעה בהן אשתו שללוט שלא האכילן מלח ועל כן נעשית נציב מלח.[26] **שדי אמר ליה לא תדחל טלייא**, זה מוסב על מה שאמרנו למעלה **עד דאנא מצלי קדם ריבוני**, והשיבו לו מן השמים אל תירא, שאני הוא שאפדה אותך ואתן פדיונך איל, כדכת׳ וירא והנה איל וגו׳.[27] **תקיף הוא אלהא.**

18 פדר״א, פל״א; ראה שפיגל, עמ׳ תפז.

19 בראשית כב ג, ות״י שם.

20 פסחים ז ע״ב ועוד; על ברכת שחיטה באגדות העקדה ראה שפיגל, עמ׳ תפ-תפא.

21 לא מצאתי את האגדה הזאת כצורתה כאן אבל יש לה מקבילות בב״ר נו ה, עמ׳ 600-601, ובתנחומא הישן, תולדות, פיסקא ב ועוד; על שמלאכי השרת נתנו הודאה ואמרו ״ה׳ אדונינו״ וכו׳ (תהלים ח י), ובכלל על מזמור ח׳ שנדרש לעניין יצחק, ראה שפיגל, עמ׳ תקכו, הערה 138.

22 ראה מה שנאמר באגדה המובאת לעיל: ״נשמו מסלות, אין אברהם מקבל את העוברים ואת השבים״.

23 כתובות סו ע״ב.

24 במדבר יח יט.

25 ויקרא ב יג.

26 ב״ר נא ה, עמ׳ 536 ובמ״י שם.

27 בראשית כב יג.

[48] ט לא תרצח

מתרג׳ אותו בתרג׳ אונקלוס ובירושלמי.[1]

עמי בני ישראל כו׳, ארום בחובי קטולייא חרבא נפיק על עלמא,[2] פי׳, בעון שפיכות דמים חרב בא לעולם כדתנן באבות, חרב בא לעולם על עובדי ע״ז ועל גילוי עריות ועל שפיכות דמים.[3] והיא מידה כנגד מידה, כמ׳ דתימ׳ שופך דם האדם באדם דמו ישפך,[4] ואם תאמ׳ זו מיתת בית דין, כבר אמ׳ חכמ׳ ז״ל אע״פ שבטלו ארבע מיתות דין ארבע לא בטלו.[5]

אלפא ביט

אתגבר בחייליה אדוניה בר חגית,[6] פי׳, הרבה נתגאה אדוניה שהיה מתנשא למלוך לפי שהיה סומך בעצת יואב בן צרויה שהיה גיבור.[7] **ביני טורייא.** פי׳, בין ההרים והמדברות, כמ׳ שנ׳ בבת יפתח וירדתי על ההרים[8] שכן דרך המקוננים ובת׳ ביואב ויקבר בביתו במדבר.[9] ויש לפרש **ביני טוריא**, בין השרים הגדולים. **גיברא הוינא וליתי דכוותי,** כלומ׳ מכל הגיבורים אשר לדוד לא היה לו אחד להנאתו שלדוד כמוני, שאילמלי יואב לא נתחזק דוד במלכות כמ׳ דתימ׳ ויהי דוד עושה משפט וצדקה לכל עמו, מה טעם, משום ויואב שר הצבא,[10] וכל הגבורות שעשיתי בעבור דוד מה הנאה יש לי מאחר שקנס עלי מיתה. **דין היתיב מלכא שלמה,** ושלמה היה משיב זאת אל לבו ואומר מה אעשה לשבועתו של אבי שציווני ולא תורד את שיבתו בשלום שאול.[11] **וכרכין ומחוזין,** ערי מבצר תרג׳ קרוין כריכין.[12] מחוזין, ספר הסמוך לים כמ׳ וינחם אל מחוז חפצם.[13] **אח עלך,** פי׳ אח׳ אוי, כמ׳ [49]
אח לראשך.[14] עלך, בשבילך, כלומ׳, תמיד אקרא אוי בשבילך. **פתח פומיה יואב כול׳,** אמ׳

1 ראה לעיל א׳, הערה 4.
2 ת״י לשמות כ׳ י״ג; ראה קומלוש, המקרא באור התרגום, עמ׳ 265-266, וראה לעיל ו׳, הערה 2.
3 אבות פ״ה מ״ט (לפנינו: ״גלות בא לעולם״ וכו׳).
4 בראשית ט ו.
5 כתובות ל ע״א-ע״ב.
6 דוידזון, א, 3197; מפורש במחזור ויטרי, עמ׳ 331-332; ראה מה שכותב על הפיוט הזה ר״ל גינצבורג, אגדות היהודים, ו, עמ׳ 278-279, במיוחד בהערה 10 שם. וראה לאחרונה במאמרו של א״א אורבך, בספר היובל לכבודו של דב סדן <ירושלים תשל״ז, עמ׳ 44-54>.
7 מלכים א א ה ואילך.
8 שופטים יא לז.
9 מלכים א ב לד.
10 סנהדרין מט ע״א.
11 מלכים א ב ו.
12 במדבר לב לו, ות״א שם.
13 תהלים קז ל.
14 מגלה יא ע״א.

יואב לבניהו שהיה רוצה להורגו, סבור אתה לנשק רוחי, כלומ׳ יש יכולת בידך בתמיה, **והלא צוארי תקיף וסייפך חליש. קץ בנייה**, פי׳, קצץ ופת׳ חתך.[15] **תמך מלכא שלמה כו׳.**

לא תנאף

מתרג׳ אותו בתרג׳ אונקלוס ובתרג׳ ירוש׳.[1]

עמי בני ישראל לא תהוון גיירין,[2] פי׳ גיירין מנאפין, ובלש׳ תלמוד גר גירא דע״ז.[3] וכן פירש רבינו שמואל זצ״ל באלף המגן, בגרות, בא גרות, בא זמן הזנות[4] שכבר יצתה מפגה בוחל והרי היא צמל כמ׳ דתימ׳ יצתה מליאה.[5] כלומ׳, שכבר מלאו ימיה, ויצתה מן הקטנות שהיא פגה, ומן הנערות שהיא בוחל, אל ימי הבגרות, כפרי המלא ומבושל כל צורכו. **ארום בחובי גיירייא מותא נפק על עלמא**, לפי שבעון המנאפין דבר בא לעולם. והכי אמרינן בבראשית רבא פרש׳ נ״ח, כל מקום שאתה מוצא דבר ערוה וע״ז אנדרולומסייא בא לעולם. פי׳, דבר בא לעולם והורגת רעים וטובים,[6] וכן מצינו על מעשה שטים ויחל העם לזנות את בנות מואב, וכת׳ ויהי המתים במגפה.[7]

אלפא ביט [50]

אית לי חד טלייא.[8] ייסד המתורג׳ על אשת פוטיפר איך היתה מספרת עם שכינותיה על עניין יוסף, שכן דרך הנשים הנואפות לספר ניאופיה אחת לחבירתה כדי לעזור זו לזו

15 ראה מה שכותב גינצבורג על זה (מובא לעיל בהערה 6) ובמיוחד על המלים ״לא תשניק רוחי״ (וכך הגיה הורוויץ במחזור ויטרי, עמ׳ 342) שלפי דעתו אין צורך להגיהן וגורס ״לא תשנק רוחך״. אבל מהנוסח שלפנינו נראה שהמפרש שלנו גרס ״רוחי״ וכך גם בפירוש שבמחזור ויטרי, עמ׳ 332, נוסף לזה כנראה בטקסט שלפני המפרש היה כתוב ״תנשק״ (במקום ״תשנק״ או ״תשניק״) וקשה לפרש גירסה זו.

1 ראה לעיל א׳, הערה 4.

2 ראה לעיל ט, הערה 2.

3 ע״ז י ע״ב; וראה בד״ס שם, עמ׳ 24 אות ע.

4 ראה ספר אגור, הוספות ותיקונים לערוך, נדפס בספר היובל לכבוד גרץ, בחלק העברי (עטרת צבי), ברסלוי 1887, ראה שם עמ׳ 35, והמהדיר, ר״ש בובר, מזכיר שם את החיבור שלפנינו, הערה רנח שם. ראה גם עמ׳ 4 ועמ׳ 9 הערה ו שם, ומייחסו לבעל שבלי הלקט, ראה מבוא, עמ׳ 8.

5 נדה מז ע״א.

6 ב״ר כו ה, עמ׳ 248-249, בשינויים. ומה שכתוב כאן שהמאמר נמצא בפרשה נ״ח טעות הוא או אולי היה כתוב פרשה כ״ה (זה סימן הפרשה בכי״א ב, ראה מ״י, עמ׳ 243) ונשתבש כ״ה לנ״ח.

7 במדבר כה ט.

8 דוידזון, א, 3196. בכמה מקורות נוסף כאן טור המתחיל ״יוסף תקיף יצריה״ (ראה דוידזון, י, 2161); ראה טל, עמ׳ 97; פירושו במחזור ויטרי, עמ׳ 333-334; ראה טל, עמ׳ 94-102 (הנוסח הארמי, תרגום עברי והערות).

בכשפיהן ובפיתוייהן. **אית לי חד טלייא**, יש לי נער אחד. פי׳ שיוסף היה אז נער, כמ׳ דתימ׳ והוא נער את בני בלהה, ובן י״ז שנה היה כמ׳ דתימ׳ יוסף בן שבע עשרה שנה.[9] **זיוויה דעבראי**, דמותו דמות עברי. **וזבינתיה מן ערבאי**, וקניתי אותו מן הישמעאלים, ארחת ישמעאלים תרג׳ ערבאי.[10] **בעיא אנא ליה למירדי בגינתי**, מבקשת אני ממנו שיחרוש בגינתי, לשון נקייה תפש המתרגם, והוא אינו רוצה ואומ׳ לי, אינו דין שיחרוש השור עם החמור, כמ׳ דתימ׳ בכור שורו הדר לו.[11] ולפי שכילכל בחכמתו את העולם בשני הרעב נקרא כן, כמ׳ דתימ׳ ורב תבואות בכח שור.[12] ובמצריים כת׳ אשר בשר חמורים בשרם,[13] ותרג׳ לא תחרוש, לא תירדי.[14] **גנומוס דידיה כסב בר שבעין שנין**, פי׳ **גנומוס** כמ׳ נימוס והוא לש׳ חוק ומנהג שלדעת.[15] כלומ׳, הוא בן שבע עשרה שנה ומנהגו כבן ע׳.[16] **דמותיה דמלכא, דולוס לית ביה**, אין בו דופי ונכל. אנשי דמים ומרמה[17] לש׳ יוון ולע״ז גרמטיקא דולוסי.[18] **הרי כמה זמנין**, הנה כמה פעמ׳ מזגתי לו הכוס, לשון נקייה על שם מים גנובים ימתקו,[19] והוא צמא לשתות ואינו רוצה. פ״א. **שזגית**, רחצתי לו הכוס. ירחץ במים תרג׳
ירושלמי ישזיג.[20] **ואמרי ליה גנבא בר גנבתא**, על שם ורחל לקחה את התרפים.[21] **מימרי** [51]
דגנבין, על שם מים גנובים ימתקו. **זעיר ומיינוק כו׳**, **דנסב הוני בגלל שופריה**, על שם ויקח אדוני יוסף אותו ויפקידהו בביתו ואת כל אשר לו נתן בידו.[22] **שופריה**, יופייו. **חינא וחסדא מלווין יתיה**. פי׳, לפי שמצינו חן וחסד ביוסף, כמ׳ דתימ׳ ויט עליו חסד ויתן חנו בעיני שר בית הסהר.[23] **למסכא**, לראות מלש׳ שהכל סכין ביופייה.[24] **טורדת אנא לך כול׳**, ואני מגזמת[25] לו לטורדו ולגרשו מתוך חצירי. **סטית**,[26] לש׳ הסרה. **יומא ולילייא נורא בלבי כול׳**, **כל ערסין דריבונך פרישין**, כל מיטות אדוניך הם מוצעות. על ראש המיטה תרג׳

9 בראשית לז ב.
10 בראשית לז כה, ות״א שם.
11 דברים לג יז; ועל כל העניין ראה מה שכתב טל, עמ׳ 98 ובמיוחד מה שמביא מב״ר פה ד, עמ׳ 1037, והשווה במ״י שם.
12 משלי יד ד; ראה תוספות ד״ה ורב תבואות, סנהדרין מב ע״א.
13 יחזקאל כג כ.
14 דברים כב י, ות״א שם.
15 ראה קרויס, *Lehnwörter*, עמ׳ 603 (בהוספות).
16 דומה למה שנאמר על ר׳ אלעזר בן עזריה, ברכות כח ע״א, אולם בב״ר פד ז, עמ׳ 1008: ״יוסף בן שבע עשרה וגו׳ בן י״ז שנה ואת אמרת והוא נער, אלא שהיה עושה מעשה נערות״ וכו׳.
17 תהלים נה כד.
18 על המלה ״דולוס״ ראה טל, עמ׳ 99, ומה שמביא שם מיוונית ויוונות בא״י לגר״ש ליברמן, עמ׳ 7; על ״לע״ז גרמטיקא״ ראה מבוא, עמ׳ 5-6; דולוסיה: dolosi באיטלקית.
19 משלי ט יז. וראה סנהדרין עה ע״א.
20 ויקרא א ט; ח כא, ובתרגום ניאופיטי שם; ראה לוי במלון לתרגומים, ערך שזג.
21 בראשית לא לד.
22 אין פסוק כזה במקרא, ומה שלפנינו הוא צירוף של בראשית ל״ט כ׳ עם ל״ט ד׳ בהשפעת ל״ט ה׳. ועיין בפסוקים.
23 בראשית לט כא.
24 מגלה יד ע״א. וזה שייך לחרוז הקודם.
25 מגזמת = מאיימת.
26 בטקסטים שלפנינו ״סניית״ או ״מנית״, ראה טל, עמ׳ 94 טור 10 ובח״נ שם.

ערסא.[27] ויישן תרג׳ ודמוך.[28] **לא בגין חד ליליא כו׳**, זו תשובת יוסף לאדונתו, אין ראוי לי בעבור יום או לילה אחד שאישן בטוב לטלטל מצעי מגן עדן. **פריסי**, לש׳ פרישת מיטה. פ"א, פרס שלי מלש׳ על מנת לקבל פרס.[29] **מפייסא אנא לכון כו׳, דתצטערון עמי**, ברי"ש, כלומ׳ שתדאגו עמי בדאגתי. ור׳ צדקיה אחי נר"ו[30] פירש **דתצעדון**, בד׳, ופת׳ שתבואו עמי. מלש׳ ויהי כי צעדו נושאי ארון וגו׳.[31] **ניכול כחדא ונשתי כחדא**, כל אילו דברי אשת פוטיפר לשכינותיה מתחילת האלפא ביתא. **סקת יתהון בגו פלטין**. פי׳, העלתה אותן על החצר והושיבה אותן על טפיטין[32] ובגדי משי. פי׳ **סגמיטין**, לש׳ לע"ז ממש סגמיטי.[33] **עבריי קרת יתיה כול׳, קטור זינך**. פי׳, אזור חלציך. **זינך**, אזורך. והוא זינר בלש׳ משנה או זונם, ובלע"ז גרמטיקא זונא.[34] **פיילין בידיה וקם ומזג להון כו׳**. פי׳ **פיילי**, צלוחית מליאה יין. השותים במזרקי יין תרג׳ דשתיין בפיילי חמרא.[35] והוא לשון לע"ז ממש, צלוחית פיאולא.[36] בלשון יוון נקרא הכוס פיילי.[37] **צפיין הוויין ליה כו׳**, פי׳ **צפיין**, לש׳ הבטה [52]
וראייה. **מכרכמן**, לש׳ כרכום. כלומ׳, שהיו תמיהות על יופייו ונבהלות מזיוו, **וכן אפיה ירקינן**,[38] שהיה יוסף מתבייש ופניו מוריקות. **קמו כולהון ונשקן על רישיה כו׳, ראיין הוויין ליה כו׳**.[39] פי׳, שהיו [ח]ותכות האתרוגין בסכין והיו מביטות אליו, ומתוך כך חותכ׳ את ידיהן. ומפורש במדרש תנחומ׳, אמ׳ חכמ׳ פעם אחת נתקבצו המצריות ובאו לראות יופייו שליוסף, מה עשתה אשת פוטיפרע, נטלה אתרוגין ונתנה לכל אחת ואחת מהן ונתנה סכין ביד כל אחת ואחת וקראה ליוסף והעמידתו לפניהן, כיון שהיו מסתכלות ביופייו היו חותכות את ידיהן, אמרה להן ומה אתם בשעה אחת כך, אני שבכל שעה ושעה על אחת כמה וכמה.[40] **שוויין עלוהי עלילה**, כלומ׳ היו משדלות אותו בדברים ומפתות אותו כדי לעשות מלאכתו. פ"א, היו מעלילות עליו ואומרות לו, אם לא תעשה הדבר הזה נאמר עליך כך וכך, וסוף סוף כן היה, כדברים האלה עשה לי עבדך.[41] **תיטול עמה למעבד עיבידתיה כו׳**.

27 בראשית מז לא, ות"א שם.

28 שם ב כא, ות"א שם ועוד.

29 אבות פ"א מ"ג.

30 ראה מבוא עמ׳ 8.

31 שמואל ב ו יג.

32 שטיחים.

33 אולי segmenti באיטלקית ופירושו: שזור בחוטי זהב.

34 ראה עה"ש, ערך זנס וערך זנר; על בלע"ז גרמטיקא ראה מבוא, 5-6; זונא: zona ברומית.

35 עמוס ו ו ות"י שם.

36 pajola באיטלקית.

37 ראה עה"ש, ערך פייל.

38 שבת קקט ע"א; כנראה שלפני המפרש היה כתוב "אפיהון מכרכמין" (מוסב על הנשים) וגם "אפיה ירקינן" (מוסב על יוסף) והאחרון אינו בטקסטים שלפנינו, ראה טל, עמ׳ 95 טור 19.

39 טור זה והבאים אחריו נמצאים במקצת המקורות במקום טקסט אחר, ראה טל, עמ׳ 95 ועמ׳ 97.

40 תנחומא הישן, וישב, פיסקא ה; ראה אגדות היהודים, ה, עמ׳ 339-340.

41 בראשית לט יט.

י״א לא תגנוב

מתרג׳ אותו בתרג׳ אונקלוס ובירושלמי.[1]

עמי בני ישראל לא תהוון גנבין כו׳, ארום בחובי גנבייא כפנא נפיק על עלמא,[2] פי׳, שבעון גזל רעב בא לעולם. דילפינן שאר גזילות מגוזל את מעשרותיו, שאינו נותנן כראוי, דכת׳ בהן וארותי את ברכותיהם.[3] וכדתנן במסכת אבות, מקצתן מעשרין ומקצתן אינן מעשרין רעב שלבצורת בא כו׳.[4] אך תמיה אני איך תפש המתרגם השיטה הזו לפרשו בגונב ממון והוא אזהרת גונב נפשות, מה מצינו דבר למד מעניינו, במה הכת׳ מדבר בדיני [53] לא תרצח, לא תנאף, אף כאן בגונב נפשות.[5] מכל מקום יש לדחוק ולומ׳, אע״פ שהוא אזהרה לגונב נפשות לא נוציאו מכל וכל שלא לפרשו כגונב ממון [ד]שם גניב אחת היא. **אריא מתילי ואחיון מתקלין,**[6] פי׳, אל האריה הן משולין ואל הנחשים דומין אותן בני אדם שהן חוטפין ולוקחים נכסי העניים. ולש׳ המקרא תפש, יארוב במסתר כאריה בסכה יארוב לחטוף עני יחטף עני במשכו ברשתו,[7] וכן דימה הגנב לנחש על שם נחש הקדמוני.[8] והם עוסקים בחשך ואפילה לגנוב בסתר, ובלילות ובחשך הן עתידין להישפט, כמפורש בפסיקתא דעשר תעשר, ומשפטיך תהום רבה, לפי שהן עסוקין בחשך כדכת׳ והיה במחשך מעשיהם, לפיכך נידונין בחשך כמ׳ דתימ׳ כי הנה החשך יכסה ארץ, אמ׳ הקב״ה תהום חשך ורשעים חשך, יבוא חשך ויכסה חשך, משל אין עושין כיסוי לגיגית לא משלכסף ולא משלזהב אלא משלחרס לפי שהוא מינו.[9] **מתילי**, פת׳ משולים. **חיון**, תרג׳ נחשים.[10] ועוד יש לפרש, חיות רעות. שכן דרך חיות רעות הטורפות... החיות והבהמות כדרך הגנב היושב... ומלסטם את הבריות. **מתקלין**, שקולים... **ובטימור קבלין**, בסתר אפילה. **גניב וח[טיף] ונס[יב] בטמרי כול׳**, פי׳ הגנב גונב וחוטף ולוקח ב[סתר]. **כ[מין] בסתרא**, על שם יארוב במסתור.[11] **ועייל בחתרי**, [ו]נכנס במחתרת והנה הוא מסתכל בכבוד העבד יותר מאדונו. כלומ׳ שהוא מסתתר מעיני הבריות ומפחד וירא שלא יראוהו האנשים, אבל מהקב״ה הרואה כל בסתר אינו ירא ואינו מפחד, כביכול, עושה עין של מעלה כאילו אינה רואה. והכי איתא בתוספתא דבבא קמא פרק ז׳, שאלו תלמידיו את רבן יוחנן בן זכיי מפני מה החמירה תורה בגנב יותר מבגזלן, אמ׳ להן גזלן השוה כבוד עבד לכבוד קונו, גנב

1 ראה לעיל א׳, הערה 4.

2 ראה לעיל ט׳, הערה 2.

3 מלאכי ב ב; לא מצאתי דרשה זו על הפסוק הנ״ל בשום מקום ואולי רבינו פירשו כך מדעתו. לעצם העניין ראה שבת לב ע״ב.

4 אבות פ״ה מ״ח.

5 מכילתא, בחדש ח, עמ׳ 232-233; סנהדרין פו ע״א.

6 דוידזון, א, 26; ראה טל, עמ׳ 28-37 (הנוסח הארמי, תרגום עברי ופירוש).

7 תהלים י ט.

8 והוא השטן, ראה תורה שלימה, בראשית ג אות י, עמ׳ רנב. וראה להלן ד״ה הלא מן קדמיי.

9 פסדר״כ, ט (שור או כשב ולא עשר תעשר כמו שצויין כאן), עמ׳ 147, בשינויים.

10 במדבר כא ו, ות״א שם ועוד.

11 תהלים י ט.

חלק כבוד לעבד יותר על כבוד קונו, כביכול עשה הגנב את עין העליונה כאילו אינה רואה
ואת האוזן שאינה שומעת שנ' הוי המעמיק' מה' לסתיר עצה וגו'.[12] **כמין**, פת' אורב, וארב
לו תרג' ויכמון ליה.[13] **חתרי**, לש' מחתרת. **דאוי יקר עבדא**, מסתכל. ובשבת סוף פרק קמא
אמר', אשכחיה דהוי קא דאוי למזרח.[14] **לעין ארעית**, עין שלמטה, כמ' ארע ממך [54]
דדניאל,[15] והוא תרג' שלמטה.[16] והוא תיקון לשון לעין שלמעלה. **סיירי**, לש' פקידה, תרג'
פוקד מסער,[17] עין... כמ' ההוא טבחא דלא סר סכיניה.[18] **הלא מן קדמיי אית [לך] למגמר
כול'.** פי', הלא תוכל להבין וללמוד מאדם הראשון שהכניסו הקב"ה לגן עדן וציווהו שלא
לגנוב מעץ הדעת... עבר(?) שחטף וטעם ממנו והמיר הציווי שנצטווה, השב על דעתך
להבין כמה בריות קנס למיתה. ולשון האגדה תפש, ר' יוסי אומ' אם נפשך לידע מתן שכרן
שלצדיקים לעתיד לבוא צא ולמד מאדם הקדמוני שלא נצטוה אלא מצוה אחת בלא תעשה
ועבר עליה, ראה כמה מיתות נקנסו לו ולדורותיו עד סוף כל הדורות, וכי אי זו מידה
מרובה מידת הטוב או מידת פורענות, הוי אומ' מידת הטוב מרובה, ומה מידת פורענ'
מעוטה ראה כמה מיתות נקנסו לו ולדורותיו ולדורות דורותיו עד סוף כל הדורות, מידת
הטוב מרובה היושב לו מן הפיגולין ומן הנותרים והמתענה ביום הכיפורים על אחת כמה
וכמה שזיכה לו ולדורותיו ועד סוף כל הדורות, בתורת כהנים סדר ויקרא פרש' י"ב.[19]
תפקיד, תרג' מצוה תפקידתא.[20] **איימר**, לש' תמורה. אינמי לש' המראה מגזרת אשר ימרה
את פיך.[21] **אנהר**, זכור כמ' נהירנא כד הון קיימין תלת סאין בסלע,[22] ובבראשית רבא פרש'
ל"ד, אמ' הקב"ה לית אתון מנהרין ליה אנא נהירנא ליה, ויזכר אלהים את נח.[23] **אקמר**,
לש' כיסוי כמ' צריך לקמור דעירובין.[24] פ"א, לש' חגור כמ' נהי דאהני לך קמרא דאבוך[25]
ופתר' אזור, חגרו שקים תרג' קמרו.[26] **זייריה דבר מעכה תלתא גנב.** פי', זרותו שלאבשלום
בן מעכה גרם לו לגנוב שלש גניבות, שגנב לב אביו ולב בית דין ולב ישראל, והיה סבור
בעניין זה למלוך. ומה גרם לו שתפשתו האֵלה בשערו ונתלה שם, לפי שהיה אבשלום
דומה בשערו לאדם הראשון ולפי שגנב שלש גניבות תקעו בלבו שלשה שבטים כמפורש [55]

12 תוספתא ב"ק פ"ז ה"ב. <הגר"ש ליברמן מזכיר את המקור שלפנינו בתוספתא כפשוטה, נזיקין, עמ' 65.>

13 דברים יט יא, ות"א שם.

14 שבת לה ע"א (וזה בפ"ב ולא בפרק קמא).

15 דניאל ב לט.

16 ראה ערך ארע ג' במלונו של לוי לתרגומים.

17 שמות כ ה, ות"א שם ועוד.

18 חולין יח ע"א. [ואולי צריך להשלים: ע"א (= עניין אחר) לש' ראייה.]

19 תורת כהנים, ויקרא פי"ב ה"י. לענין הגניבה מעץ הדעת איתא בב"ר טו ז, עמ' 140: "הוא גנבא דגנב דעתיה דברייה". הנוסח שלפנינו דומה לנוסח שבכ"י רומי, מהד' פינקלשטיין, עמ' קכ.

20 שמות כד יב, ות"א שם ועוד.

21 יהושע א יח.

22 תענית יט ע"ב (שם: ד' סאין).

23 לפנינו ב"ר לג ב, עמ' 304.

24 עירובין פ"ח מ"ט.

25 הוריות יג ע"ב.

26 איכה ב י ות"י שם.

בסוטה.[27] **זייריה**, פי׳ לש׳ זרות, כלומר זדונו וזרות לבו. **חטר מלכו**, שבט מלכות, שהיה
סבור למלוך. **למענב**, לש׳ קשירה וחיבור, תרג׳ לולאות ענובין.[29] **בוטמא**, אלה, תחת
האלה תרג׳ תחות בוטמא.[29] **במזייה**, בשערותיו. **ואשתנץ ואיענב**, לש׳ קשירה וחיבור, כמ׳
והאיכא שנאצי דפרק המצניע בשבת.[30] ופת׳, רצועות ולולאות המחוברות בכיס. **ובתלת
גיססין**, ויקח שלשה שבטים בכפו ויתקעם בלב אבשלום תרג׳ תלתא גיססין.[31] **תולייא
דליביה**, שומן הלב. **אתקנב**, לש׳ חתך, כמ׳ האי מאן דקניב סילקא דפרק כלל גדול.[32]
טמינייא וגנבייא שבעה פריטין, פי׳, אותם שהן טמונין במעשיהם וגונבין לב הבריות
המנויין בשבעה הפרושין, והן מפורשין בסוטה ובירושלמי דפרק הרואה בברכות
ובירושלמי דסוטה, שבעה פרושין הן, פרוש שכמי, מיחזי טעין מצוותה אכתפיה. פרוש
נקפי, אקף ליה ואנא עביד מצוה. פרוש קיזאי, עביר חדא חובה וחדא מצוה ומקזז חדא
לחדא. פרוש מהנכיא, מה דאית לי אנא מנכה עביד מצוה. פרוש מה חובתי ואעשנה,
היידא חובה עבדית דנעביד מצוה דכוותה. פרוש יראה, כאיוב. פרוש אהבה, כאברהם, הרי
אילו ז׳ פרושין, אין לך חביב מכולם אלא פרוש אהבה כאברהם.[33] ומה שאומ׳ **טמינייא
וגנבייא שבעה פריטין**, לצדדין קאמ׳ כמ׳ שפירשתי, זולתי פרוש אהבה ופרוש יראה, כי
החמשה האחרים הם על דרך רמאות לרמות בני אדם. ואילו שבעה פרושין משונין
במעלותן זה מזה וגזירת דינם כתוב, אבל העונש הגדול שבכולם משום שגונבין דעת
הבריות ומתכסים שחורין ומגדלין צפרניהן להטעות בני אדם. **פריטין**, פרושין. **דרגיהון**,
מעלותם. **ליבהון דברייתא מקמטין**, שגונבין דעת הבריות. עוונותיו ילכדונו את הרשע תרג׳
חובוהי׳ דרשיעא קמטין ליה.[34] **חפו גונדי**, מתכסין בגדים שחורים. בסוטה פרק היה נוטל,
בי דינא רבא ליפרע מהני׳ דחפו גונדי שאומ׳ אל תגע בי כי קדשתיך,[35] ובשבת פרק כל
כתבי הקודש. רב ענן לביש גונדא.[36] ובלש׳ לע״ז ממש גונדא.[37] **וטלפיהון פשטין**, כי [56]
מאריכין צפרניהון שיראוהו האנשים ויחשבוהו אדם כשר שאינו חושש לייפות את עצמו
ולהתקשט בבגדים יפים. פ״א, שהולכין יחיפין וחולצין מנעליהן מרגליהן, שוסעת שסע
פרסות תרג׳ מטילפי טלפייא.[38] **פשטין**, כמ׳ ופשט את בגדיו.[39] פ״א, פושטין את טלפיהן,

27 סוטה פ״א מ״ח; תוספתא שם, פ״ג הט״ז-י״ז; על ששערו של אבשלום היה דומה לשערו של אדם הראשון ראה פדר״א פנ״ג וסוטה י ע״א.

28 שמות כו ה, ותרגומים שם.

29 בראשית לה ד, ותרגומים שם.

30 שבת צב עא; ראה עה״ש ערך שנץ.

31 שמואל ב יח יד ות״י שם.

32 שבת עג ע״ב.

33 סוטה כב ע״ב; ירושלמי ברכות פ״ט ה״ז (יד ע״ב); ירושלמי סוטה פ״ה ה״ז (כ ע״ג).

34 משלי ה כב, ות״י שם.

35 סוטה כב ע״ב. הפסוק חסר בנוסח שלפנינו אבל נמצא בערוך, ראה עה״ש, ערך גנד א׳, וראה אוצר הגאונים, סוטה, עמ׳ 284.

36 שבת קיט ע״א.

37 לא זוהה.

38 ויקרא יא ג, ובתרגומים שם.

39 ויקרא ו ד.

כלומ׳ מראין את עצמן צדיקים כחזיר הזה שהוא מראה סימן טהרה שבו, כמ׳ שאמרו
רבותינו ז״ל בבראשית רבא פרש׳ ס״ה, יכרסמנה חזיר מיער, ר׳ פינחס ור׳ חלקיה בש׳ ר׳
סימון, כל הנביאים לא פירסמוה אלא שנים, אסף ומשה, אסף אמ׳ יכרסמנה חזיר מיער
ומשה אמ׳ ואת החזיר כי מפריס פרסה הוא וגו׳, למה הוא מושלה בחזיר, אלא החזיר הזה
בשעה שהוא רובץ הוא פושט את טלפיו, כלומ׳, ראו שאני טהור, כך מלכות הרשעה הזו
גוזלת וחומסת ונראת כאילו מצעת בימה וכול׳,[40] מפי׳ ר׳ מרדכי בי״ר בנימן נ״ע,[41] ועיקר.
פ״א. **טמינייא וגנבייא שבעה פריצין**, והן שבעה גנבין המנויין בתוספתא דבבא קמא פרק
ז׳, שבעה גנבין הן, הראשון שבכולם גונב דעת הבריות, המסרב בחבירו לאורחו ואין בלבו
לקרותו, המרבה לו בתקרובת ויודע שאינו מקבל, המפתח לו חנוייות[42] המכורות לחנווני,
המעוול במידות, והמשקר במשקלות, והמערב את הגידה בתלתן ואת החומץ בשמן,
אע״פ שאמרו שאין השמן מקבל דולוס לפיכך מושכין בו את המלכים, ולא עוד אלא
שמעלין עליו שאילו היה יכול לגנוב דעת העליונה היה גונב, שכל הגונב דעת הבריות
נקרא גנב שנ׳ ויגנב אבשלום את לב אנשי ישראל, מי גדול גונב או נגנב, הוי אומ׳ נגנב
שיודע שנגנב ושותק, למעלה מהן הגונב איסורי הנאה שפטור מלשלם, למעלה מהם
הגונב את השטרות ואת הקרקעות ואת ההקדישות שאינו משלם אלא הקרן, למעלה מהן
הגונב את החיה ואת הבהמה ועופות וכסות וכלים שמשלם תשלומי כפל, למעלה מהן
טבח ומכר שמשלם ארבע וחמשה, למעלה מהן גונב נפש בן חורין שנידון עליו בנפשו,
למעלה מהן הגונב כלי שרת שהקנאין פוגעין בו,[43] הרי שבעה מעלות מעלות שלגנבין
חלוקין זה מזה וכולן מפורשין לפנינו, וזה הפירוש עיקר ונכון ועתה חוזר לפרשם על סדר [57]
המשנה. **כסי ושירו מושיט ליה לחבריה במסבלי**. פי׳, האדם המושיט לחבירו כוסות שליין
ומטעמי אכילה ומכריחו להאכילו ולהשקותו כשהוא רואה שאין בדעתו לאכול ולשתות,
מי שעושה כן הקב״ה שונאו. ודומה לפניו, כביכול, שאם היה יכול זה הגנב דעתו
שלחבירו, היה גונב כמ׳ כן דעתו. זהו הגנב הראשון כמ׳ שפירשנו למעלה. **כסי**, פי׳ כוסות
יין. **שירו**, לש׳ שירותא, ופת׳ אכילה. **במסבלי**, דורון, כמ׳ השולח סבלונות לבית חמיו
דפרק מי שמת.[44] פ״א. **במסבלי**, סעודת עריי, שאינה סעודת מצוה, שאוכלין בני אדם זה
עם זה על ידי תשלומין נקראת סבלת, כדאמ׳ פרק האשה בפסחים, אפי׳ סבולת דלצוותא
בעלמא היא.[45] **מסרהב**, ממהר, כמ׳ הוי קא מסרהב ואכיל דפרק כיצד מברכין.[46] וימהרו
לשפוך דם, תרג׳ ויסתרהבון.[47] **דלא מצטבי ליה**, שאינו רוצה, מלשון די הוה צבי הוה

40 ב״ר סה א, עמ׳ 713.

41 ראה מבוא, עמ׳ 7.

42 צ״ל ״חביות״.

43 תוספתא ב״ק, פ״ז ה״ח, הי״א-הי״ג <ובתוספתא כפשוטה, נזיקין, עמ׳ 67-71, דן הגר״ש ליברמן בגירסאות של מאמר זה כמו שהוא לפנינו כאן>; השווה מכילתא, נזיקין יג, עמ׳ 294-296; לפי הנוסח שלפנינו המספר שבעה יוצא לנכון, השווה הערת הורוביץ, שם, עמ׳ 295, שורה 11.

44 בבא בתרא פ״ט מ״ה.

45 פסחים פט ע״ב.

46 ברכות מז ע״א (וזה בפרק שלשה שאכלו ולא בפ׳ כיצד מברכין).

47 משלי א טז, ות״י שם.

מחי,[48] והטי״ת יתירה כטי״ת מה נצטדק.[49] **דמי קומוי**, נראה לפניו. **בנכלי**, נכל ומרמה.
כהיל, יכול, כמ׳ האיתך כהל דדניאל.[50] **בגרמיה**, בעצמו. **הוה מפלי**, מלעיג, כמ׳ הוה מפלי
בבני ירושלים דמגילת איכה.[51] **כד זיהרין וחזוון בגנובתיה מתהני**. פי׳, כשהאדם גונב
קרקעות ושטרות, הקרן מוטל עליו לפרוע שאין כפילה בקרקעות ושטרות. דכת׳ כסף או
כלים, מה אילו מיוחדין שמיטלטלין וגופן ממון, אף כל מיטלטלין וגופן ממון, יצאו
קרקעות שאין מיטלטלין, יצאו עבדים שהוקשו לקרקעות, יצאו שטרות שאין גופן ממון.
וזה הפסוק, כי יתן איש אל רעהו כסף או כלים לשמור וגונב מבית האיש אם ימצא הגנב
ישלם שנים, בטוען טענת גנב הכת׳ מדבר ואחר כך נמצא שגנבו הוא, וכן מפורש
במיצעא[52] פרק הזהב.[53] והוצרך לומ׳ **בגנובתיה מתהני**, כלומ׳ שגנב דברים שמותרין
ליהנות מהן, אז הוא חייב לשלם. שאם היה גונב דברים האסורין בהנא׳ פטור מלשלם כמ׳
שמפורש למעלה.[54] והנה הוזכרו כאן שנים מהן, הגונב איסורי הנאה והגונב קרקעות
ושטרות. **קרנא פרע**, הקרן פורע ולא כפל כמ׳ שפירשנו. **ומיתליט דתחום משני**, והוא עומד
בארור דכת׳ ארור משיג גבול רעהו.[55] פ״א. **קרנא פרע**, הקרן נפרע ממנו. כלומ׳, קרן [58]
השמתא שהוא בארור,[56] והראשון עיקר. **לנכסין מסיימין [במ]חטפיה**, ואם גנב נכסין
מסויימין כגון מטלטלין והדומה לאותן הכתוב בפרשה, שור וחמור שה שלמה,[57] וכל
אבידה המסויימת וניכרת. **על חד תרין דיניה**, דכת׳ ישלם שנים לרעהו. **ואי לית ליה מזדבן
כול׳**, ואם אין לו ממה לשלם נמכר לשש שנים לעבדות.[58] **זיהרין**, פי׳ קרקעות כדאיתא
בהמוכר בבבא בתרא, אי אמ׳ ליה זיהרא מזבינא לך, פי׳ ירושת קרקעות.[59] **חזוון**, פי׳
שטרות, תרג׳ חזוון ראייה, שהשטרות אינם אלא ראייה בעלמא.[60] ובמקצת סידורים כת׳
מר זיהרין וחזוון, ופת׳ כמ׳ קופינא דמרא,[61] והוא מברזל וחופרין בו את הקרקע, **צפא**
בלע״ז,[62] כלומ׳ אם הוא גונב מעט קרקע מחבירו מה שהוא חופרה במרא בהכאה אחת מה
הוא נהנה שהרי חייב לשלם ועומד בארור משיג גבול רעהו.[63] **מעאן ארבע ומתור חמשה**

48 דניאל ה יט.
49 בראשית מד טז.
50 דניאל ב כו.
51 איכה רבה א יב, עמ׳ 50.
52 כן הוא בכ״י, וראה אפשטיין, מבוא לנוסח המשנה, עמ׳ 992.
53 ב״מ נז ע״ב.
54 תוספתא ב״ק, פ״ז הי״א, מובא לעיל, הערה 43.
55 דברים כז יז.
56 [שמטילין עליו שמתא ותוקעין בשופרות. ראה שבועות לו ע״א, ועיין עוד סנהדרין ז ע״ב רש״י ד״ה שופרא ומנחות לד ע״ב תוספות ד״ה טט.]
57 שמות כב ח.
58 שם ב. וראה במכילתא, נזיקין יג, עמ׳ 293: ״שומע אני לעולם, ת״ל שש שנים״ וכו׳.
59 בבא בתרא סא ע״ב. [ראה רשב״ם שם. ואולי פי׳ ״נחלה״ שבערוך ערך בסתן מלשון ירושה.]
60 גטין י ע״ב ועוד.
61 שבת קב ע״ב.
62 zappa באיטלקית.
63 דברים כז יז; עיין רמב״ם, הלכות גניבה, פ״ז הי״א: ״המסיג גבול רעהו והכניס מתחום חבירו בתוך תחומו אפילו מלוא אצבע״ וכו׳.

כול׳. פי׳, אם הגנב גונב בהמות דינו קצוב בפרשה, חמשה בקר ישלם תחת השור וארבע צאן תחת השה, ואימתי משלם ארבעה וחמשה, כששחט או מכר כדכת׳ וטבחו או מכרו,[64] אבל אם הוא חי בידו עדיין אינו משלם אלא כפל.[65] ולמה מן הצאן משלם ארבעה ומן השור ה׳, שור שביטלו ממלאכתו חמשה, שה שאין בו ביטול מלאכה משלם ארבעה. ועוד טעם אחר, צאן שנתבזה בו להוליכו על כתיפו ד׳,[66] שור שלא נתבזה להוליכו על כתיפו חמשה.[67] **נכיל**, לש׳ נכל וערמה, ויתנכלו אותו להמיתו.[68] **רפיק**, חופר כמ׳ אשכחיה דקא רפיק רפקא דמסכת תעניות.[69] **בחתר**, במחתרת. **בחשא**, לחפש ולבדוק מה שיגנוב כמ׳ [59] אדלא אבן בחשנא דשבת פרק שואל.[70] פ״א. **בחשא**, כמ׳ בחשאי, ופת׳ בסתר ובנחת, כמ׳ לשכת חשיין.[71] **לית ליה דמא כול׳**. כלומר, גנב הנמצא במחתרת אם הרגו בעל הבית אין לו דמים ואינו נהרג עליו אם ברור לו כשמש שהוא בא על עסקי נפשות, כדכת׳ אם במחתרת ימצא הגנב והוכה ומת אין לו דמים.[72] **מרי עלמין דכולא ליה גלי**, פי׳, הקב״ה שהוא אדון כל העולמים והכל גלוי לפניו. **אשקל דלא מוקים בר נשא גרמיה כול׳**, שיקל והכריע בדעתו שאין אדם מעמיד עצמו על ממונו, וכיון שאין אדם מעמיד עצמו על ממונו, הגנב משים בדעתו להורגו ונמצא רודף, והתור׳ אמ׳ הבא להורגך השכם להורגו. וזהו פי׳ אין לו דמים.[73] **אגורסנא דיליה**, על הממון שלו. כדאיתא ביבמות פרק האשה, דקא אכלה לגורסנא דבי נשא.[74] **נחת לסוף מנדעיה**, ירד לסוף דעתו שלגנב, כמ׳ שפירשנו. **שנאין גרמיהון דפלגין עם נגודין**. פי׳, מאד שונאין עצמן אותן שחולקין עם הגנבין בעלי מלקיות, לפי ששומעין כמה אלות וקללות ואינן מודין. אך סוף סוף כשיתפרסם חרפתם ובושתם בקהל או על ידי עדים גורמין לעצמן מכות ומלקיות, ומפורש בתוספ׳ בבא קמא פרק ז׳, ר׳ שמעון אומ׳ חולק עם גנב שונא נפשו אלה ישמע ולא יגיד, משלו משל למה הדבר דומה, לאחר שטען כלים מבית חבירו ויצא. מצאו אחר אמ׳ לו, פל׳ מה זו, אמ׳ לו, טול חלקך ולא תגיד. לאחר זמן מצאו בעל גניבה ואמ׳ לו, משביעני עליך אם לא ראית אדם שטען כלים מתוך ביתי ויצא. אמ׳ לו, שבועה איני יודע מה אתה שח, על זה נאמ׳ חולק עם גנב וגו׳.[75] **נגודין**, פת׳ בעלי מלקיות, כלומר [חייבין] ללקות. ויש לפרשו לש׳ משיכה, כלומ׳ הגנבים שפושטין ידיהם בממון חביריהן [למ]שכו אצלם, וזה נראה לי עיקר. **מחאתא ונגדון**, מכות ומלקיות. בברכות פרק הרואה, חלמא בישא קשי מנגדא.[76] **פריטא דמאן**

64 שמות כא לז.

65 תוספתא ב״ק, פ״ז הי״א, מובא לעיל, הערה 43.

66 בכ״י: ״חמשה״; ותוקן מעל לשורה: ״ד׳״.

67 תוספתא פ״ז ה״י.

68 בראשית לז יח.

69 תענית כג סע״א וראה בד״ס שם, עמ׳ 136, אות כ.

70 שבת קנב ע״א.

71 שקלים פ״ה מ״ו.

72 שמות כב א-ב, ות״י שם. ורש״י שם עפ״י מכילתא, נזיקין יג, עמ׳ 293, וסנהדרין עב ע״א.

73 מקורות הנ״ל.

74 יבמות קיז ע״א.

75 תוספתא ב״ק, פ״ז הי״ג, בשינויים קטנים. <וראה לעיל הערה 43.>

76 ברכות נה סע״א.

קודשא מ[כ]סא כול׳, פי׳ **פריטא** אנפרנטו (?) בלע״ז,[77] מלשון פרטיה [נ]ואף להוצא וערק
דנדרים,[78] שפת׳ פרץ גדר הקוצים, כן זה **פריטא**, פריץ. כמ׳ עיר פרוצה אין חומה.[79]
[60] כלומ׳, בן בליעל שפורץ, שגונב כלי שרת, קנאין פוגעין בו והורגין אותו כדאיתא
בסנהדרין, הגונב את הקשווא, פי׳ כלי שרת כמ׳ את קשות הנסך, קנאין פוגעין בו בשעת
מעשה ואזהרתיה מהכא, ולא יבאו לראות כבלע את הקדש ומתו.[80] כלי הקדש תרג׳ מאני
דקודשא.[81] **קנויי דנטרין כול׳**, פי׳ קנאין. כלומ׳ הצדיקי׳ המקיימין מצוות ה׳ ומקנאין
קנאת הבורא, כמ׳ דתימ׳ בקנאו את קנאתי.[82] **תפקיד ונימוסי**, פי׳, מצוות וחקים,
ובחקותיהם תרג׳ ובנימוסיהון.[83] **ציידין עליה**, פי׳, אורבין עליו, כמ׳ ואשר לא צדה.[84]
לקנסיה, לעונשו. **ומפלי בישתא ומזכי כורסיה**, ובערת הרע מקרבך[85] תרג׳ ותפלי עביד
דביש מבינך. **ומזכי כורסיה**, מטהרין את [א]רץ ישראל שנקראת כסא כבוד מרום מראשון
מקום [מ]קדשינו.[86] **קניינא קדישא [ריש] עלליה כול׳**, פי׳, ישראל שנקראו קניין כמ׳
דתימ׳ עם זו קנית.[87] ונקראו עם קדוש וראשית תבואתו שלמקום, כמ׳ דתימ׳ קדש יש׳ לה׳
ראשית תבואתו.[88] **דלאיתגורי גנביה**, שגנב נפש [אח]ד מישראל ומכרו, מה דינו. **רמו
קשיא ל[גו] רכיכא כול׳**, כלומ׳, דינו בחנק, כדכת׳ וגונב נפש מאחיו מבני ישראל והתעמר
בו ומכרו וג׳ מות יומת, וכל מיתה האמורה בתורה סתם אינה אלא חנק,[89] והיאך חונקין
אותו, נותנין סודר קשה לתוך הרך וכורכין אותו בצוארו ומושכין מיכן ומיכן וחונקין
אותו.[90] **דלאיתגורי גנביה**, והתעמר בו תרג׳ ויתגר ביה,[91] כדאמ׳ הגונב נפש אינו חייב עד
שישתמש בו, כמ׳ לא תתעמר בה.[92] **וענקין קדליה**, מלש׳ וענקים לגרגרתיך,[93] כורכין אותו
בצוארו כמ׳ ענקא. תשנוק, לש׳ חניקה, וינער תרג׳ ושניק.[94] **חיותיה מתכלי**, מכלים חייו.
שוט לא ישוטון ליה לגנבא כול׳, פי׳, בוז לא יבוזו לגנב כשהוא מתעסק לגנוב דברי תורה
שהן כמרגליות שאין להם דמים, אך שיעשה מאהבת התורה ולא להתגדל בה, אז הקב״ה

77 infranto באיטלקית.
78 נדרים צא ע״ב.
79 משלי כה כח.
80 סנהדרין פ״ט מ״ו ובבלי שם פא ע״ב ורש״י שם פב ע״א ד״ה אמר רב חסדא. וראה בתוספתא הנ״ל בהערה 43.
81 במדבר ד טו, ותרגומים שם ועוד.
82 ראה במקורות הנזכרים בהערה 80.
83 ויקרא יח ג, ות״א שם.
84 שמות כא יג.
85 דברים יג ו, ובתרגומים שם ועוד.
86 ירמיה יז יב.
87 אבות פ״ו (פרק קנין תורה) מ״י.
88 ירמיה ב ג.
89 ספרי דברים, פיסקא רעג, עמ׳ 293 ומקבילות.
90 סנהדרין פ״ז מ״ג.
91 דברים כד ז, ות״א שם.
92 ספרי דברים הנ״ל (לעיל הערה 89).
93 משלי א ט.
94 שמות יד כז, ות״א שם.

יאהב אותו והתורה מתקרבת אצלו ומשלם לו הקב״ה שכרו... [לעולם] הבא. **שוט לא** [61]
ישוטון, כמ׳ שכת׳ לא יבוזו לגנב [כי יגנב] ודרשינן באגדה, לא יבוזו לגנב כי יגנוב, דברי תורה, [למ]לא נפשו כי ירעב, למה, ונמצא ישלם שבעתיים, שא[ם] ג[רם] מזלו יזכה לתורה ונמצא ישלם שבעתיים... מזוקק שבעתיים. ואיתא בתוספתא דבבא קמא פרק [ז׳], אבל המתגנב מאחר חבירו והולך ושונה פרקו אע״פ שנקרא גנב זוכה לעצמו שנ׳ לא יבוזו לגנב כי יגנב, סוף מתמנה פרנס על הציבור ומזכה את הרבים ומשלם על מה שבידו שנ׳ ונמצא ישלם שבעתיים, אין שבעתיים אלא תורה שנ׳ אמרות ה׳ אמרות טהורות כסף צרוף בעליל לארץ מזוקק שבעתיים.[95] **מרגלין דלית להון טימי**, מרגליות דלית להון דמים, בבראשית רבא, באוני אחת ובטימי אחת.[96] **זיקין ונהור**, פי׳ אורה, **זיקין**, מלשון זיקוקי אש.[97]

י״ב אלפא ביט אחרן

אייום אפתינטין ואבזרי אורייתא כול׳,[1] פי׳ ביראת הבורא ודקדוקי התורה עיין והבין לעמוד על עיקרה להסיר מעליך דין המות, שכל הפורש מן התורה כפורש מחייו והבוחר בתורה בוחר בחיים. כמ׳ דתימ׳, כי הוא חייך וארך ימיך וגו׳.[2] ולהסיר אימה מחדרי לבך ולפכח פחדך ולבטל גזירה קשה מעליך. **אייום**, פת׳ לשון יראה, כמ׳ איום ונורא הוא.[3] ובל[ש]׳ [המ]ש[נה] כ[יצ]ד מאיימין את העדים, בסנהדרין.[4] **אפתינטי[ן]**, ...בבראשית רבא, הנהר הגדול, אפתינטין [שלנ]הר[ות].[5] **אבזר[י] אורייתא**, דקדוקי תורה, כלומ׳ כל מידי (?)... ארבעים ושמנה דברים שהתורה נקנית בהן ביי[שוב במקרא] ובמשנה וכול׳, פרק ר׳ מאיר,[6] בסנהדרין פרק בן [סורר ומורה] אינהו וכל אבזרייהו.[7] **איין**, כמ׳ עיין, [62]
כדאמ׳ ... **[עיין]** עליו.[7א] **לאפתוקי**, לעמוד על העיקר, מלש׳ אפותיקי, ... אפו תהי

95 תוספתא ב״ק, פ״ז הי״ג; מכילתא, נזיקין יג, עמ׳ 295-296 ומקבילות. ונראה שהיתה לפניו אגדה שונה במקצת בלשונה מזו שבמקורות שלפנינו, ואומר ״ודרשינן באגדה״ על הנוסח הזה ואח״כ מוסיף את התוספתא הנ״ל. <וראה בתוספתא כפשוטה הנ״ל (הערה 43) עמ׳ 72 ד״ה אבל המתגנב.>

96 ב״ר ב ב, עמ׳ 15.

97 ראה לעיל בראש הפירוש לפיוט ג׳.

1 לא מצאתי פיוט זה וגם זכרו אינו בא ברשימות; על שם מחברו ראה להלן הערה 59. <ראה לאחרונה ישראל מרדכי פלס, ״פיוט אבוד ופירושו ׳אלפביט׳ אבוד לרבינו יהודה בן בנימן מן הענויים (ריבב״ן)״, המעין מג, ד (תשס״ג), עמ׳ 25-38.>

2 דברים ל כ.

3 חבקוק א ז.

4 סנהדרין פ״ד מ״ה.

5 ב״ר טז ג, עמ׳ 144: ״אוותינטין״; וכן בכל הנוסחאות, בוא״ו.

6 אבות פ״ו (פרק קנין תורה) ונקרא פרק ר׳ מאיר על שם תחלתו.

7 סנהדרין עד ע״ב.

7א [כנראה הכוונה ליבמות כב ע״ב ומקבילות ועיין שם מה שציין שם בגליון לערוך.]

קאי.[8] פ"א. **לאפתוקי**, לאצור אותה באוצר... אוצרות ברד תראה תרג' אפותיקי.[9] **תנסיא**, מיתה בלש' יוון. בויקרא רבא, והוא ינהגנו עלמות תירג' עקילס אתנסיאה, עולם שאין בו מות. והוא לש' יוון, אה, אין. תנסיאה, מות. עלמות, אל מוות.[10] **לגזרתה**, להפריש אותה ממך, מלש' לגוזר ים סוף.[11] **בתוון**, תרג' ומחדרים אימה ומתווונייא.[12] **בעתתא לפכוחי**, להסיר פחד וגזירה הנגזרת עליך כמ' לפכוחי פחדיה דפרק אי זהו נשך.[13] **גהא ובר גהא לקיומי**, פי', התורה שבכתב ותורה שבעל פה לקיים, כדי להניח אדם נפשו תחת כסא הכבוד, היא התורה הנמשלת לשמן מבושם בריחה הנודף,[14] ולהרחיק האדם מעצמו חושך ואפילה כגבוה שמים. [**גהא ובר**] **גהא**, פי' מלשון ספר מוגה,[14א] כלומ' תורה שבכתב מפו[רשת ומדו]קדקת מפי הקב"ה. **בר גיהא**, זה תלמוד שהוא... ישראל רב מפי רב, הלכה למשה, והוא פי' תורה שבכתב. פ"א [**גהא**], כמ' גיהה ובר גיהה דמועד קטן,[15] ופת' בריכה, מעיין, על שם [שהתורה] נקראת נחל נובע מקור חכמה.[16] **גהרקא**, כסא כמ' מפקי ליה בגהרקא דדהבא דמסכת תעניות,[17] כלומר כסא הכבוד.[18] **למיצע תותיה נומיה**, להציע תחתיו מקום שכיבת בשרו, על שם והיתה נפש אדוני צרורה בצרור החיים את ה' אלהיך.[19] **תותיה**,
פי' תחותיה, עי"ן מובלעת.[19א] **נומיה**, לש' שינה. **דהנא דוורדא**, שמן מבושם שלוורד כמ' [63]
קרב לגבי דיהנא ואידהן.[20] **דיגמי**, לש' דמיון. **דהא**, לש' כהיון כדאמ' בנידה עבר או שדיהא הרי זה כתם[21] ופת' כהה. **כהוא מרי כולא אזהר**, פי', הק' שהוא אדון הכל ציוה והזהיר לאדם מממון שיהיה לחבירו להזכיר את לבו תמיד להתייאש ממנו. **ותנייא דפחדוהי**, תרג' גידי, פחדיו.[22] אפי' אם היו ביציו נבקעים והיה צריך להתרפאות בממון חבירו כדי להתיש חוליו אסור בלא ידיעת חבירו.[23] **ותתקיה לאנוחי**, חולשו להניח. **ותתקיה**, כמ' הוויין לו בנים

8 הפייטן יצר פועל מהשם אפותיקי; על פירוש השם ראה עה"ש, ערך אפתק ב'. [ועיין שם הגהת קאהוט, והיא נדחית מכאן.]

9 איוב לח כב. וראה עה"ש, ערך אפתק א'.

10 וי"ר יא ט, עמ' רמא-רמב; ראה בעה"ש, ערך אתנסיאה.

11 תהלים קלו יג.

12 דברים לב כה.

13 ב"מ סו ע"ב.

14 ראה שיה"ש רבא על הפסוק "לריח שמניך טובים" (שיה"ש א ג): "ר' אחא בשם רבי תנחום ברבי חייא, שני שמנים הם וכו', ורבנן אמרין שתי תורות הן, תורה שבכתב ושבעל פה".

14א פסחים קיב ע"א.

15 מו"ק ח ע"ב.

16 משלי יח ד. וראה מה שנדרש על הפסוק הזה במשנת רבי אליעזר, מהד' ענעלאו, עמ' 132.

17 תענית כ ע"ב.

18 ראה עה"ש, ערך גהרק, אבל רש"י בתענית הנ"ל מפרש: "תיבה תלויה בעגלה" וכו'.

19 שמואל א כה כט.

19א ראה ערוך, ערך תת ב'.

20 שבועות מז ע"ב וראה עה"ש, ערך דהן.

21 נדה פ"ט מ"ו.

22 איוב מ יז.

23 לא מצאתי מקור לדבר זה.

ותקין[24] ופת׳ חלשין. **לאנוחי**, נו״ן רפי, לש׳ מנוחה. **אסתהר**, דבר זה ברור מפי סנהדרין הנקראין אגן הסהר.[25] **זדוניה מיגנב ומינכס מענא כול׳**. פי׳, ואם הטעהו זדונו של אדם לגנוב ולטבוח [מן הצאן] שקשה הדבר על הגנב שצריך להוליכו על [כתיפו, ועוד השה] שאין בו ביטול מלאכה נתחייב לשלם ארבע [כמ׳ דתימ׳] וארבע צאן תחת השה.[26] **ענא**, תרג׳ צאן.[26א] ז... כמ׳ אזדא מני מילתא ופת׳ קשה וחזקה כפירוש ר׳ סעדיה גאון זצ״ל.[27] **חדוד**, לש׳ חידוד. **חדקי ארבע**, בעל קרנים מלש׳ חדוקות,[28] כלומ׳ ארבעה מעולים ויפים.[29] **טהרא סהדות זבין תור איכול**, פי׳, אם ברור כצהרים עדות הגנב שגנב ומכר שור, לטהר את עוונו כלפי הנגנב נתחייב לשלם חמשה בקר תחת השור וארבע צאן תחת השה. ולמה החמירה תורה בשור יותר מבצאן, לפי שלא היה לו טורח וכובד להוליכו על כתיפו ועוד שהרי מבטל אותו ממלאכתו.[30] **ייהור**, לש׳ תואר. **נירא**, תרג׳ עול.[30א] **כבלא גנב ונפיק סהדי כול׳**, **כבלא**, פי׳, חותם. כמ׳ כבלא דעבדא דפרק במה אשה.[31] כלומ׳, ממון המופקד אצל אדם או בחותם או שלא בחותם, אם גנבו בעל הבית ואחר כך יצאו עדים לאחר שנכבש בפני בית דין ונשבע שאין בידו הרי זה מתחייב כפל, אבל על טענת קרקעות אינו מתחייב כפל.[32] **לבלר כתב**, פי׳, הסופר כתב, כלומ׳, משה שנקרא מחוקק כתב בתורתו [64] מפי הקב״ה.[33] **עוף פונדיה**, להכפיל מעותיו, רבוע יהיה כפול תרג׳ עיף.[34] **פונדיה**, כמ׳ פונדיון. כדכת׳, אשר ירשיעון אלהים ישלם שנים לרעהו.[35] וכבר פירשתיו באלפ״א ביט״א שלמעלה כי כל אותה הפרשה, כי יתן איש אל רעהו בשומר שכר הכת׳ מדבר. וגונב מבית האיש, שטוען שנגנב ממנו ואחר כך נמצא שהוא עצמו גנבו ישלם שני׳, ודווקא במטלטלין אבל בקרקעות אינו משלם כפל כמ׳ שפירשתי.[36] **בגא**, בקעה שיש בה שדות וכרמים. כמ׳, הני בני בירב דדיירי בבגא, פרק קמא דפסחים.[37] **לא משתלים מדידידה**, פי׳, אינו משלם הגנב משלו כלום להוסיף עליו כפל או יותר אלא במה שגנב לבד, שכיון שאינו נותן כפל אינו נותן אלא את שלבעל הבית. **מרוס דעייל בליליא למיחתר**, פי׳, שוטה הוא הגנב הנכנס בלילה במחתרת, שאם בעל הבית יתחזק לנגדו ויהרגהו בין בעץ בין באבן בין

24 גטין ע ע״א ועוד.
25 סנהדרין לז ע״א.
26 תוספתא ב״ק, פ״ז ה״י.
26א בראשית ד ב, ובתרגומים שם ועוד.
27 דניאל ב ה, ח, ובפירוש המיוחס לרס״ג, שם.
28 חולין נט ע״ב; ראה עה״ש, ערך חדק א׳.
29 ב״ק ה ע״א: ״אמר רבי אבהו כולן כאבות לשלם ממיטב״. וראה רש״י שם ד״ה תחת נתינה כו׳.
30 תוספתא ב״ק, פ״ז ה״י.
30א במדבר יט ב, ובתרגומים שם ועוד.
31 שבת נז ע״ב.
32 ב״מ מג ע״א; שם נז ע״ב.
33 דברים לג כא. וראה סוטה יג ע״ב, ובתרגומים וברש״י לדברים שם.
34 שמות כח טז, ות״א שם.
35 שמות כב ח.
36 ראה לעיל פיוט י״א ד״ה כד זיהרין.
37 פסחים ח ע״ב: ״בבאגא״.

בברזל אין לו דמים.[38] **מרוס**, פת׳ שוטה בלשון יוון. בפסיקתא דשמעו, אמ׳ ר׳ ראובן בהדין לישנא יוונית צווחין לשטייא מורא.[39] **מתר**, פי׳ אוד שלתנור.[40] כלומ׳, בעץ או בגרזן, הוא נרגא העשוי לחתוך ולהרוג את האנשים במחתרת.[41] כלומ׳, שמתכוין ממש להורגו. **נרגוניה יתוב ברישיה**, כלומ׳, ישוב עמלו בראשו של גנב. **נרגוניה**, מלש׳ ותרגנו.[42] **עתר**, לש׳ ריבוי. כמ׳ עתרת שלום,[43] שפת׳ לש׳ ריבוי שלום. **סביל גרמי קדם סהדי כול׳**, פי׳, טוב לו לבעל הבית לסבול עצמו שלא להרוג את הגנב אם יש עדים בדבר, שאז ודאי לא הלך על עסקי נפשות. אלא סברתו של גנב היה לגנוב ממונו ואם הרגו נתחייב בנפשו וגם הוא מתחייב עליו. וזה הוא שכת׳, אם זרחה השמש עליו דמים לו, ומתרג׳ אם עינא דסהדיא נפלת עלוהי דמא ליה.[44] **פרידיה**, מרגליותיו, כלומ׳ ממונו. **עבט נפשיה**, מלש׳ לא יעבטון אורחותם, ופת׳ לש׳ עיקול כדברי מנחם בן סרוק זצ״ל.[45] **בזידי**, בזדון. **פנקט אזיל לאסבא בישא כול׳**, פי׳, הגנב ההולך בשטותו לבית המקדש לגנוב תרומות הקודש חייב [65]
להשיב הקרן והחומש.[46] **פנקט**, פי׳ היכל כדאמ׳ בריש ויקרא רבא, כשהיו שומעין האומות קול הדיבר היו נתרזין מתוך פניקטיהן.[47] לשמצה בקמיהם תרג׳ לאסבותהון שום ביש לדריהון.[48] **פנון**, מלש׳ ופנו את הבית.[49] תרומה תרג׳ אפרשותא.[50] **צניף קרנא בטופיין חומשא**, שמוסיף ענף על השו[רש]. כלומ׳, שמרבה החומש על הקרן שגזל. בראש אמיר תרג׳ בריש צנפא.[51] **בטופיין**, לש׳ ריבוי, כמ׳ עדיף טפי.[52] **קייום למישקל ותקלי תריצי כול׳**, פי׳, [לקיים] התורה הכתוב׳ במשקלות, מאזני צדק אבני צדק.[53] כי האונאה אין לה ממשות ואין לה תועלת כמ׳ קורי עכביש, כך אין תועלת והנאה בגזל. ומכניס רעב ברמ״ח איברים, כי בעון הגזל רעב בא לעולם, כאשר פירשנו למעלה בתרגום לא תגנוב.[54] אך מי שמקיים תרי״ג מצוות נוצל מכל פורענות המתרגשת ובאה לעולם. **תריצי**, תרג׳ דברי

38 שמות כב א.

39 פסדר״כ, יד, עמ׳ 246 ובש״נ שם.

40 ראה עה״ש, ערך מתרא.

41 ראה שם, ערך נרג.

42 דברים א כז.

43 ירמיה לג ו.

44 שמות כב ב, ות״א שם. וראה מכילתא, נזיקין יג, עמ׳ 293 ומקבילות.

45 יואל ב ז; ראה מחברת מנחם, מהד׳ פיליפובסקי, עמ׳ 129-130, בערך עבט.

46 ראה השגות הראב״ד להרמב״ם, הלכות גניבה, פ״ב ה״א. [ודברי המפרש תמוהים, שהרי אין מעילה אלא בשוגג ואם הלך ״בשטותו לבית המקדש״ הרי הזיד, ועיין באור שמח לרמב״ם שם.]

47 וי״ר א יא, עמ׳ כו.

48 שמות לב כה, ות״א שם.

49 ויקרא יד לו.

50 שמות כח ב, ובתרגומים שם ועוד.

51 ישעיה יז ו; בת״י מהד׳ שפרבר, ״בריש צנפא״, אבל בדפוסים הרגילים ״בריש ענפא״, ראה שם בח״נ.

52 ברכות כד ע״א ועוד.

53 ויקרא יט ל״ו.

54 בראש הפירוש לפיוט י״א.

צדיקים פתג׳ תריצין.[55] **קיון עכביתא**, תרג׳ קורי עכביש יארוגו.[56] **מאני פצי**, מי שמאנה חבירו מפצפצו ומנפצו כקורי עכביש שאין בהם ממש. מלש׳ ונפוץ הכדים,[57] ויפצפצני.[58] **ריל״ח איברין**, כמ׳ רמ״ח וכן **רית״ג** כמ׳ תרי״ג, ואם יאמר אדם מה ראה הפייטן לשנות, לפי שהיו״דין הצריכין לו, שהרי שם הפייט רמוז באות השנית שלכל שיטה ושיטה והמשכיל יבין.[59] **חצי**, לש׳ מחיצה. **פצי**, מלש׳ פצני והצילני,[60] ואינו **פצי** ראשון כפצי[61] אחרון, כמ׳ שפירשנו. **שמצא מלמישקל זיל כול׳**, פי׳ ואם תרצה ליזהר שלא לקנות שמץ רע לעצמך, צא ולמד מעכן שמעל ב[חרם], שהיה משבט יהודה שנקרא גור אריה,[62] [66] שנתכרכמו פניו ונתבייש בגורל שנפל עליו וגילה גניבתו וגם אנשי ביתו שהם ידעו הדבר ולא גילו אותו.[63] **עורזיל**, ס״א, **אורזיל**, תרג׳ עופר בשיר השירים.[64] **שמשמין אפיה**, נתכרכמו פניו. בויקרא רבא, למי חכלילות עיניים, למאן שמשמנן דעיינין.[65] **שמ... נכסי**, על הנכסים שגזל. **בורזיל**, שמש ותלמיד.[66] כלומ׳, בני ביתו שלא גילו עליו. **תני אורייתא ובה לעסוקי כול׳**. פי׳, טוב הוא שישתדל האדם ללמוד תורה ולהתעסק בה כדי שיתחדש ויאירו פניו בעולם שיני, כלומ׳ לעולם הבא, וגם בעולם הזה לקבל שכר טוב לבטל שעבוד מלכיות. על כן נאה לזקן ולבחור להעניק גרגרותיו בדברי תורה.[67] **תני אורייתא**, תרג׳ ושננתם ותתנינן.[68] **לחדותי**, לש׳ חידוש. **ולבהוקי**, לש׳ אור. **תנבת**, מלש׳ תונבא הוא דנקיט ליה.[69] וזהמתו חייתו לחם תרג׳ ומן תונבא דנקיט ליה.[70] ובלש׳ יון חולי הקרב העליון, הוא האסטמוכוס, נקרא איתוניבא.[71] **גרגרין לענוקי**, מלש׳ כי ליוית חן הם לראשך וענקים לגרגרותיך.[72]

55 שמות כג ח, ות״א שם ועוד.

56 ישעיה נט ה, ובת״י שם.

57 שופטים ז יט.

58 איוב טז יב.

59 חתימת השם, יהודה בר בנימן, מסומנת בגוף בפיוט, ראה עמ׳ 86. ואולי הוא הפייטן הנזכר ע״י צונץ, ליטג׳, עמ׳ 174, פייטן שחי במאה הי״ב.

60 תהלים קמד ז, יא.

61 בכ״י: ״לפצי״.

62 בראשית מט ט.

63 סנהדרין מג ע״ב-מד ע״א; פדר״א פל״ח.

64 שיה״ש ח יד, ותרגום שם. וראה ערך אורזילא במלון לתרגומים של לוי.

65 וי״ר יב א, עמ׳ רמט-רנ.

66 ב״ק נו ע״ב ופירוש רש״י שם, ד״ה לברזיליה.

67 השווה ספרי דברים, פיסקא י, עמ׳ 18 ומקבילות, ולענין בטול שעבוד מלכיות ראה אבות פ״ג מ״ה.

68 דברים ו ז, ות״א שם.

69 יומא פג ע״א.

70 איוב לג כ, ות״י שם.

71 הפירוש הניתן כאן אינו מובא במקורות; על הפירושים הרגילים ראה עה״ש, ערך תנבא וראה גם בערכו בתוספות הערוך.

72 משלי א ט.

י״ג לא תענה

מתרג׳ אותו בתרג׳ אונקלוס ובתרג׳ ירושלמי.[1]

עמי בני יש׳ לא תהוון משהדין כול׳, ארום בחובי שהדי שקרא ענניין סלקי[ן] כול׳,[2] פי׳, כדכת׳ נשיאים ורוח וגשם איין איש מתהלל במתת שקר, [ש]פוסלין עדותן על ידי שוחד.[3] **בצורתא,** רעב כמ׳ על דברי הבצ[רות].[4]

אלפא ביט [67]

אזדהר משהדות שקר ולישנא בישא,[5] פי׳, היזהר שלא להעיד עדות שקר ושלא לספר לש׳ הרע, כי אינך יודע כמה עונשו של לשון הרע גדול שהיא הורגת ג׳ בני האדם, המספרו והמקבלו ומי שנאמר עליו. בפסיק׳ דפרה, למה נקרא שמו של לש׳ הרע שלישי שהורג שלשה, האומרו והמקבלו ומי שנאמר עליו.[6] **בגומרהא,** גחלים תרג׳ גומרין.[7] לש׳ הכת׳ מה יתן לך ומה יוסיף לך לשון רמייה חיצי גיבור שנונים עם גחלי רתמים.[8] **לשגשא,** תרג׳ ויהם את מחנה מצרים ושגיש.[9] **דמשתעי לה,** תרג׳ ויספר ואישתעי.[10] **וצייתא,** תרג׳ האזינו אציתו.[11] **ודי עליה מתלחשא,** ומי שנאמר עליו. **גירא אתמתילת ושלהובית דרתמא כול׳,** פי׳, והלשון הרע נמשלת לחצים שנונים וגחלי רתמים, כדכת׳ חיצי גיבור שנונים וגו׳.[12] **משתרייא בארעא,** עומדת בארץ ואוכלת עד הרקיע, כדכת׳ שתו בשמים פיהם ולשונם תהלך בארץ.[13] ומי שיכול לכבוש אותה ולסכור את פיה ייקרא גיבור וכוחו ככח האריה. **גירא,** אשכיר חציי מדם תרגום ארוה גרריי מדמא.[14] **אתמתילת,** תרג׳ משל מ[ת]לא.[15] **[רתמא],** רתמים.[16] **דין לה גיברא וחילתיה דנהמי,** כלומ׳ זה [האדם] נקרא גיבור וכוחו ככח ארי נוהם, מי שיכול **לש[יצ[אי ית[ה] ולמסכר פומה, למסכר,** מלש׳ כי יסכר פי

1 ראה לעיל א׳, הערה 4.
2 ראה לעיל ט׳, הערה 2.
3 משלי כה יד, ופסוק זה נדרש על ענין עדות שקר, ראה סנהדרין כט ע״א.
4 ירמיה יד א.
5 דוידזון, א, 2185, ובמקורות הנוספים, כרך ד, עמ׳ 232 ; ראה טל, עמ׳ 38-50 (הנוסח הארמי, תרגום עברי והערות).
6 פסדר״כ, ד, עמ׳ 58.
7 ויקרא טז יב, ובתרגומים שם ועוד.
8 תהלים קכ ג-ד.
9 שמות יד כד, ות״א שם.
10 בראשית כד סו, ות״א שם ועוד.
11 דברים לב א, ות״א שם.
12 תהלים קכ ד. וראה מה שנדרש עליו בערכין טו ע״ב.
13 תהלים עג ט. וראה בערכין, הנ״ל.
14 דברים לב מב.
15 במדבר כג ז, ות״א שם ועוד.
16 תהלים קכ ד, ות״י שם.

[דו]ברי שקר.[17] **האי סהדא שקרא בשותיה דכייל כול׳**, פי׳, זה העד שמעיד שקר על חבירו בדיבורו שהוא מספר עליו, האיש המשכירו להעיד שקר קורא לו רשע, שכן מצינו באיזבל, והושיבו שנים אנשים בני בליעל נגדו וגו׳, שהיא גורמת להן להעיד שקר וקוראה אותן בני בליעל.[18] וסוף דבר, אם נודע שהוא עד שקר והוזם, ישוב עמלו בראשו[19] ועושין לו כאשר [68]
זמם לעשות לאחיו.[20] **בשותיה**, בדיבורו, כמ׳ שותיה דמר לא גמירנא דמעשה דרב יהודה בר יחזקאל בקידושין.[21] ופת׳ שעותיה, עי״ן בלועה מלש׳ ואשתעי. כי באחת ידבר אל תרג׳ בחדא שותא ימלל אלהא.[22] **דכייל**, שאומ׳, כמ׳ די אכלו קרצוהי.[23] ושרק לו תרג׳ ויכלי ליה.[24] **אגוריה**, השוכר אותו. **נכליה**, לש׳ נכל ומרמה. **בסאתא דכייל**, במידה שמודד. וימודו בעומר תרג׳ וכלו בעומרא.[25] וכן בתים לאשירה תרג׳ מכלתא.[26] **סאתא**, לש׳ סאה. ואינו דומה פתרון **דכייל** הראשון לאחרון כמ׳ שפירשתי. **זוחלא קדמאה מכולא הוה ערים כול׳**, פי׳, הנחש הראשון שהיה [ערום] מכל... כמ׳ דתימ׳ והנחש היה ערום מכל חית השדה.[27] בבראשית רבא פרש׳ י״ט, תנא בש׳ ר׳ מאיר לפי גד[ולתו שלנחש היתה] מפלתו, ערום מכל. ארור מכל.[28] **חמייה [ליקריה דרב]ייא דחלתא איתרים**, פי׳, ראה בכבודו שלאדם הר[אשון]... [ר]ביא נער, על שם שהיה בן יומו ועומד על... ונקרא חלה, כמי שמגבל את העיסה ומרים ממנה [את החלה], כך גיבל הקב״ה את עפרו והרים ממנה חלה וברא ממנו אדם, ומפורש בתנחומ׳ שלהי פרש׳ נח, נידה חלה הדלקת הנר, חלה על שגרמה מיתה לאדם הראשון שהיה חלתו שלהקב״ה.[29] **ואתקני ביה**, מלש׳ וקנאה את אשתו, זאת תורת הקנאות.[30] בבראשית רבא, אמ׳ ר׳ יהושע בן קרחה להודיעך מאי זה חט קפץ עליהם אותו רשע, מתוך שראה אותם עסוקים בדרך ארץ נתאווה לה,[31] ובסוטה פרק א׳, וכן מצינו בנחש הקדמוני כול׳, ואמ׳ אהרוג את אדם ואשא את חוה.[32] **זוחלא**, על שם זוחלי עפר.[33] **רביא**, ויגדל הילד תרג׳ ורבא רביא.[34] **איתרים**, לש׳ תרומה כמ׳ חלה תרימו [69]

17 תהלים סג יב.
18 מלכים א כא י. וראה סנהדרין כט ע״א.
19 תהלים ז יז.
20 דברים יט יט.
21 קידושין ע ע״ב.
22 איוב לג יד, ותרגום שם [וראה ערוך, ערך סר ב׳].
23 דניאל ו כה.
24 ישעיה ה כז, ות״א שם.
25 שמות טז יח, ות״א שם.
26 מלכים ב כג ז. וכן פירש הערוך, ערך כל ז׳, ומובא ברד״ק על הפסוק הנ״ל.
27 בראשית ג א.
28 ב״ר יט א, עמ׳ 170.
29 תנחומא הישן, נח, פיסקא א (וזה בתחלת הפרשה ולא בשלהי פרשת נח); ראה גם ב״ר יד א, עמ׳ 126 [ועיין עוד שם עמ׳ 168 בהערה לשורה 7. לענין כבודו של אדם הראשון ראה סנהדרין נט ע״ב].
30 במדבר ה יד, כט.
31 ב״ר יח ו, עמ׳ 168.
32 סוטה ט ע״ב.
33 דברים לב כד.
34 שמות ב י, ות״א שם.

תרומה.[35] **ואגביב**, לש' אסיפה וקיבוץ, כמ' לקשש קש לתבן תרג' לגבבא.[36] או יש לפרש' מלש' וישיבו אותנו דבר תרג' ירושלמי ואוגיבו.[37] **מילי דשקרין**, דברי שקר המפורש לפנינו, אף כי אמ' אלהים לא תאכלו וג'.[38] **טעין על טפשיתא ושדליה במיליה כול'**, פי', מה עשה הנחש הלך לו אצל חוה שהיתה [פותה] ושידל אותה בדברים.[38א] כי יפתה תרג' ארי [י']שדל[39] ... אשר בתוך הגן טעם הקב"ה ... אכלו (?) ... אשר בו בלא טורח ועמל אבל (?) ... בעמלו. כלומ' שכל מעשיו באים[40] ש... ור' משה אחי נר"ו[41] **פירש חמית בר נש דלא סני [בר עמ]ליה**, אתמהה, וכי יש אומן בעולם שאינו שונא [את בן אומנו]תו, על כן הוא אומר לכם לא תאכלו ממנו, שאם תאכלו ממנו תהיו כמותו ליכנס באומנותו, כמ' דתימ' ויפקחו עיניכם והייתם כאלהים, מה הוא בורא עולמות אף אתם תבראו עולמ'. וזה הפירוש הוא עיקר וכן מפורש בבראשית רבא.[42] **טעין**, לש' טענה. **טפשיתא**, לש' טפשות ופתיות. **מאיבא דין**, ותקח מפריו תרג' ונסיבת מאיביה.[43] **קיריס**, אדון בלש' יוון.[44] **שכליליה**, יסד אותו. **כד אתגלי קב"ה כול'**, פי', כשנגלה הקב"ה לדון את אדם וחוה על שטעו בדברי הנחש והפרו את ציווייו, עם כולם נשא ונתן, כדכת' מי הגיד לך כי עירום אתה המן העץ אשר ציויתיך לאכל וגו', ויאמר האשה אשר נתת עמדי וגו', וכן לחוה ויאמר ה' אלקים אל האשה מה זאת עשית ותאמר האשה הנחש השיאני ואוכל. אבל כשקילל את הנחש לא טען עמו כל עיקר, דכת' ויאמר [ה' א]לקים אל [הנחש כי] עשית זאת ארור אתה מכל הבהמה [וגו']. דן אות[ו ב]ל[א] טענ[ה ל]פי שהנחש היה לו להשיב [דברי הרב ודברי תלמיד] דברי מי שומעין.[45] בבראשית רבא... [ויאמר] ה' אלקים אל הנחש כי עשית זאת וגו' [עם א]דם נשא ונתן, עם חווה נשא ונתן ועם הנחש לא נשא [ונתן, אלא אמר] הקב"ה נחש זה, רשע הוא בעל תשובות. אם [אני אומר ל]ו דבר הוא יאמ', [70] אתה ציוית אותם ואני ציויתי, [למה הני]חו ציווייך והלכו אחר ציוויי, אלא קפץ עליו ופסק לו.[46] **אוגיבתא**, תשובה, וישיבו אותנו דבר תרג' ואוגיבו.[47] **למפעי**, לש' צעקה, כמ' כיולדה אפעה.[48] **חזי דינא למיצת בקיעי**, ראוי הוא בדין שישמעו הבקיאין דברי האדון

35 במדבר טו כ.
36 שמות ה יב, ות"א שם.
37 במדבר יג כו; דברים א כב. ובתרגומים שלפנינו ליתא "ואוגיבו" אלא "ויתיבו", אבל הנוסח "ואוגיבו" מובא גם בערוך, ערך גב ה', וכבר העיר שם קאהוט על הנ"ל.
38 בראשית ג א.
38א משלי ט יג. וראה להלן ד"ה טפשיתא. [ראה פדר"א פי"ג, לב ע"א ואדר"נ, פ"א, עמ' 6-7.]
39 שמות כב טו, ות"א שם.
40 מכאן ואילך בה"י לקוי ומטושטש בכמה מקומות ואי־אפשר להשלים את כל מה שחסר. את המקומות הלקויים ציינתי רק בשלש נקודות אפילו אם חסרה יותר ממלה אחת.
41 ראה מבוא, עמ' 7.
42 ב"ר יט ד, עמ' 172-173.
43 בראשית ג ו, ות"א שם.
44 ראה לעיל א, הערה 49.
45 ב"ר כ ב, עמ' 183 ובמקבילות, במיוחד בסנהדרין כט ע"א.
46 ב"ר הנ"ל.
47 ראה לעיל, הערה 37.
48 ישעיה מב יד.

ויניחו דברי העבד. ובמקצת סידורים כת׳ **חזו למיצת בקיעי**, ופת׳ ראוים לשמוע הבקיאין. **למיצת**, הסכת ושמע יש׳ תרג׳ אצית.[49] ואם ישאל השואל, אם כן שלפי שהיה לו לנחש מה להשיב לא נכנס עמו בדברים, הרי עיבר עליו מידת הדין. ישיב המשיב, שאע״פ שהיה הנחש יכול להשיב דברי הרב ודברי תלמיד דברי מי שומעין, לא היה נפטר מן הדין, שהרי מסית היה, ואין טוענין למסית. כלומ׳, שאין מקבלין טענה מן המסית לפי שלא היה לו להתחיל בדברים כלל. אלא למה לא נכנס עמו בדברים, לפי שלא רצה להרבות דבר[ים][50]... יכון לנגד עיני ...[51] **[כמא דפטר ברגז כן] אירעיה כול׳**, פי׳, פת׳ שפתח ... פוטר מים ראשית מדון[52] ופת׳ אותו ... [בראשית רבא] פרש׳ י״ט, אמ׳ ר׳ חנינא בר סנסן ארבע[ה הן פתחו באף אבדו] באף, הנחש ושר האופים ועדת קרח והמן, [נחש ויאמר אל האשה] אף כי אמר אלקים, שר האופים דכת׳ אף אני [בחלומי], עדת קרת דכת׳ אף לא אל ארץ זבת חלב ודבש [הביאתנו], המן דכת׳ אף לא הביאה וג׳.[53] **בעשרה איתליט**, שנתקלל הנחש עשר קללות.[54] **ואתקציצו כרעיה**, שנקצצו רגליו, בבראשית רבא פרש׳ י״ט, ר׳ הושעיה רבא אמ׳ דקרטוס היה עומד ורגלים יש לו,[55] ובפרשתא כ׳, בשעה שאמ׳ הקב״ה לנחש על גחונך תלך ירדו מלאכי השרת וקצצו ידיו ורגליו כול׳.[56] **ולאסתגורי גופיה**, להצטרע, תרג׳ צרעת סגירותא.[57] **ולעלמ׳ דאתי כול׳**, שגם לעולם הבא לא יתרפאו חולייו. כדאיתא בבראשית רבא פרש׳ כ׳, אמ׳ ר׳ לוי לעתיד לבוא הכל מתרפאין חוץ מנחש וגבעוני, נחש דכת׳ ונחש עפר לחמו. גבעוני, דכת׳ והעובד העיר יעבדוהו מכל שבטי [71] ישראל.[58] עשר קללות שנתקלל הנחש אילו הם, להיאלם לשונו, לקצץ רגליו, להיות מאכלו עפר, להפשיט עורו, להשית [איבה] ... [ע]ליו להורגו, להצטרע, ...ין אדם אפי׳ שאר ... [ע]פר.[59] **[מאללי ארעא על סהדות] שקרא כול׳**, פי׳, המרגלים שהוציאו ... [יש]ראל והעידו עדות שקר על עצים[60] ואבנים ... ארץ אוכלת יושביה היא,[61] נענשו ומתו ... ה]ת]אר[כ]ה ל[ש]ונן עד טבורם והיו התולעים יוצאין [מלשון ונכנסין] לטיבור ומן הטיבור ללשון,[62] כל שכן המוציא שם רע [על ח]בירו [שנ]ענש. **מאללי**, תרג׳ מרגלים.[63] **נשתרבב**,

49 דברים כז ט, ות״א שם.
50 עפ״י סנהדרין כט ע״א, [וע״ש בתוספות וביחוד במ״ש הרד״ק בפירושו לבראשית ג׳ י״ד וחידושי רבינו יונה לסנהדרין שם.]
51 סוף הפסוק בתהלים ק״א ז׳: ״לא ישב בקרב ביתי עשה רמיה דבר שקרים״ וכו׳.
52 משלי יז יד.
53 ב״ר יט ב, עמ׳ 171.
54 ראה להלן, הערה 59.
55 ב״ר יט א, עמ׳ 171.
56 ב״ר כ ה, עמ׳ 186.
57 ויקרא יג ג, ות״א שם ועוד.
58 ב״ר כ ה, עמ׳ 186-187.
59 אבות דר׳ נתן, נו״ב פמ״ב, עמ׳ 117. וראה אגדות היהודים, ה, עמ׳ 100-101.
60 בכ״י, בטעות: ״עצמם״.
61 במדבר יג לב.
62 עפ״י סוטה לה ע״א.
63 בראשית מב ט, ות״א שם ועוד.

כמ׳ אל תיקרי שיברתה אלא שירבבתה דברכות פרק הרואה,[64] ופת׳ לש׳ משיכה והארכה.
קוקני ורחשי, תולעים ושרצים, כמ׳ למאי אכלי ליה לקוקני דפרק שמונה שרצים,[65] ותרג׳
שרץ ריחשי.[66] **גייצו**, כמ׳ קצצו. **לסתרא**, מלש׳ בניין נערים סתירה.[67] **סיב לך מן הדא מילייא
למגמרא**, פי׳, על כן יש לך לקחת מוסר מאילו הדברים ללמוד ולדון קל וחומר, ומה אם
המרגלים שהוציאו שם רע על עצים ואבנים כך נענשו במיתה חמורה כזאת, המרשיע
להוציא שם רע על חבירו על אחת כמה וכמה. **פתיא דעולימתא נסיב וכביש כול׳**, פי׳, הנער
שנושא אשה ושנאה והוציא עליה שם רע לאמר [שלא היו ל]ה בתולים ואחר ... בו וענשו
אות[ו] ... כך מלקין אותו מכות.[68] [ב״ר] פרש׳ פ״ח, אמ׳ ר׳ ל[וי] בער[ביא צווחין לינוקא
פתיא][69] וקורא אותו נער על שם ... מעשה ... האמת. **עולימתא**, תרג׳ נערה.[70] **צוראי**, מנה (?) ...
פרק יש בכור, אמ׳ רב יהודה אמ׳ רב [א]ס[י] [כ]ל [הכסף האמור] בתורה סתם כסף צורי[71] והבא
כת׳ ... **דאבאיש**, על הרעה שעשה. **ומתראדיי במחאן** ... מרדות, דכת׳ ויסרו אותו.[72]
וילפינן ויסרו דהכא מן ויסרו דבן סורר ומורה ובן דסורר ומורה מבן והיה אם בן הכות [72]
הרשע.[73] **שביש**, לש׳ שבשתא דעל על.[74] **דאניס ומשדל לה לבתולתא כול׳**, פי׳, האונס
והמפתה את הבתולה חמשים כסף פורע לה, וכך היא הקצבה שלה, אבל המוציא שם רע
פורע מאה כסף כמ׳ שפירשנו,[75] ועוד מלקין אותו מכות מרדות, בוא וראה כי גדול עונש
המוציא שם רע מהעושה מעשה. **דאניס ומשדל**, פי׳, האונס והמפתה. וכי יפתה איש
בתולה תרג׳ ארי ישדל. בפרש׳ אלה המשפטים, וכי יפתה איש בתולה אשר לא אורשה וגו׳
ואם מאן ימאן אביה וגו׳ כסף ישקול כמוהר הבתולות,[76] ומשפט האונס בפרש׳ כי תצא [כי
ימצא איש נער]ה בתולה אשר לא אורשה וגו׳ ונתן [האיש][77] ... **נגדותא**, מלקות. **[קבלני
דאיתפרי]קו מדחוק פולחנא וגו׳**, פי׳, ישראל שהיו תמי[הין] ... ומלינים ומתרעמים על
הקב״ה שהוציאם מתחת [סבלו]ת מצרים מבית עבדים, בעשרה נסיונות ניסו להקב״ה ...
וחזק (?) ואעפ״כ לא נתחתם עליהם גזר דין עד ... [המ]רגלים על ידי לשון הרע.[77א] **קבלני**,

64 ברכות נד ע״ב.
65 שבת קט ע״ב.
66 בראשית א כ, ות״א שם ועוד.
67 מגלה לא ע״ב.
68 דברים כב יג-יט.
69 ב״ר פז א, עמ׳ 1061 ובח״נ שם.
70 דברים כב כג, ות״א שם ועוד.
71 בכורות נ ע״ב.
72 דברים כב יח.
73 כתובות מו ע״א.
74 פסחים קיב ע״א.
75 ערכין פ״ג מ״ד-מ״ה.
76 שמות כב טו-טז, ות״א שם.
77 דברים כב כח-כט.
77א ראה להלן, הערה 79.

פת׳ בעלי צעקות, [צעקת בני] ישראל תרג׳ קבילת בני ישראל.[78] **בעשרה נסיאו**, [בעשרה נסיונות] ניסו להקב״ה במדבר ואילו הן, ב׳ בים, א׳ ... וא׳ ... ב׳ במים, א׳ ברפידים וא׳ במרה (?), ב׳ בשליו, א׳ בשליו ראשון וא׳ בשליו האחרון, ב׳ במן, אל תותירו ויותירו, אל תצאו ויצאו, א׳ בעגל, א׳ במדבר פארן דהיינו במרגלים, הה״ד וינסו אותי זה עשר פעמים ולא שמעו בקולי, ובזאת נתחתם גזר דינם למות במדבר מה שלא היה בשאר הנסיונ׳.[79] **ורשו גזירתהון**. כמ׳ ורשום גזירתהון,[80] גזר דינם. **חוסנא**, כח. או יש לפרשו מגזרת ה׳ על עמך.[81] כלומ׳, לפי שהיה חס עליהם לא נתחתם גזר דינם עד שחטאו במרגלים. **רב רעיא דבר דאכיל עדתיה כול׳**, פי׳, דואג שהיה אביר הרועים[82] אמר לשאול המלך, שהיה משבט בנימן, שכת׳ בו בבקר יאכל עד,[83] כשהלך בנוב [עיר] הכהנים לזבוח את זבח הימים ראה
דוד ... אחימלך הכהן ושאל לו הרב ולחם,[84] אביר הרועים [תרג׳ רב] רעיא.[85] **דבר דאביל** [73]
עדתיה, של בן(?) אוכל(?) ... לשאול שבא משבט בנימן. **לנוב במתא**, ... **לאלחנן חמא**, דוד נקרא אלחנן כדכת׳ [ותהי עוד המלחמה] בגוב עם הפלשתים ויך אלחנן בן יערי [ארגים בית הלחמי], תירג׳ יונתן וקטל דוד [בר] ישי מ[חי][86] ... ובאגדת רות פרש׳ ב׳, ויך אלחנן, זה דוד [שחננו הקב״ה, בן] יערי, שהיה גדל ביער, פי׳ שהיה ... [אורגים], שהיו מעלין לו הלכה והוא אורגה.[87] **במותיה**, פי׳ בבואו. **ובעא סייפא**, חרב. **ונהם זוודתיה**, לחם צידתו. **נהמא**, לחם, צידה תרג׳ זוודין.[88] **ארכיס ושקר על רבא שמשא**, פי׳, כשראה דואג את דוד שבא וביקש מאחימלך לחם וחרב, הלך והלשין לשאול את אחימלך שהיה כהן גדול. והעיד עליו ששאל לו באפוד וגרם שנהרג אחימלך ופ״ה כהנים עמו. כדכת׳ ויאמר המלך לדואג סוב אתה ופגע בכהנים וגו׳,[89] ובעבור כן נעקר מן העולם הזה, דכת׳ אנשי דמים ומרמה לא יחצו ימיהם וגו׳,[90] ומן העולם הבא כמפורש בסנהדרין פרק חלק, אילו שאין להם חלק לעולם הבא, אחיתופל, בלעם ודואג.[91] **אר]כיס**, פי׳ הלשין, כמ׳ מרוכסי איש.[92] והוא לש׳ חיבור מגזרת ... להעמידן על ... עקיבה ... היה ... גדול ... היא לו ... כן אמ׳ ... נתחייב למיתה בור וסירה גרמו לו ... [ואבי] ראה גם ראה כנף מעילך בידי כי בכרתי את כנף מעילך ולא הרגתיך, אמ׳ ליה אבנר, מה את בע׳ מן גלגלי דדין, פי׳ ממה

78 שמות ג ט, ות״א שם.
79 אדר״נ, נו״ב, פל״ח, עמ׳ 98. וראה גם ערכין פ״ג מ״ה ובבלי שם, טו ע״א.
80 [ראה גטין פו ע״א ותוספות ד״ה רושם וב״ר פא ב, עמ׳ 971; וראה ערוך, ערך רש ד׳.]
81 צריך להשלים: ״חוסה ה׳״ וכו׳.
82 שמואל א כא ח.
83 בראשית מט כז.
84 שמואל א כב ט ואילך.
85 שם כא ח, ות״י שם.
86 שמואל ב כא יט, ות״י שם.
87 רות רבא ב ב.
88 בראשית מב כה, ות״א שם ועוד.
89 שמואל א כב יח.
90 סנהדרין סט ע״ב.
91 סנהדרין פ״י מ״ב.
92 תהלים לא כא, וראה רש״י שם.

שהוא משתבח עליך, בסירה הוערת, ... דרך גררות ... נדבקו בו קוצים ... [כיון] דאתי לגבי מעגל אמ׳ לו הלא תענה אבנר, בכנף אמרת בסירה הוערת, חנית וצפחת בסירה הוערו, אמ׳ ליה ... בבור שכחום, וזהו דכת׳ באבנר וישיבו אותו מבור ... סירה.[93] **דא הוות ליה על דלא אשלם פלוגתא**, פת׳ ולמה נענש לפי שהיה בידו למחות בשאול ולא מיחה ולא ... הניחו להשלים עם דוד.[94] **תא חמי כמה גרמא שותא**, בוא וראה כמה גדול כח הדיבור כי בכח הלשון תלוי מות [וחיים]...[95]

93 פסדר״כ, ד, עמ׳ 58-59; שם נגמר המאמר במלים ״חנית וצפחת בסירה הוערו״. למה שכתוב כאן לפנינו על הבור השוה סנהדרין מט ע״א: ״בור וסירה גרמו לו לאבנר שיהרג״. כנראה בנוסח של פסדר״כ שלפני רבינו המאמר נמשך וכלל גם את ענין הבור.

94 פסדר״כ הנ״ל.

95 משלי יח כא. וראה ערכין טו ע״ב.

נספח

[74]

כדי לתת בידי המעיין את נוסח י״ג הפיוטים הארמיים עליהם מוסבים דברי הפירוש העתקנו אותם כאן עפ״י המקורות הבאים:

א. דוידזון, אוצר, א, 7648; עפ״י טל עמ׳ 86, והיינימן עמ׳ 363-364. <ראה שירת בני מערבא (לעיל, מבוא, הערה 2), עמ׳ 110.<
ב. שם, שם, 6374; עפ״י טל, עמ׳ 103, והיינימן עמ׳ 365. <שם, עמ׳ 116.<
ג. שם, שם, 7669; עפ״י מחזור ויטרי, עמ׳ 336-337.
ד. שם, שם, 5697; עפ״י מחזור ויטרי, עמ׳ 338-339.
ה. שם, ח, 421, וראה גם ב, 166; עפ״י מחזור ויטרי, עמ׳ 337-338 ו־*REJ*, כרך 73 (1921), עמ׳ 18-19. <שירת בני מערבא, עמ׳ 120.<
ו. דוידזון, א, 5566; עפ״י טל עמ׳ 51.
ז. שם, א, 7708; עפ״י מחזור ויטרי, עמ׳ 340-341.
ח. שם, א, 5812; עפ״י טל עמ׳ 80, והיינימן עמ׳ 366-367. <שירת בני מערבא, עמ׳ 124.<
ט. שם, א, 3197; עפ״י מחזור ויטרי, עמ׳ 341-342. <שם, עמ׳ 130.<
י. שם, א, 3196; עפ״י טל עמ׳ 94-95. <שם, עמ׳ 136.<
יא. שם, א, 26; עפ״י טל עמ׳ 28-29.
יב. אינו נזכר באוצר; שוחזר עפ״י ההבאות שבפירוש.
יג. דוידזון, א, 2185; עפ״י טל עמ׳ 38-39.

א

ארכין ה׳ שמיא לסיני/ ואמר למשה מהמני תא סוק
בני פלטין לא יבהלונך/ דכבש יתהון סבך מן ריש
גומרין דאתון אדליק נמרוד/ ולא יכיל למכוי רגלוי דסבך
דבק לית הוא נורא דמלאכיי בך/ דעמך אשא אכלא אשא
הא אנא מלבש לך פורפירן דידי/ דאית ביה גברו דלא לקרוב לוותך
וקבעית קרני הודא ברישך/ דאין קריב מלאכא תנגשיניה בהון
זעירא לא תהוי באפך משה/ דלית את ידע מה חיבתך עלי
חי אנא וקיים דברייא איקוניך/ עד דלא שכללת רומא ומוכא
טירוני מרומא קמו להון תמיהין/ דין אכסנא הכא מאן הוא
יה יהב רשו לבשרא למקרב להכא/ ומן כדו אנן אנפריסין

כד חמון מלאכייא דעני כדין להון/ דין אכסנא אנא מהודע לכון
לענוותנא אתקרי משה/ רעיהון דבניי מהמנא דבייתי
מכון שמיא ורמת ארעא/ ואשתכח קאי בין חייתא
נועו מלאכין ורעוד אופנים/ רחמון למשה קאים בערפילא
סערות גופיה קמו להון כחדא/ דאיקונין דיעקב הוה מזדקף לקיבליה
עול וקריב לך רעייהון דבניי/ צווח מן כורסיה דמלכא חייא
פסל לך לוחין מן סמפירינון/ מן כורסייה דמלכא רמא
צהיל הוה ליביה דמשה וחדי/ דהוה אל רחום אפולוגוס דידיה
קריבו מלאכיא לות כורסייה דקיריס/ ואמרין בבעו לא ישלוט בן
רישא דכיפא בחוטריה הוא תבר/ ואנן קשיין ליה למנגשא
שדי אמר ליה לא תדחל טליא/ דמימרי יהי לך בסעדך
תיסב אורייתי ותיחות לך/ דלא אשכחית בנביאי כותך

ב

אנגלי מרומא פתחון לי דניעול/ אמר משה
אנן לא פתחין דלא שלטין למפתח/ אמרין מלאכיא למשה נביא
בכון אנא צווח אורנוס פתחון לי/ אמר משה
בן למה את צווח קדם קיריס למצווח/ אמרין מלאכיא למשה נביא
גבר אנא מן גינוס דאברהם צדיקא/ אמר משה
גבר בר איתא את ובאתר דנור היך תיסק/ אמרין מלאכיא למשה נביא
גיברי חילא פתחון לי גלי/ אמר משה
גליא קמי בוריין דלית רשותא בידן/ אמרין מלאכיא למשה נביא
דאי אתון לא פתחין סופיכון למפתח/ אמר משה
דאי את סליק סופך למנחת/ אמרין מלאכיא למשה נביא
וסליק משה לרקיעה ואמר למלאכיא
לית אנא נחית לית אנא נחית/ עד אורייתי אסב/ עד אצבע גבורה תכתב
עד אסב כלתי ואיזיל/ עד איסב אוריתי ואיחות
לית אנא נחית לית אנא נחית/ עד בריוני נחמה/ עד בלוחות נרמה
עד אסב כלתי ואיזיל/ עד איטיב אוריתי ואיחות
לית אנא נחית לית אנא נחית/ עד גבור אשגח/ עד גוויתכון בקרני אנגח
עד אסב כלתי ואיזיל/ עד איסב אוריתי ואיחות
לית אנא נחית לית אנא נחית/ עד דתי אייפה/ עד דאמליל פה אל פה
עד אסב כלתי ואיזיל/ עד איסב אוריתי ואיחות
לית אנא נחית לית אנא נחית/ עד השופרין תוקעין/ עד האמון בי תובעין
עד אסב כלתי ואיזיל/ עד איסב אוריתי ואיחות
לית אנא נחית לית אנא נחית/ עד ונוריד יקרה/ עד לבנים נקרא
עד אסב כלתי ואיזיל/ עד איסב אוריתי ואיחות

לית אנא נחית לית אנא אחית/ עד זׂהוא נזהא בעננא/ עד נקרב לשכינה
עד אסב כלתי ואיזיל/ עד איסב אוריתי ואיחות
לית אנא נחית לית אנא נחית / עד חׂכמה נחמה עין בעין / עד נקבל לוחות שנים
עד אסב כלתי ואיזיל / עד איסב אוריתי ואיחות
לית אנא נחית לית אנא נחית / עד טׂבעת נחזה / עד חקוקה מזה ומזה
עד אסב כלתי ואיזיל/ עד אסב אוריתי ואיחות

ג [76]

ארעא רקדא שמיא זמרו/ כד אריס קיריס לברתיה דיעקב במיפקה לחירו
באצבעתה יהב לה חמש עיזקין דנהירו/ ועל כל עיזקא ועיזקא ארבע טבעין דבהירו
גבילן בצדקא חתימן בדינא/ נקישן בחסדא טביעו בחוסנא
דהב אובריזא אינון עזקיא דאחסנא/ חמש ספרי דאורייתא מוהרא דמטרונא
הוא יהב בידה עשר יקנטייא/ מוהרא קדמאה דחביבייא
ותלת מאוון ושיתין וחמש מרגלייא/ מוהרא תניינא דמחבבותא באפרי אפרייא
זמרגזין ארבעין ותמנייא ותרתון מאון/ מתליין על צוארא דכלתי ובספוון
חטף לארוסתיה מבין בתרייא בחיזוון/ כדארתיק על תרעא והות דמכא בתוון
טען יתה על גבי נשרין/ ואוכל יתה סילווא באורתא ומנא בצפרין
ימא בזע לה גנון בסיני קטר לה בזיהורין/ מלאכיא שושבינין ומשה בר גנון בפנטירין
כליל מלכו ברישא ועל ידהא שירין/ עגילין באוזנהא וקדשיה טבע אנחירין
לבושא דריקמא מסאנא דססגורין מציירין לבוש שזיר ותיכלא הות פרזומא בשופרא
מביתא דאבוהא כד עלת למיפק/ אעלת לארוסתיה תרעין דקסמרין בעיבדתיה למירפק
נעביד ונקבל משתעיין בתריה דלא לפקפק/ ומתפרשין קדם חתנא וחדי וכלתא תידוץ כבדיוספק
סלים אתקבע לה דתיסק לגנונא/ מצורתא דאבוהא לכורסייה דחתנא
עדרין בה שבעין בתולן לשננא/ דליהוון ככמכא דחלבא על דובשנא להתלבנא
פרת למיקטר במדברא גנון נהורא לארוסתא/ גנון לגו מין גנון דליהוון צנועין בשביסתא
צואה למידמוך בינו תרי בזיתא/ וקצוותא דרססן תלייא אפותא
קמתא כתמרא כאתכלין תדיא/ ריחא דנחירו כריחא דחיזורייא
רישא ככרמלא קליעתא כארגווניא/ צוארה שעיע כעמוד דשן דפילייא
שררא לאגנא דסיהרא מעהא כגון ערימת חטין/ מקפא שושנין חניטין
תקיף עינהא כתרין בריכן דחשבון קשיטין/ ונחירא זקיף כצפיתא דדמשיק ולא מחמטין

ד [77]

אמין שיתין לרומא/ היך אריך צילמא/ כולה בושה וכלימה/ חשיב ללמא
בנתון קוטרא/ וכל זני זמרה/ איך אתון ליה מקטרא/ ומנפח הוא בכורא
גבול כמה דבליסא/ שפיך כליש עיסה/ מורקע מן כסף אוכלסא/ והוא מנפח בקורנסא

דהוא סייף וחסיל/ שאני ומתחסיל/ מתחליף ומתפסיל/ במה הועיל פסיל
הוא בוטמא ומתקליל/ יקיר וזליל/ דיוקנין מחליל/ ופום ליה ולא ממליל
ובנורא מתרמי/ לא מתגבר ולא מזמי/ פסיח הוא וסמי/ ועיינין ליה ולא חמי
זהים ומטנין ומטבע/ ובכורא מקבע/ ווי ליה דשמע/ וסגיד למאן דלא שמע
חביש בקבלא ובריח/ ומן גנבא בריח/ מתעפיש והוא סריח/ ונחיר ליה ולא מריח
טובעיה איך מתפש/ על אנפוי מתרפש/ היך יקום ולית ליה נפש/ וידויי ולא מפשפש
יתיב שמם ולא מתמליך/ ולא ידע מאן עבר ומאן מליך/ בכורכתיה מתהליך/ ורגלין ליה ולא מהליך
כפין וצחי וטעי/ ובידויי מטעי/ כלום לא בעי/ ולא משתעי
לא פשיט ידויי/ ולא מטלטל יסודויי/ ולא מודע עובדויי/ כן יהון דסגדין לויי
מן כורא לקלס עבר/ ולמחר מיתבר/ אלהנא לית אוחרן ולית ליה מתחבר
נפחית באדם קדמאי/ נשמתא מן שמאי/ דלא יימרון עימיה דבראי/ אלא אנא בעלמאי
סביל אנא בכורסאי נורא/ קדמי נהר נורא/ שטיא איך אתון לייהרא/ נור אכלא נורא
עוד כל מליך פריס/ וחמש מאה דריס/ אית להון קפצא דדריס/ דליהוו על עריס
פדון טפשי קהלי/ דאפקון שום ביש עלי/ דאמרי לדחלי/
[צורותיה דאדם ציירית]/[1] ולא אצטערית/ ברייתי ביריית/ ולא אתביירית
קנאי אנא בנאי/ ולא אתקניתי/ קבע לקיבלי ולא תחלפוני
[78] ריחמתיך ברישיך/ רחמתיך בסופיך/ שובי לאכסניך/ לנחומי עקתיך
שמע חדוותי/ שמעי ברתי/ קבילי ונטרי אורייתי
תתייבי למאן יהב לך/ ואילה אוחרן לא יהיה לך

ה

חנניה מישאל ועזריה אודעו שמיה דקודשא בריך הוא לעין כל חייא כד טעין להון ננסא והכדין אמר להו
איתו כרועו לצילמאי לולבי דתמר/ אמר להון ננסא
איתבוננו מה דעבדית לכון עד דאתון בציון
ארמאית צדיא בגו ביה גנוניה דקיריס דידכון
אית לן פטרן שמיה לא ינום/ צווחו תלתיהון
באבונן דלעיל ביה רחצונן/ אמר חנניה
ביה אנא רחיצין מן טליותן/ אמר מישאל
בנורא אנן יקדין וביה לא כפרין/ אמר עזריה
אנן לא כפרין בלא יהוי לך/ צווחו תלתיהון
גרמין אתון גרמיכון למיקד/ אמר להון ננסא
גופיכון יתעביד קטם בגו אתון נורא
גבורה ודינמיט אם אית באלהכון הוא ישיזבינכון מן ידי

1 הושלם עפ״י הפירוש, ראה שם ד״ה צורותיה וכו׳.

אית לן פטרן שמיה לא ינום/ צווחו תלתיהון
דחלתא דצילמך לית היא בליבן/ אמר חנניה
דע דפטרונו תיאורון יתך/ אמר מישאל
דמות דצילמך לית אנן פלחין/ אמר עזריה
אנן לא כפרין בלא יהוי לך/ צווחו תלתיהון
היך כפריתון בי דלא למכרוע לצילמי/ אמר להון ננסא
האידנא אתון כרעין קדם אינדרטי ואי לא יקדין
האית לכון למידרע דאתון כרעין דלא בטיבותכון
אית לן פטרן שמיה לא ינום/ צווחו תלתיהון
ומה אנן אמרין לאלהא דשמיא/ אמר חנניה
והוא גלי עמיקתא ומסתרתא/ אמר מישאל
ועימיה שרי נהורא וחשוכא ליה גליא/ אמר עזריה
אנן לא כפרין בלא יהוי לך/ צווחו תלתיהון
זריק אנא יתכון לגו אתון נורא מכפתין/ אמר להון ננסא
זעיף אנא עליכון על דאתון מרדין עלי ועל צילמי
זמן דתשמעון קל קרנא משרוקיתא ממלא כרועו קדם צילמי
אית לן פטרן שמיה לא ינום/ צווחו תלתיהון
חי וקיים הוא פטרון דידן/ אמר חנניה
חבל על בנין דכפרין באבוהון/ אמר מישאל [79]
חס לך דניכפור בנעשה ונשמע/ אמר עזריה
אנן לא כפרין בלא יהוי לך/ צווחו תלתיהון
טבחית ונכסית גוזלייא דציון/ אמר להון ננסא
טאיסנא ונהימנא כאריא כגו ביה גנוניה דקיריס דידכון
טליקית רישי מיניקיכון ולא פריק יתכון
אית לן פטרן שמיה לא ינום/ צווחו תלתיהון
ייתי ווי עלך ננסא מה את מחסד/ אמר חנניה
יאיי לך למילף מן פרעה רשיעא דקודמוי מינך/ אמר מישאל
יחיד הוא אלהנא דתיירון יתן/ אמר עזריה
אנן לא כפרין בלא יהוי לך/ צווחין תלתיהון
כולא אנא ממללא עליכון לחירן/ אמר להון ננסא
כל סנקלטין קודין וכרעין קדם אינדרטי ואיניש לא מריד
כדאתון דרמית רוחכון דלא בעיתון למכרע לצלמי
אית לן פטרן שמיה לא ינום/ צווחין תלתיהון
לית אנן משגיחין על צילמך/ אמר חנניה
לית לך חלק באלהא דבר אינש שפכיה/ אמר מישאל
לזה אלי דזמרינן בימא ואנחא דיליה/ אמר עזריה

אנן לא כפרין בלא יהוי לך/ צווחין תלתיהון[1]
מישך שדרך ועבד נגו/ אמר להון ננסא
מדאורייתא דמשה אסתכלו והגו
מבדריתו ופלחיתו סמיי ולא סגו
איתלן פטרן שמיה לא ינום/ צווחו תלתיהון
נחנא נהירין זהירין בקיימי/ אמר חנניה
נטורי פום מלכא במומי/ אמר מישאל
ניתיב גולגלי ארנוני וזימי/ אמר עזריה
אנן לא כפרין בלא יהוי לך/ צווחו תלתיהון
ספקתון בארעכון טפוסי דמשתמודעין מיהודאי/ אמר להון ננסא
סמניו צייריתון בכותלי כשדאי
סבריתון הכא למיעבד צלמי הצדאי
אית לן פטרן שמיה לא ינום/ צווחו תלתיהון
על דנא להתבותך לית אנן חשחין/[2] אמר חנניה
עילאה יכול לשיזבותנא מן ידך ומאתון שחין/ אמר מישאל
[80] עביד או לא עביד על שמיה נתרמי פשחין/ אמר עזריה
אנן לא כפרין בלא יהוי לך/ צווחין תלתיהון
פסקי וכו׳

בה שעתא[3] גזר נבוכדנצר רשיעא ואוקידו לנורא חד שבעה, ארבעין ותשעה, על די חזי למיזייה ורמו לגויה לחנניה מישאל ועזריה כפיתין. והא בגזירת אלהא אתא מלאכא גבריאל וכבה לאתונא והוו מהלכין שריין בגו נורא עם מלאכא גבריאל. באדין אסתכי מלכא מפלטוריה וחזא יתהון איך הוו מהלכין שריין בגו נורא וחבל לא הוות בהון. באדין קרא מלכא לכל שולטני מדינתא והדברי מלכא די אכלו קורציהון דיהודאי ואמר להון: הלא גברין תלתא רמינא בגו נורא מכפתין, עניין ואמרין למלכא: יציבא מלכא. ענה מלכא ואמר: הא אנא חזי גוברין ארבעה שריין מהלכין בגו נורא וחבל לא איתי להון וריוויה די רביעאה דמי לבר אלהין. באדין קריב מלכא לתרע אתון נורא יקידתא וזעיק: חנניה מישאל ועזריה, דבלשון ארמית קריתי לכון שדרך מישך ועביד נגו, עבדוהי דאלהא חייא וקיימא, פוקו ואתו מן גו נורא. ונפקו תלתיהון, חנניה מישאל ועזריה, וקמו קדם מלכא. ואיתכנשו סגניא ופחוותא אדרגזיא גדבריא דתבריה תפתיה והדברי מלכא למיחזי גיברייא אילין די לא שלט בהן נורא ושיער רישיהון לא התחרך וסרבליהון לא שנו וריח נור לא עדת בהון. באדין ספקו ידיהון מלכא והדברוהי ואמרין: דהכדין אלהא אית לישראל ואינון מתעין באלילי עממיא די לא חזיין ולא שמעין ולא יכלין להצלא. כדנא באדין כתב מלכא לכל

1 אחרי שורה זו כתוב במחזור ויטרי (עמ׳ 338): ״מכאן ואילך יסד ר׳ מאיר שליח צבור״; ראה צונץ, ליטג׳, עמ׳ 151 (ודברי צונץ נעלמו מעיני גינצבורגר, ראה מה שכתב ב־*REJ* 73 עמ׳ 18).

2 עד כאן מפורש בפירוש שלפנינו.

3 על החלק שמתחיל כאן ראה בספרות המובאת לעיל בהערה 1 ובהערה 34 לגוף הפירוש. הטקסט שלפנינו אינו אלא עיבוד קל בפרוזה של דניאל ג׳ י״ט-ל״ג.

עממיא אומייא ולישנייא די דיירין בכל ארעא: שלמכון ישגא, מיני שים טעם די כל אינש די יימר שלו על אלההון די שדרך מישך ועביד נגו הדמין יתעבד ובייתיה נוולי ישתווה, די הוא אלהא חייא וקיימא לעלמין, שולטניה שולטן עלם ומלכותיה די לא תתחבל, אתיא ותמהיא די עבד עמי אלהא חייא וקיימא שפר קדמא להחויא, אתוהי כמה רברבין ותמהוהי כמה תקיפין, מלכותיה מלכות עלם ושולטניה עם דר ודר.

הללו את ה׳ כל גוים/ אמר חנניה
שבחוהו כל האמים/ אמר מישאל
כי גבר עלינו חסדו/ אמר עזריה
ואמת ה׳ לעולם/ אמר גבריאל[4]

ו [81]

אמגן מומי לא תשתבע/ דלא תזעזע דמסתביל אארבע
בבשרך סגירו לא תקבע/ דמומי הרזא כי סלווא דמא מבע
גופך לא תחייב בממרין/ דמומי לטו חיתא גומרין
דבקא ועיילא ברמח איברין/ בהכין מניין אתהא גמרין
הלין מומתא יהבין גמרא/ במידי דאשא לא מגמרא
ובגו ביתא דמומי עיילא למישרא/ מכליא אעי ואבני סתרא
זכריה חמי ליה טייסא/ בפיתחא דהיכלא משחתה פריסא
חריתי בה מיני קנסא/ למומי ולמיימי חבריה ברוכסא
טובהון דלנפשהון מגמרין/ מלמשתבע בקשוט ולא בשקרין
יאות להון דפומהון מנטרין/ דדביק ליה ללישן מיסטר ומכירין
כד אתכבישת קרתא דדקלי/ ביום ניח איטמור שורהא בקבליה
להכי אחרים בר נון במילי/ לאקדושי ביזתא וכל סימא דלהון מתגלי
מגני שבטיה בחיסודא דכאיר/ שקר במומי וחמיד בנכסי דסאיר
נפילא גרם לדברא אאפיה ואתקטיל יאיר/ דתקיל כרובא דשררא דבפלג גופא דאיר
סהדא רבא פרסם קדמין/ בחמש דשקר חדא ליה גרמין
עדבא כבשיה ואבנין ליה מרגמין/ ורגז איתותב ואיתהפיך לרחמין
פום ממליל שחיתא וכדבין/ לנעמן אשתבע דחמיד חריטין רברבין
צת רביה ולטייה באבין/ ואסתגר הוא וגוזלוי בחובין
קושטא אשתבע דמגירתא אפיה גבה/ כד אתגבלון דינריא דינריא בלישא למטווא
ודי קנסת עלה מטא ליה בחובא/ שקרא כל דכין דעלמא מחרבא
ריפי דאנטוכיא כד אתא ננסא/ במומי דקיריס אמטייה למתניא לכורסא
טפס וסרח דלא נטרא כנימוסא/ טבחון פרחוי וטפון ליה פנסא
שרי ציבחר למימי במילין/ אי אתגרים לתיה דבר אנש בחמלין

4 ראה בהערות 42-46 לגוף הפרוש; צורתן של ד׳ השורות האחרונות כצורת הפיוט, חנניה מישאל ועזריה, שהטקסט הזה מצורף אליו.

לאתקולי בחד מהלין דאתקרון דחלין/ דאתנסו לברייהון ולא אשתכוח משתלין
תדיר ייאי לקיומי אסר וקיימי/ אוריין ועובדין טבין לאשלומי
בכן תקיף יהא בסעדך ובשופריה לך יתחמי/ ויפשינך ויסגינך ויתן לך רחמי

ז

ארקא ורקיעא ודבהון ושב ימי/ אדרע גבורתיה שכלליה בשית יומי
בעיר ורחיש וציפר וכל נשמי/ בריתי ואתקניתי לחוד בעשרא פתגמי
[82] גמירא דכולא שבתא אתרעיתי ואצטביתי לקמאי/ גזירתיה והילכתיה לאלפא ולרחומיי
דליקלעון בנייח שרכא צייתי פתגמי/ דתא לקיימא ולשעורי גרמידי תחומיי
הייא ואשור לזרוזי בתפנוקי מיכלי/ הליוסטין ובאדג כוורי ולפדא ואנומלי
ובגלימא וכסן לייקורי מעידן מעליי/ ולתלותיה שירותיה ולמיבצע אתרי חלי
זוודתיה מאדנהר לבשולי ולאטמוני ולאפויי/ זיפתא ופסול פתילתא ומשחא דלא לאקפויי
חומרא מלפפולי ברמצא וגומרי מלאחתויי/ חולא לאסופי על קודשא וטובא חדויי
טירדא וטירחא למיבטל ונפשיה לעדוני/ טעים רשוייתיה למידע דאינון תמני
יזפתא למיזף לאפושי אסקריטי וריחני/ יימאיי דאנא פרע בטופיינא לאתקוני
כלדאי בדקו על יוסף מוקר שבי/ דהוה ההוא גוי בשיבבותיה דהוו נפישי נכסיה
אמרו ליה כלדאי: כולהו נכסך אכלינהו יוסף מוקר שבי. אזל ההוא איניש זבן בהן מרגניתא וציירה בסדיניה. כד הוה עבר במברא אתא זיקא אפרחיה לסדיניה. אתא כוורא בלעיה ואסקוה צַיְדֵי. אתיוה אפנייא דמעלי שבתא, קא קרן: למזבן כוורא מאן בעי? אמרו להו: זילו לגבי יוסף מוקר שבי דרגיל דזבין, הוא יזבין יתיה. זבניה, קרעיה ואשכח ביה מרגניתא. זבנה בתלת עשרה עיליתא דדינרי.
לודקאי קצבא כד אשכח חיוא מעלייתא נטרה לשבתא לייקורי. זכה לפתור דזהב מטול תמני סרי אינשי דנטלין יתיה ועלוהי כסי וקיתונייתא וצלוחיתא ומגיסתא דדהבא קביעין ביה ועלוהי על מיני מיכלא וכל מיני משתייא. על יקרא דשבתא זכא לעותרא דין רביה.
ממלל אסיר ורעיוני שרי/ נשי וגברי מחייבי לנטורי
סכום דאתי אסיר ודחליף אשתרי לגמרי/ ענייני מצוה שפיר למיחשב ולסבורי
פנסא דטפא אסיר לטלטולי/ צפרא ופנייא לקדושי חזי ליה
קשיש ציבי במדברא אחליה/ רגז אפיש ורגימו ליה
שבייא דיליה ינטר עמי כוליה/ תוריה ואמתיה ועבדיה ועיליה.

ח

אמר יצחק לאברהם אבוהי/ מה נאה מדבחא די בניית לי אבא
בפריע פשוט ידך וסב סכינך/ עד דאנא מצלי קדם ריבוני
גלי אדרעך ואסור חרצך/ היך גבר דעביד שירותא לבריה
דין הוא יומא דיהוון אמרין/ אב לא חס על בריה ובריה לא עכב
היך תיזיל ותימור לשרה אמי/ היך תפרוש מני ותיזל לביתא

ונשיק יצחק לאברהם אבוהי/ ופקיד יתיה והיכדין אמר ליה
זרוק דמי על גבי מדבחא/ וכנוש קטמי ואוביליה לאימי
חיי ומותי כולא בידיה/ ומודי אנא ליה דהיכדין בחר בי
טובך אבא דיהוון אמרין/ דאנא אימר לעלתא דמלכא חזייא
יתקוף רוגזך וכעסך אבא/ ותהוי כגבר דלא חס על בריה
כגבר אכזרי סב סכינך/ ותיכוס יתי דלא תסאיבני
לא תהוי דידי דלא איעכבך/ דלית אנא מן ידך נסיב גרמי
מה תבכה אמר יצחק לאברהם אבוהי/ טובי דבחר בי קיריס מכל קוזמוז
ניחא רוחא דשרה אמי/ חיך נפקינן תרינן בליבא שלימה
סכינך אבא הב לי ואמושיניה/ בבעו מינך דלא תסאיבני
עיני חמיין קיסין מסדרין/ נור דליק ביום קרבני
פתח פומך ובריך אבא/ ואשמע אנא ואימר אמן
צוארי פשוט לך אבא/ מה דניחא לך קום עיבד
קמו מלאכיא ומפייסין למריהון/ בבעו מינך חוס על טליא
רחמוי דאבוי אנן מדכרין/ גבר דאכלינן מלח בביתיה
שדי אמר ליה לא תדחל טלייא/ דאנא הוא פרוקא ואפרוק יתך
תקיף הוא אלהא ותקיפין עובדוהי/ לית אוחרן כוותיה ולית דדמי ליה

ט

איתגבר בחיליה אדוניה בר חגיז כד קם בעינתי יואב בר צרוייה
ביני טורייא צווח יואב וכל ברייתא שמעון קליה
גיבר הוינא ולית דכוותי וכל גבורתי מה הנייתי
דיתיב מלכא שלמה וחשיב עלי לקטלא ולא צבי שמע לקל מילתי
הלא מדכר לי מלכא שלמה כל טבוון דעבדית עם דוד אבוהי
וכרכין ומחוזין כבישית קדמוהי נחלוי דימא ודיבישתא
זעו מיני כל רברבייא וכל גיברייא ערקו מן קדמוי
חבל על הדין עלמא אם דין הוא דינא גבר דכוותי מתקטיל בחרבא
טעם יואב כסא דמותא כד שמע אמרין לקל איתו ונקטליניה
יאי דיניכון דתקטלון יתי בתר דקטילית כל שנאיכון
כד חמא יואב דמקטלין יתיה שרי צווח ליואל בריה [8
לך יואל ברי אנא מפקד יתך אורייתא תיטר ולאחוך תרבי ולאמך תייקר
מה עבדית ליה למלכא שלמה איך הוא אכזר למיקטל יתי
נהם יואב בשעתא ההיא כד חמא גיברייא דאחדין זייניהון
סבול גרמך ולא תקטלינני דעתיד יום למיתי דתיזכר יתי
עני ליה מלכא שלמה תידכר לך דמא דאבנר בן נר ודעמשא בן יתר
פתח פומיה יואב בשעתיה ההיא ובכא עם כל חברוהי
צווח יואב בשעתא ההיא ואישתמע קליה בכל ארעא

קליה ארים מלכא שלמה והוה צווח לרחבעם בריה
רחבעם ברי קום שלוף זיינך ותידכר לך דמא דאבשלום דודך
שמעיה קליה כל ישראל שריין עיניהון דמעין מדלגין
תמה שלמה ואמר בליביה מה איעביד לשבועתא דאבא
כד שמע[1] יואב בר צרוייה שרי צווח לבניהו בן יהוידע: בנייה, בנייה, לא תשניק רוחי
צוארי תקיף וסייפך חליש ולא את יכיל למיקטל יתי
קיצץ בנייה רישיה דיואב ורישיה דיואב על לבית מלכא שלמה
שמעו עממיא דאיתקטיל יואב בפומהון חדיין ובליבהון בכיין
תווהו ובכו בני ישראל בכייא רבא על דמיתקטיל יואב בר צרוייה

י

[יוסף תקיף יצריה/ כד תבעתיה מרתיה/ וסרב למשכב לותיה/ למהוי עמה
לעלמא דאתי/ אכנישת כל שיבבתהא והכדין אמרת להון]
אית ליה חד טליא זעיר ומיינוק הוא/ זיוויה דעבריא וזבינתיה מן ערבאי
בעיא אנא דנירדי בגינתי והוא לא צבי/ ואמר לי לית אנא רדי עם תורא ועם אתנא
גנימוס דידיה כסב בר שבעין שנין/ והוא בר שבסר שנין כד זבניה יתיה
דמותיה דמלכא ומללותיה דחכם/ דולוס לית ביה ארי כבר מלכין הוא
הרי כמה זמנין שזגית לי כסא/ דצחית למשתי לא צבי למשתי
ואמרי לי גנבא בר גנבתא/ למה את בעי שתי ממוי דגנבין
זעיר ומיינוק הוא יוסף דנסיב הוני בגלל שופריה והוא עתיד למסכא לעתיק יומין
חנא וחסדא מלוין יתיה/ חד מן ימיניה וחד מן שמאליה
טרדא אנא לך מגו פלטין/ דאת סניית יתי היך זניתא
יומא ולילא נורא בלבי/ היך אילן דיקוד בשלהובית דנור
כל ערסין דריבונך פריסין/ על דאת בעי קום דמוך
לא בגין חד לילא דאדמוך יאות/ אנא מטלטל פריסין מגינתא דעדן
מפייסא אנא לכון כל חברותיי/ דתצטערון עמי בגו פלטין
ניכול כחדא ונשתי כחדא/ וגימר מילא ותימרון קושטא
סקת יתהון בגו פלטין/ ואותיבת יתהון על סגמיטין
עבדיי קרת יתיה גבירתיה דיוסף קום קטור זינך ושמש כעבדא
פיילין בידיה וקם ומזג להון/ והן הוו טענין כסא ולא טעמין ליה
צפיין הוויין ליה ואפיהון מכרכמין/ אפיה למרתיה ולביה לאבוה דשמיא
קמו כולהון ונשקו על רישיה/ ואמרין ליה לך יאי ינוק מלכותא
רחמין וחינא וחיסדא איתנגידו ליה מן שמיא
שדי יהביה ליקר ורבו בדיל יצריה דכביש

1 ראה צונץ, ליטג׳, עמ׳ 68.

תהכון באורחתיה כל ישר׳ ולא תהכון בתר גיופיא
ארי אנא סהיד אמר ה׳ בחרשיא ובגיופיא

נ״א של סוף הפיוט:

ראיין הוויין ליה ובידיהון סמנין[1] ואתרוגין לא טעמין אתרוגא וידיהן דמא מליין שוויין עלוהי עלילא ומעכבן יתיה וממללן ליה למיעבד עיבידתא תיעול עימה למיעבד עיבידתא ובתר כן תעבד רעותך.

יא

אריא מתילי ואחיון מתקלין/ דנכסי בזיזי חטפין ושקלין
בחשוכא עסקין ובטימור קבלין/ וביה דיין להון דרזין ליה גלין
גניב וחטיף ונסיב בטמרי/ כמן בסתרא ועייל בחתרי
דאוי יקר עבדא טפיה ממריה/ לעין ארעית מדמי כדלית ליה סיירי
הלא מן קדמיי אית לך למגמר/ דאיתעל לגינתא ודלא ליגנוב אזהריה דלסתמר
וחטף וטעים ותפקיד אימר/ אנהר במנדעך כמה מותא אקמר
זייריה דבר מעכה תלתא גנב/ חטר מלכו בכן סבר ליה למענב
חטפיה בוטמא במזייה ואשתטן ואיענב/ ובתלת סיגסין תיליא דליביה אתקנב
טמיניא וגנביא שבעא פריטין/ שניין דרגיהון וגזירתהון חריטין
יתירא דכולהון דליבהון דברייתא מקמטין/ חפו גונדי וטלפיהון פשטין
כסי ושירו מושיט ליה לחבריה במסבלי/ מסרהב לאברויי כד חמי דלא מצטבי ליה 8]
לברייה מסתני ודמי קומוי בניכלי/ דאי איתיה כהיל בגרמי הוה מפלי
כד זהירין וחזיין בגנובתיה מתהני/ קרנא פרע ומיתליט דתחום משני
לנכסין מסיימין במחטפיה על חד תרין דיניה/ ואי לית מזדבן לשית לפולחניה
מעאן ארבע ומתור חמשא/ אי נכסיה או זבניה הכין עונשא
נכיל ורפיק ועייל בחתר בחשא/ לית ליה דמא אם מתבריר כשמשא
מרי עלמא דכולא ליה גלי/ אשקל דלא מוקים בר נשא גרמיה אגורסנא דיליה
נחת לסוף מנדעיה דקאים לקבליה/ ודכמן אדמך קום קדים וקטליה
שנאין גרמיהון דפלגין עם נגודין/ מומי ולטו שמעין ולא מודין
עריית בישתהון בד מתפרסמא בסהדין/ גרמין לגופיהון מחאתא ונגודין
פריטא דמאן קדשא מכסי/ קנויי דנטרין תפקיד ונימוסי
ציידין עליה לקטלא לקנסיה/ ומכלי בישתא ומזכי כורסיה
קניינא קדישא ריש עלליה/ דלאיתגורי גנביה ומזבין ליה
רמו קשיא בגו רכיכא וענקין קדליה/ ובתשנוק רוח חיותיה מתכלי
שוט לא ישוטון ליה לגנבא/ מרגילין דלית להון טימי כד מגנב לחבבא

1 צ״ל ״סכינין״.

תקיף רחים ליה ואורייתא ליה מתקרבא / ומשלים ליה דעלמא דאתי זיקין וניהור ומזכי ליה לכל טבא

יב

איום אפתינטין ואבזרי אורייתא / איין לאפתוקי תנסיא לגזרתא[1]

בי ___________ תא / בי ___________ תא

(בתורן... בעתתא לפכוחי[2])

גהא ובר גהא לקיומי / גהרקא למיצע תותיה נומיה

דהנא דוורדא ___________ דיגמי / דהא ___________ מיה

הוא מרי כולא אזהר / הו ___________ הר

וותנייא דפחדוהי ______ הר / וותקיה לאנוחי ___________ אסתהר

חדוד ___________ / חדקי ארבע ___________

טהרא סהדות זבין תור אכיל ____ / טה ___________ [87]

יהור ___________ / יה ___________

(נירא[2])

כבלא גנב ונפיק סהדא ________ / כב ___________

לבלר כתב ___________ עוף פונדיה / לב _____ לא משתלים מדידיה

(בגא[2])

מרוס דעייל בליליא למיחתר ___ / מר ___________

נרגוניה יתוב ברישיה ________ / נר ___________

סביל גרמי קדם סהדי / סב ___________ פרידי

עבט נפשיה ___________ בזידי / עב ___________ די

פנקט אזיל לאסבא בישא / פנון ___________ שא

צניף קרנא בטופיין חומשא / צנ ___________ שא

קיום למישקל ותקלי תריצי / קיון עכביתא מאני פצי

ריל״ח איברין ________ חצי / רית״ג ___________ פצי

שמצא מלמישקל זיל / שמ ___________ עורזיל

שמשמין אפיה ________ זיל / שמ ___________ בורזיל

(נכסי[2])

תני אורייתא ובה לעסוקי / תנ ___________ לחדותי ולבהוקי

תנבת ___________ קי / תנ ___________ גרגרין לענוקי

1 סימן: א-ר (כפול); ש-ת (מרובע); יהודה בר בנימן (מרובע); ראה בגוף הפירוש, ד״ה ריל״ח איברין; ״כמ׳ רמ״ח וכן רית״ג כמו תרי״ג, ואם יאמר אדם מה ראה הפייטן לשנות, לפי שהיו״דין הצריכין לו שהרי שם הפייט רמוז באות השנית שלכל שיטה ושיטה והמשכיל יבין״; ראה גם בהערה 59 שם.

2 מקומן של המלים שבסוגריים אינו ברור אולם כנראה הן שייכות לשורות שמודפסות מלמעלה מהן. <ראה את שיחזור הפיוט המלא במאמרו של פלס הנזכר בהערה 1 לפירוש פיוט י״ב לעיל.>

יג

אזדהר מסהדות שקר ולישנא בישא / דלית את ידע כמה סגין עונשא
בגומרהא קטלא תלתא לשגשא / משתעי לה וצייתה ודי עליה מתלחשא
גירא אתמתילת ושלהובית דרתמא / משתריא בארבעה [צ״ל: בארעא] ומשלהבא ברומא
דין לה גיברא וחילתיה דנהמא/ לשיצאה יתה ולמסבר פומה
האי סהדא שקרא בשותיה דכייל/ רשיעא קרי ליה אגוריה ובאנפייה זייל
ועל מוחיה ניכליה נחית ועייל/ ומשתלים ליה חושבניה בסאתא דכייל
זוחלא קדמאה מכולא הוה ערים/ ולטו מכל לישניה ליה גרים
חמייה ליקריה דרביא דחלתא אתרים/ ואתקני ביה ואגביב מילי דשקרין
טעין על טפשיתא ושדלה במילי/ מאיבא דין טעם קיריס ואכליה
יקר עלמא וכל דביה בהכין שכלליה/ חמית בר נש דלא סני בר עמליה
כד איתגלי קדשא בריך הוא למידן לטעי/ עם כולהון דן וליה לא אשתעי דאוגיבתא הוה ליה למפעי
למילי דמרה ודעבדא רעי/ תפקיד דריבון חזי דינא למיצת בקיעי
כמא דפטר ברגז כן אירעיה/ בעשרה איתליט ואיתקציצו כרעיה [8
למיכל ארעא ולמגחן אמעיה/ ולאסתגורי גופיה ולעלמא דאתי לא יתאסי מרעיה
מאללי ארעא על סהדות שקרא/ על אעיא ועל עפרא
נשתרבב לישנהון ונפל על טיבורא/ וקוקני ורחשי גייצו לישנהון לסתרא
סיב לך מן הדא מילה למגמרא/ למידן בהכין קלא וחומרא
על אבנין שקרו גזירת מותניהון אתחמירא/ כל דכין על חבריה מרשע למימרא
פתיא דעולמתא נסיב וכביש/ וסני לה ומפיק עלה שום ביש
צוראי מאה קנסין ליה דאבאיש/ ומתרדי במחאן בדיל דקושטא שביש
דאניס ומשדל לה לבתולתא/ חמשין פרע לה וכן קיצותא
ודמשקר עלה מאה מתקניס ומסבינן ליה נגדותא/ תא חמי דחמיר מימרא מבישות עובדתא
קבלני דאתפריקו מדחוק פולחנא/ בעשרה נסיאו לפרוקא גיברא וחסינא
ורשו גזירתהון לא אתגמרת בחוסנא/ עד דאסהידו שקר בבישות לישנא
רב רעיא דבר דאכיל עדתיה/ לגוב במתה כד איתכניש לנכסתיה
לאלחנן חמא כד אתא תם במיתיה/ ובעא סייפא ונהם זמרתיה
ארכס ושקר על רבא שמשא/ ואסהיד עליה דשאיל ליה במאני דקדשא
ואתקטין איהו ועימיה תמנין וחמשא/ ואתעקר בשיקריה מעלמא דאתי ומהדין לאשתרושא
רב בוציניא אסתטן למותא/ וגרמו ליה גובא וסירתא
דא הות ליה על דלא אשלים פלוגתא/ איתא חמי כמא גרמא שותא
בחילא דלישן חיי ומותא/[1] דנטר גרמיה כביש יתה
שוויי שלם ואפסוקי דבבא/ שרי לשנויי מלין ולהפוכיהון לטבא
תא גמר דא מבי דינא רבא/ דאנא סיבית שני לסבא

1 עד כאן מפורש בכתב היד.

מכריזין שלמא לשנאין בקרבין/ מרי חילא לאגחא בקרבין
ובשלמנא חתימי בירכן חמודין וחביבין/ ומאן דתקוף אחסין לעמיה
יברכינון וכל ברכתא דבאורייתא כתובין

יצירתו הפיוטית של ר׳ יצחק אבן גיאת

ידיעותינו על רב יצחק בן יהודה אבן גיאת, הרי״ץ גיאת או ריצ״ג, אינן מתגליותיה של הגניזה הקהירית. גורל יצירותיו אינו דומה לגורל יצירותיהם של מחברים אחרים, במיוחד מחברים שפעלו בארצות המזרח, אשר במשך הדורות נגנזו יצירותיהם ולפעמים אף שמותיהם נשכחו ורק בדורות האחרונים העלו חכמים את זכרם מעל הדפים הבלים של כתבי־יד הגניזה. רב יצחק אבן גיאת, איש ההלכה, פוסק, מפרש ופייטן, היה ידוע מאז ומתמיד כאחד מגדולי ראשוני הראשונים. דברי רבנו מובאים תכופות בחיבוריהם של הראשונים ופיוטיו היו כלולים בסדרי התפילה של עדות ישראל במקומות מושבותיהן השונים. סדר סליחותיו ללילות האשמורות שבין ראש חודש אלול ובין יום הכיפורים והמעמד הגדול שחיבר ליום הכיפורים תופסים את המקום הראשי בספר שפתי רננות שהוא מחזור לימים נוראים לפי מנהג טריפולי וג׳רבה והערים שמסביבותיהן. מדפיסי מחזור זה, למהדורותיו השונות, הבליטו את חלקו של רבנו במנהג תפילותיהם במלים כגון אלה: ״ס׳ שפתי רננות כולל סליחות וכו׳ מרבני עולם, רבני ספרד אשר היו אחר הגאונים ועל ראשם הרב המפורסם רבנו יצחק בן יהודה בן גיאת זצ״ל״ וכו׳.[1]

אולם לצד ידיעותינו הלא מועטות על ריצ״ג השאובות ממקורות מסורתיים וטרום־גניזתיים, יש לנו היום נתונים חשובים על יצירתו המיוסדים על הגניזה. ברצוני לייחד כאן את הדיבור עד כמה שהשעה מרשה על תרומתה המיוחדת של הגניזה הקהירית לחקר פיוטי רבנו.

אחת הבעיות המסובכות העומדות בפני חוקרי פיוטי ריצ״ג היא בעיית ייחוס הפיוטים. כבר לפני התגלות הגניזה התלבטו רושמי הפיוטים בעניין זה, אבל בתקופה האחרונה התרבו הפרסומים של פיוטים מסופקים שחתום בהם יצחק סתם ושמהדיריהם ייחסו לרבנו בלי יסוד מספיק ואיתן. כפי שכתב פרופסור שירמן, היתה נטייה מצד החוקרים לייחס לריצ״ג ״כל פיוט נאה הכתוב בסגנון ספרדי״.[2] השם יצחק הוא אחד מן השמות השכיחים ביותר וגם בדורו של ריצ״ג ובמחיצתו היו כמה חכמים בשם זה, כדבריו המפורסמים של הראב״ד: ״וחזר כח התלמוד בארץ ספרד והיו שם ה׳ רבנים ושמות כלם יצחק״.[3] הוצאתם לאור של פיוטים רבים אשר חתום בהם יצחק בלי זיהוי נוסף וייחוסם המפוקפק לריצ״ג הוסיפה במידה רבה על הקושי הטמון בהפרדה זהירה של יצירות

1 בשער של שפתי רננות, ליוורנו תקע״ו.

2 ח׳ שירמן, שירים חדשים מן הגניזה, ירושלים תשכ״ו, עמ׳ 185.

3 ספר הקבלה לר׳ אברהם אבן דאוד הלוי, מהדורת ג״ד כהן, פילדלפיה תשכ״ז, עמ׳ 58 (חלק עברי).

מחברים שונים לפי בעליהם. יש להשתדל בתהליך הכנת מהדורת ביקורתית של פיוטי ריצ״ג להפנות תשומת לב מיוחדת לבעיה זו ויש לקוות שכתוצאה מזה אפשר יהיה להחזיר אבידה לפייטנים אחרים ששמם היה יצחק. ניקח לדוגמה את הפיוטים לר׳ יצחק כנזי. מפייטן זה, שהוא כנראה זהה עם ר׳ יצחק בן ר׳ שמואל הספרדי המכונה כנזי, אשר שימש בדיינות בפוסטאט בסוף המאה האחת־עשרה ותחילת המאה השתים־עשרה, יש בידינו כמה וכמה פיוטים,[4] ואחדים מהם יוחסו בטעות לריצ״ג. גם אני נטיתי להכניס לבין פיוטי ריצ״ג קינה אחת הנמצאת בגניזה ושמעליה כותרת: ״אח׳ לר׳ יצחק הרב זצ״ל נדב אמראה״.[5] הפיתוי היה קיים כי ידוע שר׳ משה אבן עזרא מונה בין סוגי השירה, שרבו, ריצ״ג, הצטיין בהם, את הנדב, את שיר האבל,[6] והיות ומספר קינותיו שהתגלו עד עכשיו קטן הוא מאד, חשבתי לייחס קינה זו לאבן גיאת. אמנם כשנתקלתי אחר כך ברשימת פיוטים הבאים מתחת לכותרת ״לרב ז״ל״[7] ונוכחתי לדעת שהם ליצחק כנזי ועם הידיעה שר׳ יצחק בן ר׳ שמואל הספרדי הנ״ל היה נקרא יצחק הרב לפי תעודות שבגניזה,[8] לא נותר ספק שאת הקינה הנ״ל אין לייחס בוודאות לאבן גיאת אלא קרוב לוודאי שהיא לר׳ יצחק כנזי. דרך אגב, הרשימות המרובות של פיוטים שנשתמרו בגניזה מכילות ידיעות חשובות שונות וכדאי בהחלט להפנות תשומת לב מיוחדת אליהן.

אם דנים אנחנו בבעיה הקשורה בשמו של מחברנו נזכיר כאן עוד חידה שחדה לנו הגניזה. תלמידו של אבן גיאת, ר׳ משה אבן עזרא, והראב״ד גם יחד, מעידים שריצ״ג נפטר בשנת ד׳ אלפים תתמ״ט, שהיא שנת 1089 למספרם.[9] והנה במכתב חשוב מאד שנכתב אל חלפון בן נתנאל בערך שלושים שנה אחרי התאריך הנ״ל נזכר לכאורה שמו של הרב יצחק אבן גיאת בין החיים. המוציא לאור של המכתב, הפרופסור גויטיין, מצביע כמובן על קושי כרונולוגי זה ומציין גם שקריאת השם אינה ברורה כל צורכה.[10] יש אולי להיעזר בתעודה נוספת לפתרון הבעיה. באוסף טיילור־שכטר בקיימבריג׳ נמצא פתק קטן שעד כמה שידוע לי לא פורסם עדיין, שנכתב אל אחד בשם חלפון הלוי מאת אחד בשם יצחק בן יוסף בן גיאת.[11] פתק זה מלמדנו על קיומם של שני אנשים בשם יצחק אבן גיאת, שאחד מהם היה בנו של יהודה, הוא ריצ״ג המפורסם שאנו דנים בו, והשני איש אחר ששם אביו היה יוסף ושלעת עתה אין לנו ידיעות עליו.

נחזור לענייננו. אין שום ספק שנצטרך להוציא מבין פיוטי ריצ״ג הרבה פיוטים שיוחסו לו בטעות. אף־על־פי־כן, יישאר מספר פיוטיו גדול מאד. קטעי הגניזה מאשרים בהחלט את מה שכתב משה אבן עזרא על רבנו: ״הרבה מכל קודמיו בענייני הפירושת והתפילות

4 ראה למשל במאמרו של ח׳ שירמן, ״סליחות מנהג ספרד״, ארשת ה (תשל״ב), עמ׳ 72-73.

5 כתב־יד קיימבריג׳ TS NS 300. fol. 30

6 משה בן יעקב אבן עזרא, ספר העיונים והדיונים, מהדורת א״ש הלקין, ירושלים תשל״ה, עמ׳ 72-73.

7 כתב יד קיימבריג׳ TS NS 325. fol. 34. [על ״הרב״, השווה עתה ש״ד גויטיין, תרביץ מה (תשל״ו), עמ׳ 64-75; מו (תשל״ז), עמ׳ 152-153.]

8 J. Mann, *The Jews in Egypt*, II, Oxford 1922, pp. 310-311, etc.

9 ספר הקבלה הנ״ל, עמ׳ 60: ספר העיונים והדיונים הנ״ל, שם.

10 ש״ד גויטיין, סדרי חינוך, ירושלים תשכ״ב, עמ׳ קסז והערה 225 שם.

11 כתב־יד קיימבריג׳ TS Misc. 35 (= Loan 1-109). fol. 93

והאבל והקינות וכו׳ והטפל אשר אצלי טיפה מימתו״ וכו׳.[12] הפרופסור שירמן, בספרו ״שירים חדשים מן הגניזה״, מתבטא בסגנון דומה: ״מן הים הגדול של יצירת יצחק אבן גיאת מובאות כאן דוגמאות מועטות בלבד״. פרופסור שירמן משער שם, לפי דעתי בצדק, שמספרם הכללי של פיוטי ריצ״ג מגיע בוודאי לארבע מאות, אם לא למעלה מזה.[13] כהשוואה גרידא נציין שמהדורת ירדן של שירי הקודש של אבן גבירול כוללת בסך הכל 244 פיוטים. למרות הפעילות החרוצה של חכמים שונים וביניהם חכם צנוע שהקדיש הרבה עמל וחיבה להוצאת שירי ריצ״ג, ר׳ יוסף מרקוס ז״ל, יש להסכים למה שכתב לאחרונה הפרופסור אברמסון: ״הרבה פיוטים חדשים של רב יצחק בן גיאת התפרסמו בשנים האחרונות ועדיין הסתור מרובה״.[14] לאמיתו של דבר, אוצרות הגניזה מכילים חומר רב הנוגע לאספקט חשוב של המחקר בפיוטי ריצ״ג שעדיין בכלל לא טופל בו. ההתעניינות בהוצאת טקסטים בודדים, בדרך כלל על־פי מקורות בודדים, בחינת הוצאת פנינים מתוך ים הקטעים של הגניזה, דחתה לגמרי את ניצול הגניזה להתקנת נוסח הטקסטים הידועים מכבר. בין כתבי־יד הגניזה יש שפע לא ישוער של העתקים מפיוטיו הרבים של ריצ״ג, הן של אלה מסדר הסליחות והמעמד המפורסמים, הן של פיוטים שיצאו לאור על־פי כתבי־יד רגילים וגם של פיוטים שנדפסו על־פי קטעי הגניזה, בלי להתחשב בהעתקים נוספים. ניצול כל החומר העומד לרשותנו היום, הוא חיוני ביותר לגבי הנוסח של המעמד ליום הכיפורים. זה הוא המעמד המתואר על־ידי אלחריזי במלים אלה: ״ובספרו אשר חבר למעמד יום הכפורים הראה נוראות/ היו לו לעד ולאות/ כי שירו צלחה עליו רוח נבואות״.[15] צונץ העריך את הסילוק המסיים את המעמד כיצירה שאף נביא לא היה צריך להתבייש בתוכנה או בסגנונה.[16] כמפורסם, מעמד זה מכיל כעין אנציקלופדיה בזעיר אנפין של ידיעות בפילוסופיה, באסטרונומיה ובאנטומיה ועוד. טקסט זה מהווה, אם כן, מקור קדום וחשוב ממדרגה ראשונה לחקר המינוח העברי של המדעים ומיצוי ההעתקים המרובים של חלקי המעמד המפוזרים לרוב בגניזה יתרום לא רק להבנת שירתו של ריצ״ג, אלא גם להרחבת ידיעותינו על מצב המדעים ומינוחם העברי בתקופתו ובארצו של המשורר. דרך אגב, עד כמה שידוע לי, היחיד שניצל את החומר שבמעמד – כמובן רק על־פי הנוסח המודפס – כמקור לתולדות המדעים, היה דוד קויפמן ששאב הרבה נתונים מעניינים מיצירה פיוטית מונומנטלית זו והכניסם לספרו על החושים, *Die Sinne*.[17] בהקשר זה עלינו להזכיר שקטעי הגניזה העשירו את ידיעותינו גם על שאר חיבורי ריצ״ג. שמו האמיתי של ספרו ההלכי, ״הלכות כלולות״, התגלה לאחרונה באחת מרשימות

12 ספר העיונים והדיונים הנ״ל, שם.

13 שירמן, שירים חדשים מן הגניזה, עמ׳ י ועמ׳ 185 הערה 3.

14 במאמרו ״פיוט לרב יצחק בן גיאת״, תרביץ מג (תשל״ד), עמ׳ 159.

15 תחכמוני, שער ג, מהדורת י׳ טופורובסקי, תל־אביב תשי״ב, עמ׳ 44.

16 L. Zunz, *Literaturgeschichte*, Berlin 1865, p. 195

17 בודאפשט 1884 עמ׳ 30 הערה 96 ועוד. אחרי סידורו של מאמר זה בדפוס הופיע מאמרו של ש׳ אברמסון, ״על ״תועלת האיברים״, סיני פב (תשל״ח), עמ׳ ז־יא, ובו מביא המחבר הרבה חומר ממעמדו של ריצ״ג.

הספרים של ר׳ יוסף ראש הסדר;[18] ובכלל התרחבו ידיעותינו על היקף ספרו זה ועל היקף פירושו למסכתות התלמוד. חיבורים אלה, או מה ששרד מהם, יחד עם פירושו הערבי על ספר קוהלת,[19] משמשים כרקע להבנת כלל יצירתו.

בירור בעיות הייחוס, הכנת רשימה מהימנה של פיוטיו, חישוף נוסף של טקסטים חדשים ובעיקר התקנת טקסט ביקורתי של כל הפיוטים על־פי כל המקורות, שבגניזה ושמחוצה לה, ופירוש נכון של השירים, יניחו את היסוד האיתן למחקר נוסף. כי בהנחת יסוד זה ייגמר רק השלב הראשון של המשימה. הבעיות האסתטיות, הליטורגיות וההיסטוריות המרובות ושאלת השפעת הגומלין בין פייטנים שונים ובין אסכולות פיוטיות שונות תוכלנה לבוא לפתרונן המלא אך ורק אחרי גמר השלב הנזכר לעיל. אולם נדמה לי, שכבר עכשיו, במצבו הנוכחי של המחקר מחויבים אנו לנגוע בכמה בעיות יסוד ולשאול כמה שאלות עקרוניות על תופעות מסוימות שבשירת ריצ״ג.

לפני התגלות הגניזה הכרנו את מעמדו ליום הכיפורים ואת סליחותיו ופיוטים בודדים ומעטים מסוג האופן, האהבה, הזולת וכדומה. גם היום אין בידינו מערכת יוצר שלמה ממנו, אולם בין קטעי הגניזה שמורים הרבה פיוטים חדשים לאבן גיאת מסוג פיוטי היוצר. בהמשך דבריי אטפל בשניים מהם והם גוף היוצר והזולת. מנחם זולאי ז״ל היה הראשון למצוא שריד של גוף יוצר אחד לריצ״ג בקטע גניזה שבמוזיאון הבריטי. טקסט זה, שהוא סופו של גוף יוצר לפרשת מקץ, נדפס על־ידי זולאי יחד עם שני גופי יוצר אחרים לחג השבועות. אחד משני היוצרות הוא לר׳ אוהב, וטקסט זה פורסם כבר קודם לכן על־ידי שירמן, והשני לר׳ ברוך. זולאי זיהה את ר׳ אוהב כר׳ אוהב בן מאיר הנשיא שורתמיקש, כמו שעשה לפניו שירמן, ואת ר׳ ברוך כר׳ ברוך בן ר׳ יצחק אלבליאה.[20] בזמן האחרון נזכרו ותוארו יוצרות אלה במאמרו של עזרא פליישר על חידושי האסכולה הפייטנית הספרדית בפיוטי היוצר.[21] גופי יוצרות אלה חוברו בתבנית זהה והם נבדלים בצורתם משאר בני מינם. שלושת יוצרות אלה מחולקים לגושים של שלוש סטרופות, כשבראש כל גוש באה כותרת, שהיא בדרך כלל פסוק או קטע של פסוק מפרשת היום. כל גוש מכיל את דיבורו הישר של אחד מגיבורי הפרשה, והכותרת מגלה את זהותו של המדבר. למשל, היוצר למקץ הוא דיאלוג בין יוסף ופרעה, עם ציון המדברים בכותרות מתחלפות: ״ויאמר פרעה אל יוסף״ או ״ויאמר יוסף אל פרעה״. מבנה מיוחד זה משרה מתח מסוים על פיוטים אלה ויוצר רושם של דו־שיח ער וחי. באוקספורד ובסדרה הישנה בקיימברידג׳, ובמיוחד בסדרה החדשה שם, נמצאים דפים לא מעטים בכתיבה זהה שהתפזרו מקונטרס אחד. כל הדפים שהתגלו עד עכשיו מכילים רק פיוטי ריצ״ג. בקטעים אלה, שלצערי הם

18 ש׳ אברמסון, ״רב יוסף ראש הסדר״, קרית ספר כו (תש״י), עמ׳ 87 הערה 47.

19 ראה לאחרונה במאמרו של ש׳ אברמסון, ״לפירוש רב יצחק בן גיאת לקהלת״, קרית ספר נב (תשל״ז), עמ׳ 156-172.

20 במאמרו ״מקור וחיקוי בפיוט״, סיני כה (תש״ט), עמ׳ מז-נב <מנחם זולאי, ארץ ישראל ופיוטיה — מחקרים בפיוטי הגניזה, בעריכת אפרים חזן, ירושלים תשנ״ו, עמ׳ 317-323>.

21 הספרות ד (תשל״ג), עמ׳ 341. <ראה עתה עזרא פליישר, היוצרות בהתהוותם והתפתחותם, ירושלים תשמ״ד, עמ׳ 499 ואילך, וראה הערה 24.>

לקויים בהרבה מקומות, שרדו מפיוטי ריצ״ג בסוג גוף היוצר, אופן, אהבה, זולת, ה׳ מלכנו והבדלה. מכל סוג נשתמרו כמה דוגמאות, והן באות בכתב־היד בזו אחרי זו, כשציונים כמו ״הבדלה אחרת״ וכדומה מבדילים ביניהן. בין קטעים אלה נמצא גם ראשו של אותו יוצר לפרשת מקץ שזולאי פרסם את סופו, ועוד יש שם שני גופי יוצרות ממש כתבנית הנ״ל, האחד לפרשת ויגש והשני לפרשת קריעת ים סוף, והוא נועד או לפרשת בשלח או לחג פסח.[22] פיוט במבנה זהה, לפרשת קרח, נמצא גם לר׳ משה אבן עזרא.[23] העובדה שפיוטים אלה הם, בלי יוצא מן הכלל, פרי עטם של משוררים שחיו בשני דורות סמוכים ובמחיצה אחת מעוררת תשומת לב. ספריהם של הרמב״ע ושל הראב״ד מעידים שר׳ יצחק אבן גיאת, ר׳ אוהב בן מאיר הנשיא, ר׳ ברוך אלבליאה ור׳ משה אבן עזרא היו קרובים זה לזה בזמן, במקום וברוח. אבן גיאת היה, לפי הרמב״ע, ״זקן החבורה והנכבד שבה ועמודה וראשה״ ובעיר אליסנה, עיר השירה, הוא היה המוציא והמביא.[24] גם הראב״ד מזכיר את השפעתו ואומר עליו שהוא ״רבץ תורה הרבה והעמיד תלמידים הרבה״.[25] אם כן, נראה לי, שקרוב לשער שיוצרו של הטיפוס החדש של גוף היוצר היה ריצ״ג, והאחרים הלכו בעקבותיו.

גם בסוג אחר, בסוג הזולת, תיקן אבן גיאת תיקון חדש ומקורי. כבר צונץ הזכיר את מתכונתם המיוחדת של כמה מזולתותיו והאריך בתיאורם.[26] הפיוטים האלה נשתמרו ברובם במקורות שמחוץ לגניזה, אולם שניים מסוג זה התגלו לאחרונה בסדרה החדשה בקיימבריג׳, והעתקם של כמה אחרים נמצא בין הדפים שהזכרתי לעיל.[27] מלבד ריצ״ג ידוע לנו רק משורר אחד שחיבר זולת אחד בצורתם של זולתות אלה והוא ר׳ יהודה הלוי.[28] החידוש הצורני בפיוטים אלה מתבטא במבנה הסטרופות, בהוספת סטרופות־ביניים ובשיטת חריזה רב־גונית. כולם, בלי יוצא מן הכלל, עשויים בדיוק בדרך אחת, וגם מבחינת נושאיהם יש בהם אחידות מוחלטת. הפייטן מונה תופעות ומאורעות המקבילים למאורע העיקרי המתואר בפרשת קריאת היום. בדרך כלל הוא בונה את פיוטו על מדרש הנותן מספר למאורעות שאירעו לאבותינו במשך הדורות ושכדוגמתם יבואו לאחרית הימים.[29] נעמוד עכשיו בקיצור על משמעותם של החידושים האלה. פרופסור פליישר, במאמרו הנ״ל, קובע שפייטני ספרד מיעטו את העשייה דווקא בשני הסוגים הנ״ל.[30] גוף היוצר והזולת בפיוט המזרחי היו ארוכים מדי והיו מיוסדים על פירוט מיכני וסטריאוטיפי

22 כתב־יד קיימבריג׳ TS NS 10 H 8. fol. 5 .TS NS 231, fol. 3. ו־TS NS 135,. fol. 4
23 כתב־יד קיימבריג׳ TS NS 133, fol. 1
24 ספר העיונים והדיונים הנ״ל, שם.
25 ספר הקבלה הנ״ל, עמ׳ 61.
26 צונץ, הנ״ל, עמ׳ 196-197.
27 ראה במאמרי: ״חמשה זולתות לרב יצחק אבן גיאת״, שי להימן — מחקרים בספרות העברית של ימי הביניים מוגשים לא״מ הברמן, ירושלים תשל״ז, עמ׳ 329-342 (להלן, עמ׳ 115-127). <ראה פליישר (לעיל הערה 21), עמ׳ 555 ואילך.>
28 ראה במאמרו הנ״ל של פליישר, שם, הערה 49.
29 ראה במאמרי הנ״ל.
30 במאמרו הנ״ל, עמ׳ 340. <ראה פליישר (לעיל הערה 21), עמ׳ 565].>

של פסוקי מקרא מפרשת קריאת היום והפטרתו, ובכלל נהפכו פיוטים אלה ליצירות מאובנות וחסרות חיות. זאת ועוד, סוגים אלה בפיוט המזרחי היו מתובלים במידה גדושה של הבאות מהספרות התלמודית והמדרשית, ומקובל במחקר שמשוררי ספרד השתדלו להתרחק ממידה זו. בקיצור, אמירת פיוטים אלה לא היתה לפי טעמם האסתטי של המתפללים בספרד. ריצ״ג, כנראה, לא היה מוכן לוותר על מנהג קדום שבתפילה, והשתדל לקיימו, ולאו דווקא בראש השנה וביום הכיפורים בלבד, אלא גם בשאר חגים ושבתות מצוינות, ותיקן בגוף היוצר ובזולת תיקונים שלפי דעתו מסוגלים היו לחדש ולרענן את פני הפיוט המאובן. מה היו הסממנים העיקריים של גוף היוצר המקובל? תלות גמורה בפרשת התורה עם שילוב הבאות מִלוליות רבות ממנה לתוך הפיוט. בא ריצ״ג והעמיד בו כּכותרות מתחלפות פסוק מהפרשה בראש כל גוש של שלוש סטרופות ועיצב אותו כדיאלוג שבין הגיבורים הראשיים המופיעים בה. ההבאות המילוליות הלקוחות מהפרשה הושמטו, ואת מקומן הוא מילא בפסוקים משאר חלקי המקרא, כשהוא מסיים בהם את המחרוזות המשולשות המסורתיות. כך דחה הדיאלוג הער והדרמטי את הפירוט הסטריאוטיפי של הפסוקים, ואולי יש לשמוע מבין טורי יוצרות אלה גם הד של השיחה המנומסת וגינוני הוויכוח שהיו רגילים על פי בני הדור ההוא. בדרך דומה הלך אבן גיאת גם בחידושיו בזולת. הוא הוסיף שני טורים מתחלפים לגרעין הרגיל של הזולת, דהיינו צורת המחרוזות המרובעות, הכניס סטרופות־ביניים וחרז אותן בשיטת חריזה עשירת צלילים ומגוונת. כתוצאה מזה נוצר זולת העושה רושם של שיר מעין אזורי, סוג פופולרי ביותר באותה התקופה. אבן גיאת שחרר את הזולת מתלותו בהפטרה והעמיד במקומה את המסגרת המדרשית. בחירת הנושא המדרשי מבטיחה את קיום צביונו של הזולת בזה, שגם המדרש דן ברעיון של הקשר בין המאורע המתואר בקריאת התורה של היום ובין מאורעות דומים שמסופר עליהם בספרי הנביאים ואף הכתובים.

כך הצליח ריצ״ג, הפייטן הפורה והמקורי, לשמור על צביונם היסודי של שני סוגי פיוט אלה, אולם יחד עם זה שחרר אותם מחבלי השגרה שהוטלו עליהם במשך הדורות. תיקוניו אלה התקבלו על דעת כמה מבני דורו הצעירים, והם המשיכו לחבר פיוטים לפי הדגם שתיקן זקן החבורה.

אסיים בהבעת התקווה שהמחקר ביצירתו הפיוטית של ריצ״ג ההולך ומתאפשר על־ידי ממצאים רבים וחשובים מתוך אוצרות הגניזה יאיר כמה וכמה פרשיות סתומות גם ביצירותיהם של שאר גדולי משוררינו הספרדים.

"לך ה׳ הגדולה" ופסוקים דומים בקדושתאות ליום הכיפורים

בעל היובל [פרופסור עזרא פליישר], פרסם מחזור גדול של פיוטים מתוך קדושתא ליום הכיפורים המיוחסת לראשון הפייטנים, יוסי בן יוסי.[1] במקומות אחרים במחקריו הוסיף והעשיר את ידיעותינו אודות קומפוזיציות מונומנטליות, מעשה ידיהם של הפייטנים הגדולים בספרד, המורכבות ממכלול של פיוטים שנועדו להיאמר בכל תפילות יום הכיפורים. קומפוזיציות אלה נקראו בשם מעמד, סדר או ספר.[2] פיוטי המעמד נותקו עם הזמן מהקשרם הראשון, ומעטים הם המעמדות ליום הכיפורים של פייטני ספרד שהגיעו אלינו בהיקפם המלא ובסדרם המקורי. יוצא מכלל זה הוא המעמד הגדול שחיבר יצחק אבן גיאת; מעמד זה שרד, פחות או יותר בשלימותו, במחזור "שפתי רננות" לפי מנהג טריפולי וג׳רבה. הראשון מבין פייטני ספרד שחיבר מעמד ליום הכיפורים היה, לפי דבריו של אלחריזי, יוסף אבן אביתור.[3] פליישר גילה, זיהה ושיחזר את מעמדו של אבן אביתור על פי מקורות ידועים זה מכבר ועל פי ממצאי הגניזה.[4] בזה הוסיף הרבה על מה שעשה בשעתו צונץ, אשר ניסה לקבוע לראשונה את תוכנם של המעמדות שחוברו בידי יוסף אבן אביתור, שלמה אבן גבירול, יצחק אבן גיאת, משה אבן עזרא, יהודה הלוי ואברהם אבן עזרא.[5] פליישר הקדיש תשומת לב גם למעמד שחיבר שלמה אבן גבירול, וגילה את סידרת הרהיטים הארוכה והחשובה השייכת למעמד זה.[6] הוא עסק אף בבעיות ההיסטוריות והספרותיות הכרוכות בתולדות הסוג הספרותי הזה ובהתפתחותו, הצביע על החידושים שהכניסו אבן אביתור ואבן גבירול אל פיוטי המעמדות שלהם, וקבע שחידושים אלה השפיעו על הפייטנים אשר באו אחריהם.[7] ואכן, אבן

1 ראה: ע׳ פליישר, "מחזורי פיוט מתוך קדושתא ליום כיפור המיוחסת ליוסי בן יוסי", קבץ על יד ס"ח ז (יז) (תשכ"ח), עמ׳ 1 ואילך [להלן: פליישר, יוסי בן יוסי].

2 ראה: יהודה אלחריזי, תחכמוני, מהדורת י׳ טופורובסקי, תל־אביב תשי"ב, עמ׳ 44-45. על מעמדו של יצחק אבן גיאת נאמר שם: "ובספרו אשר חבר ליום הכיפורים" וכו׳.

3 שם, עמ׳ 44.

4 ראה: ע׳ פליישר, יצירתו של יוסף אבן אביתור; סוגים ותבניות בפיוטיו, עבודה לשם קבלת תואר דוקטור לפילוסופיה, ירושלים תשכ"ז, א, עמ׳ 272-283, והשווה מאמרו: "בחינות בשירתו של ר׳ יוסף אבן אביתור", אסופות ד (תש"ן), עמ׳ קכח, הערה 7, שם הוא מעיר שבעבודת הדוקטור שלו לא השתמש עדיין בממצאי הסידרה החדשה של אוסף שכטר בקיימברידג׳, ושיש בממצאים אלה לשנות את התמונה הניתנת שם "בכמה נקודות חשובות".

5 ראה: L. Zunz, *Die Ritus des synagogalen Gottesdienstes*, Berlin 1859, pp. 106-115; ראה גם מאמרו של פליישר הנזכר בהערה הקודמת, עמ׳ קלו, הערה 42.

6 ראה מאמרו: "פרקי פיוט מתוך סדרת רהיטים ממעמד יום הכיפורים של ר׳ שלמה אבן גבירול", תרביץ לח (תשכ"ט), עמ׳ 136-160.

7 ראה מאמרו המובא בהערה 4 לעיל, עמ׳ קלו, הערה 42, וכן עמ׳ קלח. ראה גם מאמרו הנזכר בהערה 6, עמ׳ 137-141.

גיאת, משה אבן עזרא ואברהם אבן עזרא חיברו את המעמדות שלהם תוך שהם הולכים בעקבות אבן אביתור ואבן גבירול, הן בענייני צורה והן בענייני תוכן.

ראוי לחקור נושא זה בהרחבה ובהעמקה, על פי היסודות שהניח פליישר. ראשית כל מן ההכרח הוא לנסות ולזהות את הפיוטים השייכים לכל מעמד ומעמד. דבר זה חשוב במיוחד לגבי המעמדות של משה אבן עזרא ואברהם אבן עזרא, שכן במהדורות פיוטיהם של שני משוררים אלה לא צוין פעמים רבות שפיוט מסוים שייך למעמד זה או אחר, ומקום הניחו המהדירים לנסיונות שיחזור של מלוא היקפן של הקומפוזיציות.[8] אחרי העמדת הקורפוס על מלואו, עד כמה שהדבר הוא בגדר האפשר, כדאי יהיה להשוות זה לזה את המעמדות שחיברו הפייטנים הספרדיים הנזכרים לעיל, ולקבוע את המייחד כל אחד מהם. צעד נוסף במחקר ידרוש עיון משווה בין המעמדות הספרדיים לבין הקדושתאות ליום הכיפורים של פייטני ארץ ישראל והמזרח.[9] ולבסוף, מן הראוי לעמוד על המגמות הדתיות ועל הרעיונות הפילוסופיים והתיאולוגיים הטמונים בפיוטים אלה, אשר שימשו את בית הכנסת בתפילות היום הקדוש. עיון מעמיק בחומר הרב השקוע בחיבורים ארוכים כגון המעמדות, אשר חוברו בכוונה תחילה כיצירות שלימות ואחידות, יושיט לנו עדות נאמנה על ההשקפות הדתיות הבאות לביטוין בפיוטי קדמונינו. במיוחד אפשר יהיה ללמוד מהם על ההשקפות ששררו בקרב יהודי ספרד בתקופה קדומה של תולדותיהם, תקופה שלא שרדו ממנה חיבורים שיטתיים רבים בתיאולוגיה, ובפרט לא בשפה העברית.[10]

בהזדמנות זו רצוני לעסוק באספקט אחר של המעמדות, אספקט שלפי מיטב ידיעותי לא עסקו בו החוקרים.

כבר לראשון הפייטנים, יוסי בן יוסי, מיוחסת סידרת פיוטים ארוכה (המכונה במחקר סידרת רהיטים או מערכת רהיטים), הבנויה על פסוק או על פסוקים מן המקרא. סידרה זו היתה שייכת לקדושתא ליום הכיפורים, אשר אין אנחנו יכולים לזהותה כעת בוודאות.[11] בקדושתא ליום הכיפורים, המיוחסת במקור אחר לאלעזר הקלירי, נמצאות שתי מערכות של רהיטים,[12] וגם שרידיה של קדושתא מאת יהודה אבן קורייש מורכבים מסידרה

8 בדבר מעמדו של אברהם אבן עזרא ראה במאמר הביקורת של פליישר על מהדורתו של י׳ לוין לשירי הקודש של אברהם אבן עזרא, קרית ספר נא (תשל״ו), עמ׳ 669.

9 פליישר העיר על הקשר שבין סידרת הרהיטים המיוחסת ליוסי בן יוסי לבין ״שלשלת ארוכה של יצירות מונומנטליות״ שבאו אחריה ושחוברו לא רק במזרח אלא גם בתקופת ספרד. ראה גם פליישר, יוסי בן יוסי (לעיל, הערה 1), עמ׳ 10.

10 ראה לאחרונה: א׳ מירסקי, מחובות הלבבות לשירת הלבבות, ירושלים תשנ״ב, ושם חומר עשיר על הזיקה שבין הרעיונות הפילוסופיים והתיאולוגיים שב״חובת הלבבות״ ובין אלה שבשירת הקודש העברית בספרד. מירסקי דן בעיקרו בגלגוליהם של מוטיבים מסוימים, אבל יש מקום לדון גם במגמות כלליות ומגובשות הבאות לביטוין בפייטנות הספרדית. <ראה לאחרונה: Adena Tanenbaum, *The Contemplative Soul: Hebrew Poetry and Philosophical Theory in Medieval Spain*, Leiden 2002.>

11 ראה: פליישר, יוסי בן יוסי, עמ׳ 6, ובמיוחד במאמרו: ״חדותא בירבי אברהם — ראשון לפייטני איטליה?״, איטליה ב (תשמ״א), עמ׳ ט, הערה 11.

12 ראה: א׳ שייבר, ״פיוטי קלירי המובא ע״י קרקסאני״, גנזי קויפמן, א, בודפשט תש״ט, עמ׳ 3 ואילך ובמיוחד עמ׳ 22 ואילך.

כזו.[13] הצד השווה שבין הסדרות שהוזכרו (להוציא הסידרה הראשונה שבקדושתא המיוחסת לקלירי) הוא בניינן על הפסוקים מדברי הימים א' כ"ט י"א-י"ב: "לך ה' הגדולה והגבורה והתפארת והנצח וההוד כי כל בשמים ובארץ לך ה' הממלכה והמתנשא לכל לראש" וכו'. הפיוטים מיוסדים על מלים מפסוק זה, פיוט למלה פיוט למלה, על פי סדר הפסוק.[14]

ונשאלת השאלה: מה ענין פסוקים אלה ליום הכיפורים? ומדוע בחרו הפייטנים דווקא בהם כדי להעמיד סביבם את הקדושתאות של יום הכיפורים? כדי לענות על שאלה זו עלינו לבחון כיצד נדרשים הפסוקים בידי חז"ל. מדרש אחד אומר: "לך ה' הגדולה — זו מעשה בראשית",[15] ובמדרש אחר אנו קוראים:

> ר' ברכיה פתח: "לך ה' הגדולה... כל בשמים ובארץ". אתה מוצא כל מה שברא הקב"ה למעלן ברא למטן, למעלן זבול וערפל למטן זבול וערפל... ולא עוד אלא שחביבין כל מה שלמטן משל מעלן, תדע לך שהניח מה שלמעלן וירד בשל מטן שנאמר "ועשו לי מקדש ושכנתי בתוכם" (שמות כה ח), הוי, "כי כל בשמים ובארץ".[16]

הפסוקים מספר דברי הימים הפכו אפוא לאסמכתא מקראית בדבר הרעיון הידוע שלפיו קיימת הקבלה בין העולם השמיימי ובין העולם הארצי, כאשר מול המשכן של מעלה ניצב משכן של מטה, ומול מעשה השמים עומד מעשה המשכן שעל הארץ.[17]

דברי המדרש מתפרשים ביתר בהירות על רקע הספרות היהודית־הלניסטית. בכתבי הסופרים היהודים־הלניסטים המשכן הוא סמל העולם. פרטי מבנה המשכן וכליו ובגדי הכהן הגדול נתפסים בדרך אליגורית כסמלי היקום. בדברי פילון אנו קוראים: "כזאת היתה תלבושת הכהן הגדול... הריהי בכללותה בצלמו כדמותו של העולם, וכל חלק שבה — של כל אחד מחלקיו", והוא ממשיך ואומר: "אלה בגדי הפאר שלובש הכהן הגדול בבואו לשרת בקודש, כדי שכל אימת שיבוא פנימה לקיים את התפילות והקורבנות כמנהג אבותינו, יבוא עמו כל העולם מכוח הדמויות שבלבושו", ומסיים: "להיות הוא עצמו [הכהן הגדול] עולם בזעיר אנפין".[18] בדומה לזה מצאנו אצל יוסף בן מתתיהו: "כי מה שיחשוב על הקמת

13 ראה: ח' בראדי, "פיוט ר' יהודה בן קוריש", הצופה לחכמת ישראל ב (תרע"ב), עמ' 63-83.

14 ראה: פליישר, יוסי בן יוסי (לעיל, הערה 1), עמ' 9-10, וכן במאמרו הנזכר בהערה 6, עמ' 139 ובהערות 15, 17 ו־19 שם.

15 ראה: בבלי ברכות נח ע"א, והשווה תרגום דברי הימים: "דילך ה' רבותא דבריתא עלמא בגבורתא רבתא".

16 ראה: שמות רבה לג ד.

17 ראה: א' אפטוביצר, "בית המקדש של מעלה על פי האגדה", תרביץ ב (תרצ"א), עמ' 137-157, 257-287. <ראה לאחרונה: שולמית לדרמן, "טקסטים מקבילים בחיבור נוצרי־ביזנטי ובקטעי מדרש המיוחסים לר' משה הדרשן", תרביץ ע (תשס"א), עמ' 213-226, ותגובתו של אופיר מינץ־מנור, "הבריאה, המשכן ומשה הדרשן", שם (תשס"ב), עמ' 265-267.>

18 ראה: פילון האלכסנדרוני, על חיי משה, ב, 117 ושם 133, בתוך: כתבים, א, בעריכת ס' דניאל־נטף, ירושלים 1986, עמ' 295 ועמ' 298.

המשכן ויראה את בגדו של הכהן ואת הכלים... ימצא שכל דבר מאלה נעשה לשם חיקויו של העולם כולו ובמתכונתו".[19]

כשם שניתן לערוך השוואה אליגורית בין העולם הגדול, המקרוקוסמוס, לבין המשכן, כך יש הקבלה בין העולם הקטן, המיקרוקוסמוס, שהוא האדם, לבין המשכן. גם במדרשים נמצא רעיון זה. במקור אחד אנו קוראים: "בשעה שאמר הב"ה למשה ועשו לי מקדש, אמר היאך אני יודע לעשותו? אמר לו הב"ה אל תיבהל, כשם שבראתי העולם וגופך, כן אתה עושה את המשכן".[20] וכשם שהמדרש המובא לעיל מפרט את ההקבלה בין מה שנברא למעלה ובין מה שנברא למטה, כך אנו מוצאים במדרש אחר השוואה בין חלקי גוף האדם ובין הדברים שנבראו בארץ: "ר' יוסי הגלילי אומר: כל מה שברא הקב"ה בארץ ברא באדם... הקב"ה... בחכמתו ובתבונתו ברא את כל העולם כולו וברא את השמים ואת הארץ, עליונים ותחתונים, ויצר באדם כל מה שברא בעולמו".[21]

הרעיון היהודי־הלניסטי בדבר התאמה הרמונית ואידיאלית בין שני העולמות, העליון והתחתון, ובין האדם ושני העולמות, מגיע דרך מדרשי חז"ל גם אל הפיוטים. השימוש השכיח בפיוטי יום הכיפורים בפסוקים "לך ה' הגדולה" וכו' מקבל את הסברו הנכון והמלא על פי הבנתם במדרש, הרואה בהם אסמכתא לרעיון שהמשכן הארצי קיים מול המשכן השמיימי, דהיינו שהמשכן הארצי הוא סמל לשלימות המשכן השמיימי. המשכן או המקדש הוא, כידוע, האתר המרכזי של פולחן יום הכיפורים, ואין פלא שהפייטנים בחרו בפסוקים אלה, לפי פירושם האליגורי־מדרשי, כדי לבנות עליהם את מערכת הרהיטים שלהם ליום הכיפורים. התאמה זו של העולמות מראה על ההרמוניה ועל השלימות שבבריאה. דברי הרמב"ם על קריאת התורה של אנשי המעמד, שעניינה היה במעשה בראשית, מביעים גם הם השקפה דומה: "כי שלימות המציאות היא העבודה ואין עבודה אצלנו אלא עם הקרבנות וכך אמרו אלמלי קרבנות [או בנוסח אחר: מעמדות] לא נתקיימו שמים וארץ".[22]

הקבלה זו מוצאת את ביטויה בספרות הפיוט לעתים קרובות.[23] הפייטן יניי מביע את הרעיון בקיצור נמרץ כשהוא מפייט על ענייני המשכן: "ועשייתם כן יחשב/ במעשה בראשית".[24] גם פייטנים מאוחרים יותר, שהם כותבים על בריאת העולם ובמיוחד על בריאת השמים, עושים שימוש בדימויים הלקוחים ממעשה המשכן. סעדיה גאון, בסידרת רהיטים ליום הכיפורים, המיוסדת על פסוקים המזמור "ברכי נפשי", אומר: "כאוהל מתחתה תקרה נטויה עלי פינות ארבעה/ כתורן העליתה מנורת כוכביה כאוהל תקועה"

19 ראה: יוסף בן מתתיהו, קדמוניות היהודים, III, ז, ז, בתרגומו של א' שליט, א, ירושלים תש"ד, עמ' 92-91, ובהערות שם, ב, עמ' סח-סט.

20 ראה: בראשית רבתי, מהדורת ח' אלבעק, ירושלים ת"ש, עמ' 32.

21 ראה: אבות דרבי נתן, מהדורת ש"ז שכטר, נו"א, פרק לא (מו ע"א).

22 ראה: משנה עם פירוש רבינו משה בן מימון, מהדורת יוסף קאפח, ירושלים תשכ"ד, תענית ד, ב (עמ' שמ).

23 ראה: א' מירסקי, "מחצבתן של צורות הפיוט", ידיעות המכון לחקר השירה העברית ז (תשי"ח), עמ' 28-18, ושם כמה מקורות לרעיון זה.

24 ראה: מחזור פיוטי רבי יניי, מהדורת צ"מ רבינוביץ, א, תל אביב 1985, עמ' 331, שורה 49.

וכן הלאה.[25] מובן מאליו שמהדהד כאן פסוק מקראי,[26] אבל הקורא בדברים מתרשם בעיקר מרעיון ההקבלה שבין השמים לבין אוהל מועד. גם ב"כתר מלכות" לאבן גבירול בא ציור זה בקשר למעשה בראשית, המתואר שם לפי התורה הניאופלטונית: "וידו אהל הגלגלים מחברת/ ובלולאות היכולת יריעות הבריאות קושרת/ וכוחה נוגעת עד שפת הבריאה השפלה החיצונה היריעה הקיצונה במחברת".[27] ובדברי אבן גיאת אנו קוראים: "אל, זבול שחק מכונן אהלי/ זורחי נגהי נרות בם מעלה/ זקף מנורות לבער ויגלה/ הן כל אלה יפעל אל";[28] ועוד: "ואפאר תעצומו בדבקו שבעה גלגלים כגלדי בצלים ויהי המשכן אחד".[29]

באמצעות הפסוקים "לך ה' הגדולה" וכו' ניתנה לפייטנים האפשרות לתאר את מעשה בראשית, את נפלאות השמים והארץ, ולרמוז בזה להשקפה שלפיה ההרמוניה הקמאית והשלימות של מעשה בראשית חוזרת ביום הכיפורים אל העולם על ידי עבודת כהן גדול בקודשי הקודשים. תיאורי מעשה בראשית בפיוט הקדום ובראשית הפייטנות הספרדית היו הימנוניים, ועיקרם שבח והלל לגדולתו של הבורא. אולם ברוח החידוש שפעמה בפייטני ספרד חל שינוי בטיב פיוטים אלה. לאחר אבן אביתור החלו פייטני ספרד להכניס לפיוטיהם נושאים חדשים, שלא היו שכיחים בפיוט הישן. גם את הפסוקים "לך ה' הגדולה" וכו' החליפו באחרים. בכל זאת, גם כשאין הם עושים שימוש בפסוקי "לך ה' הגדולה" – אולי מחמת רוב השימוש בהם במשך הדורות בידי פייטנים רבים אחרים – בוחרים הם בפסוקים שגם הם מביעים התפעלות מגדולת הבורא ומן הנפלאות שבבריאת העולם. יצחק אבן גיאת משתמש בשחרית בפסוק "מה רבו מעשיך ה' כולם בחכמה עשית" (שם קד כד) ובמוסף בפסוק "אודך על כי נוראות נפליתי נפלאים מעשיך ונפשי יודעת מאד" (שם קלט יד). אבן גבירול בונה את פיוטי הרהיטים שלו לשחרית של יום הכיפורים על הפסוק "ה' מעון אתה היית לנו בדור ודור" (תהלים צ ב).[30] ויחד עם זאת, הנה בחיבורו המפורסם "כתר מלכות", שגם הוא נועד ליום הכיפורים, הוא מעמיד את הפסוקים "לך ה' הגדולה" וכו' בראש מהלליו. פסוק זה פותח את "כתר מלכות", וכפי שהעיר חיים שירמן, אבן גבירול משתמש בפסוק זה כדרך שמשתמשים הפייטנים בפסוקי סידרת הרהיטים.[31] מסיבה זו אנו מוצאים בתחילת "כתר מלכות" שורה של משפטים הפותחים במלה "לך", כגון "לך ברואי מעלה ומטה", "לך הגבורה" וכיוצא באלה. גם ההמשך שם מזכיר סידרת רהיטים, כגון הסעיפים שבהם חוזר אבן גבירול על הביטויים "אתה אחד", "אתה נמצא", "אתה חי" ודומיהם.[32]

25 ראה: מ' זולאי, האסכולה הפייטנית של רב סעדיה גאון, ירושלים תשכ"ד, עמ' קכד.

26 ישעיה מ, כב.

27 ראה: רבי שלמה אבן גבירול, כתר מלכות, ט, מהדורת י"א זיידמן, ירושלים תש"י, עמ' כד-כו.

28 ראה: שירי ר' יצחק אבן גיאת, מהדורה טנטאטיבית מאת י' דוד, ירושלים תשמ"ח, עמ' 8.

29 שם, עמ' 46.

30 ראה: פליישר (לעיל, הערה 6), עמ' 140.

31 ראה: ח' שירמן, השירה העברית בספרד ובפרובאנס, א, ירושלים-תל־אביב 1961, עמ' 257, הערה על א, 2-5.

32 והשווה בבקשתו של רב סעדיה גאון, סדור רב סעדיה גאון, מהדורת י' דוידזון, ש' אסף וי' יואל, ירושלים תש"א, עמ' מז ואילך. גם שם הוא חוזר בראש הסעיפים על "אתה הוא ה' האלקים". בעותק

נאמנותו של אבן גבירול לפסוקים ״לך ה׳ הגדולה״ וכו׳ אינה מונעת ממנו להכניס תכנים חדשים אל ״כתר מלכות״. עד כמה שאפשר לקבוע, אבן גבירול היה הראשון שכלל בתוך שירתו הדתית כעין אנציקלופדיה בזעיר אנפין של קוסמולוגיה ואסטרונומיה. ויש להבדיל בין המעמד שחיבר ליום הכיפורים לבין ״כתר מלכות״. במעמד הוא נמנע מלעסוק בנושאים אלה בפרטות, והריהו נרתע מלהכניס חומר לימודי־מדעי לתוך פיוטים הנאמרים בתפילה בציבור ביום הכיפורים. אולם בשירתו הלא־ליטורגית, הפרטית, ב״כתר מלכות״, הוא מתיר לעצמו לתת לפני היחיד המתפלל תורה שלמה מתורתו של פטולימיאוס היווני.

יוסף אבן אביתור משתמש בפסוק ״לך ה׳ הגדולה״ וכו׳ לשם בניית סידרת רהיטיו, ופיוטיו מהלכים עדיין במישור ההימנוני הידוע מן הפיוט המזרחי העתיק.[33] אבן גיאת היה הראשון שבמעמדו ליום הכיפורים, בקדושתא שלו לשחרית, כלל תיאור ״מדעי״ שלם של העולם. תיאור מדעי־אסטרונומי מפורט, הלקוח ברובו מתורת תלמי וגם מספרי ה״אחים הטהורים״ ושאר אנשי מדע ופילוסופים ערביים בני המאה העשירית.[34] אבן גיאת הרחיב את גבולות המעמד שלו, וכניסוחו של צונץ, עסק בענייני קוסמוגוניה בקדושתא שלו לשחרית ובענייני פיזיולוגיה בקדושתא למוסף.[35] בקדושתא זו נמצאת סידרת פיוטים ארוכה המכילה מידע רב על יצירת הוולד ועל האנטומיה של גוף האדם. מידע מעניין זה נשאב גם כן ברובו ממקורות ערביים ויווניים.[36] פיוטים אלה בנויים על הפסוק ״אודך על כי נוראות נפליתי נפלאים מעשיך ונפשי יודעת מאד״ (תהלים קלט יד), ומעניין הדבר שהסיפא של פסוק זה מופיע כלשונו ככותרת בראש ״כתר מלכות״, ממש לפני הפסוקים ״לך ה׳ הגדולה״ וכו׳.

החידוש הגדול של אבן גיאת הפך את סידרת הרהיטים ההימנונית למעין אנציקלופדיה מדעית. כבר תלמידו, משה אבן עזרא, התנגד לדרכו של רבו. במעמדות של משה אבן עזרא ואברהם אבן עזרא, אף שגם בהם כלולים עניינים רבים של פילוסופיה, אין נמצאים כמעט פרטי מדע אסטרונומיים או אנטומיים. משה אבן עזרא, בספרו על שירת ישראל, מסביר את הסיבה להשמטת דברים אלה כך:

> ומאלה [כלומר מהפייטנים] יש שחיברו את רוב דבריהם ביצירות לא שקולות הנאמרות בציבור ביום הצום הנכבד... ומהם... שהרבו להעביר הרבה מן

של ש׳ שפיגל של סידור רס״ג (עמ׳ מז), נמצאת הערה בכתב ידו: ״הבקשה היתה משובצת בתוך מסגרות הפסוקים נחמי׳ ט ו־ז ונועדה ליו״כ תחלה? עי׳ זולאי, אורלוגין מספר 8 עמ׳ 5״.

33 הנתונים ״המדעיים״ בפיוטיו, עד כמה שאפשר לקבוע על יסוד החומר הידוע, אינם מפורטים ומרובים והם שאובים ממקורות יהודיים־מסורתיים ולא ממקורות חיצוניים. ראה: מירסקי (הערה 10), עמ׳ 15-21.

34 החומר המדעי בפיוטי אבן גיאת לא נחקר עדיין, ראה במאמרי: “Two Philosophical Passages in the Liturgical Poetry of Rabbi Isaac ibn Giat”, *Of Scholars, Savants and their Texts: Studies... in Honor of Arthur Hyman*, New York 1989, pp. 209-213. <וראה בספר זה, בחלק האנגלי, עמ׳ *233-*238.>

35 ראה: L. Zunz, *Literaturgeschichte der synagogalen Poesie*, Berlin 1865, p. 195

36 ראה לעיל, הערה 33.

הלימודים המדויקים ובפרט התכונה השמימית לתוך התפילות האלה... עד שעברנו במעמד זה מן התפילה והתחנונים אל הויכוחים והדיונים.[37]

משה אבן עזרא מדבר כאן בפירוש על תפילות בציבור, וקרוב לוודאי שהתכוון למעמדו של אבן גיאת, ואולי גם לחיבורים דומים אחרים שאינם ידועים לנו. התנגדותו אינה מכוונת, ככל הנראה, כלפי "כתר מלכות", שנועד לתפילת היחיד.

מדברים קצרים אלה ניתן ללמוד על תמורות שונות שחלו בתימטיקה של הקדושתאות ושל המעמדות ליום הכיפורים, ויש בהם פתח לעיון מעמיק יותר בנושא חשוב זה.

37 ראה: ר' משה בן יעקב אבן עזרא, ספר העיונים והדיונים, מהדורת א"ש הלקין, ירושלים תשל"ה, עמ' 61.

"עבודה קצרה" לרב יצחק אבן גיאת

בשם "עבודה קצרה" או "עבודה קטנה" נקראים פיוטים מסוג הקיקלר[1] הכלולים בקדושתאות לשחרית יום הכיפורים מפרי עטם של פייטנים שונים. השם "עבודה קצרה" אינו קדום וכנראה צונץ היה הראשון שהשתמש בו לציון הסוג.[2] קיקלרים המתארים את סדר העבודה בקיצור נמצאים בין יצירותיהם של ר' אלעזר הקלירי[3] ושל מחברי המעמדות הגדולים ליום הכיפורים מהאסכולה הספרדית, כגון ר' יוסף אבן אביתור,[4] ר' שלמה אבן גבירול,[5] ר' יצחק אבן גיאת[6] ור' משה אבן עזרא.[7]

סוג הקיקלר לפי אופיו מכיל בסוף כל סטרופה פסוק או חלק של פסוק כלשונו;[8] ב"עבודות הקצרות", הפסוקים מסיימי הסטרופות לקוחים, דרך כלל כסדרם, מפרשת היום, דהיינו: ראשית פרשת אחרי מות. תוכן הפיוטים הוא פשוט, הפייטנים אינם משתמשים בפרטים המרובים של סדר העבודה הנמצאים בספרות חז"ל, והרושם המתקבל מהפיוטים הנ"ל הוא של פרפרזה מחורזת של פרשת היום. ר' יצחק אבן גיאת חידש חידוש בתוכן הסוג: בניגוד לקודמיו הוא מכניס לתוך פיוטו הרבה מן הענינים הנוגעים לסדר העבודה מתוך משנה יומא וגם קצת משאר מקורות חז"ל. לא זו בלבד אלא שאבן גיאת שילב הבאה כמעט מילולית ממשנה יומא פ"ז מ"ד בסוף אחת הסטרופות של פיוטו,[9] ובכך העלה את ההבאה מן המשנה לדרגה שווה עם פסוקי המקרא לגבי סיום הסטרופות של הקיקלר שלו.

קשה להסביר מה הביא את אבן גיאת לשינוי פני הקיקלר של העבודה הקצרה על ידי הוספת החומר מן המשנה. לכאורה מוטב היה להשאיר את העבודה הקצרה כמות שהיא

1 על הקיקלר בכלל ראה עזרא פליישר, שירת הקודש העברית בימי הביניים, ירושלים 1975, עמ' 148-147, וקיקלר לדוגמא שם עמ' 161-159. וראה גם מאמרו: "לחקר תכניות הקבע בפיוטי הקדושתא (קיקלר, עסטריוטא)", סיני סה (תשכ"ט), עמ' כא-מז, ומאמרו: "בירורים בדבר מקורם של מונחים אחדים בפייטנות ובשירה", תרביץ מז (תשל"ח), עמ' 189-185. על ה"עבודות הקצרות" בצורת קיקלר ראה דבריו בתרביץ לח (תשכ"ט), עמ' 144 והערה 28.

2 ראה בספרו, *Die synagogale Poesie des Mittelalters*, עמ' 80 והערה 1 שם.

3 פליישר בתרביץ ל"ח הנ"ל.

4 ראה בדיסרטציה של פליישר, יצירתו של יוסף אבן אביתור, ירושלים תשכ"ז, ח"א, עמ' 273.

5 נדפס בשירי הקדש לרבי שלמה אבן גבירול, מהד' דב ירדן, א, ירושלים תשל"א, עמ' 143-141.

6 מתפרסם להלן בגוף המאמר.

7 נדפס בשירי הקדש של משה אבן עזרא, מהד' שמעון ברנשטיין, תל אביב תשי"ז, עמ' רלז-רלט.

8 ראה פליישר, שירת הקודש העברית בימי הביניים, עמ' 147.

9 ראה בגוף הפיוט, שורה 114.

כי צירוף החומר מספרות חז״ל עלול היה לעורר בעיה שהעסיקה את הגאונים וגם את ר׳ יצחק אבן גיאת עצמו. אנו מוצאים שהגאונים התנגדו למנהג אמירת סדר העבודה בתפלות שחרית ומנחה של יום הכיפורים ופסקו שמקומו של סדר העבודה הוא בתפלת מוסף בלבד. רק בדוחק התירו את אמירת סדר העבוה בתפלות שחרית ומנחה במקומות ששם התחבב מאד המנהג על הצבור.[10] לפי דברי הגאונים עיקר חובת אמירת סדר העבודה כולל את הזכרת הווידויים וההזאות.[11] העדר הזכרת עניינים אלה בסדרי העבודה הקצרה הוציא אותם מן כלל סדר העבודה העיקרי ואולי בגלל זה לא התייחסו הגאונים בכלל לאמירת סדרים כאלה בשחרית. ההרחבה של אבן גיאת קירבה את העבודה הקצרה לאחותה הגדולה,[12] אבל בכל זאת היא נשארה בגדר הזכרת דברים בעלמא[13] ונעדרה ממנה אמירת הוידויים וההזאות. בכל אופן הצליח אבן גיאת לרענן את פני הקיקלר של העבודה הקצרה ועם זה שמר על אופיו הישן. כך היתה דרכו גם בשאר סוגי פיוט,[14] וראויה כל יצירתו הפיוטית להבחן, כדי שנוכל להכיר את אמנותו של פייטן גדול זה, שכנראה כל מגמתו היתה לחדש את פני הפיוט המסורתי לפי טעם דורו.

10 ראה אוצר הגאונים למסכת יומא, עמ׳ 18 (סי׳ לז) ועמ׳ 40-41 (סי׳ קיד-קכב) וראה בהלכות ר׳ יצחק אבן גיאת, ח״א, עמ׳ סב-סד (שערי שמחה, מהד׳ ר׳ יצחק דוב הלוי במברגר, פירטה תרכ״א).

11 ראה במקורות המובאים בספרות שצויינה בהערה הקודמת, במיוחד מה שמובא ע״י ריצ״ג עצמו, שם: ״...מתחיל לומר סדר עבודת היום ודרין שהי׳ מתודה כהן גדול ביוה״כ ואומר תחלה אנא השם עויתי פשעתי וכו׳״. וראה באוצה״ג הנ״ל, עמ׳ 18: ״יש אומ׳ שבעת ימים וי״א אזכיר סלה וכו׳ שכולן שוין ויש בהן הזאות ווידויין והן חובת היום וסדר עבודות״.

12 עד כדי כך שר׳ ישראל קמחי בספרו עבודת ישראל המכיל פירוש ארוך על סדר העבודה ביוה״כ (איזמיר תצ״ז) מביא דברים ממנה, ראה בהערה לגוף הפיוט שורות 40-41. ר׳ ישראל קמחי מביא גם ״מעבודה קצרה״ לר׳ יצחק בן ר׳ זרחיה גירונדי, ראה שם. פיוטו של ר׳ יצחק גירונדי נעשתה כדוגמתו של הקיקלר של אבן גיאת ואין ספק שהושפע ממנו. גם ר׳ יצחק גירונדי השתמש בדברי חז״ל בתיאור סדר העבודה. פיוטו של ר׳ יצחק גירונדי לא נדפס עדיין והוא נמצא בכ״י פריז מס׳ 656, דף 56 ע״א. ראה גם י׳ דודזון, אוצר השירה והפיוט, י 2766.

13 אולי לכך רומזים הדברים בראש הקיקלרים ״שעה זכרון דתי״ לר׳ שלמה אבן גבירול, ראה לעיל הערה 5: ״ובכן למדני צור דתך בזכרי סדר עבודתך״ לר׳ משה אבן עזרא, ראה לעיל הערה 7; כך גם אצל אבן גיאת, ראה להלן בראש הפיוט וראה בראש הקיקלר של ר׳ יצחק גירונדי (כ״י פריז הנ״ל): ״ובכן קחו עמכם דברים ונשובה אל ה׳ אלקינו בזכרון סדר עבודתנו״. וכבר הרגיש בזה צונץ, ראה לעיל בדבריו הנזכרים בהערה 2.

14 ראה מה שכתבתי במאמרי ״חמשה זולתות לרב יצחק אבן גיאת״, שי להימן: מחקרים בספרות העברית של ימי הביניים מוגשים לא״מ הברמן, תל אביב תשל״ז, עמ׳ 330-332; ובמאמרי ״יצירתו הפיוטית של ר׳ יצחק אבן גיאת״, תעודה א (תש״מ), עמ׳ 92-95 (לעיל, עמ׳ 93-98). וראה לאחרונה מה שכתב עזרא פליישר במאמרו ״בחינות בשירת פייטני איטליה הראשונים״, הספרות 30-31 (1981), עמ׳ 144, הערה 74.

"עבודה קצרה" — קיקלר לשחרית יוה"כ לרב יצחק אבן־גיאת

וּבְכֵן לַמְדֵנִי דָתֶךָ/ בְּזָכְרִי סֵדֶר עֲבוֹדָתֶךָ

אַחֲלַי בְּזָכְרִי צְפוּנֵי תַעֲלוּמוֹת
אִמְרֵי עֲבוֹדַת הַיּוֹם צְפוּנוֹת וּסְתוּמוֹת
בְּפָרָשַׁת אַחֲרֵי מוֹת (ויקרא טז א)
בֵּאֵר מֵאָז לְאַב הֲמוֹנָי:

בְּעֵת הָחֲדַל לְהַקְרִיב קָרְבָּנַי
וּזְכַרְתֶּם אֶת כָּל מִצְוֹת ה׳ (במדבר טו לט)
גְּמוּל זֵכֶר כְּמַעֲשֶׂה אֲקִימֶנּוּ
גַּם מִדֵּי דַבְּרִי בּוֹ לְנֶגְדִּי אֲשִׂימֶנּוּ
הָמוּ מֵעַי לוֹ רַחֵם אֲרַחֲמֶנּוּ (ירמי׳ לא יט)

יִצְדָּק חִין עֶרְךְּ קְהָלִי
כְּמַעֲשֶׂה סֵדֶר הִלּוּלִי
אֱלֹקִים יַחֲשׁוֹב לִי קָדוֹשׁ]

דִּבֵּר הַפָּרָשָׁה לְפַלְהֶדְרִין בְּהִתְחַדֵּשׁ:
דְּרוֹשׁ שִׁבְעָה סֵדֶר הַיּוֹם וְתִתְקַדֵּשׁ
בְּזֹאת יָבוֹא אַהֲרֹן אֶל הַקֹּדֶשׁ (ויקרא טז ג)

הַזּוֹת עָלָיו כָּל שִׁבְעָה וּלְכָל הַזָּאָה טְבִילָה
הָכִין וְקַחַת מִשֶּׁלוֹ לִהְיוֹת לִמְחִילָה
פַּר בֶּן בָּקָר לְחַטָּאת וְאַיִל לְעוֹלָה (שם שם)

וַעֲבוֹדַת הַיּוֹם בְּאַרְבָּעָה בִּגְדֵי לָבָן יִלְבָּשָׁם
וְטוֹבֵל חָמֵשׁ טְבִילוֹת וּבַעֲשָׂרָה קִדּוּשִׁין מְקַדְּשָׁם
וְרָחַץ בַּמַּיִם אֶת בְּשָׂרוֹ וּלְבֵשָׁם (שם ד)

יִצְדָּק [חִין עֶרְךְּ קְהָלִי
כְּמַעֲשֶׂה סֵדֶר הִלּוּלִי
אֱלֹקִים יַחֲשׁוֹב לִי קָדוֹשׁ]

זִמֵּן לְהַעֲבִיר טֶנֶף מְגוֹאָל וּמְגָאֵל
זוּג שְׂעִירִים וְאַיִל אֶ[חָד] יִקַּח כְּחֻקֵּי אֵל
מֵאֵת עֲדַת בְּנֵי יִשְׂרָאֵל (שם ה)

חַטַּאת פָּרוֹ יַקְרִיב לְחַטָּאתוֹ
חֻקֵּי וִידּוּי יַתְחִיל עָלָיו כְּחֻקָּתוֹ
בַּעֲדוֹ וּבְעַד בֵּיתוֹ (שם ו)

טָרַח וּבָא לוֹ לִצְפוֹן מִזְבֵּחַ עִם שְׁנֵי נֶאֱמָנַי
טַעַם הַגּוֹרָל עַל שְׁנֵי שְׂעִירִים כְּפִי חֶזְיוֹנַי
וְהֶעֱמִיד אֹתָם לִפְנֵי ה׳ (שם ז)

יִצְדָּק [חִין עֶרֶךְ קְהָלִי
כְּמַעֲשֶׂה סֵדֶר הִלּוּלִי
אֱלֹקִים יַחֲשׁוֹב לִי קָדוֹשׁ]

יַכְנִיס יָדָיו לְקַלְפֵּי וּבָהּ שְׁנֵי גוֹרָלוֹת יְקָרִים
יַד מַעֲלָה שֶׁל שֵׁם בַּתְּחִלָּה יָרִים
וְנָתַן עַל שְׁנֵי הַשְּׂעִירִים (שם ח)

כְּכַלּוֹתוֹ יַעֲמִיד נִשְׁחָט כְּנֶגֶד בֵּית שְׁחִיטָתוֹ
כֵּן מִשְׁתַּלֵּחַ יַעֲמִיד כְּנֶגֶד בֵּית שְׁלִיחוּתוֹ
לִפְנֵי ה׳ לְכַפֵּר עָלָיו לְשַׁלַּח אוֹתוֹ (שם י)

לְפָנָיו בָּא שְׁנִיָּה לְהִתְוַדּוֹת מַעֲלוֹ
לְכַפֵּר בַּעֲדוֹ וּבְעַד שִׁבְטוֹ מִילוּלוֹ
וְשָׁחַט אֶת פַּר הַחַטָּאת אֲשֶׁר לוֹ (שם יא)

יִצְדָּק [חִין עֶרֶךְ קְהָלִי
כְּמַעֲשֶׂה סֵדֶר הִלּוּלִי
אֱלֹקִים יַחֲשׁוֹב לִי קָדוֹשׁ]

מְקַבֵּל דָּמוֹ וְנוֹתְנוֹ לַמְּמָרֵס בְּלִי לְשַׁבֵּחַ
מַחְתָּה נוֹטֵל וְחָשׁ לִמְלַאכְתָּהּ בְּבֵית מַטְבֵּחַ
גַּחֲלֵי אֵשׁ מֵעַל הַמִּזְבֵּחַ (שם יב)

נוֹטֵל כַּף שֶׁל זָהָב רֵיקָה
נוֹתֵן לְתוֹכָהּ מְלֹא חָפְנָיו מִן הַדַּקָּה
קְטֹרֶת סַמִּים דַּקָּה (שם שם)

סוֹבֵב וּבָא בֵּין פָּרְכוֹת הֵיכַל מְעוֹנַי
סִדֵּר מַחְתָּה בֵּין הַבַּדִּים לִפְנִים וְלִפְנַי
וְנָתַן הַקְּטֹרֶת עַל הָאֵשׁ לִפְנֵי ה׳ (שם יג)

יִצְדַּק [חִין עֶרְךְּ קְהָלִי
כְּמַעֲשֶׂה סֵדֶר הִלּוּלִי
אֱלֹקִים יַחֲשׁוֹב לִי קָדוֹשׁ]

עָשָׁן מִתְמַלֵּא הַבַּיִת שֶׁלֹּא לְהִסְתַּכֵּל בִּדְמוּת
עַיִן זוֹהַר מַרְאֶה הַחוֹנֶה בִתְמִימוּת
עַל הָעֵדוּת וְלֹא יָמוּת (שם שם)

פִּלֵּל בְּצֵאתוֹ קְצָרָה שֶׁלֹּא לְהַבְעִית קְדוֹשֵׁי אָדָם
פָּנָה וְלָקַח דַּם הַפָּר וְעַל הַכַּפֹּרֶת וְלִפְנֵי בִּמְקוֹם הַדָּם
יַזֶּה עָלָיו שֶׁבַע פְּעָמִים מִן הַדָּם (שם יד)

צֵאתוֹ לִשְׁחוֹט שְׂעִיר הַחַטָּאת עִם בּוֹ יְכוּפָּר
צָעַד לִפְנִים וְהִזָּה מִמֶּנּוּ בְּמִסְפָּר
כַּאֲשֶׁר עָשָׂה לְדַם הַפָּר (שם טו)

יִצְדַּק [חִין עֶרְךְּ קְהָלִי
כְּמַעֲשֶׂה סֵדֶר הִלּוּלִי
אֱלֹקִים יַחֲשׁוֹב לִי קָדוֹשׁ]

קָם וְעָמַד בְּהֵיכָל וּבִדְמֵי שְׁנֵיהֶם
קֹדֶשׁ יְכַפֵּר בְּמִנְיָנֵי הַזָּיוֹתֵיהֶם
מִטֻּמְאוֹת בְּנֵי יִשְׂרָאֵל וּמִפִּשְׁעֵיהֶם (שם טז)

רָץ וְעָרוֹת דַּם הַפָּר לְדַם שָׂעִיר פְּעָלָיו
רָץ לַמִּזְבֵּחַ הַזָּהָב מֵעֲגָלָיו
אֲשֶׁר לִפְנֵי ה׳ וְכִפֵּר עָלָיו (שם יח)

שְׁיָרֵי הַדָּם כְּכַלּוֹתוֹ כָּל אֵל
שׁוֹפֵךְ עַל יְסוֹד מִזְבֵּחַ הַהַרְאֵל
וְטִהֲרוֹ וְקִדְּשׁוֹ מִטֻּמְאוֹת בְּנֵי יִשְׂרָאֵל (שם יט)

יִצְדַּק [חִין עֶרְךְּ קְהָלִי
כְּמַעֲשֶׂה סֵדֶר הִלּוּלִי
אֱלֹקִים יַחֲשׁוֹב לִי קָדוֹשׁ]

תַּמּוּ מֵחַטָּאת שְׁלָשְׁתָּם
תּוֹמֵךְ מִשְׁתַּלֵּחַ וּמִתְוַדֶּה עָלָיו בְּעַד קְהַל עֲדָתָם
וְנָשָׂא הַשָּׂעִיר עָלָיו אֶת כָּל עֲוֹנוֹתָם (שם כב)

יְמַהֵר תִּתּוֹ לְאִישׁ עִתִּי יָעִיר
יְקָרִים מְלַוִּין אוֹתוֹ בְּהוֹלִיכוֹ מִחוּץ לָעִיר
אֶל אֶרֶץ גְּזֵרָה וְשִׁלַּח אֶת הַשָּׂעִיר (שם שם)

צֵרוּף אֵמוּרֵי פָר וְשָׂעִיר לְהַקְטִירָם יִפְנֶה
צִיר לִשְׂרוֹף שְׁנֵיהֶם יְמַנֶּה
מִחוּץ לַמַּחֲנֶה (שם כ"ז)

יִצְדַּק [חִין עֶרֶךְ קְהָלִי
כְּמַעֲשֵׂה סֵדֶר הִלּוּלִי
אֱלֹקִים יַחֲשׁוֹב לִי קָדוֹשׁ]

חָשׁ וְחָלַץ בִּגְדֵי בָד וּגְרָעָם
חֲלִיצוֹת זָהָב לִלְבּוֹשׁ תַּחְתָּם יִנְעַם
וְיָצָא וְעָשָׂה אֶת עֹלָתוֹ וְאֶת עֹלַת הָעָם (שם כד)

קִדֵּם וּבָא לִלְבּוֹשׁ לָבָן וְצוֹעֵד
קֹדֶשׁ קָדָשִׁים לְהוֹצִיא כַף וּמַחְתָּה יִוָּעֵד
וּבָא אַהֲרֹן אֶל אֹהֶל מוֹעֵד (שם כג)

גּוֹמֵר וְחוֹלֵץ מַדֵּי בָד לְבֶשָׁם
גְּנָזָם בַּקֹּדֶשׁ שֶׁלֹּא לְאַחַר כֵּן יִלְבְּשָׁם
בְּבוֹאוֹ אֶל הַקֹּדֶשׁ וְהִנִּיחָם שָׁם (שם שם)

יִצְדַּק [חִין עֶרֶךְ קְהָלִי
כְּמַעֲשֵׂה סֵדֶר הִלּוּלִי
אֱלֹקִים יַחֲשׁוֹב לִי קָדוֹשׁ]

יִלְבַּשׁ אַרְבַּע מַחֲלָצוֹת זָהָב טְהוֹרוֹת
יַקְטִיר קְטֹרֶת בֵּין הָעַרְבַּיִם כְּחֻקּוֹת סְדוּרוֹת
בְּהֵיטִיבוֹ אֶת הַנֵּרוֹת (שמות ל' ז')

אֶת בִּגְדֵי עַצְמוֹ לוֹבֵשׁ בְּהַפְשִׁיטוֹ מַדֵּי פָז וְיַהֲלוֹם
אוֹתוֹ מְלַוִּים בְּהָלְכוֹ וַהֲלוֹם
וְיוֹם טוֹב עָשָׂה לְאוֹהֲבָיו כְּשֶׁיָּצָא בְשָׁלוֹם (יומא פז מד)

תַּמּוּ עֲבוֹדוֹת הַיּוֹם לַעֲרוֹךְ כְּפִי דְבַר צוֹפִי
תִּרְצֶה בְטוּבְךָ בְּהַקְרִיבִי בִימֵי חָרְפִּי
אֲשֶׁר פָּצוּ שְׂפָתַי וְדִבֶּר פִּי (תהלים סו יד)

יִצְדַּק [חִין עֶרֶךְ קְהָלִי
כְּמַעֲשֵׂה סֵדֶר הִלּוּלִי
אֱלֹקִים יַחֲשׁוֹב לִי קָדוֹשׁ]

חַנּוּן רָצִיתִי כְבָר מַעֲשֵׂיכֶם
חֻקֵּי עֲבוֹדָתִי אֶחֱשׁוֹב בְּהַקְרִיבְכֶם
יַעַן הַזְכַּרְכֶם (יחזקאל כא כט)

זִבְחֵי צֶדֶק זִבְחוּ וְהַעֲלוּ אֲמָרֶיךָ
זָכוֹר אֶזְכּוֹר מַהֵר וּבְאֶרֶץ מְגוּרֶיךָ
יָקֵם ה׳ אֶת דְּבָרֶיךָ (ירמ׳ כח ו)

קָרְבוּ לָבֹא יְמֵי יִשְׁעֲכֶם תָּשִׂישׂוּ
קֶרֶב הָרֵי יִשְׂרָאֵל לְחַי תִּקָּבְצוּ וְתִכָּנְסוּ
וְהַיּוֹצֵא מִפִּיכֶם תַּעֲשׂוּ (במדבר לב כד)

יִצְדַּק [חִין עֶרֶךְ קְהָלִי
כְּמַעֲשֵׂה סֵדֶר הִלּוּלִי
אֱלֹקִים יַחֲשׁוֹב לִי קָדוֹשׁ]

יִרְבּוּן צְפִירַת חֻקֵּי מוֹעֲדֵיכֶם
גְּאוּלִים יוּבְלוּ אֵלָיו לִרְצוֹנְכֶם
תַּקְרִיבוּ אֶת קָרְבַּנְכֶם (ויקרא א ב)

בְּעוֹז קָדוֹשׁ

הערות:

הפיוט מתפרסם עפ״י שלושה כתבי יד: כ״י הבריטיש מוזיאום, הרלי 5530, רשימת מרגליות מס׳ 703, דף 63 ע״ב–דף 66 ע״א (= ב); כ״י פלורנץ, פלוט׳ 27, דף 37 ע״ב, רק השורות 1-45 (= פ); כ״י אנטונין 133 (צילומו במכון שוקן בירושלים), מכיל את השורות 69 עד הסוף (= א).

הפיוט הוא חלק מן הקדושתא ״וארץ אכף״ לשחרית יוה״כ.

הפיוט נזכר באוצר השירה והפיוט של דודזון, כרך ד׳, מלואים, א 677. <כעת ראה יונה דוד, שירי ר׳ יצחק אבן גיאת (מהדורה טנטאטיבית), ירושלים תשמ״ח, עמ׳ 25 ואילך.>

הסימן: א״ב כפול, יצחק גיאת חזק (כפול). בפזמון: יצחק. בסטרופה האחרונה: יצחק גיאת. על הכותרת של הפיוט ראה הערה 13 למבוא.

חילופי נוסח:

2. צפונות וסתומות — **ב** סדורות. 7. כמעשה — **ב** כמעשה ידיו. 9. המו — **פ** והמו. 11. הלולי — **פ** מלולי. 13. לפלהדרין — **פ** בפלהדרין. 14. דרוש — **ב** דרור; ותתקדש — **פ** והתקדש. 16. ולכל — **פ** ובכל. 18. בן בקר — **פ** חסר. 19. בארבעה — **פ** בארבעת. 26. א[חד] — **פ** חסר. 27. מאת — **פ** ומאת. 29. עליו — **פ** חסר. 32. הגורל — **פ** הגרלה; בפי — **פ** כפי. 37. ידיו — **פ** ידו. 38. מעלה — **פ** יעלה; בתחלה — **פ** כתחלה. 53. נותן — **ב** ונותן (ותיקנתי לצורך הסימן). 67. שעיר — **א** השעיר. 78. וכפר — **א** לכפר. 79. ככלותו — **א** בכלותו. 85. תמו — **א** תומו. 86. משתלח — **ב** ומשתלח. 88. ימהר תתו — **ב** מהר ותתו; **א** ימהר ותתו. 97. וגרעם — **א** וגדעם. 100. ובא — **א** ושב. 104. גנזם — **א** גונזם. 113. אותו מלוים — **א** יקרים מלוין אותו. 114. כשיצא — **א** שיצא. 116. תרצה — **א** תראה. 121. חנון רציתי כבר — **א** חנון ענה כבר רציתי. 125. מהר — **א** חסר. 126. את — **א** חסר. 127. ישעכם — **א** ישע בם. 133. ירבון — **א** יכונן; מועדיכם — מזבחכם. 134. יובלו אליו לרצונכם — **א** יובלו לר[אות] (?) אליו לרצונכם; **א** יובלו אליו לחי לרצונכם.

ביאור:

1. **אחלי** – תהלים קיט ה, ותרגומו: טב לי. 4. **לאב המוני** – בגלל המשך הדברים מוכרחים לפרש כאן אב המון כמכוון למשה ולא לאברהם כרגיל עפ"י בראשית יז ד-ה. 5-7. ראה ספרי במדבר, מהד' הארוויטץ, עמ' 127 על הפסוק בבמדבר ט"ו מ': "למען תזכרו ועשיתם, לעשות זכרון כמעשה", וכאן הכוונה שאמירת סדר העבודה תיחשב כעשייתה בבית המקדש. 8. **מדי דברי בו** – לפי ירמי' לא יט וראה בשורה הבאה. 10. **יצדק חין ערך** – יזכה, ורגיל בלשון הפייטנים, ראה למשל בשבעתא לפרשת שקלים לקלירי, אשכול אווי (דוידזון, א, 8069): "ובצדק הגה ערך" וכו' ובתפלת גשם, "אר"א זכור אב" (דוידזון, ז, 91): "בְּצִדְקוֹ חוֹן" וכו'. 13. **הפְרָשה לפלהדרין** – לפי משנה יומא א א; **בהתחדש** – כנראה הכוונה להתחלת החודש, כי הפרישו את הכהן הגדול מביתו שבעת ימים קודם יום הכפורים, דהיינו בג' תשרי. 14. **דרוש שבעה סדר היום** – יומא פ"א מ"ג וראה גם מ"ו שם: "אם היה חכם דורש". ואולי פירש ר' יצחק אבן גיאת שהכהן הגדול דרש בסדר היום כל שבעה. 16. **הזות עליו כל שבעה** וכו' – ראה בבלי יומא ח ע"א, והפייטן נקט כדברי ר' מאיר: "אחד זה ואחד זה מזין עליו כל שבעה מכל חטאות שהיו שם, דברי ר' מאיר". ראה גם פרה פ"ג מ"א; **ולכל הזאה טבילה** – פרה פ"ג מ"ט. 17. **וקחת משלו** – לפי בבלי יומא ג ע"ב, וראה גם תוספתא פ"א ה"ד: "פר ושעיר שקרבו היום משל מי היו" וכו'. 19. **בארבעה בגדי לבן** – לפי ויקרא טז ד. וראה יומא פ"ג מ"ו. 20. **וטובל חמש טבילות וכו'** – לפי משנה יומא פ"ג מ"ג. 25. **טנף** וכו' – כאן במובן חטא ופשע. 26. **זוג שעירים ואיל** – ויקרא טז ה. 28-29. **חטאות פרו** וכו' **חקי וידוי** וכו' – ויקרא טז ו ויומא פ"ג מ"ח. 31. **טרח ובא לו** וכו' – יומא פ"ג מ"ט; **שני נאמני** – הסגן וראש בית אב (במשנה שם). 32. **טעם** – קשה לפרשו ואולי צ"ל טען. 37. **יכניס ידיו לקלפי** וכו' – יומא פ"ד מ"א; **גורלות יקרים** – יומא פ"ג מ"ט: "של אשכרוע היו ועשאן בן גמלא של זהב". 38. **יד מעלה** וכו' – יומא פ"ד מ"א. 40-41. **יעמיד נשחט** וכו' – יומא פ"ד מ"ב ומזה מביא ראיה בספר עבודת ישראל לר' ישראל קמחי (איזמיר תצ"ז, דף קיט ע"א) שר' יצחק אבן גיאת סבר שמה ששנוי במשנה "ולנשחט כנגד בית שחיטתו" פירושו העמדה ולא קשירה. וראה בתוספתא כפשוטה להגר"ש ליברמן, כיפורים, עמ' 757-758, המביא את דברי ר' ישראל קמחי ומזכיר את עבודתו של ריצ"ג. מדברי ר' ישראל קמחי נראה שכוונתו לקיקלר שלנו ולא לסדר העבודה הגדול של ריצ"ג. קמחי מזכיר שם גם את הקיקלר של ר' יצחק בן ר' זרחיה גירונדי והכוונה למה שכתוב בעבודה הקצרה שלו. בכ"י פריז, מס' 656, דף 56 ע"ב: "ישר והעמיד מגמת הנשחט לצפוניו" וכו'. על העבודה הקצרה לר' יצחק גירונדי ראה לעיל בהערה 12 למבוא. 43-44. לפי יומא פ"ד מ"ב. 49. **מקבל דמו ונותרו לממרס** – יומא פ"ד מ"ג; **בלי לשבח** – פירושו: כדי שלא יקרש (ראה במשנה שם) והלשון לפי תהלים סה ח: "משביח שאון ימים", ופירש ראב"ע: משקיט. 50. **מחתה נוטל** וכו' – יומא פ"ד מ"ג. 52-53. שם פ"ד מ"ד ופ"ה מ"א. 55-56. שם פ"ה מ"א. 61-63. **עשן מתמלא הבית שלא להסתכל בדמות** וכו' – משנה שם שם; בטורים אלה מהדהד הדו של הפולמוס הידוע בין הצדוקים ובין הפרושים על הקטרת הקטרת ביוה"כ. על הפולמוס ועל רקעו ראה בספרו האנגלי של רא"א פינקלשטין, הפרושים, מהד' ג', 1962, כרך א', עמ' 118-121 וכרך ב', עמ' 654-660 ובספרות המצויינת שם בהערות. 64. **פלל בצאתו** וכו' – יומא פ"ה מ"א; **קדושי אדם** – בני ישראל, לפי יחזקאל לו, לז. 65-66. יומא פ"ה מ"ג. 67. **צאתו** וכו' – שם מ"ד. 68. **צעד** וכו' – שם שם. 73-74. שם שם. 76. **רץ** וכו' – שם שם; כאן ובטורים 77, 88 ו־97 מודגשת הזריזות כמו בשאר סדרי העבודה וראה על ענין זה לאחרונה במאמרו האנגלי של ידידי ר' יוחנן מופס, בספר זכרון למ' ברברמן, *The Journal of Ancient Near Eastern Society of Columbia University*, vol. 11, 1979. <ראה עתה יוחנן מופס, אהבה ושמחה – חוק, לשון ודת במקרא ובספרות חז"ל, תרגם אביב

מלצר, ירושלים תשס״ב, עמ׳ 142 ואילך. > 77. רץ **למזבח הזהב** – שם מ״ה. 79. **שירי הדם וכו׳** – שם מ״ו. 80. **מזבח ההראל** – יחזקאל מג טו. 85. **תמו מחטאת שלשתם** – נעשו תמימים; **שלשתם** – הוא, שבטו והעם. 68. **תומך משתלח** וכו׳ – יומא פ״ו מ״ב; **תומך** – סומך. 88-89. שם מ״ג-מ״ד; **לאיש עתי** – ויקרא טז כא. 91. **אמורי פר ושעיר** וכו׳ – יומא פ״ו מ״ז. 92. **ציר לשרוף שניהם ימנה** – במשנה שם שם: ״והוציאן לבית השרפה״ ופירושו שמסר אותם להוציאם ולשרוף אותם. 97-98. **חש וחלץ** וכו׳ – יומא פ״ז מ״ג; **וגרעם** – והסירם. 100-101. יומא פ״ז מ״ד. 103-104. שם שם; ראה בבלי יומא י״ב ע״ב (ובמקבילות): ״דתניא והניחם שם מלמד שטעונין גניזה רבי דוסא אומר שלא ישתמש בהן יוה״כ אחר״. 109-110. יומא פ״ז מ״ד-מ״ה. 112. **את בגדי עצמו** וכו׳ – שם שם. **מדי פז ויהלום** – בגדי הזהב. 113. **אותו מלוים** וכו׳ – יומא שם. **בהלכו והלום** – לפי שמואל א יד טו. 116. **בימי חרפי** – איוב כט ד. 121. **רציתי כבר מעשיכם** – קהלת ט ז. 124. **זבחי צדק זבחו** – תהלים ד ו. 127. **קרבו לבא ימי ישעכם** – לפי ישעי׳ סב יא. 128. **קרב הרי ישראל** וכו׳ – לפי יחזקאל לט יז, כ״ח. 133. **צפירה** – תפארת, לפי ישעי׳ כח ה. 129. **והיוצא מפיכם תעשו** – מה שיוצא מפיכם עכשיו באמירת זכרון העבודה – תעשו כשייבנה בית המקדש.

חמשה זולתות לרב יצחק אבן גיאת

מבוא

החל מראשית פעולתו המדעית עסק בעל היובל [א"מ הברמן] בפיוטי ריצ"ג. מבכורי פרי עטו היא הרשימה של פיוטי ריצ"ג שפירסם בשנת 1929,[1] ומאז המשיך להעשיר את ספרותנו בהוצאתם לאור של פיוטי אבן גיאת.[2] מן הראוי אפוא להגיש לבעל היובל כמנחה כמה מיצירותיו הפיוטיות של ריצ"ג שלא ראו עדיין אור הדפוס.

צונץ בסגנונו התמציתי כבר קבע, שיש בין פיוטי ריצ"ג קבוצה מיוחדת של זולתות לשלש רגלים, לארבע פרשיות, לשבת חנוכה ולשבת הגדול, שנכתבו בצורה אחידה, ושמתכונת משותפת להם הן מבחינת הצורה והן מבחינת התוכן. מאז הופעת ספרו המונומנטלי של צונץ[3] לא נתגלו יותר משני פיוטי "זולת" לריצ"ג שכתובים במתכונת של הנ"ל, וגם אלה מקוטעים הם.[4] אולם לא כל הפיוטים שנזכרו ע"י צונץ נדפסו.

כידוע צונץ רשם הרבה פיוטים עפ"י כתב־יד. חלק מהם לא יצא לאור עד היום ויש מהם שנעלם מאתנו מקורם לגמרי. כך היה גם גורלם של פיוטי ה"זולת" הנ"ל; יש מהם שנדפסו ויש שנשארו טמונים בכתבי יד, ואחד מהם נעלם מקורו מעינינו לגמרי. להלן מתפרסמים בפעם הראשונה חמשה זולתות לריצ"ג, שלשה מהם שנרשמו בספרו של צונץ ושנים שנשרדו בין קטעי הגניזה ונמצאו לאחרונה. והנה רשימת כל הזולתות מסוג זה הידועים לנו:

1. פסח: "ישועות אל". צונץ, עמ' 197, 199 (דוידזון, י, 4006); נדפס להלן סי' א'.
2. שבועות: "יהִירים הודי"; צונץ, שם (ד, י, 1468); נדפס להלן סי' ב'.
3. סוכות: "יה חסד". צונץ שם (ד, י, 890); נדפס בספר יגל חזון, חמשים שירים חדשים מתקופת ספרד; י"ל... מאת אברהם יצחק כ"ץ. ירושלים תשכ"ה, עמ' 71-73.
4. חנוכה: "ישרים בשמו". צונץ, עמ' 196 (ד, י, 4260); נדפס להלן סי' ג'.

1 מזרח ומערב ג (תרפ"ט), עמ' 352-358.

2 ראה בספרו ברן יחד, ילקוט שירי תפלה, ירושלים תש"ח, עמ' מז-מט, ובספרו עתרת רננים, ירושלים תשכ"ז, שיר מס' 32, 83, 84, 85.

3 *Literaturgeschichte der synagogalen Poesie*, ברלין 1865. <וראה שם, עמ' 196-197.>

4 על אחד מהם הצביע עזרא פליישר במאמרו "חידושי האסכולה הפייטנית הספרדית בפיוטי היוצר", הספרות ד (תשל"ג), עמ' 341, הערה 49. <ראה עתה בספרו הגדול, היוצרות בהתהוותם והתפתחותם, ירושלים תשמ"ד, עמ' 555-567.> ויש להעיר שבסוף הזולת "ישועות אל" בכ"י קמברידג' (ראה בראש ההערות לפיוט א' להלן) כתוב "בקי זולת לפסח יום אפפונו וגו'", ואולי זו התחלתו של זולת נוסף לריצ"ג.

5. פרשת שקלים: "ידך תחיש". צונץ, שם (ד, י, 628); נדפס במחזור לפי מנהג קארפינטראץ. ראה הערת דוידזון שם.[5]
6. פרשת זכור: "יראיו בתום". צונץ שם (ד, י, 3768); נדפס במחזור הנ"ל.
7. פרשת פרה: "יסוד טעם". צונץ, שם (ד, י, 3082); נדפס במחזור הנ"ל.
8. פרשת החודש: "ימי חדות". צונץ, שם (ד, י, 2910); נדפס במחזור הנ"ל.[6]
9. שבת הגדול: "ימין ישע". צונץ, עמ' 196-197 (ד, י, 2965); לא נדפס, ונעלם מקורו.[6א]
10. לשבת חתן: "יענה בפה". לא נרשם ע"י צונץ ודוידזון; נדפס להלן סי' ד'.
11. קטע. נדפס להלן סי' ה'. ראה בהערות שם.

פיוטים אלה, כאמור, בנויים לפי מתכונת אחידה. כל אחד מחזיק סטרופות בנות ארבעה טורים. הטור הראשון והשני מכילים כל אחד שלש צלעיות, כשהצלעיות השלישיות חוזרות כרפרין מתחלף (אפיפורה) בסוף הטור הראשון והשני של כל סטרופה וסטרופה. הטור השלישי יש בו שתי צלעיות ומופיעה בו מלת קבע המאפיינת את נושא הפיוט. לעתים באה מלה זו כשהיא חלק משיבוץ של פסוק מקראי. הטור הרביעי הוא לרוב משולש, והוא הרפרין שחוזר בסוף כל סטרופה וסטרופה. טור זה מתחיל תמיד במלה "כן", ומביע בו הפייטן את תקוותו לגאולה העתידה לבוא. בקיצור, יש לפנינו צורה שהיא הרכב של טורים כפולים ומשולשים, ושאפשר לייחד בה יחידות של אלמנטים מרובעים מבחינת החריזה, ובזה הולך הפייטן בעקבות הצורה הקלאסית של הזולת שדרך כלל היה בנוי ממחרוזות מרובעות.[7] והנה לדוגמא שתי סטרופות רצופות מאחד הפיוטים:

ישועות אל וצדקתו/ תענה ואמונתו/ בקהל קדושים
ועל פי כל שירתו/ תתן ותהלתו/ שוררו אנשים
אנשים כבודו ספרו/ בתשע שירות שרו
כן עשירית במקדש/ ישורר עם המקודש/ לה' שיר חדש

5 כמבוא לפיוט זה בא בכ"י מונטיפיורי (רשימת הירשפלד מס' 203, דף 8) שיר קצר שקול במשקל מרובה, וזה לשונו: "לְמִי הוּא כֹל בְּטֶרֶם כָּל פְּעָלִים/ וְכֹל אַחַר כְּלוֹת הַכֹּל וְהִשְׁלִים// מְסִלַּת עוֹז וְרִנַּת מַהֲלָלִים/ נְאֻם יִצְחָק בְּפָרָשַׁת שְׁקָלִים".
צונץ, ליטג', עמ' 196, רושם את השיר כפיוט בפני עצמו לפרשת שקלים, ועל פי צונץ רשם אותו דוידזון (ל, 1097). את הבית האחרון מביא צונץ בספרו *Die synagogale Poesie des Mittelalters*, 1920[2], עמ' 122, הערה a, השווה לדברי המבוא השקולים האלה את השיר הקטן שהקדים רשב"ג ל"כתר מלכות". רי"צ גיאת הקדיש שיר קטן בראש הלכות פסחים בחיבורו "הלכות כלולות", וכן מובא שיר שלו אצל רמב"ע, ספר העיונים והדיונים, מהד' א"ש הלקין, עמ' 127.

6. דוידזון רושם את הסימן "יצחק הלוי גיאת" עפ"י הסימון שבמחזור קארפינטראץ. אולם אין שום ספק שהסימן הנכון הוא "יצחק גיאת", והאותיות ה' ל' ו' י' מצטרפות רק במקרה.

6א אחרי מסירת מאמר זה לדפוס הודיע לי ידידי ד"ר עזרא פליישר שהפיוט נמצא בכ"י של הבריטיש מוזיאום, מס' ADD 11639, ואי"ה אוציאו לאור במקום אחר.

7 ראה עזרא פליישר, שירת הקודש העברית בימי הביניים, ירושלים 1975, עמ' 227-229; הנ"ל, במאמרו המובא לעיל בהערה 4, עמ' 341.

צדקו אגיד מְדֵיי/ ימי חיי ואהודה/ בקהל קדושים
ומי כמוני מודה/ ומי כמוהו פודה/ שוררו אנשים
כליל שוררו גאוליכם/ השיר יהיה לכם
כן עשירית במקדש/ ישורר עם המקודש/ לה׳ שיר חדש

אם נעלים עין מהצלעית השלישית שבסוף כל טור ראשון ושני תשאר בידינו יחידה מרובעת צלעיות, הכוללת את האלמנט היסודי של הזולת הקלאסי.

עוד קווים אופייניים לזולתות אלה: בכולם חתום שם המחבר בראשי הסטרופות; חתימת השם היא יצחק גיאת או יצחק בר יהודה גיאת. גם מבחינת המשקל זהים הפיוטים: בכל צלעית, לרבות בצלעית המכילה שיבוץ מקראִי, יש חמש או שש הברות, והשואים הנעים והחטפים אינם במנין.

כל הזולתות האלה מספרים במעשיו הנפלאים של הקב״ה שהפליא לעמו בגאולות שונות בעבר, ושיגאל אותו גאולה שלימה לעתיד לבוא. בכמה מהפיוטים מונה הפייטן, עפ״י מדרשים שונים, סדרת מאורעות שאירעו לעם ישראל בעבר, ושהמשכם יתרחש בבוא הגאולה העתידה. כך בנוי ה״זולת״ לפסח על המדרש של י׳ שירות, לחנוכה על ז׳ חנוכות, לפרשת שקלים על ח׳ מקומות שנמנו ישראל, לפרשת פרה על י׳ פרות אדומות של הכהנים הגדולים מאהרן הכהן עד ימות המשיח.

נוסף לכך מעמיד הפייטן, דרך כלל, בכל סטרופה את גורלו של עם ישראל מול גורל שונאיו. הטיפול בנושאים שהזכרנו נעוץ באופיים הכללי של פיוטי ה״זולת״,[8] וחידושו של ריצ״ג הוא בעיקר בשטח הצורה. צורה זו שתוארה לעיל אינה מצויה, עד כמה שידוע לי, בשום פיוט מיצירותיהם של הפייטנים שקדמו לו.[9] כנראה חידש כאן אבן גיאת חידוש גדול, בהכניסו לתוך פיוטי ה״זולת״ אלמנטים שמגוונים את הצורה הקלאסית ומוסיפים לפיוט אפקט צלילי עשיר ומפתיע. הפייטן הושפע כאן מהצורות הרבגוניות של שירי האזור החילוניים, והעביר מהן לשירי הקדש שלו. קל להבין שבגלל הצורה המסובכת לא מצא ריצ״ג הרבה מחקים בין המשוררים שבאו אחריו. ידוע לנו רק ״זולת״ אחד שנכתב ממש כצורת הזולתות של ריצ״ג, והוא ״זולת״ לגדול המשוררים, רבי יהודה הלוי.[10]

8 ראה צונץ *Die synagogale Poesie des Mittelalters*, עמ׳ 62; פליישר, בספרו הנ״ל. אין ספק שהעמדת הניגוד בין ישראל ובין אומות העולם בזולתות (הנאמרים לפני התפלה ״עזרת אבותינו״) מושפעת מהלשון בגוף התפלה: ״...כל בכוריהם הרגת/ ובכורך גאלת/ וים סוף בקעת וזדים טבעת/ וידידים העברת... משפיל גאים/ ומגביה שפלים״ וכו׳.

9 ראה פליישר, במאמרו הנ״ל.

10 מובא ע״י פליישר, שם, והוא הזולת ״יום נחית גאולים״ (דוידזון, י, 1856).

א. ״ישועות אל״ לז׳ פסח

דוידזון (אוצר, י, 4006) רשם את הפיוט עפ״י צונץ, ליטג׳, עמ׳ 199. הטקסט נמצא בכ״י פריז מס׳ 658 דף 103 ב-104 א, ובקטע גניזה שחלקו הגיע לאוקספורד (D. 60, רשימת נויבאור־קולי 2846 2c, f. 10b) והמשכו הישיר לקמבריג׳ (ט״ש ס״ח 109 מס׳ 77, לפנים מס׳ 35). הקטע שבקמבריג׳ מתחיל בשורה 9 של הפיוט, במלים ״[ב]קהל קדושים.״ למעשה שייך קטע זה לקבוצת דפים מפוזרים, לרוב פגומים עד מאד, שהתפזרו מקונטרס אחד שהכיל הרבה מפיוטי ריצ״ג. דפים אלה נתגלגלו לסדרה החדשה באוסף טיילור־שכטר, ומהם העתקתי גם את הפיוטים ד׳ וה׳ להלן.

הפיוט שלפנינו נועד לשביעי של פסח (בכ״י פריז רשום עליו ״זולת ליום השירה״, ובקטע אוקספורד: ״זולת לפסח״). הסימן: ״יצחק גיאת״. המשקל: בכל צלעית שש הברות, לרבות בצלעית המכילה שיבוץ מהמקרא, והשואים הנעים והחטפים אינם במנין. הפיוט מיוסד על המדרש במכילתא דרבי ישמעאל, שירתא א, מהד׳ הארוויטץ־רבין (עמ׳ 116-118): ״את השירה הזאת, וכי שירה אחת היא והלא עשר שירות הן״ וכו׳ (ועיין שם בהערות ובחלופי גרסאות, ובמכילתא דרשב״י בשלח ט״ו א׳). בעניינו של המדרש הזה דנו אברהם עפשטיין בספרו מקדמוניות היהודים, מהד׳ א״מ הברמן, עמ׳ רנא־רנד, ורפאל Loewe בתוך: *Biblical Motifs; Origins and Transformations*, ed. by A. Altmann, 1966, עמ׳ 169-170. לאחרונה דן בנושא יהודה גולדין, במאמרו המקיף ״This Song״ בתוך: *S. W. Baron Jubilee Volume*, 1974, חלק אנגלי, כרך 1, עמ׳ 539-554. על הנושא הזה מיוסד גם פיוטו של ר׳ שמעון ב״ר יצחק ״אי פתרוס״, שהוא זולת לשביעי של פסח (פיוטי שמעון בר יצחק, מהד׳ א״מ הברמן, עמ׳ לח-מ), וראה גם את הפיוט הקטוע שנדפס ע״י ישראל דוידזון בגנזי שכטר, ג, עמ׳ 128.

יְשׁוּעוֹת אֵל וְצִדְקָתוֹ/ תַּעֲנֶה וֶאֱמוּנָתוֹ/ בִּקְהַל קְדוֹשִׁים
וְעַל פִּי כָל שִׁירָתוֹ/ תִּתֵּן וּתְהִלָּתוֹ/ שׁוֹרְרוּ אֲנָשִׁים
אֲנָשִׁים כְּבוֹדוֹ סִפְּרוּ/ בְּתֵשַׁע שִׁירוֹת שָׁרוּ
כֵּן עֲשִׂירִית בַּמִּקְדָּשׁ/ יְשׁוֹרֵר עַם הַמְּקֻדָּשׁ/ לַה׳ שִׁיר חָדָשׁ
צִדְקוֹ אַגִּיד מִדַּי/ יְמֵי חַיַּי וַאֲהוֹדֶה/ בִּקְהַל קְדוֹשִׁים
וּמִי כָמוֹנִי מוֹדֶה/ וּמִי כָמוֹהוּ פּוֹדֶה/ שׁוֹרְרוּ אֲנָשִׁים
כְּלֵיל שׁוֹרְרוּ גְאוּלֵיכֶם/ הַשִּׁיר יִהְיֶה לָכֶם
כֵּן עֲשִׂירִית בַּמִּקְדָּשׁ/ יְשׁוֹרֵר עַם הַמְּקוּדָּשׁ/ לַה׳ שִׁיר חָדָשׁ
חֲנֵסִים עָמְדוּ בְמִרְיָם/ וַיַּחֲזִיקוּ בְקָשְׁיָם/ בִּקְהַל קְדוֹשִׁים
וַיִּשְׁתַּקְּעוּ בַּיָּם/ עַל לֹא־נוֹדְעוּ אַיָּם/ שׁוֹרְרוּ אֲנָשִׁים
וּבַאֲבוֹד לֵבָב מַקְשֶׁה/ אָז יָשִׁיר מֹשֶׁה
כֵּן עֲשִׂירִית בַּמִּקְדָּשׁ/ יְשׁוֹרֵר עַם הַמְּקוּדָּשׁ/ לַה׳ שִׁיר חָדָשׁ
קְדוֹשִׁים יַחַד מִהֲרוּ/ שְׁמֹנֶה עֶשְׂרֵה סִדְּרוּ/ בִּקְהַל קְדוֹשִׁים
וְעֵת רַחֲמֵי אֵל גָּבְרוּ/ שִׁירַת הַבְּאֵר הִדְּרוּ/ שׁוֹרְרוּ אֲנָשִׁים

וְצִיר חָק בִּדְבַר מַחֲזוֹת/ אֶת הַשִּׁירָה הַזֹּאת
כֵּן עֲשִׂירִית בַּמִּקְדָּשׁ/ יְשׁוֹרֵר עַם הַמְּקֻדָּשׁ/ לה׳ שִׁיר חָדָשׁ
גְּבוּרַת הַעֲמֵד פְּלָכִים/ בְּשֶׁמֶשׁ וְסַהַר הוֹלְכִים/ בִּקְהַל קְדוֹשִׁים
וְאוֹתוֹת הַעֲבֵר נְסִיכִים/ שְׁלֹשִׁים וְאֶחָד מְלָכִים/ שׁוֹרְרוּ אֲנָשִׁים
וּבִן נוּן שִׁיר בַּהֲמוֹנַי/ אָז יְדַבֵּר לה׳
כֵּן עֲשִׂירִית בַּמִּקְדָּשׁ/ יְשׁוֹרֵר עַם הַמְּקֻדָּשׁ/ לה׳ שִׁיר חָדָשׁ
יַד יָבִין כִּי נִשְׁבְּרָה/ וַתָּשַׁר דְּבוֹרָה/ בִּקְהַל קְדוֹשִׁים
וְאִישׁ עִם אֱלֹהִים שָׂרָה/ וּמִפִּיו לִמְּדוֹ תוֹרָה/ שׁוֹרְרוּ אֲנָשִׁים
בְּהִנָּצְלוֹ מֵעֲבֵירָה/ שָׁר דִּבְרֵי הַשִּׁירָה
כֵּן עֲשִׂירִית בַּמִּקְדָּשׁ/ יְשׁוֹרֵר עַם הַמְּקֻדָּשׁ/ לה׳ שִׁיר חָדָשׁ
אַף גִּלָּה סוֹד מְכֻסֶּה/ בְּבִנְיַן בַּיִת מְנֻשָּׂא/ בִּקְהַל קְדוֹשִׁים
וְהַמַּתְחִיל בְּמַעֲשֶׂה/ וְהַמְּעַשֶּׂה הוּא הָעוֹשֶׂה/שׁוֹרְרוּ אֲנָשִׁים
לְשׁוֹרֵר לָבֹא הֵשִׁית/ שִׁיר חֲנֻכַּת הַבַּיִת
כֵּן עֲשִׂירִית בַּמִּקְדָּשׁ/ יְשׁוֹרֵר עַם הַמְּקֻדָּשׁ/ לה׳ שִׁיר חָדָשׁ
תִּקֵּן וְהוֹצִיא לְאוֹרִים/ בְּכָל מַחֲבוֹאֵי סְתָרִים/ בִּקְהַל קְדוֹשִׁים
וְלִמֵּד שְׁלֹשָׁה סְפָרִים/ יְקָרִים וְשִׁיר הַשִּׁירִים/ שׁוֹרְרוּ אֲנָשִׁים
וְנוֹרָאוֹת אֵל יֹאמְרוּ/ יוֹם יוֹם אַף יָשִׁירוּ
כֵּן עֲשִׂירִית בַּמִּקְדָּשׁ/ יְשׁוֹרֵר עַם הַמְּקֻדָּשׁ/ לה׳ שִׁיר חָדָשׁ

ב. "יהירים הודי" — לשבועות

דוידזון (אוצר, י, 1468) רשם את הפיוט עפ״י צונץ, ליטג׳, עמ׳ 199. הטקסט נמצא בכ״י פריז מס׳ 658 דף 149 בין פיוטים ליום ב׳ דשבועות. רשום עליו: "זולת לר׳ יצחק אבן גיאת ז״ל". הסימן: "יצחק בר יהודה גיאת חזק". המשקל: בכל צלעית שש הברות, לרבות בצלעית המכילה שיבוץ מהמקרא, והשואים הנעים והחטפים אינם במנין.

הפייטן מזכיר בכל סטרופה את מעמד הר סיני, ומתפלל שכשם שהופיע הקב״ה אז בקולות וברקים וקול שופר חזק כך יבוא ויגאל את עמו באחרית הימים, וישיב לאויבי ישראל את גמולם הרע.

יְהִירִים הוֹדִי נָחֲלוּ/ וְעַל שִׁבְרִי לֹא נֶחְלוּ/ בְּרֹאשׁ גּוֹלִים יִגְלוּ
צוֹעֲדִים בַּגּוֹלָה נָפְלוּ/ וְכֶעָלֶה נָבְלוּ/ בִּמְשׁוֹךְ יוֹבֵל יַעֲלוּ
כְּיוֹם שָׁוְמְעֲכֶם מִבְּזָק/ קוֹל שׁוֹפָר חָזָק
כֵּן תִּשְׁמַעְנָה אָזְנֵינוּ קוֹל שׁוֹפָר וּתְרוּעָה/ מְבַשֵּׂר יוֹם וִישׁוּעָה
חֲצֵרִים בֶּטַח שָׁכְנוּ/ עוֹשֵׂי רִשְׁעָה נִבְנוּ/ בְּרֹאשׁ גּוֹלִים יִגְלוּ
קְדוֹשִׁים בְּשִׁמְךָ כֻּנּוּ/ וְעַל יִחוּדְךָ עֻנּוּ/ בִּמְשׁוֹךְ יוֹבֵל יַעֲלוּ
כְּיוֹם לְאַחַת הִקְשַׁבְתִּי/ שְׁתַּיִם־זוּ שָׁמַעְתִּי

כֵּן תִּשְׁמַעְנָה אָזְנֵינוּ קוֹל שׁוֹפָר וּתְרוּעָה/ מְבַשֵּׂר יוֹם וִישׁוּעָה
בּוֹעֲרִים מְקוֹמְךָ סִכְּלוּ/ וּמְקוֹמָם לֹא שִׂכְּלוּ/ בְּרֹאשׁ גּוֹלִים יִגְלוּ
רְצוּיִים בְּךָ יִתְהַלָּלוּ/ וְשֵׁם קָדְשְׁךָ לֹא חִלְּלוּ/ בִּמְשׁוֹךְ יוֹבֵל יַעֲלוּ
כְּיוֹם לִקְרָאתְךָ נָסְעוּ/ חֲמִשָּׁה קוֹלוֹת שָׁמְעוּ
כֵּן תִּשְׁמַעְנָה אָזְנֵינוּ קוֹל שׁוֹפָר וּתְרוּעָה/ מְבַשֵּׂר יוֹם וִישׁוּעָה
יְסוֹדֵי בְיָדָם גִּלּוּ/ וְאֶבֶן פִּנָּה גָּלֲלוּ/ בְּרֹאשׁ גּוֹלִים יִגְלוּ
הַדְרֵי עוֹלָם נָזֹלוּ/ וִיקָרִים זָלֲלוּ/ בִּמְשׁוֹךְ יוֹבֵל יַעֲלוּ
כְּיוֹם תּוֹרָה הוֹדַעְתָּ/ מִשָּׁמַיִם הִשְׁמַעְתָּ
כֵּן תִּשְׁמַעְנָה אָזְנֵינוּ קוֹל שׁוֹפָר וּתְרוּעָה/ מְבַשֵּׂר יוֹם וִישׁוּעָה
וְזֵדִים אוֹתְךָ מָאֲסוּ/ וּבְהַבְלֵיהֶם כִּעֲסוּ/ בְּרֹאשׁ גּוֹלִים יִגְלוּ
דְּבֵקִים בְּצִלְּךָ יֶחֱסוּ/ וְאַתְּ מְנוּסָם כִּי נָסוּ/ בִּמְשׁוֹךְ יוֹבֵל יַעֲלוּ
כְּיוֹם עֵינֵיהֶם פָּגְעָה/ לְמַרְאֵה אוֹזֶן שָׁמְעָה
כֵּן תִּשְׁמַעְנָה אָזְנֵינוּ קוֹל שׁוֹפָר וּתְרוּעָה/ מְבַשֵּׂר יוֹם וִישׁוּעָה
הַגּוֹי יוֹם יוֹם נוֹעֲצוּ/ וְגוֹיֶיךָ לְעֵינְךָ יִקָּרְצוּ/ בְּרֹאשׁ גּוֹלִים יִגְלוּ
גּוֹלִים לְבֵיתְךָ רוֹצְצוּ/ בְּאִמְרֵי יוֹשֶׁר נִמְרְצוּ/ בִּמְשׁוֹךְ יוֹבֵל יַעֲלוּ
כְּיוֹם נִגְלֵיתָ מִדַּבֵּר/ וָאֶשְׁמַע אַתְּ מְדַבֵּר
כֵּן תִּשְׁמַעְנָה אָזְנֵינוּ קוֹל שׁוֹפָר וּתְרוּעָה/ מְבַשֵּׂר יוֹם וִישׁוּעָה
יָדָם לְבָרִים פָּשְׁטוּ/ וּבְמִשְׁפְּטֵיהֶם שָׁפְטוּ/ בְּרֹאשׁ גּוֹלִים יִגְלוּ
אֲמֵלִים בּוֹשֶׁת יַעְטוּ/ וְלָמוֹ רְשָׁעִים יִנָּטוּ/ בִּמְשׁוֹךְ יוֹבֵל יַעֲלוּ
כְּיוֹם שְׂפָתַי תַּבַּעְנָה/ וְאָזְנֶיךָ תִּשְׁמַעְנָה
כֵּן תִּשְׁמַעְנָה אָזְנֵינוּ קוֹל שׁוֹפָר וּתְרוּעָה/ מְבַשֵּׂר יוֹם וִישׁוּעָה
תּוֹעֵי לֵבָב אָזְרוּ/ חַיִל וְרָעוֹת גָּזְרוּ/ בְּרֹאשׁ גּוֹלִים יִגְלוּ
זְרוּיֵי קְצָווֹת נִפְזְרוּ/ בְּהִכָּשְׁלוֹ יֵעָזְרוּ/ בִּמְשׁוֹךְ יוֹבֵל יַעֲלוּ
נֶחָמוֹת נוֹדָעוּ/ בְּקוֹל שׁוֹפָר נִשְׁמָעוּ
כֵּן תִּשְׁמַעְנָה אָזְנֵינוּ קוֹל שׁוֹפָר וּתְרוּעָה/ מְבַשֵּׂר יוֹם וִישׁוּעָה

ג. "ישרים בשמו" — לחנוכה

דוידזון (אוצר, י, 4260) רשם את הפיוט עפ"י צונץ, ליטג' עמ' 196. הטקסט נמצא בכ"י פריז מס' 658 דף 240 א -241 ב, ובכ"י הוואטיקן (רוסיאנה מס' 362) דף 6 א. בכ"י פריז רשום עליו: "זולת לחנוכה ששכחתי למעלה": בכ"י וואטיקן: "זולת". הסימן: יצחק גיאת. המשקל: בכל צלעית שש הברות, לרבות בצלעית המכילה שיבוץ מהמקרא, והשוואים הנעים והחטפים אינם במנין.

הפייטן מונה שש חנוכות, ומצפה לחנוכה השביעית של אחרית הימים. ענין זה מיוסד על מה שנאמר בפסיקתא רבתי, מהד' איש שלום, דף ה' ע"א ונשנה שם דף ז' ע"ב. והנה שתי הנוסחאות זו לעומת זו:

דף ה ע"א:
וכמה חנוכות הם, שבע חנוכות
הם ואילו הן:
חנוכת שמים וארץ וכו'
וחנוכת החומה וכו'
וחנוכת של [עולי] גולה וכו'
וחנוכת הכהנים וכו'
וחנוכת העולם הבא וכו'
וחנוכת הנשיאים וכו'
וחנוכת המקדש וכו'

דף ז ע"ב:
שבע חנוכות הם
חנוכת ברייתו של עולם וכו'
חנוכת משה וכו'
וחנוכת הבית וכו'
וחנוכת בית שני וכו'
[וחנוכת החומה] וכו'
וזו של עכשיו של בית חשמונאי
וחנוכת העולם הבא וכו'

ריצ"ג אינו מונה את חנוכת החומה, ובמקומה מחלק את חנוכת הבית הראשון לשניים וסובר שגם דוד עשה חנוכה (ראה בהערות לשורות 13-15 להלן), והחנוכה השניה נעשתה כשנשלם בנין המקדש ע"י שלמה בנו. בדומה לזה נמצא גם בפיוט המיוחד לר' משה אבן עזרא "אזכרה שש חנוכות" (דוידזון, א, 2303, עפ"י מחזור חזונים דף י ע"ב): "גם מלך הודו כזית/ שירר שלישית בשומו גזית במקום שית/ מזמור שיר חנוכת הבית// מקדש צוה לבנו בן תמים וכו' דברו נצרו חכמים/ ויעש רביעית בבנות בית עולמים". פייטן זה, באמרו "בשומו גזית במקום שית" מתכוון אולי למה שנאמר על דוד המלך שחפר חפירות כדי להניח יסוד לבית המקדש (מכות יא ע"א, ירוש' סנהדרין פ"י ה"ב, ובמקבילות). המדרש של ז' חנוכות שימש נושא לפיוטים שונים, כפי שהעלה מנחם זולאי בידיעות המכון לחקר השירה העברית א, עמ' 164, הערה 14.

במיוחד קרוב פיוטנו לפיוט לשמונה עשרה לחנוכה של יעקב בר דונש (נדפס בספרו של חיים שירמן, שירים חדשים מן הגניזה, עמ' 43-45). בפיוט זה מכילה כל סטרופה טור המתחיל במלת "חנוכה" (החל בשורה 13) ובו תיאור של ישועות ה' שהביא לעמו בחנוכה ההיסטורית. אחרי טור זה בא בכל סטרופה טור המתחיל במלת "כן", ובו הבעת תקוה לעתיד לבוא. תבנית כזו מצויה גם בפיוטנו. דמיון מיוחד מצוי בטור 17 שם, שפתיחתו דומה לרפרין של הפיוט שלפנינו.

יְשָׁרִים בִּשְׁמוֹ כִּנָּה/ מִיּוֹם בָּחַר פִּנָּה/ לָתוּר לָהֶם מְנוּחָה
וְחָק בְּהִתְחַדֵּשׁ עוֹנָה/ בְּמִבְנֶה חָדָשׁ נִבְנָה/ לַעֲשׂוֹת חֲנֻכָּה וְשִׂמְחָה
  שִׂמְחַת עוֹלָם שָׂשׂוּ/ בְּשֵׁשׁ חֲנֻכּוֹת נַעֲשׂוּ
  כֵּן בִּמְהֵרָה לְעֵינַי/ שְׁבִיעִית מַקְהֵל אֱמוּנַי/ יַחְנְכוּ אֶת בֵּית ה'
צְפוּן חָכְמָה רִאשׁוֹנִית/ הוֹצִא וְדֵעָה פְּנִינִית/ לָתוּר לָהֶם מְנוּחָה
וְקָבַע בְּמַלְאֲכוּת תַּבְנִית/ כָּל מַלְאֲכוּת הַתַּבְנִית/ לַעֲשׂוֹת חֲנֻכָּה וְשִׂמְחָה
  וְשַׁבָּת נָתַן מָנָה/ חֲנֻכַּת עוֹלָם בָּנָה
  כֵּן בִּמְהֵרָה לְעֵינַי/ שְׁבִיעִית מַקְהֵל אֱמוּנַי/ יַחְנְכוּ אֶת בֵּית ה'
חֲבוּשֵׁי נוֹף בְּמַסְּעֵיהֶם/ הוּא הוֹלֵךְ לִפְנֵיהֶם/ לָתוּר לָהֶם מְנוּחָה
בְּשׁוּם שִׁכְנוֹ בֵּינֵיהֶם/ נְשִׂיאִים שָׂמוּ פְּנֵיהֶם/ לַעֲשׂוֹת חֲנֻכָּה וְשִׂמְחָה

קֵרְבוּ לְהִשְׁתַּבֵּחַ/ חֲנֻכַּת הַמִּזְבֵּחַ
כֵּן בִּמְהֵרָה לְעֵינַי/ שְׁבִיעִית מַקְהֵל אֱמוּנַי/ יַחְנְכוּ אֶת בֵּית ה׳
קְדוֹשׁ עֶלְיוֹן כַּהֲסִיבוֹ/ אֲרוֹן לוּחוֹת בִּמְסִבּוֹ/ לָתוּר לָהֶם מְנוּחָה
בְּרוּחַ אֱלֹהִים בְּקִרְבּוֹ/ הֵכִין לְשׁוֹרֵר לִבּוֹ/ לַעֲשׂוֹת חֲנֻכָּה וְשִׂמְחָה
שַׁר כַּזַּיִת/ שִׁיר חֲנֻכַּת הַבַּיִת
כֵּן בִּמְהֵרָה לְעֵינַי/ שְׁבִיעִית מַקְהֵל אֱמוּנַי/ יַחְנְכוּ אֶת בֵּית ה׳
גּוֹלֶה סְתוּמֵי עֲלוּמִים/ יֹשֶׁר עֲקוּבֵי חֲתוּמִים/ לָתוּר לָהֶם מְנוּחָה
בִּבְנוֹתוֹ כְּמוֹ רָמִים/ זְבוּל בֵּית עוֹלָמִים/ לַעֲשׂוֹת חֲנֻכָּה וְשִׂמְחָה
מִהֲרוּ וַעֲשׂוּ נְעִימִים/ חֲנֻכָּה שִׁבְעַת יָמִים
כֵּן בִּמְהֵרָה לְעֵינַי/ שְׁבִיעִית מַקְהֵל אֱמוּנַי/ יַחְנְכוּ אֶת בֵּית ה׳
יְמֵי שִׁבְעִים בִּמְלֹאותוֹ/ עַם קָרְבָה פְּקֻדָּתוֹ/ לָתוּר לָהֶם מְנוּחָה
כִּכְלוֹת בִּנְיַן בֵּיתוֹ/ חָשׁ עֶזְרָא וְסִיעָתוֹ/ לַעֲשׂוֹת חֲנֻכָּה וְשִׂמְחָה
בְּנֵי גוֹלָה בִרְנָנָה/ חֲנֻכַּת בֵּית אֱלָהָנָא דְנָה
כֵּן בִּמְהֵרָה לְעֵינַי/ שְׁבִיעִית מַקְהֵל אֱמוּנַי/ יַחְנְכוּ אֶת בֵּית ה׳
אֱמוּנִים נִתַּק עֻלָּם/ בְּעַמּוּד עָנָן גּוֹאֲלָם/ לָתוּר לָהֶם מְנוּחָה
יְמֵי שִׂמְחָתָם וְגִילָם/ נָתְנוּ חֻקַּת עוֹלָם/ לַעֲשׂוֹת חֲנֻכָּה וְשִׂמְחָה
וּמֵאָז נָחֲלוּ אֱמוּנִים/ חֲנֻכָּה שִׁבְעַת יָמִים
כֵּן בִּמְהֵרָה לְעֵינַי/ שְׁבִיעִית מַקְהֵל אֱמוּנַי/ יַחְנְכוּ אֶת בֵּית ה׳
תָּחִישׁ כְּפַעַם בְּפַעַם/ אֱסוֹף נִדָּחָם מִכָּל עַם/ לָתוּר לָהֶם מְנוּחָה
וְכִבְנוֹת בֵּית מַרְגּוֹעָם/ הֵמָּה יְחִישׁוּן וְרוֹעָם/ לַעֲשׂוֹת חֲנֻכָּה וְשִׂמְחָה
חֲנֻכַּת דִּבְרֵי חוֹזִי/ יְחֶזְקֵאל בֶּן בּוּזִי
כֵּן בִּמְהֵרָה לְעֵינַי/ שְׁבִיעִית מַקְהֵל אֱמוּנַי/ יַחְנְכוּ אֶת בֵּית ה׳

ד. "יענה בפה" – לחתן

פיוט זה לא נזכר באוצרו של דוידזון. הטקסט, שהוא כנראה בלתי שלם, נמצא בכ"י קמברידג, ט"ש ס"ח 141 מס׳ 9. קטע זה שייך גם כן לקבוצת הדפים מהקונטרס המתואר לעיל במבוא לפיוט א׳. מעל לפיוט רשום: זולת לחתן. הוא נזכר עפ"י כה"י הנ"ל ע"י עזרא פליישר, ב"הספרות", רבעון למדע הספרות, ד (תשל"ג), עמ׳ 341, הערה 49. הסימן: יצחק... המשקל: ברוב הצלעיות שש הברות, והשוואים הנעים והחטפים אינם במנין. יש דמיון מה בין זולת זה ובין הזולת לחתן לריצ"ג שהדפיס חיים שירמן בספרו "שירים חדשים מן הגניזה" עמ׳ 192 (ראה במיוחד שורות 11-12 שם: "חבל זבדך אלקים וכו׳ חלקך בארץ חיים" וכו׳; ושם שורות 17-18: וכל יענו: "אשריך יהי מקורך ברוך ושמח מאשת נעוריך". והשוה בפיוט שלפנינו שורות 1-2, 14-15).

[יַ]עֲנֶה בְּפֶה כָל יִפְנֶה/ מִשְׁכַּן חָתָן הִנֵּה/ מַה־טּוֹב וּמַה נָּעִים
מִיַּעֲלַת־חֵן מִבְנֶה/ עוֹלָם יִבָּנֶה/ בְּיַלְדֵי שַׁעֲשׁוּעִים
מִדֵּי לַיְלָה וְיוֹמָם/ זַרְעָם נָכוֹן עִמָּם
כֵּן יַעֲמֹד זַרְעֲכֶם וְשִׁמְכֶם כִּשְׁמֵי מְעוֹנַי/ לְפָנַי אָמַר ה׳
צֶאֱצָאֵי מֵעֵיהֶם/ יֹאמְרוּ כָל־רוֹאֵיהֶם/ מַה־טּוֹב וּמַה־נָּעִים
דְּרוּשִׁים לְכָל חֶפְצֵיהֶם/ הֵמָּה וּבְנֵי בְנֵיהֶם/ בְּיַלְדֵי שַׁעֲשׁוּעִים
וְנוֹדַע בְּכָל־עַם וָעָם/ בַּגּוֹיִים זַרְעָם
כֵּן יַעֲמֹד זַרְעֲכֶם וְשִׁמְכֶם כִּשְׁמֵי מְעוֹנַי/ לְפָנַי אָמַר ה׳
חָתָן מֵחֻפָּתוֹ/ יוֹצֵא כַּשֶּׁמֶשׁ בְּצֵאתוֹ/ מַה־טּוֹב וּמַה־נָּעִים
וּמַה־יָּפְיוֹ בְמַלֹּאתוֹ/ בְּיַלְדוּתוֹ אַשְׁפָּתוֹ/ בְּיַלְדֵי שַׁעֲשׁוּעִים
יְדוּעִים בְּקֶרֶב אֱמוּנַי/ זֶרַע בֵּרַךְ ה׳
כֵּן יַעֲמֹד זַרְעֲכֶם וְשִׁמְכֶם כִּשְׁמֵי מְעוֹנַי/ לְפָנַי אָמַר ה׳
קִרְאוּ כָל מְהַלְלָיו/ [זְ]מַן הִתְחַבְּרוּת אֵלָיו/ מַה־טּוֹב וּמַה־נָּעִים
וּכְטוֹב נָפְלוּ חֲבָלָיו/ הוּא וְהַחוֹנִים עָלָיו/ בְּיַלְדֵי שַׁעֲשׁוּעִים
וְזַרְעוֹ/ בְּאַרְצוֹת חַיִּים/ יִהְיֶה מְלֹא־הַגּוֹיִם
כֵּן יַעֲמֹד זַרְעֲכֶם וְשִׁמְכֶם כִּשְׁמֵי מְעוֹנַי/ לְפָנַי אָמַר ה׳

ה. קטע

הפיוט המקוטע הזה נמצא בכ״י קמברידג׳ הנזכר לעיל במבוא לפיוט ד׳. קשה לעמוד על תוכנו ועל יעודו של הפיוט, אולם כהשערה אפשר להניח שהוא זולת לחתן או לברית מילה; יתכן שהשורות 2-4 מתפרשות לענין יציר במשמעות עובר במעי אמו, ועל זה רומז הפסוק ״מושיב יחידים״ וכו׳ (תהלים סח ז) שנדרש בויקרא רבה ח׳ א׳, מהד׳ מרגליות, עמ׳ קס״ה-קס״ו, ובמקבילות, לענין זיווג איש ואשה. כמו כן ניתן לפרש את הפסוק ״קול ה׳ יחולל״ וכו׳ (תהלים כט ט) לענין זה. מאידך אפשר שלפנינו פיוט שנועד לחג השבועות, ורומז הפייטן בכמה מקומות לקולות וברקים שבמעמד הר סיני במלת הקבע ״קול״ הבאה בסוף כל סטרופה, עד שאין בידינו טקסט יותר שלם אין להכריע בדבר.

הסימן: ...ק גא... (ואולי צ״ל: גאת, אם האל״ף והתי״ו בשורה 10 בראש הצלעיות שייכות לסימן). אין שום ספק שהסימן השלם היה ״יצחק גיאת״, ויכול להיות שהסטרופה שהתחילה באות יו״ד של השם גיאת הושמטה מגוף הפיוט ע״י הסופר, כדוגמת סטרופה שלימה לעיל בפיוט ד׳ (ראה שם, הערה לשורה 9). המשקל: ברוב הצלעיות שש הברות, והשוואים הנעים והחטפים אינם במנין.

כֵּן נִשְׁמַע בְּכָל מְסִלָּה וג׳
קְשָׁרֵי יְצִיר מִתְחוֹלֵל/ קוֹשֵׁר מֵהִתְחוֹלֵל/ מוֹשִׁיב יְחִידִים
וזמן בם מ...לל/ מוּטָלִים יוֹמָם וָלֵיל/ וְהָיוּ לַאֲחָדִים

וּבִמְלֹאת יְמֵי... עולל/ קוֹל ה׳ יְחוֹלֵל
כֵּן נִשְׁמַע בְּכָל מְסִלָּה וג׳
גּוֹלָה נַפְשׁוֹ כָלְתָה/ בְּבֵית צִיר אֲסִירָיו בֵּיתָהּ/ מוֹשִׁיב יְחִידִים
לִימִין פְּזוּרִים הַפְאֵתָה/ תְּכַנֵּס לְהַר זֶה קָנְתָ[ה]/ וְהָיוּ לַאֲחָדִים
לָגוּר בְּךָ רַב וְצָעִר/ קוֹל ה׳ לָעִיר
[כֵּן נִשְׁמַע בְּכָל מְסִלָּה וג׳]
אֶל אֶרֶץ מְגוּרֵיהֶם/ תּוֹכָהּ אֲבוֹתֵיהֶם/ מוֹשִׁיב יְחִידִים
כַּיּוֹנִים אֶל אֲרֻבּוֹתֵיהֶם/ נָשָׂא אֶשָּׂא לָהֶם/ וְהָיוּ לַאֲחָדִים
וְשָׁלֵם מִכָּל מַעֲבָר/ קוֹל קוֹרֵא בַּמִּדְבָּר
[כֵּן נִשְׁמַע בְּכָל מְסִלָּה וג׳]

ברצוני להודות לידידי הפרופסור ר׳ חיים זלמן דימיטרובסקי על שהואיל בטובו להעיר לי כמה הערות חשובות לגוף הפיוטים.

הערות לשיר א׳

1 תהלים פט ו; **תענה** – תשיר, ראה הערה לפיוט ד׳ טור 1.

2 איוב לו כד. **כל** – מנוקד בקמץ בכת״י, וצ״ל חולם חסר.

3 תהלים צו ג.

4 ישעיה מב י ועוד. [מוטיב עשר שירות מצוי גם בפיוטו של נחום ברדאני ״אמנם עשר שירות״, כת״י אוקספורד e 50 דף 65. העורך, צבי מלאכי.]

5 שם נז יב. לצורה ״אהודה״ השוה תהלים כח ז ועוד.

6 עפ״י איוב לו כב.

7 ישעיה ל כט. השירה הראשונה היתה ביציאת מצרים.

9 **חנסים** – כנוי למצרים עפ״י ישעיה ל ד.

10 נחום ג יז.

11 **לבב מקשה** – פרעה; **אז ישיר משה** – שמות טו א. השירה השניה היתה בקריעת ים סוף.

13-15 סטרופה סתומה ואולי בטור הראשון שלה יש רמז לי״ח ברכות העמידה (מגלה יז ע״ב: ״שמעון הפקולי הסדיר שמונה עשרה ברכות וכו׳ אמר ר׳ יוחנן וכו׳ מאה ועשרים זקנים ובהם כמה נביאים תיקנו שמונה עשרה ברכות על הסדר״) או אולי רומז כאן הפייטן למאמר חז״ל, ״שמונה עשר יום בשנה ולילה אחד קורין בהן את ההלל״ וכו׳ (תוספתא סוכה פ״ג ה״ב, מהד׳ הגר״ש ליברמן עמ׳ 266 ומקבילות), אולם לא מצאתי שום קשר בין עניינים אלה ובין ענין אמירת שירת הבאר, שהיא השירה השלישית. במלה ״מהרו״ יש אולי רמז לאנשי כנסת הגדולה (מאה ועשרים זקנים וכו׳) שעזרא היה מהם ונאמר עליו ״והוא סופר מהיר״ (עזרא ז ו); ואמנם נדרשת פרשת הבאר לענין הזקנים והסנהדרין וכו׳ – השווה מדרש אותיות דרבי עקיבא השלם, נוסח א׳ (בתי מדרשות, ב, עמ׳ שפד-שפה) ובמקבילות: ״באר חפרוה שרים וכו׳ אין שרים אלא משה ושבעים סנהדרין וכו׳ כרוה נדיבי עם, אלו הסופרים כגון דוד ושלמה דניאל ומרדכי ועזרא הסופר״ וכו׳.

16 **וציר חק** – זה משה, שחקק את שירת האזינו, היא השירה הרביעית. חק־חקק, גזר, ראה גם להלן ג 2, ובכ״י פריז: ״חרץ״.

17 עפ״י יהושע י יב-יד; **פלכים** – גלגלים, וכך פירש הטור: יהושע העמיד את הגלגלים, שמתהלכים תמיד, ונושאים את השמש ואת הירח; לביטוי ״פלכים... הולכים״ השוה בפיוט ריצ״ג ״יציר חומר״ (כ״י אוקספורד f57, רשימת נויבאור־קולי, 14, 2852): ״ופלכים נהלכים״ וכו׳ < = יונה דוד, שירי ר׳ יצחק אבן גיאת (מהדורה טנטטיבית), ירושלים תשמ״ח, עמ׳ 381 (טור 22)>, ובדומה לזה

בפיוטו "יתר מדע" (פרסמו שרגא אברמסון, תרביץ מג [תשל"ד], עמ' 163): "בתוך פלך מתהלך וכו' חרס [שמש] וכו' ושם מעגל לו בגלגל רביעי" וכו'. <ראה שם, עמ' 423.>

18 עפ"י יהושע יב ז-כד; פירוש הטור: האנשים שוררו כשראו את המופתים שעשה יהושע בהעבירו את ל"א המלכים הנקראים גם נסיכים (השווה יהושע יג כא, על נסיכי סיחון שהוכו בידי משה); **ואותות** – בכ"י פריז: "ואותו".

19 **שיר** – בכ"י פריז: "שר"; **אז ידבר** – יהושע י יב, וזו השירה החמישית.

21 שירת דבורה – שופטים ה. זו השירה השישית.

23-22 שירת דוד, עפ"י שמואל ב כב (תהלים יח) זו השירה השביעית; **ואיש עם אלהים שרה** – עפ"י בראשית לב כט, והכוונה לדוד ששׂר עם אחיתופל (שמואל ב טו לא), שנאמר בו "ועצת אחיתפל אשר יעץ" וכו' כלומר שאחיתפל לִמֵּד תורה לדוד (השווה פרקי אבות ו ב); **בהנצלו מעבירה שר** וכו' – אולי הכוונה למה שנאמר במדרש תהלים, מהד' בובר עמ' 137: "את דברי השירה הזאת (תהלים יח א, והמשך הפסוק: "ביום הציל ה' אותו" וכו') אמר ר' סימון לא כל מי שהוא רוצה לומר שירה אומר, אלא כל מי שנעשה לו נס ואומר שירה בידוע שמוחלין לו עוונותיו" וכו'.

27-25 שיר חנכת בית המקדש, והוא השיר השמיני; השווה תהלים ל א, ומה שנדרש עליו במדרש תהלים, מהד' בובר עמ' 234-233: "מי שחשב בלבו לעשות מצוה ונאנס ולא עשאה שאני מעלה עליו כאלו עשאה, שהרי דוד חשב לבנות בית המקדש ונקרא על שמו" וכו'; **סוד מכוסה** – כנראה מיוסד על מה שנאמר בבראשית רבה א א, א ד. מהד' תיאודור־אלבק עמ' 1 ועמ' 6; "ואהיה אצלו אמון, אמון מכוסה" וכו', "ו' דברים קדמו לבריית עולם וכו' בית המקדש עלה במחשבה" וכו'; **לשורר לבא** – בשני כתבי היד "לבא", באל"ף. ואולי פירושו כאילו היה כתוב "לעתיד לבא"; אבל להלן בפיוט ג' טור 4, "לשורר לבו", בוי"ו ואולי גם כאן צ"ל "לבו".

30-39 **תקן והוציא** וכו' – מדובר על שלמה המלך החכם מכל אדם, שחבר שלשה ספרים שהם משלי קהלת ושיר השירים, והאחרון הוא השיר התשיעי, בהערה 1 למכילתא דר"י, עמ' 118; "לאורים" – בכ"י פריז: נאורים.

31 **אף ישירו** – תהלים סה יד.

הערות לשיר ב'

1 **יהירים** – כנוי לאויבי ישראל (השווה משלי כא כד); **הודי נחלו** – ירשו את הוד ישראל; **ועל שברי** וכו' – עמוס ו ו-ז.

2 **צועדים בגולה** וכו' – בני ישראל שהלכו בגולה ונפלו ונבלו כעלה (השווה ישעיה סד ה); **במשוך יובל יעלו** – שמות יט יג, וכאן הכוונה לאחרית הימים.

3 שמות יט טז; **מבזק** – מאש גדולה, השווה דברים ד יב. **בזק** – יחזקאל א יד.

4 השווה ישעיה כז יג וצפניה א טז.

5 **חצרים בטח שכנו** – כנוי לישמעאל, השווה ישעיה מב יא; **עושי רשעה נבנו** – מלאכי ג טו.

6 **קדושים** וכו' – בני ישראל ששמו של הקב"ה משותף בשמם. השווה ירושלמי תענית פ"ב ה"ו, סה ע"ד: "שיתף הקב"ה שמו הגדול בישראל". וכן בפיוט ג' שורה 1 להלן: "ישרים בשמו כנה".

7 תהלים סב יב, ופסוק זה נדרש לענין מתן תורה במכילתא דר"י, שירתא ח, מהד' הארוויטץ־רבין, עמ' 143.

9 **בוערים** – השווה יחזקאל כא לו ותהלים צד ח; **מקומך סכלו** – קלקלו והשחיתו את מקומך, השווה שמואל ב טו לא; **ומקומם לא שכלו** – כלומר לא נהרסו ממקומם, השווה בראשית לא לח.

10 **רצויים** – ישראל, השווה תהלים לד ג ועוד.

11 **לקראתך נסעו** – עפ"י שמות יט יז; **חמשה קולות שמעו** – עפ"י דברי ר' יהושע בן לוי: "זוכה לתורה שנתנה בחמשה קולות" וכו' (ברכות ו ע"ב).

13 עפ"י מיכה א ו; בראשית כט ח; תהלים קיח כב.

14 **הדרי עולם** – בני ישראל, השווה יחזקאל טו יד; **נזלו** – השווה ישעיה סג יט ועוד; **ויקרים זללו** – עפ"י איכה א יא.

15 עפ"י תהלים עו ט, והפסוק נדרש לענין מתן תורה, ראה שבת פח ע"א.

17 **אותך מאסו** – שמואל א ח ז; **ובהבליהם כעסו** – דברים לב כא.

18 **דבקים** – עפ״י דברים ד ד; **בצלך יחסו** – עפ״י תהלים לו ח; **ואת מנוסם** – ירמיה טז יט.

19 עפ״י שמות כ יח, והשוה מכילתא דר״י, בחדש ט, מהד׳ האראוויטץ־רבין, עמ׳ 235: ״רבי עקיבא אומר רואין ושומעין הנראה״; ללשון השוה איוב כט יא.

21 **הגוי וגו׳** – עפ״י תהלים פג ו; **לעיניך יקרצו** – לעיניך, ה׳, יגזרו ויחתכו את עמך. והפייטן משתמש במשחק מלים על הביטוי ״קרץ עין״.

22 **גולים לביתך רוצצו** – גולים כלשון נגלים, כלומר בני ישראל שהיו רגילים להראות בבית ה׳ רוצצו בידי האויב; **באמרי יושר נמרצו** – איוב ו כה.

23 עפ״י שמות כ יט והשוה דניאל ח יג.

25 **ידם לברים פשטו** – שלחו ידם בבני ישראל הטהורים; **וכמשפטיהם שפטו** – יחזקאל כג כד.

26 **אמלים** – חלשים, בני ישראל שנחלשו מצרות הגלות. המלה ״אמלים״ שכיחה בלשון הפייטנים, ראה בן יהודה בערכו; ״בושת יעטו״ – עפ״י תהלים פט מו; **ולמו רשעים ינטו** – אולי פירושו: והרשעים חושבים עליו, על ישראל רעות, השוה תהלים כא יב.

27 תהלים קיט קעא; ישעיה ל כא; השוה ספרי דברים, פיסקא שי, מהד׳ פינקלשטין עמ׳ 351; ״למחר עתידים ישראל להיות רואים ושומעים כשומעים מפי הקב״ה שנאמר ואזניך תשמענה״ וכו׳.

29 **תועי לבב** – עפ״י תהלים צה י.

30 **בהכשלו יעזרו** – עפ״י דניאל יא לד.

הערות לשיר ג׳

1 **ישרים בשמו כנה** – ראה לעיל פיוט ב, הערה לשורה 6; **מיום בחר פנה** – מיום שבחר בישראל וכו׳; **לתור להם מנוחה** – במדבר י לג.

2 **וחק** – חקק, גזר. ראה לעיל פיוט א׳, שורה 15. **לעשות חנכה ושמחה** – נחמיה יב כז.

4 **יחנכו את בית ה׳** – מלכים א ח סג.

7-5 מדבר על חנוכת ברייתו של עולם, בראשונה הוציא ה׳ את החכמה הצפונה ואת הדעה הפנינית, ובהן ברא ותכנן את עולמו. כשגמר את מלאכתו נתן את השבת במתנה לישראל וזו חנוכת ברייתו של עולם, והשוה ב״ר א א, מהד׳ תיאודור־אלבק, עמ׳ 1-2: ״בראשית ברא אלקים וגו׳, ר׳ אושעיא פתח ואהיה אצלו אמון וכו׳ אמון מכוסה, אמון מוצנע וכו׳ בנוהג שבעולם וכו׳ כך היה הקב״ה מביט בתורה ובורא העולם״ וכו׳. בפסיקתא רבתי הנ״ל נלמד ענין חנוכת העולם מהפסוק ״ויכלו השמים והארץ״ וכו׳ (בראשית ב א), וכנראה מכאן לקח לו הפייטן את הרעיון שחנכת העולם היא מתנת השבת, ואין ״ויכלו״ אלא לשון חנוכה לפי המדרש הנ״ל. על המלה ״פנינית״ אצל המשוררים העבריים בספרד ראה הערות י״א זיידמן ל״כתר מלכות״ לרשב״ג, עמ׳ מט במהדורתו. הביטוי נמצא כמה פעמים אצל ריצ״ג. ראה בפיוט ״מעשיך אמיץ״ (דוידזון, מ, 2057): ״מעשיך חצוב נשמה מגזרת חיים פניניה״; שם: ״וחמה פניניה בלבב קשורה < ראה אצל יונה דוד, לעיל, הערה לטור 17 שבשיר א׳, עמ׳ 104, טור 413 ושם עמ׳ 106, טור 460 >; ובפיוט ״סביביו אראלי אש״: ״פנינית צלמיהם צלם נשמה ורוח״ (ח׳ שירמן, השירה העברית בספרד ובפרובאנס, א, עמ׳ 308, שורה 13) < שם, עמ׳ 81, טור 13 >; על שבת כמנה ראה ביצה טז ע״א; **כל מלאכות התבנית** – דברי הימים א כח יט; המלים ״צפון חכמה ראשונית״ נכתבו על הגליון בכ״י וואטיקן.

11-9 מדבר על חנוכת הנשיאים; **חבושי נוף** – אסירי מצרים; **הוא הולך לפניהם** – עפ״י שמות יג כא; **בשום שכנו ביניהם** וכו׳ – עפ״י במדבר ז א ואילך, ובמיוחד פסוק פ״ד שם.

15-13 מדבר על חנוכת דוד. ראה לעיל במבוא לפיוטנו. וכל הענין עפ״י שמואל ב׳ ו׳ ואילך ובמיוחד פסוקים י״ז-י״ח, שבאחרון באה המלה ״ויכל״, מלה שנדרשת בהקשר אחר לענין חנוכה, ראה בפסיקתא הנ״ל (דף ז ע״ב): ״ואין ויכלו אלא לשון חנוכה, דכתיב ותכל כל עבודת״ (שמות לט לב) וכו׳; **לשורר לבו** – ראה הערה לפיוט א׳, טור 27; **שַׂר כזית** – השווה בפיוט המיוחס לרמב״ע, המובא במבוא לפיוטנו ״גם מלך הודו כזית״. ועל פי זה יש לפרש גם כאן: שַׂר, מלך הדומה בהודו לזית (השוה הושע יד ז, תהלים נב י); **שר** – בכ״י וטיקן: שיר; **שיר חנכת הבית** – תהלים ל א. [חנוכת דוד מתבססת כנראה בעיקר על תהלים ל׳ א׳ והשווה גם הפיוט ״איום מבראשית״ דוידזון, א, 2676. צבי מלאכי.]

19-17 מדבר על חנוכת שלמה המלך; **גולה סתומי עלומים** וכו׳ – הוא שלמה החכם מכל אדם; **בבנותו כמו רמים** וכו׳ – מלכים א ח יב ואילך; **שבעת ימים** – שם סה.

23-21 מדבר על חנוכת עולי גולה; **ימי שבעים** – עפ״י ירמיה כה יב; **בני גולה ברננה חנוכת בית אלהנא דנה** – עפ״י עזרא ו טז.

27-25 חנוכת בית חשמונאי; **בעמוד ענן גואלם** – לא מצאתי מקור לדבר זה בענין חנוכת בית חשמונאי. (מוזר שנאמר כאן ״חנוכה שבעת ימים״ ולא ״שמונת ימים״).

31-29 חנוכת בית המקדש לעתיד לבוא; ובפסיקתא הנ״ל: חנוכת העולם הבא. וכל הענין עפ״י יחזקאל לד יא ואילך.

הערות לשיר ד׳

1 שיעורו: כל מי שיפנה אל משכן החתן, כלומר החופה, יענה (ישיר ראה גם לעיל שיר א׳ 1) ויאמר ״הנה מה טוב״ וכו׳ (תהלים קלג א).

2 **מיעלת חן** – עפ״י משלי ה יט (ובפסוק שלפניו כתוב: ״ויהי מקורך ברוך ושמח מאשת נעוריך״); **מבנה עולם** – השווה את הלשון בשבע ברכות לנשואין: ״בנין עדי עד״; **בילדי שעשועים** – ירמיה לא יט.

3 **מדי לילה ויומם** – עפ״י הלשון בישעיה סו כג, ועל הפסוק הזה מיוסדת השורה הבאה: **זרעם נכון עמם** – עפ״י איוב כא ח.

4 עפ״י ישעיה סו כב-כג.

5 שם סא ט.

6 **דרושים לכל חפציהם** – תהלים קיא ב.

7 עפ״י ישעיה סא ט, ועל זה מיוסדת גם שורה 5.

9 כל הסטרופה הושמטה מגוף הפיוט והסופר הוסיף אותה על הגליון. **חתן** וכו׳ – עפ״י תהלים יט ה-ו ושופטים ה לא.

10 **ומה יפיו** – זכריה ט יז; **במלאתו** וכו׳ – עפ״י תהלים קכז ה.

11 עפ״י ישעיה סא ט הנ״ל בהערה לשורות 5, 7.

13 **זמן התחברות אליו** – בזמן שהכלה מתחברת אל החתן, או: כשחבורת בני המשתה יושבת עמו גם יחד.

14 **ובטוב נפלו חבליו** – עפ״י תהלים טז ו; **הוא והחונים עליו** – עפ״י במדבר ב ה ועוד.

15 עפ״י בראשית מה יט והשוה תהלים קטז ט.

הערות לשיר ה׳

1 אולי עפ״י ישעיה, מ ג. וראה להלן הערה לשורה 12.

2 **מושיב יחידים** – תהלים סח ז.

3 **והיו לאחדים** – יחזקאל לז יז.

4 **קול ה׳ יחולל** – תהלים כט ט.

6 עפ״י תהלים סח ז הנ״ל; **אסיריו** – נכתב בין השורות.

7 **להר זה קנת[ה]** – תהלים עח נד; **הפאתה** – אולי עפ״י דברים לב כז. ר׳ מילון בן־יהודה ערך פָּאָה עמ׳ 4804.

8 **רב וצעיר** – עפ״י בראשית כה כג; **קול ה׳ לעיר** – מיכה ו ט.

11 **כיונים** וכו׳ – ישעיה ס ח; **נשא אשא להם** – הושע א ו.

12 **ושלם מכל מעבר** – עפ״י מלכים א ה ד; **קול קורא במדבר** – ישעיה מ ג הנ״ל בהערה לשורה 1.

"מחזור בלתי נודע" וספר שפתי רננות

בספריית בית המדרש לרבנים בניו יורק נמצא טופס יחיד בעולם של מחזור קטן (10X15 ס"מ) ליום הכיפורים מדפוס ישן נושן. הספר חסר בתחילתו ובסופו. ר' ישראל דוידזון היה הראשון שהזכירו וקרא לו בשם מחזור בלתי נודע (להלן: מב"נ), תיארו בקיצור והכניס ל"אוצרו" כמה מן הפיוטים שבו.[1] ישעיה זנה הקדיש מאמר לזיהוי מחזור זה ואמר, שהוא אינו אלא חלק שני של המחזור הידוע בשם "חזונים" לראש השנה, שהוא "כמנהג המערביים שנתגוררו בסיזיליא".[2] זנה בדק את הספר מבחינה טיפוגראפית וקבע שנדפס בויניציאה בין השנים שמ"א-שמ"ג.[3] שמעון ברנשטיין ערך רשימה של כל הפיוטים שבמחזור. גם הוא ניסה לזהות את מנהגו, אך בניגוד לדעת זנה סבור היה ברנשטיין, שהמחזור הוא לפי מנהג היהודים שבצפון־אפריקה, כי פירושו של הכינוי "מערביים" אינו "אנדלוזיים" אלא יהודי צפון־אפריקה.[4]

כדי לפתור את שאלת מהותו של המחזור עלינו לעמוד על טיבו של ס' שפתי רננות (להלן: ש"ר). בהשוואת שניהם נמצא את הפתרון לזיהוי מב"נ.

במב"נ נמצאות תפילות וסליחות ליום הכיפורים. הקרובות לשחרית, מוסף ומנחה של היום הן מאת ר' יצחק אבן־גיאת (לוסינה שבספרד, 1038-1089). קרובות אלו נמצאות גם במהדורות השונות של ס' ש"ר שבו תפילות, בקשות, סליחות ותחינות לימי הסליחות, לראש השנה וליום הכיפורים לפי מנהג טריפולי וג'רבה אשר במערב והסביבה.[5] קרובות ר' יצחק אבן־גיאת ליום הכיפורים אינן נמצאות בדפוס בשום מקור אחר והנוסח של הקרובות כמעט זהה בשני הספרים.[6] עובדה זו כשלעצמה מעידה על קירבה מסוימת בין מב"נ ובין ש"ר.

1 ישראל דוידזון, אוצר השירה והפיוט, כרך ד, ניוארק תרצ"ג, עמ' 9. לפי דוידזון נדפס הספר בויניציאה בערך 1550-1560 (ש"י-ש"ך).

2 מחזור חזונים תואר בידי י' דוידזון, בתוך: ספר זכרון לכבוד הד"ר ש"א פוזננסקי, ורשה תרפ"ז, החלק העברי, עמ' נט-עז. לפי דוידזון (שם עמ' סא): בשם "מערבים" נקראו אלו שנתגרשו בסוף המאה הט"ז ממערב אירופא ונתישבו בטורקיא ובארצות המזרח.

3 ישעיה זנה, "מנהג האנדלוזים שהתגוררו בסיציליא", *Journal of Jewish Bibliography*, כרך 3, 1942, עמ' 84-89.

4 שמעון ברנשטיין: The "Unknown Mahzor" in the Library of the Jewish Theological Seminary of America, שם, עמ' 32-42.

5 בשער מהדורת ויניציאה תע"א כתוב: "כמנהג ק"ק טריפולי יע"א אשר במערב והמדינו' השכנו'". במהדורות המאוחרות נזכרה גם ג'רבה.

6 בש"ר חסרים רק הסילוקים בסוף הקרובות לשחרית ולמוסף.

בדיקה נוספת של הספרים והשוואתם מחזקות את ההשערה, ששני קובצי התפילות למנהג אחד נועדו.

בשער ש"ר, ליוורנו תקע"ו (1816), כתוב: "אשר נדפס כבר ב"פ בויניציאה ופעם ג' בליוורנו יע"א וסדר תפלות ליה"כ נדפס פעם ד' וליוקר מציאותם מלאני לבי להדפיסם זאת הפעם... בהג"ה מדוייקת... ועוד בה עשיתי לו פירוש מספיק... מידי היתה זאת... שאול הכהן בלא"א... כה"ר מוסא הכהן...".[7]

ר' שאול כהן זה שימש מורה צדק בג'רבה (המאה השמונה־עשרה-התשע־עשרה).[8] בהקדמה לפירושו לפיוטים שבש"ר כתוב: "ובס' המעמדות של ארבע תפלות של יום הכפורים הזמין עוד השם לידי ספר קטן והוא חסר בתחילתו, לא ידעתי אנה נדפס, וגם הוא יש בגליונותיו כמה הגהות ופירושים ומהם לקטתי כמה וכמה".[9]

כפי שנראה להלן אין שום ספק ש"ספר קטן" של המעמדות ליום הכיפורים שר' שאול כהן הזכירו בשער ש"ר ובהקדמה אינו אלא מב"נ.

בדף רמג, א, של ש"ר כתוב בראש הפיוט "יושיעם ויחתום": "סימן יוסף ברבי יצחק". נראה שהוא בנו של הרי"צ גיאת אלא שבדפוס ישן קטן כתוב שהוא לרבי יוסף בן אביתקר [אביתור. וכן תוקן במהדורות המאוחרות] בן שטנאס ע"כ". ודבר זה נמצא בדיוק במב"נ דף קעג, ב.

בדף רלח, א, ובדף רלט, ב, בש"ר נדפס מעל לשני פיוטים "מדפוס ישן נושן" ופיוטים אלה נמצאים במב"נ דף קג, א, וקד, ב, ולפי אוצרו של דוידזון אינם נמצאים בשום דפוס אחר.[10]

מלבד ההבאות המפורשות מ"דפוס ישן" שבש"ר מהדורת תקע"ו יש למצוא דמיון בין ש"ר דפוס ויניציאה תע"א (1171) ובין מב"נ. בשניהם נדפס בהתחלת הקרובה לשחרית יום הכיפורים בתוך מסגרת באותיות גדולות: "מעמד לליוצר לרבי יצחק ן' גיאת זצ"ל". וכן בראש תפילת מוסף: "מעמד למוסף לרי"צ גיאת זצ"ל". סדר הפיוטים שבקרובות וה"לחן" של הפזמונים שבהן שווים בדיוק בשני הספרים.[11]

במקומות אחדים יש התאמה שלימה בלשון ההוראות הניתנות לשליח צבור. בגמר סדר העבודה למוסף כתוב בשניהם: "ואחר כך אומר קדיש תתקבל ואחר כך רבי חנינא בן עקשיא וכו' אך צדיקים וגו' וקדיש דרבנן וברכו ותענו ותקובלו ברצון ואחר כך

7 זה סדר המהדורות של ש"ר: 1. ויניציאה ת"ח [1648], על פי צעדנר, עמ' 493, ושטיינשניידר, CB, טור 400, מס' 2592. דפוס זה לא עמד לרשותי. 2. ויניציאה תע"א [1711]. זו המהדורה הראשונה הרשומה על ידי דוידזון ב"אוצרו". 3. ליוורנו תקנ"ג [1793]. 4. שם תקע"ו [1816]. 5. שם תקצ"ז [1837], על פי צעדנר, עמ' 493. 6. שם תר"ד [1844], על פי שטיינשניידר, שם, מס' 2594. 7. שם תרכ"ה [1865].

8 עיין בהסכמה למהדורת תקע"ו ותרכ"ה, ועיין ח"ז הירשברג, תולדות היהודים באפריקה הצפונית, ירושלים 1965, כרך ב, עמ' 161.

9 דפוס ליוורנו תקע"ו, דף ד, א.

10 הפיוטים הם: הלא זה יום יחיד (דוידזון, ה, 638); ישראל בחירי לעם בחרתיך (ד, י, 4218).

11 מב"נ, דף סה, א, ודף קיח, א; ש"ר, דף עו, א ודף פח, א.

סליחות״.[12] בראש תפילת נעילה נדפס בלשון אחת בשניהם: ״אתחיל תפלת נעילה וצריך להתפלל אותה בעוד היום כדי שישלים אותה סמוך לשקיעת החמה״. וכאן אפילו הסידור

שפתי רננות

כולל תפלות מעולי' בקשות סליחות ותחינות

כמנהג ק"ק טריפולי

רחמים בלפון

בויניציאה

תמלא

יוסף פרץ יצ"ו.

Nella Stamparia Bragadina.
Con Licenza de Superiori.
Per Gioanni de' Paoli.

שער שפתי רננות, ויניציאה תע״א (1711)

12 מב״נ, דף קנג, א, וש״ר, דף צח, ב.

ע״ו

נדפס במצות הגביר כמ״ר רחמים בלפון יצ״ו

מעמד לליוצר לרבי
יצחק ן׳ גיאת זצ״ל

שפתי תפתח ופי יגיד תהלתך: ברוך אתה יי׳ אלהינו ואלהי אבותינו אלהי
אברהם אלהי יצחק ואלהי יעקב האל הגדול הגבור והנורא:

אל עליון קונה שמים וארץ

רשות ללמנן

וארץ אהבת לאלהי ואתחנן. אשיר עוזו רגעי וארנן. אעמוד לראות
במחשב משתונן. ואתבונן נפלאות
אל:
אל במראות דעת טורא. במו נראה ולא בעין יראה: בטרם נמצא מקום נורא.
ויקרא למקום
אל:
אל גזרו חכמות גבהו. גזר ומקוריהם גברו ולא להוו. גל עינות שכל גברו
מנהו והוא ראשית דרכי
אל:
אל דבק בלי עמל ירים דבקי גלגלים מסיבים כרחים. דברו מעידים בלי
שפתים. השמים מספרים כבוד
אל:
אל הציב. מופתיו וגלם. הפליא בהכינו. מסבות מעגלם. הם יורו כי מעולם.
ועד עולם אתה
אל:
אל ולצור פניניהם חוצבו. ומהם נמצאו ישאפו ויתאבו. והשג רצונו מעת נצבו.
ושבו ושחרו
אל:
אל זבול שחק מכונן אהלי. זורחי נגהי נרות בם מעלה. זקף מנורות לבער
ויגלה: הן כל אלה יפעל
אל:
אל חוק חג ונשא משכול. חוקותיו צופה. לנובב לא יכול. חבר רגבים ותלה
כאשכול. את כל הארצות
ה״י:
אל

שפתי רננות, ויניציאה תע״א, דף עו, א

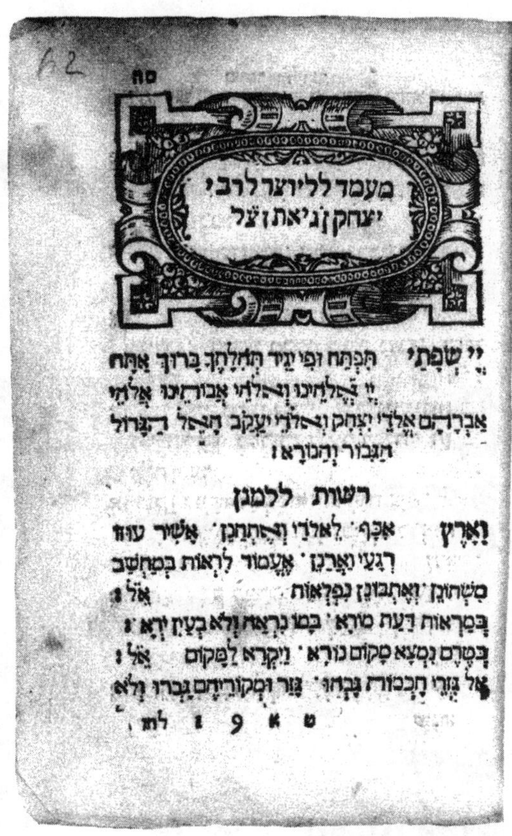

סה

מעמד לליוצר לרבי יצחק ן׳ גיאת ז״ל

יי׳ שפתי תפתח ופי יגיד תהלתך ברוך אתה יי׳ אלהינו ואלהי אבותינו אלהי אברהם אלהי יצחק ואלהי יעקב האל הגדול הגבור והנורא׃

רשות ללמנן

וארץ אכף לאלהי ואתחנן· אשיר עוז רגשי וארנן· אעמוד לראות במחשב משתונן· ואתבונן נפלאות אל׃
במראות דעת מורא· במו נראה ולא בעין יראה׃
בטרם נמצא מקום נורא· ויקרא למקום אל׃
אל גורי חכמות נבחו· גור ומקוריהם גברו ולא

[מחזור בלתי נודע], דף סה, א

הטיפוגראפי דומה, היינו ששלוש המלים הראשונות של ההוראה נדפסות בשורה אחת באותיות גדולות והמשך הטקסט בא בשורה חדשה באותיות קטנות.[13] וכן בסוף הקרובה לנעילה; הסילוק של הקרובה מנוקד בשניהם עד המלים ״וקרא זה אל זה ואמר״ ואחר כך באה הקדושה בלא ניקוד עד ״ברוך אתה ה׳ המלך הקדוש״ ואחר כך באותיות רש״י קטנות בדיוק בלשון אחת: ״וגומר התפלה ככתוב לעיל במקומו [במב״נ: דף קסט] ואחר כך יאמר ואתה שמע אלקינו עד ואנחנו הרשענו ואבינו מלכנו חטאנו לפניך וגו׳ ונופלין על פניהם ה׳ אלקי ישראל וגומר ככתוב לעיל [במב״נ נוסף: דף קז] ואם יש שהות ביום לאמר סליחות יאמר כי לא על צדקותינו עד אמונתך הודעת לו ואחר כך אומר״.[14]

מכל זה יוצא, שמהדירי ש״ר ומפרשו הכירו את מב״נ. הם השתמשו בו והביאו דברים ממנו וחיקו במקומות אחדים את הסידור הטיפוגראפי שבו. על יסוד דברים אלה ועל יסוד העובדה שהקרובות ליום הכיפורים של ר׳ יצחק אבן־גיאת נמצאות רק בשני מקורות דפוס

13 מב״נ, דף קסח, ב; ש״ר, דף ק, ב.

14 מב״נ, דף קעז, א־ב; ש״ר, דף קב, א־ב.

אלה מותר להניח, שמחזור בלתי נודע אינו אלא מחזור ליום הכיפורים לפי מנהג שפתי רננות שבו כתוב בפירוש שהוא כמנהג טריפולי וג׳רבה והקהילות אשר סביבותיהן.

כאמור לעיל, לפי השערת זנה, מב״נ נדפס בויניציאה בין שמ״א-שמ״ג. אפילו אם לא נסכים לקביעה מדויקת זאת, אין לאחר את זמן הדפסת הספר יותר משנות ש״ף-ש״ץ, מטעמים טיפוגראפיים. אם כן מתעוררת השאלה: ההיתה קהילה יהודית בטריפולי שבצפון אפריקה בתקופה זו שהיתה זקוקה למחזור נדפס? ההיו קשרים בין יהודי טריפולי ובין המרכזים הגדולים של הדפוס העברי שבאיטליה? אין לנו תשובות ברורות לשאלות אלו. אולם ידוע לנו שבשנת ש״י (1550), בערך, הגיע לטריפולי ר׳ שמעון לביא הספרדי, אירגן שם את חיי הקהילה והכניס שינויים בסדר התפילה.[15] ידוע לנו גם כן, שהמהדורה הראשונה של שפתי רננות יצאה לאור בויניציאה בשנת ת״ח (1648).[16] אין מן הנמנע שכבר כמה עשרות שנים לפני הדפסת ש״ר הזמינה קהילת טריפולי מחזור נדפס ליום הכיפורים ואפשר אולי להניח שלר׳ שמעון לביא היה חלק בהוצאתו לאור של מב״נ.[17] ר׳ שמעון היה ממוצא ספרדי ואפשר שהוא הכניס את פיוטי ר׳ יצחק אבן־גיאת הספרדי למחזורם של יהודי טריפולי. להשערות אין סוף ומי יתן שיתגלו מקורות חדשים להפיץ אור על תולדות חיי היהודים שבטריפולי ועל מנהגי התפילה שלהם, ואולי בהם נמצא גם תשובה לשאלות ששאלנו.

15 הירשברג (לעיל, הערה 8), עמ׳ 174-175, והערה שם, עמ׳ 348-349. על ר׳ שמעון לביא עיין גם *Encyclopaedia Judaica*, כרך 10, טור 540-542. נוסח השער של אחד מספרי התפילה כמנהג טריפולי: "סדר תקוני כלה לליל שבועות כמנהג ק״ק טריפולי דלברבריאה יע״ה שהובא ע״י איש חכם ורופא ואבי הקבלה כמה״ר שמעון לאבי זלה״ה שגורש מספרד מעיר קשטילייא, ויניציאה, שנת לשמע״ (ת״ם), 1680. צילום השער ב־*Jewish Encyclopedia*, כרך 12, עמ׳ 414. <ראה עתה, בועז הוס, על אדני פז – הקבלה של ר׳ שמעון אבן לביא, ירושלים תש״ס.>

16 עיין הערה 7.

17 ר׳ שמעון לביא נזכר בקשר למהדורת ש״ר דפוס ויניציאה ת״ח, עיין שטיינשניידר, מס׳ 2592.

ר׳ משה בן אלקרטבי

ר׳ יצחק אבן גיאת שלח שיר ארמי שקול לחכם אחד בשם ר׳ משה בן אלקרטבי.[1] על אודות ר׳ משה זה אין לנו ידיעות מלבד מה שאפשר ללמוד עליו משירו הנ״ל של ר׳ יצחק אבן גיאת.

משיר זה משמע שר׳ משה היה תלמיד חכם גדול, ״בר אבהן ובר אריאן״, ושהוא העמיד תלמידים ונצח בפלפולו את החכמים ושבאו אליו לבקש פתרון כל ענין סתום וקשה. חכם זה היה עני ודל, חסר בגדי־נוי ותכשיטים וכנראה התאונן על זה בפני אבן גיאת והאחרון ענה לו כי חכמתו וצדקתו הן תפארתו.

הרמב״ם בתשובותיו לחכמי לוניל על סדר פרשיות התפלין מזכיר חכם אחד בשם ר׳ משה אלקרטבי שחבר חיבור על הלכות תפלין ומוסיף: ״ואותו החיבור הוא שהטעני והטעה כל אנשי המערב מלפני״.[2]

לפי גירסת כמה כתבי יד, שם אביו של בעל חיבור תפילין היה מימון אבל כבר העיר בעל ה״כסף משנה״ שגירסה זו קרוב לודאי טעות היא ושטיינשניידר הביא על יסוד כתבי־יד אחרים שצ״ל יעקב במקום מימון.[3] שרגא אברמסון מצא בכתבי־יד הגניזה קטעים מחיבור תפלין ושם רשום שם המחבר כר׳ משה בן יוסף אלקרטבי ובמקור אחד: ר׳ משה בן מר יוסף בן אלקרטבי.[4]

מדברי הרמב״ם משמע שר׳ משה חי כמה שנים לפניו (״הטעה כל אנשי המערב מלפני״ ולפי כתבי־יד אחרים: שלפני; מלפנים) וגם שחיבורו השפיע השפעה רבה על החכמים והטעה גם את הרמב״ם עצמו. נראה שכהשערה מותר לצרף את הידיעות משני המקורות ולזהות את ר׳ משה בעל חיבור תפלין עם ר׳ משה אליו נשלח שירו של ר׳ יצחק גיאת ועל ידי השערה זו נוכל לקבוע את זמנו של בעל חיבור תפילין, דהיינו המאה הי״א, המאה בה חי ר׳ יצחק גיאת (1038-1089), וגם נלמד על פעולתו הספרותית של מקבל שירו של ר׳ יצחק גיאת.

1 נתפרסם על ידי יעקב רייפמן, מפענח נעלמים, אוצר טוב לר״א ברלינר, 1882, עמ׳ 7-8, ותרגום עברי ופירוש שם עמ׳ 28-29; וראה שם שנה 1881, עמ׳ 44. ראה מה שכתב ח׳ שירמן על מהדורתו זו של רייפמן בספר חנוך ילון, ירושלים תשכ״ג, עמ׳ 362. כתב היד שעל פיו הדפיס רייפמן את השיר היה מטושטש ובגלל זה השיר אינו שלם. <ראה עתה שרה כ״ץ, ר׳ יצחק אבן גיאת, ירושלים 1994, עמ׳ 124-133.>

2 תשובות הרמב״ם, מהדורת יהושע בלאו, ב, ירושלים תש״ך, עמ׳ 542.

3 שם, הערה 11-12.

4 שם, ג, ב״תוספות והערות״, עמ׳ 169-170. אגב אעיר שנחום גולב מביא ראיה מתשובה זו שבתקופתו של הרמב״ם היה עוד איש בשם משה בן מימון (ראה תרביץ, שנה לד, עמ׳ 289-290), אך כפי שראינו הנוסח ״משה בן מימון״ בתשובה זו טעות הוא ואין להביא ראיה ממנו.

פיוט הושענא לר׳ יוסף אבן אביתור

במהדורת ר׳ אברהם סופר [ז״ל] של ס׳ המכתם לר׳ דוד בן ר׳ לוי זצ״ל מנרבונה (ניו־יורק תשי״ט), נדפס גם פירוש להושענות לר׳ מאיר המעילי זצ״ל מנרבונה ״כפי שהוא בכ״י המכתם״ (עמ׳ 150-163). בפירוש זה מובאות פסקאות מן ההושענות, שעליהן מוסבים דברי המעילי, אבל הנוסח השלם של הפיוטים חסר היה בכתב־היד. המהדיר חיפש וחקר במחזורים נדפסים ובכתבי־יד וגילה את רוב הפיוטים המפורשים והדפיס אותם בספרו (עמ׳ 115-149). ברם עוד הניח מקום להתגדר בו, ועפ״י דברי הפירוש להושענות של יום שני (עמ׳ 152-153) עלתה בידי לגלות את עצם ההושענא, אותה פירש המעילי שם. הנוסח שמור בכתב־יד אחד של הספרייה המלכותית בקופנהאגן (מס׳ 30, דף 169-170).* כתב היד כולל פיוטים מפייטני ספרד וצרפת לשלוש רגלים. בין ההושענות ליום חמישי בא הפיוט המתפרסם כאן. בסופו חתום השם יוסף, והחוקרים מייחסים אותו לר״י אבן אביתור, אחד מחכמי ספרד הראשונים (עיין אוצר השירה והפיוט לר״י דודזון, אות ל׳, מס׳ 1142). <ראה עזרא פליישר, יצירתו של יוסף אבן אביתור, דיסרטציה, האוניברסיטה העברית, תשכ״ז, עמ׳ 414.>

אגב, אעיר כאן על מקום סתום בפיוט ״אמת אבאר הלכות סוכה״, שר״א סופר הדפיסו בעמ׳ 115 של מהדורתו הנ״ל: לשון השורה הראשונה של ההושענא ״ובהלכותיה ישנים אנדד״ – ר״ל שע״י ביאור ולימוד הלכות סוכה יעורו הלומדים בלילה, מלשון ״נדדה שנת המלך״ ז״א שיהגו בהלכות החג כל הלילה.

והנה לשון הפיוט הזה כולו.

לְמַעַן אָב[1] מֵאוּר כֶּשֶׂד שִׁוַּע וְנֶעֱנָה/ אָנָּא ה׳ הוֹשִׁיעָה נָּא[2]
לְמַעַן בָּחוּר[3] נֶעֱקַד לְעוֹלָה נְכוֹנָה/ אָנָּא ה׳ הַצְלִיחָה נָא[4]
לְמַעַן גִּבּוֹר[5] נִלְווּ לוֹ מִיכָאֵל וְגַבְרִיאֵל/ הוֹשַׁע ה׳ אֶת עַמְּךָ אֵת שְׁאֵרִית יִשְׂרָאֵל[6]
לְמַעַן דָּגוּל[7] הוֹרִיד דָּת מִשְּׁמֵי שִׁבְעָה/ עָזִּי וְזִמְרָת יָהּ וַיְהִי לִי לִישׁוּעָה[8]

* הפיוט נמצא גם בכ״י א33, 27126, של הבריטיש מוזיאום, דף 255-257, בשינויים קטנים, ואציין כאן אחדים מהם. שורה א: למען אב שוע מאור כשדים ונענה; שורה ג: למען בן נעקד לעולה מוכנה; שורה כז: למען נסתר שלשה ימים במעי דגה; שורה שלפני האחרונה: למען ישרים וסופרים מביני פתרון תבונה.

1 כלומר מאור־כשדים, הוא אברהם אבינו, ועיין תרגום יהונתן לבראשית טו ז.

2 תהלים קיח כה.

3 יצחק אבינו.

4 תהלים שם.

5 יעקב אבינו.

6 ירמיה לא ו.

7 משה רבנו.

8 שמות טו ב.

לְמַעַן הָדוּר[9] מְכַהֵן לִפְנֵי לִפְנִים בְּלֵבָב נִשְׁלָם/ הוֹשִׁיעָה אֶת עַמֶּךָ וּבָרֵךְ אֶת נַחֲלָתֶךָ וּרְעֵם וְנַשְּׂאֵם עַד הָעוֹלָם[10]

למען וָתִיק[11] מְכַפֵּר עָוֹן עוֹרְכֵי שַׁוְעוֹת/ ה׳ עוֹז לָמוֹ וּמָעוֹז יְשׁוּעוֹת[12]

לְמַעַן זָךְ[13] הֶעֱבִיר עַמְּךָ בְּמַצְלוּלֵי רֶפֶשׁ/ הוֹשִׁיעֵנוּ אֱלֹקִים כִּי בָאוּ מַיִם עַד נֶפֶשׁ[14]

לְמַעַן חָף[15] חֲקוֹתָ לוֹ בְּרִית עוֹלָם יְדוּעָה/ ה׳ צְבָאוֹת הֲשִׁיבֵנוּ הָאֵר פָּנֶיךָ וְנִוָּשֵׁעָה[16]

לְמַעַן טוֹב[17] עִם ה׳ וְעִם בָּשָׂר וָדָם/ הוֹשִׁיעָה ה׳ כִּי גָמַר חָסִיד כִּי פַסּוּ אֱמוּנִים מִבְּנֵי אָדָם[18]

לְמַעַן יָשָׁר מְנַגֵּן וִידִידְיָ׳[19] בְּמִקְדַּשׁ הֲדוֹמֶךָ/ עָזְרֵנִי אֱלֹקֵי יִשְׁעֵנוּ עַל דְּבַר כְּבוֹד שְׁמֶךָ[20]

לְמַעַן כָּלוּל[21] תִּשְׁבִּי נְבִיאֵנוּ/ ה׳ הוֹשִׁיעָה הַמֶּלֶךְ יַעֲנֵנוּ בְיוֹם קָרְאֵנוּ[22]

לְמַעַן לָמוּד[23] יָצַק מַיִם עַל יְדֵי תִשְׁבִּי בְחִילָה/ לַה׳ הַיְשׁוּעָה עַל עַמְּךָ בִרְכָתֶךָ סֶּלָה[24]

לְמַעַן מֶלֶךְ[25] הוֹסִיפוּ לוֹ חֲמֵשׁ עֶשְׂרֵה גְרוּעוֹת/ הָאֵל לָנוּ לְמוֹשָׁעוֹת[26]

לְמַעַן נִסְתָּר[27] שְׁלֹשָׁה בִּמְעֵי דָּגָה בִּמְצוּלָה/ הוֹשִׁיעָה כָּל עַנְוֵי אֶרֶץ סֶלָה[28]

לְמַעַן סְגוּפִים[29] שְׁלֹשָׁה אֲשֶׁר חִלַּצְתָּ וְתוֹשִׁיעַ/ אָתָּה אֵל מִסְתַּתֵּר אֱלֹקֵי יִשְׂרָאֵל מוֹשִׁיעַ[30]

לְמַעַן עוֹלֶה[31] גוֹלָה אֲשֶׁר מִבָּבֶל הֶעֱלָנוּ/ עוֹרְרָה אֶת גְּבוּרָתֶךָ וּלְכָה לִישׁוּעָתָה לָּנוּ[32]

לְמַעַן פְּעֻלַּת הֲדָס וּמָר דְּרוֹר[33] צִמְּתוּ צָר פּוֹשֵׁעַ/ מְהֻלָּל אֶקְרָא ה׳ וּמֵאוֹיְבַי אִוָּשֵׁעַ[34]

לְמַעַן צְנוּפֵי צְנִיפוֹת מְכַהֲנִים[35] בְּאוּרִים וְתוּמִים/ יִשְׂרָאֵל נוֹשַׁע בַּה׳ תְּשׁוּעַת עוֹלָמִים[36]

לְמַעַן קְדוֹשִׁים עֲשָׂרָה[37] נִשְׁחֲטוּ עַל שִׁמְךָ מוֹשִׁיעַ/ אֶת עַם עָנִי תוֹשִׁיעַ[38]

לְמַעַן רַבֵּי תוֹרוֹת[39] קוֹבְעֵי תַרְבֵּץ קְבוּעָה/ רְפָאֵנִי ה׳ וְאֵרָפֵא הוֹשִׁיעֵנִי וְאִוָּשֵׁעָה[40]

לְמַעַן שׁוֹקְדֵי עַל דְּלָתֶיךָ צוּר יִשְׁעִי/ מָגִנִּי וּמְנוּסִי מִשְׂגַּבִּי וּמוֹשִׁיעִי[41]

לְמַעַן תּוֹמְכֵי יִחוּדְךָ בְּכָל עֵת וְעוֹנָה/ הוֹשַׁע נָא וְהַצְלִיחָה נָּא

לְמַעַן יְשָׁרִים וְסוֹפְרִים יוֹדְעֵי מַדָּע וּבִינָה/ הוֹשַׁע נָא וְהַרְוִיחָה נָּא

9 אהרן הכהן.

10 תהלים כח ט.

11 אלעזר הכהן.

12 תהלים כח ח.

13 יהושע, שהעביר את העם את הירדן.

14 תהלים סט ב.

15 פינחס.

16 עפ״י תהלים פח כ.

17 שמואל, עפ״י שמואל א ב כו.

18 תהלים יב ב.

19 דוד ושלמה.

20 תהלים עט ט.

21 אליהו הנביא.

22 תהלים כ י.

23 אלישע הנביא, שיצק מים על ידי אליהו.

24 תהלים ג ט.

25 חזקיה המלך, עפ״י ישעיה לח ה.

26 עפ״י תהלים סח כא.

27 יונה הנביא.

28 עפ״י תהלים עו י.

29 חנניה מישאל ועזריה.

30 ישעיה מה טו.

31 עזרא הסופר.

32 תהלים פ ג.

33 אסתר ומרדכי.

34 שמואל ב כב ד.

35 לפי פירוש המעילי, מתתיהו החשמונאי ובניו.

36 ישעיה מה יז.

37 עשרת הרוגי מלכות.

38 עפ״י שמואל ב כב כה, ותהלים יח כה.

39 עיין בפירוש המעילי.

40 ירמיה יז יד.

41 עפ״י שמואל ב כב ג.

פירוש המעילי (מספר המכתם הנ״ל, עמ׳ 152-153):

חף – פי׳ נקי מלשון חף אנכי בלי פשע, וזה פינחס, ויש מפרשים חף מלשון כיסוי, כדמתרגמינ׳ ויכס וחפא, ורצונו לומר כשכיסה לבו ומחשבתו במעשה זמרי, שהיו סבורים שגם הוא לעשות כמותו נכנס, והזכיר יהושע קודם פינחס, מפני שפינחס האריך ימים אחרי יהושע, וכ״ש אם נאמר שפינחס זה אליהו, שכך אומר בכאן ״ברית עולם ידועה״, שנוכל לפרש שהוא עדיין חי, או איפשר ברית הכהונה, או אם תדקדק תוכל להפך שיהא פינחס ראשון ואחריו יהושע.

חמש עשרה גרועות – פי׳ מעלות שהם מגרעות, וכנגד אותן המעלות הוסיפו לו עוד חמש(ה) עשרה(ה) שנים.

סגופים – פירש מעונים, כדמתרגמיני׳ לענות נפש, לסגפא נפש, והם חנניה מישאל ועזריה.

צניפי צניפות מכהנים – פי׳ אלו חשמונאי ובניו.

קדושים עשרה – פי׳ עשרה הרוגי מלכות.

רבי תורות – לומדי התורה.

נפלאות בריאת העולם, יציאת מצרים, והגאולה שלעתיד לבוא, בפיוט קדום

להלן מתפרסם לראשונה הפיוט "אורי וישעי" לר' מנחם בר' מכיר, פייטן אשכנזי מהמאה הי"א,[1] על פי כתב יד של אוסף פיוטים מאשכנז מהמאה הי"ג לערך.[2]

יום טוב ליפמן צונץ הזכיר את הפיוט הזה בספרו הגדול על תולדות הפיוט, יחד עם עוד שלושה פיוטים, "אאמיר מסתתר" לר' יוסף טוב עלם,[2א] "אומץ דתותי" לפייטן בשם יוסף ו"ימי חדות" לר' יצחק אבן גיאת. בארבעתם, לפי דבריו, הציגו הפייטנים אלה מול אלה את נפלאות ה' במעשה בראשית, ביציאת מצרים ובגאולה העתידה לבוא. לפי צונץ, הקבלה זו לקוחה כנראה ממדרש אבכיר המובא בילקוט שמעוני. צונץ הזכיר גם שני פיוטי מעריב לפסח, מהפייטנים יוסף בן יעקב ויקותיאל בן יוסף, שבהם נרשמים אלה מול אלה הנִסים של גאולת מצרים והגאולה העתידה.[3] גילויו של "אורי וישעי", שלא נודע לו מקור עד כה, בספריית בית המדרש לרבנים באמריקה, כ"י 8972, דף 20 ב, סיפק הזדמנות לבדיקת הפיוטים שהוזכרו בהקשר זה על ידי צונץ והפנה תשומת לב לחקירת ביטוייה השונים של האנלוגיה הנזכרת ולחשיפת מקורותיה.

בעצם, רק שני פיוטים מתוך הארבעה זהים בבניינם ובתוכנם באשר להשוואה המשולשת הטמונה בהם. בשני היוצרות, האחד לר' יוסף טוב עלם והשני לר' מנחם בר' מכיר, ששניהם שימשו בשבתות שלפני פסח,[4] רשומים זה אחר זה הנסים והנפלאות שהתרחשו במעשה בראשית וביציאת מצרים ואלה שעתידים להתרחש בגאולה האחרונה.

1 ראה א' גרוסמן, חכמי אשכנז הראשונים, ירושלים תשמ"א, עמ' 373 ואילך.

2 ראה על כתב יד זה: ב' נרקיס, "ציורים לעשרת הדיברות במחזור אשכנזי זעיר בן המאה השלוש־עשרה", עשרת הדיברות בראי הדורות, בעריכת ב"צ סגל, ירושלים תשמ"ו, עמ' 389-407, ובמיוחד עמ' 391-393. וראה עוד במאמרי העומד להתפרסם בספר היובל לכבוד אברהם הולץ (להלן, עמ' 190-208).

2א <שולמית אליצור, "בין יוסף ליוסף – לזהות מחברו של יוצר קדום", תרביץ עא (תשס"ב), עמ' 67-86, מייחסת את הפיוט לר' יוסף אבן אביתור. כמובן, לאור מאמרה יש לבחון מחדש כמה מהעניינים שנידונו במאמר זה.>

3 ראה, L. Zunz. *Literaturgeschichte der synagogalen Poesie*, Berlin 1865, pp. 129, 158-159

4 לפי צונץ, שם, שני היוצרות הם לשבת הגדול, אבל בכתב היד של בית המדרש לרבנים שעל פיו מודפס להלן פיוטו של ר' מנחם רשום עליו: "כשיהו ב' הפסק' אז זה לשנייה". בערוגת הבשם לר' אברהם בן עזריאל, מהד' א"א אורבך, ירושלים תשכ"ג, עמ' 532, רשום מעל הפירוש לפיוטו של ר' יוסף טוב עלם: "יוצר דשבת שלפני שבת הגדול".

בשני הפיוטים האחרים[5] יש הקבלה רק בין גאולת מצרים לגאולה העתידה, בלי הזכרת הנפלאות של ששת ימי בראשית. גם ציונו של מדרש אבכיר כמקורה של האנלוגיה המשולשת אינו מדויק, כי המדרש משווה רק את הנסים של מעשה בראשית לאלה של יציאת מצרים (ובסדרה אחרת למעשה המשכן) וההשוואה לגאולה העתידה חסרה.[6]

עד כמה שיכולתי לקבוע, אין שום מקור ידוע שממנו שאבו ר׳ יוסף טוב עלם ור׳ מנחם בר׳ מכיר את ההקבלה העקיבה המשולבת והרצופה בין שלושת המאורעות, אבל אפשר לפרק את ההשוואות ולמצוא את מקורותיהן בנפרד. והנה היסודות השונים שיש להבחין ביניהם:

1. הדמיון בין הנסים של מעשה בראשית והנסים של יציאת מצרים;
2. הדמיון בין הנסים של מעשה בראשית ובין הנסים בזמן הגאולה העתידה;
3. הדמיון בין הנסים של גאולת מצרים ובין הנסים של הגאולה העתידה לבוא.

כאמור, בספרות המדרשית לא מצאנו שילוב עקיב ושוטף של כל היסודות הללו כרעיון אחיד. רק בתרגום יונתן לשמות י״ב מ״ב, ניתן לבודד גרעין של רעיון זה, אבל אין שם פירוט של הנפלאות המקבילות. וזה נוסח התרגום שם: ״ארבעה לילוון כתבין בספר דוכרניא קדם רבון עלמא: ליליא קדמאה כד איתגלי למיברי עלמא... תליתאה כד איתגלי במצרים... רביעאה כד יתגלי למפרק ית עמא בית ישראל״.[7] ואין כאן יותר.

נבדוק עתה את המרכיבים השונים של הרעיון כפי שהם מופיעים במקורות המדרשיים. נביא כמקור ראשון את דברי מדרש אבכיר, הנזכרים על ידי צונץ. וכך נמצא שם:

> [יום א]... כשם שהבדלתי בין אור לחשך, כך במצרים: ״ולכל בני ישראל היה אור״ (שמ׳ י כג).
>
> [יום ב] כשם שהבדלתי בין מים העליונים לתחתונים, אף להן אני עתיד לעשות כן, שנ[אמר]: ״והמים להם חומה מימינם״ (שם יד כב).
>
> [יום ג] בשלישי בראתי זרעים ודשאים, אף להן אני עתיד לעשות כן, ״והמן כזרע גד״ (במ׳ יא ז).

5 הפיוט ״אומץ דתותי״ מיוחס בספק לר׳ יוסף אבן אביתור, ראה ע׳ פליישר, יצירתו של יוסף אבן אביתור, עבודת דוקטור, האוניברסיטה העברית בירושלים, תשכ״ז, עמ׳ 133; הוא נדפס באוסף פיוטי ספרד בכתב יד גינצבורג, מהדורה פקסימילית בעריכת ד״ש לוינגר, ירושלים תשל״ח, עמ׳ 168-169. לפיוט ״ימי חדות מעוזכם״ לר׳ יצחק אבן גיאת ראה שירי ר׳ יצחק אבן גיאת, מהד׳ י׳ דוד, ירושלים תשמ״ח, עמ׳ 346-347. שני הפיוטים הם זולתות, וגם בזה הם נבדלים מהפיוטים של ר׳ יוסף טוב עלם ור׳ מנחם בר׳ מכיר, שהם מסוג היוצר.

6 ראה ילקוט שמעוני, א, ירושלים תשל״ג, פי״ב (בר׳ ב, רמז יז), עמ׳ 55, והערה 78 שם. ההשוואה בין בריאת העולם ובין מעשה המשכן מופיעה גם אצל ר׳ שמעיה, שחי בצרפת במאות הי״א והי״ב לערך. ראה האג (להלן, הערה 8), עמ׳ 175. על ר׳ שמעיה ראה א׳ גרוסמן, חכמי צרפת הראשונים, ירושלים תשנ״ה, עמ׳ 347 ואילך.

7 על מאמר זה ראה M. McNamara, *The Aramaic Bible: Targum Neofiti 1, Exodus*, Collegeville 1994, p. 53, n. 33. וראה R. Le Deaut, *La Nuit Pascale: Essai sur la signification de la Pâque juive à partir du Targum d'Exode XII 42 (Analecta Biblica 22)*, Roma [1963], pp. 94-100, 115-121; וראה שם פרקים ד-ה. וראה א׳ שנאן, תרגום ואגדה בו, ירושלים תשנ״ג, עמ׳ 61-62.

[יום ד] בראתי מאורות להבדיל בין יום ללילה, אף אני עתיד לעשות להם כן, "לא ימיש עמוד הענן" (שמ' יג כב).

[יום ה] בראתי עופות ודגים, אף להן "ורוח נסע מאת ה'" (במ' יא לא).

[יום ו] בראתי אדם, "ויפח באפיו" (בר' ב ז), אף להם "עץ חיים היא למחזיקים בה" (מש' ג יח).[8]

הרעיון המרכזי של המדרש מופיע כבר במדרשים קדומים, כגון במדרש הידוע המספר שבשעת בריאת העולם קבע הקב"ה בטבע את הנסים שיתרחשו בעתיד: "אמר ר' יונתן תנאין היתנה הקב"ה עם הים שיקרע לפני ישראל... אמר ר' ירמיה בן אלעזר לא עם הים בלבד התנה הקב"ה, אלא עם כל שנברא בששת ימי בראשית".[9] לפי זה, הנסים שנעשו ביציאת מצרים טמונים היו בטבע הנבראים משעת הבריאה, והם התגלו בזמן שמשה קרע את הים ועשה את שאר הנסים. וברוח זו נאמר בסדר אליהו רבה: "מיכן אמרו כל דבר שעתיד להיות בסוף [כבר] נעשה מקצתו [היום]".[10]

נושא זה העסיק כידוע את הפילוסופים של ימי הביניים, ומפורסמים הם דברי הרמב"ם בעניין זה: "ושאר הנפלאות והמופתים הושמו בטבעי הדברים אשר נעשו בו בעת העשותם תחילה, ואמרו על דרך משל שיום שני בהחלק המים הושם בטבע שיחלק ים סוף למשה". ועוד: "כי כאשר ברא ה' את המציאות הזו וטבעה כפי הטבעים הללו, שת באותם הטבעים שיתחדש בהם כל מה שנתחדש מן הנסים בזמן חדושם".[11] כראיה לדבריו מביא הרמב"ם את דברי המדרש מבראשית רבא. וכבר רב סעדיה גאון ניסח את הכלל שמן התועליות שבמעשה בראשית הוא "שנאמין במה שהוא עתיד לספר לנו על המופתים שעשה... ונאמר מי שיש לו הכח לבראם, יש לו גם הכח לחדש בהם את הדברים האלה, כגון קריעת ים סוף" וכו'.[12]

גם לרובד השני של ההיקש יש מקורות בספרות התלמודית והמדרשית, אבל עד כמה שיכולתי לקבוע אין הרצאה רצופה של המקבילות בין מה שקרה במעשה בראשית ומה שיהיה לעתיד לבוא. בספרא למשל נדרש על הפסוק "ונתנה הארץ יבולה ועץ השדה יתן פריו" (וי' כו ד): "לא כדרך שהי' עושה עכשיו, אלא כדרך שעושה בימי אדם הראשון, ומנין שהארץ עתידה להיות נזרעת ועושה פירות בן יומה, ת"ל זכר עשה לנפלאותיו (תה' קיא ד)... ומנין שהעץ עתיד להיות נטוע ועושה פירות בן יומה, ת"ל זכר עשה

8 ראה במאמרו המפורט של האג: H. J. Haag. "'Dies ist die Entstehungsgeschichte des Himmels und der Erde': Midrasch Avkir zu Gen. 2,4", *Judaica* 34 (1978), pp. 104-117, 173-179. במאמר זה האג מנתח ביסודיות את המדרש ומביא את מקבילותיו. הוא דן גם בפיוטו של ר' יוסף טוב עלם. אין הוא מזכיר את פיוטו של ר' מנחם בר' מכיר.

9 ראה בר"ר ה ד, מהד' תיאודור־אלבק עמ' 35.

10 סדר אליהו רבה, מהד' מאיר איש שלום עמ' 14.

11 פירוש המשניות לרמב"ם, אבות ה ו, ומורה הנבוכים, מהד' י' קאפח, ירושלים תשמ"ד, עמ' רלא. וראה גם בשמונה פרקים לרמב"ם, מהד' י"י גארפינקל, ניו יורק תרע"ב, עמ' 46, ובחלק האנגלי, שם עמ' 91.

12 ראה פירושי רב סעדיה גאון לבראשית, מהד' מ' צוקר, ניו יורק תשמ"ד, עמ' 223. וראה שם, עמ' 175-173 והערה 44.

לנפלאותיו" וכו'.[13] כידוע, הפסוק "זכר עשה לנפלאותיו" נהפך לכעין סִסמה טיפולוגית בתורתם של חסידי אשכנז,[14] והוא מובא בהקשר דומה גם בפיוטו של ר' יוסף טוב עלם.

לעניין זה שייך גם מאמרו המפורסם של ר' אלעזר (בבלי, חגיגה יב ע"א) שלפיו הקב"ה גנז את האור שברא ביום הראשון לצדיקים לעתיד לבוא. גם האגדה הידועה על הסעודה שהצדיקים ייהנו ממנה באחרית הימים מיוסדת על הרעיון שהקב"ה הטמין בבריאת העולם את הלווייתן ואת שור הבר, והם שמורים אצלו לארוחת הצדיקים לעתיד לבוא.[15] בספרות האסכטולוגית יש זכר לדברים נוספים השמורים מימי בראשית לצדיקים לעתיד לבוא.[16]

האנלוגיה השלישית, המדמה את הנִסים של יציאת מצרים לנסים של הגאולה האחרונה, כבר נזכרת במקרא: ביש' י"א ט"ו-ט"ז נאמר "והחרים ה' את לשון ים מצרים וכו', כאשר היתה לישראל ביום עלתו מארץ מצרים", ופסוקים אלה הובנו כנבואה על הישנות הנס של יציאת מצרים לעתיד לבוא, וכן מה שנאמר שם כ"ג ה': "כאשר שמע למצרים יחילו כשמע צור". והפסוק במיכה ז' ט"ו, מכריז על הרעיון בפירוש: "כימי צאתך מארץ מצרים אראנו נפלאות".[17]

הרעיון בא לידי ביטוי גם במדרשים. בקה"ר א' ט' (א כח) אנו קוראים: "'מה שהיה הוא שיהיה', ר' ברכיה אומר בשם ר' יצחק: כגואל ראשון כך גואל אחרון... מה גואל הראשון הוריד את המן, שנאמר 'הנני ממטיר לכם לחם מן השמים' (שמ' טז, ד), אף גואל אחרון יוריד את המן, שנאמר 'יהי פסת בר בארץ' (תה' עב טז). מה גואל ראשון העלה את הבאר, אף גואל אחרון יעלה את המים, שנאמר 'ומעין מבית ה' יצא והשקה את נחל השטים' (יואל ד יח)".[18] שורה ארוכה יותר של השוואות באה במדרש חדש לשמות:

13 ספרא, ריש פרשת בחוקותי, מהד' א"ה וייס, קי ע"ב.

14 ראה י' דן, תורת הסוד של חסידות אשכנז, ירושלים תשכ"ח, עמ' 88 ואילך.

15 ראה ח' שירמן, "הקרב בין בהמות ולויתן לפי פיוט עברי קדום", דברי האקדמיה הלאומית הישראלית למדעים, כרך שלישי, ירושלים תש"ל, עמ' 27-62. המאמר נדפס גם בספרו: לתולדות השירה והדראמה העברית, א, ירושלים תשל"ט, עמ' 66-83, בהשמטת הנספחים. וראה לאחרונה: M. Fishbane, "Rabbinic Mythmaking and Tradition: The Great Dragon Drama in Baba-Batra 74b-75a", M. Cogan et al. (eds.), *Tehilla le-Moshe: Biblical and Judaic Studies in Honor of Moshe Greenberg,* Winona Lake, Ind. 1997, pp. 273-283. המאמר נדפס כעת מחדש בספרו *The Exegetical Imagination,* Cambridge, Mass. 1998, pp. 41-55

16 ראה P. Volz, *Die Eschatologie der jüdischen Gemeinde im neutestamentichen Zeitalter,* Hildesheim 1966, pp. 114-115

17 ראה ש"א ליונשטם, מסורת יציאת מצרים בהשתלשלותה, ירושלים תשכ"ח, עמ' 16 ועמ' 103.

18 ידידי פרופסור מנחם הירשמן שלח לי בטובו את הערותיו לפסקה זו בקהלת רבא שהוא עומד להוציאו לאור במהדורה ביקורתית. הוא מביא שם את המקבילות, ומעיר על הניסוחים השונים של הרשימה וגם על דיוניהם של י' היינימן בספרו אגדות ותולדותיהן, ירושלים תשל"ד, עמ' 109 ואילך, ושל ל' גינצברג בספרו *An Unknown Jewish Sect,* New York 1976, pp. 234-235. ממדרש שמות רבה (טו כא) משמע שהפסוק בקהלת "מה שהיה הוא שיהיה" שנדרש בקה"ר הנ"ל, שימש יסוד גם לדרשה השוללת לכאורה את התחדשות הנִסים באחרית הימים: "החדש הזה לכם: הה"ד הראשונות הנה באו וחדשות אני מגיד (יש' מב ט). וכי יש לעתיד לבא חדשות? והא כתיב מה שהיה הוא שיהיה? (קה' א ט), אלא מוצאין אנו עשרה דברים עתיד הקב"ה לחדש לעתיד לבוא. הראשונה שהוא עתיד להאיר לעולם" וכו'.

"אמר ר' ירמיה כגואל ראשון כך גואל אחרון... גואל ראשון הוציא אותם למדבר כך גואל אחרון... גואל הראשון 'וה' הולך לפניהם' (שמ' יג כא), גואל אחרון 'ויעבר מלכם לפניהם' (מי' ב יג), וכשם שעשה נסים ונפלאות במצרים, כך עתיד לעשות להם באחרית הימים, שנ[אמר] 'כימי צאתך מארץ מצרים אראנו נפלאות' (שם ז טו)".[19]

כאמור, בספרות האפוקליפטית נמצאות הקבלות נוספות בין הנפלאות הראשונות והאחרונות. העניין מנוסח באופן כללי בחזון עזרא (ט, ה-ו): "כי ככל דבר אשר היה בעולם ראשיתו באחריתו ואחרית גלויה. כך גם עיתותיו של עליון: התחלותיהן נודעות במופתים ובגבורות, ואחריתן במעשים ובאותות".[20]

בספרות הפיוט אנו מוצאים גם כן רעיונות מעין אלו. י' יהלום הפנה לאחרונה תשומת לב לזיקה שבין הספרות החיצונית וספרות הפיוט.[21] אין אנו יודעים מה היו הצינורות שדרכם הגיעו רעיונות מן הספרות האפוקליפטית לפיוט הקדום, ועל אחת כמה וכמה אם היתה השפעה של ספרות זו על הפיוט האשכנזי. בכל אופן, התופעה אומרת דרשוני.

נביא כאן דוגמאות אחדות מהספרות הפיוטית שבהן יש למצוא הדים לרעיונות הנ"ל. בסדר עבודה קדום, "אז באין כול", טורים 3-4, אנו קוראים:

א <... ...> כֹּל אַתָּה חָדָשׁ לְחַדְּשׁוֹ
כִּי יְשׁוּשֶׁיךָ בְּרֵאשִׁית וּבְחוּרוֹתֶיךָ בְּאַחֲרִית[22]

טורים אלה מזכירים את מה שהובא לעיל מחזון עזרא, "כי ככל דבר אשר היה בעולם, ראשיתו באחריתו ואחרית גלויה", וכך פירושם: הדברים שיקרו בזמן מאוחר, לעתיד לבוא ("ישושיך"), כבר היו בזמן בראשית, והדברים שקרו בתחילת ההיסטוריה, בזמן מעשה בראשית ("ובחורותיך"), יקרו שוב באחרית (הימים).

במעשה היום השלישי, שם, טור 103 ואילך, מדובר על בריאת הים והיבשה, על הנסים העתידים להתחדש בקריעת ים סוף על ידי משה, ועל שאר נסים הקשורים במים שייעשו על ידי גיבורים מקראיים אחרים. גם לעתיד לבוא הקב"ה ייבש את ים מצרים ויקרעהו לשבעה נחלים (על פי יש' יא טו), ויקרה כמו שקרה בנס של יצירת מצרים:

<הַמַּיִם> לָמוֹ צִוִּיתָה אִם יָבֹא אִילֵּם [=משה]
יִתְּנוּ יְקָ<ר> <וַיַּעַמְדוּ> לִימִינוֹ
....
הִתְוִותָה עַל לְשׁוֹנוֹ לְחָתְכוֹ לְשִׁבְעָה[23]

19 J. Mann, *The Bible as Read and Preached in the Old Synagogue*, I, Cincinnati 1940, חלק עברי, עמ' ריט.

20 ספר חזון עזרא, מהד' י' ליכט, ירושלים תשכ"ח, עמ' 59.

21 ראה י' יהלום, אז באין כול – סדר העבודה הארץ־ישראלי הקדום ליום הכיפורים, ירושלים תשנ"ז, עמ' 31 ואילך. אפשר שסדר עבודה זה היה ידוע באשכנז, ראה שם, עמ' 13.

22 שם, עמ' 63. יהלום מעיר על יש' מ"ו י': "מגיד מראשית אחרית".

23 שם, עמ' 74-75, וראה בהערות שם. יהלום פירש כנראה את המילים "לשונו לחתכו לשבעה" כמוסבות על קריעת ים סוף, אבל ברור שהפייטן התכוון לעתיד לבוא, על פי הפסוק ביש' י"א ט"ו, וכפי שנדרש בפסיקתא רבתי המובא על ידי יהלום, שם.

ובדומה לזה להלן בפיוטו של ר׳ מנחם בר׳ מכיר, טור 19-20: ״וְלֶעָתִיד זוֹחֵל לְשוֹן יָם בְּהַרְעִימוֹ/ זוֹרְבוּ לְשִׁבְעָה בַּנְּעָלִים לְפַעֲמוֹ״.

גם במעשה יום הרביעי מדבר הפייטן של ״אז באין כול״ על הנסים שיתרחשו בקשר למאורות, ומזכיר את הנס שלעתיד לבוא (טור 143): ״תחדש אורם לארבעים ותשעה״;[24] ואצל ר׳ מנחם (טורים 46-48): ״וְלֶעָתִיד... חַמָּה... שִׁבְעָתַיִם״ – ומובן שזה מיוסד על יש׳ ל׳ כ״ו. וכן נזכרת בסדר העבודה הקדום סעודת לוייתן שלעתיד לבוא (שם, טור 165).[25] חשוב לציין כאן שבהרצאת האירועים של מעשה בראשית מדי יום ביומו, הפייטן רושם את הדברים שנבראו בתחילה, ומספר איך יחזרו הנסים הקדומים להתרחש בחייהם של גיבורי מקרא שונים, ואיך יארעו שוב באחרית הימים.

גם אצל יוסי בן יוסי יש זכר לרעיון זה. בסדר העבודה שלו ״אזכיר גבורות״ אנו קוראים:

11 בַּמָּרוֹם הֵכִין/ כִּסֵּא הֲדָרוֹ/ פַּרְשֵׁז עֲנָנוֹ/ וְדוֹק נָטָה לְאֹהֶל
בַּל יִצְעַן/ וּבַל יִסַּע יְתֵדוֹתָיו/ עַד בֹּא קִצּוֹ/ וְיִתְחַדֵּשׁ בְּאוֹמֶר
בֵּירַר עַל מַיִם/ עַמּוּדֵי חֶלֶד/ וְשִׁינֵּס מָתְנֶיהָ/ בְּתוֹהוּ וּבִסְעָרָה
בַּל תִּמּוֹט/ וּבַל יָמְעֲדוּ מְכוֹנֶיהָ/ עַד תִּבְלֶה כַּבֶּגֶד/ וְתוּמַר כְּמֵאָז
22 גָּדַר בַּעֲדָם/ בַּל יְכַסּוּ אֶרֶץ/ עַד נֶאֱמַן בַּיִת/ יַעֲשֵׂם גְּזָרִים
26 גְּבוּל לֹא יַשִּׂיגוּ/ וְלֶכֶת לֹא יְאַחֵרוּ/ עַד מְשָׁרֵת אֹהֶל/ יַדְמִימֵם בְּעֵמֶק
30 גָּזַר לְתוֹעֶבֶת/ עוֹף לֹא טָהוֹר/ עַד בּוֹא תִּשְׁבִּי/ וְעוֹרְבִים יְכַלְכְּלוּהוּ

ובדברו על אדם הראשון, כעין סיכום:

40 דַּעַת קִישְׁטוֹ/ וְרוּחַ חֲנָנוֹ/ לְהַשְׂכִּיל מִקֶּדֶם/ קֵץ אוֹתִיּוֹת[26]

ברור מכאן שיוסי בן יוסי ראה את מעשי בראשית כסימן ל״קץ אותיות״, לאותות ולמופתים שיתחדשו על ידי הנביאים ושאר גיבורי המקרא ובאחרית הימים.

בסילוקו המפורסם של ר׳ אלעזר בירבי קליר ״ויכון עולם״, לתשעה באב, טורים 145-146, אנו מוצאים ניסוח קצר של הרעיון:

כִּי כָל דָּבָר אֲשֶׁר מֵאָז זְמָן
הֱקִיצוֹ לְקֵץ וּזְמָן[27]

בפיוטים אשכנזיים וצרפתיים לפסח יש רמזים להשוואה דומה בין מעשה בראשית ובין יציאת מצרים מצד אחד, ובין יציאת מצרים והגאולה העתידה מצד אחר. והנה כמה דוגמאות:

24 שם, עמ׳ 78, טור 143.
25 שם, עמ׳ 80.
26 פיוטי יוסי בן יוסי[2], מהד׳ א׳ מירסקי, ירושלים תשנ״א, עמ׳ 129-134.
27 ראה שירמן (לעיל, הערה 15), עמ׳ 53.

לֵיל שִׁמּוּרִים בָּא מִבְּרֵאשִׁית...
סָכוּ לִימִין מֹשֶׁה בּוֹקֵעַ יָם/ וְהֵנִיף יָדוֹ עַל הַנָּהָר בַּעְיָם[28]

בפיוטו של יוסף ב"ר יעקב הנזכר על ידי צונץ בהקשר שלנו, מעמיד הפייטן את "פסח מצרים" מול "פסח לדורות", וגם שם יש רמז לפסוק ביש' י"א ט"ו:

פֶּסַח וְהֵנִיף יָדוֹ בְּרוּחַ בַּעְיָם/ וְהֶחֱרִים יְיָ אֶת לְשׁוֹן יָם/ פֶּסַח לֶעָתִיד

וכעין סיכום של הרעיון:

פֶּסַח יוֹסֵף עַל יְשׁוּעוֹת יְשׁוּעָה... כַּאֲשֶׁר שֵׁמַע לְמִצְרַיִם לָצוֹר נִשְׁמָעָה[29]

ובהמשך שם:

פֶּסַח חִידּוּשׁ מוֹפֵת עֲלֵי יָשָׁן... פֶּסַח לֶעָתִיד

וכן בפיוטו של יקותיאל בר יוסף שנזכר על ידי צונץ לענייננו באים אלה מול אלה הנסים של "פסח מצרים" ו"פסח לעתיד".[30]
בפיוט המתחיל "אורי וישעי על הים נגלה" לפייטן ר' מנחם ברבי יעקב איש וורמייזא שחי במאה הי"ב, נאמר:

מַפְלִיא מִקֶּדֶם נוֹרָאוֹת/ עוֹד יַרְאֵנוּ נִפְלָאוֹת...
נִדָּחִים יַדְרִיךְ בַּנְּעָלִים/ וְהִכָּה לְשִׁבְעָה נְחָלִים/ אֶת לְשׁוֹן הַיָּם
חָפְשִׁים יַדְרִיךְ שִׁירַיִם/ נִשְׁאָרִים מֵאַשּׁוּר וּמִמִּצְרַיִם/ וּמֵאִיֵּי הַיָּם
................/ ....
בְּחַצְרוֹת אֱלֹהֵינוּ יֵצְאוּ/ מַיִם חַיִּים וְיֵרָפְאוּ...
יַעֲלוּ עַל שָׂפָה/ עֲצֵי מַאֲכָל לִתְרוּפָה...
מִפְעַל נוֹרְאוֹתָיו סָפוּן מִי לְגַדְּלֵהוּ/ עוֹצֶם פְּלָאוֹתָיו אֲשֶׁר הִפְלִיא לְמַעֲנֵהוּ[31]

28 מחזור לפסח לפי מנהג בני אשכנז, מהד' י' פרנקל, ירושלים תשנ"ג, עמ' 25, ט' 3, ועמ' 31, ט' 8. הפיוט הוא לר' מאיר ב"ר יצחק ש"ץ. הרעיון שליל שימורים הוא לילה של נסים לכל הדורות נמצא בהרבה פיוטים. ראה למשל מחזור פיוטי יניי, מהד' צ"מ רבינוביץ, א, ירושלים תשמ"ה, עמ' 300. "לילה אשר בו נפדו ראשונים/ שמורים נמת יהי לאחרונים/ ומה שהיה בראשונה הוא שיהיה באחרונה/ כשמע מצרים תשמיע לצורים". כאן רציתי להפנות תשומת לב רק למקומות אחדים שבהם מופיע הרעיון בפיוט האשכנזי והצרפתי. י"י יובל, במאמרו "הנקם והקללה, הדם והעלילה", ציון נח (תשנ"ג), עמ' 38, מביא מפיוטו הנ"ל של יניי את המילים "מה שהיה" וכו' עם עוד כמה טורים כדי להוכיח שבפיוט "הארץ־ישראלי הקלאסי... עומדים הנקמה וחשבון הדמים עם אדום במרכז התיאור האסכטולוגי". התיאור האסכטולוגי שבו עסקנו במאמר זה, הן בפיוט הקלסי והן בפיוט האשכנזי־הצרפתי, שונה תכלית השוני ממה שמציע יובל. יש להעיר בהקשר זה גם על מה שנאמר בסילוק שכמה טורים ממנו מובאים בגוף המאמר (להלן, הערה 35), עמ' 604: "ועומד זרובבל ואומר לומר קדיש וכל באי עולם אחריו עונים/ ואף פושעי ישראל וצדיקי אומות העולם שבתוך גיהנם אמן נותנים/ ועת שהרשעים עונים יתגלגלו עליהם רחמי שוכן מעונים... ושבים כולם בתשובה ויתקבלו פני שכינה כחסידים הגונים". בוודאי שאין כאן תיאור של נקמה וחשבון דמים.

29 שם, עמ' 360, ט' 6, 8; עמ' 362, ט' 5.

30 שם, עמ' 373-375.

31 שם, עמ' 347 ואילך; ראה שם, עמ' 351, ט' 23-25, 27, 29; עמ' 352, ט' 7.

בשורות אלה בא זכר לנסים שייעשו לעתיד לבוא, וגם רמז לשיטה שאנו מכירים מתורתם של חסידי אשכנז, המלמדת שהנפלאות ("זכר עשה לנפלאותיו") סתומות וספונות, והן יתגלו באחרית הימים.[32]

מסר אסכטולוגי המיוסד על פסוקי המקרא ועל חזיונות אפוקליפטיים יוצא גם מפיוטו של ר' יוסף ב"ר יחיאל מפריס "יוסיף שנית":

יוֹסִיף יְיָ שֵׁנִית יֵשַׁע יְמִינוֹ בִּגְבוּרוֹת
בִּזְרוֹעוֹ יְקַבֵּץ טְלָאָיו הַחוֹנִים בַּגְּדֵרוֹת
וְהֶחֱרִים לְשׁוֹן יָם וְנָהָר וְהִכָּהוּ לְשֶׁבַע מַעְבָּרוֹת[33]

וכן נזכר "העתיד" בקדושתא לר' יוסף טוב עלם לשביעי של פסח: "וּבוֹ לְעָתִיד יְקַלְּסוּךְ", "לֶעָתִיד לָבוֹא יְחַדֵּשׁ/ שִׁיר מְפוֹאָר וּמְקֻדָּשׁ"; וכן: "כְּהֶרְאִיתַנִי נִסִּים... כֵּן תַּפְלִיא לַעֲמוּסִים".[34]

במיוחד מעניין מה שנמצא בסילוק אנונימי לשביעי של פסח:

וּכְמוֹ שֶׁהֶרְאָה אוֹתוֹת וּמוֹפְתִים וּמַפְלִיא חֲסָדָיו לָרִאשׁוֹנִים
כֵּן עָתִיד עֲשׂוֹת גְּדוֹלוֹת וְנוֹרָאוֹת לָאַחֲרוֹנִים
וּכְמוֹ שֶׁהִכָּה בְּהַכֵּה וּפָצוֹעַ וְכָל מַכָּה אֲנוּשָׁה צוֹעֲנִים
כֵּן עָתִד לְחַבֵּל וּלְהַכְחִיד כָּל שׁוֹטְמִים וְשׁוֹטְנִים
וְאָז יְרוֹמֵם אַדִּיר קֶרֶן עַם שׁוֹמְרֵי אֱמוּנִים
וִיחַדֵּשׁ אֶרֶץ חֲדָשָׁה וְשָׁמַיִם חֲדָשִׁים...
וְשִׁשָּׁה דְבָרִים יַחְזְרוּ לִמְקוֹמָן...
וְיִתְכַּנְּסוּ כָּל הַגָּלֻיּוֹת לֶכֶת לְגַן עֵדֶן לִשְׁתּוֹת מַמְתַּקִּים וְלֶאֱכוֹל מַשְׁמַנִּים
וְלִוְיָתָן וְזִיז שָׂדַי לִפְנֵי קְדוֹשִׁים מְזֻמָּנִים
וְזִיוֵיהֶם מַבְהִיקִים מִסּוֹף הָעוֹלָם וְעַד סוֹפוֹ[35]

גם כאן אנו רואים חזון אסכטולוגי המקשר את הנפלאות הקדומות אל הנפלאות העתידות לבוא, וגם כאן יש זכר לרסטורציה של דברים לעיקרם שבששת ימי בראשית. דברים שהיו טמונים מאז יתגלו לעתיד לבוא.

המלומד הנוצרי נ"א דאהל מיין את ההתבטאויות על היחס שבין "דברים ראשונים" ו"דברים אחרונים" במאמרו על הטיפולוגיה בתאולוגיה הנוצרית המקשרת את הבריאה

32 דן (לעיל, הערה 14), שם. ואולי מה שנאמר בתחילת "אאמיר מסתתר" לר' יוסף טוב עלם אינו רק מקרה, ויש לו הד בתורת חסידי אשכנז במושג ה"אל המסתתר", ראה דן, שם, עמ' 84 ואילך. לפי דן פירוש הביטוי "האל הנסתר מחושיו של אדם... אך פעולתו ונוכחותו ניכרים בעולם. בראש וראשונה בפעולת הבריאה ולאחר מכן גם בפעולות אחרות".

33 מחזור לפסח (לעיל, הערה 28), עמ' 408, ט' 1-3.

34 שם, עמ' 553, ט' 5; עמ' 557, ט' 12, ובראש הפיוט המתחיל "אדיר בעוברו".

35 שם, עמ' 603, ט' 37-43; 604, ט' 62; 601, ט' 65, 69, 171.

עם ישו ועם הכנסייה. בטיפולוגיה זו יש להבחין בין יסודות שונים, והם, בין השאר, הקבלה, ניגוד, עליונות הבריאה החדשה בזמן הישועה הבאה, השתנות, דמיון גמור, הטמנת דברים ראשונים עד אחרית הימים, הכללת הדברים העתידים לבוא בדברים שנבראו ופרה־אקזיסטנציה.[36] הדים לקטגוריות אלה נמצאים גם במדרשים וגם בפיוטים הנזכרים, וכמובן במקורות רבים נוספים שלא הוזכרו במאמר זה.

ואם יש מן הפליאה בעובדה שרק בשני פיוטים, של ר׳ יוסף טוב עלם ושל ר׳ מנחם בר׳ מכיר, יש הקבלה רצופה של הנסים של שלוש התקופות, יש גם להעיר שבכלל אין הרבה פיוטים בספרותנו שבמרכזם עומד רעיון אחרית הימים. בפיוטים המעטים שתוכנם מופנה לאחרית הימים אנו מוצאים הדים לחזון המשיחי האפוקליפטי והאכסטולוגי המתבטא במדרשי הגאולה המפורסמים.[37] בשני הפיוטים שלנו אין זכר לשני המשיחים או לקרבות עזים או לנקמה בגויים שיבשרו את אחרית הימים. התמונה המצטיירת פשוטה: העולם יחזור למצבו האידאלי שבו היה בשעת בריאתו. נפלאות הטבע הגדולות של מעשה בראשית ושל יציאת מצרים תתגלינה שוב באחרית הימים, והכול ייעשה על ידי הקב״ה בעצמו, בלי השתתפות דמויות של גיבורים נוספים.

יש להעיר בקשר זה גם על ניסוחו הקולע של עמוס פונקנשטיין המנוח: ״הפרשנות הטיפולוגית־הסמלית של המקראות ושל ההיסטוריה היתה עשירה ומגוונת בתחומיה של הנצרות, ועניה בתחומנו. ביצירה הנוצרית של ימי־הביניים, ואין צריך לומר באמנות הכנסייתית – היא תופסת מקום דומינאנטי; במקורותינו היא שולית וחיוורת״.[38] נדמה לי שחיפוש שיטתי אחרי מוטיבים טיפולוגיים בספרות היהודית של ימי הביניים עשוי לגלות מקורות נוספים, העשויים לשנות את התמונה שצייר פונקנשטיין. פונקנשטיין עסק בטיפולוגיה אצל הרמב״ן, שלפי דבריו יש לה מקבילות אצל הנוצרים. אך אפשר שיש היסטוריה ארוכה ופעילה יותר לרעיונות טיפולוגיים כאלה בספרות שלנו. מוטיבים מסוג זה אפשר שהיו תגובה לאתגרים מצד הטיפולוגיה הנוצרית אשר במרכזה עמדה דמותו של ישו הנוצרי כהתגלמות של מופתים קדומים, כולל אלה שבבריאת העולם.[39] ייתכן שגם פיוטיהם של שני המחברים הקדומים, ר׳ יוסף טוב עלם הצרפתי ור׳ מנחם בר׳ מכיר

36 ראה N. A. Dahl, "Christ, Creation and the Church", W. D. Davies and D. Daube (eds.), *The Background of the New Testament: In Honour of Charles Harold Dodd,* Cambridge 1956, pp. 422-443. וראה גם: D. S. Russell, *The Method and Message of Jewish Apocalyptic,* Philadelphia 1964, pp. 280-284. דאהל דן במאמרו, לפי מקורות נוצריים, בהתאמה שבין ה״דברים הראשונים״ וה״דברים האחרונים״, ובתפקידו של ישו בבריאת העולם ובגאולה.

37 ראה ע׳ פליישר, ״הדותה — הדותהו — חדותא — פולמוס ושברו״, תרביץ נג (תשמ״ד), עמ׳ 84 ואילך.

38 ראה ע׳ פונקנשטיין, ״פרשנותו הטיפולוגית של הרמב״ן״, ציון מה (1980), עמ׳ 35-59. וראה גם הערתו בספרו האנגלי: *Perceptions of Jewish History,* Berkeley 1993, p. 55, n. 12. אבל ראה מאמרו של פישביין הנזכר בהערה 15 לעיל, ששם הוא דן בטיפולוגיה של הדברים הראשונים והדברים האחרונים המתבטאת במסורות על התנינים, כמסופר בבבלי, בבא בתרא עד ע״ב-עה ע״א; "The Temporal sequence of the pericope thus has a mythic span from Urzeit to Endzeit, where First things correspond to Last things" (ראה שם, עמ׳ 276).

39 ראה למשל במאמרו של דאהל (לעיל, הערה 36).

האשכנזי, שניהם מהמאה הי״א,[40] חוברו כמענה לאיזו תאוריה נוצרית שנתפסה כאיום על היהודים. השערות אלה תישארנה בגדר השערות לעת עתה, ומי יודע אם נזכה לגילוי הקשרים הסמוים שהיו קיימים אולי בין ספרויות ודתות ותקופות כה רחוקות אלו מאלו.

קיצורו של דבר, במקרא, במדרש, בספרים החיצוניים, בנצרות, במחשבת ישראל, בפיוט ובספרות של חסידי אשכנז, שכיח המוטיב הטיפולוגי של "מה שהיה הוא שיהיה" בצורות שונות.

ועתה נביא את פיוטו של ר׳ מנחם בר׳ מכיר, המתפרסם כאן לראשונה.[41] מולו יועמד פיוטו הדומה (וגם השונה) של ר׳ יוסף טוב עלם לשם השוואה.[42]

ר׳ מנחם בר׳ מכיר (על פי כ״י בהמ״ל 8972, דף 20ב)	ר׳ יוסף בר שמואל טוב עלם (על פי סדר עבודת ישראל, עמ׳ 706)
אוֹרִי וְיִשְׁעִי אָגִילָה בִּישׁוּעָתוֹ	אֲאַמִיר מִסְתַּתֵּר בִּמְעוֹן חֶבְיוֹן
אֱמוּנָתוֹ וְחַסְדּוֹ זָכַר שְׁבוּעָתוֹ	אֶעֶרְכָה פְּלָאוֹתָיו זוֹ לְזוֹ בְהִגָּיוֹן
הַכֹּל עָשָׂה יָפֶה בְעִיתּוֹ (קה׳ ג יא)	אֲזַמְּרָה שֵׁם יְיָ עֶלְיוֹן (תה׳ ז יח)
בִּשְׁלוֹחַ לְתַנִּין מַלְאָכָיו וְסַרְסוּרָיו	בְּאוֹר פְּלָאָיו אַטִּיף בְּמַעַן
בְּעַד לְפַתֵּחַ בֵּיתָה אֲסִירָיו	בַּעֲשׂוֹתוֹ נוֹרָאוֹת לְרְוּוֵי לַעַן
כִּי הָיוּ בְצוֹעַן שָׂרָיו (יש׳ ל ד)	בְּאֶרֶץ מִצְרַיִם שְׂדֵה צֹעַן (תה׳ עח יב)
וְלֶעָתִיד/ גּוֹאֵל יִשְׁלַח מַלְאָכוֹ וְנִחְיֶה	גֵּאֶה הֶרְאָה נוֹרְאוֹתָיו
גּוֹלֶה וּמְפַנֶּה דֶּרֶךְ אֶהְיֶה	וְלֶעָתִיד כֵּן יַרְאֶה מִפְּעָלוֹתָיו
מַה שֶּׁהָיָה הוּא שֶׁיִּהְיֶה (קה׳ א ט)	זֵכֶר עָשָׂה לְנִפְלְאוֹתָיו (תה׳ קיא ד)

1 **אורי וישעי** – תה׳ כז א. כינוי לקב״ה. הצירוף שכיח בפתיחות של פיוטים אשכנזיים. **אגילה בישועתו** – על פי תה׳ ט טו. 2 **אמונתו וחסדו זכר** – על פי תה׳ צח ג. 3 **הכל וכו׳** – הפסוק נדרש על מעשה בראשית בבר״ר ט ב, עמ׳ 68. 4 **לתנין** – אל פרעה; על פי יח׳ כט ג, והוא כינוי שכיח בפיוט לפרעה. **מלאכיו וסרסוריו** – את משה ואהרן. הכינויים שכיחים בפיוטים. **בשלח... מלאכיו** – ראה מל׳ ג כג, ולהלן ט׳ 7. 5 **בעד** – בעבור. **לפתח וכו׳** – על פי יש׳ יד יז. 8 **גולה** – מקביל למפנה, מגלה את הדרך. **ומפנה דרך** – מלאכי שם. 9 **מה שהיה וכו׳** – נדרש בקה״ר א ט: "כגואל ראשון כך גואל אחרון" וכו׳. וראה

40 ראה גרוסמן (לעיל, הערה 1), שם, ובספרו על חכמי צרפת הראשונים (לעיל, הערה 6), עמ׳ 46 ואילך.

41 דוידסון, א, 2020. הפיוט בנוי בסטרופות משולשות, כשהטור השלישי הוא פסוק מהמקרא. ארבע מילים לטור. כל סטרופה שלישית מתחילה במילת קבע: "ולעתיד". אחרי שלוש הסטרופות הראשונות ובסוף הפיוט באות סטרופות "קדוש". סימן: א״ב כפול (מלבד האות תי״ו הבאה שמונה פעמים); מנחם ברבי מכיר חזק (יוצא מהטורים 67-77). ראה על הסימן בהערות לפיוט, טור 71.

42 דוידסון, א, 21. עשוי סטרופות תלת־טוריות, כרגיל ביוצרות, ראה ע׳ פליישר, היוצרות בהתהוותם והתפתחותם, ירושלים תשמ״ד, עמ׳ 199 ואילך, ועמ׳ 629.

מנחם בר׳ מכיר

דִּבְרֵי מוֹפְתֵי רָם וְנִשָּׂא
דִּימָּם כְּאֶחָד בִּפְלָאוֹת לְנוֹסְסָה
זֶה לְעֻמַּת זֶה עָשָׂה (קה׳ ז יד) קדוש

הֵן בָּרִאשׁוֹן בָּרָא כְּאַחַת
הַשָּׁמַיִם לְכִסְאוֹ וַהֲדוֹם הָנּחַת
בֵּין הַמַּיִם אֲשֶׁר מִתַּחַת (בר׳ א ז)

וָותִיקָיו כְּהוֹלִיךְ בִּזְרוֹעָה הַקְּדוֹשָׁה
וְהֵכִין בְּמַיִם אֶרֶץ חֲדָשָׁה
וּבְנֵי יִשְׂרָאֵל הָלְכוּ בַיַּבָּשָׁה (שמ׳ יד כט)

וְלֶעָתִיד/ זוֹחֵל לְשׁוֹן יָם בְּהַרְעִימוֹ
זוֹרְבוֹ לְשִׁבְעָה בַּנְּעָלִים לְפַעֲמוֹ
וְהָיְתָה מְסִילָּה לִשְׁאָר עַמּוֹ (יש׳ יא טז)

חִילֵּק בִּשְׁנֵי זֵידוֹנִים וְהִבְקִיעַ
חֶצְיָים נָשָׂא וְהַחֵצִי הִשְׁקִיעַ
וַיַּעַשׂ אֱלֹהִים אֶת הָרָקִיעַ (בר׳ א ז)

יוסף טוב עלם

יָזַם וְהֶרְאָה גְּבוּרוֹת מָעֻזּוֹ
סִדֵּר פְּלָאָיו זוֹ לְעֻמַּת זוֹ
בִּימִינוֹ וּבִזְרוֹעַ עֻזּוֹ (יש׳ סב ח) קדוש

דִּלָּה בָּרִאשׁוֹן זְרוֹעַ מַחְצֶבֶת
נְטוֹת יְרִיעוֹתָיו כְּעָלָה בְמַחֲשֶׁבֶת
וַיִּמְתָּחֵם כָּאֹהֶל לָשָׁבֶת (יש׳ מ כב)

הַדּוֹרִים בְּצֵאתָם מֵעַם מְסַכְסֵךְ
מַחֲסֶה מֵעֲלֵיהֶם לֹא נֶחְשָׁךְ
פָּרַשׂ עָנָן לְמָסָךְ (תה׳ קה לט)

וְלֶעָתִיד/ בְּהִשָּׁמַע קוֹל הַתּוֹר
קְנוֹת פְּזוּרָיו מִפְּלֶשֶׁת וְכַפְתּוֹר
בְּסֻכָּה יְסוֹכְכֵם לְמַחֲסֶה וּלְמִסְתּוֹר (יש׳ ד ו)

זָךְ בִּשְׁנֵי חָצָה מְצוּלוֹתָיו
חֶצְיָם בִּתְהוֹם וְחֶצְיָם בְּמַעֲלוֹתָיו
הַמְקָרֶה בַמַּיִם עֲלִיּוֹתָיו (תה׳ קד ג)

לעיל, בגוף המאמר. 10 **דברי מופתי וכו׳** – המופתים של הקב״ה שהוא רם ונשא. 11 **דימם** – השווה ביניהם. **בפלאות לנוססה** – לרומם את ישראל בנסים. ללשון השווה תה׳ ס ו. 13 **כאחת** – השווה תנחומא בובר, בראשית יט: ״כך ברא הקב״ה השמים והארץ... ללמדך ששניהם שקולין כאחת״. 14 **השמים לכסאו** – יש׳ סו א; והשווה בר״ר א יד, עמ׳ 13: ״בית שמיי אומ׳ השמים נבראו תחילה... דכת׳ השמים כסאי והארץ הדום רגלי״ וגו׳. **והדום** – ואת הארץ. **הנחת** – השפל, והוא יורד לטור הבא. ואולי יש לנקד ״הַנַּחַת״, כלומר הארץ שהיא מקום המקדש (השווה יש׳ סו א). 16 **ותיקיו** – את ישראל. **בזרועה** – צ״ל בזרוע או בזרועו. 17 **ארץ חדשה** – יבשת. הצירוף על פי יש׳ סה יז. וראה פסיקתא רבתי, קצג ע״ב: ״מה שהיה כבר הוא, ואשר להיות כבר היה (קה׳ ג טו) אמר הקב״ה עתיד אני ליבש את הים הגדול לפני גליות. מנין, שכן כתוב והחרים ה׳ את לשון ים מצרים וגו׳ (יש׳ שם)... ולא כבר עשיתי כן בעולם הזה כשיצאו ישראל ממצרים״ וכו׳. וראה קה״ר ג טו: ״אם יאמר לך אדם אפשר שהקב״ה עתיד לעשות ים יבשה אמור לו כבר היה, לא כך עשה על ידי משה, שנאמר ובני ישראל הלכו ביבשה״ וכו׳. וראה בגוף המאמר ובהערה 17. 19 **זוחל** – מפחד, מלשון ״זחלתי ואירא״ (איוב לב ו), וראה תה׳ קיד ג. **לשון ים** – ראה יש׳ יא טו. **בהרעימו** – השווה תה׳ כט ג. 20 **זורבו** – ראה איוב ו ז; ופירושו: יתייבשו. **לשבעה** – ראה יש׳ יא טו הנ״ל. **בנעלים** – על פי יש׳ שם, ״והדריך בנעלים״. לצירוף ״בנעלים לפעמו״ השווה שה״ש ז ב. 22 **חילק בשני וכו׳** – ראה בר״ר ד ד, עמ׳ 28: ״נטל הקב״ה כל מי בראשית ונתן חציים ברקיע וחציים באוקינוס״. **זידונים** – מים, על פי תה׳ קכד ה; והשווה בר״ר ד ז, עמ׳ 30. וכך הוא בתיאור מעשי יום שני בכמה סדרי עבודה קדומים. וכאן מדמה הפייטן את הרקיע המגן על העולם מהמים הזידונים אל ענני הכבוד שהגנו על ישראל ביציאת מצרים ואל הענן שיגן על ציון לעתיד לבוא. וכך הוא בפסיקתא חדתא:

מנחם בר׳ מכיר

טְנוּפִים כְּנִיעֵר נָחֵנִי שַׁאֲנָן
טִילְלַנִי עֲנָנֵי כָבוֹד לְהִתְגּוֹנָן
לֹא יָמִישׁ עַמּוּד הֶעָנָן (שמ׳ יג כב)

וְלֶעָתִיד/ יוֹמָם עָנָן וְעָשָׁן כִּבְחוֹרֵב
יְקַר חוּפָּתוֹ וְסוּכָּתוֹ הֵירֶב
מַחְסֶה מִזֶּרֶם וְצֵל מֵחוֹרֶב (יש׳ כה ד)

כִּילֵּל בַּשְּׁלִישִׁי אֲדָמָה לְהִזָּרַע
כִּלְכּוּל דָּגָן חִיטָּה לְהִשְׂתָּרַע
דֶּשֶׁא עֵשֶׂב מַזְרִיעַ זֶרַע (בר׳ א יא)

לְדַלְתֵי שְׁחָקִים פָּתַח לְעַמּוֹ
לֶחֶם אַבִּירִים הִמְטִיר בְּאָהֳלֵימוֹ
וּדְגַן שָׁמַיִם נָתַן לָמוֹ (תה׳ עח כד)

וְלֶעָתִיד/ מֵחֵלֶב כִּלְיוֹת חִיטָּה בְּמֶרֶץ
מַרְעִישׁ כַּלְּבָנוֹן פִּרְיוֹ בְתֶרֶץ
יְהִי פִיסַּת בַּר בָּאָרֶץ (תה׳ עב טז)

נִיהֵר בָּרְבִיעִי מְאוֹרוֹת בְּחַכְמָה
נֶשֶׁף יָרֵחַ וְחַמָּה בְהַשְׁכָּמָה
עוֹשֶׂה עָשׁ כְּסִיל וְכִימָה (איוב ט ט)

יוסף טוב עלם

חֲמִשִּׁים בַּעֲלוֹתָם בְּיוֹם קְרָב
בָּקַע יָם וַיַּעֲבִירֵם בְּעֻזּוֹ חָרָב
וַיִּגְעַר בְּיַם סוּף וַיֶּחֱרָב (תה׳ קו ט)

וְלֶעָתִיד/ טְרוּפִים בִּהְיוֹתָם פְּדוּיִים
בֶּאֱסוֹף נִדָּחֵימוֹ מִכֹּל אִיִּים
בַּיּוֹם הַהוּא יֵצְאוּ מַיִם חַיִּים (זכר׳ יד ח)

יָהּ בַּשְּׁלִישִׁי הִטְרִיחַ בְּרִי
הִדְשִׁיא דְשָׁאִים וְהִפְרִיא
עֵץ פְּרִי עֹשֶׂה פְּרִי (בר׳ א יא)

כְּמֵהִים בְּבוֹא עִתָּם עֵת דּוֹדִים
הֵצִיץ לְבוֹנָה וּפְרִי מְגָדִים
כְּפָרִים עִם נְרָדִים (שה״ש ד יג)

וְלֶעָתִיד/ לְהִגָּאֵל כֹּל יוּכַל
בְּצֵאת נַחַל מִמִּפְתַּן הֵיכָל
יַעֲלֶה עַל שְׂפָתוֹ מִזֶּה וּמִזֶּה כָּל עֵץ
מַאֲכָל (יח׳ מז יב)

מָרוֹם בָּרְבִיעִי הִזְרִיחַ מוֹשְׁלִים
לְאוֹר יוֹם וְלַיְלָה בְּרוּם זְבוּלִים
אֶת שְׁנֵי הַמְּאֹרֹת הַגְּדוֹלִים (בר׳ א טז)

"ביום ב׳ ברא רקיע, אף כאן פרש עליהם ענני הכבוד". ראה על זה בגוף המאמר. 25 **טנופים** – מצריים. **כניער** – על פי שמ׳ יד כז. **נחני שאנן** – השווה תה׳ עח נג: "וינחם לבטח... ואת אויביהם כסה הים". 26 **טיללני ענני כבוד** – הקב"ה היה מסכך בעדי בענני כבוד השווה תה׳ קה לט: "פרש ענן למסך". **טיללני** – הצל עלי. על פי נח׳ ג טו. **להתגונן** – להגן עליי. השווה שמ׳ יד יט. 28 **כבחורב** – כביום מתן תורה. **הרב** – הרבה; ושב אל "יקר". **יומם ענן וכו׳** – על פי יש׳ ד ה-ו. 30 **וצל מחורב** – בפסוק: צל מחרב. 31 **כילל** – עיטר. 32 **כלכול וכו׳** – להרבות מחיה ומזון לבריות. 34 **לדלתי וכו׳** – השווה תה׳ עח כג-כה. 37 **מחלב וכו׳** – דב׳ לב יד. 38 **מרעיש וכו׳** – על פי תה׳ עב טז. **בתרץ** – ברצון, ברחמים. 40 **ניהר** – הזריח. 41 **נשף** – בערב. 42 **בהשכמה** – בבוקר.

מנחם בר׳ מכיר	יוסף טוב עלם
סְגֻולָּיו בְּעַמּוּד אֵשׁ מְשַׁכֵּן סַךְ עַמּוּד שֵׁינִי שִׁיכֵּן אֶת מָסַךְ הַפֶּתַח לַמִּשְׁכָּן (שמ׳ מ ה)	נָאוֹר דְּמוּתָם לְעַם זוּ הִתְאִיר וַיַּנְחֵם יוֹמָם בְּעָנָן מַבְעִיר וְלַיְלָה בְּעַמּוּד אֵשׁ לְהָאִיר (שמ׳ יג כא)
וְלֶעָתִיד/ עֵיפַת לְבָנָה כַּחַמָּה בְסִיּוּמִים עֵין חַמָּה בִגְבוּרָה בְקִיּוּמִים שִׁבְעָתַיִם כְּאוֹר שִׁבְעַת הַיָּמִים (יש׳ ל כו)	וְלֶעָתִיד/ סְגֻלִּים בְּהִגָּאֵל כִּימֵי עוֹלָם קוּמִי אוֹרִי יַשְׁמִיעֵם גּוֹאֲלָם וְהָיָה לָךְ יְיָ לְאוֹר עוֹלָם (יש׳ ס יט)
פָּקַד בַּחֲמִישִׁי תַּנִּינֵי מַשְׁמַנֵּהוּ פּוֹרְשֵׁי יַמִּים יִרְקַק מֶנְהוּ כֹּל עוֹף כָּנָף לְמִינֵהוּ (בר׳ א כא)	עֶלְיוֹן בַּחֲמִישִׁי הִשְׁרִיץ בְּמֶרֶץ דְּגַת הַיָּם מַשְׁרִיצֵי שֶׁרֶץ וְעוֹף יְעוֹפֵף עַל הָאָרֶץ (בר׳ יא לא)
צוּר צְבָאָיו הוּגַז וְהוּנַף צִפּוֹר שְׂלָיו מִיָּם הֻכְנַף וּכְחוֹל עוֹף כָּנָף (תה׳ עח כז)	פְּדוּיִים עֵת הִתְאַוּוּ בְּמַאֲוַיִּם וַיִּתֵּן שֶׁאֱלָתָם אֵל חַי וְקַיָּם וַיָּגָז שַׂלְוִים מִן הַיָּם (במ׳ יא לא)
וְלֶעָתִיד/ קְהַל חֲבֵירִים לֶאֱסוֹף יַצְרִיחַ קְרוּאִים לְזִיז שָׂדַי וּלְהַאֲרִיחַ עַל לִוְיָתָן נָחָשׁ בָּרִיחַ (יש׳ כז א)	וְלֶעָתִיד/ צֵאת הַנַּחַל יִפְרוֹץ בִּדְגַת הַיָּם יִפְרוֹץ בְּמֵרוֹץ וְהָיָה כָל נֶפֶשׁ חַיָּה אֲשֶׁר יִשְׁרֹץ (יח׳ מז ט)
רָחַשׁ בַּשִּׁישִׁי לְגוֹלֶם הַמְּוּקְדָּם רָבוּץ בִּמְסִיבַּת אוֹדֶם וּמְאוּדָּם זֶה סֵפֶר תּוֹלְדוֹת אָדָם (בר׳ ה א)	קָדוֹשׁ בַּשִּׁשִּׁי הִשְׁלִים בְּתֶרֶץ וַיֹּאמֶר אֱלֹהִים תּוֹצֵא הָאָרֶץ בְּהֵמָה וָרֶמֶשׂ וְחַיְתוֹ אֶרֶץ (בר׳ א כד)

43 **סגוליו** – ישראל; וכך גם בפיוטו של ר׳ יוסף טוב עלם, טור 46: ״סגולים״. **בעמוד וכו׳** – שמ׳ יג, כא. 44 **סך** – סיכוך. **עמוד שיני** – של עמוד נוסף, והוא עמוד הענן, שכיסה את המשכן; השווה שמ׳ מ לד. 45 **שיכן** – השכין. 46 **עיפת לבנה** – חשכת הירח (עמוס ד יג). **כחמה** – כשמש תהיה; על פי יש׳ ל כו. **בסיומים** – על פי רצון ה׳, כהבטחתו. 47 **עין וכו׳** – ומראה השמש. הלשון על פי שופ׳ ה לא. **בקיומים** – כפי שהובטח בנבואה. ההקבלה בין המאורות שבמעשה בראשית ובין עמוד הענן (ועמוד האש) באה במדרש אבכיר; ההקבלה בין מעשה בראשית ובין אחרית הימים מצויה כבר בפסוק המובא כאן; וראה גם בגוף המאמר. 49 **פקד** – יצר. **תניני משמניהו** – את תניניו הגדולים. 50 **פורשי ימים** – דגים. **ירקק** – יברא. על פי חולין כז ע״ב ״(העופות) מן הרקק נבראו״. הטור יורד אל סוף המחרוזת. 52 **הוגז** – על פי במ׳ יא לא: ״ויגז שלוים מן הים״. **הונף** – על פי שמ׳ כט כז. 53 **הוכנף** – הועף, כדרך הפייטנים. ראה צונץ: *Die synagogale Poesie des Mittelalters*[2], Frankfurt a.M. 1920, p. 423. 55 **קהל חבירים** – את הצדיקים. הצירוף מצוי בפיוטים, ראה שירמן (לעיל, הערה 15), עמ׳ 56-57. **יצריח** – יזעק, יזמן. 56 **לזיז שדי** – תה׳ נ יא. **ולהאריח** – לארוחת הזיז והלויתן. 58 **רחש** – אמר. **לגולם המוקדם** – לאדם הראשון; השווה תה׳ קלט טז. 59 **רבוץ וכו׳** – שהושם בגן עדן שהיה מעוטר באבנים יקרות. ראה יח׳

מנחם בר׳ מכיר

שִׁבְטֵי אָדָם הַגָּדוֹל וַאֲדָנַיי
שׁוֹכְנָם בְּסִינַי עֲדוּיִים בַּעֲדָנַי
פָּנִים בְּפָנִים דִּיבֶּר יְיָ
(דב׳ ה ד)

וְלֶעָתִיד/ תּוֹרָה בִּבְרִית חֲדָשָׁה יְצַוֵּנוּ
תִּפְאַרְתּוֹ בְּמָחוֹל עַיִן בְּהַחֲוֵינוּ
הִנֵּה אֱלֹהֵינוּ זֶה קִוִּינוּ (יש׳ כה ט)

תָּם נוֹי מִפְעָלוֹ כְּהִילְכָתוֹ
תְּחוּם שְׁבִיעִי בִּקְדוּשָּׁתוֹ
בּוֹ שָׁבַת מִכָּל מְלַאכְתּוֹ (בר׳ ב ג)

תְּבוּנָתוֹ בְּמָרָה וּבְסִין הִשְׁמִיעִי
תַּרְבִּיץ אָב לַעֲנוּגֵי וּלְהַשְׂבִּיעִי
וַיִּשְׁבְּתוּ הָעָם בַּיּוֹם הַשְּׁבִיעִי
(שמ׳ טז ל)

יוסף טוב עלם

רִקֵּם יְצִיר בְּעֹז נְאָמוֹ
וְהִבְדִּילוֹ מִכָּל בְּרוּאֵי עוֹלָמוֹ
וַיִּבְרָא אֱלֹהִים אֶת הָאָדָם בְּצַלְמוֹ
(בר׳ א׳ כז)

שַׁדַּי כֵּן מִשִּׁבְעִים עֲמָמִים
חָשַׁק וְהִבְדִּיל מְעַטֵּי עַמִּים
כֵּנָם וָאַבְדִּיל אֶתְכֶם מִן הָעַמִּים (וי׳ כ כו)

תַּקִּיף כְּחָשׁ תְּנוּפַת יְמָנִית
קְנוֹת פְּזוּרָיו מִמַּאֲרִיכֵי מַעֲנִית
כֵּן יוֹסִיף יְיָ יָדוֹ שֵׁנִית (יש׳ יא יא)

תְּמִימֵי לֵב הַמְּיַחֲלִים לְגָדְלוֹ
בְּרִנָּה יְנַהֲלֵם לִמְעוֹן הֵיכָלוֹ
שָׁם יַעַבְדוּהוּ כָּל בֵּית יִשְׂרָאֵל כֻּלֹּה
(יח כ מ)

כח יג, ומה שנדרש עליו בבר״ר יח א, עמ׳ 161-162. 61-63 **שבטי וכו׳** — ישראל. **אדם הגדול** — אברהם, ראה יהושע יד טו, ומה שנדרש בבר״ר יד ו, עמ׳ 130: ״אדם [גדול] זה אברהם. **ואדניי** — השלמת הכינוי: [ושל שאר] האבות הצדיקים. ראה מנחם בר׳ מכיר השתמש בכינוי זה גם בפיוט ״אמון נוא הובא״ (ראה ערוגת הבשם, ח״ג, עמ׳ 143: ״שבטים קורא אדנים, כי הם עיקר, כמו אדני הבית״), ראה במאמרי ״פיוט אשכנזי חדש על פדיון הכלה השבויה ממצרים״, עטרה לחיים, ספר היובל לח״ז דימיטרובסקי, ירושלים תש״ס, עמ׳ 491 ואילך (להלן, עמ׳ 154-161). 62 **שוכנם** — בהיותם שוכנים. **עדויים** וכו׳ — מקושטים בתפנוקים. 64-66 **בברית חדשה** — יר׳ לא ל-לב. **תפארתו במחול** וכו׳ — לכשיראה לנו עין בעין את תפארתו במחול שלעתיד לבוא. ראה וי״ר יא ט, עמ׳ רמ-רמב, ובמקבילות: ״עתיד הקב״ה להיות ראש חולא לצדיקים לעתיד לבוא... ומראין עליו כילו (כאילו) באצבע ואומרים כי זה אלקים אלקינו״ וכו׳. בחילופי הנוסחאות ובמקבילות (שם) יש תוספת: ״ומרמזין אלו לאלו״. 67 **תם** — כלה. **נוי מפעלו** — מפעלו הנאה. 68 **תחום שביעי** וכו׳ — בתחום יום השבת וכו׳, שָׁבַת מכל מלאכתו. ואולי צ״ל ״תיחם״. 70 **תבונתו** — את תורתו. **במרה ובסין** — שמ׳ טו כג, ואילך. השבת הייתה סדורה משׁשת ימי בראשית עד שניתנה במרה; ראה מכילתא דר׳ ישמעאל, מהד׳ הורביץ־רבין, עמ׳ 59: ״מגיד שאותו היום אירעה שבת להיות, שהיא סדורה ובאה מששת ימי בראשית עד שניתנה להם לישראל״, וכו׳. 71 **תרביץ** — בכתב היד: ״נחלת״; ותיקנתי על פי צונץ (לעיל, הערה 3), עמ׳ 158, הערה 7. המילה ״תרביץ״ משלימה את חתימת הפייטן כאן, כמסומן בפנים. היא הוחלפה במקור שלנו במילה הפשוטה יותר: ״נחלת״. ו״תרביץ״, פירושה לימוד.

מנחם בר׳ מכיר	יוסף טוב עלם
וְלֶעָתִיד/ תּוֹמֵךְ יְמִינוֹ עֲדַת רַבַּת	תָּרוּם יָד מֻפְלָאָה
תָּרוֹן בְּנַחַת מֵאֵין מְשִׁיבַת	לְשַׂמֵּחַ אֹם נַהֲלָאָה
מִזְמֹר שִׁיר לְיוֹם הַשַּׁבָּת (תה׳ צב א)	בִּירוּשָׁלַיִם לְשָׁנָה הַבָּאָה
חַיִּים יְחָנֵּנוּ וְנִזְכֶּה לְתִשְׁחוֹרֶת	קוּמָה יְיָ וְחַדֵּשׁ גְּבוּרוֹת מִפְעָלֶיהָ
זְקוּקִים לִרְאוֹת בְּצִיּוֹן הַנִּבְחֶרֶת	הַמַּזְרַחַת נְגוֹהוֹת וְרַבּוּ תְעָלֶיהָ
לַמּוֹעֵד הַזֶּה בַּשָּׁנָה הָאַחֶרֶת	הַמֵּאִיר לָאָרֶץ וְלַדָּרִים עָלֶיהָ
(בר׳ יז כא) (קדוש)	(קדוש)

73 **תומך ימינו** – על פי תה׳ סג ט. **עדת רבת**: כינוי לישראל, על פי ״רבתי עם״, באיכה א א. 74 **מאין משיבת** – כנראה כמו מאין מַשְׁבִּית, מאין משיב אחור. 75 **מזמור וכו׳** – ראה משנה סוף מס׳ תמיד: ״מזמור שיר ליום השבת, מזמור שיר לעתיד לבוא ליום שכולו שבת מנוחה לחיי העולמים״. 76 **לתשחורת** – לשלטון ולשררה. לפי הפירוש במחזור ויטרי, מהד׳ ש׳ הורוויץ, נירנברג תרפ״ג, עמ׳ 513 לאבות מ יב, תשחורת הוא הממונה של מלך. 77 **זקוקים** – טהורים. **ציון הנבחרת** – השווה תה׳ קלב יג.

בולטים הדמיון וגם השוני בין שני פיוטים אלה. נתמזל מזלנו ואנו יכולים להצביע על המקור ששימש כל אחד מהם, לכל הפחות באשר להקבלה שבין מעשה בראשית ויציאת מצרים. פיוטו של ר׳ יוסף טוב עלם מיוסד על מדרש תדשא,[43] ושל ר׳ מנחם בר׳ מכיר על מדרש פסיקתא חדתא.[44]

נעמיד זה מול זה את המוטיבים המופיעים בפיוטו של ר׳ יוסף טוב עלם ובמדרש תדשא, וחסרים בפיוטו של ר׳ מנחם בר׳ מכיר ובמדרש פסיקתא חדתא:

מדרש תדשא	יוסף טוב עלם
כדמות ברייתו של עולם עשה הקב״ה	
נסים לישראל במדבר כשיצאו ממצרים,	
בראשית... יהי רקיע בתוך המים	...בראשון...
[במדבר] וענן ה׳ עליהם יומם	נטות יריעותיו...
ועוד נאמר פרש ענן למסך.	פרש ענן למסך (ט׳ 13-18)
...	
בראשית תדשא הארץ	בשלישי... הדשיא דשאים...
ובמדבר הנני ממטיר לכם לחם	[אין זכר למן]
ואומר... והנה פרח מטה אהרן	הציץ לבונה ופרי מגדים (ט׳ 31-35)

43 בית המדרש לילינק, ג, עמ׳ 167-168.

44 הנ״ל, ו, עמ׳ 38.

ההקבלות בין הפסיקתא חדתא ובין פיוטו של ר' מנחם בר' מכיר בולטות ומדויקות, ואין שום ספק שהם תלויים זה בזה. הואיל וידיעותינו על זמן התהוות מדרש פסיקתא חדתא מועטות, אין לקבוע בעצם מי שאב ממי, וכתמיד יש אפשרות ששניהם שאבו ממקור שלישי שאבד:

פסיקתא חדתא	מנחם בר' מכיר
ביום הראשון ארץ מתוך המים	הן בראשון ברח כאחת/ השמים
לכסאו	והדום
אף הוא קרע להם הים וברא להם	...
ארץ חדשה מן הים	והכין במים ארץ חדשה
ביום ב' ברא רקיע	...בשיני... ויעש אלקים את הרקיע
אף כאן פרש עליהם ענני כבוד	טיללני ענני כבוד
בשלישי ברא דשאים... זו היא החטה	בשלישי... כלכול דגן חיטה
אף כאן הנני ממטיר וכו'	לחם אבירים המטיר וכו'
ברביעי היו מאורות	ניהַר ברביעי מאורות
אף כאן נתן להם שני עמודי אש	...בעמוד אש... סך עמוד שיני...
בחמישי עופות	בחמישי... כל עוף
אף כאן נתן להם שליו	...צפור שליו
בשישי דבר עם אדם בג"ע	רחש בשישי לגולם המוקדם
אף כאן דבר עם בני אברהם הר סיני	שבטי אדם הגדול (= אברהם)... פנים בפנים דבר ה'

אין לדעת מה הסיבה שבגללה מקבילים דברי ר' יוסף טוב עלם למדרש תדשא ודברי מנחם בר' מכיר למדרש פסיקתא חדתא.[45]

45 כדאי להעיר שבקדושתא של ר' פינחס לשמיני עצרת מעמיד הפייטן אלה מול אלה את הנסים שנעשו לאבותינו בשעה שעזבו את בתיהם לעלות לרגל, ואת הנסים שיתרחשו לעתיד לבוא; ראה מ' זולאי, ארץ־ישראל ופיוטיה, ירושלים תשנ"ו, עמ' 105-108. גם הוא משתמש בלשון "(כן) תעשה לאחרונים" (ראה שם, עמ' 105).

פיוט אשכנזי חדש על פדיון הכלה השבויה ממצרים
הפיוט "אמון נוא" לר' מנחם בר' מכיר

יום טוב ליפמן צונץ, בספרו הגדול על הפיוט, העיר על הדמיון שבין כמה פיוטים העוסקים ביציאת מצרים, שבהם מתוארת כנסת ישראל ככלה והשליחים שנשלחו לפדותה, משה ואהרן, מנהלים משא ומתן עם פרעה לפדיון הכלה השבויה, שחתנה, הקב"ה, מחכה לה "להתחתן" אִתה.[1]

עזרא פליישר הפנה תשומת לב לשכיחותו של סיפור אלגורי זה של פדיון כלה, דהיינו כנסת ישראל במצרים, על ידי חתנה, הקב"ה. הראשון שכלל בפיוטו את הסיפור הזה היה ר' אמתי, הפייטן האיטלקי, שהשתמש בו בפיוט מהסוג "זולת" שכתב לחתונת אחותו. אף על פי שהרבה אלמנטים בפיוט זה מיוסדים על אגדות חז"ל, הסיפור עצמו שמסופר בו על בואם של שליחים לשכנע את פרעה בטענות הלקוחות מההלכה לשחרר את הכלה ולתת לה להתחתן עם חתנה המחכה לה, אינו נמצא בספרות התלמודית-מדרשית. אין לדעת אם בזמנו של ר' אמתי היה קיים סיפור כזה שנאבד מאתנו מאז או אולי ר' אמתי או אחד מקודמיו יצר את הסיפור באופן עצמאי. אחרי ר' אמתי באו פייטנים אחרים מאשכנז ומצרפת שפייטו גם כן זולתות על הנושא הזה. פליישר גם גילה זולת מר' יוסף אבן אביתור הספרדי שבו הוא מחקה את סיפורו של ר' אמתי. הזולתות האלה נועדו לשבת הגדול, לפסח או לשבת חתונה.[2] השימוש בפיוטים זהים לזכר יציאת מצרים ולחגיגת חתן וכלה, מראה על החשיבות הגדולה שבה התייחסו היהודים בימי הביניים לשמחות פרטיות, וגם על מרכזיותו של הרעיון של האהבה האלוהית בין כנסת ישראל ובין הקב"ה. הסיפור האלגורי של האהבה בין החתן ובין הכלה היה מתאים בעיני הפייטנים והמתפללים לציון מאורע לאומי־היסטורי ולציון מאורע פרטי. היחיד והציבור תיארו אהבה אלוהית ואהבה אנושית בתמונות ומושגים זהים והגבול בין הכללי ובין הפרטי ניטשטש בפיוטים אלה. הסיפור המסופר בחרוזים היה עממי במהותו בתיאור הגעגועים של החתן והכלה זה לזו, מרתק על ידי הצגת העימות בין המלך הרשע המחזיק כלה שבויה ובין שליחים אמיצים הבאים לפדותה, ומשעשע על ידי תיאור המשא ומתן הפלפולי שבין המלך, דהיינו פרעה, ובין השליחים, משה ואהרן. במשא ומתן זה מתווכחים המשתתפים

1 ראה L. Zunz, *Literaturgeschichte der synagogalen Poesie*, Berlin 1865, pp. 72 n. 1, 122 n. 1, 3

2 ע' פליישר, היוצרות בהתהוותם ובהתפתחותם, ירושלים תשמ"ד, עמ' 697-698, וראה מאמרו הנזכר שם בהערה 44. פיוטו של אמתי נדפס גם בשירי אמתי, מהד' י' דוד, ירושלים תשל"ה, עמ' 86-90. פליישר, שם, עמ' 698 כותב: "רבים הזולתות המרכז אירופיים השבים ומספרים את סיפורו של ר' אמתי". בהזדמנות אחרת, אי"ה, אני מתכוון לרשום אותם ולדון בהם.

בטענות הלקוחות מהלכות פדיון האמה העברייה, ופרעה מתגלה כבקי בעניינים אלה.

בכתב־יד זעיר השמור בספריית בית המדרש לרבנים באמריקה (מס׳ 8972, דף כב ע״ב) נמצא פיוט בלתי ידוע כזה מר׳ מנחם בר׳ מכיר, שחי באשכנז במאה הי״א. מנחם היה אחד מבני המכירי המפורסמים, שחיבורם ״מעשה המכירי״ הוא מקור חשוב מאוד לתורתם של חכמי אשכנז הקדומים.[3] כתב־היד הוא מאשכנז מהמאה הי״ג והוא מכיל אוסף פיוטים לשבתות מיוחדות.[4] הפיוט הוא ״זולת לשבת הגדול״. בספר ״ערוגת הבשם״ נמצא פירוש ארוך לפיוט זה, אבל היות והמקור עצמו לא היה ידוע בשעת הוצאתו של הספר, דברי הפירוש נשארו סתומים.[5] כעת, עם הפיוט בידינו, אפשר להבין גם את דברי בעל ״ערוגת הבשם״. פיוטו של ר׳ מנחם בר׳ מכיר דומה בתוכנו לשאר הפיוטים מסוג זה וגם הוא מציג דו־שיח דמיוני בין פרעה ובין משה ואהרן בעניין פדיית השבויה מהשבי המצרי. הפיוט בנוי מסטרופות בנות ארבעה טורים, כשהטור האחרון הוא פסוק מהמקרא. בכל טור שש מילים בדיוק, מלבד בטור הרביעי המביא פסוק כלשונו. הסימן האלפביתי הוא: אאב, גגד וכן הלאה. אחרי גמר הא״ב בא סימן: מנחם בן רבי מכיר חזק ואמץ בתורה לעד אמן. נראה שלפני צונץ היה טקסט שונה מזה שלנו ועל זה מראה הסימן שמובא על ידו (מנחם בן רבי... צבור לעד אמן).[6]

והנה לשון הפיוט:

אָמוֹן נוֹא הוּבָא נְזִיר אַחִים אֲדָנָיי
אָנוּס עַל פִּי הַדִּיבֵּר, רֹאשׁ אֵיתָנָיי
בָּא בְעֵמֶק חֶבְרוֹן לְקַיֵּים עֵצָה וּתְנָאי
כִּי הָיְתָה סִבָּה מֵאֵת ה׳ (מלכים א יב טו)

גָּרְמָה לַתָּם זְכוּתוֹ בְּשַׁלְשְׁלָאוֹת לֹא עֻוּנָּה
גֻּולְגַּל דָּבָר וְהוּרַד כַּלְכֹּל שָׁם רִאשׁוֹנָה
דִּמְיוֹן הָאֵם רָצָה אַחֲרֵי בֶן בִּטְנָהּ
כִּי נִכְמְרוּ רַחֲמֶיהָ עַל בְּנָהּ (מלכים א ג כו)

הָאָדוֹן הִבְטִיחוֹ הוּא וְזַרְעוֹ עֵת בוֹאוֹ
הֱיוֹת עִמָּם בְּרִדְתּוֹ מִנְיַן שִׁבְעִים יְמַלְאוּ

3 א׳ גרוסמן, חכמי אשכנז הראשונים, ירושלים תשמ״א, עמ׳ 361 ואילך; על פיוטי ר׳ מנחם, שם, עמ׳ 373; ובהערה 63 שם מזכיר גרוסמן את הפיוט שלנו.

4 על כתב־יד זה ראה מה שכתב ב׳ נרקיס, ״ציורים לעשרת הדיברות במחזור אשכנזי זעיר בן המאה השלוש־עשרה״, עשרת הדיברות בראי הדורות, בעריכת ב״צ סגל, ירושלים תשמ״ו, עמ׳ 389-407. וראה במאמרי העומד להופיע בספר היובל לכבוד הפרופסור אברהם הולץ (להלן, עמ׳ 190-208).

5 ספר ערוגת הבשם – כולל פירושים לפיוטים לרבינו אברהם ב״ר עזריאל, מהד׳ א״א אורבך, ג, ירושלים תשכ״ג, עמ׳ 143-148. וראה בהערה 25 שם: ״זולת לשבת הגדול לר׳ מנחם בר׳ מכיר ד.א. 5586. לא נדפס וגם לא נרשם ברשימת המכון לחקר השירה העברית״.

6 על הסימן ראה צונץ (לעיל, הע׳ 1), עמ׳ 298. וראה בספר ערוגת הבשם, שם, עמ׳ 148, המביא את ראשי החרוזים ואת המילים שבהם מסומן שמו של המחבר.

וּבְשֵׁשׁ מֵאוֹת אֶלֶף עֲלוֹתָם אוֹתוֹ יִמְצְאוּ
בְּתוֹכָם וּבְבוֹאָם יָבוֹאוּ וּבְצֵאתָם יֵצֵאוּ (יחזקאל מו י)

זוֹרֵז וּבָא הַמּוֹעֵד צֵאת כַּלָּה מִסִּבְלוֹתֶיהָ
זָכַר לָהּ חֲתָנָהּ חֶסֶד אַהֲבַת כְּלוּלוֹתֶיהָ
חָנְטָה פַגֶּיהָ כְּבָר וְהִיא חוֹמָה וּמִגְדָּלֶיהָ
כְּפוֹרַחַת עָלְתָה נִצָּהּ הִבְשִׁילוּ אַשְׁכְּלוֹתֶיהָ (בראשית מ י)

טָכוּס פָּנוּי לַטִּירוֹן שֵׁבֶט בְּנֵי לְוִיָּה
טוֹבִים הַשְּׁנַיִם הֵם תְּאוֹמֵי צְבִיָּיה
יְדָעָם לָרוּץ לְדַבֵּר עַל לֵב הָעִבְרִיָּיה:
הִתְפַּתְּחִי מוֹסְרֵי צַוָּארֵךְ, שְׁבִיָּה (ישעיה נב ב)

כְּבוּדָּה בַּת מֶלֶךְ פְּנִימָ[ה] סְגֻלָּתִי הַכַּלָּה
כְּבוּשָׁה חֲבוּשָׁה עִם בְּנֵי נוֹף לְשַׁכְּלָה
לֻוקְּחָה חִינָּם לְאָמָה הוּגְלַת שְׁלוּמִים כּוּלָּהּ
הַכְּצַעֲקָתָהּ הַבָּאָה אֵלַי עָשׂוּ כָּלָה (בראשית יח כא)

מַלְאָכָיו חָנֵס הִגִּיעוּ לְמוֹשֵׁל חָם הָאָשֵׁם:
"מַדּוּעַ הֶחֱזַקְתָּ בְּבַת יְדִידוּת נֶשֶׁם
נְכוֹנָה הִיא לְהִתְקַדֵּשׁ לְהִתְפָּאֵר שְׁבוֹ וָלֶשֶׁם
חָפֵץ בָּהּ הַמֶּלֶךְ וְנִקְרְאָה בְשֵׁם" (אסתר ב יד)

סִבְלוֹנוֹת הַרְבֵּ[ה] מְאֹד מֹהַר וּמַתָּן בְּתוּלָה
שָׂדוֹת וּכְרָמִים וְזֵיתִים הִנְדִּין לָהּ לְהַשְׁתִּילָה
עִיתָּהּ עֵת דּוֹדִים בַּעֲדִי עֲדָיִים חֲתוּלָה
וַיְבַהֵל אֶת תַּמְרוּקֶיהָ וְאֶת מָנוֹתֶיהָ לָתֶת לָהּ (אסתר ב ט)

פֶּתִי שִׂיחוֹת הֶעְמִיק פִּי זָדוֹת וּמַעֲקַשׁוֹת:
"פִּדְיוֹן אָמָה אַיֵּה וְאַל תַּלְאוּ בְּבַקָּשׁוֹת
צְרוֹרוֹת כֶּסֶף שִׁיקְלוּ וְחִידְלוּ מִשּׁוֹל הַקָּשׁוֹת"
וַיִּתְנַכֵּר אֲלֵיהֶם וַיְדַבֵּר אִתָּם קָשׁוֹת (בראשית מב ז)

קְדוֹשִׁים עָנוּ לַסָּכָל: "בְּלֹא עִתְּךָ תֵּאָסֵף
קוֹנֶה אֵפוֹא מְכָרָהּ הָתֵל אַל תּוֹסֵף
רְצוּצָה עֲשׁוּקָה בְאֶפֶס אָמַר לְגָאֳלָהּ בְּכוֹסֶף
יַעֲשֶׂה לָהּ וְיָצְאָה חִינָּם אֵין כָּסֶף" (שמות כא יא)

שָׁב וְהֵשִׁיב תּוֹאֲנָה: "מַה־תְּסַפְּרוּ נְדָנֶיהָ
שִׁפְחָה נֶחֱרֶפֶת לְאִישׁ אֲנִי זַנְתִּי עֲדָנֶיהָ

תּוֹלְדוֹתֶיהָ לִי הֵם כְּדַת מִשְׁפְּטֵי דִינֶיהָ
הָאִשָּׁה וִילָדֶיהָ תִּהְיֶה לַאדוֹנֶיהָ״ (שמות כא ד)

״מוֹרֶה שֶׁקֶר וְתַרְמִית״, הֵצוּ עָלָיו נְבוֹנִים
״נַעֲרָה שִׁבְחָ[הּ] לְאָב וְלַבַּעַל שְׂכַר לְבָנִים
חָתָן אָב וְאָדוֹן לָהּ וְהָפְדָּה מֶעֶלְבּוֹנִים
שַׁלֵּחַ תְּשַׁלַּח אֶת הָאֵם וְאֶת הַבָּנִים״ (דברים כב ז)

״מָה אַתֶּם וְדִבְרֵיכֶם״, נִגְרַס יָרַק יָרוֹק
״בְּדִבְרֵי שֶׁקֶר תִּשְׁעוּ וּתְשַׁעֲשְׁעוּ כִּי יִפְרוֹק
נִרְפִּים אַתֶּם נִרְפִּים״ בְּפִיו שָׁרַק שָׁרוֹק
רָשָׁע יִרְאֶה רָע וְכָעַס שִׁינָּיו יַחֲרוֹק (תהלים קיב י)

רָבוּ בוֹ עֳפָרַיִם: ״הוּפְרַע עֲצָתְךָ בִּפְרָעָה
בְּזוּת דְּבַר הַמֶּלֶךְ גְּמוּלְךָ יְשׁוּלַּם לְפוּרְעָה״
יעירה תרוץ לחוגב, אֶרֶץ לֹא זְרוּעָה
עַד אֲשֶׁר [לֹא יָבוֹאוּ יְמֵי הָרָעָה] (קהלת יב א)

״מִי ה׳ לֹא יְדַעְתִּיו״, הֵעִיז לְדַבְּרָה
״כֵּן תַּפְרִיעוּ כַּלָּה מוֹטוֹת עוֹל לְשַׁבְּרָה
יָצוֹא לֹא תֵצֵא לַמִּדְבָּר עֲבוֹר מַעְבָּרָה
וְאַתֶּם פְּנוּ לָכֶם וּסְעוּ הַמִּדְבָּרָה״ (דברים א מ)

רֵיעִים צִירֵי אֲמָנָה מְשִׁיבֵי מִלְחָמָה שָׁעְרָה
חָשׁוּ לְהָשִׁיב לְשׁוֹלְחָם דִּבְרֵי אֱמֶת לְשָׁעֲרָה:
״זְקוּקָתְךָ כְּמֵיהָה מְאֹד מִן הֶעָפָר לְנַעֲרָה
כָּזֹאת וְכָזֹאת דִּבְּרָה הַנַּעֲרָה (מלכים ב ה ד)

וּמֵאָז בָּאנוּ לְדַבֵּר בִּשְׁמֶךָ אֱלֹהֵי הָעִבְרִים
אוֹיֵב אָטַם אָזְנוֹ כְּפֶתֶן לְקוֹל חֲבָרִים
מִי וָמִי הוֹלְכִים לְכוּ נָא הַגְּבָרִים
וְהִנֵּה הוּא שָׂם לָהּ עֲלִילוֹת דְּבָרִים״ (דברים כב יד [יז])

צוּר נְגָפוֹ בְנֶאֱמָנִים זֶה בָּא וְזֶה הוֹלֵךְ
בְּתֵשַׁע נְגוּעַ וְלֹא נִפְגַּע סָחוּב וְהַשְׁלֵךְ
וְרִידּוּי אַחֲרוֹן הִכְבִּיד וַתֵּהוֹם כָּל פֶּלֶךְ
כִּי כָלְתָה אֵלָיו הָרָעָה מֵאֵת הַמֶּלֶךְ (אסתר ז ז)

לֵיל נִלְקְחָה הָאֵם וְנִתְנַגַּע בֵּית לָצוֹן
עִיתָּה – שִׁימּוּר לַבַּת הֱיוֹת מֵאָז וּלְקִיצוֹן
דָּמִים בְּסוּסָה פְּסוּחָה חֲוּפְּזָה צֵאת לְרָצוֹן
הַיָּפָה בַּנָּשִׁים צְאִי לָךְ בְּעִקְבֵי הַצֹּאן (שיר השירים א ח)

אַחַר נֶהְפַּךְ לְבָבָם לְמוֹ עַבְדוּת לְהַחְזִירָהּ
מְשָׁכָם יָם וְהִשְׁלִיכָם בְּמִידָּה שָׁוָה גְזִירָה
נְקֻודּוֹת וְתוֹרִים יְתֵרִים כְּתָרִים דּוֹד הִנְזִירָהּ
אֱלֹקִים לָנוּ מַחֲסֶה וָעוֹז עֶזְרָה בְצָרָה (תהלים מו ב)

הפיוט עשיר ברמזים לאגדות חז״ל, והפייטן שיזר אותם בפיוטו באמנות ובזריזות גדולה. להלן נשתדל לחשוף את מקורותיו ולפעמים נביא גם את דברי הפירוש שב״ערוגת הבשם״ (עה״ב) ונעיר על הגירסאות השונות משלנו המובאות שם.

1. **אמון נוא** – מצרים, השווה נחום ג ח. בעה״ב: ״ומין הדין היה לומר נוא אמון הובא׳ אך מפני כדי להתחיל בא׳ היפך״. **נזיר אחים** – יוסף, השווה בראשית מט כו ודברים לג טז. בעה״ב: ״נזיר אחיו״. **אדניי** – השבטים. בעה״ב: ״שבטים קורא אדנים כי הם עיקר כמו אדני בית״.

2-3. מיוסד על בראשית רבה פד יג, מהד׳ תיאודור־אלבק עמ׳ 1016: ״וישלחהו מעמק חברון (בראשית לז יד)... הלך [יוסף] להשלים העצה העמוקה שנתן הקב״ה בינו ובין חבר הנאה שקבור בחברון [= אברהם]: ועבדום ועינו אותם (בראשית טו יג)״; וראה סוטה יא ע״א, רש״י ד״ה וישלחהו מעמק חברון: ״ביוסף משתעי קרא כששלחו יעקב אצל אחיו והוא תחילת סיבת ירידת ישראל למצרים״. יוסף ירד למצרים כדי לקיים את מה שאמר הקב״ה לאברהם בברית בין הבתרים ״כי גר יהיה זרעך״ וכו׳ (וכך פירש בעל עה״ב). **אנוס על פי הדיבר** – כלשון ההגדה של פסח: ״וירד מצרימה – אנוס על פי הדיבור״. **ראש איתניי** – ״איתנים״ הוא כינוי שכיח לאבות ו״איתן״ הוא כינוי לאברהם אבינו, השווה פסיקתא דרב כהנא, מהד׳ מנדלבוים עמ׳ 61 ועמ׳ 464.

4. **כי היתה סיבה** – השווה בדברי רש״י המובאים לעיל (טור 2-3).

5-8. ראה שבת פט ע״ב: ״ראוי היה יעקב אבינו לירד למצרים בשלשלאות של ברזל אלא שזכותו גרמה לו״. וראה מדרש תהלים, מהד׳ בובר עמ׳ 450-451: ״ראוי היה יעקב לירד במצרים בשלשלאות של ברזל ועשה הקב״ה כמה מנגנאות [= תחבולות] כדי להורידו בכבודו... משל לפרה שהיו מבקשין למשוך אותה למקולין שלה ולא היתה נמשכת, מה עשו, משכו בנה תחלה והיתה רצה אחוריו״. השווה בראשית רבה ו ב, עמ׳ 1052-1053 ובמנחת יהודה שם (וכך פירש בעל עה״ב). **כלכל** – יוסף, ראה פסיקתא דרב כהנא, עמ׳ 61.

9-12. **האדון הבטיחו וכו׳** – עה״ב: ״כמו שנ׳ אנכי ארד עמך מצרימה״ (בראשית מו ד). ראה מכילתא דרשב״י, מהד׳ אפשטיין־מלמד עמ׳ 1: ״כשירדו ישראל למצרים, שכינה עמהם, שנ׳ אנכי ארד עמך מצרימה. וכשעלו, שכינה עמהם, שנ׳ ואנכי אעלך גם עלה (שם)״. ראה ש׳ שפיגל, אבות הפיוט, ניו יורק וירושלים תשנ״ז, עמ׳ 308 ואילך. ראה גם פרקי דרבי אליעזר פל״ט: ״וכשבאו לגבול מצרים נתייחסו כל הזכרים... הרי שבעים חסר אחת וכתיב בשבעים נפש ירדו אבותיך מצרימה (דברים י כה), מה עשה הקב״ה, נכנס עמהם, לקיים מה שנאמר אנכי ארד עמך מצרימה (בראשית מו ד). וכשעלו ישראל ממצרים נתייחסו כל הגברים ס׳ רבוא חסר אחד, מה עשה הקב״ה, נכנס עמהם, לקיים מה שנאמר אנכי ארד עמך ואנכי אעלך גם עלה (שם)״. **יבואו בתוכם** וכו׳ – שיבוץ מוצלח של הפסוק ״והנשיא בתוכם בבואם יבוא ובצאתם יצאו״ (הכתיב), והפייטן שינה את שני הפעלים ללשון רבים. סטרופה זו מהווה מעבר וכעין הכנה לסטרופה הבאה: כאן הפייטן אומר שהקב״ה יעלה יחד עם ישראל ממצרים ובהמשך יתחיל לספר את הסיפור של האהבה בין ה״חתן״ וה״כלה״.

13. **זורז ובא המועד** וכו׳ – הקב״ה קיצר את גלות מצרים. מועד הגאולה בא אחרי מאתיים ועשר שנים ולא אחרי ארבע מאות שנה כמו שנאמר לאברהם (בראשית טו יג). ראה פסיקתא דרב כהנא, עמ׳ 88. וראה להלן טור 75. **צאת כלה מסבלותיה** – על פי שמות ו ו.

14. **זכר לה חתנה חסד אהבת כלולותיה** – על פי ירמיה ב ב. בעה״ב: ״זכר לה מתנה״ ומפרש: ״וזכרתי לך חס״ד נעורי״ך אהב״ת כלולותי״ך בגימ׳ זה״ו אזכו״ר מת״ן התור״ה״. וכנראה הנוסח היה משובש כבר בזמנו ובמקום ״חתנה״ שלפנינו, שמתאים היטב לתוכן הסטרופה, היה לפניו ״מתנה״.

15-16. על פי שיר השירים ב יג, שם ח י, והפייטן משתמש בהם לציין שהכלה הביאה סימני בגרות, ורומז בזה למשנה לקידושין פ״א מ״ב: ״יתירה עליו אמה העבריה שקונה את עצמה בסימנין״. וראה

להלן טור 23 ועוד. **כפורחת עלתה נצה** – ראה הפירוש בעה"ב 144 וראה גם שם, עמ׳ 134, והוא על פי חולין צב ע"א: "והיא כפרחת, הגיע זמנן של ישראל לפרות ולרבות... עלתה נצה, הגיע זמנן של ישראל ליגאל... הבשילו אשכלותיה ענבים, הגיע זמנה של מצרים לשתות כוס התרעלה". במדרש זה יש לראות גרעין להתפתחות הסיפור שלפנינו.

17. בעה"ב מובאות שתי גירסאות, האחת: "טכוס פנוי לטירון", כמו שלפנינו; השנייה, על פי "יוצרות שכת׳ בם: טפוס לטירוג". וראה הפירוש שם. לגירסא שלפנינו השווה שמות רבה, מהד׳ א׳ שנאן עמ׳ 119: "בשעה שנגלה הקב"ה למשה טירון היה משה לנבואה"; וראה שם, עמ׳ 172-173: "שבטו של לוי פנוי היה מעבודת פרך. אמר להם פרעה: בשביל שאתם עומדים פנויים אתם אומרים: נלכה נזבחה לאלקינו (שמות ה, ח)". בלי ספק הפייטן מתכוון למקורות אלה או לדומים להם, אבל בכל זאת הטור קשה להולמו בדיוק.

18-19. **טובים השנים** וכו׳ – על פי קהלת ד ט, ושיר השירים ד ה, והכוונה למשה ואהרן וכך נדרש בשיר השירים רבה על הפסוק הנ"ל. **תאומי הצביה/ ידעם לרוץ** וכו׳ – בעה"ב (עמ׳ 141 ו־146): "כשני עפרים תאומי צבייה נדרש על משה ואהרן שהיו רצים בשליחות הק׳ צבי"; וראה מה שכתב אורבך שם, עמ׳ 141 הע׳ 97, שבשיר השירים רבה ד ה, ובאגדת שיר השירים נדרשת התחלת הפסוק על משה ואהרן, אבל אין דורשים את הדימוי לשני עפרים. **ידעם... לדבר** – השווה התפילה המפורסמת לשליח ציבור, "היה עם פיפיות" (מחזור לראש השנה, מהד׳ ד׳ גולדשמידט, עמ׳ 230): "היה עם פיפיות שלוחי עמך... הורם מה שיאמרו/ הבינם מה שידברו... ידעם היך יפארו"; וכפי שמעיר גולדשמידט, שם, הדברים מיוסדים על הפסוק הנאמר על משה ואהרן, "ואנכי אהיה עם פיך ועם פיהו" (שמות ד ט). **לב העברייה** – האמה העברייה, על פי דברים טו יב.

21. **כבודה** וכו׳ – תהלים מה יד. **סגולתי** – על פי "והייתם לי סגלה" (שמות יט ה).

22. **כבושה** – על פי ירמיה לד טז: "ותכבשו אתם להיות לכם לעבדים ולשפחות". **חבושה** – שכיח בלשון חז"ל: "חבוש בבית האסורים" (ברכות ה ע"ב ועוד). **בני נוף** – מצרים (ירמיה ב טז).

23. **לוקחה חינם** וכו׳ – על פי ישעיה נב ג-ה. **הוגלת שלומים** וכו׳ – ירמיה יג יט. בעה"ב: "והפייט שמביא זה הפסוק לזה שבתחילה ירדו דרך שלום ואחר כך החזיקו בהם עבדות והכי אמר׳ בפ׳ כל שעה (פסחים לט ע"א), מרור תחילתו רך וסופו קשה וכו׳", כלומר, שבעל עה"ב סובר שהפייטן דרש את המילה "שלומים" במובן שלום.

25. **מלאכיו** וכו׳ – על פי ישעיה ל ד. בעה"ב: "מה שעשה הפייט מלאכיו חנס הגיעו, פי׳ מלאכיו של הקב"ה הם משה ואהרן הגיעו למצרים להאשים את פרעה שהוא מושל חם".

26-27. **בבת ידידות נשם** – כמו ידידות נפש, ראה ירמיה יב ז. **שבו ולשם** – אבנים טובות (שמות כח יט). נשם היא מילה פייטנית במקום נשמה, ראה למשל בפיוט גשם לקלירי, "אף ברי" (מחזור לסכות, מהד׳ ד׳ גולדשמידט וי׳ פרנקל, עמ׳ 404), שחורז לשם עם נשם: "...בצחות לשם... לנפוחי נשם".

29-30. **סבלונות** – קידושין פ"ב מ"ו: "המקדש... ששלח סבלונות". **מהר ומתן** – בראשית לד יב. **שדות וכרמים וזיתים** – דברים ו יא; תהלים קז לז. **הנדין לה** – מילה פייטנית מלשון "נדן" והובאה על ידי צונץ כדוגמא יחידית לצורה זו מהפיוט שלפנינו, ראה *Die synagogale Poesie des Mittelalters*, פרנקפורט 1920, עמ׳ 433. לפני בעל עה"ב הייתה כנראה גירסא אחרת, משובשת: "כי דינה היה לחננה".

31. **עיתה עת דודים** וכו׳ – יחזקאל טז פסוקים ד, ז, ח. **עת** – בכתב־היד בטעות: את.

33. **פתי שיחות** וכו׳ – השווה משלי כב יד. **שיחות** – אולי צ"ל בשי"ן שמאלית: שׂיחות. בפסוק "זָרוֹת", אבל בכתב־היד: זדות; ואולי טעות היא. בעה"ב: "פתי שיח׳ העמיקה פי זרות ומעקשות". לפנינו נקוד זָדוֹת ובעה"ב זָרוֹת, ומעיר בפירושו (על ניקוד המילה במשלי הנ"ל): "צריכה דיקדוק למה לא ננקד זֵרוֹת כמו וישבה בגירות דירמיה" (מא יז). **ומעקשות** – השווה ישעיה מב טז.

34-35. **פידיון אמה איה** וכו׳ – פרעה דורש כסף בעבור פדיון האמה השבויה, ואינו מוכן לשחררה חינם. **והידלו משול הקשות** – בעה"ב שני פירושים: (א) "והחדלו מישול הקישות: תיבת משול מלשון שול תשולו לה מן הצבתים (רות ב, טז), לשו׳ השלכה, וש׳ משול נדגש, ותיבת הקישות לשו׳ השמעת קול, כמו קיש קיש קריא (בבא מציעא פה ע"ב). ופתר׳: מליצה חדלו מהשליך, השמעת קול הדיבור, כלומ׳ חדלו מלדבר דברי׳ בטלים... ולשון השלכה נופל בדיבור... והוא קרוב ללשון

נטיפה...". (ב) "וחדלו ממשול הקישות, ופי' מלמשול דברים שדבריכם אינם אלא כמשל". ואולי "הקשות" מלשון הקיש, המונח התלמודי, ופירוש הדבר: פרעה אומר למשה ואהרן שלא ישתמשו בטענות "פלפוליות" אלא ישלמו כסף ואז יהיה מוכן לשחרר את הכלה. **ואל תלאו** – השווה איוב טז ז. **צרורות כסף** – בראשית מב לה.

37. **קדושים** – משה ואהרן. **ענו לסכל בלא עתך תאסף** – השווה קהלת ז יז.

39-38. **קונה איפוא מכרה** וכו' – קשה להולמו ואולי פירושו: אל תהתל בנו להגיד שהקב"ה שקנה (קידש, אירס) את כנסת ישראל, את הכלה, אכן מכר אותה ובגלל זה הוא חייב לשלם לך כסף כדי לפדותה. זה לא ייתכן, ולכן אין צורך שהוא ישלם כסף אלא הוא יגאל אותה חינם, באפס כסף. **התל אל תוסף** – שמות ח כה. **רצוצה עשוקה** – השווה דברים כח לג. **באפס** – בלי כסף, חינם. בעה"ב: "פי אמ' הקב"ה לגאלה באפס דמים כמו שנ' חנם נמכרתם ולא בכסף תגאלו" (ישעיה נב ג). **לגאלה בכוסף** – בגעגועים של אהבה, השווה תהלים פד ג.

44-41. **שב והשיב** וכו' – פרעה השיב להם: למה לכם לדבר על הנדוניה שלה, הלא היא תישאר אצלי כשפחה ולא אשחרר אותה כי היא וילדיה שייכים לי לפי דין התורה. **תואנה** – עלילה, על פי שופטים יד ד. **שפחה נחרפת לאיש** – ויקרא יט כ. **אני זנתי עדניה** – אני פרנסתי אותה במעדנים.

45. **מורה שקר ותרמית** – משה ואהרן משיבים לפרעה: אתה מורה הוראה שלא כהלכה, דבריך הם שקר ותרמית (על פי ירמיה יד יד). **הצו** – רבו אתו, על פי במדבר כו ט.

47-46. **נערה שבחה לאב** וכו' – הקב"ה, הוא גם חתן וגם אב וגם בעל (אדון) לה, והכול מגיע לו ממנה. **נערה שבחה לאב** – על פי קידושין ג ע"ב: "כל שבח נעורים לאביה". **ולבעל שכר לבנים** – ובתור בעל שייך לו כל מה שהיא הרוויחה מעשיית הלבנים (בעבודה שעבדו במצרים). **והפדה מעלבונים** – והוא יפדה אותה מעלבונים. בעה"ב: "פי' הקב"ה חתנה ואביה ואדון לה. וי"ו והפדה שבפיוט מהפך מלשעבר להבא".

51-49. מיוסד על שמות רבה, עמ' 174: "התחיל מחרק עליהם שניו ואומר: נרפים הם". וראה שם, עמ' 177: "נרפים אתם נרפים – חרק עליהם שיניו והתחיל מחרפם". **נגרס** – איכה ג טז: "ויגרס בחצץ שני". **ירק ירוק** – במדבר יב יד. **בדברי שקר תשעו ותשעשעו** – שמות ה ט, ישעיה כט ט. ראה שמות רבה, עמ' 175, הדורש "ואל ישעו בדברי שקר" שבפסוק בשמות הנ"ל מלשון שעשועים: "אמר להם פרעה תכבד העבודה... ואל יהו משתעשעים". בכתב־היד: ותשועשעו. **כי יפרוק** – כאשר יפרוק את עולו. **נרפים אתם נרפים** – שמות ו יז. **שרק שרוק** – השווה איכה ב טז: "כל איביך שרקו ויחרקו שן".

52. הטור הוא הבאה מתהלים קיב י, אבל יש בו שינוי כי בפיוט כתוב "רשע יראה רע וכעס" ולשון הפסוק "רשע יראה וכעס".

56-53. סטרופה קשה להבנה. טור 55 אינו מנוקד בכתב־היד מכיוון שהמעתיק לא הבין את פירושו או שסירב לגלות לציבור את המשמעות החריפה של הדברים. גם בעל עה"ב מתקשה בפירושם. **רבו בו עפרים** – משה ואהרן רבו עם פרעה והטיחו דברים בפניו. עה"ב: "משה ואהרן נקראו עופרים שנ' שני שדייך כשני עפרי' תאומי צבייה, שהיו רצים בשליחות הקב"ה כצבייה. ד"א שהיו משימים עצמם כעפר, שנ' ונחנו מה כי תלינו עלינו" (שמות טז ז). ראה לעיל, טור 18. **הופרע עצתך בפרעה** – בעה"ב הגירסא: "הפרע עצתך נפרעה" ומפרשו: "רבו משה ואהרן בפרעה ואמרו לו הפרע, נתבטלה עצתך". הוא מביא את הפסוק בירמיה מ"ד ל', כיסוד לדברי הפייטן ודן בכתיב המילה "הפרע" אם בה"א או בחי"ת. **בזות דבר המלך** – אסתר א יג, יז. **גמולך ישולם** – תהלים קלז ח. **לפורעה** – כְּמובן המילה בלשון חז"ל: לשלם. בעל עה"ב מביא כאן את המדרש מילמדנו (תנחומא וארא ט ומהד' בובר אות ח, עמ' 23-24) ש"פרעה היה אחד מארבעה בני אדם שנבעלו כנשים... שהיה זכר ופרע עצמו כנקיבה". וכנראה על זה מוסב טור 55 ומובנו שפרעה שפך את זרעו לבטלה במשכב זכר. **יעירה** (?) – אינני יכול לפרשו. **תרוץ לחוגב** – על פי קהלת יב ה-ו: "ויסתבל החגב... ותרץ גלת הזהב"; וראה ברש"י שם: החגב, אלו העגבות, ותרוץ, לשון רציצה, גלת הזהב, זו האמה. **ארץ לא זרועה** – השווה בראשית לח ט; והלשון על פי ירמיה ב ב.

58-57. שמות ה ב, ד. **מוטות עול לשברה** – ויקרא כו יג. עה"ב: "כן תפריעו כלה, פי' מי [ה'] שכן תפריעו את העם ממעשיו".

59. **עבור מעברה** – על פי ישעיה י כט.

61. **ריעים** וכו׳ – משה ואהרן. **צירי אמנה** – שליחים נאמנים, השווה משלי כה יג. **משיבי מלחמה שערה** – ישעיה כח ו.

62. **חשו** – מיהרו. **לשולחם** – להקב״ה. **דברי אמת** – קהלת יב י.

63. **זקוקתך** – כלתך, על פי קידושין ו ע״א: ״הרי את זקוקה לי מקודשת״. **כמיהה מאד** – מתגעגעת מאוד, על פי תהלים סג ב. **מן העפר לנערה** – ישעיה נב ב.

65. **ומאז באנו לדבר בשמך** – שמות ה כג. **אלהי העברים** – שם ה ג.

66. **אויב אטם** וכו׳ – תהלים נח ה-ו. **לקול חברים** – משה ואהרן. עה״ב: ״לקול חברים שעשה פייט, פי׳ בשביל קול חברים שלא ישמעם, כמו ואמר פרעה לבני ישרא׳״ (שמות יד ג, שגם שם הפירוש: בשביל ישראל).

67. **מי ומי** וכו׳ – שמות י ח, יא. 68. פרעה האשים את משה ואהרן שהם אינם אומרים את האמת, ראה שמות רבה, עמ׳ 259: ״מי שאומר דבר זה [בנערינו ובזקנינו נלך] אין דעתו אלא לברוח״.

69. **בנאמנים** – המכות, השווה דברים כח נט. זה **בא והולך** – עה״ב: ״פי׳ לא היה הולך עד שהיה בא אחר תחילה״.

70. **ולא נפגע** – עה״ב: ״כמו אין שוטה נפגע״ (שבת יג ע״ב). **סחוב והשלך** – ירמיה כב יט.

71. **ורידוי אחרון** – המכה האחרונה; ״רידוי״ היא מילה פייטנית, ראה צונץ (לעיל בהערות לטורים 29-30), עמ׳ 396. **ותהום כל פלך** – על פי רות א יט.

73-74. **ליל נלקחה** וכו׳ – ראה פרקי דר׳ אליעזר פכ״ו: ״באותו הלילה שנלקחה שרה אמנו אותו הלילה ליל פסח היה והביא הקב״ה על פרעה ועל ביתו נגעים גדולים להודיע שכן הוא עתיד להכות את מצרים בנגעים גדולים שנא׳ וינגע ה׳ את פרעה נגעים גדולים (בראשית י״ב י״ז)״. **בית לצון** – ביתו של פרעה. בשמות רבה, עמ׳ 257, מובא הפסוק ״אם ללצים הוא יליץ״ (משלי ג לד) בקשר לפרעה. **עיתה שימור לבת** וכו׳ – עה״ב: ״שבאותו לילה יצאו ממצרים. ודרשו רבותינו, ליל שמורים אחד במצרים ואחד לעתיד. בפ״ק דראש השנה (יא ע״ב) לילה המשומר לעתיד לבוא״. וראה בהערות אורבך, שם. **ולקיצון** – ולעתיד, מלשון קץ.

75. **דמים בסוסה** וכו׳ – על פי יחזקאל טז ו, והשווה מכילתא דר׳ ישמעאל, מהד׳ הורוביץ־רבין עמ׳ 14: ״נתן להם הקדוש ברוך הוא שתי מצות דם פסח ודם מילה שיתעסקו בהם כדי שיגאלו שנאמר ואעבור עליך ואראך מתבוססת בדמיך״ (יחזקאל שם). **חופזה צאת** – הקב״ה מיהר את הגאולה, ראה לעיל, טור 13.

76. **היפה בנשים** וכו׳ – פסוק זה נדרש בשיר השירים רבה על יציאת מצרים.

77. **אחר נהפך לבבם** וכו׳ – שמות יד ה. עה״ב: ״לרדוף אחריהם, להחזירם לעבדות״.

78. **משכם ים והשליכם במידה** וכו׳ – הגירסא בעה״ב היא ״משנסים השליכם״ ופירש: ״מלשון וישנס מותניו (מ״א י״ח מ״ו), פי׳ מצרים שהיו [משנסים] עצמם על ישראל השליכם לים, מידה כנגד מידה שהשליכו זכוריהם למים״. **גזירה** – רמז ללשון ״לגזר ים סוף לגזרים״ (תהלים קלו יג) וגם ללשון ״גזירה״, שהקב״ה גזר עליהם במידה שווה, במידה כנגד מידה.

79. **נקודות ותורים יתרים** וכו׳ – עה״ב: ״הוא שנ׳ תורי זהב נעשה לך עם נקודות הכסף (שיר השירים א׳ י״א) ודרשו רבותי׳ תורי זהב, זה ביזת הים, עם נקודות הכסף, זו ביזת מצרים, על כן אמרו גדולה ביזת הים מביזת מצרים וזהו שיסד ותורים יתירים... כשעלו מן הים לקחו יותר ממה שלקחו כשיצאו ממצרים״. וזה מיוסד על מכילתא דר׳ ישמעאל, עמ׳ 47, וראה בעה״ב ובהערות שם. **כתרים דוד הנזירה** – הקב״ה עיטר אותם בכתרים, השווה שבת פח ע״ב: ״כל דיבור ודיבור שיצא מפי הקב״ה קושרים לו שני כתרים״. אבל לא מצאתי את העניין של קשירת כתרים בשעת קריעת ים סוף.

80. **עזרה** – מעבר לתפילת ״עזרת אבותינו״ ששם שולב ״זולת״ זה בתפילה.

פיוט על ביזת היהודים

תלונות על העוני ועל המסים והקנסות הכבדים שהוטלו על היהודים על ידי הגויים ידועות היטב מספרות חז״ל ומימי הביניים. ר״א מרמורשטיין אסף את המקומות המדברים על עניין זה מהספרות התלמודית והמדרשית, והגר״ש ליברמן דן במקורות אלה על רקע שלטון רומי.[1] תלונות אלה מוצאות הד חזק בפיוטי ימי הביניים, במיוחד בפיוטי סליחות. י״ל צונץ, בספרו הגדול על שירת הקודש של ימי הביניים, פותח את דיונו בפרק על הסבל המתואר בספרות הפיוט, ובראש פרק זה עומדת רשימה של מקורות מתקופות וממקומות שונים שמדובר בהם על העול הכספי הקשה שנשא עם ישראל במאות הי״א ואילך באירופה בעקבות המיסוי והפקרת הנכסים שהטילה עליו הכנסייה.[2] לעתים קרובות מנסחים הפייטנים את דבריהם על נושא מכאיב זה בלשון חז״ל, כפי שמשתמע כבר מדברי צונץ שם. והרי מספר מצומצם של דוגמאות המאפיינות את ההתייחסות לעניין זה:

נִלְאֵתִי נְשׂוֹא עוֹל מַדְהֵבָה
נוֹאֶמֶת מְדוֹד וְהָבֵא הֲבָאָה־רַבָּה[3]

לִשְׁלוֹל וְלָבוֹז עֲמַל יָדֵימוֹ
...
רְאֵה כִּי־אָזְלַת־יָד וּמִכִּיס תַּם הַכֶּסֶף[4]
כְּנוֹס מַס וְחָמָס וַעֲנִיֵּיךְ יְרוֹשֵׁשׁוּ[5]

נְקוֹם הַדָּם וּנְקוֹם הֶחָמָס... חֵפֶץ פְּרוּטָה מִכִּיס אָזְלָה[6]

1 במאמרו של מרמורשטיין, תרביץ ג (תרצ״ב), עמ׳ 175-177, ובמאמרו של ליברמן, *JQR* 36 (1946), עמ׳ 344-370 (= Saul Lieberman, *Texts and Studies*, New York 1974, pp. 127-153)

2 L. Zunz, *Die synagogale Poesie des Mittelalters*, 2nd ed., Frankfurt am Main 1920, pp. 9-10

3 ר׳ גרשום מאור הגולה, סליחות ופזמונים, יוצאים לאור על ידי א״מ הברמן, ירושלים תש״ד, עמ׳ ח (= סדר הסליחות כמנהג פולין, מהד׳ ד׳ גולדשמידט, ירושלים תשכ״ד, עמ׳ מג, ושם הראה שהוא מיוסד על המאמר בשבת קמט ע״ב).

4 שם, עמ׳ יג-יד (= סליחות, עמ׳ קעח-קעט).

5 פיוטי שלמה הבבלי, מהד׳ עזרא פליישר, ירושלים תשל״ג, עמ׳ 342 (= סליחות, עמ׳ נא).

6 פיוטי רבי שמעון ב״ר יצחק, יוצאים לאור על ידי א״מ הברמן, ברלין־ירושלים תרח״ץ, עמ׳ קע-קעא (= סליחות, עמ׳ נה-נו).

אֵין תְּשׁוּרָה לְהָבִיא כִּי הַכֶּסֶף אָזַל
בַּמֶּה יְקַדֵּם פְּנֵי מֶלֶךְ עָשׁוּק וְנִגְזָל
...
מוֹרֶה מְאֹד עַמְּךָ יִשְׂרָאֵל נִתְדַּלְדַּל
סָגוּר וּמְעֻנֶּה נִבְזֶה וְאִישִׁים חֲדַל
מִשְׁמַן בְּשָׂרוֹ רָזֶה וּכְבוֹד יַעֲקֹב דַּל
עָנִי כִּי יַעֲטֹף כְּלַפָּיו הַטֵּה בְדַל
...
פַּרְנָסָה מוּעֶטֶת בְּאֵין פָּקוֹלִין וּמָעוֹת וְאִיסָרִים
...
רָץ אַחַר פַּרְנָסָתוֹ וְאֵין יָכוֹל לְהַגִּיעַ[7]

קוֹנְסוֹת לִמְדוֹד וְהָבֵא זִימִיּוֹת וַאֲרְנוֹנִיּוֹת
רוֹעֲצוֹת וְרוֹצְצוֹת וְגוֹבוֹת מֶנוּ מִסִּיּוֹת[8]

סוֹב נָא בְרַחֲמִים עַל גּוֹזַל הַנִּגְזָל
...
רְצוּצֵי עֲנִיֶּיךָ כֵּן תָּחִישׁ לִפְקוֹד
בְּזוּיֵי אַרְנוֹן יָרִימוּ קָדְקֹד[9]

גָּבָה מֶנִי פִּרְעוֹן חוֹבוֹת[10]

דִּלְדְּלוּ גִּלְגְּלוּ עֲנִיּוֹת בִּמְקוֹם עֲשִׁירוּת
...
הֶעֱשִׁירוּ גָּדְלוּ עָלוּ...
וּמִיַּחֲלֶיךָ מְעִידֶיךָ מָטָה יָדָם לְהִשְׁתַּבְּרָה
וְנִזְדַּלְזְלוּ וְנִדַּלְדְּלוּ וְצָלְלוּ לְהִשְׁתַּקֵּעַ כַּאֲבָרָה[11]

בּוֹסְסִים חוֹמְסִים נַחֲלַת חֶבְלְךָ רוֹמְסִים נוֹגְשִׂים וְהוֹלְמִים
יְגִיעֵנוּ חוֹטְפִים וְטוֹרְפִים וְעָלֵינוּ סוֹד מַעֲרִימִים
רוֹדְפִים וּמְרַדְּפִים וּמְגַדְּפִים וּמְאַיְּמִים
זֶה מַכֶּה וְזֶה מְדַכֵּא וְזֶה מְנַכֶּה בְּדָמִים[12]

7 ר׳ מאיר בר יצחק ש״ץ, ראה לקט פיוטי סליחות, מהד׳ ד׳ גולדשמידט וא׳ פרנקל, ירושלים תשנ״ג, עמ׳ 379-380. על שכיחות נושא זה בפיוטיו ראה שם, עמ׳ 796.

8 פיוטי רש״י, יוצאים לאור על ידי א״מ הברמן, ירושלים תש״א, עמ׳ יא. וראה בהערות שם שזה על פי המאמר בשבת קמט ע״ב הנ״ל ועפ״י ויקרא רבא, סוף פל״ג (מהד׳ מרגליות, עמ׳ תשסט).

9 ״תהיינה עיניך פקוחות״ לר׳ יוסף ברבי יצחק (המאות הי״א-י״ב), מחזור שד״ל, א, עט ע״א.

10 ר׳ יצחק בר יקר, לקט פיוטי סליחות (לעיל, הערה 7), עמ׳ 347.

11 הנ״ל, שם, עמ׳ 349-350.

12 ר׳ אלעזר מוורמייזא, שם, עמ׳ 79 (= שירת הרוקח – פיוטי רבי אלעזר מוורמייזא, מהד׳ יצחק מיזליש, ירושלים תשנ״ג, עמ׳ 111).

בְּאוֹנָאַת דְּבָרִים וּבְמָמוֹן לְעָנְשִׁי[13]

בִּקְשׁוּ לְהַעֲנִישִׁי לִמְנוֹעַ חֻקִּי וְלַחְסוֹר מְזוֹן טַפִּי

...

טָחֲנוּ דִכְּאוּ עֲנִיֵּי הַצֹּאן כְּרֶכֶב רֵיחַיִם קֶמַח

...

פּוֹרֵעַ חוֹבוֹת לֹא לִי מִמֶּשְׁכָּן לְכָל-עַוָּל[14]

בּוֹזְזַי נוֹאֲמִים הָאוֹכְלִים אוֹתִי וּמַדְקִים:
אֲכַלְתִּיךָ כַּמָּה שָׁנֵי חֲזָקָה וְיֵשׁ חֲזָקָה לַנְּזָקִים,
עוֹלֵל לָמוֹ כַּאֲשֶׁר עוֹלַלְתָּ לִי בְּשֶׁקֶל דַּנְקִים[15]

וּמַדּוּעַ אַנְפְּרוּת רַבָּה וְגוֹבִין מִן הַמְּחוֹרְרִין[16]

צָרוֹת כַּמָּה מִסִּים אֵיךְ אוּכַל שְׂאֵת
מִדֵּי שָׁנָה בְשָׁנָה מַתָּן אֶשָּׂא מַשְׂאֵת[17]

זָהָב זָהָב זָהָב יַחְשְׁבוּ עֹזְרֵי רָהַב
הָאוֹמְרִים לִי הַב הַב[18]

ואפשר להוסיף כהנה וכהנה.

הציטטות הנ״ל ודומותיהן נמצאות בפיוטים שבהם הפייטן מתלונן על אספקטים שונים של הגלות והרדיפות. הביזה והמיסוי והעוני הם רק חלק מכלל הסבל שהפייטן מקונן עליו. בפיוט המתפרסם להלן בפעם הראשונה, הנושא העיקרי הוא הלחץ הכספי מחמת המסים הכבדים והפחד מהשלטונות שבאים ומחרימים את רכושם של היהודים. לא ידוע לי שום פיוט אחר המוקדש לנושא זה באופן בלעדי. יש בפיוט גם רמז, כנראה, שהשלטונות ביטלו את החובות שהנוצרים היו חייבים ליהודים (טורים 9-10), וכמובן הפסידו על ידי זה הרבה כסף. הפחד של היהודים מהתקפות פתאומיות (טור 7) מתואר בצבעים חיים.

אין בפיוט עצמו שום נקודת אחיזה למקום או לזמן שנגזרו על היהודים גזרות אלה. בתור רקע אפשרי, ברצוני להצביע על מה שידוע על גזרות כאלה בצרפת ובאנגליה במאה הי״ג. במיוחד מלא ידיעות חשובות הוא החיבור ״מלחמת מצוה״ המיוחס לר׳ מאיר ב״ר

13 לפייטן בשם אליעזר, ראה לקט פיוטי סליחות (לעיל, הערה 7), עמ׳ 46.

14 פיוטי אליה בר שמעיה, מהד׳ יונה דוד, (ניו יורק) תשל״ז, עמ׳ 34-35.

15 ״פיוטי רבי אפרים ב״ר יעקב מבונא״, מהד׳ א״מ הברמן, ידיעות המכון לחקר השירה העברית ז (תשי״ח), עמ׳ 258, וראה שם בהערות.

16 ר׳ מאיר בר יצחק מאורליאנס, לקט פיוטי סליחות (לעיל, הערה 7), עמ׳ 401 ושם בהערות. לזהותו של פייטן זה ראה שם, עמ׳ 802-813.

17 לר׳ צדקיהו בן בנימן מהענוים, מבחר השירה העברית באיטליה, י״ל ע״י חיים שירמן, ברלין תרצ״ד, עמ׳ ק.

18 לר׳ יצחק הלוי גירונדי, ראה א״מ הברמן, עתרת רננים, ירושלים תשכ״ז, עמ׳ 178.

שמעון המעילי מנרבונה. חיבור זה הוא איגרת למלך צרפת, לואי התשיעי, המכונה "הקדוש". האיגרת נכתבה כתגובה לגזרות המלך באמצע המאה הי"ג על היהודים, שבהן אסר עליהם את ההתעסקות בהלוואת כספים. בתעודה זו נזכרים התאריכים 1245 ו־1270. ר' מאיר מדבר על העוני המעיק על בני ישראל בעקבות החקיקה החדשה של המלך, וכותב שהחוק שודד מהיהודים כל מה שיש להם. ר' מאיר מתאונן במיוחד על שהמלך ציווה שלא הקרן ולא הריבית של החובות שהגויים חייבים ליהודים יהיו נתונים לגבייה, וכל זה נוסף על המס הגדול שהטילו המלך ואבותיו על היהודים.[19] החוקרים[20] ניתחו את התעודה הזאת בעיון, ויש ללמוד ממנה הרבה על המצב הכספי של היהודים לאור הגזרות של אמצע המאה הי"ג. לא רק בצרפת היו גזרות כאלה, גם באנגליה נשלל רכושם של היהודים במאה הי"ג כמה פעמים על פי גזירות שונות של המלכים, ואף כאן יש בידינו תיעוד מפורט על הצעדים שנקטו השלטונות לשדוד רכוש יהודי כדי לצמצם את הפעילות המסחרית שלהם.[21] בפיוט שלפנינו מדבר הפייטן גם על מסירת נפש על קדושת השם (טור 15 וטורים 26-27). כידוע, הפקרת הנכסים והטלת מסים וקנסות היו מלוות לעתים בהריגת יהודים. כך קרה, למשל, בבריסטול שבאנגליה בשנת 1210 וכמה פעמים לפני שנה זו ולאחריה.[22]

הפיוט "שוקלי דמם" (כנראה צ"ל "שוקלי המס"), המתפרסם להלן, עוסק, בלי שום ספק, בנושא הנ"ל. הפיוט הוא מעין אזורי (סוג שיר סטרופי), בכל טור יש ארבע מילים, והוא חתום "שלמה", פעמיים, בראשי הטורים של המחרוזת הראשונה ובראשי שאר המחרוזות. לא יכולתי לזהות מי הוא שלמה זה.[23] הפיוט הוא מסוג הגאולה[24] והוא היה נאמר באחת השבתות שבין פסח לשבועות, שבהן קהילות אשכנז היו רגילות להוסיף לתפילות הקבועות פיוטי יוצר. בפיוטים אלה קוננו הפייטנים על הרדיפות, בעיקר אלה

19 ראה ספר המאורות לרבינו מאיר ב"ר שמעון המעילי מנרבונה... על מסכתות ברכות ופסחים, יוצא לאור על ידי משה יהודה הכהן בלוי, ניו יורק תשכ"ד, עמ' יד-כ. וראה בהערה הבאה.

20 Robert Chazan. "A Jewish Plaint to Saint Louis", *HUCA* 45 (1974), pp. 287-305; וראה הספרות הרשומה שם, בהערה 2. ראה גם: Kenneth R. Stow, "Papal and Royal Attitudes toward Jewish Lending in the Thirteenth Century", *AJSreview* 6 (1981), pp. 161-184

21 דיון מפורט על המיסוי, הביזה והקנסות וביטול החובות שהוטלו על היהודים בצרפת ובאנגליה במאה הי"ג נמצא בספרים הבאים: William Chester Jordan, *The French Monarchy and the Jews: From Philip Augustus to the Last Capetians*, Philadelphia 1989; H. G. Richardson, *The English Jewry under Angevin Kings*, London 1960; Zefira Entin Rokeah, *Medieval English Jews and Royal Officials*, Jerusalem 2000

22 ראה בספרות הנרשמת בהערה הקודמת. וראה לאחרונה במאמרה המפורט של סוזן איינבינדר – Susan L. Einbinder, "Meir b. Elijah of Norwich: Persecution and Poetry Among Medieval English Jews", *Journal of Medieval History* 26 (2000), pp. 145-162

23 פליישר במהדורתו לפיוטי ר' שלמה הבבלי (לעיל, הערה 5), עמ' 369, מזכיר את הפיוט ואת סימנו על פי צונץ וכ"י מינכן ופריס (ראה להלן), וכותב שאי אפשר לייחסו לר' שלמה הבבלי "בשום פנים". על זהותו האפשרית של הפייטן ראה להלן בהערות לטור 27 של הפיוט.

24 בכ"י פריס, כתוב בסופו "בגלל אבות תושיע בנים", המעבר הרגיל מפיוטי גאולה לברכת גאולה. בכ"י מינכן רשום עליו "גאולה". בכ"י ניו יורק בא אחריו פיוט שרשום עליו "גאולה".

שבעקבות מסעי הצלב, שאירעו בחודשים אייר וסיון, בימי ספירת העומר. הטקסט עצמו לא היה ידוע עד כה, ורק פירוש עליו היה כלול בספר "ערוגת הבשם".[25] בלי הטקסט דברי בעל "ערוגת הבשם" אינם מובנים כל צורכם. עכשיו, שהטקסט של הפיוט עומד לפנינו, מתבהרים דברי הפרשן.

הפיוט נשתמר בשלושה כתבי יד: 1 – כ"י ספריית בית המדרש לרבנים, מס' 8972, דף 242ב, שהוא אוסף פיוטים מאשכנז מסוף המאה הי"ג.[26] כתב יד זה מנוקד; 2 – כ"י מינכן, ספריית המדינה של באווריה, כ"י עברי 88, דף 107א, על הגיליון. יש בו פירוש מילים קשות בין השיטין. לפי קטלוג שטיינשניידר, החלק הישן של כתב היד, שהוא מחזור אשכנזי, נכתב במאה הי"ג (מ);[27] 3 – כ"י פריס, הספרייה הלאומית, כ"י עברי 646, דף 108ב, לפי הקטלוג של זוטנברג, מחזור אשכנזי מהמאה הי"ד (פ).[28] הפיוט נדפס על פי כתב היד שבספריית בית המדרש לרבנים וחילופי הגרסאות יובאו על פי שני כתבי היד האחרים ששניהם אינם מנוקדים.

שׁוֹקְלֵי דמם עַל הַיִּחוּד
לָכֵן שְׂכַרְכֶם בְּיוֹם־זֶה אָחוּד
מַה־לָּכֶם אֲנוּחִים לְבַבְכֶם פָּחוּד
הוּא קַל־יוֹשַׁת מְנַדֵּיכֶם כָּחוּד
בִּטְחוּ בוֹ בְּכָל־עֵת וַעֲנוּ בְּפַחַד
ה' אֱלֹקֵינוּ ה' אֶחָד

לְשַׁעֲטַת פְּרָסוֹת שַׁדַּי יִתַּר
לִבִּי סְחַרְחַר בְּקִרְבִּי נִיתַּר
בְּשׁוּרִי יְגִיעַי בְּיַד־אִישׁ נִיתַּר
דִּיבֵּר וְאָמַר מוּתָּר מוּתָּר
צוּרִי, אַל־נָא פָּנִים תִּסְתַּר
מְמוֹנוֹ לָבַז וְטִירָיו לְהַחְתַּר

25 ספר ערוגת הבשם לרבינו אברהם ב"ר עזריאל, מהד' א"א אורבך, ירושלים תרצ"ט-תשכ"ג, חלק שלישי, עמ' 539-541.

26 לכתב יד זה, ראה: ב' נרקיס, "ציורים לעשרת הדיברות במחזור אשכנזי זעיר בן המאה השלוש־עשרה", עשרת הדיברות בראי הדורות, ערך בן ציון סגל, ירושלים תשמ"ו, עמ' 389-407; מאמרי בעטרה לחיים – מחקרים בספרות התלמודית והרבנית לכבוד פרופסור חיים זלמן דימיטרובסקי, ירושלים תש"ס, עמ' 491-500, וראה שם, הערה 4 [לעיל, עמ' 155].

27 Moritz Steinschneider, *Die hebraieschen Handschriften der K. Hof-und Staatsbibliothek in München*, 2nd ed., München 1895, p. 55. אני מודה לד"ר בריגיטה גולת (Brigitte Gullath) על שהואילה בטובה לשלוח לי צילום הפיוט.

28 H. Zotenberg, *Catalogues des manuscrits hebreux et samaritains de la Bibliotheque Imperiale*, Paris 1866, pp. 93-94

וּבְנֵי אֵיתָן יַעֲנוּ בְּפַחַד
[ה׳ אֱלֹקֵינוּ ה׳ אֶחָד]

מָסַרְתִּי עַצְמִי עַל־קְדֻשַּׁת הַשֵּׁם
וְגַם־אֲנִי נֶאֱלַח חוֹטֵא וְאָשֵׁם
דַּאֲגַת לְבָבִי במורש רושם
וַאֲנִי בְּכָל־זֹאת מִכְּרָם נושם
יְרוּחַם עֲבָדַי מְיוּחָס בְּשֵׁם
וְגוֹבֵי הַמַּס תְּנִיעֵם תְּרוֹשְׁשֵׁם
וְיֵדְעוּ כִּי אַתָּה אֵל הַמְּיוּחָד
[ה׳ אֱלֹקֵינוּ ה׳ אֶחָד]

הָגֵן בְּחַסְדְּךָ אֱמוּנִים נְכוֹנִים
יְסוֹדֵי זֶרַע שְׁלֹשֶׁת אֵיתָנִים
שְׁבוּעַת אֲבוֹתָם יִהְיוּ מְגִינִּים
וְנוֹחֵל כְּלִימָּה יִרְאֶה קְנְיָינִים
בִּלְבוּשׁ צְבוּעִים גְּוָנִים גְּוָנִים
וְכֻלָּם מְיַחֲדִים אֵל הַמְּיוּחָד
ה׳ אֱלֹקֵינוּ ה׳ אֶחָד

חילופי גרסאות:

1. דמם – מ פ המס 2. לכן – מ פ לכם. ביום – מ יום. 3. לבבכם – פ ולבבכם. 8. לבי סחרחר בקרבי – פ לבי בקרבי סחרחר. ניתר – מ ויתר (?). 11. תסתר – מ נסתר. 12. ממונו לבז – פ תנה הונו לבז. וטיריו – מ פ וטירותיו. 16. פ חסר. וגם – מ גם. 19. עבדי – מ עברי פ עבדך. 20. וגובי המס – מ וגוביו (?) חמס פ וגובהי (?) חמס. 27. צבועים – מ פ מוצבע.

פירוש:

1-2 **שוקלי דמם וכו׳** – הגרסה הנכונה היא כנראה **שוקלי המס**, כפי שהיא בכ״י מ, ובכ״י פ ובערוגת הבשם (מכאן ואילך: עה״ב), ושם פירושו: ״אומ׳ שליח ציבור מכנסת ישר׳ השוקלים מס לאומות העולם ומייחדים שמו של הק בממונם״. **לכן שכרכם וכו׳** – בעה״ב (כמו בכ״י מ וכ״י פ): **לכם שכרכם**. ופירש עה״ב: ״כלומ׳ לכם אמור על ידי ישעי׳ הנביא ששכרכם אחוד ומיוחד לעתיד לבוא על כך, שנ׳: ׳ונוגשייך צדקה׳ (יש׳ ס יז)״. והשווה: ״וא״ר אלעזר: בזמן שבהמ״ק קיים, אדם שוקל שקלו ומתכפר לו. עכשיו, שאין בהמ״ק קיים, אם עושין צדקה מוטב, ואם לאו באין עובדי כוכבים ונוטלין בזרוע, ואעפ״כ נחשב להן לצדקה, שנ׳: ׳ונוגשיך צדקה׳״ (בבא בתרא ט ע״ב). והשווה פסיקתא דרב כהנא, מהד׳ ד׳ מנדלבוים, ראש פרשת כי תשא (פרשת שקלים), עמ׳ 17. המדרש מעמיד שם את מצוות השקלים מול המיסוי של עשו הרשע. בכל אופן, הפייטן רואה במסירת הרכוש לגויים ייחוד השם, בדומה למסירת הנפש, ואולי דבר זה מסביר את חילוף הנוסח המס – **דמם**, שיש במילה ״דמם״ הד למילה ״דמים״, דהיינו כסף. **ביום זה** – כנראה הכוונה לעתיד לבוא (ראה עה״ב; אבל ראה להלן, טור 3). **אחוד** – עה״ב: ״אחוד ומיוחד״, כנראה ראה במילה ״אחוד״ נרדפת למילה ״מיוחד״. 3. **מה לכם וכו׳** – עה״ב: ״מה לכם כנסת ישר׳ בגלות, שאתם אנוחים, לבבכם פחוד מדי יום יום מאימת אויבים״. ואולי הבין את הצירוף ״ביום זה״ שבטור הקודם

כמוסב לטור הזה. 4. **הוא קל יושת** – עה"ב: "כלומ' האויב יושת לכלימה וקלות על שמפחד אתכם בגזרותיו וגוזל ממון מכם". **מנדיכם כחוד** – השווה ישע' סו ה. עה"ב: "ושונאכם ומנדיכם יהיו כחוד מן העולם". ללשון, השווה בסליחה לר' יוסף טוב עלם: "טאט ממיריך בכחד", לקט פיוטי סליחות (ראה לעיל, הערה 7), עמ' 285. 5. **בטחו בו בכל עת** – תהלים סב ט. **בפחד** – ביראה. 6. **ה' אלקינו וכו'** – דברים ו ד. 7. **לשעטת פרסות** – השווה ירמיהו מז ג. עה"ב: "ישרא' אומ': כשאנו שומעים קול שעטת חבורת פרסות סוסים של אומות העולם קופצי' ודוהרים. ופי': באותה שעה סבורים אנו שעלינו נרעשים. ושעט לשו' רעש ודוהר הוא, ופ"ה [= ופסוק הוא] בירמיה". **שדי יתר** – בכ"י מ מעל למילים אלה: "לש' שבר". עה"ב: "שדי לשו' שבר. פ"ה: יומם ולילה תכבד עלי ידך נהפך לשדי (תהלים לב ד), וחברו מנחם עם: סלף בוגדים ישדם (משלי יא ג)". ופירש רש"י בתהלים הנ"ל: "ומנחם חבר לשון שדידה". דברי עה"ב "שבר עולי מיותר", אינם מובנים לי, וגם החלק השני של הטור קשה. 8. **לבי סחרחר בקרבי ניתר** – תהלים לח יא; איוב לז א. 9. **בשורי וכו'** – יגיעי, עמלי, רכושי, הוני, על פי יחזקאל כג כט, הנזכר הרבה פעמים בפיוטים, ראה לעיל: יגיענו חוטפים וטורפים (ליד ציון הערה 12); כחנו יגיענו הן גזלו (לקט פיוטי סליחות, ראה לעיל, הערה 7, עמ' 13); ואוכלים יגיעותי וכל מחמדים יקרים (שם, עמ' 283) ועוד. עה"ב: "פי': ביד איש הותר ממוני לו. כדכת': ראה ויתר גוים (חבקוק ג ו). ראה הק' ז' מצות שקיבלו עליהם בני נח ולא קיימום, עמד והתיר להם ממון ישר' (בבא קמא לח ע"א)". וראה הערת רא"א אורבך שם, הערה 77, המעיר שלשון הגמרא היא שונה, "עמד והתיר ממונן לישראל", והוא אומר: "ובודאי שגם המחבר הביא את המאמר בלש"ז, אלא שחסרות מלים אחדות בהם הוא מפרש את דברי הפייטן, המתלונן שממון ישראל הותר לגויים". אבל יותר נראה שבעל עה"ב הביא את הגמרא מבבא קמא רק כדי להוכיח ש"ויתר" הוא לשון התרת ממון (ולא כדעתו של ר' מתנה, ולפיה "ויתר" לישנא דאגלויי [גלות] הוא). והוא לא דייק בהבאת המאמר, ולא חסר כלום מדברי המפרש. בהמשך כתוב בעה"ב: "פ"א: **ביד איש ניתר**, כלומ' איש נתגאה ונתנשא, כמו: יתר שאת (בראשית מט ג), וכמו: מה יתרון לאדם (קהלת א ג)". 10. **דיבר ואמר מותר מותר** – עה"ב אינו מפרש טור זה, ואולי בנוסח שלפניו היה חסר. ונראה שפירש: האויב אמר (הכריז, הוציא צו) לבטל את החובות של הגויים שהיו חייבים ליהודים, התיר את ההתחייבות שלהם, שהייתה כמו נדר, וביטל אותה. ראה הספרות הרשומה לעיל, הערות 20-21. כידוע, "מותר מותר" משמש להתרת שבועות ונדרים, לצד הפורמולה המשולשת (מותר לך, מותר לך, מותר לך) הנפוצה יותר. ראה ספר האשכול, מהד' שלום אלבעק, ח"ב, עמ' 25, הערה ד. אני מודה לידידי הפרופסור נחמן דנציג על שהפנה את תשומת לבי למקור זה. 11. **אל נא פנים תסתר** – תהלים כז ט ועוד. הניקוד בא לצורך החריזה, וכך נקוד בכ"י בהמ"ל (ראה לעיל, בראש הפיוט). 12. **ממונו לבז וטיריו להחתר** – **וטיריו** – כ"י מ וכ"י פ: טירותיו. כנראה פירושו: בקשת ישראל שה' יתן את ממונו של האויב לבז, וטירותיו (מבצריו, ארמנותיו) יהיו נחתרות. השווה שמות כב ב ועוד. **ממונו לבז** – עה"ב: "לבזוז ולשלול ממונו". מה שכתוב בעה"ב: "ממונו לבד המשילנו עליו" משובש, ובמקור היה ממונו **לבז** (כדיבור המתחיל) ובעל עה"ב הוסיף פירושו: "המשילנו עליו". זאת אומרת יתן אותנו מושלים על האויב. 13. **ובני איתן** – איתן הוא אברהם, ראה בבא בתרא טו ע"א. **בפחד** – באימה וביראה. 15. **מסרתי עצמי על קדושת השם** – עה"ב: "אז בשע' גזירה כשבאו עלי אויבים". 16. **וגם אני נאלח חוטא ואשם** – עה"ב: "כלומ', אע"פ שאני נאלח, חוטא ואשם, אעפ"כ לא נסוגותי אחור לפרוש כפי לא' זר, כדרך שדרשו רבותי': כפלח הרמון רקתך (שיה"ש ד ג), אפילו ריקנין שבידך (צ"ל: שבך) מלאים מצות כרימון (עירובין יט ע"א). ומצינו גם שפי' אפי', כמו: הכל סג יחדיו נאלחו אין עושה טוב אין גם אחד (תהלים יד ג)". וראה הערות רא"א אורבך, שם. 17. **דאגת לבבי במורש רושם** – קשה לפרשו. בעה"ב מפרש: "כלומ', לבבי דואג על ירושת הרושם הגדול הנעשה אז בישר', שירשתי הרושם הזה אחרי הנהרגים על קידוש שמך. וירש לבבי דאגות ומכאובות". 18. **ואני בכל זאת מכרם נושם** – בכ"י מ, בין השיטין: "פי' כמו: או מי מנושיי" (ישעי' נ א). בעה"ב: "כלומ', אני כנסת ישר' בכל זאת הצרה שעברה עלינו, ואינך זוכר לי לזוכרינו ולגאלינו מן הגלות בזכותם, אלא עדיין אני מכרם של אומות העולם. **נושם**, לשו' הפסוק הוא: מי מנושי אשר מכרתי אתכם לו (ישעי' נ א). והיה לו להקדים **נושם למכרם**, כדרך הפסו', אלא בעבור החרז היפך. ופי' כאדם המלוה אל חברו על המשכון, ואין לו במה לפדות לו משכנו, כך אנו בין אומות העולם כמה שנים כבר ואין אנו נפדים, אלא נושה את מכרם" [הבאתי את דברי עה"ב בשינוי של הפיסוק – מח"ש]. 19. **ירוחם עבדי מיוחס בשם** – בנוסח שלפני עה"ב כנראה בא טור זה אחרי טור 20. הוא מסביר "מיוחס בשם" עפ"י הפסוק בבראשית ל"ב כ"ח, וקושר את הטור עם מה שנאמר בטור 21,

ומפרש שכאשר ייקראו בני יעקב בשם המיוחס והמעולה, ישראל, "אז ידעו כי אתה אל המיוחד על ידי גאולתם". 20. **וגובי המס** – ראה בחילופי הגרסאות. בעה"ב "גובין חמס", ופירש: "פי' לוקחין לשקר, הם אומות הגובין את ישר' לעבדים בחמס, כי לא נמכרנו להם, שנ': איזה ספר כריתות אמכם אשר שלחתיה או מי מנושי אשר מכרתי אתכם לו (ישעי' נ א)" וראה לעיל, טור 18. **תניעם תרושש** – עה"ב (בטעות: ותדושם): "לאומות העולם, וילכו נע ונד וירושו, כמו רוששנו (מלאכי א ד)". 23. **הגן בחסדך אמונים נכונים** – אמונים – בני ישראל, ישעי' כו ב ועוד. 24. **יסודי זרע שלשת איתנים** – עה"ב: "את ישר', שהם יסודי זרע שלשלת [כנראה בטעות, במקום שלשת] איתנים תקיפים, כמו שנ': והאיתנים מוסדי ארץ (מיכה ו ב)". האיתנים הם האבות. ראה ראש השנה יא ע"א. 25. **שבועת אבותם יהיו מגינים** – "יהיו" מוסב כנראה על "אבותם" ולא על "שבועת", והמובן ברור. 26. **ונוחל כלימה יראה קניינים** – השווה יחזקאל לד כט. עה"ב: "פי': יראו קניין עולם הבא". השווה עבודה זרה י ע"ב: "יש קונה עולמו בשעה אחת". לפי עה"ב, הכלימה היא שנהרגו על קידוש השם. אבל כנראה הכוונה גם על הבושה והכלימה שהיהודים סבלו בעקבות הרדיפות בכלל והפקרת ההון והמיסוי בפרט. ויש על זה רמז בסוף הטור: "יראה קניינים = הון (במקום נטילת ה"קניינים" שלקחו הגויים מהיהודים). 27. **בלבוש צבועים גוונים גונים** – בעה"ב, כמו בכ"י מ ובכ"י פ: "בלבוש מוצבע". בעה"ב: "ושנים גוונים" במקום "גוונים גונים" והפירוש שם: "בלבוש הריגתם שנמצא עליו כמה גווני דמים". והמהדיר מעיר שם לכתובות קיא ע"ב, ותוספות שם, ד"ה בלבושיהן, ויפה עיניים, והמקורות שצויינו שם, ומאמרו של ג' שלום, "לבוש הנשמות וחלוקא דרבנן", תרביץ כד (תשט"ו), עמ' 290 ואילך. שלום מביא שם (עמ' 291-292) את דברי הרמב"ן (על הפסוק בבראשית מ"ט ל"ג. וראה הערות במהד' חיים דב שעוועל, ירושלים תשי"ט, עמ' רעו-רעז): "כי נפשות הצדיקים צרורות בצרור החיים, וזו תחופף עליו כל היום, לובשת לבושת השני" וכו'. ואולי יש איזה קשר בין דברים אלה ("לבושת השני") ובין הגירסה של בעל עה"ב, "ושנים גוונים", אלא שהשתבשו הדברים ואינם מובנים כעת. גם בפיוטים וזכרונות שעל גזרות אשכנז וצרפת, יש זכר למלבושים שהקדושים מתלבשים בהם בעולם הבא. ראה גזירות אשכנז וצרפת, מהד' א"מ הברמן, ירושלים תש"ו, עמ' פב: "נפשותם צרורות בצרור החיים בתוך היכל המלך, מלובשים כל אחד מהם שמונה בגדים של ענני כבוד" (מדברי ר' אליעזר ב"ר נתן). וראה הערות הברמן, שם, עמ' רנב; שם, עמ' פז: "שפע טוב הצפון תשלום שכרם/ שמונה בגדי כבוד" וכו' (מהנ"ל); שם, עמ' קכג: "ועניין החסידים ההרוגים על יחוד השם נדרש במדרש 'מה רב טובך', בלקח טוב ובשוחר טוב, שלכל אחד שמונה בגדים ככהן גדול" וכו' (מתוך ספר זכירה לר' אפרים ב"ר יעקב מבונא). וראה *The Jews and the Crusaders: The Hebrew Chronicles of the First and Second Crusades*, Translated and Edited by Shlomo Eidelberg, The University of Wisconsin Press, Madison 1977, pp. 132, 179. המלבושים הנזכרים כאן הם כנראה לבנים, כך משתמע מהביטוי "בגדים של ענני כבוד" ואמנם הכהן הגדול לבוש בגדי לבן (אבל גם בגדי זהב), ובפיוט שלפנינו מדובר על בגדים צבעוניים, וכך גם משמעו של "לבוש השני" הנ"ל, וכנראה היו רווחות מסורות שונות בעניין זה. בפסק הלכה, המובא בשם רבינו יחיאל מפריס, כתוב שלא הלבישו בתכריכין להרוגים על קידוש השם, "ולא שינו כסותם", אלא השאירו אותם בבגדים שבהם נהרגו. וזה כמו שכתוב בעה"ב הנ"ל: "בלבוש הריגתם שנמצא עליו כמה גווני דמים". וראה אברהם דוד, "פרעות ביהודי צרפת בעת מסע הרועים של שנת י"א (1251)", תרביץ מו (תשל"ז), עמ' 251-257 (אני מודה לד"ר סוזן איינבינדר על שהפנתה את תשומת לבי אל מאמר זה). דוד, במאמרו הנ"ל, מציע השערה שאולי פיוט אחד מפייטן בשם שלמה בן יוסף מדבר גם כן על אותה הפורענות שרבינו יחיאל מפאריס מדבר עליה (ראה שם, עמ' 256-257). ומי יודע אם שלמה בן יוסף זה אינו זהה לשלמה, מחבר הפיוט שלפנינו? 28. **וכולם מיחדים אל המיוחד** – עה"ב: "שבשעת הגזירה אמ': שמע ישר' ה' אלקינו ה' אחד".

פיוט מעריב בלתי ידוע לשמיני עצרת שמחת תורה

במנהגי התפילה השונים בימי־הביניים היו נפוצים פיוטי מעריב שעיטרו את קריאת השמע וברכותיה בלילי החג. פיוטי מעריב כאלה, שנקראו "מעריבים" או "מעריבות", היו שכיחים ואהובים מאוד במנהג אשכנז וצרפת ונמצאו גם במנהגי איטליה ורומניא. תחילתו של סוג פיוטי זה היא בתקופה הקלאסית של הפייטנות בארץ ישראל, והסוג זכה ליצירה מרובה בימי־הביניים במרכז־אירופה. מספר פיוטי המעריב גדול; לליל שמיני עצרת בלבד ידועות שמונה מערכות שונות במנהג אשכנז וצרפת.[1] בין מחברי פיוטי מעריב נמנה גם רבנו תם,[2] שבעל היובל [יונה דוד] עומד להוציא לאור את פיוטיו.

כאן מוגש מעריב בלתי ידוע לשמיני עצרת שמחת תורה ששם מחברו היה משה, כמו שחתום בטורים 23, 66-68 של הפיוט, אך איננו יכולים לזהותו בוודאות עם שום פייטן ידוע.[3] הפיוט נמצא, יחד עם שאר פיוטים מהסוג הזה, ובכלל אלה פיוט המעריב הנ"ל של רבנו תם, בכתב־יד של בית המדרש לרבנים באמריקה, מס' 8972, דף 163 ע"ב.[4] הפיוט

1 על פיוטי מעריב בכלל ראה עזרא פליישר, שירת הקודש העברית בימי־הביניים, ירושלים 1975 (להלן פליישר), עמ' 243 ואילך ועמ' 463 ואילך. על פיוטי מעריב בסוכות וכו' במנהג אשכנז וצרפת ראה מחזור לסוכות, שמיני עצרת ושמחת תורה, לפי מנהגי אשכנז לכל ענפיהם וכו', מוגה מעובד ומבואר בידי דניאל גולדשמידט, הושלם בידי יונה פרנקל, ירושלים תשמ"א (להלן מחזור לסוכות), עמ' כז-לא.

2 ראה מחזור לסוכות עמ' 46 ואילך ועמ' 315 ואילך.

3 בטורים 24-25 יש כמה אותיות שאפשר שמצטרפות לשם בר י[...]סף. על חכם בשם משה בר יוסף שחי בנרבונה במאה הי"ב ראה במאמרו של ב"ז בנדיקט, תרביץ יט (תש"ח) עמ' 19 ואילך. אין בידינו שום ראיה לזהות אותו עם מחבר הפיוט שלפנינו.
פרופסור עזרא פליישר, כאשר קרא את המאמר, גילה שבתוך הפיוט חתום גם שם אביו של הפייטן (דבר שנעלם ממני): **חסדאי** (טורים 24-25, 34-40: **חוסיך** (או: סחופים)... דלות מאוים; מעון שכלל... היכלו... בישע[ך] נגיל... חיזיון ספון... דשוש איים. לפי זה יש לתקן את מה שכתבתי בביאור לטור 40. כפי שהודיע לי פרופסור פליישר, משה בר חסדאי הוא החכם המפורסם ר' משה תקו, בעל ס' כתב תמים, שעד עכשו היו ידועים ממנו רק שני פיוטי סליחות, ראה צונץ, ליטרטורגשיכטה, עמ' 317. הוא העיר גם שהמחבר אולי חתום גם בטורים 26-27, 30-32: **קרוב** או **קרובה** וחזן או **החזן**: קבץ, רחומיך, ובקשם, הנאור, חוק [זמן], נערצים. תודתי העמוקה נתונה לו על הערותיו החשובות והמאלפות. על ר' משה תקו ראה בספרו של א"א אורבך, בעלי התוספות, ירושלים תש"ם, עמ' 420-425.

4 ראה על כתב יד זה בצלאל נרקיס, "ציורים לעשרת הדיברות במחזור אשכנז זעיר בן המאה השלוש־עשרה", עשרת הדיברות בראי הדורות, בעריכת בן־ציון סגל, ירושלים תשמ"ו, עמ' 389 ואילך; וראה גם מה שכתבתי בס' עטרה לחיים: מחקרים בספרות התלמודית והרבנית לכבוד פרופסור חיים זלמן דימידרובסקי, ירושלים תש"ס, עמ' 492. דרך אגב ברצוני להעיר שבנוסח פיוטו של רבנו תם שבכתב

אינו מנוקד, אף על פי שרוב רובם של הפיוטים שבכתב היד מנוקדים. יש ללמוד מכך שכבר בזמן כתיבת כתב היד אמירת הפיוט לא הייתה שכיחה ולכן השאיר אותו הסופר בלי ניקוד. מעניין גם שהסופר העתיק את טור 19 בלי החרוז השני הדרוש שם, מפני שכנראה כבר בימיו, בערך במאה הי"ג, לא הכירו את הטקסט בשלמותו.

בניין הפיוט זהה למה שידוע לנו משאר הפיוטים של הסוג: "בתים קצרים, בני ארבעה טורים, לכל פסקה, ופיוט יותר רחב להכנסה בתוך ברכת הגאולה" – כניסוחו הקצר של דניאל גולדשמידט.[5] כמו בהרבה פיוטי מעריב אחרים בא בברכת הפורס פיוט שצורתו שונה משאר הפיוט, והוא נקרא במקורות "תוספת".[6] סימן הא"ב משתרע על חלקו הראשון של הפיוט, עד טור 22, ואחריו באה כאמור חתימת השם משה. בטורים 41-26 אין סימן, ומטור 42 ואילך הפייטן מתחיל סימן א"ב חדש. בסוף הפיוט חתום "משה חזק". כנהוג בפיוטים מסוג זה, בטור האחרון שלפני חתימת הברכה או הפסקה משתמש הפייטן בלשון הרומזת על מטבע הברכה או על נוסח הקבע של הפסקה, כגון בטור 4, "ולילה ללילה", הרומז ללשון הברכה "ומעביר יום ומביא לילה"; כמו כן המילה "אהבה" בטור 8 מגשרת אל מטבע הברכה שבא אחריה: "אוהב עמו ישראל"; וכן בטורים 29, 33, 37, 41,[7] 71. מספר המילים בבתים בני ארבעה הטורים אינו קבוע, אבל לרוב יש בטור ארבע מילים. בהרחבת הפיוט שבאה אחרי שני הבתים הראשונים יש מילות קבע בתחילת כל טור ("שמיני") ובסופו ("ביום השמיני"), כנהוג.[8] בחלק הזה מחולק הטור לשני חלקים חורזים, והחלק השני של הטור הוא לרוב פסוק מהמקרא. סימן הא"ב המתחיל בטור 1 של הפיוט נמשך לאורך ההרחבה הזאת. התופעה הזאת אינה שכיחה בפיוטי המעריב האשכנזיים והצרפתיים, והיא צורה ארכאית, כי בדרך כלל מתחיל סימן חדש עם ההרחבה.[9] כמו בשאר ההרחבות בפיוטי מעריב, אשכנזיים וצרפתיים, גם כאן מזכיר הפייטן את ענייני החג והלכותיו.[10]

היד (דף 159 ע"ב) יש שינויים לגבי הטקסט הנדפס במחזור לסוכות והנה כמה מהם: לעמ' 315, טור 1: בעצרת אום עצום ימינך מאדרת; לטור 3: תשועות; לעמ' 316, טור 7: זה היום נכבד בעשרת; לטור 18: בחק-חסר; לטור 19: קדש ללינה לשלשים ידחם; לעמ' 317, טור 20: ראוי לקרבן עצמו להכשיר; שם, לטור 5: בהשקט ובבטחה; לטור 6: קטורת לפניך תיכון שיחה; לטור 8: ברוב תנחומיך.

5 ראה במאמרו, "מעריב לליל שביעי של פסח לרבי יוסף טוב עלם", הנ"ל, מחקרי תפילה ופיוט, ירושלים תשל"ט, עמ' 381.

6 ראה מחזור לסוכות (לעיל, הע' 1), עמ' כז ולהלן הערה לטור 19 של הפיוט.

7 בלי ה"תוספת" (טורים 42-71) כאן הייתה צריכה לבוא החתימה של הברכה האחרונה של קריאת שמע וברכותיה שבתפילת מעריב, דהיינו: "הפורס סוכת שלום" וכו'. כדי לרמוז לברכז זו בחר הפייטן בחרוז "-לום" וסיים במילה: "לשלום". אולם חתימת הברכה "האמיתית" מופיעה רק אחרי גמר ה"תוספת", ובמילה "ירושלים" בטור האחרון של הפיוט רומז הפייטן שוב ללשון הברכה המעבירה ל"הפורס סוכת שלום... ועל ירושלים". מעברים "מדומים" כאלה נמצאים גם בסוגי פיוט אחרים, ראה למשל על "סטרופות-סיום מדומות" אצל פליישר (לעיל, הע' 1), עמ' 145. כך הוא גם בפיוטי מעריב אחרים, ראה מחזור לסוכות (שם), עמ' 9-10, 23-27 ועוד.

8 ראה פליישר (לעיל, הע' 1), עמ' 245, 465. מילות קבע דומות נמצאות גם בשאר פיוטי המעריב לשמיני עצרת, ראה מחזור לסוכות (שם), עמ' 311, 315, 325, 328.

9 ראה על תופעה זו במחזור לסוכות (שם), עמ' כח והערה 18 שם, וראה פליישר, עמ' 465.

10 ראה פליישר, שם.

ב״תוספת״, כאמור, יש סימן א״ב וחתימה ״משה חזק״, והיא בנויה על מחרוזות בנות שישה טורים כשהטור האחרון הוא פסוק מהמקרא.

סגנון הפיוט פשוט בדרך כלל, אבל בכמה מקומות, כפי שצוין בהערות לגוף הפיוט, יש ניסוחים שהבנתם קשה. נושא הפיוט הוא שמיני עצרת ושאר דברים הקשורים למספר שמונה, כגון ברית מילה. כרגיל בפיוטים דומים, הפייטן מזכיר את העניינים שבהם מצטיין חג זה, כמו שמבואר בבבלי מסכת סוכה מז ע״ב - מח ע״א ובמס׳ יומא ב עב - עג ע״א ששמיני עצרת רגל בפני עצמו הוא לענין פז״ר קש״ב, דהיינו: פיס, זמן, רגל, קרבן, שיר וברכה; וראה רש״י שם. רמזים לכך נמצאים בפיוט שלפנינו, בטורים 20-22.[11] בטורים האחרונים של השיר מדבר הפייטן על חג שמחת תורה. בדרך כלל בפיוטי מעריב לשמיני עצרת אין זכר מיוחד לחג זה ו״הם מתחלקים בין שני הלילות ללא כל אבחנה״.[12] מבחינת החריזה יש לשים לב לחריזת העיצורים בי״ת רפה וו״ו בטור 11.[13]

הפיוט

אֱלֹהֵי צִדְקִי אֲקַוֶּה
בְּחוֹגְגֵי שְׁמִינִי לִי חַסְדּוֹ יְצַוֶּה
גְּבוּרוֹתָיו מַזְכִּירִים יְחַלֵּץ וְיַרְוֶה
דְּבַר יוֹם בְּיוֹמוֹ וְלַיְלָה לְלַיְלָה יְחַוֶּה בא״י המעריב ערבים

הוֹפַעְתָּ מֵאָז בְּאַלְפֵי רְבָבָה
וּמִימִינְךָ אֵשׁ דָּת כְּתוּבָה
זְכוּת סְגוּלִי[ם] לְרוֹמְמָה וּלְשַׂגְּבָהּ
חִכָּה יְשׁוּעָתְךָ חוֹלֵה אַהֲבָה בא״י אוהב עמו ישראל

שְׁמִינִי טֵכֵּס לִשְׁמוֹר/ אֶת אַבְרָהָם לֵאמוֹר בַּ[יוֹם] הַ[שְּׁמִינִי]
שְׁ[מִינִי] יָסַף לְחַדֵּשׁ בְּבֵית בִּנְיָינוֹ/ וַיָּמָל אַבְרָהָם אֶת יִצְחָק
בְּנוֹ בַּ[יוֹם] הַ[שְּׁמִינִי]

1. עפ״י תהלים ד ב, ישעי׳ נא ה, בראשית מט יח. 2. שמיני – שמיני עצרת (ושמחת תורה). **חסדו יצוה** – עפ״י תהלים מב ט. 3. **גבורותיו מזכרים** – בשמיני עצרת מזכירין גבורות גשמים (ראו משנה תענית א א). **יחלץ וירוה** – עפ״י ישעי׳ נח יא, כלומר, יגאל וישביע את אלה המזכירים את גבורות הגשמים, דהיינו את ישראל. 4. עפ״י שמות ה יג ועוד, ותהלים יט ג. 5. עפ״י דברים לג ב ובראשית כד ס. 6. **ומימינך** – בכה״י ״וממיניך״, והטור עפ״י דברים לג ב. 7. **סגולי[ם]** – ישראל, עם סגולה. **ולשגבה** – עפ״י תהלים כ ב. 8. **חולה אהבה** – בפסוק ״חולת אהבה״, שיה״ש ב ה. 9. **טכס לשמור וכו׳** – נערך, סודר לשמור את מצוות מילה ביום השמיני, עפ״י בראשית יז ט ואילך, וכן ויקרא יב ג. **את אברהם לאמור** – בראשית כג ה. 10. **שמיני יסף לחדש בבית בניינו** – המובן אינו ברור לגמרי, אבל כנראה הפייטן התכוון לקשר את העניין של שמונה ימי מילה עם שמיני עצרת, כמו שנדרש הפסוק ״יספת לגוי״ וגו׳ בפסיקתא דרב כהנא, מהד׳ דב מנדלבוים, עמ׳ 421-422 על שני העניינים: ״׳ביום השמיני עצרת תהיה לכם׳ וגו׳. ׳יָסַפְתָּ לַגּוֹי ה׳ יָסַפְתָּ לַגּוֹי׳ (ישע׳ כו טו). אומות העולם את נותן להם בן זכר וכו׳ אבל ישראל את נותן לאחד מהם בן זכר והוא מונה

11 ראה מחזור לסוכות (שם), עמ׳ 293, 303, 311, 316, 325 (וההערה לטור 2 שם).

12 ראה שם, עמ׳ ל.

13 ראה על תופעה זו בפיוטי בני אשכנז וצרפת במאמרה של שולמית אליצור, ״חריזת הפיוטים ודרכי ההגייה של בני צרפת ואשכנז הקדומים״, לשוננו 58 (תשנ״ד-תשנ״ה), עמ׳ 325.

שְׁ[מִינִי] כִּיהֵן וְחִסֵּר וְקֵירֵב/ וְהָיְתָה לּוֹ וּלְזַרְעוֹ אַחֲרָיו בַּ[יוֹם] הַ[שְּׁמִינִי]
שְׁ[מִינִי] לֶעָתִיד בְּכִינּוֹר לַעֲלוֹת/ לַמְנַצֵּחַ בִּנְגִינוֹת בַּ[יוֹם] הַ[שְּׁמִינִי]
שְׁ[מִינִי] מִבְחַר זֶבַח לְמַגִּישַׁי/ יֵרָצֶה לְקָרְבַּן אִשַּׁי בַּ[יוֹם] הַ[שְּׁמִינִי]
שְׁ[מִינִי] נְאֻם שַׁבָּת לְהַקְדִּימָהּ/ בִּבְרִית זכר [...] בַּ[יוֹם] הַ[שְּׁמִינִי]
שְׁ[מִינִי] סְפוּת עֲצֶרֶת חֶמְדָּתְךָ/ יָסַפְתָּ לַגּוֹי נִכְבַּדְתָּ בַּ[יוֹם] הַ[שְּׁמִינִי]
שְׁ[מִינִי] עַל שִׁבְעִים לְהַקְרִיב קָרְבָּנוֹ/ תַּחַת אַהֲבָ[ה] יִשְׂטְנ[וּ] בַּ[יוֹם] הַ[שְּׁמִינִי]
שְׁ[מִינִי] פַּר הִקְרִיבוּ עַל עַצְמֵיכֶם/ עֲצֶרֶת תִּהְיֶה לָכֶם בַּ[יוֹם] הַ[שְּׁמִינִי]
שְׁ[מִינִי] צֵטת מִסּוּכָּה לְבָתֵּיהֶם/ עֲרוֹךְ שׁוּעַ עַל גִּשְׁמֵיהֶם בַּ[יוֹם] הַ[שְּׁמִינִי]
שְׁ[מִינִי] קוֹדֶשׁ מוֹעֵד לְהֵחָשֵׁב/ אוֹתוֹת בְּתוֹסֶפֶת [...] בַּ[יוֹם] הַ[שְּׁמִינִי]
שְׁ[מִינִי] רְאִיַּית רֶגֶל פְּנוֹת בֹּקֶר לְאָהֳלוֹ/ וְשָׁלְמוּ יְמֵי אֶבְלוֹ בַּ[יוֹם] הַ[שְּׁמִינִי]
שְׁ[מִינִי] שִׁיר מְיוּחָד לְהַזְמִינִי/ לַמְנַצֵּחַ עַל הַשְּׁמִינִית בַּ[יוֹם] הַ[שְּׁמִינִי]
שְׁ[מִינִי] תְּפִילָּה וְזִימּוּן יְבָרְכוּ/ מְבָרְכֵי אֶת הַמֶּלֶךְ וַיְבָרְכוּ בַּ[יוֹם] הַ[שְּׁמִינִי]
שְׁ[מִינִי] מִמָּרוֹם שַׁוְעָתִי הַקְשִׁיבָה/ אֶת שְׁבוּתֵי[נוּ] ה׳ הָשִׁיבָ[ה] בַּ[יוֹם] הַ[שְּׁמִינִי]

לשמונה ימים ומל אותו" וכו׳. **וימל אברהם** וכו׳ – בראשית כא ד. 11. **שמיני כיהן** וכו׳ – בכל ימי חג הסוכות חיסר, הפחית הכהן ממספר הקרבנות שהקריב, ראה במדבר כט יב ואילך. **והיתה לו** וגו׳ – שם כה יג. 12. **לעתיד** וכו׳ – לעתיד לבוא יעלו לירושלים בשמיני עצרת וינגנו בכינור וישוררו "למנצח בנגינות". ראה תהלים ו א והשווה דה"י א טו כא. 13. עפ"י ויקרא כב כז והשווה מלאכי א יא. 14. אחרי המילה "זכר" באות בכתב היד עוד שתי מילים שהסופר כתב אותן בקיצור ("וקר׳ בה׳") ואיני יכול להשלימן. 15. **שמיני ספות** וכו׳ – הוספת את יום השמיני כעצרת. **יספת לגוי** וגו׳ – ישעי׳ כו טו, והפסוק הזה נדרש על שמיני עצרת. ראה לעיל ביאורו לטור 10. 16. **על שבעים** וכו׳ – שבעים פרים שהקריבו ישראל בחג הסוכות הן כנגד שבעים אומות העולם, ראה פסיקתא דרב כהנא, עמ׳ 433 ומקבילות. **תחת אהבה** וגו׳ – תהלים קט ד. הפייטן שינה את לשון הכתוב למען החרוז, ורצונו לומר שישראל מקריב קרבנות למען האומות, והן במקום לאהוב את ישראל על כך שונאים אותו. 17. עפ"י במדבר כט לה-לו. הפר שהקריבו בשמיני עצרת בא על עצמם, על עם ישראל. 18. **צאת** וכו׳ – בשמיני עצרת יוצאים מן הסוכה וחוזרים לבתיהם. **ערוך שוע** וכו׳ – עפ"י איוב לו יט, עורכים תפילה (על הגשם). וראה מחזור לסוכות (לעיל, הע׳ 1), עמ׳ 172, הערה לטור 1 של הפיוט "אערך שועי". 19. **קודש מועד** וכו׳ – שמיני עצרת נחשב כמועד בפני עצמו וכמקרא קודש. **אותות בתוספת** – אחרי המילה "תוספת" יש מקום ריק בכתב היד למילה אחת ובאמת חסירה כאן המילה החורזת על "להחשב". המילה "תוספת" נזכרת בהקשר דומה בפיוט מעריב לשמיני עצרת לפייטן עלום שם, ראה מחזור לסוכות, עמ׳ 311 טור 2. 20. **ראיית רגל** וכו׳ – מי שעולה לרגל חייב ללון בירושלים ורק בבוקר הוא יכול ללכת אל ביתו. **ושלמו** וגו׳ – ישעי׳ ס כ. הרגל מבטל את האבלות. השווה בפיוט המעריב של רבנו תם, מחזור לסוכות, עמ׳ 316 טור 19. בטור זה ובשני הטורים הבאים הפייטן רומז ל"פז"ר קש"ב", יומא ב ע"ב, ראה במבוא לעיל. 21. **שיר מיוחד** וכו׳ – הכוונה לשיר מיוחד שהלוויים היו אומרים ביום זה. **למנצח על השמינית** – תהלים ו א. "להזמיני/ השמינית" אינן חורזות והפייטן כנראה "ויתר" על החריזה למען הבאת הפסוק כלשונו. ולעניין זה השווה בפיוט מעריב במחזור לסוכות, עמ׳ 312 טור 6: "שמיני ועד בשיר להשיחו/ על השמינית בנצוחו", ובהערות שם. 22. **תפילה** וכו׳ – בשמיני עצרת מזכירים בתפילה ובברכת המזון שהוא יום שמיני עצרת, כלומר שהוא חג בפני עצמו. **מברכי** וגו׳ – מל"א ח סו. ומדובר שם על יום

שְׁ[מִינִי] בָּרֵךְ חוּסֵךְ פַּלֵּט / יִקְרָא בְּשֵׁם ה׳ יִמָּלֵט   בַּ[יוֹם] הַ[שְּׁמִינִי]
שְׁ[מִינִי] סְחוּפִים דַּלּוֹת מַאֲוָיִם / לְהָשִׁיב בִּמְצוּלוֹת יָם   בַּ[יוֹם] הַ[שְּׁמִינִי]

שְׁ[מִינִי] קַבֵּץ רְחוּמֶיךָ וּבַקֵּשׁ מֵעַמִּים
בִּיטָה אֶנְקָתָם וּזְכוֹר תְּמִימִים
מַלֵּא שִׁמְךָ הַנִּכְבָּד וְכִסְאֲךָ מְרוֹמִים
עֲנוֹת שִׁירָה כְּשָׁר עוֹבֵר אָורחוֹת יַמִּים   בגילה מלכותך

הַנָּאוֹר חוֹסֶן וּבָרֵךְ נֶצַח מְבָרְכִים
חוֹק וְקוֹדֶשׁ שַׁבָּתוֹן מְקַיְּימִים וּמִסְתּוֹכְכִים
נַעֲרָצִים תּוֹשִׁיעַ מִיַּד פּוֹרְכִים
עוֹשֵׂי דְבָרְךָ שִׁמְךָ מְיַחֲדִים וּמְבָרְכִים   זה צור ונ׳ כי פדה

מָעוֹן שַׁכְלֵל והתכלל הֵיכָלוֹ
מְשִׁיחָיו קְרָ[א] וְיָדָיו רָב לוֹ
עַמְּךָ תְּרַחֵם מָגִינִּי וּתְמוֹךְ גּוֹרָלוֹ
אַחֲרֵי נִמְכַּר גְּאוּלָּה תִּהְיֶה לוֹ   בא״י גאל ישר׳ השכיבנו

בִּישְׁעֲ[ךָ] נָגִיל וְאַל תִּתְעַלֵּם עֵלוֹם
חִיזָּיוֹן סָפוּן גַּלֵּה וְאַל תִּגְלוֹם
דִּשׁוּשׁ אִיִּים הוּשַׁמָּה שְׁכִינָתְךָ בָּהּ לַהֲלוֹם
תְּנַחֵם עִיר קָודְשֶׁךָ וְקָרָא[תָ] אֵלֶיהָ לְשָׁלוֹם

השמיני של החג. 23. **שועתי הקשיבה** – עפ״י תהלים ה ג. **את שבותי[נו]** וגו׳ – תהלים קכו ד. 24. **חוסך פלט** – השווה תהלים לא ב. **יקרא וגו׳** – יואל ג ה. 25. **סחופים וכו׳** – בני ישראל שהיו סחופים בגלות מקומים שיגאלו ביום זה. **להשיב וגו׳** – תהלים סח כג (בפסוק: ״ממצולות״). 27. **ביטה** – הביטה. 28. **מלא שמך** – עפ״י פסחים נ ע״א: ״א״ר נחמן בר יצחק לא כעולם הזה העולם הבא, העולם הזה נכתב ביו״ד ה״י ונקרא באל״ף דל״ת אבל לעולם הבא כולו אחד״ וכו׳, ועפ״י פסיקתא דרב כהנא, עמ׳ 53: ״ר׳ לוי בשם ר׳ הונא בר׳ חנינא כל זמן שזרעו של עמלק קיים בעולם לא השם שלם ולא הכסא שלם, אבד זרעו של עמל׳ מן העולם, השם שלם והכסא שלם״. וכן גם בפיוטו של ר׳ שמעון בר׳ יצחק: ״שם יקרא ככתיבתו/ מחציתו תתמלא תיבתו// עוד תתנשא מלכותו/ וכסאו יכון במלאתו״; ראה מחזור פסח לפי מנהג בני אשכנז לכל ענפיהם... מוגה מעובד ומבואר בידי יונה פרנקל, ירושלים תשנ״ג, עמ׳ 504. **וכסאך מרומים** – ישעי׳ ו א. 29. **כשר עובר אורחות ימים** – כמו שהיה שר משה רבנו, ״אז ישיר משה״ וגו׳. **עובר וגו׳** – תהלים ח ט. 30. **הנאור חוסן** – הקב״ה, השווה תהלים עו ה וישעי׳ לג ו. **וברך וכו׳** – ותברך את אלה שמברכים אותך. 31. **חוק וקודש וכו׳** – מקיימים את השבת ואת חג הסוכות כיום קדוש כחוק, והשווה שמות טו כה שפירשוהו על השבת (״חק זה השבת״, מכילתא דרבי ישמעאל, מהד׳ הורוביץ־רבין עמ׳ 156). 32. **נערצים** – ישראל, כדוגמת נקדשים. **פורכים** – המצרים, עפ״י שמות א יג. **עושרי דברך וכו׳** – ישראל. 34. **מעון** – בית המקדש, עפ״י תהלים כו ח. **והתכלל** – אולי כמו משתכלל. 35. **וידיו רב לו** – דברים לג ז. 36. **מגיני** – הקב״ה. **ותמוך גורלו** – של ישראל, עפ״י תהלים טז ה. 37. **אחרי וגו׳** – ויקרא כה מח. 38. **בישע[...] נגיל** – ישע׳ כה ט. **ואל תתעלם** – תהלים נה ב. **עלום** – כנראה כמו עילום, במובן לעולם, ראה דה״י ב לג ז. 39. **חזיון ספון** – החיזיון הסתום, השווה דניאל ח כו. **ואל תגלום** – אל תכסה. 40. **איים** – ארצות. אבל הטור מגומגם ואולי ת״ל ״דרוש עיים (בעי״ן) הושמה״, עפ״י תהלים עט ב: ״שמו את ירושלים לעיים״. אבל גם כך יישאר מובן הטור מעורפל. **הושמה שכינתך בה להלום** – ״הלום״ לשון מלכות, עפ״י זבחים קב ע״א: ״ואין

אֲבָרֵךְ אֶת ה׳ חָזָק גּוֹאֲלֵינוּ
בַּגּוּף נִגְלָה תַּנִּין לְצַמֵּת בִּגְלָלֵינוּ
גְּדוֹלוֹת בְּדָורְכוֹ בַּיָּם רָאוּ וַיַּאֲמִינוּ
דְּגָלָי[ם] נָסְעוּ מִן שָׁמַיִם לָקְטוּ וְטָחֲנוּ
הוֹפִיעַ בְּרֶכֶב רִבּוֹתַיִים תְּמִימָה לְהַנְחִילֵנוּ
[ו]מָה אַדִּיר שִׁמְךָ ה׳ אֲדוֹנֵינוּ

זְבוּל מִשְׁכְּנוֹת מִקְדָּשׁוֹ נַחַל מְטַהֵר נְטָעָם
חֶלְקִי ה׳ חֶלְקוֹ חֶבֶל מֻונְעָם
טוֹבוּ אוֹהָלִים עוֹלֵי רְגָלִים בְּהַגִּיעָם
יְפֵה נוֹף מְשׂוֹשֵׂינוּ לְהֵרָאוֹת בְּשִׁילוּשׁ פַּעַם
כְּבוֹד הַלְּבָנוֹן רֶגֶשׁ רִינָּה בְּהָרִיעָם
לִפְנֵי ה׳ בְּהִתְאַסֵּף רָאשֵׁי עָם

מִצִּיּוֹן מִכְלַל יוֹפִי בְּרָכָה גְאוּלָּה הופעת
נֶחָמוֹת תּוֹרָה חַיִּים יְשׁוּעוֹת
סְעָדֵינוּ אֱלֹקִים יֶשַׁע תחיה (?) מְחַכִּים בְּשִׁבְטְךָ רְעוֹת
עַד אָנָה פָּנֶיךָ תַּסְתִּיר תְּאַמֵּץ בִּרְכַּיִם כּוֹרְעוֹת
פְּדוּת לְנַפְשִׁי שְׁלַח שחה ברכות רעות
צֶמַח תַּצְמִיחַ אֵל דֵּיעוֹת
קְרָא דְרוֹר לִשְׁבוּיֶיךָ בַּשֵּׂר שְׁנַת גְּאוּלַי

הלום אלא מלכות״; וראה גם עבודה זרה מד ע״א: ״כל הראוי למלכות הולמתו״. **שכינתך** – בכ״י ״שכינך״. **בה** – אולי צ״ל בהם (ה״איים״). 41. **וקרא[ת] אליה לשלום** – דברים כ י. 42. **חזק גואלינו** – עפ״י לשון התפילה ״כי גואל חזק אתה״. 43. **בגוף נגלה** – אולי פירושו עפ״י מה שנאמר במכילתא דרבי ישמעאל, עמ׳ 129: ״׳ה׳ איש מלחמה ה׳ שמו׳, ר׳ יהודה אומר... מגיד שנגלה אליהם הקב״ה בכל כלי זיין, נגלה עליהם כגבור חגור חרב״ וכו׳. ושם בהמשך: ״׳ה׳ איש מלחמה׳, שהוא נלחם במצרים״. **תנין** – מצרים, ראה יחזקאל כט ג. **לצמת** – להכרית. 44. **בדורכו בים** – חבקוק ג טו. **ראו ויאמינו** – שמות יד לא. 45. **דגלים** – במדבר י יד. **מן שמים וכו׳** – במדבר יא ח. 46. **הופיע וכו׳** – עפ״י דברים לג ב, תהלים סח יח. 47. **ומה וכו׳** – תהלים ח ב. בפסוק ״מה״, בלי וי״ו, והתוספה כאן לצורך הא״ב. 48. **זבול וכו׳** – אולי פירושו בית המקדש בנוי ליד נחל שבו נובעים מים טהורים לטהרת הטמאים; השווה זכרי׳ יד ח. 49. **חלקי ה׳** – איכה ג כד. **חבל מונעם** – עפ״י תהלים טז ו. 50. **טובו וכו׳** – במדבר כד ה. ופירוש הטור: עולי הרגל מגיעים לירושלים שבה ״טובו אוהלים״. 51. **יפה נוף** – תהלים מח ג. פירוש: בשלוש הרגלים ה׳ הראה לעולי רגלים את ירושלים, יפה הנוף, קריית משושנו, השווה ישעי׳ סו י. 52-53. **כבוד הלבנון** – ישעי׳ לה ב. **רגש** – תהלים נה טו. **בהריעם לפני ה׳** – עפ״י תהלים צח ו, והמשפט ״פוסח״ מטור לטור. **בהתאסף** וגו׳ – דברים לג ה. 54. **מציון מכלל יופי** – תהלים נ ב. **ברכה גאולה** – אולי צ״ל ברכת גאולה. **הופעת** – קשה, כי החרוז דורש ״־עות״ ואולי צריך לנקד ״הוֹפַעַת״ והיא קשורה לטור הבא: מציון יוצאת הופעת נחמות וכו׳. 56. **סעדינו אלקים ישע** – השווה תהלים יח לו. **תחיה(?)** – קשה להבין. **מחכים בשבטך רעות** – בני ישראל מחכים לכך שהקב״ה ירעה אותם בשבטו, השווה מיכה ז יד. 57. **עד אנה וכו׳** – תהלים יג ב. **תאמץ וכו׳** – ישעי׳ לה ג. 58. **פדות לנפשי שלח** – תהלים קיא ט. **שחה ברכות רעות** – פירושו נעלם ממני. 59. **צמח תצמיח** – ירמי׳ לג טו. **אל דיעות** – שמ״א ב ג. 60. **קרא דרור** – ויקרא כה י. **שנת גאולי** – ישעי׳ סג ד.

רֵיעִים יְרוּדִי[ם] מִקֶּרֶב דּוֹחֵק בְּפִילּוּלַי
שׁוֹמֵעַ שַׂמַּח מֵרוֹם מַאֲזִין מִילּוּלַי
תְּפִילָּתִי יִקַּח נוֹדְךָ לְהָשִׁיב גְּבוּלַי
מָכוֹן כּוֹנֵן לְשַׁנֵּן שְׁבָחַי בְּהִילּוּלַי
אָשִׁירָה לַה׳ כִּי גָמַל עָלַי

מַהֵר זְמַן בִּינְיַין בֵּית קָודְשִׁי וְתִפְאַרְתִּי
שְׁתוּלִים לְהַעֲלוֹת בִּמְנוּחָה בִּיכּוּרֵי אַדְמָתִי
הָפֹךְ נִסְכֵי פָר לְגַלְגֵּל בְּחִיבָּתִי
חַדֵּשׁ יָמֵינוּ זְכוּת שִׂמְחַ[ת] תּוֹרָתִי
קוֹרְאִים וְגוֹמְרִים וּמַתְחִילִים זֹאת בְּרִיתִי לְרַוְחָתִי
אַעֲלֶה יְרוּשָׁלַיִם עַל רֹאשׁ שִׂמְחָתִי בא״י פורס סוכת יתגדל ויתקדש

61. **רעים ירודי[ם]** – בני ישראל בגלות. **מקרב דוחק** – תוציא את בני ישראל מקרב דוחק הגלות. **בפילולי** – בתפילתי. 62. **שומע וכו׳** – אולי שיעורו: הקב״ה השומע ומאזין לדברי תפילתי ישמח אותנו מהשמים. 63. **תפילתי יקח** – תהלים ו י. **נודך להשיב גבולי** – אולי פירושו: את עמך, שהיו נעים ונדים, תשיב לגבולם; והשווה ירמי׳ לא טז-יז. 64. **מכון כונן** – כונן את מכונך, את בית המקדש, השווה שמות טו יז. **לשבח שבחי בהילולי** – שנוכל לשנן את הקב״ה בהלל ובזמירות. 65. **אשירה וגו׳** – תהלים יג ו. 66. **בית קדשי תפארתי** – ישעי׳ סד י. 67. **שתולים** – תהלים צב יד. **ביכורי אדמתי** – שמות כג יט. 68. **הפך וכו׳** – אולי פירושו: הפך את זמן הגלות לזמן הגאולה ונסכי הפר של החג שוב יגלגלו עלינו את חיבת הקב״ה. 69. **חדש ימינו** – איכה ה כא. **זכות שמח[ת] תורתי** – מסיים בהזכרת חג שמחת תורה. 70. **קוראים וגומרים ומתחילים זאת בריתי** – בשמחת תורה גומרים את קריאת התורה השנתית ומתחילים לקרוא בה מחדש. **זאת בריתי** – התורה, השווה ישעי׳ נט כא. **לרווחתי** – איכה ג נו. 71. **אעלה וגו׳** – תהלים קלז ו.

שירי פתיחה וחתימה בספר ״יחוסי תנאים ואמוראים״ לר׳ יהודה בן קלונימוס משפירא

אחד החיבורים המופלאים והמרשימים ביותר שחכמי אשכנז יצרו בימי הביניים הוא הספר האנציקלופדי הגדול שנקרא היום בפי כל ״יחוסי תנאים ואמוראים״ (להלן: יתו״א).[1] מחברו של יתו״א חי בסוף המאה הי״ב ותחילת המאה הי״ג וזוהה, על פי עדויות וראיות שונות, כר׳ יהודה בן קלונימוס בן מאיר משפירא, אע״פ ששמו או שם ספרו[2] אינם נזכרים בפירוש בחלקי החיבור שנשארו בידינו. הראשון בחקר המודרני שהקדיש תשומת לב מלאה לספר זה היה אברהם עפשטיין ורוב הידיעות על המחבר ועל חיבורו נקבעו על ידו.[3] א״א אורבך דן במחבר בפרוטרוט ומתאר את גדולתו בתורה ואת הערך הרב של חיבורו, והוא מציין גם ש״חוקרים חשובים בימינו הסתייעו בחומר״ שבספר ומזכיר ביניהם במיוחד את הגר״ש ליברמן.[4] יעקב זוסמן העיר לאחרונה על אופיה המיוחד של תורתם של חכמי שפירא שפעולתם הספרותית כללה נושאים שדרך כלל היו חסרים ברפרטואר של שאר חכמי הראשונים.[5] יתו״א מוצאו בחוג חכמי שפירא ותכונותיו מתאימות לתיאור זה. ואמנם מפליא הדבר שחיבור חשוב זה כמעט נעלם לגמרי במשך הדורות, ורבותינו הראשונים והאחרונים אינם מזכירים אותו ואפילו בימינו טמונים עוד חלקים ממנו בכתבי יד. הערכים המרובים של האות יו״ד ומה ששרד מהאות כ״ף לא ראו עדיין את אור הדפוס, וזה גורלו גם של השיר שבא בסוף הערכים של האות יו״ד.[6] לכבודו

* בן דודי היקר, הרב חיים שמלצר, רבה של סנט-גלן בשוויץ, העיר לי כמה הערות מאירות עיניים, ותודתי נתונה לו גם בזה.

1 מהדורה י״ל מימון עם מבוא מאת מ״ח קצנלבוגן, ירושלים תשכ״ג.

2 לפי עפשטיין אולי היה שם החיבור ״שם הגדולים״, אבל אורבך דוחה את השערתו של עפשטיין. בכל אופן כדאי לשים לב לכך שבשירים שנדון בהם להלן המחבר כותב: ״להצליחי שמות הגבורים״ (שיר ב): ״סיעני לחדשים שמות נגידים נדיבים וראשים״ (שיר ו) – ואולי יש מזה קצת אסמכתא לדעתו של עפשטיין. וראה A. Epstein, “Das talmudische Lexicon יחוסי תנאים ואמוראים und Jehuda b. Kalonymus aus Speier”, *MGWJ* 39 (1895), p. 399; א״א אורבך, בעלי התוספות, א, ירושלים תש״ם, עמ׳ 370, הערה 51.

3 עפשטיין (שם), עמ׳ 398-403, 447-460, 507-513.

4 אורבך (לעיל, הערה 2), עמ׳ 361-378, וראה עמ׳ 372 שם.

5 י׳ זוסמן, ״מסורת לימוד ומסורת נוסח של התלמוד הירושלמי״, כתבי האקדמיה הלאומית הישראלית למדעים – החטיבה למדעי-הרוח, מחקרים בספרות התלמודית: יום עיון לרגל מלאת שמונים שנה לשאול ליברמן, ירושלים תשמ״ג, עמ׳ 14, הערה 11.

6 השווה מה שכתב אורבך על ״ספר הישר״ לרבנו תם, דהיינו שבמשך הדורות יצא הספר מכלל

של בעל היובל [פרופסור יצחק ברזילי] אפרסם כאן את השיר הנמצא בין האות יו״ד ובין האות כ״ף, שיר המשמש כפתיחה וכחתימה לערכים של האותיות האלה, ואדון גם בשאר השירים הדומים לו שנדפסו במהדורה החלקית של יתו״א.

יש בספר בסך הכל שבעה שירים.[7] בכולם באה הבעה של שבח והודייה לה׳ על שנגמרו ערכי אות אחת ובקשת עזרה מה׳ להתחיל ולגמור את הערכים של האות הבאה ואת אלה של שאר האותיות. כפי שקבע עזרא פליישר, פתיחות שיריות, כמו אלה הנמצאות במדרש פתרון תורה ושהמפורסמות שבהן הן הפתיחות במדרש הגדול, לא שימשו, כמובן, בתפקיד ליטורגי כל שהוא.[8] הם נכתבו על ידי מחבריהם מפני שהם רצו לבקש רשות מה׳ לחבר את הספר והביעו בהם את תודתם על הסייעתא דשמיא שהיתה להם בכתיבתו. כמובן, גם השירים שביתו״א אינם משמשים מטרות ליטורגיות ובכל זאת יש להצביע על דמיון מה ביניהם לבין הרשויות לחתן שהיו נפוצות באשכנז.[9] רשויות אלה נאמרו בבית הכנסת כשהחתן עלה לתורה והיה להן מטבע קבוע. ברשויות לחתן תמיד יש ארבעה חלקים המכילים בקשת רשות מה׳, מהתורה, מחכמי התורה ומהקהל,[10] ובהרצאת הדברים מרבה הפייטן לדבר בשבח התורה ולומדיה. שבח לאותם גורמים נמצא גם בשירים שבספר יתו״א. נוסף לדמיון שבתוכן, יש להעיר שברשויות אין למצוא מבנים סטרופיים מגובשים, ושאורכם של כל אחד מארבעת חלקי הרשות, המחורז בפני עצמו בחרוז אחיד, אינו קבוע ומאפיין אותו בלבד. כך הוא המצב גם בשירים שבס׳ יתו״א. עוד צד שווה בין שני הסוגים, והוא ששניהם חוברו לציון מאורעות קונקרטיים: הרשויות לכבוד חתן וכלה, והשירים הנדונים כאן מציינים את ההתקדמות בחיבור הספר, ומעטים הם השירים שנתחברו בימי הביניים באשכנז בנסיבות אישיות משמחות. אך עם כל הדמיון יש להדגיש את השוני, והעיקר הוא, כאמור, שהשירים שבס׳ יתו״א, כמו השירים שבס׳ פתרון תורה ומדרש הגדול ודומיהם,[11] אינם משמשים שום מטרה ליטורגית.

שימוש מפני ש״חיבוריהם של אחרונים קלטו את תורתם של הראשונים״ עד כדי כך שרק שני כתבי יד נשארו מהחיבור והוא לא נדפס עד שנת תק״ע – אורבך (לעיל, הערה 2), עמ׳ 160. ואולי בדומה לכך קרה גם לספר יתו״א. החיבור כולו עומד להופיע במהדורת ידידי ד״ר מאיר רבינוביץ, בהוצאת מכון אופק.

7 שיר א: בין בי״ת לגימ״ל, יתו״א (לעיל, הערה 1), עמ׳ לה; שיר ב: בין ה״א לו״ו, שם, עמ׳ סח-סט; שיר ג: בין ו״ו לזי״ן, שם, עמ׳ עא; שיר ד: בין זי״ן לחי״ת, שם עמ׳ רי-ריא; שיר ה: בין חי״ת לטי״ת, שם, עמ׳ תמב-תמג; שיר ו: בין טי״ת ליו״ד, שם, עמק תפז-תפח; שיר ז: נדפס להלן.

8 ע׳ פליישר, ״ציונים לנחלתו הפייטנית של רב האיי גאון – פתיחות השיר במדרש ׳פתרון תורה׳״, מחקרי ירושלים בספרות עברית י-יא [אסופת מאמרים לזכר דן פגיס] (תשמ״ח), עמ׳ 661-681.

9 ראה את האוסף היפה, רשויות לחתן, תל־אביב תרצ״ו; ועל הסוג ראה: ע׳ פליישר, שירת הקודש העברית בימי הביניים, ירושלים 1975, עמ׳ 472.

10 פליישר (שם).

11 אולי היה כדאי פעם לייחד את הדיבור על השירים שמחברים ומעתיקים חיברו על ספרים. שירי ספרים כאלה היו נפוצים מאוד, ואביא כאן רק דוגמאות בודדות ומקריות לסוג זה כדי להראות את תפוצתם בכל הדורות ובכל המקומות: השיר בסוף ספר הערוך (דוידזון, נ, 527); מדרש החפץ (ראה לאחרונה: מ׳ חבצלת ״לעניין הפתיחות והחתימות ב׳מדרש החפץ׳ על התורה לר׳ זכריה בן שלמה

בדיקת שבעת השירים שבספר יתו"א מעלה שאין להם מבנה מגובש. שיר א׳ וג׳ הם קצרים מאד, והאחרים ארוכים, וכאמור, באף אחד מהם אין מבנה סטרופי אחיד. החריזה משתנה כמה פעמים לאורך השיר ויוצרת חטיבות שאורכן אינו שווה. רק בשיר אחד יש סימן (שיר ז׳) והוא א"ב פשוט. גם מבחינת המקצב יש חוסר עקביות: בהרבה טורים יש ארבע מלים אבל בדרך כלל מספר המלים בטור אינו קבוע.[12] לפעמים משתמש המחבר בחרוז פנימי, כגון בשיר א׳: העמל/ואמל, שם: באהבתו/וחמלתו; בשיר ב׳: בוזרים/צוברים; בשיר ה׳: להעלות ארוכה/לפרוכה/מדוכה; שם: להבליג שפויה/רפויה/שבויה; שם: לשובבה/לסובבה/לנובבה; שם: אמריו/דבריו; בשיר ו׳: חסידיו/בסודיו.

מעניין הוא שבכמה מקומות נדמה כאילו המחבר חותם שם ברוך בתוכם. בשיר א׳: יברך מבורך; בשיר ב׳: וברוך צורי; בשיר ד׳: ברוך הוא באמרי נועם; בשיר ה׳: וברוך מבורך אשר חזק עצמותיי; שיר ז׳ טור 29: ולמען שמך המבורך. מובן מאליו שבהחלט אפשרי שרק מקרה הוא לפנינו, אבל הופעת המלה בחמשה מתוך שבעת השירים וגם

הרופא", קרית ספר סא [תשמ"ו-תשמ"ז], עמ׳ 587-588); ספר התרומה (ראה אורבך [לעיל, הערה 2], עמ׳ 348-349 והערה 23 שם); ספר ראבי"ה (ראה מבוא לספר ראבי"ה לר"א אפטוביצר, ירושלים 1938, עמ׳ 95: "וחוץ מן הפתיחות והחתימות הפיוטיות שבראשי התשובות וסופיהן מתובל כל הספר במליצות ולשונות חדות ונעימות"); שני שירים לר׳ יעקב בר׳ שמשון (מחזור ויטרי, נירנברג תרפ"ג, מבוא, עמ׳ 186-187); ספר כריתות; ספר שבלי הלקט; ספר ציוני על התורה; פירוש ר׳ יוסף בכור שור על התורה (העיר לי על זה פרופסור אברהם גרוסמן); שיריו של שמואל הנגיד על ספרו "הלכתא גבראתא" (דיואן שמואל הנגיד, מהדורת ד׳ ירדן, ירושלים תשכ"ו, עמ׳ 89-96); וראה לאחרונה: ש׳ אברמסון, "כתיבת המשנה (על דעת גאונים וראשונים)", ר׳ בונפיל, מ׳ בן־ששון, וי׳ הקר (עורכים), תרבות וחברה בתולדות ישראל בימי הביניים – קובץ מאמרים לזכרו של חיים הלל בן־ששון, ירושלים תשמ"ט, עמ׳ 40-41; שירו של הרד"ק על פירושו לתהלים (ראה מהדורת א׳ דרום, ירושלים 1967, עמ׳ ח); ומפורסמים הם שיריו של ר׳ אברהם אבן עזרא בפתיחות ספריו ובסופיהם (והם מקובצים בדיואן ראב"ע, מהדורת ד׳ רוזין, ברסלוי 1885, עמ׳ 16-84); שיריו של הרמב"ן לפתיחות חיבוריו (כתבי רבינו משה בן נחמן, מהדורת ח"ד שעוועל, א, ירושלים תשכ"ג, עמ׳ תג-תכא); שירים רבים מסוג זה כתב ר׳ זרחיה הלוי, בעל "המאור" (ראה: שירת המאור – פיוטי רבי זרחיה הלוי, מהדורת י׳ מייזליש, ירושלים תשמ"ד, עמ׳ 8-9 ועמ׳ 137-159). ובקשר לזה יש להזכיר גם את השירים השקולים הקצרים המופיעים בראש "כתר מלכות" לר׳ שלמה אבן גבירול ובראש אחד מפיוטיו של ר׳ יצחק אבן גיאת, וכן בראש הלכות פסחים בחיבורו "הלכות כלולות" (ראה במאמרי, "חמשה זולתות לר׳ יצחק אבן־גיאת", צ׳ מלאכי [עורך], ש׳ להימן – מחקרים בספרות העברית של ימי הביניים מוגשים לא"מ הברמן, ירושלים תשל"ז, עמ׳ 330, הע׳ 5 [לעיל, עמ׳ 116]), על שירים של מעתיקים כתב בקצרה מ׳ שטיינשניידר, ראה: הרצאות על כתבי יד עבריים, ירושלים 1965, עמ׳ 63, 67; וראה לאחרונה: מ׳ ריגלר, "הקולופון בכתבי יד עבריים מימי הביניים כמקור היסטורי", עבודת דוקטור, האוניברסיטה העברית בירושלים, תשנ"ה, עמ׳ 37 ובהערות בעמ׳ 298-299; על פורמולות בחרוזים בספרי תימן ראה: י׳ רצהבי, במעגלות תימן, תל־אביב תשמ"ח, עמ׳ 86-96; וראה את שירו של אליהו הבחור על דפוס וניציאה 1538 של פירוש רש"י על התורה במאמרי, "Rashi's Commentary on the Pentateuch and on the Five Scrolls, Venice, Bomberg, 1538"; י׳ ברלין (עורך), ספר היובל לכבוד יצחק קיוב, ניו־יורק תשל"ב, חלק אנגלי, עמ׳ 433-525 [להלן, עמ׳ *98-*99]. בשירים אלה טמונים נתונים מעניינים על המחברים ועל הספרים ולפעמים גם על עניינים אחרים, וגם ערך ספרותי יש באחדים מהם.

12 גם ברשויות לחתן יש מקצב חפשי – ראה פליישר (לעיל, הערה 9), עמ׳ 472.

בצירוף כפול, "ברוך מבורך" בליווי "חזק" כמעט תיכף אחריו, יש בה כדי לעורר קצת חשד שמחבר בשם "ברוך" רצה לרמוז כאן לשמו.[13] היות ויחוס הספר לר' יהודה בן קלונימוס ודאי הוא ומקובל במחקר, אי אפשר להניח ששם המחבר היה ברוך. בכל מקום, הופעתו האפשרית של השם ברוך דורשת פתרון. פשוט ביותר לשער שהמחבר, יהודה, חתם את שמו של מישהו אחר, אולי קרובו, בתוך השירים. מנהג זה של חתימת שם קרוב או בן היה ידוע בין הפייטנים.[14] אפשרות שנייה לכאורה היא שהשם ברוך היה שמו של הסופר, ולא של המחבר, אך דבר זה אינו מתקבל על הדעת, במיוחד מפני השימוש בלשון "סודר" המתייחס למעשה הספר, כגון "ואני העלוב סודר גיבוריו" (שיר ד'), ועוד, ביטוי שבא לעתים קרובות בגוף הספר לציון פעולת המחבר בכתיבת ספרו.[15] ואולי הפתרון הוא: הספר חובר על ידי כמה מחברים, אחד מהם, המחבר העיקרי, היה ר' יהודה, אבל תרם לחיבור הספר, בתור עורך, מלקט או חבר, גם חכם בשם ברוך ושמו הוא שנרמז בשירים; ואולי ברוך זה בעצמו חיבר את השירים ולא יהודה. על תופעה זו של חיבור ספר ע"י מחברים שונים תעיד ההבאה הבאה מס' יתו"א עצמו: "כל זה העתקתי מכתיבת גלילי ידי רבנא שמואל בן רבנה קלונימוס הזקן זקיני אבי אב אמי זל"ע ומעט מזער משלי ומשום דודנו רבנא קלונימוס בן רבנא יהודה פי'... ואחי הרב ר' מאיר חיבר והוסיף את אלה שאכתוב...".[16] אנו רואים כאן יצירה קולקטיבית של כמה מחברים, שניים בכתב ושניים בעל פה ואולי גם בחיבור יתו"א השתתפו כמה מחברים.[17] כמובן כל הדברים הללו

13 מעניין שהפייטן רבינו ברוך בר שמואל ממגנצא שיזר את שמו בכמה מקומות בפיוטיו (נוסף לחתימות הרגילות שבהם), ראה למשל הזמר לשבת המפורסם שלו, "ברוך אל עליון אשר נתן מנוחה", א"מ הברמן, "פיוטי רבינו ברוך בר שמואל ממגנצא", ידיעות המכון לחקר השירה העברית ו (תש"ז), עמ' נח, טור א, ושם, עמ' עא, טור מט: "גם ברוך יהיה", ושם, עמק' עג, טור פב: "יברכוך הכל ברוך הבא", ועוד.

14 פליישר (לעיל, הערה 9), עמ' 440 (על פייטני אשכנז ואיטליה).

15 ראה: עפשטיין (לעיל, הערה 2), עמ' 399, וראה במבוא לספר יתו"א (לעיל, הערה 1), עמ' 8, 12; אורבך (לעיל, הערה 2), עמ' 370. אמנם יש מקום סתום בספר, שבו משתמש המחבר בשורש "סדר" לגבי מה שנראה העתקה, ובכל זאת רוב רובו של השימוש בלשון "סדר" מוסב על חיבור הספר ולא על העתקתו. וראה יתו"א (לעיל, הערה 1), עמ' שמה (ומובא במבוא [שם], עמ' 16): "ואגב שטפאי משכתני מחשבת ההלכות וכתבתי חנן בן אבשלום כאן ולא היה לי לכותבו אלא על זה כתיבה לא זזה ממקומה עד נעתיק המתנדב להעתיק ויסדיר", וכו'.

16 ראה: עפשטיין (לעיל, הערה 2), עמ' 451; עפשטיין מביא את הדברים על פי כ"י אוקספורד 2199; בכ"י בית המדרש לרבנים באמריקה בניו יורק Rab. 2348 ההבאה נמצאת בדף 154 ע"ב. החיבור שמדובר כאן עליו הכיל "תבות שדרשום רבותינו אחת לשתים", ראה כתבי ר' אברהם עפשטיין, א, ירושלים תש"י, עמ' רסח. אם כן, גם חיבור זה של ר' שמואל היה כעין מילון, ובזה היה דומה קצת לאופיו האנציקלופדי־המלוני של יתו"א.

17 אורבך משתמש בביטוי "יצירה ספרותית קולקטיבית" לגבי התוספות – ראה אורבך (לעיל, הערה 2), עמ' 32. איבן מרקוס מזכיר דעות חוקרים שדיברו על פעולה קולקטיבית בקשר ל"ספר חסידים" – ראה: I. Marcus, *Piety and Society: The Jewish Pietists of Medieval Germany*, Leiden 1981, p. 136; יצירה קולקטיבית של ליקוטים, של עריכות שונות, וכו', היתה כנראה נחלת יהדות אשכנז. ביטוי זה מתאים לספרי דבי רש"י השונים, כגון מחזור ויטרי (דרך אגב, אפטוביצר חשב שהיו שני ספרים בשם זה, ראה מבוא לספר ראבי"ה [לעיל, הערה 11], עמ' 415; ולעומת זה ראה אורבך [לעיל, הערה 2],

אינם אלא בגדר השערה בעלמא, ואין אנו יכולים לקבוע אם באמת "ברוך" בשירים אלה רומז לשם אדם או לאו, ואם כן מי הוא היה. לעיתים קרובות מזכיר המחבר בשירים את הספר עצמו ועניינים הנוגעים בחיבורו. את פעולת המחבר הוא רואה כזה של "סודר", ואת מטרת החיבור – בהבאת דברי התנאים והאמוראים בסדר המתאים, כל איש ותורתו לחוד, כדי שלא לערבב תורתו של אחד בזו שלחבירו ולבאר ולישב את דבריהם ולפלפל בהם ב"פלפול ישר".[18] הוא רואה את החיבור ככרם שבו נטועות שורות מסודרות. הוא מזכיר את מספרם של הערכים לפי האותיות השונות הוא גדול או קטן. את התנאים ואת האמוראים הוא מכנה בכינויים כמו גבורים, אדירים, חסידים, תמימים, נגידים וכו'. והנה המקומות שבשירים הנוגעים בעניין הספר עצמו:

שיר א:

...
ולגמור ולסיים שאר האותיות כסדרן
...
בסדר גימל יגמליני
...

שיר ב:

...
בין הבדים בוזרים צוברים[19]
לזכותו[20] להצליחי שמות הגבורים[21]
אדירי חפצי בהם בחיבורים

עמ' 135), הפירושים השונים לפיוטים, ספרות המנהגים ועוד. ואולי גם לדרך חיבורו של הספר "מעשה המכירי" יש עניין לכאן. הספר חובר בהשתתפות ארבעה אחים, בני מכיר – ראה א' גרוסמן, "בני מכיר וספרם מעשה המכירי", תרביץ מו (תשל"ז), עמ' 110 ואילך; הנ"ל, חכמי אשכנז הראשונים, ירושלים תשמ"א, עמ' 361 ואילך. וראה את דבריו הקולעים של י' תא־שמע, "על כמה ענייני מחזור ויטרי", עלי ספר יא (תשמ"ד), עמ' 89: "וכך הלך הספר [מחזור ויטרי] הלוך והשתכלל גם במהלך המאה הי"ג, בעיקר ע"י תוספות מדבי ר' ברוך בעל ספר התרומה, ועוד במפנה המאות שימש הספר מרובה־הבגדים הזה כמצע ותשתית לייסד אליו את בניינה של ספרות המנהגים האשכנזית, מן דבי מהר"ם מרוטנבורג. אלא שזהו נושא גדול בפני עצמו. דוגמא נאה לפנינו לדרך מסירתה ושימורה של המסורת אצל האשכנזים. הישן מתעדכן תדיר ע"י החדש בן־הזמן, אולם לעולם אין החדש בא להחליף את הישן, למרוד בו או לירש את מקומו, אלא 'להוסיף' עליו בלבד, וההתקדמות נעשית מאליה, כמעט מבלי משים, אלא שגם זה נושא גדול הוא בפני עצמו".

18 ראה הערה לגוף הפיוט, טור 9.

19 כפי שמעיר המהדיר בספר יתו"א (לעיל, הערה 1), עמ' סח, הערה 2, הכוונה לקטורת, על פי בבלי כריתות ו רע"ב, ויש לפרש את הדברים כמוסבים על מאמרי חז"ל המפוזרים בכל הספרות התלמודית, ובא המחבר וצבר ואסף אותם יחד תחת שמות אומריהם.

20 אולי צ"ל "לזכותי".

21 ראה לעיל, הערה 2.

לישבם לשתלם[22] בכנם[22א] בביאורים
וברוך צורי עזרני בחמישי
...
... ויחזקני ויאששי
בשאר האותיות עם הששי
אשר ענפיו מרובין ושרשיו מעוטין
משאר כל השטין הנחרתין ונפרטין
חוץ מן הצדי היחיד כעוללה בלקט הפרטים

שיר ג:

...
במתן בשישי/ ירבה את משושי/ ובאות השביעי/ טובו להשביעי

שיר ד:

...
ואני העלוב סודר גיבוריו
חסידיו תמימיו נבריו יזכני למערכת כביריו
המישרים אמריו דבריו כסדר לנוטעם
בשורות מטעם/ מראיה ומטעם[23]
...
וכאשר חזקני באות השביעי
...
באות השמיני להחזיק בימיני
...
להרימני כל שאר האותות לבאר
...

שיר ה:

...
ובא השמיני סייעני
...
... גמלני לסדר חסידיו
ויזכני לסודיו ודוברי רפסודיו[24]

22 הוא משתמש בביטוי זה גם בשיר ו׳: ״לשותלם בלי ערב״.

22א ראה בראשית מ יג, ועוד.

23 ראה בהערה לטור 5 של שיר ז׳.

24 צירוף של הלשונות משני פסוקים: מלכים א ה כג (״ואני אשימם דברות בים״, וראה רש״י שם) ודברי־הימים ב ב טו (״ונביאם לך רפסֹדות על ים יפו״); ואולי הכוונה למנהיגי אניות, קברניטים, ראה בבלי בבא בתרא צא רע״ב.

ושיתי יסודיו/ לערוך מערכת מעשה ידיו
...
בשאר אותיות עם התשיעי

שיר ו:

...
בכל מיני שבחות עשיריים[25] נערכים
...
ובאות תשיעי סייעני להרשים
שמות נגידים נדיבים וראשים
חסידיו בסודיו גילו תעלומה בפירושים
ובעשירי אשר מחנהו מאד רב
יעצימני אליו לקרב/ וילמד ידי לקרב
לשותלם[26] בלי ערב/ ושיחי עלי יערב
כל רב ורב/ גבולו לא יחרב
וטוב ומטיב בשאר האותות ילמדני
...
בסדר צדיקיו לצמדני...
...
... בפלפול ישר לחדדני...

שיר ז:

...
טעמי טובו קלה וחמורה/ ילמדנו תורתו כל מצוה במאמרה
כערכה כחוקה כהילכתה כביאורה/ ללמוד וללמד לשמור ולעשות כביר[ה]
מישרי תפוחים ומשכיות אופנם בסברה/ נגד מלכים ובעלי תריסין להתגברה
סעד וסמך וסייג לאמתן לדברה/ עדת אבירים שמות הגבורים לחברה
פתור חידותם במליצה כחמה ברה/ צירוף שמותם לככרם נטוע כשורה
קצירי יונקותם כפרי יופיים להתאשרה/ רבי התעודה במלאכת הפרדס להתכש[רה][27]
...
באות העשירי רב מחנהו/ פעל עמי למענהו
...
ותרום (?) ידך עמדי לרשום אות עשתי עשר...

25 אולי על פי תהלים צב ד, "עלי עשור", וכמובן רומז כאן לאות העשירית, יו"ד.
26 ראה גם בשיר ב': "לישבם לשתלם בכנם בביאורים".
27 ראה להלן בהערות לשיר, טורים 5-10.

בשירים מדובר גם על צרות הפרט והכלל. המחבר היה כנראה חולה אנוש והתרפא, כפי שמשתמע מן הטורים 15-12 שבשיר ז׳; וראה גם בשיר ב׳: ״וירא תשושי/ ויחזקני ויאששי״; ובשיר ה׳: ״וברוך מבורך אשר חזק עצמותי הנבהלות/ בכמה בלהות ומחלות... ואני כואב לעני״ כו׳. את הצרות שעברו על הכלל הוא מזכיר שם בטורים 27-25;[28] וראה גם בשיר ג׳: ״וירא עלבוני/ ויגוני ודאבוני/ ויריב יריבני/ ויבנה חורבני״; ושיר ד׳: ״להעלות ארוכה לפרוכה מדוכה בפלגי תעלותיו/ להבליג שפיה רפויה שבויה ממכלאותיו/ לשובבה לסובבה לנובבה בנאות מעלותיו״.

את עבודתו בחיבור הספר הוא מדמה לקטורת ולקורבנות, וכמו שבדרך כלל אומרים על התפלה שהיא שילום פרים, דהיינו שהיא באה במקום הקורבנות, כך רואה כאן המחבר את העיסוק בתורה, המתבטא בחבור הספר, כתחליף לקורבנות; ראה בשיר ב׳: ״נדבת שפתי כשילום פרים/ מחים ניחוחים ממרקים מכפרים/ לריח ערב נרדים כפרים/ מור וקציעה ויתר נספרים/ בין הבדים בוזרים צוברים/ לזכותו להצליחי שמות הגבורים״. ובדומה בשיר ה׳: ״ויערב שיחי כל ראשי בשמים עם מר ואהלות/ וכמנצחי על נחילות בתופים ומחולות״; ובשיר ו׳: ״הודיתי ותורתי ככלי ואשים/ כקטורה באפיו לרצון ישים״; וכן גם בשיר ז׳, המובא להלן, טורים 19 ואילך.

להלן הטקסט של השיר השביעי, עפ״י שני כתבי יד: כ״י בית המדרש לרבנים באמריקה בניו יורק, .Rab מס׳ 2348, דף 176 ע״א וכ״י אוקספורד 2199, חלק ג׳, דף 403 ע״א-ע״ב.

אוֹדֶה שִׁמְךָ גָּדוֹל וְנוֹרָא/ בְּיוֹדוּ רָמוּז בִּגְבוּרָה וּמוֹרָא
גָּנוּז וְחָבוּי בְּתַעֲלוּמָה שְׁמוּרָה/ דָּגוּל מֵרְבָבָה כַּחֲטִיבַת אֲמִירָה
הוֹדוּ לַמְסַיְּים בִּצְבָאוֹתָיו בִּזְמִירָה/ וְהוֹ אֱלֹקֵינוּ בְּאֵין תְּמוּרָה
זוּלָתוֹ אֶפֶס בְּדֵיעָה גְמוּרָה/ חֶלְקִי וְגוֹרָלִי ה׳ נַפְשִׁי אָמְרָה
טַעֲמֵי טוּבוֹ קַלָּה וַחֲמוּרָה/ יְלַמְּדֵנוּ תוֹרָתוֹ כָּל מִצְוָה כְּמַאֲמָרָהּ
כְּעֶרְכָּהּ כְּחֻקָּהּ כְּהִלְכָתָהּ כְּבֵיאוּרָהּ/ לִלְמוֹד וּלְלַמֵּד לִשְׁמוֹר וְלַעֲשׂוֹת כַּבִּירָ[ה]
מְיַשְּׁרֵי תַפּוּחִים וּמַשְׂכִּיּוֹת אוֹפַנָּם בִּסְבָרָה/ נֶגֶד מְלָכִים וּבַעֲלֵי תְרֵיסִין לְהִתְגַּבְּרָה
סַעַד וְסֶמֶךְ וּסְיָיג לַאֲמִתָּן לְדַבְּרָה/ עֲדַת אַבִּירִים שְׁמוֹת הַגִּבּוֹרִים לְחַבְּרָה
פָּתוֹר חִידוֹתָם בִּמְלִיצָה כַּחַמָּה בָרָה/ צֵירוּף שְׁמוֹתָם לְכַכֶּרֶם נָטוּעַ כְּשׁוּרָה
קְצִירֵי יוֹנְקוֹתָם כְּפִרְיֵי יוֹפְיָים לְהִתְאַשְּׁרָה/ רַבֵּי הַתְּעוּדָה בִּמְלֶאכֶת הַפַּרְדֵּס לְהִתְכַּשְּׁ[רָה]
שָׁמְרָה נַפְשָׁם עֵדוֹתֶיךָ בְּתוֹרָתְךָ נִקְשְׁרָה/ תְּמִמֵי דֶרֶךְ הוֹרוּ אוֹרַח יְשָׁרָה
וּמִי אָנֹכִי הֲלוֹם הֲבִיאוֹתָנִי/ אִישׁ יְדוּעַ חֹלִי וּמַכְאוֹב הֲשִׁיבֹתָנִי לְאֵיתָנִי
שִׁוַּעְתִּי וְשִׁיוְעוּ רַבִּים וְרִפֵּאִיתָנִי/ נַפְשִׁי מִשְּׁאוֹל וּמִשַּׁחַת הֶעֱלִיתָנִי
מִיָּרְדִי בוֹר חִיִּיתָנִי וְהִצַּלְתָּנִי/ וְתִגְרַת יָדְךָ כִּמְעַט כִּילִיתָנִי
וּמִידַּת חֶמְלַת חֲנִינָתְךָ כִּלְכַּלְתָּנִי/ וּמִדַּלָּה תְּבַצְּעֵנִי וְהֶחֱלַמְתָּנִי וְהֶחֱיִיתָנִי
וְכַמָּה מַעֲלוֹת טוֹבוֹת עָלַי/ עָשִׂיתָ עִמָּדִי וְלֹא כְמַעֲלָלַי

28 הדברים מובאים על ידי אורבך (לעיל, הערה 2), עמ׳ 376-375.

גְּמַלְתָּנִי חֲסָדֶיךָ וְקָטֹנְתִּי וּמְעוּטִים פְּעָלַי/ וַאֲנִי גֶבֶר בְּאֵין אֱיָלַיי
וְאַתָּה תוֹחַלְתִּי תִקְוַת חֵילַיי/ עֲזַרְתַּנִי וְנִחַמְתַּנִי כְּבָרִיא אוּלַיי
בְּאוֹת הָעֲשִׂירִי רַב מַחֲנֵהוּ/ פָּעַל עִמִּי לְמַעֲנֵהוּ
זֶה אֵלִי בְּמָה אַנְוֵיהוּ/ שָׁמֵם וְחָרֵב וְצָדוּ נָוֵיהוּ
מִזְבְּחוֹ הָרוּס חִישׁ יְרַפְּאֵהוּ/ וְעַל מְכוֹנוֹ וִיסוֹדוֹ יִבְנֵהוּ
וְכָל יִשְׂרָ[אֵל] וִיהוּדָה אַחֲרָיו יִנְהוּ/ בְּהֵיטִיבוֹ צִיּוֹן וִירוּשָׁלַיִם כִּרְצוֹנֵהוּ
זֶה הַיּוֹם הַהוּא נְחַכֶּה וּנְקַוֵּיהוּ/ בְּעוֹלוֹת מֵחִים זִבְחֵי צֶדֶק נְחִיחֵהוּ
יִזְלוּ בְשָׂמָיו לְרֵיחֵהוּ

וְעַתָּה אַתָּה וּמֵעוֹלָם אַתָּה אָבִינוּ/ תֹּאמַר דַּי לְצָרוֹתֵינוּ וּכְאֵיבֵינוּ
וְשִׁבְעָתַיִם הָשֵׁב לְחֵיק מַכְאִבֵינוּ/ כִּי מִמְּךָ לֹא נִסְתְּרוּ אַנְחוֹת דַּאֲבוֹנֵינוּ
נְגִיעֵי לְבָבֵינוּ מַדְוֵינוּ וְעֶלְבּוֹנֵינוּ
וְתָרוּם (?) יָדְךָ עִמָּדִי לִרְשׁוֹם אוֹת עַשְׁתֵּי עָשָׂר/ וּבִשְׁאָר הָאוֹתוֹת אָבִי אַתָּה רוֹעִי לֹא אֶחְסָר
וְרוּחֲךָ הַטּוֹבָה תַּנִּיחֵנִי/ וּלְמַעַן שִׁמְךָ הַמְבוֹרָךְ תְּנַהֲלֵנִי וְתַנְחֵ[נִי].

הערות לשיר:

1 **אודה שמך גדול ונורא** – על פי תהלים צט ג: "יודו שמך גדול ונורא", ושם נח ח: "אודה שמך". **ביודו רמוז** – יש כאן רמז לאות יו"ד כי שיר זה בא בסוף הערכים המתחילים ביו"ד, אבל עיקר כוונתו למה שנאמר בגוף הספר: "ואמר יודו שמך גדול ונורא קדוש הוא. בפסוק רמוז שם בן ארבע אותיות בתחלתו ובסופו. ונאמן רוח יכסה דבר שכיסה עתיק יומין ברוך שמו לעולם ועד"; מובא על ידי אורבך (לעיל, הערה 2), עמ' 376, על פי כ"י אוקספורד קנט ע"א (בכ"י ניו יורק חסרים הדפים [אחרי דף 80] שהכילו ערך זה).

3-2 **גנוז וחבוי בתעלומה שמורה** – הכוונה למה שנאמר לעיל שכיסה עתיק יומין וכו'. **שמורה** – מלשון "ואביו שמר את הדבר", בראשית לז יא. **דגול מרבבה... למסיים בצבאותיו** – השווה בבלי חגיגה טו ע"א: "מאי דרש? [רש"י: מהיכן הבין (ר' עקיבא) מקום השכינה שנזהר שלא הציץ שם] אמר רבה בר בר חנה אמר רבי יוחנן ואתה מרבבות קודש (דברים לג ב) אות הוא ברבבה שלו, ורבי אבהו אמר דגול מרבבה (שיר השירים ה י) דוגמא הוא ברבבה שלו וריש לקיש אמר ה' צבאות שמו (ישעיהו מח ב) אדון הוא בצבא שלו"; והשווה מכילתא דר"י, מסכתא דשירה, בשלח א (הורוביץ־רבין, עמ' 120 [ומקבילות]): "מהו צבאות? אות הוא בתוך צבא שלו". וראה תחילת שיר ה': "חסין יק' מי כמוך בכל הצבאות/ בדגלי איומים דגול בצבאות/ כגדודים אין מספר לרבבות וריבואות/ כתי כתות פליאות כסויי במחבואות" וכו'. וראה בפיוטו של ר' מאיר ב"ר יצחק ש"ץ: "רדו מלאכי צבאות שנונים בחרבם/ רשם ואות רבם מסויים בקרבם" ("אדיר ונאה בקודש", יוצר לשבועות או לשבת אחר שבועות, סדור עבודת ישראל, עמ' 761 ואילך, ובדיסרטציה של א"פ לוין [Lavin], "פיוטי מאיר בר יצחק ש"ץ", עבודת דוקטור, בית המדרש לרבנים באמריקה, ניו־יורק 1984, עמ' 36, טורים 77-76); וראה גם בפיוטי רבינו ברוך בר שמואל ממגנצא: "מאד רב הוא במחנהו ואל אות הוא בצבאותיו" (מהדורת א"מ הברמן [לעיל, הערה 13], עמ' פב, טור סו); "רכב ערבות ואות בצבאות" (שם, עמ' קו, טור סז [דוידזון, י, 3527]). **כחטיבת אמירה** – ראה בבלי ברכות ו ע"א; חגיגה ג ע"א: "את ה' האמרת היום וה' האמירך היום (דברים כו יז), אמר להם הקב"ה אתם עשיתוני חטיבה אחת בעולם" וכו'. ורש"י פירש: "האמרת: לשון חשיבות ושבח" (ברכות שם); "חטיבה אחת: שבח אחד, שבח מיוחד לומר אין כמוך" (חגיגה שם). ומובא בערוך בשם רב האי גאון: "ציור אחד בעולם

כלומר דבר הניכר שאין כמותו (ערוך השלם, ערך אמר, עמ׳ 126). ולפי זה ״אמירה״ שבטור זה מקבילה ל״זמירה״ שבטור הבא. **והו[!]** – כך בכ״י ניו־יורק אבל בכ״י אוקספורד ״והוא״, ואולי הגירסה של כ״י ניו־יורק, ״הו״, על פי ״אני והו הושיעה נא״ במשנה סוכה ד, ה. **באין תמורה** – השווה פיוטו של רבינו אפרים ב״ר יצחק מרגנשבורק המתחיל ״אשר אין לו תמורה והוא יהיה והיה״ (מהדורת א״מ הברמן, ידיעות המכון לחקר השירה העברית ד [תחר״ץ], עמ׳ קנט.

4 **זולתו אפס** – על פי ״אפס זולתו״ שב״עלינו לשבח״. **חלקי וגורלי וכו׳** – על פי איכה ג כד; תהלים טז ח.

5 **טעמי טובו** – על פי תהלים לד ט: ״טעמו וראו כי טוב ה׳״; וכאן מוסבים הדברים על התורה. וראה גם בשיר ד׳: ״יזכני למערכת כביריו המישרים אמריו דבריו, בסדר לנוטעם בשורות מטעם, מראיה ומטעם״; שתי המלים ״מראיה ומטעם״ מיוסדות גם כן על הפסוק הנ״ל ״טעמו וראו״.

6 **ללמוד וללמד לשמור ולעשות** – כמו בברכת אהבה רבה.

7 **טעמי טובו וכו׳** – על פי משלי כה יא, ונדרש במדרש שיר השירים ב ה (גרינהוט, עמ׳ נב): ״ומנין שנמשלו דברי חכמה בתפוחים שנאמר תפוחי זהב במשכיות כסף דבר דבור על אופניו (משלי כה יא)״. ואולי כוונתו שתלמידי חכמים מיישרים את הקשיים, וכאילו כל הר וגבעה (תפוחים) מתיישרים לפניהם, וראה מה שהובא משיר ד׳, לעיל, בביאור לשורה 5: ״המישרים אמריו״ וכו׳. **נגד מלכים** – תהלים קיט מו. **ובעלי תריסין** – בבלי ברכות כז ע״ב. וראה בשיר ו׳: ״וילמד ידי לקרב״. והשווה בפיוטו של ר׳ יהודה בן קלונימוס בן יהודה ממגנצא: ״בעלי תריסים משיבי מלחמה מלמדים״ (רשויות לחתן, תל־אביב תרצ״ז, עמ׳ כ), ובפיוט ״ארזי הלבנון״ לר׳ מאיר בן יחיאל (דוידזון, א, 7564): ״בעלי תריסין במלחמתה״ וכו׳.

8 **עדת אבירים** – תהלים סח לא. המחבר מכנה את הרוגי מלכות בשם זה, ראה אורבך (לעיל, הערה 2), עמ׳ 375, ובהערה 77 שם הוא מביא מפיוט אחד: ״עשרת אבירי ברית״. ואולי ״עדת אבירים״ כאן רמז לעשרה הרוגי מלכות, כי עדה היא עשרה, כידוע, ראה בבלי סנהדרין ב ע״א. **שמות הגבורים** – שמואל ב כג ח.

9 **כחמה ברה** – שיר השירים ו י; תהלים יט ט. **לככרם נטוע כשורה** – החכמים דומים בישיבתם לשורות הכרם, ראה בפירוש המשניות לרמב״ם על עדויות ב, ד: ״כרם – שם לקבוץ החכמים שנתקבצו ביבנה וזה לפי שהם דומים בישיבתם שורות שורות כשורות הכרם והשם יתברך קרא כנסת ישראל כרם שנאמר כרם היה לידידי (ישעיה ה א)״; וראה בשיר ד׳: ״כסדר לנוטעם בשורות מטעם״; ובסוף שיר ב׳: ״כעוללה בלקט הפרטים״ (המושג ״לקט״ שייך בקשר לכרם, ראה ויקרא יט י) והשווה ויקרא רבה לו ב (מרגליות, עמ׳ תתלו); ״מה הגפן הזאת אין נוטעין אותה ערבוביה אלא שורות שורות״.

10 **קצירי יונקותם** – תהלים פ יב. **רבי התעודה** – הכוונה לרבי התורה, לחכמי התורה. **במלאכת הפרדס** – אולי הכוונה לפירוש דברי התורה בארבע שיטות: פשט, רמז, דרש, סוד.

11 **שמרה נפשם עדותיך** – תהלים קיט קסז. **נפשם... נקשרה** – בראשית מד ל. **תמימי דרך** – תהלים קיט א. **הורו אורח ישרה** – על פי תהלים כז יא. ״הורו״: בכ״י אוקספורד, ״הוא״.

12 **ומי אנכי הלום הביאותני** – שמואל ב ז יח. **איש ידוע חלי ומכאוב** – על פי ישעיה נג ג. **השבתני לאיתני** – על פי שמות יד כז.

14-13 **שועתי וכו׳** – על פי תהלים ל ג-ד; לט יא. **שועתי ושיועו רבים** – כנראה הכוונה שהמחבר התפלל וגם התפללו רבים, הציבור, בעדו, ותפילת רבים ותפילתו הביאו לו רפואה; ותפילת רבים כוחה גדול, ראה למשל רש״י סוטה לג ע״א, ד״ה יחיד: ״אינו מואס בתפלתן של רבים״.

15 **ומדלה תבצעני** – ישעיה לח יב, ולפי פירושו של ר׳ יוסף קרא: ״כמו דלות ורעות תאר (בראשית מא יט), כלומר מחסירות בשר שהיה לי מחמת החולי, יבצעני: ישלימני, כמו והיה כי יבצע ה׳ את כל מעשהו (ישעיה י יב)״. **והחלמתני והחייתני** – ישעיה לח טז.

16 **וכמה מעלות טובות** – כלשון ההגדה: ״כמה מעלות טובות למקום עלינו״. **ולא כמעללי** – השווה תהלים קג י.

17 **גמלתני חסדיך וקטנתי** – על פי ישעיה סג ז; בראשית לב יא. **גבר באין אייליי** – תהלים פח ה. ״גבר״: כ״י אוקספורד, ״הגבר״.

18 **ואתה תוחלתי תקות חיליי** – על פי תהלים לט ח. **עזרתני ונחמתני** – תהלים פו יז. **כבריא אוליי** – תהלים עג ד.

19 **באות העשירי** – באות יו"ד. כ"י אוקספורד: "באות עשירי". **רב מחנהו** – יואל ב יא. וכוונתו שיש הרבה ערכים בספר המתחילים ביו"ד. וראה גם בשיר ו׳: "ובעשירי אשר מחנהו מאד רב". **פעל עמי למענהו** – משלי טז ד.

20 **זה אלי במה אנויהו** וכו׳ – שמות טו ב. והשווה במכילתה דר"י, מסכתא דשירה, בשלח ג (הורוביץ־רבין, עמ׳ 127): "ואנוהו, ר׳ ישמעאל אומר וכי אפשר לבשר ודם להנוות לקונו וכו׳ ר׳ יוסי בן דורמסקית אומר אעשה לפניו בית מקדש נאה, אין נוה אלא בית המקדש שנא׳ ואת נוהו השמו (תהלים עט ז)" וכו׳. וראה תרגום שם: "וית בית מקדשיה אצדיאו".

21 **מזבחו הרוס** וכו׳ – מלכים א יח ל. **ועל מכונו** וכו׳ – על פי עזרא ב סח; תהלים קד ה.

22 **וכל ישראל** וכו׳ – שמואל א ז ב. **בהיטיבו** וכו׳ – תהלים נא ב.

23 **זה היום** – תהלים קיח כד. **היום ההוא** – ירמיה ל ז. **נחכה ונקויהו** – ישעיה ח יז. **בעולות מחים** – תהלים סו טז. **זבחי צדק** – תהלים נא כא. **נחיחהו** – צ"ל "ניחחהו".

24 **יזלו בשמיו** – שיר השירים ד טז.

25 **ועתה אתה** וכו׳ – השווה בראשית כו כט; ישעיה סד ז. אצל אורבך (לעיל, הערה 2), עמ׳ 375, "ועתה אחד", אבל בשני כתבי היד: "ועתה אתה". **תאמר די לצרותינו** – ראה בראשית רבה צב א (תיאודור־אלבק, עמ׳ 1138 [על הפסוק "ואל שדי יתן לכם רחמים" בראשית מג יד]): ""מי שהוא עתיד לומר לייסורים די" וכו׳; וברש"י (על הפסוק הנ"ל): "ויאמר די לצרותי".

26 **ושבעתים** וכו׳ – תהלים עט יב. **כי ממך לא נסתרו** וכו׳ – תהלים לח י. בכ"י אוקספורד: "כי ממך לא נסתר ואנחות".

28 **לרשום אות** – כ"י אוקספורד: "לרשום את אות"; וראה בשיר ו׳: "ובאות תשיעי סייעני להרשים". **אות עשתי עשרה** – היא אות כ"ף. **אבי אתה** – תהלים פט כז. **רועי לא אחסר** – תהלים כג א.

29 **ורוחך הטובה תניחני** – תהלים קמג י. **ולמען שמך** וכו׳ – תהלים לא ד; כג ב.

מעשה ר׳ אמנון והסליחה "תא שמע"

הפרופ׳ אברהם נפתלי צבי רות, שהייתי מתלמידיו בבודפשט, עוקב במאמרו "ונתנה תוקף והעיר מגנצא", שנדפס ב"הדואר", גליון ל"ו, אחרי התפתחותו של הסיפור הידוע על ר׳ אמנון והפיוט "ונתנה תוקף". ברצוני להעיר כאן על פרט אחד, שלפי מיטב ידיעותיי לא נתנו עליו החוקרים את דעתם בעניין אגדת ר׳ אמנון.

יש סליחה בארמית לעשרת ימי תשובה, המתחילה "תא שמע מרי עלמא". סימן הסליחה "תשר"ק, א"ב, אפרים ברבי יעקב חזק", והיא חוברה ע"י רבינו אפרים בר יעקב מבונא (עיין דוידזון, ת, מספר 4). הפיוט נדפס לאחרונה על־פי כתבי־יד ודפוסים עתיקים ובליווי הערות על־ידי אברהם מאיר הברמן, ידיעות המכון לחקר השירה העברית ז (תשי"ח), עמ׳ 283-291.

אותה הסליחה באה בסדר סליחות דפוס פראג שמ"ז, דף סו ע"א ואילך, בתוך הסליחות לעשרת ימי תשובה. הואיל וסדר סליחות זה נדיר הוא מאוד, אעתיק כאן מקצתו של תוכן השער: "סליחות מסודר כפי סדר ומנהג בני מדינת אשכנז ולועזים יזי"א עם פירוש שהתחיל לחבר הגאון מהר"ר מרדכי ב"ר יודא ז"ל הנקר׳ ר׳ מארדוש... וחתנו הגאון מהר׳ צבי בן מהר"ר חנוך ז"ל מלא מקומו להשלים אותו... וגם אנחנו המדפיסים... העיר ה׳ את רוחנו... לחפש ולבדוק ולעיין בספרים ישנים...". הספר נדפס ע"י המדפיס ר׳ מרדכי בן גרשם הכהן.

בראש הפיוט נדפס הסיפור דלקמן: "שמעתי שהמחבר הזה חכם ועשיר גדול היה ואהוב לאדונו ופעמים רבות רמז לו על דבר ההמרה ושמו אמנון...". ובהמשך הדברים נאמר שם, שר׳ אמנון שגה ואמר להגמון שיתן לו זמן לחשוב על ההמרה ומייד התחרט על דבריו והחליט לקדש את השם ברבים על כי "בגדתי באלקי ישראל בפי ולשוני לקחת זמן לחשוב מחשבות". אז ציווה השר "ויוציאו לשונו ויעקרו פיו וינקרו עיניו וישברו רגליו וישם אותו בכלי גדול עם כל איבריו וי"כ (יום כיפור) היה ויתחנן הצדיק עוד אל אדונו ויאמר שלחיני אל ב"ה (בית הכנסת) ויחמול האדון עליו ויעש לו כן, ובהיותו בבית הכנסת בקש שישימו אותו לפני ארון הקודש אצל החזן ויסד על פה זה הפיוט ("תא שמע" הנ"ל) וגם ונתנה תוקף, והחזן אמרו וישורר בו ומאז נקבע לתפלת קבע".

סיפור זה על מסיבות חיבורה של הסליחה "תא שמע" לא מצאתי בשום מקום אחר, וגם לא ראיתי שייחסו את הפיוט לר׳ אמנון במקום לר׳ אפרים מבונא. הפרופ׳ רות במאמרו הנ"ל מעיר, שמקורו העתיק ביותר של הסיפור הוא ס׳ "אור זרוע" לר׳ יצחק מווינא, ושם

כתוב בזו הלשון: ״מצאתי מכתב ידו של ה״ר אפרים מבונא בר יעקב שר׳ אמנון ממגנצא יסד ונתנה תקף״. כנראה הכירו מסדריו או מפרשיו של סדר סליחות דפוס פראג הנ״ל את דברי ה״אור זרוע״, המובאים בשם רבינו אפרים מבונא וצירפו אותם אל פיוט הסליחה של ר׳ אפרים ובטעות ייחסו את הפיוט עצמו לר׳ אמנון, גיבור האגדה המסופרת ע״י ר׳ אפרים.

תוכן הסליחה ״תא שמע״ נאה הוא לסיפור על קידוש השם, שהרי מחברה מקונן בה על הרדיפות התכופות ועל הצרות הקשות העוברות על ישראל.

מכל מקום, יש עניין בדבר שכרכו את מעשה ר׳ אמנון לא רק עם הפיוט ״ונתנה תוקף״, אלא גם עם פיוט אחר – לפחות על־פי מקור אחד.[1]

1 <על סיפור ר׳ אמנון נכתבו מספר דברים מזמן פירסום דברַי, ויש להזכירם – ראה: י׳ יהלום, פיוט ומציאות בשלהי הזמן העתיק, הקיבוץ המאוחד 1999, עמ׳ 237, 243-245; י״י יובל, ״שתיקת ההיסטוריון ודמיון הסופר – ר׳ אמנון ממגנצא ואסתר־מינה מוורמייזא״, אלפיים 15 (תשנ״ח), עמ׳ 132-137; ח׳ מאק, ״ויהי ביום הדין בראש השנה, ויבואו כיתות מלאכים לפני ה׳״, הארץ, 26.9.2003, תרבות וספרות, עמ׳ 4; איבן (ישראל) מרקוס, ״קידוש השם באשכנז וסיפור רבי אמנון ממגנצא״, קדושת החיים וחירוף הנפש, קובץ מאמרים לזכרו של אמיר יקותיאל, בעריכת י׳ גפני וא׳ רביצקי, ירושלים תשנ״ג, עמ׳ 131-147; ע׳ יסיף, ״אגדה והיסטוריה – היסטוריונים קוראים באגדות עבריות מימי הביניים״, ציון סב (תשנ״ט), עמ׳ 192-200; שם סה (תש״ס), עמ׳ 222. וראה להלן בחלק האנגלי, עמ׳ *230-*232.>

משהו על פיוטים לנישואין באשכנז

התדמית של היצירה הפייטנית באשכנז (ובצרפת) בימי הביניים מצטיירת בעיני הציבור, ואפילו בעיני חוקרים לא מעטים כפייטנות מקוננת, מלאת צער ויגון, שעיקר מטרתה ותפקידה לשרת את צורכי התפילה בימי אבל ותענית וכמעט כולה מביעה רק זעקת קינים והגה והי. פייטנות זו נחשבת כעדות על רדיפות וכתגובה עליהן ולא כיצירה אמנותית־ספרותית, ובייחוד לא כשירה שיש בה שמחת חיים ועליזות. הסליחות והקינות המרובות ששרדו מהמאות האחת עשרה והשתים עשרה ואילך העיבו על העובדה שהיו גם פיוטים מסוג אחר, ואלה נועדו למאורעות של שמחה שנחוגו לא רק בבית אלא גם על ידי אמירת פיוטים מיוחדים בתוך סדר התפילה בציבור בבית הכנסת. היצירה הפייטנית באשכנז הייתה אינטנסיבית לא רק בחיבור סליחות אלא דווקא בסוגי פיוט אחרים שהקהילות השתמשו בהם לציון שמחות, ובפרט חתונות.[1] בתקופות קדומות אלה, כשחיי הציבור היו בסכנת רדיפות ואיומי שמד ומספר היהודים היה קטן, נחשבו כנראה כל לידה וכל חתונה כמאורע שראוי לחגוג לא רק בחיק המשפחה אלא גם במסגרת התפילה של כל הקהל בבית הכנסת.

הסיבה העיקרית להיעלמות הפיוטים לימי שמחה מתודעת הציבור הייתה השתנות מנהגי התפילה וטקסי השמחה הביתיים והציבוריים במרוצת הדורות. בזמן ששמרו הקהילות על אמירת סליחות וקינות בימי תענית, הושמטו כמעט כליל הפיוטים של ימי שמחה פרטיים, כגון ברית מילה ונישואין, מתוך סדר התפילה. יש להניח שהסליחות והקינות על מאורעות ומצבים שהשפיעו על חיי הציבור כולו נשארו בסדר התפילה מפני שהיו עדויות על צרת רבים, אולם השמחות של היחיד, בייחוד בתקופות מאוחרות יותר, כשהאוכלוסייה היהודית גדלה, לא נחשבו ראויות לציון בתוך סדר תפילת הציבור ולא היו חשובות דיין כדי לשנות את סדר התפילה הרגיל. ההבדל בגורלם של שני הסוגים נגרם גם בשל מקומן של ההוספות הפיוטיות בתוך התפילה: בתקופה שאנו דנים בה נאמרו הסליחות בנפרד, בסדרי סליחות מיוחדים, ולא היוו הפסק בתפילות הקבע. כפי שנראה להלן, לפחות כמה מן ההוספות הפיוטיות לימי חתונה נכנסו באמצע תפילות הקבע, בקריאת שמע וברכותיה ובקדושה למוסף, ואולי בגלל ההתנגדות להפסק בתפילה החליטו

1 במהדורות הרבות של סדרי סליחות לפי מנהג אשכנז לענפיו יש מאות רבות של פיוטי סליחות, וראה במבוא לסדר הסליחות כמנהג פולין, מהדורת דניאל גולדשמידט, ירושלים תשכ״ה, עמ׳ 6-8, ובמבוא למהדורתו של מחזור יום כיפור, ירושלים תש״ל, עמ׳ יב-יד. וראה עתה גם לקט פיוטי סליחות מאת פייטני אשכנז וצרפת (אוסף מכתבי יד דניאל גולדשמידט; הגיה, עיבד וביאר אברהם פרנקל), ירושלים תשנ״ג. בקובץ זה כלולים 356 פיוטי סליחות. על היצירה בסוגים אחרים ראה להלן.

הקהילות להשמיט את ההוספות. הסיבה החשובה ביותר להסרת הפיוטים מתפילת הציבור בשבת שלאחרי החתונה הייתה, קרוב לוודאי, השינוי שחל בימים שבהם התקיימו חתונות בימי הביניים באשכנז. החל מתקופות קדומות התקיימו הנישואין באשכנז בערבי שבתות וכל השמחות הקשורות לחתונה נחוגו תיכף ומיד אחר כך, בשבת. שבת זו הייתה שבת החתונה ובה נאמרו הפיוטים שנועדו לציון השמחה. החל מסוף ימי הביניים השתנה המנהג והחתונות התקיימו בימי רביעי. השמטת הפיוטים מסדר התפילה הייתה קשורה כנראה לשינוי זה. שרידים למנהג הישן נשארו באשכנז עד לתקופה החדשה.[2] כך או כך, בסדרי התפילה האשכנזיים נתמעטו במשך הדורות הפיוטים שנאמרו לכבוד חתונות וטקסי ברית מילה, ובתקופה המודרנית הם נעדרו כמעט לגמרי.

עזרא פליישר, במחקריו השונים, תיאר את החידושים הרבגוניים של פייטני אשכנז וקבע שהם עסקו הרבה בחיבור פיוטים מסוג היוצרות והרשויות. הם כתבו פיוטים להזדמנויות ליטורגיות שונות, הכניסו לפיוט הקונבנציונלי סוגי פיוט חדשים והוסיפו פיוטים בתפילות הקבע במקומות שבמסורת הפיוט הקלאסית לא היו רגילים לעטרם בפיוט. בין החידושים האלה יש קישוטים פיוטיים לפסקאות "המלך היושב" ו"שבח נותנים לו" בתפילת שחרית לשבתות, וכן לפסקה "אלהיכם" שבקדושת מוסף. פייטני אשכנז הִרבו לפייט גם לקריאת התורה, לאמירת התרגומים הארמיים שנתלוו לפרשיות חגיגיות שבתורה, כגון שירת הים, עשרת הדיברות ופטירת משה, ולעלייתם של החתנים לתורה, הן חתנים של ממש והן "חתני תורה" ו"חתני בראשית" שעלו לסיום התורה והתחלתה מחדש בחג שמחת תורה.[3]

בדיקה רופפת של כמה כתבי יד של מחזורים, סידורים ואוספי פיוטים אשכנזיים מימי הביניים, מראה שראוי להקדיש תשומת לב לנושא זה של פיוטים למאורעות משמחים, משום שבכתבי יד אלה טמון חומר רב למדי שעדיין לא נדפס. כתב יד אחד, הנמצא בספריית בית המדרש לרבנים באמריקה (מס' 8972), עשיר בפיוטים לכבוד חתן וכלה, שנאמרו בבית הכנסת בשבת שלאחרי הנישואין. החוקרים התעניינו בכתב יד זה בגלל המיניאטורות הצבעוניות הבלתי רגילות שבו, המעטרות טקסטים פיוטיים נדירים. בצלאל נרקיס הקדיש מאמר מפורט לצד האמנותי של כתב היד והביא תיאור קודיקולוגי מדויק שלו.[4] נרקיס מכנה את כתב היד בשם "מחזור אשכנזי זעיר" וקובע את זמן כתיבתו למאה השלוש עשרה – וליתר דיוק, שנת 1295 לערך – ואת פרנקוניה שבמרכז גרמניה כמקום מוצאו. כבר אלכסנדר מארכס, שרכש את כתב היד עבור ספריית בית המדרש לרבנים באמריקה, בשנת 1928, העיר על חשיבותו. הוא שתיאר אותו לראשונה, כדרכו תמיד

2 ראה דיון מפורט ויסודי בעניין זה בתוך מנהגים דק"ק וורמייזא לרבי יוזפא שמש, מהדורת בנימין שלמה המבורגר ויצחק זימר, ירושלים תשנ"ב, ח"ב, עמ' נב-נז.

3 עזרא פליישר, היוצרות בהתהוותם והתפתחותם, ירושלים תשמ"ד, עמ' 607 ואילך, ובייחוד עמ' 611-610, 626-625. ראה גם בספרו שירת הקודש העברית בימי-הביניים, ירושלים 1975, עמ' 433 ואילך, ובייחוד עמ' 460-463, 448-449.

4 בצלאל נרקיס, "ציורים לעשרת הדיברות במחזור אשכנזי זעיר בן המאה השלוש עשרה", עשרת הדיברות בראי הדורות, בעריכת בן-ציון סגל, ירושלים תשמ"ו, עמ' 389-407.

בקיצור ובדייקנות, וקרא לו "אוסף פיוטים לשבתות מיוחדות וקצת חגים". מארכס הדגיש שכתב היד כולל פיוטים חלופיים ליום אחד, דהיינו החזן היה רשאי לבחור מתוך קבוצת פיוטים שונים שנועדו למאורע ליטורגי מסוים, כפי שהיה נהוג בתקופה שהמנהג האשכנזי היה גמיש והפיוטים וסדריהם עדיין לא קפאו. לפי מארכס, כתב היד נכתב בשנת 1300 לערך באוסטריה.[5] כתב היד היפה הוצג כמה פעמים בתערוכות פומביות ובקטלוגים של תערוכות אלה תואר, פחות או יותר, על פי דבריו של מארכס.[6] בתוכן של כתב היד לא עסקו החוקרים בכלל, עד שבא לאחרונה אברהם פרנקל ופרסם מתוכו פיוט בלתי ידוע לר' שלמה הבבלי. לפי פרנקל כתב היד הוא "סידור 'אוסטרייך' משנת 1300 לערך".[7]

הפיוטים לנישואין בכתב היד הזה (דף 94א-107ב) מתחלקים לשתי חטיבות, ואולי יש להוסיף עליהן עוד חטיבה אחת (85א-93ב). בכל כתב היד יש להבחין בקלות בין החטיבות השונות: הייעוד הליטורגי של כל חלק ברור מאוד ובדרך כלל הוא מסומן בפירוש, החלקים נבדלים זה מזה גם באמצעות דפים ריקים ובאמצעות המלה "סליק", ופעמיים מופיעים גם קולופונים של הסופר בסוף החטיבה או בתחילתה.[8] כך למשל מכיל החלק הראשון והגדול ביותר של האוסף פיוטי יוצר לשבתות מיוחדות של השנה, ובראש כל פיוט ציין המעתיק את סוג הפיוט ובאיזו שבת נאמר (2א-107ב). החטיבה המכילה פיוטי נישואין מתחלקת, כאמור, לשני חלקים. הייעוד של הפיוטים ברור לגמרי. בחלק הראשון (94א-98א) נמצאת הקומפוזיציה הפיוטית המפורסמת של ר' שמעון ב"ר יצחק, "אייחד שם שוכן תרשישים" (דוידזון, א, 2730), פיוט יוצר לשבת חתן הנמצא בהרבה כתבי יד וספרי דפוס.[9] בחלק השני (99א-107ב) נמצאים פיוטים רבים לטקס עלייתם לתורה של החתן ושל השושבינין. אולם בחלק הקודם לזה (85א-93ב) המצב מסובך יותר. בניגוד לשאר חלקי האוסף חסרים כאן ציונים מפורשים לייעודיהם של הפיוטים, ורק שֵׁם הסוג ניתן לפעמים. לכאורה נדמה שלפנינו קבוצת פיוטים "נייטרליים" המתאימים לכל הזדמנות ושליח הציבור יכול לבחור ממנה פיוט לעת מצוא, לעיטור התפילות כרצונו. כך הם פיוטי "נשמת", "אופן", "מאורה" וכו', המופיעים בחלק זה בלי שנאמר עליהם

5 Alexander Marx, *Bibliographical Studies and Notes on Rare Books and Manuscripts in the Library of the Jewish Theological Seminary of America*, ed. Menahem H. Schmelzer, New York 1977, pp. 100-101

6 *The People and the Book: The Background of Three Hundred Years of Jewish Life in America: A Tricentennial Exhibition at the New York Public Library*... compiled Joshua Bloch, New York 1954, pp. 56-58 ("Hebrew Hymnal"); *Illuminated Hebrew Manuscripts from the Library of the Jewish Theological Seminary of America,* The Jewish Museum, New York 1965, #18 ("Siddur")

7 אברהם פרנקל, "האופן 'שש כנפים כנופים' לר' שלמה הבבלי", תרביץ סו (תשנ"ז), עמ' 131-136.

8 סליק: 89ב, 91א, 98א ועוד. דפים ריקים: 79, 98, 107. קולופונים: 166ב: "נשלמו מעריבים/ שבח ליושב הכרובים/ ועושה רביבים/ ירפאני ממכאובים/ ויוציא טלאים וכשבים/ מתוך חזירי/ וכלבים"; 172ב: "בעזרת ה' משיב הרוחות/ אחל לכתוב סדר סליחות/ וה' בעל גבורות וכוחות/ יוציאנו מצרות לרוחות/ וה' אלקי' בוחן כליות וטוחות/ יהפוך אבלותינו לשמחות/ ויסיר מארצו יגון ואנחות".

9 מהדורה ביקורתית של הפיוט כלולה בתוך פיוטי רבי שמעון ב"ר יצחק, י"ל בידי אברהם מאיר הברמן, ירושלים-ברלין 1938, עמ' נו-סא.

בפירוש, ובלי שיתברר מתוכנם, לאיזה מאורע נועדו. אולם בדיקה מדויקת יותר מוכיחה שפיוטים רבים למדי בחלק הזה נועדו לשבת נישואין. מסקנה זו יוצאת מתוכנם של כמה פיוטים וגם מההשוואה למקורות אחרים שבהם פיוטים המופיעים כאן סתם, בלי ציון ייעודם, באים כשנאמר עליהם בפירוש שהם מיועדים לשבת חתונה. כבר הפיוט הראשון, העומד בראש חלק זה, הוא לכבוד חתן וכלה. כדי להדגים את תוכנו, את מקומו בליטורגיה ואת סגנונו, אביא כאן את הטקסט של הפיוט במלואו:

[1]

נִשְׁמַת יְשָׁרִים יְחִילוּךָ לְאוֹר זוֹרֵחַ
יִיחוּדֶךָ יַאֲמִירוּ יְדִידִים מִתְאַוִּים בְּקוֹל צוֹרֵחַ
יִפְרַח בְּיָמָיו צַדִּיק וְרוֹב שָׁלוֹם עַד בְּלִי יָרֵחַ (תהלים עב ז)

נִשְׁמַת וָתִיקִים מְלַוִּים הֶחָתָן מִמְּכוֹן נְוָותוֹ
וִועוּדֶיךָ יְבָאֲרוּ ויהַלְלוּ שִׁמְךָ כְּצֵאת הַשֶּׁמֶשׁ בִּגְבוּרָתוֹ
וְהוּא כְּחָתָן יוֹצֵא מֵחֻפָּתוֹ (תהלים יט ו)

נִשְׁמַת שָׂשִׂים וּשְׂמֵחִים בְּרוֹב עוֹז וּתְהִלָּה
סִילוּדֶיךָ יַגְבִּירוּ שִׁירוֹת בְּרִינָה וְצָהֳלָה
קוֹל שָׂשׂוֹן קוֹל שִׂמְחָה וְקוֹל חָתָן וְקוֹל כַּלָּה (ירמיהו ז לד)

נִשְׁמַת פִּרְחֵי עֲדָתֶךָ הֲמוֹנֵי קְהָלֶיהָ
פִּלוּלֶיךָ יְדַבְּרוּ פּוֹצְחִים בְּרֶנֶן וְצִילְצוּל הִילוּלֶיהָ
כֶּחָתָן יְכַהֵן פְּאֵר וְכַכַּלָּה תַּעְדֶּה כֵלֶיהָ (ישעיהו סא י)

נִשְׁמַת הַמַּשְׁכִּימִים הַיּוֹם עִם הֶחָתָן לָבוֹא
הִילוּלֶיךָ יְהַדְּרוּ הַיּוֹשְׁבִים מִפֹּה וּמִפֹּה סְבִיבוֹ
בְּיוֹם חֲתֻנָּתוֹ וּבְיוֹם שִׂמְחַת לִבּוֹ (שיר השירים ג יא)

נִשְׁמַת קְהִילוֹת יַעֲקֹב הָעוֹמְדִים בְּבֵית מַאֲוַויָּם
הֵם וּבְנֵיהֶם וְגִיזְעָם ואפיריים
אוֹמְרִים אִילוּ פִינוּ מָלֵא שִׁירָה כַּיָּם

פיוט זה הוכנס לתפילת נשמת לפני הפסקה "אילו פינו" וכו'. יש בו סימן "יוסף ה..." כפול וכל טור שלישי בכל סטרופה הוא פסוק מן המקרא. הפיוט מיוחס לפייטן הספרדי, יוסף אבן אביתור.[10] בתקופה זו, במאה השלוש עשרה, לא היה זה נדיר שפיוטים ספרדיים

10 ראה דוידזון, י', 4266, שרושם את התחלת הפיוט בנוסח "ישרים יחלוך" ומייחסו לאבן אביתור, על פי צונץ. פליישר מכניסו גם הוא בין פיוטי אבן אביתור, ראה עזרא פליישר, יצירתו של יוסף אבן אביתור, חיבור לשם קבלת תואר דוקטור לפילוסופיה, האוניברסיטה העברית, ירושלים תשכ"ז, עמ' 349, מס' 24. ייתכן שהפיוט מס' 1 (עמ' 346) המובא שם זהה לפיוט שלפנינו. לא הייתה לי הזדמנות לבדוק

הופיעו באוספי פיוטים אשכנזיים וצרפתיים. כך המצב גם בקונטרס הפיוטים הנלווה אל מחזור ויטרי הנדפס,[11] וכך בכתב היד שלפנינו בחלק זה, כפי שנראה להלן. אף על פי שלכאורה אין להטיל ספק בייחוס הפיוט לאבן אביתור, יש להעיר שיש דמיון בין כמה ביטויים שבפיוט ובין ניסוחים דומים בטקסטים אשכנזיים וצרפתיים. בפיוט שלפנינו מתואר ליווי החתן מביתו לבית הכנסת במלים אלה: "ווֹתיקים **מלווים** החתן ממכון נוותו" (טור 4), "המשכימים היום עם החתן לבוא/ ... **היושבים** מפה ומפה **סביבו**" (טורים 13-14). בדומה לזה, בחלק העוסק בענייני נישואין במחזור ויטרי נכתב:

> ובשבת שחרית לאחר שהשלים הסדר עם הציבור הולך לבית הכנסת ושושבינין אחריו ומתעטף בציצית ויושב בצד הארון והשושבינים **יושבים** להם **סביבותיו**.

ועוד:

> השלימו סדריהם יוצאים מבית הכנסת יוצא החתן תחילה ושושבינין אחריו ילווהו.[12]

וכך מתואר גם בפיוטי רשויות שונים למחברים אשכנזיים:

> ושושביניך **ילווּך**[13]
> ויעמדו **מסביב** קהל תמימים... ושושביניך לבד עמך כתאומים/ עמוד ואליך מצודדים מכל צדדים[14]
> צעדיו כדרך המלך ילך ושושביניו אחריו... בעלותך למגדל **ילווּך**[15]
> יוצאים ובאים אתך ועוטרים **סביבותיך**[16]

ברם, הנוהג ששושבינים מלווים את החתן ומקיפים אותו אינו ייחודי לאשכנז; גם בשירי הכלולות של ר׳ יהודה הלוי נמצאים תיאורים הדומים לאלה שהובאו לעיל ממקורות אשכנזיים: "בואו וראו הוד חתן והוד שושביניו **סביבו**", "והצבא אשר יצא לשרת פני חתן ולראות החתנה/ ושבעת כוכבי שחק כאחים **סבבוהו**...", "יפרח חתן כשושן... כהדסים עומדים **סביביו** והוא עומד בין ההדסים".[17] הציורים המטאפוריים של ר׳ יהודה הלוי

בכתבי יד ולברר דבר זה. הפיוט רשום גם בדוידזון, נ, 767, ושם נזכר שהוא נדפס (כנראה רק פעם אחת) עם פירוש קצר בסידור שער השמים, שהוא המהדורה הראשונה של סידור השל"ה, אמסטרדם 1717, ח"ב, עמ׳ 134. הסטרופה האחרונה כנראה אינה שייכת לפיוט זה אלא מתוספת גם לשאר פיוטי "נשמת", וראה דברי פליישר, שם, עמ׳ 331. "ואפיריים" (טור 17): כנראה טעות סופר במקום "פריים".

11 מחזור ויטרי, מהדורת שמעון הלוי הורוויץ (מהדורה ב) נירנבערג תרפ"ג, בסוף הספר נוסף "קונטרס הפיוטים הנלווה אל המחזור ויטרי כתב יד לונדון... העתקתיו... חיים בראדי".

12 מחזור ויטרי, עמ׳ 593, 599.

13 פיוטי ר׳ שמעון ב"ר יצחק (לעיל, הערה 9), עמ׳ קפז.

14 רשויות לחתן, ירושלים תרצ"ו, עמ׳ יג, רשות לר׳ יצחק סגן לויה.

15 רשות לחתן לר׳ אפרים מבונא, שם, עמ׳ ל (ידיעות המכון לחקר השירה העברית [תשי"ח], עמ׳ 281).

16 רשות לחתן לר׳ יצחק נקדן, רשויות לחתן, עמ׳ מו.

17 שירי הקדש לרבי יהודה הלוי, מהדורת דב ירדן, ד, ירושלים תשמ"ו, עמ׳ 965, 979, 994.

משקפים כנראה נוהג קונקרטי של ליווי החתן על ידי שושביניו המקיפים אותו, ובכל זאת התיאורים במקורות האשכנזיים־צרפתיים נראים ממשיים ומפורטים יותר. הם דומים למתואר בפיוט שלפנינו אבל בכל זאת אין בזה כדי לשלול את הבעלות על הפיוט מר׳ יוסף אבן אביתור.

הפיוט שופע אווירה של שמחה ושל שירה ורינה. בפיוט הקצר באים זה אחר זה ביטויי ששון וצהלה: ״ויהללו שמך״, ״ששים ושמחים ברוב עוז ותהלה״, ״יגבירו שירות ברינה וצהלה״, ״פוצחים ברנן וצילצול הילוּליה״, ״הילוליך יהדרו״. סגנון זה מתאים היטב לתחושת השמחה של הזוג הצעיר. מלת הפתיחה ״נשמת״ מקשרת את הנושא להימנון ״נשמת״ הנאמר בתפילות השחרית של שבתות וחגים והמלים המצטרפות אל מלת פתיחה זו (ישרים, ידידים, וותיקים, פרחי עדתך [= הצעירים], המוני קהליה, המשכימים היום, קהילות יעקב) מציינות את השתתפות הקהל בשמחת היחיד ואולי גם רומזות לכך שרגשות שמחה אלה נובעים מתוך נשמתם של המשתתפים.

הפיוט הבא בחטיבה זו גם הוא פיוט מסוג ״נשמת״. התחלתו: [2] ״נשמת מלומדי מורשה״ (דוידזון, נ, 779), והיו רגילים לאמרו בתפילת שחרית של שמחת תורה לפי מנהג אשכנז ופולין. הוא מפורסם כפיוט היחידי מסוג זה במחזור אשכנז, אף על פי שהסוג היה נפוץ מאוד במסורת הפיוטית של ספרד ופרובאנס.[18] כפי שכבר העיר צונץ, פיוטים מסוג זה נמצאים במנהג אשכנז רק לשמחת תורה ולשבת נישואין.[19] במקרה של פיוטי רשות לחתן תורה ולחתן בראשית לשמחת תורה, גם במקרה של פיוטי ״נשמת״ יש להניח שפיוטי שמחת תורה הם חיקויים לפיוטים לחתנים ממש.[20] ל״נשמת מלומדי מורשה״ אין שום קשר לנישואין, כמובן, וברור מתוכנו שהוא נכתב לכבוד התורה ולומדיה.

אחרי שני פיוטי ״נשמת״ אלה בא פיוט שרשום עליו ״למי ידמה לך״, דהיינו הפיוט מיועד לפִסקת ״מי ידמה לך״ שבתפילת ״נשמת״.[21] פייטני אשכנז היו רגילים לעטר את תפילת ״נשמת״ בפיוטים או להשתמש במקום זה בפיוטים ספרדיים, כפי שהראה פליישר.[22] מלבד פיוטים שהוכנסו לפני הפסקה ״אילו פינו״, חוברו פיוטים גם לפסקה ״המלך היושב על כסא רם ונשא״ וגם ל״אל ההודאות״, והשניים האחרונים הם מחידושי אסכולת הפייטנות האשכנזית. פיוט ל״מי ידמה לך״, כמו זה שלפנינו, אינו ידוע לי ממקור אחר. והנה לשונו:

[3]

1 מִי יִדְמֶה לָּךְ/ וּמִי יִשְׁוֶה לָךְ
שָׁמַיִם לֹא זַכּוּ לְמוּלָךְ/ אַף כִּי נֵצֶר נִתְעָב נִשְׁלַךְ
הוּא לְדֵרָאוֹן וְאַתָּה בְּגוֹרָלֶךְ/ ה׳ מֶלֶךְ ה׳ מָלָךְ

18 ראה מחזור סוכות שמיני עצרת ושמחת תורה לפי מנהג אשכנז לכל ענפיהם... מוגה וכו׳ בידי דניאל גולדשמידט, הושלם בידי יונה פרנקל, ירושלים תשמ״א, עמ׳ 331-332, וראה שם במבוא, עמ׳ לד.

19 L. Zunz, *Die Ritus des synagogalen Gottesdienstes,* Berlin 1989, p. 83

20 ראה פליישר, שירת הקדש (לעיל, הערה 3), עמ׳ 472.

21 ראה על זה להלן.

22 פליישר, שם, עמ׳ 461-463.

מִי יָצַר שַׁחַק וְכֹכָב צַר וָאוֹר
אֶרֶץ וְכָל עָלֶיהָ וְרוֹבַע יְאוֹר
הֲלֹא אַתָּה ה׳ אַדִּיר וְנָאוֹר
עַיִן עַל מָרוֹם וְעָפָר מֻשְׁלָךְ/ ה׳ מֶלֶךְ ה׳ מָלָךְ

מִי חִילֵּק שֵׁשׁ עִיתֵּי שָׁנָה
הַחֲיּוֹת כָּל חַי אֶרֶץ כּוֹנְנָה
הֲלֹא אַתָּה ה׳ קֶדֶם מְעוֹנָה
לָכֵן כָּל יְצִיר יְקַדֵּם לְהַלֶּלָךְ/ ה׳ מֶלֶךְ ה׳ מָלָךְ

מִי קָץ וּמָאַס בְּעוֹבְדֵי תְמוּנָה
בָּחַר בְּאַבְרָהָם לְשָׁלִישׁת שָׁנָה
הֲלֹא אַתָּה ה׳ אֲשֶׁר לָךְ הִקְנָה
מְכוֹן שִׁבְתְּךָ וַהֲדוֹם רַגְלֶךָ/ ה׳ מֶלֶךְ ה׳ מָלָךְ

מִי קוֹל יַעֲקֹב לְקָשׁוֹב הִרְגִּיל
עַמּוֹ בְּצָרָה מְשַׂמְּחוֹ אֶל גִּיל
הֲלֹא אַתָּה ה׳ עָלָיו מַרְגִּיל
אַהֲבָה מַה מְאֹד טוֹב רַגְלֶךָ/ ה׳ מֶלֶךְ ה׳ מָלָךְ[23]

פיוט זה אינו ידוע וזכרו לא בא במקורות הרגילים. שם מחברו היה יצחק, כפי שחתום בראשי הסטרופות, אחרי מלת הקבע "מי". אף על פי שעניין חתן וכלה אינו נזכר בפיוט בפירוש, יש רגליים לדבר שהשתמשו בו לכבודם. הפיוטים שפייטני אשכנז חידשו לפסקאות "נשמת" היו בשימוש בשבתות נישואין;[24] אולי גם בטור 17 – "עמו בצרה משמחו אל גיל" – יש רמז דק לשמחה כזו.

23 טור 2: על פי איוב טו טו-טז. טור 3: על פי דניאל יב ב, יג. טור 4: על פי ישעיהו ה ל. טור 5: **וכל עליה** – לא ברור בכתב היד. **רובע יאור** – אינני יודע פירושו. טור 6: על פי ירמיהו יד כב ועוד. תהלים עו ה. טור 7: פירושו: עינו של ה׳ גם על צבא השמים (המרום) וגם על בני האדם (עפר מושלך). טור 8: בראשית ח כב, וראה פירוש רש״י שם. טור 9: ישעיהו מה יח. טור 10: דברים לג כז. טור 12: **בעובדי תמונה** – עובדי עבודה זרה, על פי שמות כ ד. טור 13: אברהם היה בן שלוש כשהכיר את בוראו, ראה בראשית רבה ל ח, עמ׳ 273-274. טורים 14-15: בראשית יד יט, כב, שמות טו יז, ישעיהו סו א. אברהם הכריז שה׳ הוא קונה (לך הקנה) שמים (מכון שבתך) וארץ (הדום רגלך). והשווה תנחומא, בובר, בהר ג, עמ׳ 105: "כיון שראה הקב״ה היאך חיבב אברהם את המצות, התחיל מקנה לו העליונים והתחתונים". טור 16: ה׳ רגיל לשמוע את קול יעקב. טור 17: תהלים צא טו, איוב ג כב. טור 18-19: ישעיהו נב ז, ואולי יש כאן משחק מלים על הפסוק "דגלו עלי אהבה" (שיר השירים ב ד).

24 Philipp de Haas, *Ungedruckte Stücke aus den Breslauer deutschen Machzor-Handschriften*, Breslau 1906, pp. 67-69

והנה רשימת הפיוטים הבאים אחרי הפיוט שהובא לעיל:

4 שבעה שחקים לא יכלכלוך, לר׳ שלמה אבן גבירול (דוידזון, ש, 285). ״לפני קדיש ראשון״.
5 שאי עין יחידתי, לר׳ שלמה אבן גבירול (ש, 64). ״לנשמת״.
* 6 יבהלוני סעפי חזיוני, סימן: יהודה. ״לנשמת״.
7 שחרתיך בכל שח [צ״ל שחרי] ונשפי, ל׳ שלמה אבן גבירול (ש, 865). ״אחר לנשמת״.
8 יעירוני בשמך רעיוני, לר׳ יהודה הלוי (י, 3149). ״לנשמת דר׳ יהו׳ קשטל׳״.
* 9 הגדול בכבוד שמך שיר לא יקוש ממך, סימן: יצחק.
10 המלך שיר נדבות, סימן: שלמה (ה, 775). ״להמלך היושב״.[25]
11 יחדו לב נשלם, ליוספיה הגר (י, 2464). ״לברכו״.
12 יחדיו בשיר מעלות, לר׳ יוסף (קמחי?) י, 2454).[26]
*13 ימים והרים דוק וגיאות, ״לשבח נותנים לו״.
14 שבח מי יגמור ליוצר אור לאמור, לשמואל (ש, 226). ״אחר״.
*15 מחנות מחנות שרפי אל, סימן: יוסף.
16 יקר אדון הנפלאות, לר׳ יהודה הלוי (י, 3628).
17 ישעך יזכרו עם בך יכתירו, לר׳ יהודה הלוי (י, 4188). ״אופן״.
18 אלי אהללך בבור לבב, לר׳ אברהם אבן עזרא (א, 4892).
19 יאתה שדי לך מלוכה וגדולה, לר׳ יהודה הלוי (י, 74).
*20 יקודי אש גוייתם, סימן: יצחק.
21 ארוממך כי נשגב כבוד שמך, לר׳ אברהם אבן עזרא (א, 7547).
*22 יודוך ה׳ מלכי עת אשר תפנה דרכי, סימן: יעקב. ״מאורה״.
23 יודעי הפיצוני ימי עוני, לר׳ יהודה הלוי (י, 1567). ״אהבה״.
24 יודעי יגוני יספו להציב אש לבי כידוד [צ״ל: יודעי יגוני יספו באש לבי כידוד], לר׳ יהודה הלוי (י, 1569). ״אהבה״.
25 אמרות האל טהורות, לר׳ יהודה הלוי (א, 5909). ״מאורה״.
26 התנערי מעפרים לבשי עוזך שביה, לר׳ מאיר מרוטנברג (ה, 1241).[27]
*27 השמים שמים לה׳ יעוררו רחמיך לקרא׳[ת] רצוני, בלי סימן.
28 שלח אמתך ואורך, לשמשון (ש, 326).
29 שלשים ושתים נתיבות שבילך [כל ברואי מעלה], לשלמה (כ, 282).

25 נדפס בספרו של פליישר, שירת הקודש (לעיל, הערה 3), עמ׳ 461-462. האאס (לעיל, הערה 24) מביאו ממחזור בכתב יד שהיה שמור בברסלוי, כפיוט לשבת חתונה, ראה שם, עמ׳ 67-69. האאס מביא שם עוד שני פיוטים ל״המלך היושב״, על פי כ״י המבורג 37 ו־42. באחד יש סימן, יצחק חזק, והשני מיוחס לר׳ אלעזר בן יהודה בן קלונימוס מוורמש, על פי צונץ (L. Zunz, *Literaturgeschichte der synagogalen Poesie*, Berlin 1865, p. 318). לפי צונץ חיבר ר׳ אלעזר מוורמש שני פיוטים גם ל״שבח נותנים לו״ (צונץ, שם).

26 ראה על פיוט זה בתוך מנהגים דק״ק וורמיישא (לעיל, הערה 2), עמ׳ נג, הערה 32.

30 מסילות לבבי אחת עולה, למרדכי (מ, 1931).
31 יה אנא אמצאך, לר׳ יהודה הלוי (י, 770).
32 אלהיכם אני פצתה צרור המור (א, 4572).[28]
33 אלהיכם שכנו שם, לשמואל (א, 4601).
34* אלהיכם סביביו נסערה, בלי סימן. ״אחר״.
35 אלהיכם יחיד בעולמו, סימן: יושף חזק (א, 4583).[29] ״אחר״.
36 אלהיכם יוסיף ידו שנית (א, 4578).[30] ״אחר״.
37 אלהיכם אני זוכר הברית (א, 4571). ״אחר״.
38 אלהיכם יזריח שמשו, סימן: יהודה חזק (א, 4581).
39 קוראים בלבב שלם, לר׳ יהודה הלוי (ק, 244).
40 יפרח לנוחי ושר משיחי [צ״ל: שר], ליהוספיה הגר (י, 3437).[31] ״אחר לשים שלום״.
41* אדון עוזי פודי מגוזי, סימן: יוספיה.
42 יה שמך ארוממך, לר׳ יהודה הלוי (י, 1143). ״לקדיש אחרון״.
43 יה צור מחסי עוז מגדל, ליצחק (י, 1061). ״אחר לקדיש אחרון״.[32]

הפיוטים המסומנים בכוכב אינם ידועים, עד כמה שיכולתי לקבוע. מלבדם יש גם אחדים שעדיין לא נדפסו, אף על פי שהם נזכרים במקורות (מס׳ 32, 35, 36, 40).

בחלק זה של כתב היד, כפי שעולה מן הרשימה, יש בעיקר שני מיני פיוטים: פיוטים בסוגים שכיחים של משוררים מפורסמים מספרד, ר׳ שלמה אבן גבירול, ר׳ יהודה הלוי ור׳ אברהם אבן עזרא, ופיוטים בסוגים נדירים, של מחברים שזהותם בלתי ידועה פחות או יותר והרבה מפיוטיהם עדיין לא נדפסו, ואפילו אלה שנדפסו כלולים בפרסומים מדעיים ולא בסדרי התפילה האשכנזיים המודפסים. הפיוטים לתפילת ״נשמת״ ולפסקאות השונות שבה, לפסקה ״שבח נותנים לו״ שבתוך ההימנון ״אל אדון״ הכלול בברכה הראשונה שלפני קריאת השמע בתפילת שחרית לשבת, ולפסקה ״אלהיכם״ שבקדושת מוסף בשבת ובחגים – נאמרו ברובם בשבתות נישואין.[33] לפנינו כנראה אוסף של פיוטים ששימש כעין

27 נדפס על ידי פליישר, היוצרות (לעיל, הערה 3), עמ׳ 681-682, פליישר כתב שם שפיוטו של ר׳ מאיר מרוטנבורג הוא חיקוי לפיוטו של ר׳ יהודה הלוי, ״אמרות האל״. בכתב היד שלנו באים שני הפיוטים זה אחר זה. הגרסה אצל פליישר: ״התנערי מעפרים לבשי ציון שבייה״.

28 לפי צונץ (לעיל, הערה 25), עמ׳ 85, זהו פיוט אנונימי ישן. בכתב היד שלפנינו הוא אינו שלם וכנראה חסר כאן דף בכתב היד.

29 לפי צונץ (שם), עמ׳ 569, נועד פיוט זה לשבת חתונה והוא נמצא בכתב יד ״Orat, 37״, סימנו היום: כתב יד עברי של הספרייה הלאומית בפאריס, מס׳ 647.

30 לפי צונץ (שם), עמ׳ 272, גם פיוט זה נועד לשבת חתונה ומחברו הוא יוסף בן נתן חזן.

31 ראה מחזור לפסח, מהדורת יונה פרנקל, ירושלים תשנ״ג, עמ׳ 246, וראה גם במבוא, עמ׳ מב.

32 על הפיוט ״האל העירה וראה״ ל״קדיש אחרון״ שהיה נהוג באשכנז עוד בתקופה המודרנית ראה מנהגים דק״ק וורמיישא (לעיל, הערה 2), עמ׳ נז, הערה 69.

33 הפיוטים ״המלך שיר נדבות״ (10), ״מסלות לבבי״ (33), ״ארוממך כי נשגב כבוד שמך״ (21), ״שבח מי יגמור״ (14), ״שלח אמתך ואורך״ (28), נועדו לשבת חתונה בכתב יד אחר של מחזור שהיה

אנתולוגיה פיוטית לחזנים שממנה בחרו יצירות לחגיגות לעת מצוא. ״אנתולוגיה״ זו הייתה מורכבת מהפיוטים המפורסמים של משוררי ספרד שתוכנם הכללי והנייטרלי התאים לכל מאורע, וידוע שבסדרי התפילה לפי המנהגים השונים הם נאמרו בהזדמנויות שונות. לחלק זה נכנסו גם פיוטים של מחברים בני המקום, שביצירותיהם הנדירות השתמשו הקהילות כדי לציין מאורעות אינדיבידואליים, בעיקר בשבתות חתונה וקצת לכבוד טקסי ברית מילה.[34]

החטיבה הבאה אחרי ״אנתולוגיה״ זו מכילה, כאמור, את יצירתו של ר׳ שמעון ב״ר יצחק,[35] שהיא יוצר קלאסי לשבת חתונה. הקומפוזיציה הפיוטית של ר׳ שמעון היתה חלק קונבנציונלי של סדר התפילה, לעומת הפיוטים הכלולים בחלק הקודם, ששימשו יותר כעיטורים לעת מצוא ואמירתם הייתה תלויה במנהג המקום, בבחירת החזן ובטעמם של המתפללים.

בחטיבה הבאה נמצאת סדרת פיוטים הקשורים לטקס קריאת התורה בשבת, כאשר קראו לחתן ולשושביניו לעלות לתורה. היה נהוג באשכנז להוסיף פרשה קצרה לקריאה הרגילה כשעלה החתן לתורה, והיא הפרשה בספר בראשית כ״ד א׳-ד׳: ״ואברהם זקן בא בימים״. גם הפטרה מיוחדת הייתה לחתן, והיא נלקחה מישעיהו ס״א י׳ עד ישעיהו ס״ג ט׳: ״שוש אשיש בה׳״.[36] עליית החתן לתורה נחגגה בטקס גדול ובאמירת רשויות, פיוטים וברכות (״מי שברך״).[37] מדור גדול של אמירות כאלה נשמר במחזור ויטרי הנדפס[38] והיה כדאי וראוי לבדוק את החומר הפיוטי לנישואין הנמצא בשאר כתבי היד של מחזור ויטרי במקורות אחרים.

להלן נמשיך ברשימת הפיוטים שבתוך כתב היד, וכאן יבואו התחלות הפיוטים הנועדים לקריאת התורה:

44 אהלל ברעד לשם פה, ליוסף (דוידזון, א, 1462). ״רשות לכהן״.

45 יבוא לגני צור לבבי, ליוסף (י, 95). ״רשות ללוי״.

46 מרשות שוכן עד וקדוש, לר׳ שמעון ב״ר יצחק (מ, 2512). ״לחתן״.

47 אתניה שבחיה (א, 8967).

48 במקהלות ברכו בני ברית, לר׳ ברוך בן שמואל (ב, 809).[39]

49 יה בשר שר צבאך, ליהוספיה הגר (י, 806).

בברסלוי, ראה האאס (לעיל, הערה 24), עמ׳ 67-81. וראה מה שכתב פליישר, היוצרות (לעיל, הערה 3), עמ׳ 610-611, ובמיוחד הערה 12 שם ועמ׳ 625-626 והערה 40 שם.

34 הפיוט ״אלהיכם אני זוכר הברית״ (37) נועד לברית מילה.

35 לעיל, הערה 9.

36 על קריאת התורה, ובייחוד על קריאת ההפטרה בשבת חתונה, ראה מנהגים דק״ק וורמיישא (לעיל, הערה 2), עמ׳ נו-נז, הערה 65; יצחק (אריק) זימר, עולם כמנהגו נוהג, ירושלים 1996, עמ׳ 273-280.

37 ראה פליישר, שירת הקודש (לעיל, הערה 3), עמ׳ 472.

38 מחזור ויטרי, עמ׳ 596-600.

39 ראה ״פיוטי רבינו ברוך בר שמואל ממגנצא״, מהדורת אברהם מאיר הברמן, ידיעות המכון לחקר השירה העברית ו (תש״ו), עמ׳ עו.

50 דבוק חתן בדתיך, לדונש (ד, 11).

*51 נער ישראל ואהבתיו, בלי סימן.

*52 ממים רבים תמשני, בלי סימן.

53 יפרח חתן כשושן, לר׳ יהודה הלוי (י, 3434).

*54 נבחר מעם ריע שעשועים, בלי סימן

*55 אגביר קולי ברמה, סימן: אברהם.

*56 יערב שיחי לבי ישיש, סימן: יוסף (?).

*57 יה מתי רוח ממרום יערה, סימן: יהודה.

*58 יעור לבי משנת ודם, בלי סימן.

*59 אלוה אבי עד שיתהו לעד, סימן א-ח.

60 ואני נשארתי לבדי (ו, 60). ״לשבעת שרי המלך״.[40]

גם בחלק זה נמצאים זה על יד זה פיוטים שכיחים, כמו פיוטי הרשות של ר׳ שמעון ב״ר יצחק, ופיוטים נדירים ובלתי ידועים. כדי להדגים את סגנון הפיוטים האלה ואת רוח השמחה והשעשועים השורה עליהם, אביא את הפיוט הראשון (מס׳ 44) ואת הפיוט האחרון (מס׳ 60) שבסדרה.

[44]

אֲהַלֵּל בְּרַעַד לְשָׁם פֶּה
בּוֹרֵא אֶרֶץ מַבִּיט וְצוֹפֶה
גּוֹלֶה עֲמֻקוֹת מוֹחֵץ וְרוֹפֵא
הַכֹּל עָשָׂה יָפֶה (קהלת ג יא)

דַּהֲרַת עֻזּוֹ בְּרוּם גְּבוֹהִים
הַלְלוּהוּ בְמוֹרָא צְבָאוֹת נִמְהָרִים
וְהַדְּרוּ זַמְּרוּ עַם כְּמֵיהִים
תְּנוּ עוֹז לֵאלֹהִים (תהלים סח לה)

זָוִיּוֹת גַּיא תִּיקֵּן וְשִׁיפֵּר
חַיּוֹת וּשְׂרָפִים בְּלִי מִסְפָּר
טָסִים וּמְעוֹפְפִים וְרוֹעִים בָּאֵפֶר
הַכֹּל הָיָה מִן הֶעָפָר (קהלת ג כ)

40 על מספר השושבינים ראה מנהגים דק״ק וורמיישא (לעיל, הערה 2), עמ׳ נד, ובהערות 36-35 שם. בסדרה שלפנינו יש ט״ו חרוזים לקריאת השושבינים ואולי בחר החזן מאלה כרצונו אבל כל מספר הקרואים היה רק שבעה, כפי שכתוב בראש הסדרה: ״לשבעת שרי המלך״ (על פי אסתר א); וכמובן, ״המלך״ כאן פירושו ״החתן״, וכך כתוב גם בחרוז הראשון (ראה להלן): ״שבעת שרי החבורה״.

יֵצֶר כַּף רֵיקָם לִזְבוֹד
כְּנֶגְדּוֹ הִשְׁוָה עֵזֶר לוֹ הוֹד
לִשְׁמוֹ נֶצַח בְּחִיל לַעֲבוֹד
תְּנוּ לֵאלֹהֵיכֶם כָּבוֹד (ירמיהו יג טז)

מֵאָז שִׁיפֵּר מְרֻקָּם בְּאֶשְׁכּוֹל
נְתָנוֹ בְּשֶׁקֶל כֹּל יָכוֹל
סִדֵּר לוֹ זוּג לִשְׁקוֹל הַכֹּל
כַּאֲשֶׁר לַכֹּל (קהלת ט ב)

קֶרְבוּ לִשְׁמוֹעַ שׁוֹפְכֵי עֲתִירָה
טַעֲמֵי שֶׁבַח לְשֹׁכֵן סִתְרָה
נוֹרְאוֹתָיו סַפְּרוּ קְהִלָּה מוּכְתָּרָה
וְהַכֹּל תְּנוּ כָבוֹד לַתּוֹרָה.[41]

[60]

א וַאֲנִי נִשְׁאַרְתִּי לְבַדִּי מֵחֲבוּרָה
וְאֵין קוֹרֵא עִמִּי בְּתוֹרָה
עֲלֵיכֶם אִישִׁים אֶקְרָא

41 דודזון בערכו רושם את הפיוט כפתיחה לקריאת התורה סתם ונותן את סימנו כ-א-ט, קטן [יוסף], על פי צונץ (לעיל, הערה 25, עמ׳ 723). צונץ מצא את הפיוט סמוך לפיוט ״יבוא לגני״, כמו בכתב היד שלפנינו, והיות שפיוט זה (״יבוא לגני״) חתום בו יוסף, ייחס לו גם את ״אהלל ברעד״. צונץ רושם אותם על פי כתב יד Ms. B. Niederhofheim. הפיוט נמצא גם בכ״י שוקן, מס׳ 131160 דף 63א, גם שם רק עד ט׳. הפיוט מיוסד על הפִסקה ״הכל הבו גודל לאלוקינו/ ותנו כבוד לתורה״, שמשתמשים בה לקריאת העולים לתורה. על הנוהג לשיר ״על הכל״ בימים מיוחדים ראה להלן, הערה 45. טור 1-2: תהלים ב יא; שמות ד יא; בראשית א א; תהלים קד לב; משלי טו ג. טור 3: איוב יב כב; דברים לב לט. טור 6: תהלים ב יא. **נמהרים** — עם ישראל, על פי ישעיהו לה ד. טור 7: **עם כמיהים** — על פי תהלים סג ב. טור 9: **זויות גיא** — פינות העולם. טור 10-11: אולי הכוונה למלאכים ולבני אדם (רועה באפר, על פי ישעיהו מב כ) ואולי הכוונה למלאכים (חיות ושרפים), לעופות ולבעלי כנף (טסים ומעופפים) וכן לחיות ולבהמות (רועים באפר). בכתב היד שלפנינו: ״ורועות״; בכ״י שוקן: ״ורועים״. טור 13: אולי על פי תהלים קלט ה, וקשה לפרשו. טור 14: בראשית ב כ. טור 17: **מרוקם** — האדם, ראה תהלים קלט טו; **באשכול** – אולי הכוונה לארץ, על פי הפסוק ״וקמתי בתחתיות ארץ״, ובמלה ״אשכול״ משתמשים הפייטנים לציון ״תבל״ ו״ארץ״, ראה למשל ר׳ יצחק אבן גיאת, וארץ אכף, סטרופה ח: ״חבר רגבים ותלה כאשכול את כל הארצות האל״ (פיוטי ר׳ יצחק אבן גיאת, מהד׳ יונה דוד, ירושלים תשמ״ח, עמ׳ 8) וכן שירי הקדש לרבי שלמה אבן גבירול, מהד׳ דב ירדן, ירושלים תשל״ג, עמ׳ 453, הערה לטור 3, וכן שירי השירים אשר לשלמה, לשניאור זק״ש, פאריש 1868, עמ׳ קמז-קמט. טורים 18-19: אינני יודע פירושם ואולי הכוונה שאיש ואשה יחד שולטים על כל הארץ, כפי שכתוב בבראשית א כח. טור 21: **שופכי עתירה** — שופכי תפילה. טור 22: **לשכן סתרה** – ה׳ השוכן בסתר, על פי תהלים צא א. טור 23: תהלים קמה ו, והשווה בפיוט המפורסם ״אל נא לעולם תערץ״: ״נוראותיו שיחו/ ספרו עזו״; וראה פליישר, שירת הקודש (לעיל, הערה 3), עמ׳ 146. **מוכתרה** — שמוכתר בכתר תורה.

שׁוֹשְׁבִינֵי הַמֶּלֶךְ וְהַגְּבִירָה
שִׁבְעַת שָׂרֵי הַחֲבוּרָה
רוֹאֵי פְּנֵי הַמֶּלֶךְ בַּהֲדָרָ[ה]
עמ׳ עמ׳ עמ׳ פלו׳ ב״ר פלו׳ מְהֵרָה
וַעֲלֵה אֵלַי הָהָרָה

ב רַגְלְךָ בָּטוּחַ בְּךָ יחוץ (?)
שֶׁבֶת מוֹשָׁבְךָ לָחוּץ
אוֹיֵב עָלֶיךָ שָׁחוּץ
נָגוּף יִהְיֶה וּמָחוּץ
עע״ע פב״פ בְּגִיחוּץ
טְהוֹר יָדַיִם וְרָחוּץ
דְּבַר הַמֶּלֶךְ נָחוּץ
לָמָּה תַעֲמוֹד בַּחוּץ

ג לְךָ בָּחוּר וְטוֹב בִּקְהָלֶיךָ
עֵינֵי כָּל יִשְׂרָ[אֵל] עָלֶיךָ
סַדֵּר וַעֲרוֹךְ מִלּוּלֶךָ
וְהַשְׁמִיעֵנִי אֶת קוֹלֶךָ
עע״ע פב״פ בְּחֵילֶךָ
הַיְשֵׁר צֶדֶק מַעְגָּלֶיךָ
דְּבַר סֵתֶר לִי עָלֶיךָ
וַעֲמוֹד עַל רַגְלֶךָ

ד טוֹב אַתָּה וַחֲמוּדִי בְּעֵינָי
צֵאתְךָ וּבוֹאֲךָ בְּמַחֲנָי
יוֹדֵעַ סֵדֶר עִנְיָנָי
שׁוֹנֶה הֲלָכוֹת בִּסְבְרוֹנַי
עע״ע פב״פ מַשְׂכִּיל בִּנְבוֹנָי
לְהוֹדוֹת לְשׁוֹכֵן מְעוֹנָי
עֲמוֹד בְּבֵית ה׳

ה וַהֲדָרְךָ נָעִים בְּוִיעוּדֶךָ
צְלַח רְכַב הוֹדֶיךָ
מְאֹד נַעֲלָה כְּבוֹדֶיךָ
בְּיוֹפִי מַעֲשֵׂה יָדֶיךָ
עע״ע פב״פ בְּמַעֲמַד[ךָ]
קְרַב הֵנָּה בְּוִיעוּדֶיךָ

צוּר לְבָרֵךְ בְּכָל מְאוֹדֶיךָ
עֲמוֹד עַל עוֹמְדֶיךָ

ו בְּעָמְדִי ...מו צְבִי מֻוגְבָּר
תַּרְתֵּי גֶּבֶר נָקִי וּבָר
שְׁפַל בֶּרֶךְ מְדֻוּבָּר
עַל כָּל רוֹאָיו גָּבַר
עע״ע פב״פ חָכָם וְסָבַר
מֵבִין לְכָל דָּבָר
עוֹז ה׳ לְהִתְגַּבָּר
קוּם כִּי עָלֶיךָ הַדָּבָר

ז וּבִינוֹתִי וּבְחֶמְדָּה חֲטוּבָה
חֲבוּרָה נְכוֹנָה וַחֲבִיבָה
טַעֲמֵי תוֹרָה רְבוּבָה
הֵיכַל קֹדֶשׁ עֲנוּ בָהּ
עע״ע פב״פ בַּשְׂגוּבָה
יָקַרְתָּ בְּעִינוּי בְּחִיבּוּבָהּ
בִּרְכוֹת שָׁמַיִם לְגוֹבְבָהּ
עָרְכָה לְפָנַי וְהִתְיַצְּבָה

ח רְאֵה קְרָאתִיךָ בְּשֵׁם
דָּמְתָה לַעֲרוּגַת הַבֹּשֶׂם
יָקַרְתָּ כְּאַחְלָמָה וְלֶשֶׁם
נָקִי מִבְּלִי אָשָׁם
עע״ע ופב״פ וְהָרֵם נֶשֶׁם
לְפָאֵר לְמוֹרִיד הַגֶּשֶׁם
וּבַגּוֹיִם יֵצֵא לְךָ שֵׁם
בְּתִתְּךָ בְּרָכָה וְהוֹדָאָה לְשֵׁם[42]

ט בַּחוּר מֵעָם לְךָ טַל יַלְדוּתְךָ
פְּתַח פִּיךָ בְּבִרְכוֹתֶיךָ
וְהִתְיַצֵּב פֹּה עַל עֲלוֹתֶיךָ
וִיטִיבְךָ לִבְּךָ בְּאַחֲרִיתֶךָ
עע״ע פב״פ מִתּוֹךְ עֲדָתֶיךָ
וְקוּם עַל מִשְׁמַרְתֶּיךָ

42 מעל לחרוז זה רשום ״וזה יאמר לשושבין עשירי״. על מספר השושבינים ראה לעיל, הערה 40.

וְיֵטִיבוּ אֹהָלֶיךָ וּמִשְׁכְּנוֹתֶיךָ
וִיבַלּוּ בִּנְעִימִים שְׁנוֹתֶיךָ

י בָּרֵךְ אֶתֵּן לְךָ וְלֹא אֲשִׁיבֶנָּה
יְבָרֶכְךָ שׁוֹכֵן מְעוֹנָה
בְּהַרְבּוֹתְךָ לִיתֵּן מַתָּנָה
לִכְבוֹד הַתּוֹרָה וְהַחֲתוּנָּ[ה]
עע״ע פב״פ וּקְרַב הֵנָּה
וַעֲלֵה אֵלַי בְּגִיל וּרְנָנָה
לְבָרֵךְ בְּקוֹל רָם אֵל אֱמוּנָה
הֲלֹא אָצַלְתִּיךָ בְּרָכָה לְמָנָה

יא הִנְּךָ יָפֶה אַף נָעִים
רְאֵה קְרָאתִיךָ יֶלֶד שַׁעֲשׁוּעִים
חִיבַּבְתִּיךָ בְּשֵׁם גַּעְגּוּעִים
וִיכַבְּדוּךָ רָשִׁים וְשׁוֹעִים
עע״ע פב״פ הַנָּעִים
וּבָרֵךְ תְּמִים דֵּעִים
בְּצֶדֶק גְדוּדִים וּנְטוּעִים

יב אֵת שֶׁאָהֲבָה נַפְשִׁי רְאִיתִיךָ
מִתּוֹךְ עַם הֲרִימוֹתִיךָ
אֶת קוֹלִי שְׁמַעְתִּיךָ
מִיּוֹם יְדַעְתִּיךָ
עע״ע פב״פ כִּי שַׂמְתִּיךָ
לְנֵזֶר בִּקְהַל עַם שִׁמַּשְׁתִּיךָ
וְגַם טֶרֶם קְרָאתִיךָ
אָצַלְתִּי לְךָ בְּרָכָה וּבֵרַכְתִּיךָ

יג חֲמֵשׁ עֶשְׂרֵה תֵיבוֹת
בְּבִרְכַּת כֹּהֲנִים כְּתוּבוֹת
כִּיוַּנְתִּיךָ כְּנֶגְדָּם לִקְרֹא בְּחִיבּוֹ
וּבָהֶם תִּתְבָּרֵךְ מִי עֲרָבוֹת
עע״ע פב״פ וַעֲלֵה בִקְרָבוֹת
וְתֵן שְׁבָחוֹת עֲרֵבוֹת
וְתִתְבָּרֵךְ בְּרִיבּוּי טוֹבוֹת
בְּלִי מִסְפָּר קְצוּבוֹת

יד סוּרָה אֵלַי אַל תִּירָא
פְּאַר הַחֲבוּרָה
אֲשֶׁר בְּאֶמֶת וּבְצֶדֶק גְּדוּרָה
קוּמָה נָא מִלְעֲצָרָה
עע״ע פב״פ לִקְרוֹא בַתּוֹרָה
וְתַשְׁמִיעַ אֶת קוֹלְךָ בְּהַדְרָהּ
וִיבָרֶכְךָ עוֹטֶה אוֹרָה

ט״ו טַל יָלִין בִּקְצִירָךְ
נָוֶה וּמְעוּלֶּה בְּחִבּוּרָךְ
כַּאַיֶּלֶת הַשַּׁחַר זִיו תּוֹאֲרָךְ
כְּאוֹר הַחַמָּה זוֹהֳרָךְ
עע״ע פב״פ אַב וְרַךְ
וּבָרֵךְ אֶת ה׳ הַמְבוֹרָךְ
בְּמַאֲמָרָךְ וּבְדִיבּוּרָךְ
וְתִזְכֶּה לִדְבַר ה׳ בְּאֶרֶץ הֲדָרָךְ[43]

כאמור לעיל, מנהגים אלה של אמירת פיוטים שונים בשבת נישואין נשתכחו בחלקם או ברובם כבר בסוף ימי הביניים, ובתקופה החדשה הם נעלמו כמעט כליל, אולם נשאר זכר לאמירת הפיוטים במקומות השונים בתפילת השחרית של שבת נישואין. במנהגים דק״ק וורמיישא אנו קוראים כך:

> בריילפט הוא שבת שיש בו נישואין. אז בשבת שחרית, כשמגיעין בנשמת למי ידמה לך שותק המנגן, ואז הרב יוצא מב״ה, והקהל אחריו ובאין לפני פתח בית החתן והחתן יוצא... והרב אחרי החתן, והקהל אחריו. וכן הולכין עם החתן

43 צונץ (לעיל, הערה 25) עמ׳ 628-629, מזכיר סדרה זו ומביא שם את החרוז הראשון והאחרון. לפי צונץ (שם עמ׳ 549) הייתה ידועה עוד סדרה כמו זו שלפנינו וחלקים ממנה נשמרו בכתבי יד. הסגנון בחרוזים שלנו הוא קל ומשתעשע ועממי. חרוז א: **ואני נשארתי לבדי וכו׳** – השושבינים נקראו לתורה אחרי ששאר הקרואים גמרו את קריאת הפרשה כרגיל, והשושבינים חזרו וקראו את הפרשה או חלק ממנה, בדומה למנהגנו בשמחת תורה; וראה מנהגים דק״ק וורמיישא (לעיל, הערה 2), עמ׳ נד הערה 36. **ועלה אלי ההרה** – לשון שעשועים לקריאה לעלייה על הבימה. חרוז ב: המובן אינו ברור; **למה תעמוד בחוץ** – שוב קריאה מתבדחת לעולה לתורה. כך גם בחרוז ג: **דבר סתר לי עליך ועמוד על רגלך**, ובחרוז ט: **והתיצב פה על עלותיך**, משחק מלים על במדבר כג ג: ״התייצב על עולתך״. הקורא מחלק מחמאות לשושבינים ומהלל את מידותיהם הטובות ואת חכמתם בתורה: ״טהור ידים ורחוץ״ (חרוז ב), ״בחור טוב״ (חרוז ג), ״טוב אתה וחמודי [אולי צ״ל וחמוד] בעיני... יודע סדר עינייני/ שונה הלכות בסברוני... משכיל בנבוני״ (חרוז ד), ״מאד נעלה כבודיך/ ביופי מעשה ידיך״ (חרוז ה), ״גבר נקי וברך/ שפל ברך... חכם וסבר/ מבין לכל דבר״ (חרוז ו), ״נקי מבלי אשם״ (חרוז ח), ״הנך יפה אף נעים/ ...ויכבדוך רשים ושועים״ (חרוז יא), ״פאר החבורה״ (חרוז יד), ״נוה ומעולה בחבורך״ (חרוז טו). כמובן, השושבינים מקבלים גם ברכות ותודה על המתנות המרובות שהם נודרים לתת (חרוז י).

לב״ה. והחתן יושב על מקום המיוחד לכל החתני׳, שהיא בראש הכנסת, ואז המנגן פסוקי דזמרא מתחיל מי ידמה לך וגומר נשמת.[44]

כפי שראינו לעיל, בכתב היד שלפנינו יש פיוט מיוחד שנועד לשבת חתונה. פיוט זה נאמר במקום הזה בתפילת נשמת (מספר 3). יש להניח שבתקופות הקדומות נאמר הפיוט בזמן שהגיע החתן לבית הכנסת והחזן התחיל בפסקה ״מי ידמה לך״. עם הזמן הוסר הפיוט מן התפילה אבל ציון המקום בתפילה וכניסת החתן בנקודה זו נשארו. גם במקומות אחרים היו החזנים רגילים לציין בניגון ובקול רם פסקאות מסוימות בשחרית של שבת חתונה. המקומות האלה זהים למקומות שבהם נאמרו הפיוטים בתקופות הקדומות. כך נמסר בספר המנהגים הנזכר על אמירת ״שבח נותנים לו״ ו״על הכל״ בקול רם על ידי החזן, ונוהג זה מתאים למה שראינו לעיל, כלומר שפיוטים מיוחדים נועדו להיאמר בשבתות חתונה בפסקאות אלה.[45] שוב, הפיוטים נשכחו אבל החזנים המשיכו לשמור על ציון הפסקאות שבהן היו רגילים לאמרם.

כתב היד המצויר המיניאטורי שמשך את תשומת לב חוקרי האמנות היהודית של ימי הביניים[46] עשיר אפוא גם מבחינת תוכנו הספרותי. עיון נוסף בו ובשאר כתבי יד של פיוטי אשכנז וצרפת יחשוף בלי ספק יצירות חדשות שגילויין וניתוחן יתרמו לציור תמונה שלמה ומאוזנת של הפייטנות העברית באשכנז ובצרפת בימי הביניים.

רשימת הפיוטים לפי סדר הא״ב:

אגביר קולי ברמה 55
אדון עוזי 41
אהלל ברעך 44
אלהיכם אני זוכר הברית 37
אלהיכם אני פצתה 32
אלהיכם יוסיף ידו 36
אלהיכם יזריח שמשו 38
אלהיכם יחיד בעולמו 35
אלהיכם סביביו נסערה 34
אלהיכם שכנו שם 33
אלוה אבי עד 59
אלי אהללך בבור לבב 18
אמרות האל טהורות 25

44 מנהגים דק״ק וורמיישא (לעיל, הערה 2), עמ׳ נב-נג.

45 ראה שם, עמ׳ נד, וראה גם מנהגות וורמייזא לר׳ יודא ליווא קירכום, מהד׳ ישראל מרדכי פלס, ירושלים תשמ״ו, עמ׳ פ. דיון רחב בעניין ״ימי שירת ׳על הכל׳״ נמצא אצל בנימין שלמה המבורגר, שרשי מנהג אשכנז, בני ברק תשנ״ה, עמ׳ 152-157. ל״שבח נותנים לו״ נועדו הפיוטים מס׳ 13-14, ול״על הכל״ – פיוט מספר 44.

46 לעיל, הערה 4.

אליעזר אריה הלוי פינקלשטיין
חכם, חוקר, מגשים וחולם

בערב שבת, כ״ב בכסלו תשנ״ב, בגיל 96, שבק פרופסור אליעזר אריה (לואיס) פינקלשטיין חיים לכל חי. עד לימיו האחרונים עסק בתורה ובחכמה, למד, חקר וכתב כמו שהיה רגיל כל ימיו. במשך חייו הארוכים, שחפפו כמעט את כל המאה העשרים, הטביע פינקלשטיין את חותמו על יהדות אמריקה ועל חכמת ישראל, הן בתרומתו המדעית והן במנהיגותו הרוחנית והציבורית. משהו מיוחד היה במפעלו הרבגוני: פעילותו השפיעה על מחקריו ואלה נתנו אותותיהם בדרכו הציבורית. דבר זה יש שירצו לדרשו לשבח ואולי גם לגנאי: לשבח, מפני שלמדנותו ותורתו השתקפו תמיד בכל מה שעשה כמנהיגו של ציבור גדול בישראל, ולגנאי, מפני שבמחקריו נתן ביטוי לחזונותיו ולא שמר תמיד על הגבול בין ״המדע הטהור״ ובין השקפותיו הפוליטיות, הדתיות והחברתיות. פינקלשטיין לא הסתייג מלערב את שני התחומים ומלנסות לשלבם בהרמוניה. הוא ראה עצמו, ביודעין ובלא יודעין, כממשיכה של מסורת רבנית היסטורית, שמייצגיה איחדו בתוכם ידיעות עמוקות ורחבות בתורה ובחכמה עם התמסרות בכל לב ובכל מרץ לצרכי הציבור ולהדרכתו. בבואנו להעריך את פינקלשטיין כחוקר וכגאון בתורה ובחכמה, עלינו לראות בו התגשמות מודרנית של דגם קדום: מנהיגים רבניים גדולים, שהקדישו את חייהם ללימוד התורה, להגדלתה ולהאדרתה, ובעת ובעונה אחת עסקו בהנהגה ציבורית אמיצה ולפעמים מהפכנית. ראייה זו עשוייה להסביר תופעות מגמתיות שונות במחקריו של פינקלשטיין ולאפיין את מפעלו המחקרי לשלביו ולמרכיביו הרבים.

אליעזר אריה פינקלשטיין נולד בארצות הברית, בעיר סינסינטי (בכ״ב בסיון תרנ״ה), לאביו ר׳ שמעון יצחק הלוי (רש״י) פינקלשטיין. הבן השאיר שתי תעודות מעניינות על אביו. האחת, מבוא ל״סדר תפילה עם ביאור שיח יצחק״ (ירושלים 1968). הוא תיאר שם את אביו כרב ליטאי טיפוסי, שהיגר לאמריקה ופעל שם בקהילות שונות. הוא היה תלמיד חכם גדול, שידע את הש״ס בעל פה אפילו בעת זקנתו. הוא עדיין שמע תורה מפיו של ר׳ ישראל סלנטר והיה קרוב לר׳ יצחק אלחנן ספקטור. אף על פי שר׳ שמעון יצחק התנגד מאוד להשקפות הרפורמה, היה אייזיק מ׳ וייס, ראש תנועת הרפורמה בארצות הברית, בין באי ביתו. באותו מקום סיפר פינקלשטיין גם על אמו, ש״סבלה הרבה מדרך החיים באמריקה״. היא עודדה אותו, אולי עוד יותר מאביו, שילמד בהתמדה, ושלחה אותו, אף בימי שלג וסופה, ללמוד בבית המדרש. התמונה המתקבלת מקווים ביוגרפיים אלה מראה אנשים בני הדור הישן, שעיקר מטרתם היתה להעביר לבניהם את דרך החיים ״הליטאית״.

התעודה השנייה היא אוטוביוגרפיה של האב, בניסוחו של הבן, שהופיעה בקובץ *American Spiritual Autobiographies: Fifteen Self-Portraits* (ניו־יורק 1948). כאן מתגלה האב כאדם שקשור מאוד לאמריקה, החש רגשות גאווה כל פעם שהוא משמיע את המשפט "אני אמריקני", וכמי שלא יכול לתאר לעצמו שיבה לסלובודקה אחרי שטעם את טעם הדמוקרטיה והחירות. שני יסודות אלה – מורשת ליטא ורוח החירות האמריקנית – התמזגו בפינקלשטיין והשפיעו על אישיותו כל ימי חייו.

יסוד שלישי, לא פחות חשוב, היה התקשרותו עם בית המדרש לרבנים באמריקה בניו־יורק, ששניאור זלמן שכטר עמד אז בראשו. פינקשטיין הצעיר נכנס למוסד כתלמיד בשנת הלימודים 1913-1912 ומאז ובמשך כל ימי חייו נשאר קשור עמו כסטודנט, כמורה, כאיש מינהל ובראש המוסד. שכטר ועמיתיו, לוי גינצברג ואלכסנדר מארכס, פתחו בפני הסטודנט הצעיר את עולמה של חכמת ישראל, במיוחד בצורה שהיתה מקובלת בגרמניה. מאביו הוא קיבל את דרך הלימוד המסורתית, מ־City College ומאוניברסיטת קולומביה בניו־יורק את האידיאל האמריקני ואת ההשכלה הכללית, וממוריו בבית המדרש לרבנים את ההתעניינות במדעי היהדות.

מאמריו הראשונים כבר העידו על כשרונותיו, ידיעותיו, כח דמיונו וחריפותו. במאמרו הראשון סקר ספרים חדשים העוסקים בספרות ההלניסטית ובמאמר השני סקר כמה ספרים חדשים בתיאולוגיה.[1] את מאמרו השלישי, שעסק בבעיית ההלכה בספר היובלים, כתב כתלמיד בבית המדרש לרבנים. הוא הופיע לראשונה ב־*Harvard Theological Review* (כרך 16, 1923), ונדפס מחדש באוסף מאמריו: *Pharisaism in the Making* (1972). במבואו לאוסף זה הדגיש פינקלשטיין כי על אף שיותר מחמישים שנה חלפו מאז נכתב המאמר, הנה כמעט וכל הטענות המדעיות שהעלה בו נשארו שרירות וקיימות.

נכונותו של פינקלשטיין לקבל ביקורת בנוגע לפרטים מסוימים בכתביו, יחד עם נאמנות להשקפת עולמו המדעית הכללית למרות ביקורת חריפה, מאפיינות את גישתו. מצד אחד, החזיק בדעותיו ובשיטותיו הראשונות ולמרות הביקורת לא חזר מהן. על אמונתו באמיתות שיטותיו הצהיר כבר בצעירותו, כגון בתשובתו לביקורת שפירסם יצחק בער על ספרו *Jewish Self-Government in the Middle Ages* (*MGWJ*, כרך 74, 1930), ויותר מאוחר גם במבוא למהדורת ספרי על ספר דברים (1939), בהוספות למהדורה השלישית של ספרו *The Pharisees* (1962) ובספרו *New Light from the Prophets* (1969). במבואו לספרי דברים כתב: "אודות השטה שהחזקתי בנסוח הספרי כבר נשאו ונתנו חכמים וחוקרים אחדים... אי אפשר לי להסכים ולהיות תמים דעה אתם". כאישיות חזקה הבטוחה בעצמה, הגיע פינקלשטיין למסקנותיו הכלליות אחרי עיון ודיון שקול וממושך, ולא זנח את עיקר שיטתו כל ימי חייו. מצד שני, בעניין הפרטים של דיוניו ופירושיו קיבל ברצון את

1 ביבליוגרפיה של כתבי פינקלשטיין יצאה לאור בשנת 1977 ובה רשימה של ספריו ומאמריו עד שנת 1974: *A Bibliography of the Writings of Louis Finkelstein* (להלן: ביבליוגרפיה). הוספות, בשכפול, הוכנו על ידי אורה המלסדורף בשנת 1985. מאז הופיעו כמה מאמרים שלו (בספרי היובל לכבודם של ארתור היימן ושל סימור כהן). בימיו האחרונים עוד הספיק לאשר את תוכן הכרך החמישי ממהדורתו: ספרא דבי רב והוא ספר תורת כהנים, ירושלים תשנ"ב.

דעות חבריו ותיקן את דברי עצמו בנימה של הכרת טובה והערצה לאלה שחולקים עליו. כך, למשל, במבוא להוצאה השנייה של ספרי על ספר דברים (1969), הביע את צערו על שבגלל טרדותיו המרובות בצרכי ציבור אין בידו לתקן את מה שצריך תיקון בספר. הוא הזכיר את מאמרי הביקורת של י"נ אפשטיין ושל ש' ליברמן על ההוצאה הראשונה, וקבע כי "הלומד חייב להשתמש בהם".

המאמר הרביעי שפירסם הוא מחקרו המבריק, המהפכני והשנוי במחלוקת, על התפתחות תפילת העמידה ("The Development of the Amidah").[2] פינקלשטיין היה בן שלושים כשמאמר זה הופיע, והוא קנה לו מיד שם בקרב חכמי ישראל. מאמריו הראשונים בספרות הלניסטית, בתיאולוגיה מודרנית, בתולדות ההלכה הקדומה ובהתפתחות התפילה היהודית בראשיתה, הם הניצנים הראשונים לעבודתו המדעית הפוריה בנושאים אלה במשך למעלה מיובל שנה.

רק פעמיים סטה פינקלשטיין מעיסוקו המדעי העיקרי: חקר הספרות הרבנית העתיקה. בשנת 1924 הוא פירסם את ספרו *Jewish Self-Government in the Middle Ages* (מהדורה שנייה: 1964). ספר זה כלל בתוכו מהדורה ביקורתית של תקנות רבינו גרשם מאור הגולה ורבינו תם ושאר תקנות מאשכנז של ימי הביניים, בליווי תרגום לאנגלית. לספר צורפו גם כמה תקנות מאיטליה ומקורפו, מתוך כתבי יד שההדיר כאן לראשונה. שיטתו במהדורת הטקסטים הושפעה ממורו אלכסנדר מארכס. מלבד איסוף כל כתבי היד וספרי הדפוס שאפשר היה להשיגם אז, פינקלשטיין גם מיין את המקורות למשפחותיהם וניסה לקבוע את יחסן זו לזו. מעניינות במיוחד הן מסקנותיו לגבי האוטונומיה הפנימית של הקהילה היהודית בימי הביניים. תופעת ההתארגנות העצמית של עם נרדף, שהתגורר בין ריבונויות שונות הנלחמות זו בזו, נראתה בעיניו דבר חשוב הראוי לתשומת לב. הוא שיבח את יהדות אשכנז על דבקותה בלימוד התורה ובשמירת ערכי היהדות, שהושגו, לדעתו, תודות לארגון הקהילות. פינקלשטיין גם רמז על ההקבלה בין התפקיד שמילאה העיר יבנה אחרי חורבן הבית השני ובין תפקידן של התקנות האשכנזיות אחרי חורבן ישיבות סורא ופומבדיתא. מתקבל הרושם שפינקלשטיין התכוון להציג את יהדות אשכנז כאות וכמופת ליהדות אמריקה, כשם שעשה אחר כך ביחס לפרושים. הספר נחשב לחיבור יסודי, חשוב ומקורי עד היום, וזוכה תדיר לדיון ולהתייחסות בקרב טובי החוקרים של דורנו.[3]

ספר זה לידתו היתה בתחרות שנערכה בבית המדרש לרבנים, לכתיבת מסה בהיסטוריה יהודית. בערך באותו זמן עבד פינקלשטיין על עבודת הדוקטור שלו באוניברסיטת קולומביה. עבודתו היתה מוקדשת למהדורה ביקורתית של פירוש הרד"ק על ארבעים הפרקים הראשונים של ספר ישעיה והיא יצאה לאור בשנת 1926 (מהדורה שנייה: 1966). גם כאן השתמש פינקלשטיין בכתבי היד ובדפוסים הראשונים של הפירוש, חיבר מבוא מפורט ובנוסף הדפיס לראשונה את פירושו האליגורי של רד"ק לבראשית. מלבד ערכה

2 ביבליוגרפיה, מס' 5, 321, 338.

3 ראה, למשל אברהם גרוסמן, חכמי אשכנז הראשונים, ירושלים תשמ"א, עמ' 135 ואילך.

המדעי של הוצאה זו, יש עניין גם בדברי המבוא היפים של פינקלשטיין. הוא הביא את דברי הגמרא ״לא הגלה הקב״ה את ישראל לבין האומות אלא כדי שיתוספו עליהם גרים״ (פסחים פז ע״ב), ודרש אותם כלפי ״גיורם״ של ערכי תרבות ורוח, שאותם אימצו היהודים בכל ארצות פזוריהם. מכאן עבר לדיון בהשפעות הזרות השונות על מפרשי המקרא בספרד והבדיל בין האסכולה הפרשנית הספרדית לבין זו הצרפתית, תוך שהגדיר את הראשונה כפילולוגית־פילוסופית ואת השנייה כתלמודית־מסורתית. מפרשי פרובאנס הצליחו להגיע לידי הרמוניזציה בין שתי הגישות ואין לך דוגמא נאה יותר מן הרד״ק עצמו, שבו נפגשו שני הזרמים בזיווג מושלם. תפיסה זו מסבירה אולי מה היתה הסיבה להימשכותו של פינקלשטיין לעיסוק מדעי בפירושו של הרד״ק. ואכן, כפי שנראה עוד להלן, פינקלשטיין השתדל בכל פעולותיו ליצור הרמוניה בין זרמים שונים, שלכאורה עמדו בסתירה זה לזה.

מכאן ולהבא התרכז פינקלשטיין במחקר הספרות הרבנית העתיקה. ספריו, מאמריו ומהדורותיו נגעו כולם, באופן ישיר ועקיף, בתולדות הפרושים, במדרשי ההלכה, בספרות התנאים, בתולדות התפילה ובקשר ההדוק, שהוא ראה, בין עולם הנביאים לבין עולמם של החכמים.

יצירתו בתחום זה היתה פוריה באופן יוצא מן הכלל, במיוחד לאור העובדה שלמן שנות השלושים כבר משך בעול הנהלת בית המדרש לרבנים, תחילה כעוזרו הראשי של כורש אדלר, ומשנת 1940 ועד פרישתו בשנת 1972 כראש המוסד, בראשונה כנשיא ואחר כך כנגיד. והנה, דווקא בשנים אלה הופיעו רוב חיבוריו הגדולים.

נפתח בספריו על הפרושים. בשנת 1938 יצאה לאור המהדורה הראשונה של ספרו: *The Pharisees: The Sociological Background of their Faith*. המהדורה השלישית של הספר, בצירוף תוספת ארוכה, הופיעה בשנת 1962. בנושא זה עסק גם בספרו העברי ״הפרושים ואנשי כנסת הגדולה״ (1950), ובספרו הקלאסי *Akiba: Scholar, Saint and Martyr*, שנדפס לראשונה בשנת 1936 ואחר כך כמה פעמים וגם בתרגום רוסי.[4] בספרו *New Light from the Prophets* (1969), סיכם פינקלשטיין הרבה מטענותיו הקודמות בעניין הפרושים, והקדים את תורת החכמים לתקופת הנביאים ואפילו לתקופה שלפני גלות בבל, וייחס לנביאים עצמם מאמרים שנשתמרו בתורתם של החכמים ולא בספרי המקרא. אוסף מחקרים פרי עטו, שעסקו בפרושים ובנושאים קרובים, ובצירוף מבוא, הופיע בשנת 1972 בשם *Pharisaism in the Making*.

בספרים אלה יש להבחין בכמה רבדים. ראשית כל, מכילים הם מספר רב של דיונים במאמרי חז״ל שמשתקפים בהם חילוקי הדעות בין הפרושים לבין הצדוקים. למשל, במהדורה השלישית של *The Pharisees* הוא דן, בין השאר, בעשרים ושלושים עניינים שהכתות נחלקו עליהם. ב״הפרושים ואנשי כנסת הגדולה״, הוא אסף את המקורות על אנשי כנסת הגדולה ודן בהם. כן נמצא סוגיות ומאמרים רבים שפינקלשטיין פירשם בחריפות גדולה, באופן חדשני ומבריק. בדיונים אלה הוא טיפל בסוגיות ועניינים קשים,

4 ביבליוגרפיה, מס׳ 49, 249, 320, ובהוספות של המלסדורף, מס׳ 351, 361, 369 ועוד.

כגון הלכות טומאה וטהרה והלכות קרבנות, ובשקלא וטריא שלו הוא נשא ונתן הן בדברי רבותינו הראשונים והאחרונים והן בדברי החוקרים החדשים. פינקלשטיין בירר את השיטות של תנאים שונים ותיאר את השקפותיהם כמגובשות וכאחידות. אך העיקר בדיוניו הוא הנסיון לשחזר את עולמם הרוחני, המוסרי, התרבותי, הדתי, החברתי והכלכלי של הכתות והזרמים השונים שפעלו בעם ישראל, ואת עולמם האישי של החכמים, במיוחד החל מתקופת המכבים.

כאן הגיע פינקלשטיין לתוצאות מרחיקות לכת, בסגנון מרומם, ספוג שירה ומלא רגש אמיתי. הוא תיאר את הפרושים בכלל, ואת נציגיהם הגדולים הלל ור׳ עקיבא (וגם אחרים) בפרט, כחלוצים שהגשימו בחייהם (ובמותם) את הערכים הנשגבים של צדק ויושר, חירות ואינדיבידואליות. בספרו *The Pharisees* הקדיש פרקים לתורת השארות הנפש, כבוד האדם, שלום, שוויון האנושות וכדומה, וייחס לפרושים תפקיד ראשוני בהתפתחות רעיונות אלה. לפי פינקלשטיין כת הפרושים היתה האחראית לצמיחת הרעיונות הללו, ולכן מחוייבים אנו לשנות את דימויים של הפרושים, שהיה מקובל במיוחד בין לא יהודים. הפרושים היו אנשים נעלים, תורתם עסקה באידיאלים הכי נכבדים של התרבות המערבית והם־הם שהשפיעו על הציוויליזציה המערבית במידה הגדולה ביותר. פינקלשטיין לא היסס לקבוע כי למעשה כל תרבות העולם המערבי מושפעת מתורת הפרושים. נביא כאן, בתרגום מאנגלית, את המשפטים הראשונים מספרו *Akiba*: ״עקיבא בן יוסף, גיבורו של ספר זה, עומד בשורה אחת עם האישים הכי מצויינים של המסורת היהודית, משה וישעיה הנביא מבין הנביאים, הרמב״ם, חסדאי קרשקש ושפינוזה מבין הפילוסופים. הוא היה שווה להם בעומק שכלו, ברוחב הבנתו ובבהירות חזונו״. ובהמשך: ״אבל במובן יותר רחב, הפילוסופיה שלו [=של ר׳ עקיבא] השפיעה באופן כללי על קווי המיתאר של המחשבה המערבית״. ההזדהות השלימה עם השקפות חז״ל, תפיסת הרעיונות שבדבריהם כערכים מוסריים עליונים והראייה ההיסטורית של עולם החכמים כגורם חשוב בהתפתחות הציוויליזציה המערבית, הביאו את פינקלשטיין לידי התלהבות אמיתית, שהתבטאה גם בסגנון הציורי המאפיין במיוחד את ספרו *Akiba*.

מפורסמת מאוד היא שיטתו הסוציולוגית של פינקלשטיין, לפיה היו הצדוקים נציגי הכהונה האריסטוקרטית והפרובינציאלית, ולעומתם ייצגו הפרושים את חוגי האומנים והסוחרים הפליבאים של ירושלים. על פי הבחנה זו נתפרשו לו הרבה מהמחלוקות שבין החכמים. בכל כתיבתו הוא ראה את הפרושים יושבי הערים, ובייחוד את יושבי ירושלים, כאנשים בעלי אופק רחב ודיעות אוניברסליות, שהתנגדותם לשלטון האריסטוקרטיה נבעה מהשקפותיהם הדמוקרטיות. שלושה דברים עשה פינקלשטיין ביחס לפרושים ולתורתם: ראשית, האריך את תקופת פעולתם וקבע את תחילתה בתקופת הנביאים ואת המשכה ביהדות בת זמננו. שנית, מצא ברעיונותיהם עומק פילוסופי והרחיב את תחום השפעתם על פני כל תרבות העולם המערבי. בתפיסה נועזת זו יש, מחד גיסא, מן הפולמוס נגד ההשקפה הנוצרית הקלאסית שעל פיה הפרושים, דהיינו היהודים, הם כת צרה ובודדת שתורתם פחותת ערך בהשוואה לאידיאלים המקראיים של הנביאים (וכמובן גם בהשוואה לאידיאלים של הנצרות). מאידך גיסא, יש בתפיסה זו גם מגמה של חיזוק כבודם העצמי

של היהודים בהיותם שותפים ב"מסורת היהודית־הנוצרית" (מונח שבשנות החמישים והשישים היה נפוץ מאוד בארצות הברית). ושלישית, שתורת הפרושים היא המקור לאידיאלים הנשגבים של אמריקה החופשית והדמוקרטית. כאילו שינה פינקלשטיין את המאמר הידוע וגרס: יפיפותו של שם נכנסה לאהלי יפת! שיטה זו, שפינקלשטיין הפיץ בין בחיבוריו המדעיים ובין במאמריו הפופולריים ובנאומיו הרבים, תרמה תרומה עצומה להעלאת קרן היהדות באמריקה. לא זה המקום לעקוב אחרי חדירת רעיונות אלה לתודעה העממית האמריקנית של שנות החמישים והשישים, אבל בלי שום ספק הכבוד הגדול שנפל בחלקו של פינקלשטיין מאת נשיאי ארצות הברית, מנהיגי ממשלה, שופטים ואנשי רוח, נבע מהפצתה המוצלחת והיעילה של תורה זו.

כשם שהאמין בהשפעה החיובית של היהדות על העולם, כך האמין שערכי התרבות של העמים שבקרבם התגוררו היהודים העשירו את היהדות. מי שרוצה להבין את מקום היהדות בעולם צריך להיות בקי בכל התרבויות, החל מכנען העתיקה ועד לתרבות המורכבת של תקופתנו. ביטוי אמיץ לתפיסתו את ההשפעות ההדדיות הללו נתן בספרו הגדול *The Jews: Their History, Culture, and Religion*. פינקלשטיין יזם וערך את הספר, שבמהדורתו הראשונה (1949) יצא בארבעה כרכים ואחר כך הופיע במהדורות ובצורות שונות.[5] הספר מכיל מחקרים וסקירות של טובי החוקרים של היהדות ושל היהודים. המדורים שבספר הם: תולדות היהודים והיהדות; תפקיד היהדות בתרבות העולם; הסוציולוגיה והדמוגרפיה של היהודים; הדת היהודית. בין המשתתפים היו מלומדים כמו ויליאם פוקסוול אולברייט, אליאס ביקרמן, ססיל רות, ישראל היילפרין, בן־ציון דינור, יצחק בן־צבי, שלום שפיגל, אברהם יהושע השל, אלכסנדר אלטמן, אברהם הלקין, מרדכי קפלן, אריק ורנר, רחל וישניצר, ורבים אחרים. המחקרים השונים מתארים את היהדות ואת תרומת היהודים מבחינות רבות, כולל מוסיקה, אמנות, רפואה ומדעים. לחידוש גדול נחשב בזמנו העיסוק המדעי בסטטיסטיקה, סוציולוגיה ודמוגרפיה של היהודים. כמה מהמאמרים מיוסדים על מחקר מקורי, וחשיבותם עומדת עד היום. פינקלשטיין עצמו חיבר סקירה על האמונות והדעות ועל המנהגים של היהדות. הסקירה היא קצרה, אבל באופן מפליא שלימה בידיעות מעשיות על היהדות וכתובה בצורה שאפילו אלה שאין להם שום ידיעה במנהגי הדת יכולים להבינה. מגמתו של פינקלשטיין, להראות בספר אחד את כל ההיבטים של היהדות ושל היהודים, מפורשת ומנומקת במבואו, שנוסח כמכתב אל יוסף מאיר פרוסקואר, מנהיג יהודי מפורסם בזמנו ושופט בבית המשפט העליון של מדינת ניו־יורק. פינקלשטיין הצליח לשתף במפעלו את העידית היהודית האינטלקטואלית והציבורית וגם בדרך זו תרם להפצת ידע חיובי של היהדות ועל היהודים בקרב שכבות רחבות.

לצד חיבוריו הכוללים, פירסם פינקלשטיין מאמרים רבים ובין אלה ראוי לייחד את הדיבור לשורת מאמריו על הליטורגיה היהודית. כבר נזכר מאמרו על תפילת העמידה (1925). על זה התוספו במשך השנים מאמרים על ברכת המזון (1929), על ראשית בית

5 ביבליוגרפיה, מס' 194, 234, 325.

הכנסת (1930), על הקדושה (1932, 1978), על עשרת הרוגי מלכות (1938), על ההגדה של פסח (1938 ו־1943), על המונח "פורס על שמע" (1942), על ההפטרות לפי מנהגי ארץ ישראל, ביזנטיון והקראים (1943), על ההלל (1951), על מלכויות, זכרונות ושופרות ("לביאורה של משנה סתומה", 1974).[6] כמה ממאמרים אלה נכללו בקובץ *Pharisaism in the Making* (1972). גם באחד ממאמריו האחרונים (The Impact of the Roman" "Emperors on the Synagogue Liturgy, בספר לכבודו של הרב סימור כהן, 1991), הוא שב ודן בענייני ליטורגיה. מחקרים אלה, במיוחד המאמרים על העמידה ועל ההגדה של פסח, גרמו להתרגשות גדולה ולסנסציה בין המלומדים. ראשית כל, פינקלשטיין הקדים מאוד את התהוות הטקסטים הליטורגיים האלה. הוא ייחס אלמנטים מדרשיים מההגדה לתקופה הקדם־חשמונאית ואת תפילת העמידה הקדים לתקופת הנביאים! שנית, הוא ראה בטקסטים אלה תגובה אקטואלית למאורעות פוליטיים שונים; ושלישית, הוא ניסה למצוא את הניסוח הראשוני של הטקסטים. כך, למשל, הוא ניסה לשחזר את הנוסח המקורי של ברכות העמידה. בעניין זה הבחין בין סגנונות שונים: יש ברכות העושות שימוש בצירוף "ה' אלוקינו", אחרות בכינוי "אבינו", ויש שבכל ברכה באות שבע מלים בדיוק. לפי קריטריונים סגנוניים אלה הציע פינקלשטיין תאריכים מסוימים להתהוות הברכות השונות. הרבה מבקרים קמו לשיטתו, ביניהם יצחק משה אלבוגן, דניאל גולדשמידט ויוסף היינימן. בכל זאת, זכותו המדעית של פינקלשטיין, גם בתחום זה, גדולה היא מאוד. הוא עורר שאלות שעד היום מתלבטים בהן חכמי ישראל. הוא ניתח את מקורות חז"ל בחריפות והפנה תשומת לב לקשר שבינן לבין תפילות שונות והעמיד את החוקרים על חשיבות הרקע ההיסטורי והפוליטי בהבנת תופעות וטקסטים ליטורגיים. ולבסוף, הוא אסף וערך את הנוסחאות של טקסטים יסודיים של הליטורגיה היהודית ממנהגי תפילה שונים, מקטעי הגניזה הקהירית וגם מסידורי תפילה שבכתבי יד ובדפוסים. כך עשה, למשל, וביסודיות גדולה, בקשר לעמידה ולברכת המזון. למרות הביקורת, פינקלשטיין המשיך להחזיק בדעותיו, ובמבוא לקובץ מאמריו *Pharisaism in the Making* ובספרו *New Light from the Prophets*, חזר והדגיש, שהוא משוכנע בקדמוניות טקסטים אלה. דעתו, כי חלקים בהגדה הם תגובה לשלטון התלמיים במצרים ולשלטון הסלבקים בסוריה במאה השלישית לפנה"ס, התפשטה עד כדי כך, שהיא נכנסה לכמה מהדורות עממיות של ההגדה של פסח.[7] ומי מן החוקרים המודרניים יכול להשתבח בכך שאחד ממאמריו נכלל במחזור לימים נוראים, כמו פינקלשטיין שפתיחת מאמרו על עשרת הרוגי המלכות נתקבלה במחזור שערך מ' סילברמן.

עלינו לסכם עוד מפעל נוסף וענקי שלו, שאולי בו הגיע לשיא גדולתו כחוקר. הכוונה לעבודתו הממושכת, החל משנת 1932 וכמעט עד ליומו האחרון, בההדרת מדרשי הלכה ובעיון מעמיק בהם. זכינו ולאחרונה נקבצו מאמריו החשובים בנושא זה בכרך החמישי של מהדורתו לספרא (1991). כאן ימצא הלומד את מאמריו הקלאסיים באנגלית, על הכללים

6 ביבליוגרפיה, מס' 15, 18, 28, 60, 62, 110, 117, 118, 170, 345, 362 (בהוספות של המלסדורף).

7 Lawrence A. Hoffman, *Beyond the Text*, Bloomington and Indianapolis 1987, pp. 90-91

לההדרת טקסטים של המכילתא ושל הספרי לצד מחקרים אחרים, רובם בעברית, על תיקוני נוסח בספרא ובספרי ומאמרים העוסקים בסוגיות היסטוריות וטקסטואליות הקשורות במדרשי הלכה. במאמרים אלה, וגם בספרו "מבוא למסכתות אבות ואבות דרבי נתן" (1950), יש רשימה שלימה של המקורות, הן אלה שבקטעי הגניזה ובכתבי יד והן אלה שבדפוס, וגם עדויות ממקורות אחרים, כגון הבאות בספרות הראשונים. פינקלשטיין דן בטיבו של כל מקור ומקור, מיין את המקורות לפי השתייכותם למשפחות וניסה להפריד בין הטקסט המקורי לבין ההוספות השונות שנתוספו עליו במשך הדורות. בי"ד נקודות סיכם את הכללים לפיהם צריכים לגשת לההדרת טקסט תנאי,[8] ולמרות התפתחויות וגישות חדשות במקצוע, עדיין לא פג תוקפם של כללים אלה.

עבודות אלה היו הכנה למהדורות ביקורתיות של שני מדרשי תנאים: "ספרא הוא תורת כהנים" ו"ספרי לספר דברים". יש להניח שרוב החוקרים יסכימו, שמהדורות אלה הן גולת הכותרת של מפעלו בחכמת ישראל. פינקלשטיין עצמו ראה בהוצאתן לאור את עיקר תפקידו המדעי. הרבה מחיבוריו האחרים שנזכרו לעיל צמחו מתוך עיסוקו הממושך בההדרת טקסטים אלה ובפירושם. בשנת 1939, כבר אחרי פרוץ מלחמת העולם השנייה, נגמרה הדפסתו של ספרי לדברים. הספר היה כלול ב־*Corpus Tannaiticum*, מפעל ביוזמת האירגון הגרמני־יהודי לקידום מדעי היהדות (*Gesellschaft zur Förderung der Wissenschaft des Judentums*). מעניין הדבר, שחכמי ישראל בגרמניה פנו אל מלומד צעיר בארצות הברית כדי שהוא יגמור את המהדורה שבהכנתה החל החכם והחוקר הגדול חיים שאול הורוביץ.

יש הרבה סמליות בעובדה, שאחד המפעלים המדעיים החשובים והאחרונים שעסקו בו בגרמניה, נגמר על ידי פינקלשטיין באמריקה. הוא ראה את עצמו בפרט, ואת בית המדרש לרבנים בניו־יורק בכלל, כהמשך למרכז היהודי־המדעי שנהרס באירופה. כידוע, רוב הטפסים של מהדורת הספרי לדברים אבדו בזוועות שבגרמניה הנאצית ורק עותקים אחדים מן הספר הגיעו לישראל ולארצות הברית. בשנת 1969 הופיע הספר שנית, מלווה בהקדמה חדשה מאת פינקלשטיין, שהביע את צערו על שאין בידו "לתקן את הטעויות שנפלו בהעתקת השינויים; וגם את הנוסח במקום שהעזתי פני להגיה את נוסח הפנים נגד כל הנוסחאות המקובלות, וכן לא יעשה, ילדות היתה בי".

מהדורת הספרי לדברים השתבחה בדברי שאול ליברמן, שכתב: "פינ[קלשטיין] ציין והבליט את היחס ההדדי בין כתה"י, את היחס בין כתה"י לראשונים, הִרבה להביא את פיסקאות הראשונים, ציין במדה מרובה לספרות המקצועית, סימן את המאמרים השונים בספרות העתית, ציין למקבילות בספרות החיצוניים, תיקן מסורת מלאה ומקיפה של הספרות התלמודית. ובראש וראשונה ראוי פינ[קלשטיין] לתודה ולברכה בעד זה שהתעכב בהערותיו על כל מה שראוי להתעכב והבליט בכל מקום את הצד ההיסטורי, הפולקלורי, האגדתי וההלכי בחומר שעיבד. ואם מטרת כל ספר ממין זה היא להעשיר אותנו בערכי תרבות חדשים, הרי השגנו את מבוקשנו, והוצאה זו תתפוס אחד מן המקומות הראשיים בספרותנו.[9]

8 ראה ספרא, ה, עמ' 50-52.

9 <ראה עתה: שאול ליברמן, מחקרים בתורת ארץ־ישראל, בעריכת דוד רוזנטל, ירושלים תשנ"א, עמ' 578.>

ואחרון אחרון חביב, כמה מלים על מפעלו של פינקלשטיין בהוצאת "ספרא דבי רב הוא תורת כהנים". לפנינו מונחים היום חמישה כרכים של הוצאה זו (1983-1991), כרך א: מבוא; כרך ב: ברייתא דרבי ישמעאל ופרשת ויקרא — דיבורא דנדבה ודיבורא דחובה, בצירוף מסורת הספרא ופירוש קצר; כרך ג: שינוי נוסחאות; כרך ד: פירוש ארוך הנקרא "שם משמעון" (רמז לשם אביו!); כרך ה: מפתחות לכרכים הקודמים ומבחר מאמרים במדרשי הלכה. שנים רבות לפני שהופיעה הוצאה זו פירסם פינקלשטיין פקסימילה של כתב יד רומי של תורת כהנים, עם מבוא ארוך (1956). על עיסוקו בספר זה כתב: "שמתי את לימוד ספר תורת כהנים לעיקר משנתי" (הקדמה לכרך ב). הוא קיווה להוציא את הספר בשלימות, אבל הרגיש שלא יעלה הדבר בידו והחליט להדפיס את החלקים שהיו מוכנים אצלו (הקדמה לכרך א). אפילו בצורתה הנוכחית מהדורה זו היא למופת, מכל הסיבות שמנינו כבר לעיל בקשר לספרי. במהדורה זו נכללו גם צילומי קטעי גניזה רבים של הספרא (כרך א), ובפירושו הארוך נשא ונתן בפירוט רב בדברי ראשונים, אחרונים וחוקרים מודרנים, עד שקשה לתאר שיש איזה מקור הנוגע לספרא, קדום או חדש, שנעלם מעיניו.

יש לשער שבעזבונו של פינקלשטיין נותר חומר רב לשאר חלקי הספרא. בנו, ר' עזרא פינקלשטיין, אישר בפני את הדבר והוסיף, שאביו עבד גם על ספר גדול העוסק בתורת השארות הנפש ביהדות. הוא מסר לי שאביו ציווה, שכל החומר שייצא לאור מעזבונו צריך להופיע בשמו של המוציא לאור ולא תחת שמו הוא. פינקלשטיין הסביר זאת בכך, שהוא עצמו כבר לא יוכל לעבור על החומר, לתקנו ולשנותו כדרך שנהג בכל פירסומיו האחרים. ואולי יש לפרש את רצונו זה על פי האידיאל שהוא תיאר במאמרו: "The Ethics of Anonymity among the Pharisees".[10] — וכך כתב שם: "Apparently to the ancient Hasideans posthumous fame seemed an irrational goal in life" (כנראה, בעיני החסידים הראשונים תהילה שלאחר המוות נחשבה מטרה בלתי הגיונית). ובהמשך הביע את דעתו כי אנונימיות היא הביטוי הקיצוני של אהבת ה'. כל חייו של פינקלשטיין היו אכן מוקדשים לעבודת ה' ולאהבתו.

בסקירתנו הקצרה עסקנו רק בהיבט אחד של מפעלו. לא הרחבנו את הדיבור על כל שעשה למען בית המדרש לרבנים באמריקה, וכיצד הפך אותו לאחד המרכזים הגדולים והחשובים של מדעי היהדות בעולם, שממנו יצאו מלומדים חשובים, שמשמשים היום במוסדות לימוד גבוהים בישראל ובארצות הברית. לא טיפלנו בפעולתו למען דו־שיח של נציגי היהדות עם נציגי דתות אחרות, או בתרומתו להרמת קרן היהודים באמריקה. עוד יסופר וייכתב על פעולתו הרבגונית של פינקלשטיין, על שיטתו ותורתו ועל תרומותיו על רקע ההיסטוריה של המאה העשרים. אך בראש ובראשונה, ר' אליעזר אריה בן ר' שמעון יצחק הלוי פינקלשטיין ראה את עצמו כממשיך תורתם של נביאים, חסידים ראשונים, פרושים, ורבנים שבאו אחריהם, ועיקר חלומו היה להגשים את האידיאלים הנשגבים של תורת ישראל בתקופת התוהו ובוהו המודרנית שבה חי ופעל.

10 ביבליוגרפיה, מס' 226, 338.

בקטע גניזה אחד של אבות דרבי נתן אנו מוצאים נוסח שזה לשונו: ״רבן גמליאל אומ׳ שלוש [מדות] בתלמידי חכמים... אבן פשיפס (כן בכת״י) כאיזה צד? זה תלמיד חכמים ששנה מדרש הלכות והגדות בזמן שתלמיד אחר ניכנס אצלו, שאלו במדרש אומר לו, בהלכות אומ׳ לו, בהגדות אומ׳ לו, בשיחת של מושלים אומ׳ לו, זה הוא אבן פסיפס שיש לה ארבעה פנים מארבעה צדדים״.[11] בספרי לספר דברים מובאת דרשה על הפסוק ״הבו לכם אנשים חכמים ונבונים״ וגו׳ (דברים א יג): ״אנשים, בחתיכה ובפסיפס״. פינקלשטיין בהערותיו פירש כך: ״פסיפס הוא כינוי לת״ח שמראה פנים מכל צד ובקי בכל התורה כולה״; והמשיך: ״ות״ח הוא איש המצויין ומחותך מכל צד בחכמה ובציור כאבן של פסיפס״.[12] אם נדרוש בדרך צחות את המלים (שחסרות בשאר המקורות) ״בשיחת של מושלים אומר לו״ כמוסבות על פינקלשטיין, שנוסף לחכמתו ב״מדרש הלכות ואגדות״ ידע גם לייצג את היהדות בפני נשיאים ומושלים, נמצא בכל מה שנאמר כאן תיאור מתאים של פינקלשטיין ומפעלו.

פינקלשטיין היה רגיל להביע את תודתו לקב״ה, על שזכה להיות ״מחובשי בית המדרש ולהגות בתורתו״. זכינו אנחנו ויזכו הדורות הבאים אחרינו ליהנות מתורתו ומחכמתו.

11 ראה בספרו של פינקלשטיין, מבוא למסכת אבות ואבות דרבי נתן, עמ׳ קפב.

12 ספרי, מהדורת פינקלשטיין, עמ׳ 21.

אלכסנדר שייבר והמחקר היהודי בהונגריה

לפני זמן קצר הגיע לידינו ספרו החדש, בשני כרכים, של פרופ׳ אלכסנדר שייבר מבודפשט.[1] המחבר רכש לו שם עולמי במפעליו המדעיים והציבוריים השונים. יש בהופעת ספרו החדש כמה דברים המעוררים תשומת לב מיוחדת.

ראשית כל, נזכיר את מקום הדפסתו של הספר. חיבורו של שייבר יצא לאור בהונגריה ע״י האירגון המרכזי של יהדות המדינה. במדינות מזרח אירופה ואפילו בכמה מדינות באירופה המערבית אין כמעט כיום שום פעולות מדעיות מחקריות יהודיות, ואם יש איזה חכם נסתר במקומות אלה שיוצר במקצוע זה, קשה לתאר שימצא לו אכסניה המוכנה לפרסם את דבריו. לא כך המצב בהונגריה, שבה קיימת במה קבועה להוצאתם לאור של ספרים על היהודים ועל היהדות. מי שמכיר במקצת את המצב השורר באירופה המזרחית יידע להעריך ככל הראוי את המאמצים המרובים ואת הכשרון הגדול הדרושים להחזקת פעולות מדעיות בחכמת ישראל בארצות אלה. מחבר הספר שלפנינו דואג לכך, שעד כמה שתנאי המקום מאפשרים זאת, תתקיים שם מסגרת לעבודה מדעית ולפרסומים מדעיים.

פרופ׳ שייבר משתדל בכל כוחו להמשיך במסורת הגאה של חכמת ישראל בהונגריה והוא חושב את עצמו כחוליה, אולי החוליה האחרונה, בשרשרת הארוכה של חוקרים גדולים שהעשירו את כל ענפי מדעי היהדות במחקריהם הקלאסיים. די להזכיר את שמותיהם של דוד קויפמן, יצחק יהודה גולדציהר, בנימין זאב בכר, עמנואל לעף ויהודה אריה בלוי, כדי לעמוד על התרומה הגדולה שיהדות הונגריה תרמה לחכמת ישראל. השראת חכמים אלה ממריצה את שייבר לעסוק כל ימיו במחקר היהדות ובהשראה זו הוא טורח ועמל בשדה הפולקלור היהודי, בתולדות הפיוט, בחקר הגניזה, בתולדות האמנות היהודית, בביבליוגרפיה, בתולדות הספר העברי ובשאר מקצועות.

בד בבד עם פעולתו המדעית האישית ראה שייבר כהכרח השעה את הצורך להקים גל-עד ליהדות ארצו, שבמשך כאלף שנים פעלה על אדמת הונגריה, ושחייה נגדעו באכזריות על-ידי הצר הצורר בשואה הנאצית. אחרי המלחמה הוא התחיל להתרכז באיסוף חומר לתולדות היהודים בהונגריה והוא העושה והמעשה בחשיפת התעודות ונתונים השונים הדרושים לכתיבת ההיסטוריה הרוחנית והפוליטית של יהדות זו.

מפעל האיסוף יכול להיעשות רק במקום שרוב החומר המדעי שמור ושיש בו מומחים המבינים לתת לו משמעות ולפרש אותו בהקשרו הנכון. שייבר אירגן קבוצה שלימה של מלומדים, יהודים ושאינם יהודים, שחיפשו בארכיונים ובספריות בכל המדינה ושגילו גם

1 S. Scheiber, *Folklór és Tárgytörténet*, I-II, Budapest 1974 [מהד׳ ב׳: 1977, בשלושה כרכים.]

מימצאים ארכיאולוגיים של אתרים יהודיים מימי הביניים. כתוצאה מפעולה זו יצאו לאור כמה ספרים על תולדות קהילות שונות. נוסף על כך ט״ו כרכים של אוסף תעודות, בעריכתו של שייבר, המכילים תעודות בלטינית, בהונגרית, בגרמנית, בסלאבית ובמקצת אף בעברית וביידיש. תעודות אלה נוגעות לחייה הכלכליים ומעמדה הפוליטי של יהדות הונגריה. שייבר עצמו תרם בשטח זה שני ספרים רבי ערך. באחד מהם הוא נותן לפני הקורא אוסף של קטעי כתבי יד שנשרדו בכריכות ספרים בספריות השונות בהונגריה; ובספר השני מקובצים טקסטים של כתובות עבריות, שהקדומה ביניהן מוצאה מהתקופה הרומית, תקופה בה התיישבו היהודים הראשונים בקולוניה הרומית פנוניה (היום – מערב־הונגריה).

מלבד עבודתו במדעי היהדות ובאיסוף חומר לתולדות יהודי הונגריה יש לשייבר התעניינות נוספת והיא: חשיפת המקורות של המוטיבים המקראיים והיהודיים הטמונים בכתבי סופרים הונגריים. אין שום ספק שגם בעיסוק זה רואה שייבר כעין הקמת זכר לתרומות הרבות שיהודי הונגריה תרמו לתרבות המקום. רק מלומד כמוהו, שהוא בן־בית בספרות ההונגרית וידיו רב לו בספרות היהודית, מסוגל לגלות את ההשפעות היהודיות הנמצאות ביצירותיהם של גדולי סופרי הונגריה. הוא הצליח לגלות מוטיבים כאלה, שנכנסו לספרות ההונגרית ביודעין ובלא יודעין, בעיקר בשירי המשורר הלאומי הגדול של המאה הי״ט, ארני יאנוש (Arany Janos).

עלינו להוסיף, שיחד עם פעולות אלה, שייבר הוא מנהלו של בית המדרש לרבנים שבבודפשט, מעמיד תלמידים רבים, שכותב הטורים האלה הוא אחד מהם, ומנהיג את קהילתו באהבה ובהבנה גדולה. פעולותיו הציבוריות הן חלק בלתי נפרד של עיסוקו הרבגוני בכל מה שנוגע ליהדות הונגריה ולקשריה לכלל ישראל.

עתה נחזור לספרו החדש, שהתחלנו לדבר עליו בראש המאמר. גוף הספר, שכולו כתוב בהונגרית, מכיל מאמרים שיצאו לאור במשך כשלושים שנה בכתבי־עת ובקבצים שונים. עשרים ואחד מאמרים עוסקים בפולקלור היהודי ובהם הוא מייחד את הדיבור על נושאים כגון: האגדות על בנות לוט, על מגדל בבל, על העשן העולה מהקרבנות שקין והבל הקריבו, על שמשון הגיבור העוקר אילן, על מעשיות בחיבורו של הקראי יהודה הדסי, על תפקידו של השופר בטכסי אבלות, על הפורמולה הידועה בקולופונים של ספרים עבריים ״עד שיעלה חמור בסולם״ וכו׳ וכו׳. מאמרים אחרים דנים בפעולותיהם המדעיות של חוקרים יהודיים מהונגריה בתחום הפולקלור היהודי. במאמרי־הערכה אלה הוא כותב על עמנואל לעף, מחברו של הספר המונומנטלי ״פלורה דר יודן״ (Flora der Juden); על דוב הלר, חוקר מופלג של האגדה, ושל המעשיה היהודית ועל שני מלומדים צנועים, ששמותיהם אינם מוכרים מחוץ לגבולות הונגריה והם ברטלן קולבך (Bertalan Kolbach) ויצחק פייפר. פייפר מסר את נפשו, בראש קהילתו, על קידוש השם בשנת תש״ד.

בכרך השני של הספר ארבעים וחמישה מאמרים, ובכולם הוא מטפל בבעיית חשיפת מקורותיהם של מוטיבים יהודיים בכתבי סופרים הונגריים, החל מהמאה הט״ז וכלה באמצע המאה העשרים. במאמר האחרון שייבר מגיש לפני הקורא רשימה של מחזות,

שירים, רומנים וסיפורים הונגריים המיוסדים על נושאים מקראיים, שהופיעו בין השנים 1973-1945. רשימה זו מוכיחה בעליל שגם בתקופה האחרונה המשיכו סופרי הונגריה, מבני ברית ומשאינם בני ברית, ליצור את יצירותיהם הספרותיות בהשפעת ספר הספרים.

הספר נגמר ברשימה ביבליוגרפית של כתבי שייבר, שחוברה על־ידי תלמידו, רוברט דן. דן משמש היום כפרופסור באוניברסיטת בודפשט והוא בעצמו כתב לאחרונה ספר מעניין על הידיעות בשפה העברית בחוגי הנוצרים בהונגריה בתקופת הריפורמציה ולאחריה. ביבליוגרפיה זו מכילה 1142[1] פריטים של פרסומים בהונגרית, באנגלית, בגרמנית, בעברית ובשאר שפות שראו אור בהונגריה, באנגליה, בצרפת, בארצות־הברית ובמדינת ישראל. במאמריו שנאספו בספר זה, כמו בכל מאמריו, מראה המחבר את כוחו הגדול באיתור מוטיבים ומקורותיהם על־ידי ידיעות כוללות בספרות העולמית, ההונגרית הקלאסית, ואחרון אחרון, בספרות העברית.

מטרת פעולתו המדעית והציבורית של פרופ׳ שייבר היא להראות לעולם את יופיה והדרה של יהדות גדולה, שתרמה כל־כך הרבה לתרבותו של העם ששכנה בתוכו ולתרבות היהודית הכללית גם יחד. יצירה פוריה זו נפסקה כשרוב רובה של גלות יהודי ארץ הגר נשמד ונהרס בידי הנאצים ועמיתיהם ההונגריים. ואם עדיין לא כבה אישה של יהדות זו לגמרי, ואם עדיין יש עוד זכר להישגיה המרובים, עלינו להודות על כך לאדם גדול צנוע ומסור זה, שמקדיש את כל חייו לשמירת הגחלת...

1 <במהדורה השנייה רשומים 1569 פריטים.>

מפתחות

מפתח המקורות

* את המפתחות ערך מר דוד קירשן. המספר שמשמאל ללוכסן הוא מספר של הערה.

תהלים (המשך)

ספרות בתר-תלמודית

מפתח התחלות הפיוטים

* לפיוטים נוספים ראה עמ׳ 197-208

מפתח אישים

חכמים ומשוררים*

* נזכרים כאן חכמים ומשוררים מימי הביניים

חוקרים*

* נזכרים כאן חוקרים שיש במאמרים התייחסות לדבריהם

מפתח כתבי יד

רשימת הקבצים וכתבי העת שהמאמרים נדפסו בהם לראשונה

"פירוש אלפביטין על י"ג פיוטים ארמיים" — מחקרים ומקורות, בעריכת ח"ז דימיטרובסקי, ניו יורק תשל"ח, עמ' 274-169

"יצירתו הפיוטית של ר' יצחק אבן גיאת", תעודה א (תש"מ), עמ' 95-89

"'לך ה' הגדולה' ופסוקים דומים בקדושתאות ליום הכיפורים", כנסת עזרא — אסופת מחקרים מוגשת לע־רא פליישר, בעריכת ש' אליצור ואחרים, ירושלים תשנ"ה, עמ' 291-285

"'עבודה קצרה' לרב יצחק אבן גיאת", יד להימן — קובץ מחקרים לזכר א"מ הברמן, בעריכת צ' מלאכי, לוד תשמ"ד, עמ' 169-154

"חמשה זולתות לרב יצחק אבן גיאת", שי להימן — מחקרים בספרות העברית של ימי הביניים, מוגשים לא"מ הברמן [הימן הירושלמי] במלאות לו שבעים וחמש שנה, התקין וערך צ' מלאכי בהשתתפות י' דוד, ירושלים תשל"ז, עמ' 342-329

"'מחזור בלתי נודע' וספר שפתי רננות", ארשת ה (תשל"ב), עמ' 130-125

"ר' משה בן אלקרטבי", תרביץ לה (תשכ"ה), עמ' 194

"פיוט הושענא לר' יוסף אבן אביתור", הדאר, שנה ארבעים ושתים, גליון לט, ט' בתשרי תשכ"ד, עמ' 764-763

"נפלאות בריאת העולם, יציאת מצרים, והגאלה שלעתיד לבוא, בפיוט קדום", מאה שערים — עיונים בעולמם הרוחני של ישראל בימי הביניים, לזכר יצחק טברסקי, בעריכת ע' פליישר ואחרים, ירושלים תשס"ג, עמ' 86-71

"פיוט אשכנזי חדש על פדיון הכלה השבויה ממצרים — הפיוט 'אמון נוא' לר' מנחם בר' מכיר", עטרה לחיים — מחקרים בספרות התלמודית והרבנית לכבוד פרופסור חיים זלמן דימיטרובסקי, בעריכת ד' בויארין ואחרים, ירושלים תש"ס, עמ' 500-491

"פיוט על ביזת היהודים", נטיעות לדוד — ספר היובל לדוד הלבני, בעריכת י' אלמן ואחרים, ירושלים תשס"ה, עמ' שטו-שכד

״פיוט מעריב בלתי ידוע לשמיני עצרת שמחת תורה״, תעודה יט (תשס״ג), עמ׳ 273-281

״שירי פתיחה וחתימה בספר ׳יחוסי תנאים ואמוראים׳״, לר׳ יהודה בן קלונימוס משפירא, בין היסטוריה לספרות — ספר יובל ליצחק ברזילי, בעריכת ש׳ נש, הקיבוץ המאוחד 1997, עמ׳ שיט-שכח

״מעשה ר׳ אמנון והסליחה ׳תא שמע׳״, הדאר, שנה ארבעים ושלוש, גליון מא, כ״ד במרחשון תשכ״ה, עמ׳ 734

״משהו על פיוטים לנישואין באשכנז״, מחקרים בספרות ישראל מוגשים לאברהם הולץ, בעריכת צביה בן־יוסף גינור ז״ל, ניו יורק תשס״ג, עמ׳ 31-52

״אליעזר אריה הלוי פינקלשטיין — חכם, חוקר, מגשים וחולם״, מדעי היהדות 32 (תשנ״ב), עמ׳ 37-45

״אלכסנדר שייבר והמחקר היהודי בהונגריה״, הדאר, שנה חמישים וחמש, גליון ד, כ״ד בכסלו תשל״ו, עמ׳ 53-54

אנו מודים למערכות הקבצים וכתבי העת על הרשות להדפיס את המאמרים.